Elementary Children's Literature

THIRD EDITION

Elementary Children's Literature

INFANCY THROUGH AGE 13

Nancy A. Anderson
University of South Florida

Allyn & Bacon

Boston   New York   San Francisco
Mexico City   Montreal   Toronto   London   Madrid   Munich   Paris
Hong Kong   Singapore   Tokyo   Cape Town   Sydney

Executive Editor: Aurora Martínez Ramos
Series Editorial Assistant: Jacqueline Gillen
Marketing Manager: Krista Clark
Production Editor: Mary Beth Finch
Editorial Production Service: Omegatype Typography, Inc.
Composition Buyer: Linda Cox
Manufacturing Manager: Megan Cochran
Electronic Composition: Omegatype Typography, Inc.
Interior Design: Omegatype Typography, Inc.
Cover Administrator: Linda Knowles

For related titles and support materials, visit our online catalog at www.pearsonhighered.com.

Between the time website information is gathered and then published, it is not unusual for some sites to have closed. Also, the transcription of URLs can result in typographical errors. The publisher would appreciate notification where these occur so that they may be corrected in subsequent editions.

Library of Congress Cataloging-in-Publication Data

Anderson, Nancy A.
  Elementary children's literature : infancy through age 13 / Nancy A. Anderson.—3rd ed.
      p. cm.
  Includes bibliographical references and index.
  ISBN–13: 978-0-13-715143-1 (pbk.)
  ISBN–10: 0-13-715143-8 (pbk.)
  1. Children's literature—History and criticism. 2. Children's literature—Study and teaching (Elementary) 3. Children—Books and reading. I. Title.
    PN1009. A1A464   2009
    809'.88282—dc22

                                                                    2008045039

Printed in the United States of America

10 9 8 7 6 5 4 3 2   HAM   13 12 11 10 09

Credits appear on pp. 383–385, which constitute an extension of the copyright page.

Allyn & Bacon
is an imprint of

www.pearsonhighered.com

ISBN 10: 0-13-715143-8
ISBN 13: 978-0-13-715143-1

To my adopted family—Yen, Justin, Jason, and Jim

Contents

Preface   xv

Part One   Entering the World of Children's Literature   1

Chapter 1

Introduction to the World of Children's Literature   1

Defining Literature for Children   2

The Birth of Modern Children's Literature   4

Book Illustrations   7

The Genres of Literature   8

The Dewey Decimal System   9

Book Formats   11
- Picture Books   11
- Easy-to-Read Books   12
- Illustrated Books   13
- Graphic Novels   13
- Chapter Books   14
- Hardcover Books   14
- Paperback Books   15
- Grocery Store Books   15
- Series Books   17

The Value of Children's Literature   18

Prereading Schema Building   20
- The Process of Schema Building   20
- Modeling the Process   22

Summary   24

Chapter 2

Elements of Quality Children's Literature   26

Book Awards   27
- Newbery Medal   27
- Caldecott Medal   27

Laura Ingalls Wilder Medal   28
Hans Christian Andersen Award   29
Children's Choices and Teachers' Choices   29

Literary Elements   30
Characters   31
Point of View   31
Setting   34
Plot   35
Theme   37
Style   38
Tone   39

Responding to Literature   39

Reader Response Theory by Gloria Houston   40

Literature Circles   42

Developing a Classroom Library by Susan E. Knell   42
Summary   44

Chapter 3

The Art of Illustration   46

Evaluating Illustrations   47

The Union of Art and Text   47

Visual Elements of Artistic Design   48
Space   48
Line   49
Shape   49
Color   49
Texture   50
Scale and Dimension   51
Composition   51

Artistic Styles   52

Artistic Media and Techniques   55
Painting   55
Drawing   56
Other Techniques   56

Integrating Visual Art and Literature by Janet C. Richards   58
Summary   60

Chapter 4

Early Childhood Books   62

Books of Early Childhood   63
    Board Books   63
    Concept Books   64
    Pattern Books   74
    Wordless Picture Books   75

Motivating Children to Become Lifelong Readers
    by Susan E. Knell   77

Summary   79

Chapter 5

Traditional Literature   80

Evaluating Traditional Literature   81

History   82

Characteristics   84

Themes of Traditional Literature   87

The Subgenres of Traditional Literature   89
    Myths   89
    Fables   92
    Ballads and Folk Songs   94
    Legends   96
    Tall Tales   97
    Fairy Tales   98
    Traditional Rhymes   107

Summary   110

Part Two   **The Boundless World of Fiction   111**

Chapter 6

Modern Fantasy   111

Evaluating Modern Fantasy   112

The Beginnings of Fiction and Modern Fantasy   **113**
  Hans Christian Andersen   113

Types of Fantasy   **115**
  Animal Fantasy   116
  Literary Fairy Tale   116
  Animated Object Fantasy   118
  Human with Fantasy Character   121
  Extraordinary Person   122
  Enchanted Journey   125
  High Fantasy   128
  Supernatural Fantasy   132
  Science Fiction   134
  Unlikely Situation   137

Summary   **139**

Chapter 7

Animal Fantasy   144

Evaluating Animal Fantasy   **147**

Milestones in Animal Fantasy   **147**
  1877: *Black Beauty: The Autobiography of a Horse* by Anna Sewell   147
  1894: *The Jungle Book* by Rudyard Kipling   147
  1901/1902: *The Tale of Peter Rabbit* by Beatrix Potter   148
  1903: *The Call of the Wild* by Jack London   148
  1908: *The Wind in the Willows* by Kenneth Grahame   148
  1929: *Bambi: A Life in the Woods* by Felix Salten   149
  1939: *Rudolph the Red-Nosed Reindeer* by Robert L. May   149
  1941: *Make Way for Ducklings* by Robert McCloskey   150
  1942: *The Poky Little Puppy* by Janette Lowrey   150
  1952: *Charlotte's Web* by E. B. White   150
  1957: *The Cat in the Hat* by Dr. Seuss   150

Types of Animal Fantasy   **151**
  Type I: Anthropomorphic Animals in an All-Animal World   152
  Type II: Anthropomorphic Animals Coexisting with Humans   156
  Type III: Talking Animals in Natural Habitats   160
  Type IV: Realistic Animals with Human Thinking Ability   162

Summary   **164**

Chapter 8

Multicultural Literature   168

Evaluating Multicultural Literature   170

Categories of Multicultural Books   171
Culturally Neutral Books   171
Culturally Generic Books   172
Culturally Specific Books   172

Misrepresentation of Culture   173

Latino Literature by Alcione N. Ostorga   176

African American Literature by Sabrina A. Brinson   181

Asian American Literature by Ni Chang   186

Native American Literature   192

Literature of Religious Cultures   195

International Literature   196

Summary   200

Chapter 9

Contemporary Realistic Fiction   201

Evaluating Contemporary Fiction   202

Characteristics of Contemporary Realistic Fiction   202

Censorship by Jenifer Jasinski Schneider   203
Selecting versus Censoring   205

Themes   206

Bibliotherapy by Dan T. Ouzts and Mark J. Palombo   208
The Purpose of Bibliotherapy   209
Guidelines for Using Bibliotherapy   209

Families   212
Traditional Families   212
Nontraditional Families   214
Dysfunctional Families   215
Abandoned Children   215

Friendship   216

Humor   218

Adventure   219

Mystery   222

Social Reality   224
  War   224
  Homelessness   225
  Poverty and Child Labor   226
  Gangs and Crime   226
  Racism   226

Personal Issues   227

Animals   229

Summary   230

Chapter 10

Historical Fiction   234

Evaluating Historical Fiction   235

Characteristics of Historical Fiction   235

Biographic Historical Fiction   236

Researching Historical Fiction   238

Scott O'Dell Award   239

Periods Depicted in Historical Fiction   239
  Ancient Times   239
  Medieval Times   240
  Colonial Times   241
  Revolutionary Era   242
  Early Frontier Era   243
  Civil War Era   247
  Post–Civil War Frontier Era   248
  World War I Era   250
  Great Depression Era   251
  World War II Era   253
  Post–World War II Era   255
  Civil Rights Movement   255

Enhancing Curriculum with Historical Fiction by Sharon Smith   259

Summary   261

| *Part Three* | **Discovering the World through Nonfiction** | **264** |

Chapter 11

Biography and Autobiography   **264**

Evaluating Biography   266

Reading Biographies for Pleasure   267

Types of Biography   268
    Authentic Biography   268
    Fictionalized Biography   272

Forms of Biography   273
    Complete   273
    Partial   274
    Picture Book   275
    Collective   275

Integrating Biography with the Study of History   276

Enhancing Curriculum with Biography by Sharon Smith   276

Summary   **279**

Chapter 12

Informational Books   **281**

Evaluating Informational Books   283

Characteristics of Informational Books   284

Enhancing Curriculum with Informational Books   285

Building a Foundation for Content Area Reading   287

Graphic Organizers   288

Summary   **294**

Chapter 13

Poetry and Verse   **296**

Evaluating Poetry and Verse   298

Characteristics of Poetry and Verse   298
    Rhythm and Rhyme   298
    Language   299

Forms of Poetry   300

Poetry in Our Culture   302

NCTE Award for Excellence in Poetry for Children   303

Developing Love (or Hate) for Poetry   303
Ways to Teach Kids to Hate Poetry   303
Ways to Encourage Kids to Love Poetry   304

Types of Poetry Books   306

The Value of Poetry in the Classroom by Georgann C. Wyatt   306

Summary   309

Chapter 14

Teaching Reading through Literature   312

Reading Aloud to Children   313
Questioning Guidelines   314
Listening–Prediction Activity   314

Sustained Silent Reading   317

Reading Instruction with Trade Books   317

Children's Oral Reading   319
Individual Oral Reading   319
Group Oral Reading   320

Guided Silent Reading   321
Reading–Prediction Activity   321
Guided Reading Activity   322

Implementing a Yearlong Literature Program   325
Organizing Reading Instruction by Genres   325
Organizing Reading Instruction Thematically   326

Summary   332

Glossary   333

References   343

Name and Title Index   349

Subject Index   377

I first taught children's literature in 1980 when I was a graduate assistant at the University of Southern Mississippi, home of the extensive de Grummond collection of children's books. Through the years, I have searched for just the right textbook to teach children's literature. I wanted one that was brief, so my students could spend most of their reading time with children's books, and I wanted one that was limited to preschool and elementary literature, because a brief text could not adequately cover that realm and young adult literature as well. I also wanted a textbook that integrated pedagogy and applications my students could explore in class. I never found the elusive "just right" textbook, so I spent many years collecting books, information, and resources for my students. When I was asked to teach my course over the Internet, I decided to pull all my books, information, and resources into a "just right" textbook, which would be appropriate for both traditional instruction and distance learning courses.

Elementary Children's Literature: Infancy through Age 13 is designed as an introductory text for preservice teachers of elementary, early childhood, and special education. It is also appropriate for noneducation majors who are taking children's literature as a liberal arts requirement. Most of my noneducation students either are or intend to be parents, and I believe they will be more purposefully involved in their children's learning after reading this text. In writing this book, I did not assume readers had prior knowledge of contemporary children's literature or were fluent in "educationese." Each literary and education term is defined in the text the first time it is used and also appears in the end-of-book glossary. To further optimize readability, I wrote in a conversational tone, speaking directly to readers.

This textbook is organized around genres, and it includes a complete chapter on each major genre plus the subgenres of fiction. Genre chapters contain ample bibliographies of books in print, most with annotations. Each genre chapter also includes a list of evaluation criteria. In addition to the inclusion of multicultural literature in each chapter, there is a separate chapter on multicultural literature that is largely written by minority literature specialists who present inside views of their cultures and provide annotated lists of books *by* minority authors and illustrators (rather than just books *about* minorities).

Instructional and curriculum tie-ins are woven within the text, plus they appear in literature response boxes at strategic places in the chapters. At least one activity per chapter is a technology application. The final chapter, Teaching Reading through Literature, is a pedagogical overview of how teachers and parents can apply their knowledge of literature to help children grow in their language and reading abilities. Another unique feature of this book is the overview of the Dewey decimal system, which is discussed in the first chapter and reinforced with brief directions for locating books at the beginning of each genre chapter.

Several features of this text that are continued from the first edition make it especially appropriate for teachers and parents of preschool and elementary school children.

- The text is easy to read and comprehend.
- The information is relevant for teachers and parents—education majors and nonmajors.
- Curriculum tie-ins are woven within the text and also appear in Literature Response boxes, Literature and Technology boxes, and Issues in Literature boxes.
- A full chapter is dedicated to animal fantasy.
- A full chapter features early childhood picture books, and picture books are included in all the other chapters as well.
- A full chapter is devoted to teaching reading through literature.
- A chapter on the art of illustration provides information on the visual elements of artistic design, artistic styles, and artistic media and techniques.
- A glossary of more than 200 literary terms appears at the end of the book.

Features New to This Edition

- **End-of-chapter summaries** recap the most important information in each chapter, allowing readers to refine their schema of new information gained.
- A six-page insert of **full-color illustrations** allows readers to appreciate the art of illustration in children's books.
- In each genre chapter, I designate my **favorite books,** selected after reading more than 1,000 children's books, which can guide readers if they have difficulty deciding where to start reading.
- **Outstanding authors and illustrators** in each genre are featured in boxes that highlight their works, guiding students in finding exemplary works.

Supplements for Students

A companion website is available at www.pearsonhighered.com/anderson3e. It includes direct links for referenced Internet sites, a self-test, essay assignments, and an interactive version of each of the following activities: Character Continuum (p. 32), Story Mapping (p. 37), Cultural Literacy on Mythology (p. 91), Harry Potter Wizardspeak (p. 131), Readers Theater (p. 153), Mystery Clues (p. 222), Character Mapping (p. 253), Biography Timeline (p. 266), KWL Chart (p. 289), and Question Levels (p. 315).

Supplements for Teachers

A 110-item multiple-choice electronic test bank is available to instructors through their sales representatives. The companion course is available on CD in the Black-Board format for instructors whose institutions support this Internet course delivery platform. You may request the CD from me at the e-mail address below.

Acknowledgments

I thank Aurora Martínez Ramos, my Allyn and Bacon editor, for allowing me to prepare this third edition, and for providing valuable suggestions on what needed to be added.

I am indebted to my esteemed colleagues who wrote segments on their areas of expertise for this book, and I gratefully acknowledge them: Sabrina A. Brinson, Ni Chang, Melissa DuBrowa, Gloria Houston, Susan E. Knell, Mary Lou Morton, Alcione N. Ostorga, Dan T. Ouzts, Mark J. Palombo, Suzanne M. Flannery Quinn, Shannon L. Quinn, Janet C. Richards, Jenifer Jasinski Schneider, Sharon Smith, Donna Stewart, B. Ruth Sylvester, and Georgann C. Wyatt. This book is much stronger because of them.

I also acknowledge the following reviewers for their valuable ideas on how to improve this book: Traci P. Baxley, Florida Atlantic University; Linda S. Estes, St. Charles Community College; Susan Garness, Minot State University; Jill Hughes, Casper College; Vanessa J. Morris, Clarion University of Pennsylvania; Harold Nelson, Minot State University; and Nancy L. Peterson, Utah Valley State College.

—Nancy A. Anderson
naa@mail.usf.edu

Elementary Children's Literature

Introduction to the World of Children's Literature

1

This pen and ink illustration is an example of the surrealist style.

From *Alice's Adventures in Wonderland,* written by Lewis Carroll and illustrated by Sir John Tenniel.

*O*ne of my warmest childhood memories is of my mother reading *Miss Pickerell Goes to Mars* (MacGregor) to my older sister and me. We were in elementary school and quite capable of reading it ourselves, but we had grown accustomed to having our mother read to us each night before bedtime. Stories sounded so much better when she read them. Another happy memory is of my sixth-grade teacher, Mr. Conway, reading a chapter a day from *The Adventures of Tom Sawyer* (Twain). The books he read that year helped pass the afternoons in the hot portable classroom. Each day we begged him to read one more chapter or even just two more pages because we could not wait to find out what happened next.

Do you have similar memories of your parents' and teachers' reading to you? Because you are reading this book, you are most likely a teacher or a parent, or you intend to become a teacher or parent. This book will introduce you to the vast and wonderful world of children's literature, so you will be prepared to create such memories for the children in your classroom or your home. In this textbook, when I talk about *your children,* I am referring both to students and to your own children.

Within these pages I will acquaint you with numerous books appropriate for children from birth through age 13—the preschool and elementary school years. This textbook is intentionally brief; after all, most of your reading should be children's books—not a book *about* children's books. Therefore, I will not attempt to cover the many fabulous books available for middle school and high school students; several other good textbooks do focus on literature especially for adolescents and young adults (e.g., Donelson & Nilsen, 1997, and Brown & Stephens, 1995).

Defining Literature for Children

A few definitions will help outline the scope of this book. You might think *children's literature* could be easily defined as "books for kids." However, there are many different definitions of children's literature and even varying definitions for *literature* and *children!*

What is literature? Are all books literature? Are only stories considered literature? One definition of literature requires that the work be of good quality (Hillman, 1999). Hillman describes some signs of poor quality—stodgy writing, plots that are too predictable, too illogical, or too didactic. However, there is little agreement on what constitutes good quality. For example, the first time I taught an undergraduate multicultural literature course, I assigned *Ishi, Last of His Tribe* (Kroeber) for the biography reading. I selected it because the book had affected me deeply, moving me to tears when the last members of Ishi's family died. However, my students were nearly unanimous in their reaction to the book: "It stinks!" I learned that quality is in the eyes of the beholder.

I consider all books written for children to be literature—excluding works such as comic books, joke books, cartoon books, and nonfiction works that are not intended to be read from front to back, such as dictionaries, encyclopedias, and other reference material. It is true that some books are of better quality than others are, but one person cannot dictate to another what he or she ought to perceive as high quality. It is an individual perception, which will develop as you read this textbook and some of the children's books that I believe are high quality. (I'm hoping you don't think any of them stink!) To assist you, I describe many of the elements of quality children's literature in the next chapter. Additionally, the beginning of each genre chapter contains a set of evaluative questions you may ask yourself as you read the books. The information in Chapter 2 and the evaluation questions will help you refine your ever-developing judgment of quality books.

Some people consider children's literature to span the age group of birth through 18. However, no junior high or high school students I know consider themselves children. Therefore, I define literature for youth ages 13 to 18 as adolescent or **young adult literature,** and literature for youth from birth through age 13 as **children's literature.** Traditional elementary schools enroll children through sixth grade, and typically children are 12 or 13 years old when they complete elementary school.

It is easy to distinguish between a kid in elementary school and one in middle or junior high school; it is even easy to distinguish between a 13-year-old and a 14-year-old, simply by asking them. But it is not so easy to distinguish between children's and adolescent literature. The definitions and dividing line are arbitrary at best, and sometimes children will surprise you when they cross over these lines with their reading selections.

When my adult students ask me how to determine what age or grade level a book would be suited for, I usually tell them that any book a reader likes is appropriate for that reader. When they do not accept that answer (which is most of the time), I tell them that one rule of thumb (also known as the "quick and dirty" rule) is that the author often makes the main character the age of the intended audience. Like most quick and dirty rules, this one is not always true. For example, the best-selling book *Shane* (Schaefer) is narrated by a young boy. However, the book's subject matter and readability are suited for young adults, and there was a great motion picture made about the book in the 1950s that appealed to all ages.

Some book publishers print an approximate reading level somewhere in their books. For example, Bantam indicates the level in the upper section of the copyright page, and Scholastic puts it on the lower portion of the back cover. In either case, look for the letters RL (Reading Level) followed by a numeral. For example, RL2 indicates a second-grade reading level. The level is written in this code so as not to turn away a child in an older grade who might wish to read the book.

Keep in mind that reading levels are approximations determined by readability formulas that take into account only average lengths of words and sentences. Because the formulas cannot measure readers' prior knowledge of the content or interest in the subject, they are often invalid. For example, after my graduate students read *The Devil's Arithmetic* (Yolen), a book about the Holocaust, they engaged in a heated discussion about how early to introduce the book. Some argued sixth grade, but others said definitely not before eighth grade. Then one of the students raised her hand and said, "I read it in third grade." That was the end of that discussion.

I used to think that although some children were not able to read on their grade level, their interest level would be the same as that of their peers. One summer I took a group of preservice teachers to an inner-city school to tutor children in summer school. For the first session, tutors were to read aloud to the children, so I told my students to take four books on different reading levels and let the children choose which book they wanted to hear. When we collected the children from their classrooms, one stood out from the rest. He was about 12, and taller than his tutor; he looked like he might soon be able to play halfback for the Tampa Bay Buccaneers. "I hope his tutor brought some sports books," I thought to myself. But I later discovered that the book he picked for his tutor to read was Arnold Lobel's *Days with Frog and Toad!*

Therefore, in this text I do not attempt to pigeonhole books by assigning them to grade levels. The elementary children I have encountered like a wide range of books, from picture books to young adult novels. Assigning grade levels to books actually discourages children from reading many fine books. As mentioned, children are reluctant to select a book that has been labeled for a lower grade level. Worse, if children learn they are able to read only books designated for lower grade levels, their self-esteem is damaged, especially when their classmates find out. Often these children choose not to read at all rather than read a book on the primary level. When given varied choices, such as they find in a school or public library, children will select books appropriate to their interests and reading abilities. Read to your children from books that you like and from books they request. You will soon find out if the topic is not interesting because it is too babyish (or too sophisticated), and you can make another selection.

The Birth of Modern Children's Literature

Some schools of library science offer graduate courses on the history of children's literature. In one such school, a sage professor told me, "I don't know why they offer that course. I don't think children's literature has any history!" I laughed, but I did wonder why she said it. After all, every children's literature textbook I had read contained a chapter on history. When I asked the professor, she replied that children's literature as we know it today began in 1865 when Charles Dodgson (under the pen name of Lewis Carroll) wrote *Alice's Adventures in Wonderland*. It was the first novel written especially for children that was purely entertaining, with no instructional purpose. The book has a dreamlike quality: Alice follows a white rabbit down a rabbit hole and finds herself in a fantasyland where animals speak, objects come alive, and people change sizes.

What did children read before the publication of *Alice?* Children have always listened to and enjoyed folklore, and after the development of the printing press in the late 1400s, they were able to read folk literature. Because traditional literature is presented in Chapter 5, I will reserve the discussion of its history for that chapter, and briefly discuss the development of children's novels here.

Before 1865, children in the English-speaking world read and enjoyed adult novels, such as *Robinson Crusoe* (Defoe, 1719), *Gulliver's Travels* (Swift, 1726), *The Swiss Family Robinson* (Wyss, 1812), *A Christmas Carol* (Dickens, 1843), and *Journey to the Center of the Earth* (Verne, 1864). If you review the unabridged versions of these works, you will find them very advanced reading, so I think these books must have been read by older, more capable children who perhaps shared them with their younger siblings.

The earliest books written for children were entirely religious, instructional, or for the improvement of their morals and manners. In the latter half of the eighteenth century, however, an English publisher named John Newbery published books for children to *enjoy*. One such book, *The History of Little Goody Two Shoes* (Newbery, 1765), is considered the first novel written especially for children. Newbery's books were also highly moralistic, but at least someone had recognized that children needed to be entertained as well as indoctrinated. Young children read and enjoyed these books, of course, because there was little else for them to read. However, those early books would not entertain children today. When I reviewed some of them, I found them to contain all the flaws of "nonliterature" identified by Hillman: "stodgy writing, plots that are either too predictable or too illogical, and socially conscious themes that outweigh the slender story that supports them" (1999, p. 3).

Imagine the delight of children when they first read *Alice's Adventures in Wonderland*. "What made this story absolutely unique for its time was that it contained not a trace of a lesson or a moral. It was really made purely for enjoyment" (Huck, Hepler, Hickman, & Kiefer, 1997, p. 96). Charles Dodgson was a mathematics lecturer and ordained deacon at Christ Church College of Oxford University in England. He often entertained the young daughter (Alice Liddell) of the dean of his college by telling stories about Wonderland. Later he published the stories under the pseudonym of Lewis Carroll in *Alice's Adventures in Wonderland* and the sequel *Through the Looking-Glass and What Alice Found There* (1871).

Alice was the **prototype**—the first of its kind—of modern children's literature. Other good books that were widely read by children also appeared during the remainder of the nineteenth century. Not all were specifically intended for children, and certainly not all were free from moralism. (Even today, a common criticism of children's literature is that too many books are moralistic, with implicit lessons built in.) However, these books were primarily entertaining, and most contained child characters. Box 1.1 presents a partial list of the books considered **children's classics**—not because they were all written for children, but because the children of the nineteenth century read and treasured them. These books are classics because they are still in print, and readers still enjoy them more than a century after their first publication.

Box 1.1

Children's Classics of the Nineteenth Century

1812	*The Swiss Family Robinson* by Johann Wyss
1843	*A Christmas Carol* by Charles Dickens
1864	*Journey to the Center of the Earth* by Jules Verne
1865	*Alice's Adventures in Wonderland* by Lewis Carroll (Charles Dodgson)
1865	*Hans Brinker or the Silver Skates* by Mary Mapes Dodge
1868	*Little Women* by Louisa May Alcott
1869	*Twenty Thousand Leagues under the Sea* by Jules Verne
1871	*Through the Looking-Glass* by Lewis Carroll (Charles Dodgson)
1872	*Around the World in Eighty Days* by Jules Verne
1876	*The Adventures of Tom Sawyer* by Mark Twain (Samuel Clemens)
1877	*Black Beauty* by Anna Sewell
1883	*Treasure Island* by Robert Louis Stevenson
1883	*The Adventures of Pinocchio* by Carlo Collodi (Carlo Lorenzini)
1884	*Heidi* by Johanna Spyri
1886	*Kidnapped* by Robert Louis Stevenson
1886	*Little Lord Fauntleroy* by Frances H. Burnett
1894	*The Jungle Book* by Rudyard Kipling
1900	*The Wonderful Wizard of Oz* by L. Frank Baum

Responding to Literature

Comparing Book and Movie Versions of a Classic   Read one of the children's classics and list the elements of the story that might have attracted children in the nineteenth century. Most of the classics have been made into movies (some several times). View a video of the story and compare it to the book. Make a Venn diagram (see Chapter 12, Figure 12.4) showing the similarities and differences. Determine whether the book or the movie would be most appealing to children today, and explain why.

Because of their age, all the classic books are in the **public domain,** meaning they are not protected by copyright laws. Therefore, you need to be cautious when you check them out of the library or purchase them because there are many poorly adapted or condensed editions on the market. However, the full texts of these classics are accessible online for viewing or downloading at www.gutenberg.net.

Integrating Literature and Technology

eBook Readers   Just what do people do after they download an electronic book (or eBook) from Project Gutenberg or an Internet bookstore? Reading it on a computer screen might be hard on the eyes, and even a laptop would limit its portability. Printing it out would not only take time and money for ink and paper but would be bulky compared to a paperback edition. Today there are lightweight reading devices that hold hundreds of books and permit thousands of page views before the batteries run out. The newest eBook readers provide sharp text, readable from nearly any angle and in dim light (just like the printed page). Amazon's new wireless reading device, the Kindle, allows readers to purchase and download books from Amazon's online store in less than a minute, anywhere there is cell phone reception! Audio books are also becoming increasingly popular. Using Google or another search engine, type in *free children's audio books* to find a plethora of stories your children will enjoy.

Book Illustrations

The development of illustrated books for children is also an interesting story. Children's books were usually illustrated with crude woodcuts, if at all, until Sir John Tenniel delightfully illustrated *Alice* in pen and ink in 1865. That same year, a talented English printer named Edmund Evans perfected the photographic engraving process and solicited gifted artists to create the first colored illustrations for children's books. Among the artists he encouraged and supported were Walter Crane, Randolph Caldecott, and Kate Greenaway. The types of books they illustrated included traditional literature, verse, and alphabet books. As you can imagine, Evans's beautiful books were tremendously popular, and they ushered in the modern era of color illustrations in children's books, something we take for granted today.

Kate Greenaway was perhaps the most popular of the three artists, judging by the sheer volume of books sold. Her scenes of happy children in peaceful landscapes charmed the public. (See her illustration at the beginning of Chapter 2.) Greenaway was so popular that dressmakers began styling children's clothing to emulate the dress of the children in her pictures. However, Randolph Caldecott, with his unique way of depicting humor and lively characters in action, is often recognized as the most talented of the three artists.

The nineteenth century produced some lovely illustrated books; however, the pictures served only as decorations. The modern picture storybook did not emerge until the beginning of the twentieth century in England. Six publishers rejected Beatrix Potter's manuscript of *The Tale of Peter Rabbit,* but she was determined to see her illustrated story made into "a little book for little hands." In 1901 Potter withdrew her own savings of 11 pounds and printed 450 copies of the book, which became the prototype of modern picture storybooks. One of the unique qualities of this book was created when Potter matched her illustrations with the text, using the pictures to share in the storytelling process. You probably remember the main character, Peter, the errant young rabbit who—against his mother's admonition—goes to eat in Mr. McGregor's garden and is nearly caught and eaten himself.

The copies Potter had printed quickly sold and gained the attention of Frederick Warne and Company, who published the second and many subsequent printings. In *Peter Rabbit,* and in her twenty-two other books that followed, Potter used clear watercolors to illustrate woodland animals dressed as ordinary country folk. Her union of enchanting stories with expertly drawn pictures became models for the authors and illustrators of the numerous picture storybooks that followed.

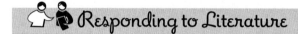

Responding to Literature

Analyzing Potter's Illustrations   Compare photographs of real rabbits with Potter's illustrations in *The Tale of Peter Rabbit.* Read a biography of Potter, such as *At Home with Beatrix Potter* (Denyer), and discover why she was able to draw the animals with such anatomical accuracy.

The Genres of Literature

Many thousands of good children's books are available from libraries, stores, and book clubs, so people often do not know how to begin learning about literature. Literature is best studied if it is organized into categories called *genres* (zhän'rəz). Genres are groupings of books with similar style, form, or content. The term *genres* also applies to other types of media, such as music, movies, plays, television shows, and artwork.

Although one can classify and study literature according to genres, not all books fit into one and only one category. Some books fit well in two categories, and some books fit into none! For example, I am never sure whether to shelve my copy of *The Very Hungry Caterpillar* (Carle) with animal fantasy or counting books. And my copy of *Miss Nelson Is Missing* (Allard) has been moved several times because it has aspects of both realistic fiction and fantasy.

Not everyone organizes literature genres in exactly the same way, but a common organization is outlined in Box 1.2 along with the chapters in which the genres are presented in this textbook. I have categorized literature into six major genres: early childhood books, traditional literature, fiction, biography and autobiography, informational books, and poetry and verse. Notice that some of the genres have subcategories. Four chapters of this textbook are devoted to the subcategories of fiction, and the remaining five genres are covered in one chapter each.

Box 1.2

Literary Genres of Children's Literature

Early Childhood Books	**Chapter 4**	**Fiction**	
Concept		Fantasy	**Chapter 6**
Alphabet		Animal fantasy	**Chapter 7**
Counting		Contemporary fiction	**Chapter 9**
General		Historical fiction	**Chapter 10**
Pattern picture books			
Wordless picture books		**Biography and Autobiography**	**Chapter 11**
Traditional Literature	**Chapter 5**	**Informational Books**	**Chapter 12**
Myths			
Fables		**Poetry and Verse**	**Chapter 13**
Ballads and folk songs			
Legends			
Tall tales			
Fairy tales			
Traditional rhymes			

The Dewey Decimal System

Libraries also use genres to organize books on shelves so people can easily find them. Although nearly all university and other large libraries now use the Library of Congress classification system, most school and public libraries still use the **Dewey decimal system,** named after the Columbia University librarian Melvil Dewey, who in 1876 pioneered this practical system to facilitate classification of books.

Have you ever been frustrated because you made a thorough card catalogue or computerized search, only to find that the book you wanted was not on the shelf? By learning the simple Dewey decimal system, you can walk to the appropriate section and see what books are available. For example, if you need a children's biography of Dr. Martin Luther King, Jr., you can walk to the section of the library where the biographies for children are shelved—J920. Then you can quickly scan the books until you get to the *K*s, where books about King are located.

A short overview of the Dewey decimal system follows, and more specific information is provided at the beginning of each genre chapter.

The Dewey decimal system gets its name because books are shelved by subjects that are grouped into ten main classes. See Box 1.3 for the Dewey decimal system of classification. Each class has ten subdivisions, and each subdivision may be broken down further by adding a decimal point and more numbers. This allows very

---

Box 1.3

Dewey Decimal System of Classification

000–099   General Works
Computers, encyclopedias, reference books, periodicals

100–199   Philosophy and Psychology
Personal improvement

200–299   Religion and Mythology
Mythology, Christianity, Judaism, Islam, Bible stories

300–399   Social Sciences
Traditional literature, family, government, community life, conservation, transportation, law, holidays, costumes, etiquette

400–499   Language
Dictionaries, English language, other languages

500–599   Natural Sciences and Mathematics
Mathematics, astronomy, physics, chemistry, earth science, dinosaurs and prehistoric life, trees, flowers, animals

600–699   Applied Sciences, Useful Arts, and Technology
Medicine, health, diseases, human body, safety, machines and inventions, space and aeronautics, gardening, manufacturing, building, pets, sewing

700–799   Fine Arts, Sports, and Recreations
Architecture, coins, pottery, drawing, handicrafts, painting, photography, music, hobbies, games, sports, magic, "how to" books

800–899   Literature
Fiction, poetry, plays

900–999   History, Geography, Biography, and Travel
Biography, travel, atlases, United States history, world history, geography

---

specific subjects to be shelved together. The following example illustrates this very well:

973	United States History
973.7	Civil War
973.73	Battles of the Civil War
973.738	Appomattox

Dewey categorized fiction works in the 800 section; for example, American fiction was 813, and British fiction was 823. Today, the vast majority of school and public libraries have a separate section for fiction in which books are shelved alphabetically by authors' last names. Storybooks or juvenile novels are typically shelved in a section titled *J FIC,* and all the subcategories—fantasy, science fiction, animal fantasy, contemporary realistic fiction, and historical fiction—are intermingled.

Picture books are found in a special section. The **spine** of a picture book—the part you see when it is on the shelf—usually has an *E* with the first letters of the author's last name underneath. (*E* is supposed to stand for *Easy,* but it should really stand for *Everyone* because everyone can enjoy picture books.) The books are typically arranged alphabetically by the author's last name. In busy public libraries, however, you may encounter the picture books in bins, one for each letter of the alphabet. Be aware that young children are sometimes quite fickle with picture books, pulling out one to inspect it and then tossing it back, not necessarily where they found it. Therefore, you may find books in the wrong bins. Even in the most meticulous school libraries, where books are lined up neatly on the shelves, I have heard librarians groan about the hours they spend reshelving misplaced books.

Book Formats

Genre has to do with the content of a book—what it is about—but there are other ways to categorize and compare books. One example is **book format**—the way a book is put together or the way it looks. I have already used several terms that refer to format—for example, *picture book.* What is the difference between a picture book and a storybook? And is there such a thing as a picture storybook?

Picture Books

Norton (1999) explained that "most children's books are illustrated, but not all illustrated children's books are picture books" (p. 214). What makes a picture book distinctive is that it conveys its message through a series of pictures with only a small amount of text (or none at all). The illustrations are as important as—or more important than—the text in conveying the message. Books that have no text at all are called *wordless picture books* or textless books. Picture books for young children, including wordless books, are presented in Chapter 4, which deals with early childhood books such as concept books and pattern books.

Picture storybooks are picture books with a plot, with the text and illustrations equally conveying the story line. "In a picture storybook, pictures must help to tell the story, showing the action and expressions of the characters, the changing settings, and the development of the plot" (Huck et al., 1997, p. 198). Most people simply call these picture books as well, not drawing a distinction on whether the text conveys a story. In fact, the umbrella term *picture book* is commonly used to refer to any book that has more illustrations than text.

Picture books of all kinds are easy to recognize because of their size and length. They are usually larger than storybooks, and their shapes are varied. The number of pages is fairly uniform. The majority of picture books (excluding unusual formats such as board books or pop-up books) have thirty-two pages, counting both sides of the leaves and including all the pages that come before and after the story. Books of this length typically do not have page numbers. Longer picture books have forty-eight or sixty-four pages. The length of all books is usually a multiple of sixteen because of the way presses print the paper.

Some children's literature specialists combine all picture books in a separate genre and study them as one vast group. However, when people refer to a picture book, they are usually referring to its format. It looks so distinctively different that I could hold up a picture book and a juvenile novel across the room, and you could easily distinguish between the two without looking inside either one. Though all picture books have a distinctive format, they have content as well, and the content can be categorized by genre. To do justice to this vast and appealing group, I present a selection of picture books in each of the genre chapters.

Easy-to-Read Books

If you selected a hundred picture storybooks at random and reviewed each for the length and complexity of its sentences and the difficulty and number of syllables of its words, you would see that most of these books are intended to be read *to* rather than *by* young children (Chamberlain & Leal, 1999). However, a format specifically designed to give beginning readers successful independent reading experiences has the generic name **easy-to-read books**. Some publishers have their own trademarked names for their easy-to-read series—for example, "I Can Read" and "Ready to Read" books.

The uniqueness of easy-to-read books makes them simple to recognize. First, because they are read independently by children, the books are smaller than regular picture books. In addition, the pages look very different. The illustrations are designed to give clues to the meanings of the words, but the pictures are smaller and less profuse, allowing the text to take up a greater proportion of each page. A liberal amount of white space is achieved by larger print, more space between lines, and lines that end with the phrase rather than running flush to the right margin. Perhaps the most significant characteristic of easy-to-read books is the restricted vocabulary. Usually fewer than 250 different words appear in a book, and these are arranged in short simple sentences, often with word patterns, repeated text, and even rhyming lines to make decoding new words easier. The difficulty of the vocabulary is also controlled, with the majority of the words having only one syllable.

Beginning readers tire easily, and their comprehension is taxed when they have to remember the plot of a book that they are not reading straight through. Authors of many easy-to-read books take this into consideration and break their books into separate stories or short episodic chapters. These books have a table of contents with the title of each story or chapter. Young children gain experience in using a table of contents, and they feel accomplishment in reading a book with "chapters." Young readers often call these "chapter books," though they are more aptly called transitional books because they are a bridge between picture books and storybooks.

The relatively short history of this format is interesting. After twenty years of publishing picture storybooks for children, Theodore Seuss Geisel (Dr. Seuss) published the first easy-to-read book, *The Cat in the Hat,* in 1957. Else Holmelund Minarik's *Little Bear* immediately followed. Both authors wrote several sequels to those early books. Other authors who have enjoyed great success with this format include Arnold Lobel with *Frog and Toad Are Friends* and Cynthia Rylant with *Henry and Mudge: The First Book of Their Adventures*. Both of these books were also followed by popular sequels.

The majority of the early easy-to-read books were animal fantasy, but they are now available in all genres. Good stories, simple text, and well-matched illustrations make these books appealing to beginning readers of all ages. Remember the 12-year-old halfback from earlier in this chapter? At the beginning of the summer, he read at the primer level; by the end of the summer, he could independently read the Frog and Toad book he picked out the first day.

Illustrated Books

As children grow from infancy to adolescence, they will notice that the books targeted for them have increasingly fewer illustrations. Books for very young children are primarily illustrations with little or no text (picture books). As children develop, books made for them have illustrations that convey part of the message, but the text is needed for the complete story line (picture storybooks). As they begin to read independently, their books have illustrations that add to the story, but there are fewer of them, and the text itself could stand alone. These books are called **illustrated books**. Though the illustrations depict what is happening in the story, they do not provide new information. The text is clearly more important than the illustrations (Glazer, 1997).

Graphic Novels

Graphic novels are not new, especially for adults. However, in recent years, they have become enormously popular with children and adolescents. The definition of graphic novels is still evolving, but as a literature format, I define them as novels whose stories are told through a combination of text and illustrations. They are longer than picture books (about 64 to 128 pages), and instead of full-page illustrations, the story is most often presented in illustrated panels similar to comic books. Most graphic novels are illustrated with the same artistic quality of modern picture books, and some fans of this format even consider them a unique art form. Though many graphic novels are fantasy, they can be found in all genres of literature, and the tone can be humorous or serious.

The text of graphic novels presents a complete story line with a distinct plot, whereas comic book series and the Japanese version of graphic novels called *manga* both contain episodic stories. A single comic book or *manga* might start a story, begin in the middle of things, or end a story. Readers cannot read just one to gain the whole story. Conversely, graphic novels may have sequels, but each contains a new, complete plot. Unlike comic books, graphic novels are typically bound in longer and more durable formats and are available in bookstores and libraries. Like other novels, graphic novels are given an International Standard Book Number (ISBN), which further differentiates them from serials, such as magazines and comic books.

Some graphic novels, such as *Diary of a Wimpy Kid: A Novel in Cartoons* (Kinney), have appeared on coveted best-seller lists. Additionally, some graphic novels are based on traditional (text only) best-selling novels. A visual learner or a reluctant reader may be more likely to pick up the graphic version of a story than the original version that is several hundred pages long. Following is a list of recommended graphic novels (see the end-of-chapter Books Cited section for publication information).

Colfer, Eoin, & Andrew Donkin. *Artemis Fowl: The Graphic Novel.*
Holm, Jennifer L. *Babymouse: Heartbreaker.*
Jacques, Brian. *Redwall: The Graphic Novel.*
Kinney, Jeff. *Diary of a Wimpy Kid: A Novel in Cartoons.*
MacHale, D. J., & Carla Speed McNeil. *The Merchant of Death: Pendragon Graphic Novel.*
Nickel, Scott. *Billions of Bats: A Buzz Beaker Brainstorm.*
Pilkey, Dav. *The Adventures of Captain Underpants: An Epic Novel.*
Rogers, Gregory. *Midsummer Knight.*
Selznick, Brian. *The Invention of Hugo Cabret: A Novel in Words and Pictures.*
Siegel, Siena Cherson. *To Dance: A Ballerina's Graphic Novel.*
Trondheim, Lewis. *Tiny Tyrant.*

📖 Issues in Literature

Are Graphic Novels Real Literature?   Read one of the books in the preceding section and tell whether you think it is more like a comic book or more like a novel.

Make an argument for or against graphic novels being considered true literature.

Chapter Books

As children approach adolescence, the books targeted for them become longer and have even fewer illustrations. Sometimes the only illustration is the picture on the book jacket or cover. This format is commonly referred to as the **juvenile novel** or junior novel. Of course, children do not restrict their reading to fiction novels. They also read nonfiction works such as biography and informational books; I call nonfiction books in this category **chapter books**. This term connotes that they are lengthy enough for the author to divide into chapters. Lynch-Brown and Tomlinson (1999) describe the nonfiction chapter book as a format that features a large amount of text organized into chapters. In nonfiction chapter books, graphics and illustrations are common but are still less important than the text. Almost all biographies, with the exception of picture book biographies, appear in this format.

Hardcover Books

So far, I have primarily discussed the format of books in terms of size, shape, ratio of illustrations to text, and difficulty of text. Format also refers to aspects of the physical makeup of a book such as the quality of binding and paper. The publishers' hardcover editions are the highest-quality books. Covers are usually constructed of heavy-duty cardboard covered with quality glossy paper. The pages of the book are sewn together, and they are held inside the cover by sturdy **endpapers** that are glued to the inside of the front and back covers. Designs that pertain to the book's subject or theme colorfully decorate the endpapers of many hardcover picture books.

Hardcover books are durable, and the high-quality paper ensures the best color reproduction of illustrations. This is the best format for books that are going to be read repeatedly, such as picture books. However, hardcover books are expensive, and it is a major loss if classroom copies become misplaced or "permanently borrowed." Also, from a teacher's practical point of view, they are heavy to carry and take up a lot of shelf space.

Paperback Books

Most books are first issued in hardcover and later are issued in paperback to reach a new market of buyers looking for less costly books. Usually the pages of softcover books are made of somewhat lower-quality paper. Instead of being sewn, the pages are glued together and then glued to a stiff paper cover. Quality paperback books can be identified because they have a spine. That is, when you place them on the shelf, you can see the back edge of the book where the title and names of author, illustrator, and publisher are printed. Paperback editions can have their shelf life extended with Mylar book tape that holds the binding together. Paperback is probably the best format for juvenile novels and chapter books that children may read only once.

Several popular book clubs, such as Carnival, Scholastic, Troll, and Trumpet, are marketed in schools nationwide. Teachers distribute order forms to their pupils and then collect and tally the orders. The ordering process can be time-consuming, but the companies are liberal with free books for the teachers. Because of this, many teachers have built large classroom libraries without ever purchasing a book. Book club editions are the least costly because they are mass-produced. Quality of paper diminishes with the price, and the colors in illustrations are not always true to the originals. Picture books are usually stapled in the center, rather than being glued with a spine; juvenile novels and chapter books are often smaller in size, which results in smaller print. However, book clubs have made great literature available and affordable for all children. An added bonus is that some new books appear in a book club edition long before the bookstores get them in the paperback edition because authors sell hardcover rights, paperback rights, and book club rights separately to publishers.

Grocery Store Books

One year I taught in a paraprofessional training program at a community college. All the students were in their 20s or 30s, and most had children. One of their early assignments was to select a children's book, read it to the class, and ask appropriate questions. One by one the students stood up and read books that were about cartoon, comic book, TV, and movie characters. Not one student had selected a quality children's book—what kids often call "library books." I realized they would need guidance in selecting appropriate children's books to use in classrooms.

These future paraprofessionals had selected **grocery store books,** which incidentally can now be found in drugstores and large discount chain stores as well. They are much less likely to be found in libraries or bookstores. A large portion of these books are called **merchandise books** in the publishing trade because their primary purpose is to sell something—movie tickets, dolls and toys, backpacks, admission to theme parks, and countless other things. Merchandise books are so ubiquitous that a majority of parents surveyed in twenty-two states said these were the types of books they read to their preschool children on a regular basis (Warren, Prater, & Griswold, 1990). Books about Care Bears, Smurfs, and Star Wars were often named in the survey.

There is no doubt these books are popular. Golden Press (publisher of Little Golden Books) published five of the top eight books on the list of all-time best-selling children's hardcover books (Roback, 2001). These best-sellers are *The Poky Little Puppy* (Lowrey), *Tootle* (Crampton), *Pat the Bunny* (Kunhardt), *Saggy Baggy Elephant* (Jackson & Jackson), and *Scuffy the Tugboat* (Crampton). Perhaps you remember reading these books as a child. They represent some of the better stories that are published by Golden Press. They do not have cartoon characters, and their purpose is to entertain rather than to sell something (other than books, of course). When I was a child, my mother bought these books at the grocery store for 25 cents. They cost much more than that now, but when you compare their format to that of a regular hardcover book, you can see the differences in quality. The edges of the cardboard cover are exposed, and the cover is stapled to the pages, rather than being sewn and attached by endpapers. More importantly, I hope you will notice the differences in the quality of story and illustrations as you begin to read the books introduced to you in this textbook.

Why do these grocery store books, including merchandise books, sell so well? Perhaps it is because they are readily accessible; most families include someone who goes to the grocery store each week. In addition, these books are relatively inexpensive—partly because of the way they are constructed, but also because of the mediocre quality of the content. There is no doubt they appeal to young children, especially when their characters are familiar faces from Saturday morning cartoon shows or the latest Disney movie.

May (1980) provides a harsh criticism of Disney books. She believes that

> Disney's greatest contributions to American popular culture lie in his use of total merchandising techniques to promote cute, stereotyped characters, his use of familiar children's literature titles, and his misuse of those books' plots, themes, and characterization in order to create a product. (p. 213)

My adult students often complain when I tell them they cannot use grocery store books for their assignments in my literature or reading courses. To help them understand my reasoning, I use the following analogy.

Imagine that when you were a young child, every evening after supper (or dinner, if you lived in the South), your parents gave you a chocolate cupcake with white frosting that they bought at the grocery store. It was delicious! Each evening, you could hardly wait to finish your peas and carrots so you could get your cupcake. It was something you could count on 365 days a year, and you loved those chocolate cupcakes with white frosting.

Now imagine that when you started school, you went to the cafeteria to get your lunch on the first day, and when you got your tray, you found spice cake for dessert. Every day there was something different. One day it was banana pudding and another day cherry pie. Once, when your class went on a field trip to the mall, you visited a bakery. This bakery sold carrot cake with cream cheese frosting, German chocolate cake with pecan and coconut frosting, beautifully decorated white cakes, cheesecake, key lime pie, apple pie, and numerous little pastries with a variety of fillings and toppings. The teacher let you go in the store and buy whatever you wanted.

That grocery store cupcake satisfied you before you knew there were other desserts to be had, but after you found out about the abundance and variety of freshly baked cakes and pies and pastries, the grocery store cupcake was never quite as satisfying again.

By the same token, I believe that after you indulge yourself in quality literature, you will never be satisfied with grocery store books again. I must add one disclaimer. In recent years I have seen some grocery stores, drugstores, and large discount chain stores carry regular books along with merchandise books that tie in to cartoons, comic books, TV shows, and movies. As your knowledge of quality literature grows, you will be able to distinguish the good from the mediocre or poor, and you might pick up some great bargains in the discount stores.

Series Books

Have you ever read a book that was so good you felt disappointed when you were finished because you wanted to know what would happen next to the characters? That is why authors write **sequels**. When a sequel to a sequel is written, it makes a **trilogy**. If the author writes a fourth related book, it becomes a **series**. All the books in a series will have some unifying element, such as characters or theme. Series also exist among nonfiction books, such as the biographies published by Crowell. Some series are delightful and of high literary quality, among them J. K. Rowling's Harry Potter series and Barbara Park's Junie B. Jones series. Many series, however, are written according to a formula, and they vary only slightly from one book to the next.

Formula books are often found for sale with the grocery store books. Perhaps that can partially explain their enormous success—they are readily accessible to parents and children. Formula series include Nancy Drew (Stratemeyer), Hardy Boys (Stratemeyer), American Girl (Pleasant), Magic Tree House (Random), and Mary-Kate and Ashley (HarperEntertainment). Despite their mediocre quality, formula books tend to have uplifting themes, and these books may help reluctant readers discover pleasure in reading—if the books are actually read. There is indication that some children merely collect series books as they would Barbie dolls or "any other childhood collectible—amassed for the sheer joy of having the latest one, counting them up, or trading them" (Mesmer, 1998, p. 108). Another genuine criticism is that even "'modern' serial books continue to exude a Dick and Jane white bread aura" in which the theme, tone, language, culture, and recurring heroes are not identifiable to any minority group (Oldrieve, 2003, p. 18).

📖 Issues in Series Books

What Should Children Be Allowed to Read? Young children like to hear their favorite picture books read again and again. Adults like to hear their favorite songs and pieces of music numerous times. When older kids read formula books, they are encountering familiar characters and themes, and they are not so different from the young children and adults who have favorite works they wish to enjoy more than once.

Make arguments both for and against allowing children to read as many formula books as they desire.

However, educators and concerned parents want their children to read books that are entertaining *and* enlightening, and often series books are only entertaining (Hillman, 1999). Perhaps the best way to teach children to be discriminating readers is to read good literature to them and help them select books from the library, rather than from a grocery store. Generate discussion comparing a strong central character in a quality book to a flat one that shows no growth or change throughout the series, such as Kristy Thomas in the Baby-sitters Club or Nancy Drew in the long-running mystery series. Eventually, most young readers will become saturated with the predictability of the series and move on to other books. But in the meantime children miss a lot of wonderful literature and, depending on their age when they outgrow the series books, they may then feel that the great books seem too childish.

👥 Responding to Literature

Analyzing Series Books Read two books from any popular children's series. Describe the formula used by the author. List the elements of the books that children would find appealing. Then list several elements or characteristics that might cause literature critics to say the books are of poor literary quality.

The Value of Children's Literature

You now have a basic understanding of children's literature. As you begin to read the children's books that are discussed in this textbook, I believe you will find most of them enjoyable for children and adults alike. Children are never too young to be read to. In fact, some mothers start reading to their children before they are born. What is remarkable is that research indicates unborn babies hear their mothers and react to their voices (see DeCasper, Lecanuet, Busnel, & Granier-Deferre, 1994). In addition to building a bond between parent and child, daily reading to preschool children may be the single most important thing parents can do to improve their children's chances for success in school. Children's book editor Janet Schulman (1998) described the educational and emotional benefits of reading to children with her metaphor that "books help give children a leg up on the ladder of life" (p. vi). Of course, nurturing parents should continue to read to their children after they start school and for as long as they will listen—which, if all goes well, will be throughout the elementary school years.

Children are never too old to be read to either. I remember working with a talented student teacher who was placed in a challenging classroom of sixth graders, all of whom had been identified as being at risk of failing or dropping out of school. The student teacher did an excellent job with them, though they were often rowdy. One day when the classroom teacher was out, I walked into the classroom, and the first thing I noticed was that I could hear only *one* voice, and the kids were all awake! In fact, they had their eyes glued on the student teacher, who was reading them *Stone Soup* (Brown), a picture book fairy tale.

Unfortunately, not all parents read to their children on a regular basis. First, not all parents read. Also, some parents must work more than one job, leaving little time to read to their children. Others have the time and ability to read aloud, yet do not see the advantages—both affective and cognitive—of reading to children. Some parents are eager to read to their children but do not know where to start, so they resort to grocery store books. I recommend reviewing *Best Books for Beginning Readers* (Gunning, 1998) and *Read to Me: Raising Kids Who Love to Read* (Cullinan, 1992). These books and others at your library or bookstore will not only provide descriptions of numerous quality children's books but also tell you how to maximize your reading time.

Following are a few of the specific benefits children derive from reading and listening to books:

- Strengthening a bond between the child and adult reader
- Experiencing the pleasure of escaping into a fantasy world or an exciting adventure
- Developing a favorable attitude toward books as an enrichment to their lives
- Stimulating cognitive development
- Gaining new vocabulary and syntax
- Becoming familiar with story and text structures
- Stimulating and expanding their imaginations
- Stretching attention spans
- Empathizing with other people's feelings and problems
- Learning ways to cope with their own feelings and problems
- Widening horizons as they vicariously learn about the world
- Developing an interest in new subjects and hobbies
- Understanding the heritage of their own and other cultures
- Acquiring new knowledge about nature
- Bringing history to life
- Stimulating aesthetic development through illustrations
- Exploring artistic media used in illustrations

Some educators teach reading through trade books—children's literature—instead of using the reading textbooks known as **basal readers** (see Chapter 14). In such classrooms, all the children may read the same book, or they may select their own literature to read. Some teachers provide a list of books from which children can choose. Children's literature is surely more interesting to read than basal readers, which typically contain only excerpts of books or picture book stories minus most of the pictures, and children's literature is definitely more interesting than the basal reading programs' workbooks, worksheets, and board work (read "bored work"). Children learn to read by reading, and what better for children to read than the literature created just for them?

Prereading Schema Building

In this last section, I introduce you to a strategy that will help readers better comprehend and enjoy the books they read. It is grounded in reader response theory, which posits that in order to interact with text, the reader must bring something to the reading process. This something is called **schema**, "a system of cognitive structures stored in memory that are abstract representations of events, objects, and relationships in the world" (Harris & Hodges, 1995, p. 227). **Schemata** (the plural of *schema*) are more generally referred to as background experience or prior knowledge. In order to comprehend (and therefore fully enjoy) a book, readers must be able to integrate or connect new information in the text with their networks of prior knowledge. Reading then becomes an active process of constructing meaning.

If children have little or no prior knowledge of the subject of a book, comprehension and enjoyment are seriously impaired. Perhaps you can relate to the following story.

My eighth-grade English teacher assigned the class to read *Ivanhoe* (Scott), a book with a medieval setting first published in 1820. My library copy had no illustrations—not even on the cover! While slowly reading the first page, I asked myself, "What the heck are they talking about?" I reread the first page. I knew the meanings of nearly all the words, but I could not decipher the sentences. I looked at the back and saw the book was 352 pages! In tears, I went to my older (and smarter) sister and said, "I can't understand this!" She gave me a brief description of the plot and told me to reread the first page once more. This time, when I started reading, I knew where and when the story took place and who the main characters were, and things began to make sense. When I finally finished the book, I actually liked it!

The Process of Schema Building

I had been overwhelmed because my English teacher had failed to help her students build a schema to enable them to comprehend *Ivanhoe*. Fortunately, I had an older sister to collaborate with, but not all the kids in my class had someone to help them. Teaching readers to construct their own schema before reading is quick and easy, and I suggest you use it for all the books you read to your children. Most importantly, I hope you will teach this process to your children and encourage them to use it each time they read a new book. It is probably the single most important thing you can do to enhance children's understanding and appreciation of a fiction book. I call it the **prereading** schema-building process, and it can be used with either picture books or juvenile novels. The purpose is to activate the reader's prior knowledge as well as to build a scaffold for new knowledge such as vocabulary and historical or cultural setting.

I. Begin at the End. Please, do not read the end of the book first! However, starting with the last text page, look at each page until you reach the back cover. These last pages often contain critical information for understanding the book, such as glossaries, maps, or afterwords that will provide helpful information you can refer to while reading. You also may find information about the author. Usually books do not mention that these aids are provided at the end. I have had students who struggled to read a work of historical fiction that contained many foreign words, such as *Ishi, Last of His Tribe* (Kroeber), only to discover the glossary after finishing the book.

II. Cover the Cover. Sometimes information such as a brief biographical sketch of the author is printed on the inside back cover of a paperback book, so always look. If nothing is there, turn the book over and look at the back cover. Most paperbacks will have a short synopsis of the story there. The ending is not revealed, but information such as the name and age of the main character and where and when the story takes place is usually provided. Sometimes there are excerpts from reviews, and these may add a bit of additional information, such as the theme. (On hardcover books, the synopsis and reviews are on the inside flaps of the book jacket. Information about the author and illustrator is also provided there.)

Next, look at the front cover. On a paperback book, or on the jacket of a hardcover book, you should find an illustration. If the book jacket is missing, turn to the first illustration in the book. Think like a detective and look for clues as to what the story might be about. Here are some questions that will help you make predictions:

- What clues can you find that tell about the setting of this story—where and when it happened?
- What do you think the characters might be doing?
- What does the title tell you about the story? Predict what kind of story it might be (fantasy, realistic, humorous).
- What do you think might happen in this story? Why do you think so?
- What do you think the illustrations or designs on the colored endpapers or title page mean? What additional information about the story can be found in these illustrations?
- Do these clues remind you of events in your own life or events in other books you have read?

III. Finish at the Front. The final stage of building a story schema is reviewing all the front matter—the pages that precede the first text page. Locate the title page that shows the title, author, and publisher. The back of this page lists publication information, including the copyright date. (In a few picture books, the copyright page is at the end.) There may be more than one edition of the book, so look for the year of original publication. This gives you an idea of when the author wrote the story. It is sometimes important to know the decade in which a book was written—particularly in the case of contemporary fiction, which may not seem contemporary to readers who are younger than the book. Look for a dedication or acknowledgment that might contain clues about the author. Some authors include a foreword that provides information to help readers understand and enjoy the book. Reading titles of chapters may provide an overview.

The information you gain by previewing the end pages, the back and front covers, and the front matter should give you enough background to allow your full enjoyment of the book. After reading the first few pages, stop and confirm or disprove your earlier predictions.

Modeling the Process

The following is an example of a think-aloud activity in which you can teach the process of previewing a book for comprehension. Using the paperback edition of *The Voyage of the Frog* (Paulsen), I describe here my thoughts as I preview the book.

> The name of this book is *The Voyage of the Frog*. It sounds like an animal fantasy story where a frog takes a trip. Following the last page of text is a map. This is probably where the story takes place. The map shows the Pacific Ocean off the coast of Lower California and Mexico, and it outlines the route of the voyage. That's a long way for a frog to swim! There's a lot of detail and notes on the map, but I'll skip it now and look back at it while I read the book to follow where all the events happen.
>
> On the inside of the back cover is a photograph, probably of the author. He looks a little like my father with his beard and jacket and baseball cap (except he is holding a dog, and my father doesn't like dogs). The author must really like dogs to have one in his picture. Underneath the photograph I see the author's name—Gary Paulsen. The paragraph under the picture says he has won lots of awards. It also lists the names of some of his other books. I've read *Hatchet!* It was great. I hope this book is just as good. The paragraph says he has homes in New Mexico and on the Pacific. The map showed the Pacific area, so he must be writing about one of the places where he lives.
>
> On the back cover of the book, I see an excerpt from the story, a short summary, and some excerpts of reviews. Reading the back cover gives me a lot of information. The main character is named David Alspeth, and he is 14 years old. The *Frog* is the name of a sailboat—not a character. There is a storm at sea, and David is stranded with little food and water and no radio. (He should have taken a cell phone with him.) One of the reviewers said this is a survival story. *Hatchet* was a survival story also, so I think I'm really going to like this book.
>
> On the front cover is a picture of a small sailboat in a stormy sea. The size of those waves makes me remember when my family went on a cruise, and I got so sick. I feel sorry for the boy inside the boat because the sky looks dark, and the storm might last a long time. In the picture I can't see the boy, but the boat looks modern, so it looks like this is a realistic story that takes place in modern times.
>
> On the title page, I see the book was published in 1989. That explains why the boy didn't take a cell phone. Everybody didn't carry them around back then. The table of contents doesn't tell me much, but after it is a diagram of the sailboat with all the parts labeled. I don't know much about boats, so I'll look back at this while I'm reading when I don't know what a term means. The next page contains only a quote from someone

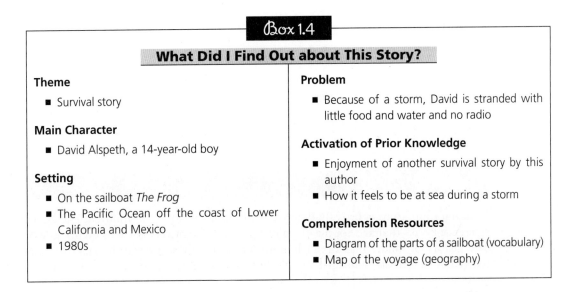

Box 1.4

What Did I Find Out about This Story?

Theme

- Survival story

Main Character

- David Alspeth, a 14-year-old boy

Setting

- On the sailboat *The Frog*
- The Pacific Ocean off the coast of Lower California and Mexico
- 1980s

Problem

- Because of a storm, David is stranded with little food and water and no radio

Activation of Prior Knowledge

- Enjoyment of another survival story by this author
- How it feels to be at sea during a storm

Comprehension Resources

- Diagram of the parts of a sailboat (vocabulary)
- Map of the voyage (geography)

named Joseph Conrad: "Only the young have such moments." I don't know what that means, but I'll look at it again after I read the book to see if I understand it then.

And now, I'm ready to read.

Box 1.4 lists the information I gained by using the prereading schema-building process before reading *The Voyage of the Frog*. In Box 1.5, I have provided the steps for the process. (By the way, if you do the strategy with this textbook, you will discover a glossary of all the key terms that appear in boldface type in the textbook.)

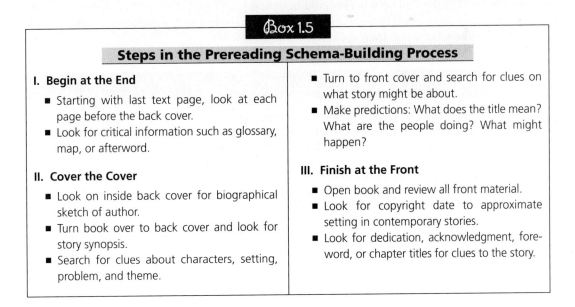

Box 1.5

Steps in the Prereading Schema-Building Process

I. Begin at the End

- Starting with last text page, look at each page before the back cover.
- Look for critical information such as glossary, map, or afterword.

II. Cover the Cover

- Look on inside back cover for biographical sketch of author.
- Turn book over to back cover and look for story synopsis.
- Search for clues about characters, setting, problem, and theme.

- Turn to front cover and search for clues on what story might be about.
- Make predictions: What does the title mean? What are the people doing? What might happen?

III. Finish at the Front

- Open book and review all front material.
- Look for copyright date to approximate setting in contemporary stories.
- Look for dedication, acknowledgment, foreword, or chapter titles for clues to the story.

♟ Literature Activity: Building Schema

Select a popular picture book or juvenile novel, and use the prereading schema-building process to deduce as many clues as you can about the story before reading it. After you finish reading, check your list of clues to see if they were all accurate. If not, determine what led you to form a misconception.

Summary

Children's literature is broadly defined as all books written for children, excluding reference books that are not meant to be read in their entirety (such as dictionaries). The history of modern children's literature is relatively short, dating back to 1865 when Lewis Carroll published *Alice's Adventures in Wonderland*—the first novel written specifically for children that was purely entertaining. The prototype of the modern children's picture storybook is *The Tale of Peter Rabbit,* published by Beatrix Potter in 1901.

Literature is most easily studied in genres or categories with similar characteristics. The literary genres are early childhood books, traditional literature, fiction, biography, informational books, and poetry. These categories are typically used to determine where books are shelved in libraries. Children's books are available in a variety of formats: picture books, easy-to-read books, illustrated books, graphic novels, chapter books, hardcover books, paperback books, grocery store books, and series books.

The prereading schema-building process can be used with all genres and formats of books to build background knowledge for readers to comprehend and enjoy reading new books on their own.

Children's Books Cited in Chapter 1

Alcott, Louisa May. *Little Women.* Scholastic, 1868/1995.
Allard, Harry. *Miss Nelson Is Missing.* Illus. James Marshall. Houghton Mifflin, 1977.
Baum, L. Frank. *The Wonderful Wizard of Oz.* TAB Books, 1900/1958.
Brown, Marcia. *Stone Soup.* Atheneum, 1989.
Burnett, Francis H. *Little Lord Fauntleroy.* Buccaneer, 1886/1981.
Carle, Eric. *The Very Hungry Caterpillar.* Philomel, 1969.
Carroll, Lewis. *Alice's Adventures in Wonderland.* Illus. John Tenniel. BHB International, 1865/1998.
Carroll, Lewis. *Through the Looking-Glass and What Alice Found There.* Illus. John Tenniel. Morrow, 1871/1993.
Colfer, Eoin, & Andrew Donkin. *Artemis Fowl: The Graphic Novel.* Hyperion, 2007.
Collodi, Carlo. *The Adventures of Pinocchio.* Philomel, 1883.

Crampton, Gertrude. *Scuffy the Tugboat*. Illus. Tibor Gergely. Western, 1946.

Crampton, Gertrude. *Tootle*. Illus. Tibor Gergely. Golden Books, 1945.

Defoe, Daniel. *Robinson Crusoe*. Knopf, 1719/1992.

Denyer, Susan. *At Home with Beatrix Potter: The Creator of Peter Rabbit*. Abrams, 2000.

Dickens, Charles. *A Christmas Carol*. Creative Edition, 1843/1995.

Dodge, Mary Mapes. *Hans Brinker or the Silver Skates*. Amereon, 1865/1940.

Holm, Jennifer L. *Babymouse: Heartbreaker*. Random House, 2007.

Jackson, K., & B. Jackson. *Saggy Baggy Elephant*. Western, 1947.

Jacques, Brian. *Redwall: The Graphic Novel*. Philomel, 2007.

Kinney, Jeff. *Diary of a Wimpy Kid: A Novel in Cartoons*. Amulet Books, 2007.

Kipling, Rudyard. *The Jungle Book*. Illus. Jerry Pinkney. Morrow, 1894/1995.

Kroeber, Theodora. *Ishi, Last of His Tribe*. Houghton Mifflin, 1964.

Kunhardt, Dorothy. *Pat the Bunny*. Golden Books, 1940.

Lobel, Arnold. *Days with Frog and Toad*. HarperTrophy, 1979.

Lobel, Arnold. *Frog and Toad Are Friends*. HarperTrophy, 1970.

Lowrey, Janette Sebring. *The Poky Little Puppy*. Golden Books, 1942.

MacGregor, Ellen. *Miss Pickerell Goes to Mars*. Whittlesey, 1951.

MacHale, D. J., & Carla Speed McNeil. *The Merchant of Death: Pendragon Graphic Novel*. Aladdin, 2008.

Minarik, Else Holmelund. *Little Bear*. Illus. Maurice Sendak. Harper & Row, 1957.

Newbery, John. *The History of Little Goody Two Shoes*. Newbery, 1765.

Nickel, Scott. *Billions of Bats: A Buzz Beaker Brainstorm*. Stone Arch, 2007.

Paulsen, Gary. *Hatchet*. Viking Penguin, 1987.

Paulsen, Gary. *The Voyage of the Frog*. Orchard, 1989.

Pilkey, Dav. *The Adventures of Captain Underpants: An Epic Novel*. Scholastic, 1997.

Potter, Beatrix. *The Tale of Peter Rabbit*. Frederick Warne, 1902.

Rogers, Gregory. *Midsummer Knight*. Roaring Brook, 2007.

Rylant, Cynthia. *Henry and Mudge: The First Book of Their Adventures*. Illus. Suçie Stevenson. Aladdin, 1987.

Schaefer, Jack. *Shane*. Houghton Mifflin, 1949.

Scott, Sir Walter. *Ivanhoe*. New American Library, 1820/1987.

Selznick, Brian. *The Invention of Hugo Cabret: A Novel in Words and Pictures*. Scholastic, 2007.

Seuss, Dr. *The Cat in the Hat*. Random House, 1957.

Sewell, Anna. *Black Beauty*. Grammercy, 1877/1998.

Siegel, Siena Cherson. *To Dance: A Ballerina's Graphic Novel*. Atheneum, 2007.

Spyri, Johanna. *Heidi*. Grammercy, 1884/1998.

Stevenson, Robert Louis. *Kidnapped*. Random House, 1886/1989.

Stevenson, Robert Louis. *Treasure Island*. Everyman's Library, 1883/1992.

Swift, Jonathan. *Gulliver's Travels*. Price Stern Sloan, 1726/1989.

Trondheim, Lewis. *Tiny Tyrant*. Roaring Brook, 2007.

Twain, Mark. *The Adventures of Tom Sawyer*. Courage, 1876/1991.

Verne, Jules. *Around the World in Eighty Days*. Amereon, 1872/1987.

Verne, Jules. *Journey to the Center of the Earth*. Reader's Digest, 1864/1999.

Verne, Jules. *Twenty Thousand Leagues under the Sea*. Indiana University Press, 1869/1992.

Wyss, Johann. *The Swiss Family Robinson*. Price Stern Sloan, 1812/1977.

Yolen, Jane. *The Devil's Arithmetic*. Viking Penguin, 1988.

Elements of Quality Children's Literature

2

TOMMY was a silly boy.
  "I can fly," he said ;
He started off, but very soon
  He tumbled on his head.

His little sister Prue was there,
  To see how he would do it ;
She knew that, after all his boast,
  Full dearly Tom would rue it !

The original of this illustration was engraved with four-color plates, which accounts for the bold outlines of the shapes.

From *Under the Window*, written and illustrated by Kate Greenaway.

There are literally thousands of good children's books in print. Some are obviously better than others, but how do you find the best? This chapter will explore different ways to identify and appreciate excellent children's literature. For example, one way is to choose an outstanding author or illustrator and read some of her or his books. Another way is to review the books that some knowledgeable people believe to be superior—so superior that they deserve an award.

Book Awards

Award-winning authors and books are a good place to start, so let me introduce you to the most prestigious awards. Some are given for a specific book, and others are awarded to authors and illustrators for their complete works.

Newbery Medal

In 1921 Frederick G. Melcher, editor of *Publishers Weekly,* proposed a way to honor distinguished contributions to children's literature. The Association for Library Service to Children (ALSC) of the American Library Association agreed to judge and award a medal named after John Newbery, the English publisher who first made books that were both instructional and entertaining available to young people. The Newbery Medal is the oldest of many book awards given today and therefore is the best known and most prestigious in the United States. This award is given to the author of the most distinguished contribution to literature for children published in the United States during the preceding year. Additional guidelines stipulate that the author must be a citizen or permanent resident of the United States.

In 1922 the first Newbery Medal was awarded to Hendrik Willem van Loon for *The Story of Mankind,* an informational book. Additionally, five noteworthy books were given a Newbery Honor, which is much like a "runner-up" award. Each year since, one author has been awarded a gold Newbery Medal, and usually several silver honor medals have also been awarded. (There is no set number.) Often you can distinguish Newbery books by the foil or printed medallion on the book jacket or cover. Remember that the gold medallion is for the Newbery winner, and the silver is for an honor book. However, not all copies of Newbery-winning books will be so designated. None of the books printed and sold in the first year will have the medallions because the award is not bestowed until the year following publication. In addition, book jackets—where the foil medallions are usually placed—may be missing from books.

Caldecott Medal

Sixteen years after the first Newbery Medal was awarded, Frederick G. Melcher established the first award for book illustration. It was named after Randolph Caldecott, an English artist who was one of the first to create color illustrations in children's books. Like the Newbery, the Caldecott Medal is awarded by the ALSC. The first gold Caldecott Medal was awarded in 1938 to Dorothy Lathrop for her illustrations in *Animals of the Bible* (Fish). Two honor books were also named the first year, and one or more honor books have been recognized each year since. The guidelines for the Caldecott winner also require that the book be published in the United States in the preceding year and that the illustrator be a citizen or permanent resident of the United States. However, the illustrator need not be the author of the book. Gold foil or printed medallions also adorn the book jackets or covers of Caldecott winners, and silver medallions indicate honor books. Look for the words "Caldecott Medal" to distinguish this award from the Newbery Medal because the medallions are similar.

To date, several hundred books have won Newbery, Caldecott, and honor book awards—too many to name in a brief textbook. Many of the early winners would not appeal to children today. Additionally, some recent Newbery winners are geared more for adolescents than for children. Therefore, I have included the names of award-winning books that would appeal to elementary school children in the appropriate genre chapters.

Integrating Literature and Technology

Association for Library Services to Children: www.ala.org/ ala/alsc   This website provides comprehensive, up-to-date lists of award-winning books. Type the award name in the "Search" textbox and click "Go." This site also has a link to the ALSC "Great Web Sites for Kids," which has the following categories: animals, the arts, history and biography, literature and languages, reference desk, mathematics and computers, sciences, and social sciences. All main categories have subcategories to refine your search further. The next time your children need to write a report, have them start by looking for information at this site.

Laura Ingalls Wilder Medal

In 1954 Laura Ingalls Wilder was the first recipient of the award that bears her name. Wilder authored the series of books based on her life in the American frontier known as the "Little House" books. This award is given to an author or illustrator who, like Wilder, has made a lasting contribution to children's literature through her or his body of work. The ALSC also sponsors this award. The winners of the Wilder Medal, now given every two years, are shown in the following list.

- Laura Ingalls Wilder (1954)
- Clara Ingram Judson (1960)
- Ruth Sawyer (1965)
- E. B. White (1970)
- Beverly Cleary (1975)
- Theodor Seuss Geisel (Dr. Seuss) (1980)

- Maurice Sendak (1983)
- Jean Fritz (1986)
- Elizabeth George Speare (1989)
- Marcia Brown (1992)
- Virginia Hamilton (1995)
- Russell Freedman (1998)
- Milton Meltzer (2001)
- Eric Carle (2003)
- Laurence Yep (2005)
- James Marshall (2007)

Hans Christian Andersen Award

Perhaps the most prestigious award is the one international prize, the Hans Christian Andersen Award, named after the Danish storyteller and author who is lauded as the father of modern fantasy. (More is said about Andersen's accomplishments in Chapter 6.) Like the Wilder Award, the Andersen Award is given in recognition of individuals whose complete bodies of works have made an outstanding and lasting contribution to children's literature. Since 1956 the Hans Christian Andersen Award has been given to a living author every two years by the International Board on Books for Young People. Since 1966 an award has also been given to a living illustrator. Queen Margrethe II of Denmark is the patron of these biennial awards, but the panel of five judges is composed of individuals from five different countries.

Since the first awards were given in 1956, only the following five authors and one illustrator from the United States have won this highest international distinction:

- Meindert DeJong (1962)
- Maurice Sendak (1970)
- Scott O'Dell (1972)
- Paula Fox (1978)
- Virginia Hamilton (1992)
- Katherine Paterson (1998)

Sendak, the only U.S. illustrator to win this award, and Hamilton were also honored with the Laura Ingalls Wilder Award, which—like the Hans Christian Andersen Award—is given for a person's life work.

Adults select the recipients of all the awards named thus far. There is no doubt that these selections are outstanding books produced by talented authors and illustrators, but do children like the same books that adults do? Do they read and enjoy the books that adults believe are the best?

Children's Choices and Teachers' Choices

Some lists of outstanding books are selected by children. In 1975 the Children's Choices list became the first such recognition. The International Reading Association

(IRA) and the Children's Book Council (CBC) cosponsor this project. Each year, publishers select the books to be evaluated from their titles published in the previous year. The number of books selected can be as many as 700. The books are grouped into five reading levels, and then all are sent to five review teams of educators located in different regions of the United States. Each team is responsible for getting the books to 2,000 children in elementary school classrooms; therefore, throughout the school year, the books are read to or by approximately 10,000 children. These children vote for their favorites, and the top 100 titles are announced at the IRA's annual conference. The list is also published each year in the October issue of *The Reading Teacher*.

Since 1989 the IRA's Teachers' Choices list has spotlighted outstanding books that teachers find to be exceptionally useful in the curriculum. Approximately 30 titles are selected from more than 300 recently published books. Books are field-tested throughout the United States, with each book read by at least six teachers or librarians in each of seven regions. The educators then vote for the books they believe have the highest literary quality plus potential for use across the curriculum. The list of top books is published each year in the November issue of *The Reading Teacher*.

In addition to general awards given to authors and illustrators, there are several awards that are genre specific, such as the Orbis Pictus Award for nonfiction. Genre-specific awards are described in the appropriate genre chapters of this text.

Issues in Book Awards

Adults select all the award-winning children's books and lifetime awards given to authors and illustrators. Even the Children's Choices Awards are given to books that adults have preselected. (Children simply narrow down the search.)

Using the information presented in this section, make a case for whether you do or do not think Newbery and Caldecott Award–winning books have greater appeal for children than other quality books that have not won an award.

Literary Elements

Reading books by award-winning authors and illustrators is one way of discovering some of the best books available. However, there is a multitude of children's books in print, and more than 5,000 new ones are published each year. The list of award-winning books is minuscule compared to what is available. How can you select the best from this mountain of possibilities? One way to assess the literary merit of fiction books is to analyze and evaluate the **literary elements** or various parts of a fiction story: characters, point of view, setting, plot, theme, style, and tone.

Characters

Characters are *who the story is about,* and the action revolves around them. Brown and Stephens (1995) believe that "the effective development of the main character may be the single most important element of the work" (p. 170). Authors develop characters primarily from three sources: (1) from the narrator's description of physical appearance and personality; (2) from other characters—what others think of characters and what others' actions are toward them; and (3) from the characters themselves—what they think, what they say, and what they do. Expect the latter to be the most revealing. "Actions, we all know, speak louder than words, and it is through actions that the most convincing evidence about character is revealed" (Russell, 1997, p. 61).

Main characters, especially the central character or **protagonist,** must be fully developed; that is, the readers should learn of the characters' many traits—their strengths as well as their weaknesses. These complex characters are called **round characters.** It is essential that readers relate to them; and when an author has created a well-developed character, the reader can imagine what might happen to her or him if the book continued (Glazer, 1997). "The main characters in an excellent work of fiction for children are rounded, fully developed characters who undergo change in response to life-altering events" (Lynch-Brown & Tomlinson, 1999, p. 29). This capacity for change defines such characters as **dynamic.**

Supporting characters are less well developed than the main characters; only a few of their traits may be revealed. Sometimes they are **flat characters** who exhibit only one side of their personality. Flat characters are often **stereotypes** who possess only the traits considered typical of their particular group. Flat characters are usually static, undergoing no change in personality throughout the book.

Rothlein and Meinbach (1996) provide a dozen excellent activities for learning about characterization. One of these, the *character continuum,* appears in Box 2.1. To help children gain a deeper understanding of a particular character, encourage them to analyze the inner qualities of the character as they determine where on the character continuum he or she would fall. With the exception of stereotyped characters (often found in traditional literature), most characters should fall somewhere between the continuum's extremes. This activity encourages readers to use higher-order thinking skills to view characters as neither all good nor all bad, but as having some desirable traits and some not so desirable—just as real people do.

Point of View

A book's **point of view** is the perspective from which an author presents a story—a perspective shaped by *who is telling the story* and how much this narrator knows. Though the author writes the book, the story is not typically told from the author's point of view. Before the author begins writing, he or she must determine what point of view to use, because it will permeate the entire book. In a good book, the point of view can usually be determined in the first page or two, and the author is consistent in using this point of view throughout.

Box 2.1

Character Continuum

Title of Book: _____

Name of Character:_____

friendly————————————————————————— unfriendly

happy ———————————————————————————— sad

wise ————————————————————————————— foolish

adventurous ——————————————————————— cautious

outgoing ————————————————————————— shy

unselfish ————————————————————————— selfish

honest——————————————————————————— dishonest

brave ——————————————————————————— fearful

leader ——————————————————————————— follower

mature ——————————————————————————— childish

Instructions: Analyze the inner qualities of this character using the pairs of opposite words. Place an **X** on the line where you think the character falls on each dimension. Most characters will fall somewhere between the two extremes.

Source: Adapted from Liz Rothlein and Anita Meyer Meinbach, _Legacies: Using Children's Literature in the Classroom._ New York: HarperCollins, 1996.

First Person. When the narrator is one of the characters in the story and refers to himself or herself as _I_ and _me,_ the author is employing the **first-person point of view**. With this point of view, the reader will see events unfold through the eyes and thoughts of the narrator, and only of the narrator. Therefore, the reader cannot learn what other characters are doing or saying if they are not in sight of the narrator. Because the reader can never learn what is in the minds of other characters, an author using the first-person point of view might contrive for the narrator to do a bit of eavesdropping. With this kind of device, the author can reveal essential information through other characters as well. For example, a child might be able to hear the adults in her family talking when she climbs out her bedroom window to the porch and listens outside the living room window. In this way, the author can move the story line along without changing narrators.

Readers of realistic fiction will find first person the primary point of view for that genre. However, when a story is told only through events the narrator has experienced, the reader should expect the narration to be quite subjective. A good example of a book using this point of view is Judy Blume's _Are You There God? It's Me, Margaret._ This story is told through the eyes of a young girl. An interesting way for the first-person narrator to reveal a realistic story is through letters and diaries. Some good examples are *Dear Mr. Henshaw* (Cleary) and *Absolutely Normal Chaos* (Creech).

Alternating Point of View.   Sometimes an author will write a story that is told in first person accounts by two or more characters, called **alternating point of view.** Often, the author shifts narrators each chapter, and a single incident is sometimes told from two or more points of view. Katherine Applegate used this style in *Animorphs: The Andalite's Gift*. The main characters are five children—one of whom has permanently "morphed" (become transformed) into a falcon—who are fighting evil aliens, and each chapter is the first-person account of one of these main characters. Avi with Rachel Vail authored *Never Mind! A Twin Novel*, which consists of chapters with alternating points of view between a male and female twin. In a most unique writing collaboration, Avi wrote the chapters narrated by the male twin and Vail wrote those narrated by the female.

Omniscient.   The omniscient and all other points of view are told in third-person narrative, in which the narrator refers to all characters as *he, she, it,* or *they*. The narrator with an **omniscient point of view** is not a book character but rather an all-knowing and all-seeing voice that can relate events that are occurring simultaneously. In this point of view, readers are able to learn what all the characters are doing and thinking, what has happened in the past, and even what will occur in the future. A classic example of a book using an omniscient point of view is *Charlotte's Web* (White).

Limited Omniscient.   When a story is narrated through a **limited omniscient point of view,** the story unfolds through the viewpoint of only one of the characters. However, the story is told not *by* the character but by the omniscient narrator, who enters the mind of this character and reveals her or his experiences, actions, speech, thoughts, and history. The reader knows only what that particular character can see and understand. An example is *Little House on the Prairie* (Wilder).

Objective.   In the **objective point of view,** the reader learns about characters only through their actions and speech. The narrator does not enter the minds of any of the characters, but rather takes a reporter's view, presenting only the facts. The narrator tells but does not comment on or interpret what is happening in the story. The reader learns nothing about characters when they are not in the author's narrative or dialogue. Their actions must speak for themselves as they unfold in the story. *Frog and Toad All Year* (Lobel) is an example of a book using the objective point of view.

   First person and omniscient are the two points of view used most often in children's fiction. One way to help distinguish them is to think about which characters are being described. When a story is told by an omniscient narrator, *all* the characters are described through the perspective of the narrator. However, when a story is told in the first person by one of the characters, he or she fully describes the other characters but is not likely to describe himself or herself. Rather, the reader begins gradually to understand the narrator by what he or she says and does.

Some nuances of point of view can even be revealed though illustration. In *Why Mosquitoes Buzz in People's Ears* (Aardema), artists Leo and Diane Dillon show the frightened monkey leaping through trees to warn the other animals. A dead limb breaks and falls, killing an owlet. However, four pages later, when Mother Owl (who did not witness the accident) gives her account, the illustrations depict a vicious killer monkey standing on the nest, clutching the baby owl, and beating it with a stick! This book is a great vehicle for showing children how the retelling of a real-life experience changes when it is told by more than one person.

Responding to Literature

Changing Point of View   Read your children a book with several characters. Have the children select a particularly interesting or exciting incident. Ask them to write a letter or journal entry describing the incident from the viewpoint of different characters. You might first want to read them *The True Story of the 3 Little Pigs* (Scieszka) and *The Pain and the Great One* (Blume) to show how different points of view can change stories dramatically.

Setting

Setting is *where and when the story takes place*. Every story occurs in some time period at some geographical location(s). Setting can include topography, climate, and weather when these are integral to the story. Setting "may play a significant role that has an impact on every other aspect of the book, it may be inconsequential and barely mentioned, or it may not be mentioned at all" (Brown & Stephens, 1995, p. 175). Setting can be a realistic time and place that the reader recognizes, such as the New Jersey suburb in Blume's *Are You There God? It's Me, Margaret*. Settings can also be quite abstract, perhaps in an imaginary world with a time period that does not correspond to earth time, as in *The Lion, the Witch and the Wardrobe* (Lewis). The story could cover a time span of only one day, as in *Finding Buck McHenry* (Slote), or it could span decades, as in *The Rifle* (Paulsen). When the title of a book names its setting, expect the setting to be a major element of the story, as in *Little House on the Prairie* (Wilder). In addition, the setting serves a major function in survival stories, in which the conflict is person against nature, as in *Hatchet* (Paulsen).

Setting is more important in some stories than others; therefore, there are two types of settings—backdrop and integral. The **backdrop setting** is relatively unimportant to the story. The name is derived from traditional theater where flat, nondescript painted scenery was dropped from the ceiling at the back of the stage. This is the type of setting often found in traditional literature that begins with a literal or implied "once upon a time." Traditional literature is nearly always set in an indeterminate past time and in an unspecified place, such as a queen's castle, a peasant's hut, a dark forest, or a barnyard. It is not surprising that fantasy, which has its origins in traditional literature, also employs the backdrop setting frequently, as in *Frog and*

Toad Together (Lobel). Some authors deliberately leave time and place vague in order to emphasize the universality of their stories, as in *Sounder* (Armstrong).

The **integral setting** is essential to the story, meaning that the story could not have taken place anywhere but in the setting specified by the author. According to Lukens (1999), "We say a story has an *integral setting* when action, character, or theme are influenced by the time and place" (p. 155). The integral setting is most often used in realistic fiction, especially historical fiction, as in *Johnny Tremain* (Forbes). Perhaps the most difficult setting for authors to write about is a time before they were born. Both the author and the illustrator of historical fiction must undertake painstaking research in order to present an authentic setting. However, authors can go overboard in developing the setting. Settings should be introduced to the reader subtly, through things the characters see, say, and do within the story. Authors should not rely on multiple pages of tedious description.

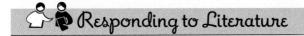 Responding to Literature

Finding Picture and Text Clues   Select a historical fiction picture book such as *Uncle Jed's Barbershop* (Mitchell) or *The Year of the Perfect Christmas Tree* (Houston). Tell your children to look in the illustrations for clues that show the events took place in the past. Read the book aloud and ask the children to tell you the clues they saw in the illustrations. Next, tell them to listen for clues in the story, and read the book again. Make a chart of all the visual and verbal clues that were found.

Plot

"**Plot** is the sequence of events showing characters in action" (Lukens, 1999, p. 103). In other words, it is *what happens in a story*. In order to keep readers involved, the plot must tell a good story; the lives of the characters in a book should be more exciting or more interesting than the readers' lives. There are four primary types of plots: cumulative, linear, episodic, and circular.

Cumulative. **Cumulative plots** are most often found in traditional literature and pattern books. In cumulative plots there is repetition of phrases, sentences, or events with one new aspect added with each repetition. "The Gingerbread Man" is a good example of a story with a cumulative plot. Young children love to join in on its refrain.

Linear. **Linear plots** are popular in realistic fiction and fantasy, as in *Swimmy* (Lionni). The plot should be constructed logically; that is, events should happen logically and not by coincidence. There are three major parts to a progressive linear plot:

1. In the *beginning,* the characters and setting are introduced, and the central problem of the story is revealed. Usually the main character sets a goal to overcome a problem.

2. In the *middle,* the main character attempts to overcome the problem and usually meets with obstacles, or the main character participates in a series of events that lead to a solution of the problem.
3. In the *end,* either the problem is resolved or the main character learns to cope with it.

Episodic. **Episodic plots** are most often used in easy-to-read books or transitional books, such as *Frog and Toad All Year* (Lobel). Although the characters and setting are usually the same throughout, there is no central problem that permeates the book. Rather, each chapter has a miniplot complete with introduction, problem, events, and resolution. Books with episodic plots are good for children with short attention spans or for children with limited reading ability. In either case, if children listen to or read only one chapter a day, they do not have to remember what was read the day before to enjoy the book.

Circular. **Circular plots** have the same components as linear plots, but the resolution or end of the story shows that the characters are in the same situation as when the story started. For example, in *Once a Mouse . . .* (Brown), a hermit's pet mouse is successively changed from a mouse to a cat to a dog to a tiger—and then, because of his vanity, back to a mouse. In *Ox-Cart Man* (Hall), the pioneer family works hard all year to grow and make goods for the father to take to a distant market in the oxcart he built. Once at the market, the man sells everything, including the cart and the ox. He returns home with the necessities and gifts he has purchased with the money earned, and the family begins to make and grow the goods to be sold at next year's market.

Naming the components of plot, or **story mapping,** is an activity that will help children follow and understand the structure of a story, either while children are reading a book or, with shorter books, after they finish. Figure 2.1 is an example of a story map of the chapter titled "Cookies" from the episodic book *Frog and Toad Together* (Lobel).

Two elements that can be used to move a plot along are flashback and exposition. In a **flashback** the narrator recounts an earlier event to "give the reader background information that adds clarity or perspective to the plot, but does not fit into the chronological flow of the plotline" (Brown & Stephens, 1995, p. 173). Flashbacks that explain important relationships or the past history of a character will keep the reader from getting bogged down in detailed descriptions or history at the beginning of the book. A device similar to flashback is **exposition**—passages in which the narrator briefly tells (rather than recreates in scenes) what has happened before the story opens. The opposite of flashback is **foreshadowing**—passages in which a forthcoming event is hinted at. The author gives these clues to the readers to prepare them for a coming event in the story and to build anticipation.

Conflict is the interaction of plot and character or the opposition of two forces. Tension is a necessary result of conflict. Without sufficient conflict and tension, a book is dull; but with well-developed conflict, the story will create **suspense,** a sense

FIGURE 2.1 **Story Map**

Title: "Cookies" from *Frog and Toad Together*   **Author:** Arnold Lobel

<u>Beginning</u>

Main characters:	Toad and his friend Frog
Setting—Place:	Frog's house in a garden
—Time:	Summertime in the present day
Problem:	Frog and Toad cannot stop eating the cookies Toad baked.
Goal:	They want to have willpower to stop eating cookies.

<u>Middle</u>   ⇩

Events/attempts to reach the goal:

1. They put the cookies in a box.
2. They tie the box with string.
3. They put the box up on a high shelf.

<u>End</u>   ⇩

Resolution: Frog takes the cookies off the shelf and gives them to the birds.

of anxiety, because the reader is uncertain of the outcome. There are four primary types of conflict:

- Character against self (e.g., *Wringer* by Jerry Spinelli)
- Character against another character (e.g., *Harry Potter and the Sorcerer's Stone* by J. K. Rowling)
- Character against society (e.g., *The Giver* by Lois Lowry)
- Character against nature (e.g., *Hatchet* by Gary Paulsen)

One outcome of a good plot is that children are better able to understand their own problems and conflicts by reading about the conflicts of the characters.

Theme

The **theme** of a book is its central idea, the underlying message the author is conveying to the reader. Other definitions include a significant truth, a value-laden statement, a broad and powerful idea that has universal application, or more simply, the moral of the story. Sometimes the theme is explicit or stated directly by the narrator or a story character. For example, in *Knee-Knock Rise*, Uncle Anson says that "if your mind is made up, all the facts in the world won't make the slightest difference" (Babbitt, p. 111). More often, the theme is implicit. Readers have to infer the meaning from what happens in the story. I find theme to be the most obscure and elusive of the literary elements. To complicate this, some books have a secondary theme or even multiple themes, and others have themes that are so vague they are difficult to express in words.

A theme is more easily understood if it is stated in a complete sentence. For example, "remember" is a word. "Important to remember" is a phrase that adds a little more meaning. However, "It is important to remember the history of your culture" is a sentence and thus a complete thought. It is also the theme of *The Devil's Arithmetic* (Yolen).

To determine the theme of a book, ask yourself these questions:

- What is the underlying meaning or significance of this story?
- What was the author's purpose in writing the story?
- What did the author say to me through the story?
- What are the comments the author makes about beliefs, fundamental truths, human nature, life, society, human conditions, or values?
- What is the common idea that ties the story together?

 *Responding to Literature*

Determining the Themes of Lionni's Books   To gain a better understanding of theme and how to determine it, read a picture book by Leo Lionni, such as *Frederick*. Lionni's themes are usually morals and are easy to detect. Write the theme of each book in a complete sentence.

Style

Style cannot be isolated from the words of the story and is often challenging to detect. It is the manner in which a writer expresses his or her ideas to convey a story. It permeates every sentence of the work and sets the mood of the story. Style has to do with the *writing* as opposed to the *content* of a book. It is *how* an author says something as opposed to *what* she or he says. Authors have many ways to use words to express their ideas. Some of these are tone (discussed next), use of imagery, figurative language, allusion, irony, selection of vocabulary, grammatical structure, symbolism, and dialect—as well as the devices of comparison, sound, and rhythm. Style is what makes an author's work distinctive from other writers' works.

Children often select multiple books by the same author because they like the author's distinctive style, such as the styles of Judy Blume and Gary Paulsen. However, most authors will vary their style when writing for different age groups or when they feel a certain story warrants it. Style is truly the author's personal choice, depending on the characters, setting, and plot of the story.

To determine the style an author used in a book, ask yourself these questions:

- What kinds of words and sentences did the author choose to tell the story?
- Was there any distinctive language, choice of words, or sentence construction? What mood did this create?
- What effect might the author be trying to achieve?

Tone

Tone involves the author's attitude toward the book's subject, characters, and readers. However, tone is often quite subtle and may not be easy to pinpoint. In addition, an author may change the tone as the main character or the supporting characters change. Some examples of appropriate tones used in books for children include serious, humorous, moralistic, hopeful, sympathetic, wondrous, longing, loving, satirical, and nostalgic.

Russell (1997) named several tones that he deemed *inappropriate* for child readers. These include

- *Condescending:* talking down to the reader as an inferior
- *Sensational:* horror laden or thrill seeking
- *Sentimental:* overly emotional, conveying an overly sweetened view of the world
- *Didactic:* preachy and overly moralistic

Children's literature is particularly likely to have a didactic tone. The literary elements truly suffer when the story has been created around a message instead of having a message flow naturally from the story.

Like style, tone is developed through the author's choice of words and through the way all the elements of the story work together. Because tone influences the meaning of a story, it is important for children to grasp it in order to comprehend the story. For example, consider the misconceptions that would arise if a child read a tall tale such as the story of Paul Bunyan and believed the author's tone was serious rather than humorous.

Responding to Literature

Not all children love books. I remember Carla, a fifth grader who transferred to my classroom at midsemester. When she first made the weekly trip to the library with my class, I noticed she was the only one who did not check out a book. I inquired why and she exclaimed, "Because I *hate* book reports!" Apparently, the only time Carla had read a library book was to do an assignment, so she associated books with work.

There are so many ways to respond to and extend literature that I hope teachers are not still requiring their pupils to do written book reports. An alternative is to have a child show some of the illustrations and briefly describe the book to other children in the class or in a small group. This is called a **book talk,** and it is a good way to get children interested in reading a variety of books. (Book talks are explained in more detail in Chapter 14.) A great resource for teachers is *Book Talk and Beyond: Children and Teachers Respond to Literature* (Roser & Martinez, 1995). This book contains information on a variety of activities, such as focus units, language charts, webbing, grand conversations, literature circles, dramatizing, and literature journals. These and other activities are introduced throughout this text. If you would like to look ahead at these, you may find the list and page numbers in the Subject Index under "Literature responses and activities."

Gloria Houston, the author of several historical fiction books, has studied reader response theory for many years. Her explanation and application of reader response follows.

Reader Response Theory

by Gloria Houston

Louise Rosenblatt (1995) is arguably the best known theorist of **reader response** and is certainly the most influential in the contemporary field of teaching children's literature. Her transactional theory is grounded in the belief that meaning is not inherent in the text; rather, the reader/listener creates meaning in an active mental process when the reader and text converge.

In this constructivist theory, a response to literature is a private inner reaction that is not observable by an outsider. The reader's response begins during the act of reading and may continue well after the reading is finished because reading is an active creative experience. Rosenblatt named two categories of reader response—efferent and aesthetic. An **efferent** (from the Latin *efferre*—to carry away) **stance** is appropriate when a reader's attention is focused on information, facts, or instructions that will be retained after the reading. Therefore, it is the stance of choice for reading nonfiction, such as textbooks, reference books, informational books, and biographies.

An **aesthetic stance** is the appropriate stance for reading fiction. It is more difficult to define because the most important goal of the aesthetic stance is to have a lived-through experience—which Rosenblatt calls an **evocation**. The aesthetic stance may be extended across an entire continuum of responses, from reliving the reading experience to imagining or picturing characters, settings, or events from the story. With aesthetic responses, the reader interacts with the emotions and ideas that the text evokes to create an individual experience. In essence, the reader is living through the experience with the story—an evocation.

Teachers and parents should not assume that young readers will automatically adopt the appropriate stance for a particular text, especially for fiction. Because everything else in the curriculum requires an efferent stance, readers often take that stance when reading fiction as well, even when they are not faced with end-of-chapter questions! Students have been taught the efferent stance for so long (both by implication and through experience) that if we do not introduce the aesthetic stance and the concept of reading for pleasure, many will never get it. In a way, we must unteach the efferent stance to unsophisticated readers if many of them are ever to understand the aesthetic stance.

Rosenblatt suggests that, beyond the socially agreed-upon meanings of words (e.g., a *cow* is not an *airplane*), *there is no one right way to know what a text means.* Because responses are personal, a wide range of responses should be both accepted and encouraged. This theory, according to Rosenblatt, suggests that all interpretations of the meaning of a work are valid meanings. *Meaning* is not in text, and meaning is certainly not in teachers. Meaning is in *readers*. The teacher cannot know what a scene in a book may evoke in the reader's imagination, because the teacher is not privy to the reader's background and emotions. A text will not be the same experience for any two readers, and the meaning of a particular text may change even for the same reader when the work is reread at a later time.

Responses do not need to be active or overt, such as discussing, writing, dramatizing, or drawing. With literature, the most fundamental response is the reader's emotional interaction with the characters and events of the book. One way to enhance this interaction is to engage children with questions during and after reading. (Some sample questions are presented in Box 2.2.)

Although it is acceptable to discuss the story while it is being read, any serious analysis needs to come only after the reader has had time to mentally live through the experience or evocation. Evocation and analysis cannot occur at the same time. Therefore, it is essential for adults to wait for children to internalize the story before formally analyzing it or its elements to avoid the risk of imposing their own or someone else's analysis of the story. During this time for internalizing, I suggest the teacher do something different with the story, such as reading something else that relates to the story or connecting the story to another subject area such as social studies by talking about the setting. After a minimum of one day, teachers can return to the book. At that time, children should be able to analyze the book informally and spontaneously.

One way for the teacher to initiate analysis is to ask children to draw a scene as they visualize it while hearing a passage or after they read. This is a most productive activity for all ages, because much will be revealed that the teacher could learn in no other way. Asking children to tell you about their drawings will help them verbalize their personal meanings. Following the drawings and verbalizations, small or large

---

Box 2.2

Story Questions

Questions to Ask While You Read

1. What do you think this character might be thinking? What clues help you to know?
2. How do you think this character feels? What clues help you?
3. Why did _____ finally decide to _____ ?
4. What was the reason for _____ ?
5. What do you think might happen next? Why do you think so?

Questions to Ask After You Read

1. What does the title of the story mean to you now?

2. What caused the problem faced by the main character?
3. What words describe the personalities of the characters?
4. What did the main character learn at the end? What did the other characters learn?
5. What do you think is the most important idea the author might want you to remember about this story?

group discussions will allow readers to share their various meanings. This sharing allows readers to learn to respect the opinions of others, to ask questions for clarification, and to extend their individual meanings if they so choose. It is usually necessary for the teacher to model for children how to show respect for the interpretations and opinions of others, which is only possible if the teacher genuinely accepts diverse opinions.

Literature Circles

A great way to turn kids on to books, allowing them to respond to what they read by sharing their thoughts with others, is literature circles. These are small temporary discussion groups that have chosen to read the same book. More is said about literature circles in Chapter 14, but here I offer a brief outline based on *Literature Circles: Voice and Choice in the Student-Centered Classroom* (Daniels, 1994):

- Students choose their own reading materials.
- Small temporary groups are formed, based on book choices.
- Different groups read different books.
- Groups meet on a regular schedule to discuss their reading.
- Students use notes to guide both their reading and discussion.
- Discussion topics come from the students.
- Group meetings aim to be open, natural conversations generated through personal connections, digressions, and open-ended questions about books.
- In newly formed groups, students play a rotating assortment of task roles.
- The teacher serves as a *facilitator,* not as a group member or instructor.

Developing a Classroom Library
by Susan E. Knell

Imagine wanting to be an excellent basketball player, chef, or musician and not having the tools around that you need to succeed. To become accomplished at anything, you must have practice tools at hand, such as a basketball hoop in the driveway, cookbooks in the kitchen, or music books at the piano. The same is true with children learning to read. They need the tools nearby that will help them practice to become proficient readers

Good classroom libraries are not a luxury; they are vital to children's success in becoming lifelong readers. In many schools, classes make only one thirty-minute visit to the school library weekly, and children are typically limited to checking out two books. What happens if they finish their books before the next weekly trip, discover their books are too difficult or easy, or simply find they do not like them well enough to finish? Individual trips back to the library may cause children to miss part of their free reading period.

So, what does a good classroom library include? It should contain books from all genres, including nonfiction. In fact, I suggest that at least 40 percent of your collection consist of nonfiction because it can increase children's world knowledge base while expanding their curiosity. Be sure to include picture books, quality series books, magazines, newspapers, and reference books (such as atlases, dictionaries, and a space-saving encyclopedia on CD-ROM). Books the children have written and bound should also be included.

The most inviting and attractive rooms are those where books are displayed prominently throughout. Your classroom library should look more like a bookstore where books are displayed everywhere, arranged in interesting ways to encourage children to pick them up and start reading. Wherever possible, display book covers facing the children. A great way to do this is by installing inexpensive rain gutters made of enameled reinforced plastic found at home improvement stores. They are easily cut to any size, and the plastic support brackets can be screwed into almost any wall, including concrete blocks. (See Jim Trelease's website at www.trelease-on-reading.com and click on Rain Gutter Bookshelves.)

Following are more ideas for effective book displays:

- Bookshelves on wheels that can be moved to create various learning environments and centers
- Colorful plastic cartons that are labeled for easy identification by titles, authors, themes, genres, or topics
- Baskets of various sizes and shapes
- Empty desks
- Chalkboard trays
- Small tables underneath author or genre bulletin board displays
- Clothes-drying racks for big books, magazines, and newspapers

I suggest starting with about 300 trade books, depending on the children's ages and diversity of reading levels. You may certainly begin with fewer books—just set a goal to add at least two more books per child each year. Building your classroom library takes some time, but it need not take a lot of money. You can borrow books from your school or public library. Though these will not be a permanent part of your collection, they add many choices for children. Most school libraries do not have a checkout limit for teachers, so periodic trips can keep your collection new.

School book clubs give free books to teachers, according to the dollar amount ordered. Prices are reasonable and titles include both classic books and new best-sellers, so get your children and their families involved in ordering books.

At the beginning of the school year, send a letter home to parents suggesting they donate books in honor of children's birthdays and in lieu of holiday or end-of-year presents for you. If parent groups conduct school book fairs, ask them to donate proceeds for classroom libraries or purchase books directly. Paste a bookplate or label in each, acknowledging the person who donated it. (You can print them with any art software program, such as Print Artist.)

Buy used books at garage sales, flea markets, and library sales. You may find books in good condition at a very cheap price. Also, look for bargains in the large discount chain stores, where good titles can often be found among the grocery store books. And if you are lucky enough to live in an area that has a Book Warehouse outlet, you can find new books for half price! Some may be a bit shopworn, but most are publisher overruns or bookstore leftovers that are in new condition.

Alma Flor Ada tells a wonderful story of her son's third-grade teacher who implemented a yearlong program called "The One Thousand Book Classroom" (see *A Magical Encounter,* 2003, pp. 18–25). The children in this classroom wrote letters requesting books from publishers, authors, school board members, legislators, and community leaders. They later extended the letters to state, national, and international levels. By the end of the school year, they far exceeded their goal of 1,000 books!

To identify new titles for your collection, you must keep current in the field of children's literature. Frequent the children's section of local bookstores to see what is newly published. Most will allow you to read books without buying them. Read book reviews in professional journals and online (Amazon Internet bookstore at www.amazon.com has reviews of nearly every book in print). Attend professional conferences such as International Reading Association and the National Council of Teachers of English to hear authors speak, browse the book exhibits, and attend sessions on children's literature. Communicate frequently with your school and public librarians to discover new books, to find out which books the children are reading, and to learn new trends in children's literature.

Make building your classroom library a priority that continues throughout your teaching career. Being excited about your library will be contagious, and children will revel in the reading choices they have right in their own classroom—the enjoyable tools they need to learn.

Summary

There are numerous awards given to quality children's books, many of which are genre specific and will be discussed within the genre chapters. Some coveted awards that are not genre specific include (1) the Newbery Medal for the year's most distinguished contribution to literature for children, (2) the Caldecott Medal for the year's most distinguished book illustrations, (3) the Laura Ingalls Wilder Medal for an author or illustrator who has made a lasting contribution through his or her body of work, (4) the international Hans Christian Andersen Award for authors and illustrators whose complete bodies of work have made a lasting contribution, and (5) Children's Choices (voted on by students) and Teacher's Choices (for being exceptionally useful in the curriculum).

Readers can analyze seven major literary elements in fiction stories. (1) Characters are who the story is about. (2) Point of view is determined by who is telling the story. (3) Setting is where and when the story takes place. (4) Plot is what happens in the story. (5) Theme is the author's underlying message or central idea of the story. (6) Style is the manner in which a writer expresses himself or herself. (7) Tone reflects the author's attitude toward the book's subject and the readers.

In her reader response theory, Louise Rosenblatt contends that the meaning of a book is not inherent in the text; rather, the reader creates the meaning in an active mental process based on his or her background experiences. Therefore, reading a particular book will not evoke the same response in any two readers; all interpretations of the meaning of a book are valid in this theory.

Children's Books Cited in Chapter 2

Aardema, Verna. *Why Mosquitoes Buzz in People's Ears*. Illus. Leo D. Dillon & Diane Dillon. Puffin, 1978.

Applegate, Katherine A. *Animorphs: The Andalite's Gift*. Scholastic, 1997.

Armstrong, William H. *Sounder*. Harper & Row, 1969.

Avi, & Rachel Vail. *Never Mind! A Twin Novel*. HarperCollins, 2004.

Babbitt, Natalie. *Knee-Knock Rise*. Sagebrush, 1999.

Blume, Judy. *Are You There God? It's Me, Margaret*. Atheneum, 2001.

Blume, Judy. *The Pain and the Great One*. Illus. Irene Trivas. Atheneum, 2003.

Brown, Marcia. *Once a Mouse . . . : A Fable Cut in Wood*. Aladdin, 1989.

Cleary, Beverly. *Dear Mr. Henshaw*. HarperTrophy, 2000.

Creech, Sharon. *Absolutely Normal Chaos*. HarperTrophy, 1997.

Fish, Helen Dean. *Animals of the Bible*. Illus. Dorothy Lathrop. Lippincott–Raven, 1937.

Forbes, Esther. *Johnny Tremain*. Houghton Mifflin, 1943.

Hall, Donald. *Ox-Cart Man*. Illus. Barbara Cooney. Puffin, 1983.

Houston, Gloria. *The Year of the Perfect Christmas Tree*. Illus. Barbara Cooney. Puffin, 1996.

Lewis, C. S. *The Lion, the Witch and the Wardrobe*. HarperCollins, 1994.

Lionni, Leo. *Frederick*. Knopf, 1990.

Lionni, Leo. *Swimmy*. Dragonfly, 1992.

Lobel, Arnold. *Frog and Toad All Year*. HarperTrophy, 1984.

Lobel, Arnold. *Frog and Toad Together*. HarperTrophy, 1979.

Lowry, Lois. *The Giver*. Houghton Mifflin, 1993.

Mitchell, Margaree King. *Uncle Jed's Barbershop*. Illus. James Ransome. Aladdin, 1998.

Paulsen, Gary. *Hatchet*. Viking Penguin, 1987.

Paulsen, Gary. *The Rifle*. Laurel Leaf, 1997.

Rowling, J. K. *Harry Potter and the Sorcerer's Stone*. Scholastic, 1998.

Scieszka, Jon. *The True Story of the 3 Little Pigs*. Illus. Lane Smith. Puffin, 1994.

Slote, Alfred. *Finding Buck McHenry*. HarperCollins, 1993.

Spinelli, Jerry. *Wringer*. HarperTrophy, 1998.

van Loon, Hendrik Willem. *The Story of Mankind*. Liveright, 1921.

White, E. B. *Charlotte's Web*. Illus. Garth Williams. Harper & Row, 1952.

Wilder, Laura Ingalls. *Little House on the Prairie*. Illus. Garth Williams. HarperTrophy, 1935.

Yolen, Jane. *The Devil's Arithmetic*. Puffin, 1990.

The Art of Illustration

3

The artist used woodcuts to create this
illustration, which gives a stained-glass effect,
characteristic of the fauvist (expressionist) style.

From *Drummer Hoff,* adapted by Barbara
Emberley and illustrated by Ed Emberley.

𝒴oung children *do* judge a book by its cover (and all the pictures between the covers). Even adults, when they first pick up a book or magazine, tend to look at the pictures before they read the words. That is why many advertisers put attractive pictures and minimal print in their ads.

In the last chapter, I discussed determining the quality of children's books through major book awards and by analyzing the various literary elements. I concluded the chapter with an explanation of reader response theory, which allows us to understand why all of us (including our children) have somewhat different—but ever developing—opinions on what constitutes quality literature. In this chapter, I discuss determining the quality of children's books through their artistic aspects.

Evaluating Illustrations

Ask yourself these questions to judge the appropriateness of illustrations in a book.

- Are the illustrations appealing to children?
- Do the illustrations enhance the story?
- Are the pictures a reflection of the tone of the story?
- Are all the pictures and details in harmony with the text?

The Union of Art and Text

Art and text were forever bonded when Beatrix Potter published *The Tale of Peter Rabbit* in 1901. Today, artistic excellence is increasingly apparent and appreciated in children's literature, thanks to visual artists such as Leo and Diane Dillon, Chris Van Allsburg, and Maurice Sendak. "Illustrators of children's books realize the importance of conveying, through illustrations, the excitement, beauty, and meaning of the story" (Rothlein & Meinbach, 1996, p. 326). In picture storybooks (commonly shortened to "picture books"), the two arts of storytelling and illustration are combined. Thus, both are required to convey the story because neither could carry the story line alone. Just like the printed words of the story, illustrations have both meaning and content.

Also like words, pictures are representations of concrete things, and the meanings of these representations must be learned. This is not an automatic process with young children, especially when the drawings are not intended to convey what an object actually looks like. Therefore, parents and teachers need to encourage a young child's capacity to obtain meaning from pictures. As children learn to construct meaning from pictures, they are developing their **visual literacy**—the ability to interpret graphic stimuli. Just as children learn to read by reading, it only makes sense that children learn visual literacy by viewing.

The ability to interpret and communicate through visual symbols in art is one aspect of visual literacy. Long before children are able to read (i.e., to construct meaning from print by interpreting written symbols), they are able to obtain ideas and meaning from pictures, and they should be encouraged to express these ideas. Parents and teachers enhance visual literacy when they focus children's attention on the illustrations as part of sharing books. Even after children learn to read, illustrations continue to aid their comprehension. Among the many components of a child's visual world (which includes television, movies, DVDs, video games, and computers), book illustrations are a beautiful medium through which to learn about their world.

Responding to Literature

Comparing Illustrations in Folktales   Select two picture books that are different versions of the same folktale—for example, "Snow White" or "Hansel and Gretel." Carefully compare the illustrations in the different versions, and tell which pictures you believe most enhance the tale. Explain the reasons for your choice.

Visual Elements of Artistic Design

Good illustrations evoke a variety of emotions from both the child and adult viewer. Visual artists use certain methods to create the effects that stimulate these emotions, and examining the elements helps children appreciate the artist's skill in creating a final effect (Stewig, 1980). Just as our alphabet is the basis for our verbal literacy, the visual elements—including space, line, shape, color, texture, scale, dimension, and composition—are central to our visual literacy and our comprehension of artistic design.

In this chapter, I refer to the various pieces of artwork that appear at the beginning of each chapter as well as to artwork in the color insert that follows page 52 for examples of the various artistic elements, styles, and media presented in the following sections.

Space

To achieve their desired effects, artists use both **positive space** (the areas objects take up) and **negative space** (the white or blank areas that surround shapes and forms). For example, notice that Thomas Locker uses only positive space (no blank areas) in illustrating the nature scene that opens Chapter 13 (p. 296).

Artists use space to draw viewers' attention to the elements they wish to emphasize. A page with considerable negative space draws a viewer's immediate attention to the objects or characters depicted. However, a page with little negative space will divide the viewer's attention. Space can also create emotional effects. For example, an illustration with generous use of negative space may suggest emptiness, loneliness, and isolation; whereas an illustration with only positive space can evoke feelings of claustrophobia, confusion, or chaos.

Line

Line is a horizontal, vertical, angled, or curved mark made by a tool across a surface. Lines are used to define the shape of objects and to suggest movement and distance. Heavy lines can boldly define forms and create shapes, such as in Kate Greenaway's illustration on page 26, or lines can be thin and delicate. They can also appear static or convey movement. See Mary Grandpre's use of diagonal lines to show the rapid descent of both Harry Potter and the elusive golden snitch on page 111.

Lines need not be regular throughout an illustration. For example, see the various types of lines Arnold Lobel uses in his illustration of Frog and Toad on page 144. Artists also use the element of line to suggest certain emotional responses. Some examples are using curved lines to suggest calmness, zigzagged lines to suggest excitement, horizontal lines to suggest stability, vertical lines to suggest strength, and diagonal lines to suggest confusion.

Shape

Shape refers to the two dimensions of height and width arranged geometrically. Shape is usually created when spaces are contained by a combination of lines. Yet some visual art forms, such as collage, consist almost entirely of shapes with little or no use of singular lines. A shape can appear flat and two-dimensional, such as in Tomie dePaola's illustration of Tom and Tommy in the color insert. Alternatively, through an artist's shading techniques (with a buildup of small strokes), a shape may appear fully rounded and three-dimensional, such as Trish P. Watts's illustration of Bud on page 312.

Sutherland (1997) contrasts shapes as "distinct or vaguely suggested, simple or ornamented, free-flowing or rigid" (p. 116). Various types of shapes in an illustration are used to depict a variety of emotions. Lighter, more delicate shapes may suggest freedom, movement, and grace. Angular shapes are used to elicit an excited response from the viewer. Rounded shapes are used to achieve a sense of warmth, coziness, and security. Large grouped shapes may suggest stability, but also depict confinement and awkwardness, depending on the artist's purpose. Note how Jerry Pinkney uses large shapes to depict the confinement of Blanch in the chicken coop in the color insert.

Artists employ specific shapes to affect the viewer's perception. Squares may evoke a sense of dullness or lack of imagination. Triangles may be interpreted as agitation or conflict, whereas circles imply reassurance and importance. A circle is a virtual visual trap, and anything placed inside is perceived as significant (Stonehill, 1998).

Color

The **colors** in the rainbow are different hues in the visible spectrum of light. In visual art, color is achieved through pigments and light. An artist can make many colors from the pigment of a single **hue** (pure color) by adding differing amounts of *white* to achieve variations of **tints,** or by adding differing amounts of *black* to achieve variations of **shades.** Colors can be bold and brilliant or subtle and vaporous. Illustrators may use little color—for example, black ink on white paper, as in Sir John Tenniel's illustration of Alice and the Cheshire cat on page 1 and Ray Cruz's illustration of Felita's family on page 168. An artist may even employ monochrome techniques with a variety of tints and shades of a single hue.

Have you ever noticed how certain colors can evoke moods and feelings? For example, reds, yellows, and oranges are perceived as warm colors that suggest excitement and happiness. Greens and blues are cool colors and suggest calm, quiet, peaceful, or melancholy feelings. Darker shades are associated with gloominess and can induce a somber mood, whereas lighter shades are associated with cheeriness and can induce a feeling of happiness.

There are various theories on why specific colors bring certain emotions to mind. For example, red is the color of blood, and this color is often used to depict anger and other strong emotions, including passion. The ocean and sky appear blue, indicating coolness and passivity. The sun appears yellow, and this color commonly depicts warmth and cheerfulness. Snow is white, and this color is used to portray innocence. Night appears black, and this color often symbolizes evil (e.g., the clothing worn by burglars, witches, and vampires). Artists sometimes use these nonverbal cues to present subliminal messages to viewers and convey the tone of the book.

Texture

Some artists skillfully give the impression of three-dimensional texture on a two-dimensional canvas. Have you ever thought about how your eyes "feel" an object before you pick it up? For example, you can predict that a piece of lava rock will be rough before you touch it. Artists use the viewer's ability to predict tactile experiences to create optical **texture**—the illusion of a tactile surface by the skillful application of colors, lines, and shading that imply variations in dimension.

Collage is particularly effective in depicting textural contrast, and watercolor—when applied as a thin wash—is used to depict delicate textures such as a diaphanous fabric, a vapor of fog, or even the glimmer of candlelight. (I know; the latter is not a texture, but definitely a tactile experience if you stick your fingers in it!)

Russell (1997) commented, "An artist who wants to emphasize the realistic quality of a picture may pay greater attention to texture" (p. 119). For example, the shiny shirt that Bud wears in the realistic illustration on page 312 gives the illusion of smoothness. Diane Stanley used shading in the clothing worn by Cleopatra and Mark Antony to give the illusion of fullness on page 264. Barbara Cooney used the various elements to depict many textures in her illustration of the nativity play on page 234.

Responding to Literature

Analyzing Optical Textures   Using what you have learned about the various artistic elements, describe how Barbara Cooney achieves the following textures in *The Year of the Perfect Christmas Tree* (Houston): the hard stove, the soft sheep, the frilly dress, the prickly tree, the plump pianist, and the glowing candlelight.

Scale and Dimension

We live in a three-dimensional world, yet we are able to perceive a two-dimensional representation as realistic if an artist can imply linear perspective. Stonehill (1998) explained it in the following manner:

> The technical convention of linear perspective is a Renaissance invention. It is a systematic, formalized method of representation that allows the artist or designer to simulate depth with a few scant lines. It operates on the premise that objects appear progressively smaller the farther away they are. Lines that extend out into space converge at one or more vanishing points on the horizon line, which coincides with eye level. (p. 2)

Visual scale deals with the apparent relative size of objects, and it acts to show relations among them, especially their proximity. It is commonly used to create the illusion of depth (or distance) on a two-dimensional plane, because objects diminish in apparent size as the viewer moves away from them. In Ed Young's illustration on page 80, contrast the small size of the wolf in the lower left of the illustration with the larger size of the girls at the top of the illustration. This gives the perception of distance (and the reader senses that the girls' lives depend on maintaining that distance). At the top of Diane Stanley's illustration on page 264, notice the fleet of ships and the lighthouse known as the Pharos of Alexandria, whose very small sizes give the perception of distance between the two lovers and the seaport. Artists' skillful use of scale makes the viewers forget they are looking at a flat picture.

The illusion of **dimension** goes beyond scale. Because light travels in straight lines, it does not curve around an object. Therefore, not all parts of an object are equally illuminated from a single light source. To represent the variations of reflected light from an object's surface, artists use shading to make a flat shape appear to have dimension (e.g., making a circle appear to be a sphere). This includes using dark shading to depict shadows. For example, in Mary Grandpre's illustration of Harry Potter on page 111, note that through shading and the appearance of shadows, the light source appears to be behind Harry as he flies under the portico to catch the golden snitch.

Composition

Composition is the combination and arrangement of the elements in an illustration. Varying the placement of focal points and the angles from which a scene is viewed conveys different moods. A well-composed illustration shows unity and focus, and all the elements are in balance.

Another important aspect of composition is **point of view**, the vantage point from which the viewer is looking at the objects or events depicted. When the vantage point is close, the viewer is brought into the scene and is mentally engaged in the action or mood. When the vantage point is far away, the viewer is more detached. Notice how Ed Young's placement and sizing of objects in the illustration on page 80 give the viewer the children's perspective of the wolf far below.

Point of view is an important aspect both in the composition of an illustration and in the literary elements, which were discussed in the last chapter. Keep in mind that the events depicted in an illustration, as well as in a story, are understood differently when they are seen from different points of view. For example, a scene can be depicted from a small child's viewpoint looking up (sometimes called the worm's-eye view because it is from ground level) or from the panoramic viewpoint of a bird flying over the scene. Artists use point of view to imply dimension. For example, from the worm's-eye view, the lines of a tall building would be diagonal and appear wider at the base, progressively growing narrower at the top. Conversely, from the bird's-eye view, the same building would be wider at the top and grow progressively narrower at the base.

Responding to Literature

What Do I See? What Do I Think? What Do I Wonder?   Richards and Anderson (2003) developed a visual literacy strategy to help emergent readers focus attention on picture storybook illustrations. It is called "What do I see? What do I think? What do I wonder?" or STW. In this activity, children carefully view the book cover or first illustration and tell what they see in the picture. Record this on a chart (see example in Figure 3.1) in the first column, titled "What I see." Next, they tell what they think might be happening in the picture, and this is recorded in the second column, "What I think." Last, they form a question about the characters or setting depicted, and this is recorded in the third column, titled "What I wonder." Children then read the beginning of the book until they reach the next significant illustration and repeat the process.

Artistic Styles

Another way to enhance children's appreciation of illustration artwork is to look at the techniques artists use to create their work. **Folk art** is based on designs and images that are characteristic of a specific culture. Because there are innumerable cultures, there are also innumerable folk art styles, each attempting to recreate the atmosphere or pervasive mood of a specific culture. Folk art is most often characterized by imaginative use of color, repeated stylized patterns, lack of dimension, simple childlike forms, and flat patterns (absence of spatial depth). Mitsumasa Anno made use of these effects along with atypical scale in *Anno's Counting Book* on page 62. For example, the flowers are as tall as the adjacent trees, and the people are nearly as tall as the buildings.

Artists who use the **realistic** style depict objects realistically with recognizable shapes, realistic color, and proper perspectives and proportions. Because realistic art endeavors to depict the world as we see it, it is often the easiest style to recognize.

With pencil and watercolors, the artist created large crowded shapes to show the character's confinement in the chicken coop (from *The Talking Eggs,* written by Robert D. San Souci and illustrated by Jerry Pinkney).

The artist employed the realistic art style to illustrate a fantasy book (from *The Littlest Angel,* written by Charles Tazewell and illustrated by Paul Micich).

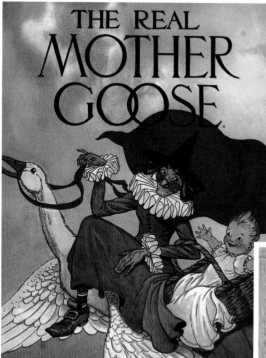

Notice the location of Mother Goose's cape, the child's hair, and the goose's wings, which give the illusion of movement through the air (from *The Real Mother Goose,* illustrated by Blanche Fisher Wright).

The artist used cut paper, crayons, and colored pencils to create this illustration (from *Leaves! Leaves! Leaves!* written and illustrated by Nancy Elizabeth Wallace).

The three-dimensional collage for this book was created by Sculpy clay, acrylic paints, wood, fabric, and a variety of found objects (from *Snapshots from the Wedding,* written by Gary Soto and illustrated by Stephanie Garcia).

The artist used simple forms and flat patterns that are characteristic of folk art (from *Tom,* written and illustrated by Tomie dePaola).

Both acrylic and oil paints were used by the artist to achieve the deep color of this illustration that uses only positive space (from *My Life with the Wave,* written by Octavio Paz and Catherine Cowan and illustrated by Mark Buehner).

Watercolor washes were used to create fluid shapes in this whimsical illustration (from *Tell Me Again about the Night I Was Born,* written by Jamie Lee Curtis and illustrated by Laura Cornell).

Mommy, Daddy, tell me again about the night I was born.

in the napping house, where no one now is sleeping.

Notice that the point of view in this illustration is above the ground (from *The Napping House,* written by Audrey Wood and illustrated by Don Wood).

The artist employed visual scale to create the illusion of distance from the main house to the outhouse (from *When I Was Young in the Mountains,* written by Cynthia Rylant and illustrated by Diane Goode).

Notice the artist's unusual depiction of free-standing leaves (at the top of the trees) that are not connected by twigs or small branches (from *Ox-Cart Man,* written by Donald Hall and illustrated by Barbara Cooney).

In this illustration from a wordless book, you can look at the facial expression of the frog to determine what it is thinking (from *Tuesday,* written and illustrated by David Wiesner).

The artist made use of multiple colors to depict the festivity of the occasion (from *Radio Man,* written and illustrated by Arthur Dorros).

The artist used digital art to create this illustration (*from Walter the Farting Dog,* written by William Kotzwinkle and Glenn Murray and illustrated by Audrey Colman).

FIGURE 3.1   STW Chart on *Snow-White and the Seven Dwarfs*
(Illustrated by Nancy Ekholm Burkert)

What I See	What I Think	What I Wonder
A beautiful woman standing under some leaves	Something is behind her because she is looking in back.	Is someone chasing her?
The woman running through the forest with animals everywhere	She likes animals because she is smiling, but the animals are afraid because they are running away.	Is she lost?
The woman fixing dinner for some little people	This is a happy place because they are smiling, there are flowers on the table, and the dog looks nice.	Does she work for these little people?
The woman on the ground and a person in black outside the house	The person in black hurt the woman because she is running away instead of helping her.	Will the beautiful woman get better?
A person dancing with a red ball in her hand	This is a scary person because her room has bats, a picture of a skeleton, and a black spider.	Is she going to hurt the beautiful woman again?
The little people and a man riding a horse next to the beautiful woman in a glass box	The woman is dead because her eyes are closed and the little people look so sad.	Is the man going to take her back to the forest?
The woman and man walking up some steps to a party with the little people	They are the king and queen because they are wearing crowns.	Will the little people live with the king and queen in a palace?

This style is by far the most common choice for book covers in young adult literature. Trish P. Watts used the realistic style in creating the art for the cover of *Bud, Not Buddy* (Curtis) on page 312. Yet while both the objects in the front (Bud and his suitcase) and the object in the back (the poster that is Bud's only clue to his father's identity) look realistic, the composition with one overlying the other gives an unusual effect.

The **impressionist** style uses an interplay of color and light created with blots, splashes, speckles, or dots of paint (as opposed to longer brush strokes) to create a dreamlike, romantic effect—often a view from afar—such as Thomas Locker's illustration from *Thirteen Moons on Turtle's Back* (Bruchac & London) on page 296. Artists using the impressionist style are concerned with the transient appearance, "the way things momentarily look in particular circumstances of light and shade" (Nodelman, 1996, p. 229). For example, see Ed Young's artwork in *Lon Po Po: A Red-Riding Hood Story from China* on page 80.

The **expressionist** style leans toward the abstract, focusing on depicting emotions. It employs the artistic elements in a highly individual and subjective manner in which the artists paint what they feel, rather than simply what they see. It includes deliberate distortion and exaggeration. Expressionism has several variations. *Cubism* juxtaposes various geometric shapes, for example, Lois Ehlert's illustrations (not depicted) in *Thump, Thump, Rat-a-Tat-Tat* (Baer). *Fauvism* employs bold black lines and richly contrasting colors, sometimes with a stained-glass effect, for example, the artwork by Ed Emberley in *Drummer Hoff* at the beginning of this chapter (p. 46).

Artists who employ the **surrealist** style distort and play with images to convey a fantasy quality. Surrealism represents the artist's intellectual (as opposed to emotional) response to a subject. It depicts unrealistic situations in a way that makes the impossible seem strangely possible. That is, objects can be rendered quite realistically, but they are sometimes juxtaposed unnaturally with contrasting objects to create a world that is surprising, puzzling, and even shocking. For example, Sir John Tenniel's illustration on page 1 from *Alice's Adventures in Wonderland* (Carroll) depicts a realistic-looking girl gazing up a realistic-looking tree. However, among the slim branches is an overly large cat with a bizarre (and not very catlike) expression on his smiling face!

It is not surprising that surrealistic art most often appears in books of fantasy, such as *Harry Potter and the Sorcerer's Stone* (Rowling). On the cover of this book, Mary Grandpre masterfully composes a picture that includes the most interesting items of the story—the golden snitch, Hogwarts castle, the three-headed dog, and a unicorn—all encircling Harry, who is swiftly diving on his broomstick in a game of Quidditch, shown on page 111.

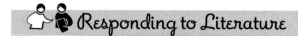

Responding to Literature

Using Book Cover Art to Make Predictions   Book jackets on hardcover copies of the Harry Potter series (American editions only) contain mural-type illustrations that encompass both the front and back. Carefully view all the elements in the mural before reading the book, recording your predictions on how each might contribute to the story. After reading the book, look back at the cover and discuss how each character, object, and setting contributed to the plot.

In the **cartoon** style, drawings are reduced to their essentials with simple lines and primary colors. (Resist an automatic association with comic books, or you will have difficulty recognizing this style in children's literature.) The simplified figures and exaggerated proportions used in the cartoon style are particularly effective in achieving movement and humor. Dr. Seuss made this style popular with his gross exaggerations and zany creatures that create hilarious effects in his many children's books. Shel Silverstein also uses the cartoon style in pen and ink to illustrate his books.

The classic artistic styles gradually developed through artistic movements of the past, so they are time oriented. They are directly linked to where the artists lived and studied art, which masters they researched, and the mentors and peers with whom they interacted. Classic styles, such as the impressionist and expressionist, are rarely found in their purest form in artwork for children. Although today's artists are likely influenced by the classic styles, most use their own hybrid styles, which I discuss in the next section.

Artistic Media and Techniques

Many artists consistently employ their own unique styles that, when combined with their favorite technique and medium, makes their work easily recognizable. For example, Tomie dePaola's characteristic folk art style in watercolor is his signature (see the color insert), and Eric Carle's signature style is collages of transparent tissue papers, which he lightly streaks with paint. Other artists, such as Ed Emberley, prefer versatility and use different combinations of style, technique, and media, depending on how they want to express a particular story.

The materials that artists use to make the original artwork for illustrations are called *media*. Artists select media carefully in order to give optimal expression to their ideas; otherwise, the images they wish to create could be limited. For example, woodcuts are bold, but they rarely reveal texture. Collage can easily depict texture but seldom gives the perception of depth. Black ink on white paper can be used to achieve depth, but it will not convey the moods of the story the way color can. Tempera can be used to achieve myriad colors, but it will not create the impression of light the way translucent watercolor does.

Painting

Watercolor is the most popular medium for book illustrations. In this medium, artists add varying amounts of water to either a dry form of pigment or a pigment bound with a water-soluble solution of gum arabic and glycerin. Watercolor is used to produce a fluid, loose, sometimes transparent effect when a greater amount of water is added, or a highly controlled effect with strong colors when it is mixed with less water. The color itself can define the form; for example, see the artwork by David Wiesner from *Tuesday* in the color insert. Alternatively, ink or pencil lines can be added to produce definition; for example, see the artwork by Gail Gibbons in *Frogs* on page 281. The ink/pencil lines may be formed before the watercolor is applied or after, depending on the desired effect.

Tempera consists of pigment mixed with egg yolk or a gelatinous or glutinous substance. It is less transparent than watercolor, so it can be used to produce brilliant hues. Gouache is powdered paint similar to tempera, but it is mixed with a white base, resulting in an opaque color.

Oil paints combine color pigment with a linseed oil base and turpentine or other thinner. These paints are usually opaque, and layering can produce effects of depth and dimension. Trish P. Watts used oil paint to create the book cover art for *Bud, Not Buddy* (Curtis) on page 312.

In **acrylic paints**, liquid acrylic plastic (polymer) is used to bind color pigment. Acrylics can be used to produce brilliant and even shocking colors. Like oil paint, acrylic dries slowly, and it can be manipulated, changed, or covered with varnish or gel for myriad effects. Mitsumasa Anno used acrylic paints to achieve the vivid colors in *Anno's Counting Book* on page 62.

Drawing

Drawing is a linear art technique accomplished with instruments such as pencil, pen and ink, charcoal, marker, or crayon. Lead or colored pencils can be used to create strong lines, shaded areas, smudged shadows, and details. For example, see how Diane Stanley combines colored pencils with watercolor in her illustrations for *Cleopatra* (Stanley & Vennema) on page 264.

Pen-and-ink drawings can be rendered with different shapes and types of pen points and with either black or colored ink. Pen and ink is often used to give definition in watercolor washes, but it can be used alone with no colors, as in the drawings by Ray Cruz in *Felita* (Mohr) on page 168.

Pastels are soft-colored chalks for drawing, but they can also be applied by hand in their powdered form. Pastels produce opaque images; for example, see the artwork by Ed Young in *Lon Po Po* on page 80.

Other Techniques

Artists use a variety of other techniques (though not all are depicted in this textbook). **Woodcut** is the oldest medium for making art prints. More recently, linoleum has been substituted for hardwood because it is easier to cut. (*Block print* is a more appropriate term when wood is not used.) The artist cuts away the background of the picture, applies ink or color to the surface, and presses the block against paper. Ed Emberley employed this technique to illustrate *Drummer Hoff* on page 46.

Airbrushing is a form of stenciling in which artists use a compressed-air atomizer to spray paint on a surface. This technique was used by Leo and Diane Dillon in *Why Mosquitoes Buzz in People's Ears* (Aardema) (not depicted).

Collage, first made famous by Pablo Picasso, is a technique of cutting or tearing paper or fabric shapes that are then assembled and glued on a surface. Ezra Jack Keats made this form popular in children's books with *The Snowy Day*, and artists such as Leo Lionni, Eric Carle, and Nancy Elizabeth Wallace carry on the tradition. See an example of Wallace's cut paper collage from *Leaves! Leaves! Leaves!* in the color insert.

Also in the color insert is a most unusual form of three-dimensional collage. In *Snapshots from the Wedding* (Soto), Stephanie Garcia used Sculpy clay, acrylic paints, wood, fabric, and a variety of found objects to create dioramas that were then photographed.

Integrating Literature and Technology

Illustrating Scenes from Storybooks

by B. Ruth Sylvester

Children may illustrate a favorite scene from a storybook by using computer art programs, such as Microsoft Paint or AppleWorks. From the program's "toolbox," children have access to a variety of drawing tools such as a virtual "pencil" or "spray can" for an airbrushed effect. Lines and shapes drawn with these tools can be thickened and colored, depending on the desired effect; and perfect circles, ovals, and straight lines are achievable with computer art. Young artists can color their illustrations by selecting basic colors from the palette on the menu bar or by creating custom colors with just a few clicks of the mouse. In addition, the image can be altered by flipping it horizontally or vertically, by inverting the colors, or by stretching or skewing the image.

Digital photography may be the answer for children who are not confident in their artistic abilities. With a simple (and inexpensive) digital camera, children may collaborate with friends to stage scenes from a story with props found in the classroom or brought from home. Once the scenes are captured with the camera, files can be inserted into any photo program and enhanced. Some elaborate graphics-editing programs, such as Adobe Photoshop, have more than 100 filter choices to transform illustrations that were created with crayons, photographs, or any other media. Some of the filters' effects are watercolor, line drawing, mosaic, stained glass, and blurred.

Additionally, thousands of images in the form of clip art, photographs, and illustrations may be captured from search engines such as Google. Go to www.google.com, and select "Images." In the textbox, type in a keyword to search. Be prepared for the voluminous results (over 148,000 images are located when the word "ladybugs" is entered)! Images are located at numerous websites, some of which may be copyrighted, so for each desired image, you must visit the originating website and carefully review it for guidelines on using the material. Images in the public domain can easily be saved to your computer by right clicking on the image and selecting "Save Picture As . . ." from the menu. Then save it in your Pictures folder for future projects. To add a graphic to a Microsoft document, first click on the area where you want it to appear. Next, go to the "Insert" menu, and select "Picture." Click on "From File," and then double click the selected filename or thumbnail image.

Children's art no longer needs to be restricted to drawing and coloring with pencils, crayons, markers, and paint. By giving children time to explore the unlimited options of technology-created art, you provide them with engaging opportunities to create images that are fun, sophisticated, and attractive. And if they take a risk and do not like the results, they can easily remedy it by clicking the undo button!

📖 Issues in Illustration

What Is True Art?   Photography has been called the art of composition, but some critics have questioned it as an artistic technique because they consider it more of a technical skill than an artistic ability. It was made popular by Tana Hoban, who used a combination of her artist's eye and photographer's skill to produce illustrations in her many concept books, such as *Cubes, Cones, Cylinders & Spheres*. Other photographer–illustrators of children's books include George Ancona and Bruce McMillan. Today, computer-generated graphics constitute the newest technology-based art form in children's picture books. Digital art was pioneered by J. Otto Seibold with *Mr. Lunch Takes a Plane Ride*. Lisa Desimini used computer-generated graphics to illustrate *Love Letters* (Adoff), and veteran illustrators Don and Audrey Wood now work exclusively as digital artists; for example, see *Alphabet Adventure*.

Select a book that is illustrated by either photography or computer-generated graphics (or view Nina Crews's *The Neighborhood Mother Goose*, which employs both). Referring to specific illustrations in the book, develop an argument either for or against the selected medium as a true artistic style.

Integrating Visual Art and Literature
by Janet C. Richards

Thousands of years ago, humans etched paintings on cave walls. Today's toddlers scribble and draw (occasionally on walls) before they can speak. Five-year-olds make chalk images on sidewalks. Adolescents passionately spray paint intricate portrayals of their emotions and experiences on bridges, buildings, and highway exits. There is no doubt that visual art is a primary form of human expression and communication. Therefore, it makes sense to integrate visual art with children's literature.

Integrating visual art with literature is supported by the twenty-first-century visions of literacy that extend definitions of language far beyond reading and writing. Committees for both the National Standards for Arts Education (U.S. Department of Education, 1994) and the Standards for the English Language Arts (National Council of Teachers of English, 1996) endorse connecting visual arts with literature. Art and literature connections are also validated by reader response theory (Rosenblatt, 1993) and multiple intelligences theory (Gardner, 1999).

At the most basic levels, integrating the visual arts helps children become more motivated about reading and listening to literature, and it helps them visualize and remember stories. At higher levels, connecting visual art to literature allows children to evoke and represent their feelings and emotions about story characters and their actions. Children also become more aware of a story's setting, problem, and solution when they can draw or use clay to sculpt their ideas about these elements. In addition, children can show their understanding of critical story scenes and underlying story themes by devising group murals and dioramas. At a much deeper level, children who translate their understanding of literature into another literacy sign system, such as visual art, have opportunities to explore, imagine, reflect, and express their ideas in new ways. Equally important, visual art provides learning opportunities that are not related to children's social class, ethnic background, school ranking, or Standard English proficiency (Richards, 2002).

Numerous resources offer suggestions for teachers and parents to help children connect the arts with literature. I suggest reading Chapter 4 in *Integrating Multiple Literacies in K–8 Classrooms: Cases, Commentaries, and Practical Applications* (Richards & McKenna, 2003). Other valuable readings are Chapter 5 in *The Arts as Meaning Makers: Integrating Literature and the Arts throughout the Curriculum* (Cornett, 1999) and *Art Works! Interdisciplinary Learning Powered by the Arts* (Wolf & Blalock, 1999).

These resources discuss ways to expand children's understanding of literature through visual art. For example, 4- and 5-year-olds might listen to the story *Snow-White and the Seven Dwarfs* (Burkert), as they fashion a papier-mâché poisoned red apple. Eight-year-olds might read Eric Carle's *The Very Hungry Caterpillar* and make an edible caterpillar using sliced banana for body parts; dried coconut for body fuzz; raisins for eyes, nose, and mouth; and tall, thin cookies for antennae. Older children might read *The Watsons Go to Birmingham—1963* (Curtis) and depict their aesthetic responses (i.e., personal perceptions, attitudes, and opinions) to the tragic Alabama church bombing by combining sophisticated media, such as watercolors, markers, and pastels.

Multimedia visual arts activities are also options. For example, children might read *Gregory Cool* (Binch) in which a boy visits his grandparents on the island of Tobago. Then they might create a large tissue-paper ocean and sand beach with shells and papier-mâché crabs. After reading *My Great-Aunt Arizona* (Houston), they might use watercolors, crayons, fine-line markers, computer graphics, and magazine cutouts to depict their personal dream travels. An ecologically focused book, such as *The Great Kapok Tree: A Tale of the Amazon Rain Forest* (Cherry), might inspire children to use cardboard, tissue paper, bark, grass, construction paper, wallpaper scraps, cotton balls, and other media to create a rain forest complete with animals.

Classroom teachers will also find abundant ideas for integrating art and literature in *Art Projects Plus* (Blount & Webb, 1997). I hope you will sustain your children's in-born artistic abilities by encouraging them to respond to literature with visual art.

Responding to Literature

Designing Book Covers

by Donna Stewart

Select a book your children have not heard before and cover the outside with heavy paper, such as from a brown grocery bag. This example uses *Alexander and the Wind-Up Mouse* by Leo Lionni, but any picture book with strong characters will work. Tell the children to visualize the characters and setting as you read the text (but do not show the illustrations). After you finish reading, ask them to close their eyes and form a mental picture of Alexander the mouse, the wind-up mouse, the lizard wizard, the kitchen, and the garden. Next, tell the students to pretend they have been hired to illustrate the book, and their first job is to design a cover that incorporates an important event from the story. It should include the title and author. Encourage them to select from a variety of media: watercolor, tempera, chalk, Cray-pas, collage, charcoal, or colored pencils. When finished, create a bulletin board with the students' book covers. Last, reread the book, sharing all the illustrations.

Summary

Just as there are literary elements, there are also artistic elements. Space consists of the areas that objects take up. Line is a horizontal, vertical, angled, or curved mark made by a tool across a surface. Shape refers to the two dimensions of height and width arranged geometrically. Colors are different hues in the visible spectrum of light. Optical texture is the illusion of a tactile surface by the application of colors, lines, and shading that imply variations in dimension. Visual scale deals with the apparent relative size of objects. Dimension is an illusion created by shading to make a flat shape appear to have depth. Composition is the combination and arrangement of the elements in a piece of art.

Artistic styles found in children's books include folk art, realistic, impressionist, expressionist, surrealist, and cartoon. Artistic techniques include painting (watercolor, tempera, oil, and acrylics), drawing (lead or colored pencils, pen and ink, and pastels), and various other methods (such as woodcutting, airbrushing, and collage).

Children's Books Cited in Chapter 3

Aardema, Verna. *Why Mosquitoes Buzz in People's Ears*. Illus. Leo D. Dillon & Diane Dillon. Dial, 1975.

Adoff, Arnold. *Love Letters*. Illus. Lisa Desimini. Blue Sky Press, 1997.

Anno, Mitsumasa. *Anno's Counting Book*. Thomas Y. Crowell, 1977.

Baer, Gene. *Thump, Thump, Rat-a-Tat-Tat*. Illus. Lois Ehlert. HarperCollins, 1989.

Burkert, Nancy Ekholm. *Snow-White and the Seven Dwarfs*. Farrar, Straus, & Giroux, 1987.

Binch, Caroline. *Gregory Cool*. Dial, 1994.

Bruchac, Joseph, & Jonathan London. *Thirteen Moons on Turtle's Back*. Illus. Thomas Locker. Philomel, 1992.

Carle, Eric. *The Very Hungry Caterpillar*. Philomel, 1969.

Carroll, Lewis. *Alice's Adventures in Wonderland*. Illus. Sir John Tenniel. Henry Altemus, 1865.

Cherry, Lynne. *The Great Kapok Tree: A Tale of the Amazon Rain Forest*. Harcourt Brace Jovanovich, 1990.

Crews, Nina. *The Neighborhood Mother Goose*. Amistad, 2003.

Curtis, Christopher Paul. *Bud, Not Buddy*. Illus. Trish P. Watts. Delacorte Press, 1999.

Curtis, Christopher Paul. *The Watsons Go to Birmingham—1963*. Delacorte Press, 1995.

dePaola, Tomie. *Tom*. Putnam, 1993.

Emberley, Barbara. *Drummer Hoff*. Illus. Ed Emberley. Simon & Schuster, 1967.

Gibbons, Gail. *Frogs*. Holiday House, 1993.

Hoban, Tana. *Cubes, Cones, Cylinders & Spheres*. Greenwillow, 2000.

Houston, Gloria. *My Great-Aunt Arizona*. Illus. Susan Condie Lamb. HarperCollins, 1992.

Houston, Gloria. *The Year of the Perfect Christmas Tree*. Illus. Barbara Cooney. Dial, 1988.

Keats, Ezra Jack. *The Snowy Day*. Viking, 1962.

Lionni, Leo. *Alexander and the Wind-Up Mouse*. Knopf, 1969.

Lobel, Arnold. *Frog and Toad Together*. HarperTrophy, 1971.

Mohr, Nicholasa. *Felita*. Illus. Ray Cruz. Dial Books, 1979.

Potter, Beatrix. *The Tale of Peter Rabbit*. Frederick Warne, 1901.

Rowling, J. K. *Harry Potter and the Sorcerer's Stone*. Illus. Mary Grandpre. Scholastic, 1998.

Seibold, J. Otto, & Vivian Walsh. *Mr. Lunch Takes a Plane Ride*. Viking, 1993.

Soto, Gary. *Snapshots from the Wedding*. Illus. Stephanie Garcia. Putnam, 1997.

Stanley, Diane, & Peter Vennema. *Cleopatra*. Illus. Diane Stanley. William Morrow, 1994.

Wallace, Nancy Elizabeth. *Leaves! Leaves! Leaves!* Marshall Cavendish, 2003.

Wiesner, David. *Tuesday*. Clarion, 1992.

Wood, Audrey. *Alphabet Adventure*. Scholastic, 2001.

Young, Ed. *Lon Po Po: A Red-Riding Hood Story from China*. Putnam & Grosset, 1989.

Anno's Counting Book

This illustration was created in the folk art style that characteristically does not employ the elements of dimension or scale.

From *Anno's Counting Book*, written and illustrated by Mitsumasa Anno.

Library location   **Section E—Easy reading picture books**

Shelved alphabetically by author's last name

ave you ever had a young child turn a page too early while you were reading a picture book? When you say, "Wait, I'm not finished reading this page!" the child looks up quizzically and thinks, "Well, *I* am!" Young children believe that the illustrations, rather than the printed words, tell the story. When you read to them, they conceptualize that you are *telling* a story from the pictures. Indeed, a good picture book does tell a story through its art. After listening to a book once and looking at the pictures, most young children can retell the story.

Recall the definitions of books with illustrations presented in Chapter 1.

- *Picture books* convey their message through a series of pictures with only a small amount of text (or none at all). The illustrations are as important as— or more important than—the text in conveying the message.
- *Picture storybooks* are picture books with a plot, and the text and illustrations equally convey the story line. (Most people simply call these picture books as well.)
- *Illustrated books* are for older children. The illustrations are fewer and more limited in color, sometimes only black and white. The illustrations are extensions of the text and may add to the story, but they are not necessary to convey its meaning.

Keep in mind that *picture book* is a format. It is found in all genres and all forms of books. The illustrations in a children's book (or lack thereof) play an important part when younger children select books. Therefore, it is important that illustrations appeal to young readers and complement the text in telling a story.

Books of Early Childhood

What are your earliest memories of books? Did you have access to picture books before you entered school? Being regularly read to and having access to appropriate books before school age make a big difference in children's achievement once they start school. Children who have listened to many readings of books and who have been encouraged to look through the books and retell the stories have a much greater likelihood of becoming good readers.

Board Books

I have stressed that it is never too early to begin reading to your own children, and I suggest you start with the books made especially for the very young. Little ones not only love to look at books—they also like to gnaw, throw, and pull at them, so these books must be sturdy.

In **board books,** the content and format are designed for very young children. These durable books usually consist of twelve to thirty-two sturdy cardboard pages that have a glossy wipe-off finish on each side. They range in size from three to twelve inches square, and all corners are rounded to prevent a poke in the eye. Usually each page is illustrated with a clear and simple picture, sometimes with just a one-word caption. Some board books may tell a simple story, but many are concept oriented and have labels for familiar objects. Also, best-selling picture books sometimes are published in a board book version. Following is a list of some of the most popular first books. (Note the icon designating my favorite book in this list, *The Going to Bed Book.*)

Recommended Board Books

Aigner-Clark, Julie. *Puzzling Shapes: A Puzzle Book.* Illus. by Nadeem Zaidi. Baby Einstein, 2002.

Aigner-Clark, Julie. *See and Spy Counting.* Illus. by Nadeem Zaidi. Baby Einstein, 2001.

Bentley, Dawn. *Good Night, Sweet Butterflies: A Color Dreamland.* Illus. Heather Cahoon. Little Simon, 2003.

Boynton, Sandra. *Barnyard Dance!* Workman, 1993.

Boynton, Sandra. *Moo Baa La La La.* Little Simon, 1982.

Boynton, Sandra. *The Going to Bed Book.* Little Simon, 1995.

Brown, Margaret Wise. *Goodnight Moon.* Illus. Clement Hurd. HarperCollins, 1947.

Brown, Margaret Wise. *The Runaway Bunny.* Illus. Clement Hurd. HarperFestival, 1942.

Christelow, Eileen. *Five Little Monkeys Jumping on the Bed.* Clarion Books, 1989.

Falconer, Ian. *Olivia's Opposites.* Atheneum, 2002

Fox, Mem. *Time for Bed.* Illus. Jane Dyer. Red Wagon, 1997.

Kunhardt, Dorothy. *Pat the Bunny.* Golden Books, 1940.

Martin, Bill, Jr., & John Archambault. *Chicka Chicka ABC.* Little Simon, 1993.

Martin, Bill, Jr. *Brown Bear, Brown Bear, What Do You See?* Illus. Eric Carle. Henry Holt, 1996.

McBratney, Sam. *Guess How Much I Love You.* Illus. Anita Jeram. Candlewick, 1994.

Melmed, Laura Krauss. *I Love You as Much . . .* Illus. Henri Sorensen. HarperFestival, 1993.

Rathmann, Peggy. *Good Night, Gorilla.* Putnam, 1994.

Van Fleet, Matthew. *Tails.* Red Wagon, 2003.

Wilkinson, Bruce H., & Melody Carlson. *Secrets of the Vine for Little Ones.* Tommy Nelson, 2002.

Zelinsky, Paul O. *The Wheels on the Bus.* Dutton, 1990.

Concept Books

Concept books are picture books that present numerous examples of a particular concept. Because children are never too young to listen to and look at books, they are also never too young to learn about the world around them. One of the most delightful ways children learn about their world is through concept books, which

Featured Author

Sandra Boynton

Undoubtedly, Sandra Boynton is my favorite author of early childhood books! In addition to authoring and illustrating numerous board books, she composes music, designs thousands of greeting cards, and creates art that appears on collections of wallpaper, T-shirts, balloons, plush toys, stationery items, and mugs. Her oddball humor makes her board books extra-appealing to children and adults alike. Her signature style features whimsical and hilariously zany animals, such as the elephant, moose, and pig in *The Going to Bed Book*. Children might find their own bedtime routines more fun after they see these animals prepare for bed by taking a bath (in one big tub), finding their pajamas, brushing their teeth, and finally rocking to sleep in the ark. In her classic, *Moo Baa La La La*, enchantingly silly animals entertain children with their oddball antics while making the traditional animal sounds—all except for the three dancing pigs who sing "La La La." In *Barnyard Dance!* a bespectacled cow plays the fiddle while a pig twirls a sheep at a boisterous, knee-slapping square dance. Readers will want to sing along as the animals do-si-do in the barnyard. In *Oh My Oh My Oh Dinosaurs!* learning opposites is fun with Boynton's sassy and energetic dinosaurs. Through activities such as singing, sunbathing, painting, dancing, and playing volleyball, a gang of personable dinosaurs demonstrates concepts such as *good* and *bad, happy* and *sad, early* and *late,* and *plump* and *lean.* The simple rhymes, goofy animals, and sweet lyrics in all of Boynton's books make for memorable reading experiences.

focus on a particular body of knowledge. They could be considered informational books for the very young and do much to help children discover labels of familiar objects and living things. Good concept books also present beautiful images and entertaining language to attract young listeners and readers. These books help activate children's thinking, and they are a stimulus for children to construct schemata for new concepts through their own mental relationships. Some of the common concepts presented in these books include

- Letters of the alphabet (e.g., a, b, c)
- Counting numbers (e.g., 1, 2, 3)
- Colors (e.g., red, yellow, blue)
- Shapes (e.g., circle, square, triangle)
- Opposites (e.g., hot/cold, fast/slow)
- Size relationships (e.g., big/small, short/tall)

Alphabet Books. Alphabet books, also called ABC books, are concept books that present the letters of the alphabet. These are often a young child's first introduction to the symbols that represent our language. It is desirable for alphabet books to present the letters in alphabetical order in both lower- and uppercase forms (or little and big letters, as children call them). Commonly, one **two-page spread** (two facing pages in a book) is devoted to each letter. For example, the featured letter and one or more words that begin with that letter are on one page, and an illustration depicting the things named is on the facing page.

Russell (1997) identified three patterns of alphabet books. Potpourri books have no uniformity in subject matter. For example, the featured objects in *From Acorn to Zoo* (Kitamura) range from armadillo, airplane, balloon, and book to yo-yo, yogurt, zoo, and zebra.

Sequential story books have a continuous story line throughout. Finding a word for each letter of the alphabet to fit in the story line can be quite difficult, and the examples sometimes appear contrived. *Albert B. Cub & Zebra* (Rockwell) is one such book, containing only a very loose story line. However, the illustrations are colorful and invite conversation between a child and adult.

Themed books depict objects that are linked by a theme or topic, as in *Ashanti to Zulu: African Traditions* (Musgrove). These books can be helpful when you are teaching thematic units to children of all ages. The bibliography at the end of this section includes alphabet books with themes of animals, bugs, coral reef creatures, dinosaurs, and flowers—to name a few. Themed books are a colorful and interesting way to convey information. However, as with sequential story alphabet books, finding an appropriate example for each letter is challenging, and sometimes authors resort to words from other languages. For example, *Eating the Alphabet* (Ehlert) contains the words *jalapeno* and *jicama* for the letter *J*. Both vegetables are native to Mexico, and their names are pronounced as if the *j* were an *h* (hah-lah-PAY-nyoh and HEE-cah-mah). This could be confusing to young children who are just beginning to match letters with the language sounds they represent.

Because many alphabet books are available, teachers and parents can afford to be quite discriminating when selecting them. I mentioned that it is desirable for books to depict both forms of the alphabet—uppercase (capital) and lowercase (small) letters. At least 90 percent of the letters young children encounter in print are lowercase, so it is the most desirable form to learn first. Unfortunately, many otherwise excellent alphabet books present only the uppercase letters.

Annie's abc (Owen) is a potpourri book that exclusively depicts lowercase letters. With hundreds of small pictures to match with words and sounds, it provides both an exercise in observation and a way for the adult to introduce the letters and their corresponding sounds. It also presents an excellent example of a clear, nonornamental typeface that is easily recognizable to young children. Even the manuscript forms of lowercase *a* and *g* (ɑ and ɡ) are utilized instead of the printed forms found in nearly all other books.

Ed Emberley's ABC (Emberley) uniquely shows how to form uppercase letters. Each letter is presented on a two-page spread that is divided into four frames, showing animals engaged in a variety of activities that demonstrate the sequence of strokes that form each letter. For example, the letter *B* is formed by a beetle that takes blueberries out of a basket and places them on a table in front of a bear. At the end of the book, all the letters are labeled with the numbered sequence and direction of the strokes. Another book that uses graphics to present the letters is *Alphabatics* (MacDonald), in which letters are reshaped through a series of frames to form a picture of the object named. For example, the lowercase letter *m* reshapes to form a mustache. These books are good for children who are strong visual learners.

In addition to presenting the sequence of letters and the unique forms of each, ABC books introduce other concepts of our alphabetic language. Nearly all children (and adults) say that "letters make sounds" (e.g., "What sound does the letter *B* make?"). In actuality, people make speech sounds, and *letters represent sounds*. A grasp of which letter (or letter cluster) represents which sounds is known as **letter–sound correspondence.** By listening to and experimenting with the **phonemes** (sounds) that letters represent, children grow in their phonemic awareness that spoken words are made up of various sounds. Children who are adept in phonemic awareness are better able to decipher the code of our written language and become independent readers.

For children to grasp letter–sound correspondence in alphabet books, it is essential that the featured words and their corresponding illustrations be within the child's realm of knowledge. For example, "*A* is for apple" is preferable to "*A* is for anvil" (Anno). Even if children have never eaten an apple, most likely they have seen one. However, young children probably do not have a mental schema for *anvil*, because they have had no experience with one. Nor would they likely be able to grasp the meaning if it were explained, because the use of anvils is quite limited today.

Books such as Maurice Sendak's *Alligators All Around,* which uses abstract examples (e.g., "forever fooling," "never napping," and "quite quarrelsome"), are limited in their use for nonreaders. However, they do make delightful reading experiences for older children who enjoy alliteration. Cefali (1995) provides an annotated list of alphabet books suitable for children who have already mastered the alphabet.

To help young children make the connection between letter and sound, the featured letter should represent the first sound in the illustrative word. For example, "*P* is for puppy" is far preferable to "*P* is for lip." This rule is not simply for consistency or for the delight of alliteration. Beginning readers initially learn to segment the first phoneme of words. Once that is mastered, they learn to segment the last phoneme. Finally, they learn to segment the phonemes in between.

Because all vowels in the English language represent more than one sound, they are a particular challenge to authors of alphabet books. In *Dr. Seuss's ABC* (Seuss), the author is masterful in his representation of the vowel *o*. Seuss ingeniously represented this vowel in five ways—short vowel (*O*scar and *o*strich), long vowel (*o*nly), *r*-controlled vowel (*o*range), and both diphthong vowels (*oi*led and *ow*l).

Consonants are more consistent than vowels in their representation of sounds. However, there are a few that commonly represent more than one sound. Both C and G represent *hard* and *soft* sounds. *Dr. Seuss's ABC* demonstrates this with *camel* on the *ceiling*. In *From Acorn to Zoo*, Satoshi Kitamura uses *girl, grass,* and *goat* to illustrate the hard sound of G and illustrates the soft sound with *giraffe* and *ginger*.

However, most books do not contain examples of both the soft and hard sounds for these two letters.

The letter *X* represents different sounds when it appears in the beginning, middle, or end of words. (Listen for these sounds when you say *xerography, exit,* and *fox.*) Few common words begin with *X*, so *xylophone* has been the classic word to exemplify this letter, because it is within most children's realm of knowledge. However, in recent years, authors have become creative, particularly in themed books. Examples are

- *xenotarsosaurus*—a small meat-eating dinosaur that walked on two legs (Dodson)
- *Xhosa*—an African tribe (Musgrove)
- *xigua*—the Chinese name for watermelon (Ehlert)

Good alphabet books present more than letter forms, letter sequence, and letter–sound correspondence. Vocabulary growth can be encouraged when an adult reads the book with a child, pointing out and naming the various things in each picture. Some potpourri books—such as *From Acorn to Zoo: And Everything in Between in Alphabetical Order* (Kitamura)—have numerous objects on all pages with a small label conveniently placed under each item. Others, such as *Albert B. Cub & Zebra* (Rockwell), do not label the targeted objects on the page, but the reader can turn to the back of the book to find the names. In addition to the main animal depicted, each page of *Animalia* (Base) contains multiple other objects that are spelled with the same beginning letter, so children can play a game of finding and naming as many as possible.

Some alphabet books, such as *Ashanti to Zulu: African Traditions* (Musgrove), are obviously not geared for early childhood, but rather for more able readers. Often these are themed books that present considerable content on a particular topic, such as *The Underwater Alphabet Book* (Pallotta), and therefore are similar to informational books. However, these books were included in this chapter because they are alphabet books.

Recommended Alphabet Books

Ada, Alma Flor. *Gathering the Sun: An Alphabet in Spanish and English.* HarperCollins, 1997.

Anno, Mitsumasa. *Anno's Alphabet.* Crowell, 1975.

Base, Graeme. *Animalia.* Abrams, 1987.

Dodson, Peter. *An Alphabet of Dinosaurs.* Scholastic, 1995.

Ehlert, Lois. *Eating the Alphabet: Fruits & Vegetables from A to Z.* Harcourt Brace Jovanovich, 1989.

Emberley, Ed. *Ed Emberley's ABC.* Little, Brown, 1978.

Gaiman, Neil. *The Dangerous Alphabet.* Illus. Gris Grimley. HarperCollins, 2008.

James, Helen Foster. *S Is for S'Mores: A Camping Alphabet.* Illus. Lita Judge. Sleeping Bear, 2007.

Johnson, Stephen T. *Alphabet City.* Puffin, 1999.

Kitamura, Satoshi. *From Acorn to Zoo: And Everything in Between in Alphabetical Order.* Farrar, Straus & Giroux, 1992.

MacDonald, Suse. *Alphabatics.* Bradbury, 1986.

Martin, Bill, Jr., & John Archambault. *Chicka Chicka Boom Boom.* Illus. Lois Ehlert. Aladdin, 2000.

Martin, Steve, & Roz Chast. *The Alphabet from A to Y with Bonus Letter Z!* Flying Dolphin, 2007.

Micklethwait, Lucy. *I Spy: An Alphabet in Art.* HarperTrophy, 1996.

Musgrove, Margaret. *Ashanti to Zulu: African Traditions.* Dial, 1976.

Owen, Annie. *Annie's abc.* Knopf, 1987.

Pallotta, Jerry. *The Underwater Alphabet Book.* Charlesbridge, 1991.

Rockwell, Anne. *Albert B. Cub & Zebra: An Alphabet Storybook.* Crowell, 1977.

Schafer, Kevin. *Penguins ABC.* North Word, 2004.

Sendak, Maurice. *Alligators All Around.* HarperCollins, 1962.

Seuss, Dr. *Dr. Seuss's ABC.* Random House, 1963.

Van Fleet, Matthew. *Alphabet.* Simon & Schuster, 2008.

Counting Books. **Counting books,** sometimes called number books, are concept books that present the counting numbers. Like alphabet books, they can be used to prepare young children for school while offering many enjoyable reading experiences. These concept books typically devote one or two pages to each of the counting numbers 1 through 10, and they include illustrations of objects for counting. Many of these books are themed, such as Pattie L. Schnetzler's delightful *Ten Little Dinosaurs,* in which a pair of wacky plastic eyeballs are built into the back cover of the book. Through the holes in the pages, the eyeballs jiggle from page to page and dinosaur to dinosaur.

Other counting books may follow a story line. Eric Carle's *The Very Hungry Caterpillar* is my favorite counting storybook. A tiny (and hungry) caterpillar pops from an egg, and the readers follow as he satisfies his appetite throughout the week with one apple, two pears, three plums, four strawberries, five oranges, and ten pieces of junk food! At the end of the week, he is neither tiny nor hungry, but there is something wonderful in store for him—metamorphosis into a beautiful butterfly. In Carle's signature style, there are pages of differing sizes with die cuts to represent holes where the caterpillar has eaten through the food. (In Carle's other books—featured in Chapter 7—look for the unusual: different page sizes and shapes, die cuts in the pages, textures, microchips for sound effects, and even tiny blinking lights!)

In counting books it is important that featured objects on each page be familiar, so children can readily identify them; and the relationship of the objects should be obvious. To make it easier to select objects for counting, the illustrations should not be visually overloaded. It is desirable for counting books to depict all of the following concepts:

- Numbers—the amount of things to be counted (e.g., *, **, ***)
- Numerals—the symbolic representation of numbers (e.g., 1, 2, 3)
- Number words (e.g., *one, two, three*)

A book that meets all these criteria is *Over in the Meadow,* an old nursery counting rhyme that was adapted and illustrated by Paul Galdone. It opens with "Over in the meadow in the sand in the sun, lived an old mother turtle and her little turtle one."

There are some excellent counting books that do not contain the number words because their targeted audience is prereaders. An example is Eric Carle's *My Very First Book of Numbers.* This appealing book is spiral bound, and the sturdy pages are cut in half. The top parts of the pages contain the numerals 1 to 10, each with the appropriate number of small black squares for a child to point out and count. The challenge is to turn the bottom parts of the pages and match the numeral on the top part with the correct number of colorful objects on the bottom part by achieving one-to-one correspondence.

There is variety in the numbers depicted in counting books; they are not restricted to the first ten numbers. Tana Hoban used photographs of common objects and events to illustrate the numbers 1 through 100 in *Count and See.* However, some books for younger children include only the first five or six numbers. Two examples are Eileen Christelow's *Five Little Monkeys Jumping on the Bed* and Jeffie Ross Gordon's *Six Sleepy Sheep.* Once children have learned to count from 1 to 10, it is fun to share books that count backward, such as Molly Bang's *Ten, Nine, Eight.*

In counting books children can identify the counting numbers and discover seriation (i.e., the order of numbers). In addition, when adults or older siblings sit with children while they view the books, they can tell children the names (labels) for all the items depicted in the illustrations and engage the children in conversation about what they see. This is a fun way for children to expand their vocabularies.

After children master the counting numbers, they can enjoy books that introduce more sophisticated math concepts. One such book is *Anno's Counting Book,* which depicts the changing seasons (represented by the twelve months) with beautiful watercolor paintings that progressively show the growth of a rural village. It begins with zero and extends to twelve. Zero is a critical concept for understanding place value in our base-ten number system, and yet it is overlooked in nearly all other counting books. Anno also depicts one-to-one correspondence by means of a stack of cubes at the left of the pictures and the corresponding numerals at the right of the pictures. Older children can be introduced to set theory through the multiple sets of objects on each two-page spread (e.g., buildings, animals, children, adults, and trees). Each set corresponds with the featured number, and each set increases by one on the following page.

In *Sea Squares,* Joy N. Hulme uses the theme of sea creatures to depict the numbers 1 to 10 and the squares of these numbers, for example, "Ten squirmy squids squirting ten inky trails / Pulling ten tentacles like ten wagging tails / When *10* squids retreat so fast, / *100* tails go swishing past." In *The Butterfly Counting Book,* Jerry Pallotta describes butterflies and uses the odd numbers to count from 1 to 21 by *twos* (e.g., 1, 3, 5, 7). In a similar manner, Elinor J. Pinczes counts from 5 to 30 by *fives.* In a cumulative fashion, she describes the animals that have come to view the Northern Lights in *Arctic Fives Arrive.*

In *One Hundred Hungry Ants,* Elinor J. Pinczes tells a humorous story of 100 ants that are marching in rows to a picnic. By showing the ants in lines of varying numbers, she introduces the factors of 100 (i.e., 1 and 100, 2 and 50, 4 and 25, 5 and 20, 10 and 10). This is a clever and fun way to discover the math concepts of factoring and multiplication.

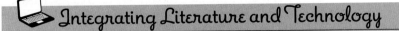

Integrating Literature and Technology

Gayle's Preschool Rainbow: www.preschoolrainbow.org This colorful site contains many preschool education activities and early childhood education lesson plans for teachers to use to enrich classroom curriculum. (Topics are arranged by themes.) Plus, it contains easy and fun learning games for parents to do at home. On the side "Navigation" bar, click on "Rhymes, Songs, and Fingerplays" to find counting rhymes. Select a favorite rhyme and illustrate it, making your own counting book.

Recommended Counting Books

Anno, Mitsumasa. *Anno's Counting Book.* HarperTrophy, 1975.
Bang, Molly. *Ten, Nine, Eight.* Greenwillow, 1983.
Bentley, Dawn. *The Rubber Duckies.* Illus. Heather Cahoon. Robin Corey, 2008.
Berkes, Marianne. *Over in the Jungle: A Rainforest Rhyme.* Illus. Jeanette Canyon. Dawn, 2007.
Carle, Eric. *Count with the Very Hungry Caterpillar.* Grosset & Dunlap, 2006.
Carle, Eric. *My Very First Book of Numbers.* HarperCollins, 1974.
Carle, Eric. *Ten Little Rubber Ducks.* HarperCollins, 2005.
Chizuwa, Masayuki. *My First Book of Money: Counting Coins.* Kumon, 2007.
Christelow, Eileen. *Five Little Monkeys Jumping on the Bed.* Clarion, 1989.
Galdone, Paul. *Over in the Meadow.* Simon & Schuster, 1986.
Giganti, Paul. *Each Orange Had 8 Slices.* Illus. Donald Crews. HarperTrophy, 1999.
Gordon, Jeffie Ross. *Six Sleepy Sheep.* Puffin, 1991.
Hoban, Tana. *Count and See.* Macmillan, 1972.
Hulme, Joy N. *Sea Squares.* Hyperion, 1991.
Jay, Alison. *1-2-3: A Child's First Counting Book.* Dutton, 2007.
Krebs, Laurie. *We All Went on a Safari: A Counting Journey through Tanzania.* Barefoot, 2004.
Martin, Bill, Jr., & Michael Sampson. *Chicka Chicka 1 2 3.* Illus. by Lois Ehlert. Simon & Schuster, 2004.
Pallotta, Jerry. *The Butterfly Counting Book.* Scholastic, 1998.
Pallotta, Jerry. *One Hundred Ways to Get to 100.* Illus. Rob Bolster. Scholastic, 2003.
Pinczes, Elinor J. *Arctic Fives Arrive.* Houghton Mifflin, 1996.
Pinczes, Elinor J. *One Hundred Hungry Ants.* Houghton Mifflin, 1993.
Rose, Deborah Lee. *The Twelve Days of Kindergarten.* Illus. Carey Armstrong-Ellis. Abrams, 2003.
Schnetzler, Pattie L. *Ten Little Dinosaurs.* Accord, 1996.
Sierra, Judy. *Counting Crocodiles.* Illus. Will Hillenbrand. Voyager, 2001.

Other Concept Books.   In addition to the alphabet and counting numbers, there are numerous other concepts presented in books for the very young. One popular topic for concept books is color. Authors and illustrators have imaginative ways to introduce colors to young readers. Ann Jonas uses lovely watercolors in *Color Dance* to reveal the primary (red, yellow, and blue), secondary (orange, green, and purple), and tertiary (vermilion, marigold, chartreuse, aquamarine, violet, and magenta) colors as the children in her illustrations dance with translucent scarves. Shelly Harwayne in *What's Cooking?* uses a combination of painting crayons and water to illustrate a story about the cooking sprees of the kids in Mrs. Peabody's class, who prepare meals of yellow, red, and green foods.

Some books are designed to present more than one concept. In *Planting a Rainbow,* Lois Ehlert uses graphic designs with bold colors on a white background to show the primary and secondary colors through a variety of plants and flowers. The author's use of labels introduces children to the concepts of both colors and flowers.

Concept Books on Color

Bentley, Dawn, & Heather Cahoon. *Good Night, Sweet Butterflies: A Color Dreamland.* Little Simon, 2003.
Ehlert, Lois. *Planting a Rainbow.* Harcourt Brace Jovanovich, 1988.
Harwayne, Shelley. *What's Cooking?* Mondo, 1996.
Horacek, Petr. *Butterfly Butterfly: A Book of Colors.* Candlewick, 2007.
Jonas, Ann. *Color Dance.* Greenwillow, 1989.
Lloyd, Sam. *What Color Is Your Underwear?* Cartwheel, 2004.
Wood, Audrey. *The Deep Blue Sea: A Book of Colors.* Illus. Bruce Wood. Blue Sky, 2005.

In addition to color, **shape** is a concept that children are expected to understand before starting first grade. *Shapes* by Rosalinda Kightley presents the basic shapes and lines: circle, square, rectangle, triangle, diamond, semicircle, straight line, right angle, zigzag, and wavy line. Each shape is introduced on a full page with a white background, and facing it is a graphic illustration that contains several sizes and colors of the featured shape. For example, the illustration for *triangle* is a Christmas tree with gifts. Children are challenged to find the two dozen or more triangles in the illustration. However, the picture also includes circles, squares, and rectangles, which were previously introduced, so children will have an opportunity to practice their visual acuity in distinguishing among the shapes.

In Eric Carle's *My Very First Book of Shapes,* young children can be shown how to match a black shape with an object that has a similar shape. For example, the circle matches an illustration of the sun; the square matches a framed picture; a triangle matches a teepee. As in *My Very First Book of Numbers,* Carle designed a spiral-bound book with sturdy pages cut in half, so the young viewer can flip through the bottom parts of the pages to find an object to match the black shape on the top part of a page.

In Tana Hoban's characteristic style, attractive colored photographs adorn the pages of *Dots, Spots, Speckles, and Stripes.* In this book Hoban portrays the circles and straight lines that the world contains. For example, circles (dots, spots, and speckles) are found in her photographs of polka-dotted dresses, freckles, and sunflowers. Straight lines are represented by a striped dress, slats in patio furniture, and a zebra.

Concept Books on Shapes

Carle, Eric. *My Very First Book of Shapes.* HarperCollins, 1974.
Franco, Betsy. *Bees, Snails, & Peacock Tails: Shapes Naturally.* Illus. Steve Jenkins. McElderry, 2008.
Hoban, Tana. *Dots, Spots, Speckles, and Stripes.* Greenwillow, 1987.
Kightley, Rosalinda. *Shapes.* Little, Brown, 1986.
Micklethwait, Lucy. *I Spy Shapes in Art.* Greenwillow, 2004.
Murphy, Chuck. *Shapes: Slide 'n' Seek.* Little Simon, 2001.
Walsh, Ellen Stoll. *Mouse Shapes.* Harcourt, 2007.

Words and their relationships are additional concepts that are important for young children. Prepositions are particularly challenging, because they are not as concrete as many familiar nouns or verbs. *Rosie's Walk* (Hutchins) depicts illustrations of Rosie the hen going *across, around, over, past, through,* and *under* things during her walk. Unbeknownst to Rosie, however, a fox is trying to catch her for dinner. In the clever and humorous illustrations, the fox encounters some mishap each time he tries to grab her. For example, as Rosie walks across the yard, the fox lands on the prongs of a rake, which smacks him in the head. Each two-page spread illustrating a preposition (e.g., around the pond) contains a picture clue that readers can use to predict the mishap that will befall the fox on the following page. When children are listening to this book for the first time, be sure to stop and ask them to predict what might happen next to the fox. This will encourage their search for picture clues to aid comprehension.

Inside, Outside, Upside Down by Stan and Jan Berenstain is also a good book for helping children explore the meanings of prepositions. This book shows a young bear in relation to a large box he has hidden in. In the process of the box being transported, the following prepositions and relationships are illustrated: in/out, on/off, inside/outside, upside down/right side up.

Reading books about antonyms will encourage children to think about many different concepts in our language (e.g., knowing what one word means, such as *high,* and finding a word that represents an opposite concept, such as *low*). Many enjoyable books introduce antonyms and help children gain mastery of their language.

Concept Books on Words

Beall, Pamela Conn, & Susan Hagen Nipp. *Wee Sing & Learn Opposites.* Price Stern Sloan, 2007.

Berenstain, Stan, & Jan Berenstain. *Inside, Outside, Upside Down.* Sagebrush, 1999.

Carle, Eric. *Eric Carle's Opposites.* Grosset & Dunlap, 2007.

Doudna, Kelly. *Pronouns.* Sandcastle, 2001.

Hutchins, Pat. *Rosie's Walk.* Simon & Schuster, 1968.

Martin, Justin McCory. *The Planet without Pronouns.* Scholastic, 2004.

Scarry, Richard. *Best Word Book Ever.* Golden, 1991.

Seeger, Laura Vaccaro. *Black? White? Day? Night?* Roaring Brook, 2006.

In addition to books about the alphabet, numbers, colors, shapes, antonyms, and parts of speech, concept books abound for many other topics. Look for entertaining and enlightening books for young children on many other essential concepts, such as plants, animals, time, and holidays. Anita Lobel's *One Lighthouse, One Moon* (2000, Greenwillow) cleverly presents concepts on days of the week, months of the year, seasons, colors, and numbers in her three-chapter picture book of a little girl and her cat who live near the sea.

Pattern Books

Pattern books are picture books that contain repetitive words, phrases, questions, or some other structure that makes them predictable. The repeated element helps listeners remember what comes next so they can join in as you read aloud. These simple books are easily committed to memory, making them useful in initial reading instruction. My favorite pattern book is *The Wheels on the Bus* (Kovalski), an adaptation of a traditional song. The first verse is

> The wheels on the bus go round and round,
> Round and round, round and round.
> The wheels on the bus go round and round,
> All around the town.

Each subsequent verse follows the pattern:

> The wipers on the bus go swish, swish, swish.

> The people on the bus hop on and off.

> The horn on the bus goes toot, toot, toot.

Pattern books make great **lap reading.** When a child sits in an adult's lap, the adult can talk about and point to things in the text and illustrations. When lap reading with a familiar pattern book, encourage children to focus on the printed words and join in on parts they recognize or remember. For example, you can pause at the end of a sentence or line and allow the child to complete it. If you point *under* each word as the child says it, that will help the child learn the **concept of word:** the idea that a written word is a string of letters bounded by spaces. Once children can match spoken words to their written counterparts, they have made an important discovery called **speech-to-print match,** and most children will then begin to learn some of the words by sight.

Some of the advantages of lap reading can be obtained for groups of children when teachers use **big books**—books that are enlarged to about four times their normal size. Big books are great for teaching emergent readers the **concepts of print:** the conventions that a page is read from top to bottom, lines are read from left to right, and books are read from front to back. (Not all written languages are arranged in this manner.) For more ideas on using early childhood books to develop children's beginning reading processes, see "Developing and Assessing Emergent Literacy through Children's Literature" in *Literacy Assessment for Today's Schools* (Anderson, 1995).

Pattern books are wonderful for initial reading instruction because they are predictable, the vocabulary is limited, and the illustrations reinforce the text. Though they usually contain characters, setting, and a few events, most do not have full plots. Therefore, like concept books, they can rarely be used to teach story structure. However, children who have listened to a book several times can usually recite it by looking at the illustrations. This practice is helpful later when children begin reading independently and realize they can look to illustrations for clues on unknown words. It is also important because when children have a simple pattern book memorized, an adult can help them focus on the printed words by pointing under each word as they say it. Through this process children can add these words to their sight vocabulary and become ready to tackle harder books.

Recommended Pattern Books

Carle, Eric. *Mr. Seahorse.* Philomel, 2004.
Emberley, Barbara. *Drummer Hoff.* Illus. Ed Emberley. Simon & Schuster, 2005.
Hutchins, Pat. *The Doorbell Rang.* Live Oak, 2004.
Kovalski, Maryann. *The Wheels on the Bus.* Kids Can, 1990.
Martin, Bill, Jr. *Panda Bear, Panda Bear, What Do You See?* Illus. Eric Carle. Henry Holt, 2003.
Root, Phyllis. *One Duck Stuck.* Illus. Jane Chapman. Candlewick Press, 2003.
Wood, Audrey. *The Napping House.* Illus. Don Wood. Harcourt Brace Jovanovich, 2004.

Wordless Picture Books

In **wordless picture books,** also known as textless books, the story is revealed through a sequence of illustrations with no—or very few—words. Wordless picture book is a format, so it is found in all genres. In these books, skillful illustrators develop a full plot through their artwork, making printed words unnecessary. In the preface to his wordless book *Sing, Pierrot, Sing: A Picture Book in Mime,* Tomie dePaola wrote, "The words, as in all mime, are in the eyes of the listener."

Wordless books first gained popularity in the late 1960s. In 1980 John Warren Stewig found the value of wordless picture books so significant that he devoted an entire chapter to them in his children's literature textbook. Stewig asserted it was not a new idea that pictures alone could reveal a story. He cited examples of the pictures in cave dwellings, medieval tapestries, and cathedral stained-glass windows that portrayed stories hundreds and even thousands of years ago. Stewig named several advantages of making wordless picture books accessible to children:

- They aid the development of visual literacy—the language of images.
- They can be interpreted and enjoyed by children who do not read well (or do not read at all), such as preschool children, children who are learning disabled in reading, and children with limited English proficiency.
- They can help parents and teachers assess and develop children's thinking and language abilities.
- They can serve as a stimulus for a language experience account (LEA) that can be used for early reading instruction.
- They develop imagination by stimulating an oral or written interpretation of the plot.

Cianciolo (1973) was one of the first to extol the value of wordless picture books in enhancing visual literacy. Believing that pictures tell a universal language, she purported that viewers "must be able to bring meaning and significance to the shapes, positions, and movements that are depicted by the book artist as he tells his stories in pictures" (p. 226). She encouraged using wordless books to help children express a verbal translation of objects or situations in illustrations.

D'Angelo (1981) elaborated on the use of wordless picture books to develop language. She asserted that "interpreting pictures in wordless books can provide opportunities for developing the child's vocabulary and syntax by naming objects, inventing dialog, making comparisons, describing and interpreting actions, and predicting and evaluating outcomes" (p. 37).

📖 Issues in Picture Books

Do Literature Books Have to Contain Words?   Some people do not consider wordless picture books to be literature. They say that a book has to tell a story, and how can a book tell a story if there are no words? Groff (1974) issued a caution not "to wrongly accredit pictures as literature. Nor to give way to wishful thoughts that wordless books will motivate children to read and appreciate literature" (p. 303). However, others like Stewig (1980) believe that artists have the ability to develop all the components of a good story (setting, characterization, plot, and theme) through their illustrations.

Select a wordless picture book from the following bibliography. Using the story map format provided in Figure 2.1, outline each of the elements of story structure that you identify from the illustrations. Do you believe this book qualifies as literature?

Recommended Wordless Books

Briggs, Raymond. *The Snowman.* Penguin, 2000.
Day, Alexandra. *Puppy Trouble.* Farrar, Straus & Giroux, 2002.
Fleishman, Paul, & Kevin Hawkes. *Sidewalk Circus.* Candlewick, 2004.
Henterly, Jamichael. *Good Night, Garden Gnome.* Dial, 2001.
Jenkins, Steve. *Looking Down.* Houghton Mifflin, 2003.
Lehman, Barbara. *The Red Book.* Houghton Mifflin, 2004.
Mayer, Mercer. *Frog Goes to Dinner.* Dial, 2003.
McCally, Emily Arnold. *Four Hungry Kittens.* Dial, 2001.
Spier, Peter. *Noah's Ark.* Dragonfly, 1992.
Weitzman, Jacqueline Preiss, & Robin Preiss Glasser. *You Can't Take a Balloon into the Museum.* Dial, 2002.
Wiesner, David. *Tuesday.* Scott Foresman, 1997.

Motivating Children to Become Lifelong Readers

by Susan E. Knell

Wouldn't it be wonderful if we could wave a magic wand and turn all reluctant readers into engaged ones? What is it that motivates children to want to read and to continue to read, even when there is no reward, grade, or condition for doing so? Unfortunately, there is no one program, strategy, or reward that will make children want to read. However, Gambrell's (1996) research with first-, third-, and fifth-grade children revealed five essential areas that promote engaged reading.

1. **Engaged readers tend to have classrooms and homes that are rich in a variety of books.** Classroom and home libraries are important, and they should include books from a variety of genres, topics, and reading levels.
2. **Engaged readers like prior experiences with books.** Children love to read and interact with books more than once.
3. **Engaged readers want to choose their own books.** Choice is vital to reading engagement. As children learn to self-select their reading materials, they become discriminating and independent readers.
4. **Engaged readers need opportunities for social interaction.** Have you ever had a friend tell you that you just *had to* read a particular book because it was so fabulous? Children also need opportunities to tell their friends *and* teachers how books made them feel.
5. **Engaged readers view *books* as the best reward.** If we want children to be motivated readers who read for their own purposes, we need to rethink extrinsic reward programs (see Knell, 1999). There is no research base indicating that any organized reading management or incentive program promotes reading motivation. In fact, such programs can actually *decrease* intrinsic motivation to read, and they take a great deal of your time, money, and energy (see Lamme, Fu, & Allington, 2002). If you desire to use incentives, use free books instead of candy, prizes, or points for rewards.

Following are some guidelines that research reveals *do* promote reading motivation.

Read aloud to your children. You should read aloud to your children every day, regardless of their age. Reading aloud promotes bonding and instills a greater desire for children to read to themselves. Moreover, it can be the most enjoyable part of the day for you and your children.

Provide many and varied opportunities for children to interact with books. Children need various ways to respond to books, such as writing in journals, dramatizing scenes, creating works of art, and simply talking about books. These interactions promote further appreciation of books.

Use interest surveys with children. Discover their attitudes about reading and where their interests lie, then find books accordingly. Reading engagement increases when children find books about their favorite interests.

Give book talks regularly. Advertise newly acquired books by keeping them in a designated basket or decorated box. After giving book talks on each, let children know that they may peruse them during the day. Don't be surprised if, by the end of the day, the basket is empty! A good website for information on book talking is www.nancykeane.com.

Provide a conducive environment for quiet reading. Designate a special reading center with comfortable spots for curling up with a good book. Author centers, book arrangements, and collections of children's responses to favorite books should look inviting and show visitors that books and reading are valued.

Provide daily time for children's recreational reading. Allow children to read *anything* of their choosing for a sustained period each day. During this time, you can either read or confer with individuals about their reading selections.

Integrate technology with reading. Share multiple websites on authors, illustrators, book reviews, and best-sellers.

Stock your classroom library with great books. Keep current by visiting bookstores, reading reviews in journals and online, talking to librarians, attending professional conferences, and visiting publisher and author websites.

Share your own love of books. Bring your personal books to the classroom, so your children can see you reading them during independent reading time. Tell children what you are reading now and what you plan to read next. When you finish a book, tell them how it made you feel. Explain to them how reading books taught you about the world, helped you better understand other people, and showed you how to do new things.

Try the psychological phenomenon of "blessing" the book. Gambrell (1997) relates that when you have introduced a book, read portions of it aloud, and "gushed" over it, your children will want to read it themselves. Adults have strong influential power with their children, and they should use this in a positive and motivating way.

All too often, I have literature students who admit that they never liked to read, and they may never have read an entire book before taking my course. When I ask them why, most respond that they never found any books that interested them. Because children's books cover nearly every subject, this means no adult ever introduced them to the right book. One of the most important jobs you have is to find just the right book for the right child at the right time. Then all your children can be motivated to read.

Summary

Board books are specially designed to be children's first experience with literature. They are constructed with sturdy cardboard pages with a wipe-off finish and have little text. Concept books are designed for preschool children and emergent readers. They present numerous examples of concepts, such as letters of the alphabet, the counting numbers, common colors, geometric shapes, and opposites. Pattern books are popular with beginning readers because they contain repetitive words, phrases, questions, or refrains that make them very predictable. Nonreaders and readers of all ages can enjoy wordless picture books, also known as textless books because they contain no—or very few—words. In wordless books, the story is revealed through a sequence of illustrations.

Traditional Literature   5

Using pastels in the impressionist style, the artist employed the element of scale to suggest distance between the girls and the wolf.

From *Lon Po Po: A Red Riding Hood Story from China,* translated and illustrated by Ed Young.

Library locations | **Myths, J292; all other traditional literature, J398**

Stories, songs, and rhymes with unknown authorship that were passed down orally from one generation to the next before being written down

*P*eople have always told stories; it is the oldest form of remembering. In ancient times, long before written language was developed, people told stories to preserve the history, traditions, desires, and taboos of their social groups. Each generation told their stories to the next, which in turn told the stories to the youth of the generation that followed them.

Since prehistory, all cultures have passed along such tales through the **oral tradition,** and they have always been an essential part of our humanness (Yolen, 1981). Some stories were told just for entertainment. Others were used to share the history of a group of people and also to teach lessons and transmit values and beliefs. Still others were intended to explain natural phenomena—such as the changing of the seasons and the cycle of night and day—and usually involved the people's gods and other religious beliefs. Certain stories were accompanied by music and were sung instead of recited. These stories remained in a constant process of variation, depending on the memory, talent, or purpose of the storytellers.

Evaluating Traditional Literature

Because of its antiquity and multicultural origins, **traditional literature** (also known as folk literature) is a unique genre, and a special set of evaluation criteria should be applied (Norton, 1999). The following questions can guide you as you select traditional literature books:

- Does the book help children better understand the nonscientific traditions of early cultures?
- Will it help children appreciate the culture and art of a different country?
- Does it familiarize children with another dialect or language of the world?
- Can it be used to stimulate creative drama, writing, and other forms of artistic expression?
- Will it help children realize that people from another part of the world have inherent goodness, mercy, courage, and industry?
- Is it void of unwholesome ethnic and racial stereotyping?
- If adapted, does the language retain the flavor of the older form, or is it oversimplified?
- Do the illustrations complement and extend the narrative while maintaining the heritage of the tale?
- Does the reteller tell where and how the tale was obtained, if/how it was altered, and the purpose for any adaptation?

History

Stories, songs, and poetry passed from one generation to the next in the oral tradition are collectively called **folklore.** Historically, folklore was not intended specifically for children but was for the enjoyment and enlightenment of the whole family. The origin of each tale has been lost in antiquity. Indeed, each tale had a multitude of contributors, for in the course of retellings, the tales were altered as storytellers modified them to suit their own times and audiences. This modification process continues today, making folklore an ever-changing body of work. Rosemary Sutcliff (1981) wrote in her author's note to *The Sword and the Circle,* "No minstrel ever follows exactly the songs that have come down to him from the time before. Always he adds and leaves out and embroiders and puts something of himself into each retelling" (p. 8).

Even after written language was developed and paper was invented, stories continued to be transmitted through the oral tradition because books had to be hand copied. This slow process made books rare and valuable. Few people were literate because there was so little available for the general population to read. After the development of the printing press in the late 1400s, books became more affordable and accessible, and there was then a greater reason to learn to read and write. Many children were schooled to become literate, but not all, especially not children from poor families or those living in rural areas. So the oral tradition of storytelling continued for many more years.

Then, in 1697 a Frenchman named Charles Perrault did a remarkable thing. He recorded the tales his nursemaid had told him as a child and published eight of them in a book he titled *Stories or Tales from Past Times with Morals.* This book included classic stories such as "The Sleeping Beauty," "Little Red Riding Hood," and "Cinderella." Perrault's book was enormously popular in Europe, both in French and in English editions. Soon after, another Frenchman named Antoine Galland translated Asian and North African traditional tales into French, and in 1704 Galland published the first volume under the title *The Arabian Nights, or Tales Told by Sheherezade.* This collection included such well-known tales as "Aladdin and the Wonderful Lamp," "The Seven Voyages of Sinbad the Sailor," and "Ali Baba and the Forty Thieves." The books published by Perrault and Galland were prototypes of the traditional literature genre.

Some of the most enduring tales were collected by two German brothers, Jacob and Wilhelm Grimm. Their first volume, *Nursery and Household Tales,* was published in 1812, and a second volume followed in 1815. Favorites from this collection included "Hansel and Gretel," "Rumpelstiltskin," and "Snow White." Early readers of the collection criticized the tales as gruesome, violent, and not appropriate for children. However, the collection had begun as a linguistic—rather than a literary—project to preserve the old German language. The Grimms' goal was to create a national identity for the German people by presenting the common people's voice through the culture's folklore.

The Grimms soon realized there was considerable difference between what an entertaining tale is in oral form and what an entertaining tale is in written form. As they prepared newer versions of their collection, they altered the original tales, which were somewhat disjointed without the benefit of the body language, intonation, pacing, and audience participation that storytellers relied upon. The Grimms combined variants of stories to devise their own "best" versions, and they edited the newer stories to make them more readable and dramatic.

As time passed, the Grimms reissued the stories with greater alterations to appeal to parents who wished to use them to teach children values, such as obedience, hard work, and humility. To make them more acceptable, they continued to rewrite the stories, making moral messages more explicit, omitting sexual scenes, and toning down violent episodes (which meant far milder forms of punishment for the villains). However, by combining the best elements of several versions to arrive at a product that would have greater appeal, the stories became increasingly further removed from their folk origins. Today compilers of folktales continue to adapt many of the Grimms' stories for children by further toning down the violence.

Responding to Literature

Storytelling   After reading several folktales, try your hand at being a storyteller. Use the following steps to get started.

1. Select a story that is easy to remember. Traditional tales are good choices, especially fables or cumulative fairy tales.
2. Read the story several times over several days.
3. Select simple props (such as puppets or toys) to use, especially if they will help you remember all the characters and events in a tale.
4. Stand in front of the mirror and tell the story, paying attention to your body language.
5. Tell the story to a family member or friend, and ask him or her to comment on your oral skills.
6. Practice in front of a mirror again, this time focusing on the art of pausing—to create suspense, to underline an image, or to invite a laugh.
7. Add gestures (especially face and hand movements) to your story, and add sounds effects, such as a monster growling or a door creaking.
8. Tell the story into a tape recorder and analyze your performance to see how you might improve.
9. Tell your story to an audience!

In 1841 Peter Asbjørnsen and Jorgen Moe published a compilation of the popular lore of Norway. Their joint collection, *Norwegian Folk Tales*, included such favorites as "The Three Billy Goats Gruff" and "East of the Sun and West of the Moon." In 1845 Asbjørnsen published an additional collection titled *Norwegian Fairytales and Folklore*.

Because the United States is a relatively young country, little true folklore in the oral tradition had time to develop. One major collection of American folklore was recorded by Joel Chandler Harris. In 1881 Harris published a volume of African American traditional stories, which he titled *Uncle Remus, His Songs and Sayings.* The escapades of Brer (short for brother) Rabbit and his nemeses, Brer Fox and Brer Bear, are hilarious. "The Tar Baby" was my favorite as a child. Unfortunately, Harris wrote the tales in a nearly undecipherable dialect that was his exaggerated attempt to reproduce the language of the elderly former slaves from whom he had heard the tales in rural Georgia. Harris presented the tales within a loose story he created of an old slave named Uncle Remus, who is telling stories to the child of his white "master." The stories themselves are delightful and entertaining. However, the context in which they were presented is replete with racist remarks, which has resulted in the book's being banned from most school libraries and from many public libraries as well. Fortunately, adapted versions of the stories are now available in picture books retold by such talented writers as Julius Lester (1987, 1990) and Van Dyke Parks (Harris, Parks, & Jones, 1986; Harris & Parks, 1987).

Other significant works include the collections of Scottish scholar and folklorist Andrew Lang, who published *The Blue Fairy Book,* the first of twelve volumes, in 1889. Joseph Jacobs's collection of English and Irish tales, titled *English Fairy Tales,* was published in 1898. Some well-known stories included in Jacobs's collection were "The Three Little Pigs," "Henny Penny," and "Jack and the Beanstalk."

Characteristics

What makes traditional stories different from other types of stories? How can they be so readily identified? The major difference between a traditional story and all the other stories you will be reading about in this textbook is that its *authorship is unknown.* Each traditional tale is so ancient that it has had a multitude of contributors, all of whom helped craft the story as you read it today, which also explains why there are many variations of each tale. For example, there are both French and German versions of "Cinderella." In fact, several hundred Cinderella-type stories have been found in Europe, and more than a hundred have been identified in other parts of the world as well. Indeed, there is much similarity in folklore throughout the world.

When students ask me to identify the original version of a particular tale, I explain that the closest we can come to the "original" is to read the oldest recorded version—a version captured by one of the early compilers of traditional literature, such as Aesop, Asbjørnsen, Bechstein, Galland, Grimm, Jacobs, La Fontaine, Lang, Moe, or Perrault.

The easiest way to identify traditional literature is to look in the J398 section of a library that uses the Dewey decimal system of classification. (Nearly all school libraries do.) Every book with J398 marked on the spine should be traditional literature. To identify traditional literature in a store or private collection, look for the following characteristics:

1. **Unknown authorship.** Words such as *retold by* or *adapted by* usually appear on the book cover or title page, or you may recognize the "author" as one of the early

compilers of traditional literature. Clues may also be found in the book jacket copy, in phrases such as *an old tale*. If there is an identifiable author—meaning that the story is the product of a single person's mind—it is *not* traditional literature.

2. **Conventional introductions and conclusions.** The phrases *Once upon a time* and *They lived happily ever after* represent the conventional introductions and conclusions that are either explicit or implied in most tales of traditional literature. The stories are timeless, and the reader has the "secure knowledge that no matter what happens, love, kindness, and truth will prevail—and hate, wickedness, and evil will be punished" (Huck et al., 1997, p. 271).

3. **Vague settings.** Backdrop settings are used; as readers we are not told when the story took place, nor are we usually told where it took place. An indeterminate past time at an unspecified location is sometimes the best description of the setting of a traditional tale. The illustrations will probably reveal the most information, such as a castle, forest, peasant village, and the like.

4. **Stereotyped characters.** Because characters represent values and attributes, not real humans, they are stereotyped. These flat characters are either all good or all evil. Following are some of the most common types:

- *Beautiful daughter:* There are rarely any plain-looking daughters in traditional literature. Daughters who are good are beautiful, and daughters who are beautiful are good. Intelligence or any other virtue is rarely mentioned. Examples are the female protagonists in "Sleeping Beauty," "Snow White," "Rapunzel," and "Beauty and the Beast."
- *Handsome prince:* When there are beautiful daughters in distress, there are usually handsome princes to save them. They appear in all the "beautiful daughter" stories just mentioned. There are rarely any ugly princes who save the day—if you do not count the ones under evil spells, as in "The Frog Prince" and "Beauty and the Beast." Even they eventually turn into handsome princes.
- *Evil stepmother:* Quite often, the handsome prince saves the beautiful daughter from the evil stepmother, as in "Cinderella," "Snow White," and "Rapunzel." The evil stepmother is often a witch as well. (I hope my stepdaughter is not reading this.)
- *Weak father:* Of course, when there is an evil stepmother, there is usually a weak father who wimps out and does not help his daughter, as in "Snow White" and "Hansel and Gretel." But sometimes the father wimps out on his own, even without a second wife, as in "Rumpelstiltskin" and "Beauty and the Beast."
- *Simpleton:* A boy who is mentally challenged or walks to the beat of a different drummer is the simpleton. He is often abused by family members or others in the community, though he usually comes out ahead in the end. Some examples of this type character are found in "Jack and the Beanstalk," "Hans in Luck," and *Strega Nona* (dePaola).

5. Anthropomorphism. In traditional literature, human characteristics are frequently attributed to animals, plants, and objects. Some examples of **anthropomorphic** characters are the hungry wolf in "Little Red Riding Hood," who talks and dresses in Grandmother's clothing; the lively cookie in "The Gingerbread Man," who talks and runs away; and the magic mirror in "Snow White," which not only talks but is omniscient, possessing knowledge of things happening far away.

6. Cause and effect. Cause-and-effect relationships are quite apparent in traditional literature. Good characters prevail and are rewarded. Evil characters get their just punishment, which is frequently banishment or even, in the older versions of tales, a painful death. For example, the evil Queen in "Snow White" meets a dreadful end.

> The looking-glass answered, "Oh Queen, although you are of beauty rare, the young bride is a thousand times more fair." Then she railed and cursed, and was beside herself with disappointment and anger. First she thought she would not go to the wedding; but then she felt she should have no peace until she went and saw the bride. And when she saw her she knew her for Snow-white, and could not stir from the place for anger and terror. For they had ready red-hot iron shoes, in which she had to dance until she fell down dead. (Crane, 1922, p. 102)

7. Happy ending for the hero. The ending is always a happy one for the good characters, who are often rewarded by great wealth or marriage to royalty. For example, in "Hansel and Gretel" the father and stepmother leave the two children in the forest because there is not enough food for them all. The children fall prey to an evil witch, but they outsmart and kill her. Then they fill their pockets with her treasures and find their way back to their father's house.

> Then they ran till they came up to it, rushed in at the door, and fell on their father's neck. The man had not had a quiet hour since he left his children in the wood; but the wife was dead. And when Gretel opened her apron the pearls and precious stones were scattered all over the room, and Hansel took one handful after another out of his pocket. Then was all care at an end, and they lived in great joy together. (Crane, 1922, p. 44)

8. Magic accepted as normal. One reason children love traditional literature is that the element of magic is a foundation in most stories. No one questions the logic when wolves talk, pigs build houses, little men spin straw into gold, cookies run away, or rags are turned into a ball gown because the magical element is anticipated in traditional tales.

9. Brief stories with simple and direct plots. It was necessary for traditional tales to be brief and simple, so storytellers could more easily remember them. As a result, these stories are appealing to children, who find them easy to comprehend. Although traditional tales were originally for the whole family, today they are found almost exclusively in the children's sections of libraries and bookstores, because the stories are brief, simple, and direct.

10. **Repetition of actions and verbal patterns.** Another way storytellers remembered their tales—and made them memorable—was by reciting them in a cumulative manner, with repetition of actions and verbal patterns. An example of this type of *cumulative tale* is "The Gingerbread Man." A runaway cookie escapes from the little old woman who baked him, and he continues to run on past the little old man, some apple pickers, some reapers, a cat, a dog, and a pig before he meets his demise with a fox. Each time he escapes another character, he calls out a refrain and repeats the names of the characters he has evaded so far.

> Run, run, run as fast as you can. You can't catch me. I'm the gingerbread man. I ran away from the little old woman, and the little old man, and some apple pickers, and . . . I can run away from you too, I can.

Although not an exhaustive list, this summary has covered the more common characteristics of traditional literature. However, be aware that you may encounter some stories that, although they contain many of these characteristics, are not true traditional literature—because they were not orally passed from one generation to the next. Rather, they were written by an individual as the product of his or her creative mind. These stories are called literary tales, and they belong to the fantasy genre. There are literary fairy tales, literary myths, literary fables, literary ballads, and even literary nursery rhymes. Keep in mind that when you see the term *literary* in front of *any* category of traditional literature, it means the story was written by an individual.

The first author to successfully employ the literary style of writing was Hans Christian Andersen, starting in 1835. His original stories are often confused with the traditional ones because he emulated fairy tales so well. Indeed, you are most likely to find Andersen's stories in the traditional literature section rather than the fiction section of the library. In addition, his works are frequently included in anthologies of traditional literature. Further discussion of Hans Christian Andersen appears in Chapter 6, Modern Fantasy, where his stories more appropriately belong.

Themes of Traditional Literature

Recall from Chapter 2 that the *theme* of a story is its central idea or underlying message. Often this message is a significant truth, a value-laden statement—or more simply, the moral of the story. Because one of the purposes of folklore was to transmit cultural values and beliefs, the theme is usually quite apparent. Several common themes in traditional literature follow.

- **Triumph of good over evil.** Good versus evil is surely the most prevalent theme in all literature, regardless of genre. In traditional literature the good prevails, sometimes with the help of a magical being, such as the fairy godmother in "Cinderella," but sometimes because of the characters' ingenuity, as in "Hansel and Gretel." It is unfortunate that stepmothers are nearly always portrayed as evil (Warner, 1991).

- **Trickery.** The theme of trickery sometimes constitutes the reverse of the first theme. In trickery the protagonist is successful—not because he is good, but because he is a clever deceiver. For example, in "Puss-in-Boots" the cat kills other animals without mercy, deceives the king, threatens to chop the field workers into small pieces, and steals a vast estate for his master, who is the son of a poor miller. For his deeds, the cat is made a great lord when his master marries the king's daughter. However, not all tricksters scheme for gain; some do so to preserve their lives, as in the case of Brer Rabbit in "The Tar Baby." Trickster characters are usually small, resourceful animals, such as Anansi the Spider in West African tales and Coyote and Raven in Native American tales.

- **Hero's quest.** Stories with the **hero's quest** theme feature a protagonist who is on a long journey fraught with trials and impossible tasks, in which he or she is searching for something of great importance or value. The character may be searching for riches, a specific treasure, wisdom, a loved one, or even his or her own identity. In *Jason and the Golden Fleece* (Naden), the hero searches for the fleece that was shorn from Hermes' magic ram. In *The Fool of the World and the Flying Ship* (Ransome), the simpleton protagonist seeks a flying ship so he can marry the princess. In *Arrow to the Sun* (McDermott), the boy is seeking the father he has never seen.

- **Reversal of fortune.** In the rags-to-riches theme, a story usually begins with a downtrodden underdog character who becomes blessed with luck and good fortune through a series of unpredictable events. Examples of stories with this theme are "The Elves and the Shoemaker," "Puss-in-Boots," and "Hansel and Gretel." Occasionally the reversal of fortune may be from richer to poorer, as in "Hans in Luck." Hans, being burdened by a large lump of gold to carry, successively trades with passersby until he has nothing but a stone. The greed of the wife in "The Fisherman and His Wife" causes the couple to go from poverty to great wealth and back to poverty.

- **Small outwitting the big.** The theme of the victorious little guy is especially appealing to children, who readily identify with small characters. Quick-wittedness, rather than brawn, makes the protagonists successful in stories such as "Jack and the Beanstalk," "Hansel and Gretel," "Puss-in-Boots," and "Tom Thumb." The Brer Rabbit stories (Harris & Parks; Harris, Parks, & Jones) always show the rabbit pitted against larger animals and repeatedly outwitting them. This theme is also known as the "triumph of the underdog."

Children's Books Cited in Preceding Sections

Crane, Lucy. *Household Stories from the Collection of the Bros. Grimm.* Avenel Books, 1922.

dePaola, Tomie. *Strega Nona.* Simon & Schuster, 1975.

Harris, Joel Chandler, & Van Dyke Parks. *Jump Again! More Adventures of Brer Rabbit.* Illus. Barry Moser. Harcourt Brace Jovanovich, 1987.

Harris, Joel Chandler, Van Dyke Parks, & Malcolm Jones. *Jump! The Adventures of Brer Rabbit.* Illus. Barry Moser. Harcourt Brace Jovanovich, 1986.

Lester, Julius. *More Tales of Uncle Remus: Further Adventures of Brer Rabbit, His Friends, Enemies, and Others.* Illus. Jerry Pinkney. Dial, 1990.

Lester, Julius. *The Tales of Uncle Remus: The Adventures of Brer Rabbit.* Illus. Jerry Pinkney. Dutton, 1987.

McDermott, Gerald. *Arrow to the Sun.* Puffin, 1974.

Naden, Corinne J. *Jason and the Golden Fleece.* Illus. Robert Baxter. Troll Associates, 1980.

Ransome, Arthur. *The Fool of the World and the Flying Ship.* Illus. Uri Shulevitz. Farrar, Straus & Giroux, 1968.

Sutcliff, Rosemary. *The Sword and the Circle.* Puffin, 1981.

The Subgenres of Traditional Literature

The bulk of traditional literature consists of *folktales,* the generic term for the various kinds of narrative literature found in the oral traditions of the world. These tales convey the legends, customs, superstitions, and beliefs of people in past times. Dividing this large genre into smaller categories or **subgenres** makes the field easier to study and ensures that nothing important is overlooked. The subgenres of folktales are (1) myths, (2) fables, (3) ballads and songs, (4) legends, (5) tall tales, and (6) fairy tales. Nursery rhymes (which are closer to poetry than to tales), along with other **traditional rhymes,** make up a final category of traditional literature.

Before you begin reading about the various categories of traditional literature, it is important to remember two things. First, to be true folk literature, a story must have *no known author.* I stress this once again because many good books appear to be traditional literature and share some of the same characteristics; these books may even have a term such as "legend," "fable," "ballad," or "myth" in the title. But if the story is the idea of one person (i.e., not passed orally from one generation to the next), then these stories are literary folktales, which are a form of fiction and are presented in Chapter 6, Modern Fantasy.

Second, for the time being, suspend your own definitions of terms such as *fairy tale, myth, fable,* and *legend.* In everyday language we often use these terms to mean any highly imaginative story. However, folklorists define these as distinct forms of folktales. Even when you are certain a story is true traditional literature, you cannot always count on the title to let you know what form it is—because even authors sometimes use the terminology interchangeably. However, by the time you finish this chapter, you will understand the distinctions and will be able to recognize the various forms of traditional literature.

Myths

With one exception, all traditional literature is shelved in the J398 section of the library. The exception is mythology, which is shelved in J292. In the Dewey decimal system, the 200 section is for books about religion, and **myths** belong here because they deal with the religious beliefs of past cultures.

This is a good place to address a question I am often asked by preservice teachers: "Is it legal to use literature books about religion in public schools?" The answer is *yes.* Please see Box 5.1 for clarification on this question, provided by former president Bill Clinton. I hope that after you read it, you will be encouraged to share mythology, Bible (and other scripture) stories, and stories about various religions with your pupils. Two books I highly recommend are *Celebrate! Stories of the Jewish Holidays* (Berger) and *Tomie dePaola's Book of Bible Stories.* More books on religion are presented in Chapter 8 under religious cultures and in Chapter 12 under informational books on religion. Also, I encourage you to look through the books about various religions in the J200 section of your library.

Mythology was perhaps the earliest form of folklore because it filled an essential need. Humans have always sought to understand the world and its inhabitants, and myths provided an explanation for otherwise unexplainable events. The plots of myths usually include heroes and supernatural beings, including gods who control natural forces such as the seasons and death. The intent of myths was to offer interpretations of natural phenomena and other mysteries of life as acts (or influences) of deities. For example, all cultures had myths of the creation of the world and of the origins of the first man and woman. The mythology of many cultures is lengthy and

Box 5.1

Excerpt from President Clinton's Statement of Principles on Religious Expression in Public Schools

Teaching about Religion

Public schools may not provide religious instruction, but they may teach ABOUT religion, including the Bible or other scripture: The history of religion, comparative religion, *the Bible (or other scripture)-as-literature* [italics mine], and the role of religion in the history of the United States and other countries, all are permissible public school subjects.

Similarly, it is permissible to consider religious influences on art, music, *literature* [italics mine], and social studies. Although public schools may teach about religious holidays, including their religious aspects, and may celebrate the secular aspects of holidays, schools may not observe holidays as religious events or promote such observance by students.

Student Assignments

Students may express their beliefs about religion in the form of homework, artwork, and other written and oral assignments free of discrimination based on the religious content of their submissions. Such home and classroom work should be judged by ordinary academic standards of substance and relevance, and against other legitimate pedagogical concerns identified by the school.

Note: The president's statement does not have the force of law. However, it was promulgated to summarize court holdings on religion in the schools, and former Secretary of Education Richard Riley sent it to all 15,000 public school districts in the United States. This excerpt relates to literature, but the full statement is available in the July 13, 1995, issue of the *New York Times,* which can be accessed through the Lexis-Nexis Academic Universe database. These guidelines were reaffirmed with minor changes in May 1998, and again in December 1999 through a letter from former Secretary Riley that was mailed to all principals.

complex, with episodic plots and continuing characters, in contrast to other types of folktales. However, individual stories from collections have been adapted into picture books appropriate for elementary children.

Gerald McDermott used a colorful picture book format in *Raven: A Trickster Tale from the Pacific Northwest,* which tells of a time when the men and women of earth lived in cold darkness. Raven becomes the boy child of the Sky Chief's daughter in order to steal the sun and give it to the people.

Classic myths are narratives with a serious and reverential tone. Children may find it easier to enjoy and comprehend myths if you read them aloud. Also, keep in mind that like all folklore, myths were not originally intended just for children. Although they may be shelved in the children's section, they are not always appropriate for children. Some involve violent acts such as murder, rape, and incest. It is a good rule to preview *everything* before you read it to children or make it available for their independent reading.

Although Greek, Roman, and Norse myths are likely the most familiar, myths from all cultures are worth exploring. They can be included in studies of ancient cultures to provide insight into the people's religion and philosophy, as well as into their ideas, modes of life, and the nature of their civilization (Evslin, Evslin, & Hoopes, 1966). Myths also lend themselves as models for creative writing. For example, you may encourage children to write their own modern creation myths, such as the origin of computer viruses.

Mythology's influence in modern culture is quite evident. There are constant allusions to mythological characters and plots in daily speech, literature, and advertisements. Myths have given us the names of the planets, constellations, days of the week (for example, Thursday is derived from "Thor's day"), and months of the year, as well as the names of some elements/chemicals and scientific concepts. The following quiz will test your knowledge of how mythology has enhanced our modern English language.

♟ *Literature Activity:* Testing Your Cultural Literacy

In our language, many terms, names, and figures of speech were derived from the names of characters in Greek and Roman mythology. Test what Hirsch (1987) calls your *cultural literacy* by naming a mythological character for each of the following. (No character is used more than once.) Answers are available at www.pearsonhighered.com/anderson3e.

1. Early space mission
2. Company that repairs auto exhaust systems
3. Reverberation of the voice
4. Candy bar
5. Liquid metal
6. Vain self-centered person
7. Disney canine character
8. The inner self or mind
9. Name of a large planet and a small automobile

10. Name of (real) ill-fated passenger ship
11. Planet next to Earth
12. A process to strengthen rubber

Recommended Books of Mythology

Evetts-Secker, Josephine. *Father and Son Tales.* Illus. Helen Cann. Barefoot Books, 1999.

Fu, Shelley. *Ho Yi the Archer and Other Classic Chinese Tales.* Illus. Joseph F. Abboreno. Shoe String, 2000.

Green, Jen. *Myths of Ancient Greece.* Raintree, 2001.

Kimmel, Eric A. *Ten Suns: A Chinese Legend.* Illus. Yongsheng Xuan. Holiday House, 1998.

Lee, Fran. *Wishing on a Star: Constellation Stories.* Gibbs Smith, 2001.

McDermott, Gerald. *Raven: A Trickster Tale from the Pacific Northwest.* Voyager, 2001.

Osborne, Mary Pope. *Favorite Norse Myths.* Illus. Troy Howell. Sagebrush, 2001.

Strauss, Susan. *When Woman Became the Sea: A Costa Rican Creation Myth.* Illus. Cristina Acosta. Beyond Words, 1998.

Wolfson, Margaret Olivia. *Marriage of the Rain Goddess: A South African Myth.* Illus. Clifford Alexander Parms. Sagebrush, 2001.

Zeitlin, Steve. *The Four Corners of the Sky: Creation Stories and Cosmologies from around the World.* Illus. Chris Raschka. Henry Holt, 2000.

Fables

Fables, like myths, were likely one of the earliest forms of folklore—because they, too, served an essential purpose. They taught lessons about behavior, thereby transmitting cultural values from one generation to the next. Although fables appear to be simple beast stories, they are allegorical. You may need to generate discussion to help younger children understand the underlying meaning of fables. The fables encountered in traditional literature today come from a variety of cultures, but most of them share several distinct characteristics.

- They are very brief, simple narratives, usually less than one page long.
- The tone is didactic, because the purpose was to instruct the listener in a universal moral truth, often a lesson on how to behave.
- Typically, the characters are anthropomorphic animals that are unnamed. Characters are simply called by what they are, such as Fox, Crow, or Mouse. Occasionally a human ("The Boy Who Cried Wolf") or even an element of nature ("The Wind and the Sun") can be a character.
- The setting is a rural area in the distant past.
- Plots generally involve only one event, usually a conflict between animal characters portraying human faults, that provides a simple example of right from wrong.
- The intended moral is often stated at the end of the story, though some fables have only an implied moral.

Undoubtedly, the most popular fables today are those attributed to Aesop, a freed slave from Thrace who purportedly lived in Greece during the sixth century B.C., though he originally may have been from Africa. His name became attached to a collection of beast fables that had long been transmitted through oral tradition. With his sharp wit, the legendary Aesop added his own flair as he retold the fables, and they continued to be transmitted in the oral tradition for several more centuries. They were written down around 300 B.C. by Demetrium Phalerus, founder of the library at Alexandria and again by Greek and Roman writers around the first century A.D. Because the tales had long been in the oral tradition before they were ever recorded, the originator is certainly not verifiable, and the tales would more aptly be called Aesopic fables. One of the first printed books in English was *Aesop's Fables,* published in 1484 by William Caxton. Along with the Greek versions, fables from India's *The Panchatantra* and *The Jataka Tales* commonly appear in anthologies labeled "Aesop's Fables," which may now be accessed online at http://AesopFables.com.

In Europe, France was the most voluminous producer of fables. A common character in these stories is a wily fox known as Reynard. Jean de la Fontaine (1661–1694) is believed to be the greatest of all French fabulists. His fables, written in verse, were extensively imitated by later writers from many countries.

Even older children can enjoy fables from collections such as Charles Santore's *Aesop's Fables,* in which twenty-four animal tales are beautifully illustrated. Younger children can enjoy fables in a simple picture book format with Ed Young's *Seven Blind Mice,* which is an adaptation of the Indian fable, "The Blind Men and the Elephant." It is charmingly illustrated in cut paper collage and can be used as a concept book for colors, days of the week, and ordinal numbers (first, second, third, etc.). Fables from a variety of cultures are available in picture book format—for example, *Once a Mouse* (Brown), *Chanticleer and the Fox* (Chaucer), and others in the bibliography that follows this section.

Cultural Literacy. Numerous figures of speech have come from the morals of fables. From the Greek fable "The Boy Who Cried Wolf" comes the phrase "crying wolf," which refers to the notion that giving false alarms will keep people from believing you when a real problem arises. "The Fox and the Grapes" gave rise to the expression "talking sour grapes"—that is, speaking in a derogatory manner about something you were not able to obtain. Fables and all other folklore constitute an essential part in the process of learning one's culture—what Hirsch (1987) called **cultural literacy.** Houston (2004) speaks to the importance of cultural literacy.

> For instance, the term, *a wolf in sheep's clothing,* conveys the image of a person who is not what he seems to be. The image is drawn from *Aesop's Fables.* If we know the story, we understand the allusion. . . . Lack of knowledge [of cultural literacy] is a handicap in communication in many situations.
>
> The set of stories we assume our listeners/readers know becomes the shorthand of a culture. That is, a great deal of information can be conveyed in just a word or phrase taken from one of these stories. It is quite possible that students who do not know the stories are handicapped in reading the required canon of books in high school and therefore handicapped on standardized tests, the effects of which may reach on to adulthood. (p. 9)

Throughout this chapter, titles of stories that are italicized refer to specific published books. However, titles of stories encased in quotation marks are common folktales that can be found in print in several versions. When I use these general folktales as examples of concepts, I have assumed you are familiar with these tales. In other words, I have assumed you are culturally literate in terms of these stories. However, if there are titles in quotation marks you are not familiar with, I urge you to locate copies in your library and read them.

Recommended Books of Fables

Brett, Jan. *Town Mouse, Country Mouse.* Putnam, 1994.
Brown, Marcia. *Once a Mouse . . . : A Fable Cut in Wood.* Aladdin, 1989.
Chaucer, Geoffrey. *Chanticleer and the Fox.* Illus. Barbara Cooney. HarperTrophy, 1982.
Climo, Shirley. *The Little Red Ant and the Great Big Crumb: A Mexican Fable.* Illus. Francisco X. Mora. Clarion, 1999.
MacMillan, Ian C. *Khala Maninge: An African Fable—The Little Elephant That Cried a Lot.* Illus. Eric G. MacMillan. ManingeMali, 2003.
Orgel, Doris. *The Lion and the Mouse and Other Aesop's Fables.* Illus. Bert Kitchen. Dorling Kindersley, 2000.
Pinkney, Jerry. *Aesop's Fables.* SeaStar, 2000.
Santore, Charles. *Aesop's Fables.* Random House, 1997.
Ward, Helen. *The Hare and the Tortoise.* Millbrook, 1999.
Yolen, Jane. *A Sip of Aesop.* Illus. Karen Barbour. Scholastic, 2000.
Young, Ed. *Seven Blind Mice.* Puffin, 1992.

Ballads and Folk Songs

Not all folktales were told or recited; some stories, called **ballads,** were sung as narrative poems. Folk ballads are one of the newer forms of traditional literature, having developed across Europe in the late Middle Ages. Wandering minstrels earned their living by traveling from village to village and from one manor house to another, performing and entertaining the occupants with popular ballads and news from other regions. Coffin (1999) gives high praise to this form of folklore: "Aesthetically, the ballad is considered by many to be the most remarkable and beautiful art form that the folk traditions of the world have developed" (p. 2).

The Middle Ages spawned ballads of the legendary Robin Hood, who lived around the fourteenth century as a chivalrous outlaw who was reported never to allow women to suffer injustice. Though he did indeed plunder the rich to give to the poor, his great popularity arose because he stood for the yeoman's love of freedom and resistance to the king's oppressive laws—after the Norman Conquest, a person could get hanged for hunting in the king's forests, which included much of England, including towns and fields.

English and Scottish ballads were first compiled by Bishop Thomas Percy in 1765, and from 1882 to 1898, Francis James Child published five volumes of English and Scottish popular ballads, which remain the definitive canon of ballads for that region. Though the Robin Hood ballad collections consist of detailed narratives with full plots, many ballads are simple stories sung in rhymed stanzas, such as "On Top of Old Smoky." A number of popular ballads and other folk songs have been retold in picture book format, usually with musical scores in the back.

Because ballads are songs, they are best enjoyed with music. If you are musically challenged (like me), obtain a recording from the library, so you can help your children grow in cultural literacy by learning the songs of their culture. In addition, learning American ballads and folk songs can be a fun way to learn about U.S. history.

Integrating Literature and Technology

KIDiddles Musical Mouseum: http://kididdles.com/lyrics   This website was developed especially for children, and it contains nearly all lyrics of children's songs in the public domain plus a few copyrighted songs that have permission to be posted on the site. Many of the song lyrics link to MIDI files of simple tunes for you and your children to sing along with. The songs are organized both by alphabetical order as well as by the following categories: traditional (including ballads and folk songs), lullabies, finger plays and jump rope rhymes, learning (including alphabet and counting), humorous, food, animals, nature, inspiration (including self-esteem), international, and new (copyrighted) songs.

Recommended Books of Ballads and Folk Songs

Berry, Holly. *Old MacDonald Had a Farm*. North-South, 1994.

Delacre, Lulu. *Arroz con Leche: Popular Songs and Rhymes from Latin America*. Sagebrush, 1999.

Hoberman, Mary Ann. *I Know an Old Lady Who Swallowed a Fly*. Megan Tingley, 2004.

Hoberman, Mary Ann. *Yankee Doodle*. Megan Tingley, 2004.

Kidd, Ronald. *On Top of Old Smoky: A Collection of Songs and Stories from Appalachia*. Illus. Linda Anderson. Ideals, 1992.

Langstaff, John. *Frog Went A-Courtin'*. Illus. Feodor Rojankovsky. Sagebrush, 1999.

Malcolmson, Anne, & Grace Castagnetta. *The Song of Robin Hood*. Illus. Virginia Lee Burton. Houghton Mifflin, 2000.

Owen, Ann. *I've Been Working on the Railroad*. Illus. Sandra D'Antonio. Picture Window, 2003.

Owen, Ann. *She'll Be Coming Round the Mountain*. Illus. Sandra D'Antonio. Picture Window, 2003.

Silverman, Jerry. *Ragtime Song and Dance: Traditional Black Music*. Chelsea House, 1995.

Spier, Peter. *The Erie Canal*. North Country, 1999.

Legends

Legends are unverifiable (and typically unreliable) historical and/or biographical accounts that were told by professional poets whose function was to recite the great deeds of their culture's heroes. They are written in an earnest tone because they were believed to be true. They are set in historic times and focus on the lives of extraordinary humans and events, often with a kernel of truth. However, the truth is distorted; attributes of courage, goodness, wisdom, or beauty are often highly exaggerated.

The term *legend* was first applied to stories about the lives of the Christian saints, such as St. Patrick, who brought Christianity to Ireland. Another legendary saint was St. George, a martyred Roman Christian soldier from 300 A.D. who died near Lydia in Palestine. It is believed that in the legend, *Saint George and the Dragon* (Hodges), the princess symbolized the church, and the dragon represented the evil throughout Europe at that time. The plot of this story is common to most legends; it contains a challenge, a quest, enchantment, and a battle with an evil force—with justice finally triumphing.

A legend differs from a myth by portraying a human hero rather than a god or goddess. In addition, whereas myths are set in a remote time, legends are set in a specific place and time, especially when the protagonist is a historical hero. The specific setting distinguishes the legend from all other forms of folktales. Legends can overlap with ballads when the ballads are about legendary people. The difference is not in the subject but in the format: Ballads are songs, and legends are narratives (stories or tales).

One of the most popular legends in the English language is of King Arthur, leader of the Knights of the Round Table who searched for the Holy Grail and avenged wrongs throughout Britain. The real Arthur (if he existed at all), was not likely a king, but rather a sixth-century medieval Celtic war leader who gallantly resisted the Saxon takeover of Britain. French nobility adopted his legends 600 years later, and they were recited at the courts of kings and noblemen by specially trained troubadours (called bards in England) who greatly romanticized the stories.

A number of interesting legendary characters are subjects of children's books. Hua Mu Lan was a brave Chinese woman who disguised herself as a man and took the place of her elderly father when he was called to war. The Swiss hero William Tell fought for freedom and independence. Rabbi Löw of Prague created the Golem from clay to help the Jewish people of the city who were being persecuted. John Henry was a former slave who drove steel into mountainsides to help blast a passage for the railroad tunnels in the Allegheny Mountains of West Virginia.

Recommended Books of Legends

Brooks, Felicity, & Anna Claybourne. *King Arthur and His Knights.* EDC Publishing, 2002.
Chin, Charlie. *China's Bravest Girl: The Legend of Hua Mu Lan.* Illus. Tomie Arai. Children's Book Press, 1997.
Fisher, Leonard Everett. *William Tell.* Farrar, Straus & Giroux, 1996.
Hastings, Selina. *Sir Gawain and the Loathly Lady.* Illus. Juan Wijngaard. HarperTrophy, 1987.

Hodges, Margaret. *Saint George and the Dragon.* Illus. Trina Schart Hyman. Little, Brown, 1990.

Lester, Julius. *John Henry.* Illus. Jerry Pinkney. Puffin, 1999.

Mayer, Marianna. *Women Warriors: Myths and Legends of Heroic Women.* HarperCollins, 1999.

Paterson, Katherine. *Parzival: The Quest of the Grail Knight.* Puffin, 2000.

Siegelson, Kim. *In the Time of Drums.* Illus. Brian Pinkney. Jump Sun, 1999.

Wisniewski, David. *Golem.* Clarion, 1996.

Tall Tales

The United States is a comparatively young country, and there was little time for a large body of stories to develop in the oral tradition; however, in the 1800s the U.S. frontier spawned the **tall tale,** making it the youngest form of folktales. Tall tales emerged through the storytelling of ordinary people and the imaginations of professional writers of eastern newspapers, inexpensive novels, and periodicals. It is impossible to disentangle the oral from the written stories, because these tales moved in and out of the literary and oral modes.

Tall tales are delivered with grand assertion of unbelievable exploits told with great exaggeration and hyperbole. Yet, they also rely on understatement for their humorous effect by sometimes minimizing the enormity of an object or feat. In all regards, the tone is humorous with exaggerated feats of gigantic, extravagant, restless, and flamboyant characters (*American Tall Tales,* Osborne). Some of the tales describe the courage and endurance of real historical heroes, such as frontiersman Davy Crockett, firefighter Mose Humphreys, keelboat man Mike Fink, and pioneer John Chapman (Johnny Appleseed)—whose prowess continued to grow long after they died. Other heroes of tall tales are imaginary, composite characters that embody an entire trade, such as the cowboy Pecos Bill, logger Paul Bunyan, steel worker Joe Magarac, sailor Stormalong, farmer Febold Feboldson, and frontierswoman Sally Ann Thunder Ann Whirlwind. Mary Pope Osborne's collection of American tall tales gives many interesting historical facts behind the tales of these real and imaginary heroes.

Whereas Native American tales represent the folklore of the indigenous people in the Americas, tall tales represent the folklore of the Euro-American pioneers who set out to win the continent (from the Native Americans, unfortunately). At one time, tall tales were presented to city dwellers as true pictures of life out west, supposedly to dupe naive readers because the stories were absurdly exaggerated. For example, the behemoth lumberjack Paul Bunyan was so quick on his feet he could blow out a candle and leap into bed before the room became dark. He was so big that he combed his beard with the top of a pine tree. No wonder that Paul managed to dig the Great Lakes and gouge out the Grand Canyon, despite the hardships he and his crew of lumberjacks encountered—such as a blizzard that lasted for several years.

American legends overlap with tall tales when the subject is a real person, such as Davy Crockett. However, the tall tale version of a person is preposterous because of its exaggerations ("Davy killed him a bear, when he was only three"), whereas the legendary version is believable but romanticized. It is interesting to note that the African American steel driver, John Henry, has been the subject of ballads, legends, and tall tales.

Recommended Books of Tall Tales

Brimner, Larry Dane. *Captain Stormalong*. Compass Point, 2004.

Johnson, Janet P. *Keelboat Annie: An African-American Legend*. Illus. Charles Reasoner. Troll, 1999.

Kellogg, Steven. *Johnny Appleseed*. HarperCollins, 1996.

Kellogg, Steven. *Mike Fink*. HarperTrophy, 1998.

Kellogg, Steven. *Paul Bunyan*. HarperTrophy, 1985.

Kellogg, Steven. *Pecos Bill*. Rayo, 1995.

Metaxas, Eric. *Mose the Fireman*. Rabbit Ears, 2004.

Nolen, Jerdine. *Big Jabe*. Illus. Kadir Nelson. Amistad, 2003.

Osborne, Mary Pope. *American Tall Tales*. Illus. Michael McCurdy. Knopf, 1991.

Schanzer, Rosalyn. *Davy Crockett Saves the World*. HarperCollins, 2001.

Fairy Tales

Fairy tales are by far the most abundant folktales, but are difficult to define because they are so varied. To make matters more confusing, most fairy tales do not contain fairies, which is why folklorists prefer to call this category by its German name—Märchen. I usually tell my students to use the rule of exclusion—meaning that if it *is* a folktale and it is *not* a myth, fable, ballad, legend, or tall tale—then it *must* be a fairy tale.

Fairy tales constitute a wide variety of folk narratives that express the wishes, hopes, desires, and fears of ordinary people. The protagonists are most frequently poor people and humble tradesmen, though there is a fair share of royal supporting characters. The original purpose of most fairy tales was to enchant listeners with stories of supernatural events in a wonderland setting filled with magic and strange, fantastical characters. They serve the same purpose for children today.

Fairy tale characters may be anthropomorphic animals ("The Three Little Pigs"), imaginary beings with magical powers ("Rumpelstiltskin"), plants ("The Tale of Three Trees"), inanimate objects ("The Gingerbread Boy"), and of course humans ("Snow White"). In American fairy tales, a boy named Jack is a common human character.

Imagined characters that appear in fairy tales include banshees, brownies, dwarves, elves, gnomes, goblins, imps, pixies, trolls, and of course fairies. The latter can be good or evil, but even good fairies are prone to play pranks on humans. Bad fairies can cause the sudden death of cattle, bewitch children, and even substitute changelings, ugly fairy babies, for human infants. (Now you know why your sibling might be so different from you and the rest of your family!)

Coffin (1999) described a typical fairy tale plot as involving "an underdog hero or heroine who is put through great trials or must perform seemingly impossible tasks, and who with magical assistance secures his or her birthright or a suitable marriage partner" (p. 5). Because fairy tales are the largest subgenre of traditional literature, they can best be examined and appreciated when grouped by commonalities. There are seven major groups with recognizable literary patterns: beast stories, trickster tales, simpleton tales, pourquoi tales, cumulative tales, realistic tales, and wonder stories.

Beast Stories. **Beast stories,** also called animal stories, have anthropomorphic animals as characters. Perhaps the best-known beast tale is "Goldilocks and the Three Bears." The animal characters act, talk, and reason as humans do, though they may retain a few animal traits as well. In a Native American tale, *The Story of Jumping Mouse* (Steptoe), a young mouse journeys to reach the land of his dreams. Though retaining all his animal habits, he is able to talk with other animals, and he portrays the human emotions of desire, discontent, dismay, hope, sadness, courage, unselfishness, and compassion.

A common theme, especially in African lore, is a smaller animal outwitting a larger animal or other foe. Because the trickster character is most often portrayed as an animal, most of the trickster tales described in the next section are also beast stories. In addition, many cumulative tales, such as "The Three Pigs," are also beast stories.

Trickster Tales. The mischievous survivor who is the protagonist of **trickster tales** is often portrayed by an animal such as a spider, coyote, fox, or rabbit. He uses his wits to gain some advantage or to get out of trouble. Sometimes he is the bringer of good things, such as light, stories, healing, or fire, and he even may speak up for underdog characters. Other times, he is selfish and reprehensible, trying to get something for nothing, taking advantage of others, stirring up trouble just for the fun of it, trying to make others look foolish or get into trouble—ever scheming but never remorseful!

The trickster is greedy, impulsive, and full of tricks, which are sometimes clever and sometimes foolish. He always defies conventions, being ever inventive and resilient, looking for a meal to swipe or some way to secure something with little or no effort. He even engages in fantastic lying contests. He is known as Iktomi, Coyote, or Raven by Native American tribes, Ananse by African tribes, Reynard by Europeans, Hodja by Turks, Brer Rabbit by African Americans, and Bugs Bunny to children (though the last is not a folktale character).

The trickster's opponents are usually stronger, meaner characters, and he often defends himself against becoming their dinner. Trickster tales teach children that they must be on guard constantly for others' tricks, but the trickster serves an even greater purpose. He is a role model for survival, one who maintains resistance in the face of oppression or hardship. His indomitable spirit is to be admired when he comes out ahead because of his wits rather than his physical strength or station in life.

In *Jump Again!* (Harris & Parks), when Brer Rabbit is captured, he pleads repeatedly, "'Please, Brer Fox, don't fling me in that briar patch.' Of course, Brer Fox wants to hurt Brer Rabbit as bad as he could, so he caught him up and flung him into the middle of the briar patch" (p. 11). But that was exactly where Brer Rabbit wanted to go because he was "bred and born in a briar patch," and there was no place he loved better. This is an example of how a trickster uses shrewd thinking to save his life.

The trickster is an exception to the stereotyped characters in traditional literature who are either all good or all bad. Tricksters are typically amoral—neither good nor bad. Sometimes they are wise and helpful, but they can also be sly and mischievous. However, they are always charming and likeable, and they always manage to escape severe punishment.

In Native American lore, the trickster is often Coyote, and Susan Strauss provided several good examples in *Coyote Stories for Children*. According to Medicine Hawk Wilburn (1998), the tales of Coyote serve a number of valuable purposes for humankind.

> He shows us our weaknesses. He teaches us how to be wily and aware of our surroundings. He teaches us by reverse example how to behave; how to act; how to treat others. He reflects our selfish ways back to us. He brings us face to face with our dark (or lighter) side. Most of all, Coyote teaches us how to laugh at the world, and therefore laugh at ourselves.

Simpleton Tales. The foolish protagonist in **simpleton tales** is often called the noodle head or numskull. He is humorously impractical, does not take the obviously logical action, and often takes others' words literally. However, in the end, he may turn out to be wiser than he appears. He is often portrayed as a likeable, childlike character without common sense, such as in the Puerto Rican *Juan Bobo Goes to Work* (Montes).

Simpletons typically make a mess of things with their absurd mistakes—as does Big Anthony in *Strega Nona* (dePaola), who makes the town overflow with pasta because he cannot figure out how to turn the magic pasta pot off.

Sometimes, however, simpletons succeed where people who are more intelligent do not. In *The Fool of the World and the Flying Ship* (Ransome), two clever brothers and one foolish brother set out on the same quest. The two clever brothers are never heard of again, but the foolish brother finds the flying ship, takes it to the Czar, and—after succeeding at numerous trials—marries the princess. The ancient and magical man who first befriended him reveals the theme to this tale: "You see how God loves simple folk. Although your own mother does not love you, you have not been done out of your share of the good things."

Pourquoi Tales. *Pourquoi* (poor-QWAH) means "why" in French. **Pourquoi tales** answer questions about the way things are, such as cultural customs, natural phenomena, and animal traits and characteristics. These tales often relate how various animals developed their familiar characteristics because of mistakes they had made. They were designed to teach children socially acceptable behavior in a fanciful short story with an implicit, rather than explicit, moral. They are lighthearted, humorous explanations such as "How Turtle's Back Was Cracked" (Ross), an allegory of human behavior that provides a lesson on appropriate conduct. Today these stories are still used by Native Americans as a way of passing on cultural values to their children.

Rainbow Crow: A Lenape Tale (Van Laan) is a beautiful story, both in text and in illustrations, that explains why the courageous crow changed from a lovely bird of rainbow colors and pleasing voice to the bird it is today. These tales can also explain human customs. *Tikki Tikki Tembo* (Mosel) explains why Chinese parents give their children short names. Pourquoi tales should not be confused with myths that explain natural phenomena as actions or influences of deities (gods and goddesses); rather, animals typically bring things about in pourquoi tales.

Cumulative Tales. In **cumulative tales,** the same event repeats itself with successively more characters or events added, such as in *The Gingerbread Boy* (Galdone). This means that each time the refrain is repeated, a new item is added to the story, and the list of events or participants expands. However, cumulative tales can have as few as three repetitive events, as in "The Three Little Pigs." Others sound like a chant, where only one new phrase or sentence is added, and the full refrain is repeated each time, such as in the Nandi tale, *Bringing the Rain to Kapiti Plain* (Aardema).

Some cumulative tales are called **chaining tales,** because each part of the story is linked to the next. Cullinan (1989) explained, "The initial incident reveals both the central character and problem; each subsequent scene builds onto the original one. In some stories, the chain builds up and then unwinds until the original cause of the problem is resolved. The accumulation continues to a climax and then unravels in reverse order" (p. 239). In *One Fine Day* (Hogrogian), a fox drinks an old woman's milk, so she cuts off his tail. In order to get her to sew his tail back on, he must replace the milk. He goes from one character to another, but each requires the fox to give something, until he meets a kind miller who "gave him the grain to give to the hen to get the egg to pay the peddler to get the bead to give the maiden to get the jug to fetch the water to give the field to get the grass to feed the cow to get the milk to give the old woman to get his tail back."

Realistic Tales. Perhaps the smallest group of fairy tales, the **realistic tales** concern characters, settings, and events that are realistic. That is, although the plots may be far-fetched, they follow all the laws of the physical world. Because there are no elements of fantasy, realistic tales are void of talking animals, fantasy creatures, and magical objects or beings. Uri Shulevitz presents a humble old man as the protagonist in *The Secret Room,* in which an old man wins the favor of the king through his clever and wise responses (no magic), and he is made the king's chief counselor.

Wonder Stories. Enchantments and other magic abound in **wonder stories.** These stories' characters include supernatural beings such as fairy godmothers, helpful elves, and evil trolls. Magical objects, such as mirrors, cloaks, oil lamps, and rings are common. The plots of wonder stories center on common people who need supernatural assistance in order to solve their problems. Often these stories involve adventure, romance, and unusual characters, such as the princes in *Beauty and the Beast* (Brett) and *The Frog Prince* (Blair), both of whom were turned into ugly animals by evil enchanters.

In wonder tales, dreams come true—literally. In *The Mud Pony* (Cohen), the boy's clay horse comes to life. Baba Yaga's dream comes true when she is adopted as a *babushka* (grandmother) by a young boy in *Babushka Baba Yaga* (Polacco). Duffy gets a life of ease and marries the squire when an impish creature does her spinning for her in *Duffy and the Devil* (Zemach).

Virtue and wisdom are rewarded in wonder tales. In *The Talking Eggs* (San Souci), the younger sister is respectful and obeys an old woman, for which she is rewarded with magic eggs that provide her with many riches. In *The Fourth Question* (Wang), a young man unselfishly gives up his one chance to have the Wise Man answer his pressing question. Instead, he asks three questions for three people who befriended him—and, because of this, his own problem is solved.

It is common to illustrate fairy tales in a setting near the time the story first appeared in print. However, some artists have taken traditional tales and illustrated them with contemporary settings. This approach may appeal to older children who think they have outgrown fairy tales. Anthony Browne's illustrations of the Grimms' *Hansel and Gretel* depict the brother and sister as impoverished children living in a dirty, run-down two-story brick house. The pictures are artfully drawn and amusing, from the bottle of Oil of Olay and panty hose on the dresser to the stepmother's heavy makeup and the flowered wallpaper in the witch's kitchen.

Traditional literature is the original multicultural literature, and nowhere is this more evident than with fairy tales, the largest category of traditional literature. Following are recommended books from a variety of cultures. Bold entries denote Cinderella-type stories, which are discussed in the next section.

African Fairy Tales

Aardema, Verna. *Bringing the Rain to Kapiti Plain.* Illus. Beatriz Vidal. Puffin, 1993.

Aardema, Verna. *Misoso: Once Upon a Time Tales from Africa.* Illus. Reynold Ruffins. Knopf, 1994.

Aardema, Verna. *Why Mosquitoes Buzz in People's Ears.* Illus. Leo D. Dillon & Diane Dillon. Dial, 1990.

Bryan, Ashley. *Beautiful Blackbird.* Atheneum, 2003.

Cummings, Pat. *Ananse and the Lizard: A West African Tale.* Henry Holt, 2002.

Haley, Gail E. *A Story, a Story: An African Tale.* Sagebrush, 1999.

 Steptoe, John. *Mufaro's Beautiful Daughters: An African Tale.* Amistad, 1987.

American Fairy Tales

Compton, Joanne. *Ashpet: An Appalachian Tale.* Illus. Kenn Compton. Holiday House, 1994.

Haley, Gail E. *Mountain Jack Tales.* Parkway, 2001.

Hamilton, Virginia. *Her Stories: African American Folktales, Fairy Tales, and True Tales.* Illus. Leo D. Dillon & Diane Dillon. Blue Sky, 1995.

Harris, Joel Chandler, & Van Dyke Parks. *Jump Again! More Adventures of Brer Rabbit.* Illus. Barry Moser. Harcourt Brace Jovanovich, 1987.

Hunt, Angela Elwell. *The Tale of Three Trees: A Traditional Folktale.* Illus. Tim Jonke. Chariot Victor, 2004.

Lester, Julius. *The Tales of Uncle Remus: The Adventures of Brer Rabbit.* Illus. Jerry Pinkney. Puffin, 1999.

San Souci, Robert D. *The Talking Eggs: A Folktale from the American South.* Illus. Jerry Pinkney. Dial, 1989.

Native American Fairy Tales

Bruchac, Joseph. *Flying with the Eagle, Racing the Great Bear: Stories from Native North America.* Sagebrush, 2001.

Cohen, Caron Lee. *The Mud Pony.* Illus. Shonto Begay. Sagebrush, 1999.

Pollock, Penny. *The Turkey Girl: A Zuni Cinderella Story.* Illus. Ed Young. Little, Brown, 1996.

Powell, Patricia Hruby. *Frog Brings Rain.* Illus. Kendrick Benally. Salina Bookshelf, 2006.

Ross, Gayle. *How Turtle's Back Was Cracked: A Traditional Cherokee Tale.* Illus. Murv Jacob. Dial, 1995.

Strauss, Susan. *Coyote Stories for Children: Tales from Native America.* Illus. Gary Lund. Beyond Words, 1991.

Van Laan, Nancy. *Rainbow Crow: A Lenape Tale.* Illus. Beatriz Vidal. Dragonfly, 1991.

Asian Fairy Tales

Meeker, Clare Hodgson. *A Tale of Two Rice Birds: A Folktale from Thailand.* Illus. Christine Lamb. Sasquatch Books, 1994.

Mosel, Arlene. *The Funny Little Woman.* Illus. Blair Lent. Puffin, 1993.

Mosel, Arlene. *Tikki Tikki Tembo.* Illus. Blair Lent. Holt, 1989.

Rinpoche, Ringu Tulku. *The Boy Who Had a Dream: A Nomadic Folk Tale from Tibet.* Findhorn, 1997.

Wang, Rosalind C. *The Fourth Question: A Chinese Tale.* Illus. Ju-Hong Chen. Holiday House, 1991.

Young, Ed. *Lon Po Po: A Red Riding Hood Story from China.* Penguin, 1996.

Young, Ed. *Yah-Shen: A Cinderella Story from China.* Putnam, 1996.

British Fairy Tales

Faulkner, Matt. *Jack and the Beanstalk.* HarperTrophy, 1997.

Galdone, Paul. *The Gingerbread Boy.* Clarion, 2001.

Greaves, Margaret. *Tattercoats.* Illus. Margaret Chamberlain. Frances Lincoln, 1990.

Greene, Ellin. *Billy Beg and His Bull: An Irish Tale.* Illus Kimberly Bulcken Root. Holiday, 1994.

Huck, Charlotte. *The Black Bull of Narroway: A Scottish Tale*. Illus. Anita Lobel. Greenwillow, 2001.

Zemach, Harve. *Duffy and the Devil*. Illus. Margot Zemach. Sunburst, 1986.

French Fairy Tales

Brett, Jan. *Beauty and the Beast*. Sagebrush, 1999.

Muth, Jon J. *Stone Soup*. Scholastic, 2003.

Perrault, Charles. *Cinderella*. Illus. Marcia Brown. Aladdin, 1997.

Perrault, Charles. *The Complete Fairy Tales of Charles Perrault*. Clarion, 1993.

Perrault, Charles. *Little Red Riding Hood and Other Stories*. Illus. Sarah Moon. Creative, 2002.

Perrault, Charles. *Puss in Boots: A Fairy Tale*. Illus. Fred Marcellino. Sunburst, 1998.

Perrault, Charles. *Sleeping Beauty*. Illus. Trina Schart Hyman. Little, Brown, 1983.

German Fairy Tales

Blair, Eric. *The Frog Prince*. Picture Window, 2004.

Brett, Jan. *Goldilocks and the Three Bears*. Putnam, 1996.

Grimm, Jacob, & Wilhelm Grimm. *Cinderella and Other Tales by the Brothers Grimm*. HarperFestival, 2005.

Grimm, Jacob, & Wilhelm Grimm. *Hansel and Gretel*. Illus. Anthony Browne. Walker, 1995.

Grimm, Jacob, & Wilhelm Grimm. *Rapunzel*. Illus. Paul O. Zelinsky. Puffin, 2002.

Grimm, Jacob, & Wilhelm Grimm. *Rumpelstiltskin*. Illus. Paul O. Zelinsky. Sagebrush, 1999.

Grimm, Jacob, & Wilhelm Grimm. *Snow-White and the Seven Dwarfs*. Illus. Nancy Ekholm Burkert. Sunburst, 1987.

Latino Fairy Tales

Ada, Alma Flor. *Mediopollito / Half-Chicken*. Illus. Kim Howard. Random, 1997.

Anaya, Rudolfo. *Farolitos for Abuelo*. Illus. Edward Gonzales. Hyperion, 1999.

Anaya, Rudolfo. *Farolitos of Christmas*. Illus. Edward Gonzales. Hyperion, 1995.

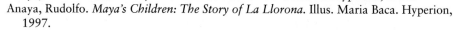 Anaya, Rudolfo. *Maya's Children: The Story of La Llorona*. Illus. Maria Baca. Hyperion, 1997.

dePaola, Tomie. *Adelita: A Mexican Cinderella Story*. Putnam, 2002.

Gonzalez, Lucia M. *The Bossy Gallito*. Illus. Lulu Delacre. Scholastic, 1999.

Montes, Marisa. *Juan Bobo Goes to Work: A Puerto Rican Folktale*. Illus. Joe Cepeda. HarperCollins, 2000.

Russian Fairy Tales

Martin, Rafe. *The Language of Birds*. Illus. Susan Gaber. Putnam, 2000.
Mayer, Marianna. *Baba Yaga and Vasilisa the Brave*. HarperCollins, 1994.
Oram, Hiawyn. *Baba Yaga and the Wise Doll*. Illus. Ruth Brown. Penguin, 1998.
Polacco, Patricia. *Babushka Baba Yaga*. Philomel, Sagebrush, 1999.
Ransome, Arthur. *The Fool of the World and the Flying Ship*. Illus. Uri Shulevitz. Sunburst, 1987.
Robbins, Ruth. *Baboushka and the Three Kings*. Houghton Mifflin, 1986.
Vagin, Vladimir. *The Enormous Carrot*. Scholastic, 1998.

Scandinavian Fairy Tales

Asbjørnsen, Peter Christen. *Norwegian Folk Tales*. Egmont, 1998.
Asbjørnsen, Peter Christen, & Jorgen Moe. *East of the Sun and West of the Moon and Other Norwegian Fairy Tales*. Illus. George Webbe Dasent. Dover, 2001.
Braekstad, H. L. *Swedish Fairy Tales*. Hippocrene, 1998.
Finch, Mary. *The Three Billy Goats Gruff*. Illus. Roberta Arenson. Barefoot, 2001.
Phelps, Ethel J. *Tatterhood and Other Tales: Stories of Magic and Adventure*. Illus. Pamela Baldwin Ford. Sagebrush, 1989.
Shepard, Aaron. *The Maiden of Northland: A Hero Tale of Finland*. Atheneum, 1996.
Shepard, Aaron. *The Princess Mouse: A Tale of Finland*. Atheneum, 2003.

Additional Fairy Tales

Claire, Elizabeth. *The Little Brown Jay: A Tale from India*. Illus. Miriam Katin. Mondo, 1994.
Climo, Shirley. *The Egyptian Cinderella*. Illus. Ruth Heller. HarperCollins, 1992.
Climo, Shirley. *The Persian Cinderella*. Illus. Robert Florczak. HarperTrophy, 2001.
dePaola, Tomie. *Days of the Blackbird: A Tale of Northern Italy*. Putnam, 1997.
dePaola, Tomie. *Strega Nona* (Italy). Sagebrush, 1999.
Hausman, Gerald. *Doctor Bird: Three Lookin' Up Tales from Jamaica*. Illus. Ashley Wolfe. Philomel, 1998.
Hogrogian, Nonny. *One Fine Day* (Armenian). Sagebrush, 1999.
Jaffe, Nina. *The Way Meat Loves Salt: A Cinderella Tale from the Jewish Tradition*. Illus. Louise August. Holt, 1998.
Leeson, Robert. *My Sister Shahrazad: Tales from the Arabian Nights*. Frances Lincoln, 2002.
Rose, Deborah Lee. *The People Who Hugged the Trees* (India). Roberts Rinehart, 2001.
San Souci, Robert. *Cendrillon: A Caribbean Cinderella*. Sagebrush, 2003.

Schwartz, Howard. *Elijah's Violin & Other Jewish Fairy Tales.* Illus. Linda Heller. Oxford University Press, 1994.

Shulevitz, Uri. *The Secret Room* (Middle East). Sunburst, 1996.

Zemach, Margot. *It Could Always Be Worse: A Yiddish Folk Tale.* Sunburst, 1990.

Cinderella Stories. "Cinderella" is perhaps the best-known fairy tale, and this is likely why Walt Disney chose it to make his famous animated movie, which was an adaptation of both Perrault's French version titled "Cendrillon" and the Grimms' German version titled "Aschenputtel."

The oldest known version is the Chinese "Yeh-Shen," which has been traced to the ninth century (Wolkomir & Wolkomir, 2004). More than 700 other versions of this enchanting tale have been identified from various world cultures. (See Northrup [2004] for annotations of 29 versions published in the English language.) The Cinderella stories were likely spread through the migration of people to other countries and by trade caravans. However, in 1697 Charles Perrault published the version that is most familiar to children in our culture. Marcia Brown used the Perrault version for *Cinderella, or the Little Glass Slipper,* which was awarded the Caldecott Medal in 1955.

In many American versions of the tale, the protagonist is illustrated as blonde, blue eyed, and fair skinned. Yet less than half our population is of Northern European origin (Lurie, 2004), meaning most children will not share these same physical attributes. Reading Cinderella-type stories from a variety of cultures will allow your children to find a protagonist with whom they may relate.

In addition, it is fun to compare the various **motifs** in the books. Motifs are recurring elements within traditional stories found in various combinations across stories and cultures, such as magic objects or helpers, tests of character or strength, and transformations (human to animal or animal to human). For example—depending on which version you read—Cinderella may lose a glass slipper, a black silk shoe, or a carved leather strap from her sandal. Likewise, the magical helper may be a ten-foot-long fish instead of a fairy godmother. In addition, Cinderella is not always female. In the Irish tale, *Billy Beg* (Greene), the protagonist is a boy!

Responding to Literature

Comparing Story Motifs and Artwork in Cinderella-Type Stories   Read at least two versions of Cinderella-type stories from different cultures. (Some examples are listed in boldface type in the preceding bibliographies.) Then compare the following motifs typically found in this story: (1) protagonist, (2) evil person, (3) siblings, (4) magical helper, (5) type of celebration, (6) protagonist's attire at celebration, (7) male of high status, and (8) lost article. Next, analyze the illustrations for culture-specific details, such as animals, architecture, artwork, clothing, dwellings, foods, landscapes, plants, and other artifacts.

Featured Author

Ed Young

Ed Young was born in Tienstin, China. He grew up in Shanghai, later moved to Hong Kong, and finally settled in the United States. He has illustrated more than eighty books for children and was awarded the 1990 Caldecott Medal for *Lon Po Po: A Red Riding Hood Story from China* (see the illustration at the beginning of this chapter). He also was awarded Caldecott Honors for *The Emperor and the Kite* and *Seven Blind Mice.* In addition, he has twice been nominated for the international Hans Christian Andersen Award. In his books, he often uses three-picture sequences, which resemble traditional Chinese decorative panels.

His most popular books include *Lon Po Po,* in which three girls are left home when their mother goes to visit their grandmother. The wolf, Lon Po Po, shows up at their door dressed as their granny, and the girls must use their wits to keep from being eaten. In another favorite, *Cat and Rat: The Legend of the Chinese Zodiac,* the Emperor challenges all the creatures to race through forests and rivers, saying he will name each of the twelve years in the cycle after the winners. Rat comes in first, but only by being a trickster.

In *I, Doko: The Tale of a Basket,* the narrator is a *doko,* a Nepalese basket designed to tote heavy loads. Over the decades, Doko carries many things for his owner Yeh-Yeh: crops, his baby, the dowry of his son's wife, his grandchild, and his aged wife's body to the grave. Finally, the son uses Doko to carry the feeble Yeh-Yeh to the temple steps because he does not want to care for his aged father, and Yeh-Yeh's grandchild must step in to remind his father that the same consequences could befall him unless Yeh-Yeh is returned home. In *The Lost Horse,* the changing nature of life is exemplified. A man's horse runs away, but the man does not mourn. The horse later returns with a mare, but he does not celebrate. His son is thrown from the mare's back and breaks his leg, but the man does not consider this bad. When his son's injury prevents him from going to war and thus saves him from a likely death, the man knows he was right to trust in the fortunes of life.

Traditional Rhymes

Nursery rhymes are traditional verses intended for very young children. Often these simple rhymes are a child's first contact with literature. Most of the rhymes are nonsensical, but they have several features that make them enjoyable. Their musical language, often created with strong rhythm, makes them appealing to children, and they contain action, humor, and entertaining incidents.

Most likely, the nursery rhymes you heard as a child were of British origin and were called **Mother Goose** rhymes. There are several explanations of how the term

Mother Goose became associated with these rhymes, but I will provide the one I find most plausible. In 1729, an English translation of Perrault's fairy tales was published and became very popular in England. In addition to the enchanting tales, it contained nursery rhymes. The book was subtitled "Tales of My Mother Goose," and the **frontispiece** (the illustration preceding the title page) depicted an old woman. A caption within the illustration read "Mother Goose's Tales." Some believe the woman was a Ms. Goose, perhaps the nursemaid who first told Perrault the fairy tales. (At that time, "Mother" was added to the names of women as a sign of respect.) Interestingly, the term Mother Goose became associated with the nursery rhymes rather than with the fairy tales in the book.

Among the subjects of nursery rhymes are festivals, vocations, courtship, marriage, and death—topics that more closely match adults' interests. However, long before these rhymes were recorded, they were entertainment for adults as well as children, as is true for all folklore. Most nursery rhymes do not make sense today, but they have historical links to their originating cultures. Many developed from humorous verses that were based on real people, events, or customs. Some of the sources for the rhymes were old proverbs, street cries, games, ballads, and even tavern songs. Others were political satires, masked by allegory to lampoon political and religious leaders. The popular "Ring-a-Ring o' Roses" is said to have its origins in the history of England.

> Ring-a-ring o' roses,
> A pocket full of posies;
> A-tishoo! A-tishoo!
> We all fall down.

Chisholm's (1972) research led her to conclude that this rhyme originated during the time of the Great Plague in England in 1664. The first symptom of the plague was a rosy rash that broke out on the victim's face and body, which the rhyme refers to as "roses." The "pocket full of posies" means the herbs or flowers people carried in their pockets in an effort to ward off the plague. "A-tishoo! A-tishoo!" refers to the next symptom, which was violent sneezing, followed by death, described as "We all fall down."

All cultures have nursery rhymes—including the United States. There are two great collections of American rhymes. *A Rocket in My Pocket: The Rhymes and Chants of Young Americans* (Withers) includes hundreds of jump rope rhymes, jingles, chants, riddles, and tongue twisters. *The Rooster Crows* by Maud and Miska Petersham contains nursery rhymes, skipping rhymes, counting-out rhymes, finger games, and jingles.

For the British collections, I especially like *Hey Diddle Diddle and Other Mother Goose Rhymes* by Tomie dePaola. This book is very appealing to young children because the illustrations are colorful and uncluttered as well as enchanting. In addition to collections, individual nursery rhymes can be subjects of picture books. Maurice Sendak used two nursery rhymes with only twelve lines to write and illustrate the picture book *Hector Protector and As I Went over the Water*. Understandably, many of the pages contain only Sendak's charming illustrations. Following are suggested books of traditional rhymes from various cultures.

Recommended Books of Traditional Rhymes

Benjamin, Floella. *Skip across the Ocean: Nursery Rhymes from around the World*. Illus. Sheila Moxley. Orchard, 1995.

Crews, Nina. *The Neighborhood Mother Goose*. Amistad, 2003.

Griego, Margot C. *Tortillas Para Mama and Other Rhymes in Spanish and English*. Illus. Barbara Cooney. Holt, 1988

dePaola, Tomie. *Hey Diddle Diddle and Other Mother Goose Rhymes*. Putnam, 1998.

Grover, Eulalie Osgood. *The Original Volland Edition of Mother Goose*. Illus. Frederick Richardson. Derrydale, 1997.

Jaramillo, Nelly Palocio. *Grandmother's Nursery Rhymes / Las Nanas de Abuelita*. Illus. Elivia Savadier. Sagebrush, 1999.

Petersham, Maud, & Miska Petersham. *The Rooster Crows*. Sagebrush, 1999.

Sendak, Maurice. *Hector Protector and As I Went over the Water*. Di Capua, 2001.

Withers, Carl. *A Rocket in My Pocket: The Rhymes and Chants of Young Americans*. Illus. Susanne Suba. Scholastic, 1990.

Wright, Blanche Fisher. *The Real Mother Goose*. Scholastic, 1994.

Issues in Traditional Literature

Is Folk Literature Too Violent?   Critics have argued that traditional literature is too violent to share with children. Inasmuch as the genre was not specifically intended for children, this is a claim worth investigating. First, let us look back at some of the literature I have discussed in this chapter. Snow White's wicked stepmother had to dance in red-hot iron shoes until she fell down dead. The gingerbread boy was eaten alive by a fox. Puss-in-Boots killed other animals without mercy and threatened to chop the field workers into small pieces. Some myths contain events that include murder and rape. And, although I failed to mention this earlier, in older versions of "The Frog Prince," the Frog was not kissed by the beautiful princess—he was thrown against the wall! (But he turned into a prince anyway.) Not even nursery rhymes can be excluded from this investigation. Consider the words to the familiar rhyme "Goosey, Goosey Gander."

> Goosey, goosey gander,
> Whither shall I wander?
> Upstairs and downstairs
> And in my lady's chamber.
> There I met an old man
> Who would not say his prayers,
> I took him by the left leg
> And threw him down the stairs.

Violence in nursery rhymes and folktales was taken for granted in past centuries (including the twentieth century), but people today are more conscious of children's exposure to violence, given the frequent news reports of violent crimes committed by children against both children and adults.

However, another side of the argument contends that because of most children's viewing habits, television and video game violence has far more influence than children's literature. By the time the average child graduates from high school, he or she will have spent more time viewing television than being in school. Traditional literature is an ever-changing body of works, and most of the popular tales have been adapted for younger children. To withhold the entire genre of traditional literature from children is to deprive them of cultural literacy.

Explain why you do or do not advocate that children should be exposed to the violence in traditional literature.

Summary

Traditional literature consists of stories, songs, and rhymes with unknown authorship that were passed down orally from one generation to the next before being written down. In addition to unknown authorship, traditional tales typically have conventional introductions and conclusions, vague settings, stereotyped characters, anthropomorphic figures, apparent cause-and-effect relationships, happy endings for the heroes/heroines, magical elements, and simple plots. Many of the tales have repetition of actions and verbal patterns. Themes of this genre include triumph of good over evil (by far the most prevalent), trickery, hero's quest, reversal of fortune, and the small character outwitting bigger characters.

Traditional literature can be divided into a number of subgenres. Myths convey the religious beliefs of past cultures; fables are very brief stories that teach lessons about appropriate behavior, usually with animal characters; ballads relate a story through song, often about legendary characters; legends are seemingly historical and biographical accounts about a culture's heroes that are unverifiable; tall tales originated on the U.S. frontier as vastly exaggerated accounts of flamboyant fictional characters; fairy tales are folk narratives, typically about ordinary people. Among the major groups of fairy tales are beast (or animal) stories, trickster tales, simpleton tales, pourquoi tales, cumulative tales, realistic tales, and wonder stories.

The final subgenre of traditional literature, traditional rhymes, is also called nursery rhymes. The European collections of traditional rhymes are called Mother Goose; however, traditional rhymes exist in all cultures.

Modern Fantasy

6

The artist of this surrealistic illustration used diagonal lines to imply the character's rapid descent and shading to make the character appear three-dimensional.

From *Harry Potter and the Sorcerer's Stone*, written by J. K. Rowling and illustrated by Mary Grandpre.

Library locations   **J (Juvenile) for junior novels; E (Easy) for picture books**

Fiction: A literary work that is designed to entertain, the content of which is produced by the imagination of an identifiable author

Modern fantasy: A fiction story with highly fanciful or supernatural elements that would be impossible in real life

This is the first of four chapters on **fiction.** This chapter will explore modern fantasy; Chapter 7, animal fantasy; Chapter 9, contemporary realistic fiction; and Chapter 10, historical fiction. All fiction books, regardless of genre, are typically located in the *unnumbered* section of the library. Storybooks or juvenile novels are separated from picture books and have a *J* (Juvenile) on the spine. (A few libraries use *F* for Fiction.) Picture books have an *E* (Easy) on the spine. Both J and E books will have the first letters of the author's last name underneath, and both are shelved alphabetically by *authors'* last names.

Fantasy was the inevitable offspring of traditional literature. Today, because both genres still share so many elements, we distinguish them by referring to them as traditional fantasy stories and **modern fantasy** stories. What is it that makes fantasy so different from other forms of fiction? Fantasy contains some type of unreality or enchantment—what children call magic. The story elements break the natural physical laws of our world without explanation. When you were a child (or maybe even an adult), did you pretend your pets could talk or your toys came to life? Did you ever pretend you could fly or become invisible? Did you wish you had a fairy godmother who would take you to wonderful places, or that you lived with both parents happily ever after? Did you ever wish you could acquire great riches (like win the lottery)? In fantasy people can live out their desires, but to fully enjoy fantasy, readers must suspend their disbelief of the impossible and accept that anything is possible within the covers of a book.

Evaluating Modern Fantasy

The following questions can guide you as you select modern fantasy books:

- Is the theme worthwhile for children?
- Is the plot original?
- Are the fantasy elements of the story well developed?
- Is the setting authentic and integral to the story?
- Does the author's characterization allow readers to suspend disbelief?
- Is the story logical and consistent within its chosen format?
- Is the point of view consistent?

- Does the author use appropriate language that is believable and consistent with the story?

For high fantasy:
- Is the main character truly heroic?
- Are all the characters plausible in their own settings?
- Is the secondary world believable?
- Is the quest purposeful?

For science fiction:
- Is the technology convincing?
- Are purposeful questions about the future raised?

The Beginnings of Fiction and Modern Fantasy

In the late 1400s, the development of the printing press using movable metal type made the mass publication and circulation of literature possible. Once reading materials were readily available, more people became literate. When people could read stories, listening to and telling stories became less important, and the ancient art of storytelling gradually diminished. Had it not been for the efforts of the early compilers of traditional stories, the tales might have been lost entirely.

Storytellers of the new era—such as Perrault, Galland, and Grimm—recorded old tales in print. Their published stories ultimately reached a far greater audience than was possible in the oral tradition. The new literate population clamored for more stories to read, and storytellers began to write their own tales, albeit still with the heavy influence of folktales. Eventually, the literary storytellers deviated from the folktale mold and became increasingly more individual in their subject matter and writing styles. These unique stories were the early beginnings of children's fiction and modern fantasy.

Hans Christian Andersen

Hans Christian Andersen was born in 1805 in Odense, Denmark, the son of a poor cobbler who died when Christian (as his mother called him) was eleven years old. Andersen never showed any interest in shoemaking—his desire was to be a performer. He ran away to Copenhagen when he was fourteen and nearly starved trying to work as a singer, dancer, and actor—all with little success—before realizing his talent was for writing. Jonas Collin, director of the Royal Theater, recognized Andersen's potential and procured a royal scholarship for him, which permitted him to continue his studies for many years.

Andersen began his career as a storyteller, retelling traditional tales that were fashioned with his own creative wit. However, the bulk of his published works are original stories that did not exist in the oral tradition. Andersen published the first of his 210 short stories in a series of pamphlets in 1835 and continued to write until his death in 1875.

In Denmark, Andersen also had success publishing novels, plays, poems, songs, and nonfiction works. However, his enchanting short stories gained him international fame and made him immortal. Andersen's short stories are among the most widely read works in world literature. Translations of his stories exist in more than 150 languages.

Andersen's name is typically associated with **literary fairy tales,** a subgenre that draws from the elements and motifs of traditional folk literature, yet is the product of a single author rather than the outcome of a multitude of unknown storytellers. However, I believe that Andersen's stories are far more than simply literary fairy tales—they are the prototype of the modern fantasy genre.

Many of Andersen's stories do bear characteristics of literary fairy tales—for example, both his stories and literary fairy tales have themes that are common to traditional literature. For example, a vain character is tricked in "The Emperor's New Suit," good triumphs over evil in "The Wild Swans," a hero's quest is successful in "The Snow Queen," a poor person becomes rich in "The Tinder-Box," and the underdog triumphs in "The Ugly Duckling."

Yet while some literature specialists may be content to clump Andersen's stories within the single fantasy subgenre of literary fairy tales, Eitelgeorge and Anderson (2004) argue that within the body of his work, there exist stories that have characteristics of all the subgenres of modern fantasy. In the next section, I discuss the ten themes that categorize the subgenres of modern fantasy, and I will introduce each with one of Andersen's tales that served as a prototype. Andersen's stories offered models that paved the way for future authors to venture beyond the scope of traditional tales into the many subgenres that have evolved to become today's world of modern fantasy.

Close analysis of Andersen's tales reveals characteristics that deviate considerably from both traditional tales and modern literary fairy tales. The most significant of these elements include use of original plots, well-rounded main characters, specific settings, humor through satire, and realistic—sometimes sad—endings. Additionally, the themes of his stories convey universal truths through expression of deep feelings and experiences, often with much melancholy.

Andersen's main characters are typically well rounded and quite vivid. Examples are the little mermaid who fell in love with a mortal, the fir tree that learned too late that it should have been happy with its life the way it was, and the persecuted little duckling.

Humor through satire is evident in "The Emperor's New Suit," where only a child will tell the vain and gullible emperor that he is quite naked! Andersen's use of irony and satire is perhaps most evident in "The Top and the Ball"—a one-sided love story of a mahogany toy top's adoration for a Moroccan leather ball, which is an allegory of Andersen's own life experience of being spurned by a woman and seeing her years later with her husband. The story concludes:

> He spoke not a word about his old love; for that soon died away. When the beloved object has lain for five years in a gutter, and has been drenched through, no one cares to know her again on meeting her in a dust-bin.

Unlike traditional literature and literary fairy tales, Andersen's tales deal with the universal truths and deep feelings of love, remorse, longing, and the agony of death. "The Brave Tin Soldier" exemplifies the selfless nature of love. "The Fir Tree" is a poignant story of the remorse of learning one should be satisfied with one's station in life. "The Ugly Duckling" expresses the longing to be accepted, and for more than 160 years, parents have used this beloved story (which was based on Andersen's own experience as a gangly and homely young man) to teach the value of perseverance and humility. The following excerpt exemplifies these truths:

> Then he felt quite ashamed, and hid his head under his wing; for he did not know what to do, he was so happy, and yet not at all proud. He had been persecuted and despised for his ugliness, and now he heard them say he was the most beautiful of all the birds.

Even the agony of death is discussed in some of Andersen's most beloved tales. This is where Andersen's style departs dramatically from traditional stories and literary fairy tales, which always have a happy ending for the hero. Consider the following endings of some of his more popular stories. In "The Little Mermaid," the protagonist throws herself from the ship into the sea, and her body dissolves into foam. In "The Brave Tin Soldier," a little boy throws the tin soldier into the stove, and he melts away. In "The Fir Tree," the little Christmas tree is chopped into pieces and set ablaze. "The Little Match-Seller" ends with the little girl frozen to death on the last evening of the year.

Young readers of Andersen's tales learn that life does not always have a happy ending, and that death is inevitable. Indeed, the universal truths and deep feelings expressed in these tales often have serious moral implications.

Hans Christian Andersen wrote with wisdom that reinforces kindness and sympathetic understanding. Yet, he also wrote with a deliberate simplicity that stirred the imagination. For nearly seventeen decades, these endearing qualities have appealed to children and adults throughout the world. For a complete collection of his tales with contemporary translations by Eric Christian Haugaard, I recommend *Hans Christian Andersen: The Complete Fairy Tales and Stories*. Many of Andersen's individual stories are also available in picture book format, notably *The Little Match Girl*, illustrated by Rachel Isadora, and *Thumbelina*, illustrated by Arlene Graston. English translations of Andersen's tales are found online at http://hca.gilead.org.il.

As evidence that Andersen fathered the modern fantasy genre, I provide examples in each subgenre section in this chapter to demonstrate how he laid a foundation for the writers of fiction who followed him—most notably Charles Dodgson. Under the pen name of Lewis Carroll, Dodgson published the first entertaining novel for children in England in 1865, *Alice's Adventures in Wonderland,* which ushered in the era of modern children's literature.

Types of Fantasy

The genre of fantasy is vast, particularly for preschool and primary-grade children, so I have broken it into ten groups:

1. Animal fantasy
2. Literary fairy tale
3. Animated object fantasy

  4. Human with fantasy character
  5. Extraordinary person
  6. Enchanted journey
  7. High fantasy
  8. Supernatural fantasy
  9. Science fiction
  10. Unlikely situation

Animal Fantasy

In animal fantasy the main—and often all—characters are anthropomorphic animals. They possess human speech and can think and express emotions like humans. Often they live like humans, wearing clothing, living in houses, cooking food, and the like. Examples of Andersen's stories in this category include the persecuted Swan in "The Ugly Duckling" and a beautiful songbird in "The Nightingale." Modern personified animal characters are found in *Frog and Toad Are Friends* (Lobel), *The Very Lonely Firefly* (Carle), and *Berlioz the Bear* (Brett).

Animal fantasy is so popular with younger children that when you look through the picture book sections of bookstores and libraries, about half of the books have fantasy animal characters. Because of its popularity with children, I have devoted all of the next chapter to animal fantasy.

Literary Fairy Tale

A literary fairy tale follows the patterns set by the oral tradition of folklore but is written by an identifiable author. Hans Christian Andersen's "Little Claus and Big Claus" and "The Tinder-Box" are both unique tales that follow the formula of traditional tales. Literary fairy tales may be the oldest category of fantasy, but even today some authors choose this style for both picture books and juvenile novels.

Ella Enchanted (Levine) is a novel-length Cinderella fantasy. At birth, Ella of Frell had inadvertently been cursed by Lucinda, an imprudent fairy who bestowed a spell of obedience on her. Ella must obey anything anyone tells her to do, no matter what the consequences are. When her beloved mother dies, her avaricious father takes a loathsome new wife with two daughters, who all make Ella serve them in her father's long absence. The fairy godmother in this story has cared for Ella since birth, playing the role as cook in the manor home where she lives. The prince is a long-time family friend, and he and Ella share a deep mutual respect before falling in love. There are grand balls, a pumpkin coach, glass slippers, and a search for the slippers' owner, but Levine weaves them into a new story that will touch the hearts of readers of any age.

The most enchanting and absorbing literary fairy tale I have read is undoubtedly *The Moorchild* by Eloise Jarvis McGraw. Set in medieval times, this novel opens with, "It was Old Bess, the Wise Woman of the village, who first suspected that the baby at her daughter's house was a changeling" (p. 3). Old Bess's granddaughter had indeed been stolen by the Moor fairies, and in her place a half-fairy, half-human baby had been left—a changeling. Saaski grows into a child who is considered a freak because of her unusual appearance and strange behaviors, not the least of which is her ability to play haunting melodies on the bagpipes without instruction. Her memory and perception of the Fairy Folk gradually return. After being driven from the village, Saaski and her only friend, Tam the goatherd boy, embark on a quest. They attempt to find her parents' real child—for which she was exchanged—and to return the child to them.

In Katherine Paterson's *The King's Equal* (1992), a vain and cruel young king must leave his kingdom and live as a goatherd for one year before he is able to marry the woman he loves. He is befriended by a talking wolf who helps him learn humility and kindness.

As a young boy, Tomie dePaola learned the traditional story of Strega Nona from his Italian grandmother. The story of the Grandma Witch and her noodle-head helper, Big Anthony, was so popular that dePaola followed it with several original stories. When Strega Amelia threatens to put Strega Nona out of business, Big Anthony goes to work for the competition and, with his usual bumbling, ends up putting the competitor out of business in *Strega Nona Meets Her Match.*

Teresa Bateman's original Irish tale, *The Ring of Truth,* has all the charm of a traditional Irish tale with leprechauns, magic, and gold. The leprechaun king punishes Patrick O'Kelley for his fibbing and boastfulness with a magic ring that will forever make him tell the truth. However, the truth is stranger than his blarney, and no one believes the story.

Pete Seeger got the idea for his story-song *Abiyoyo* while reading to his children from a book of South African lullabies. In this story a little boy with a ukulele and his magician father come up with a plan to rid the town of the fearsome giant Abiyoyo. The boy plays a song to make the monster dance, and when Abiyoyo falls down exhausted, the father touches him with his magic wand and makes him disappear.

In addition to literary fairy tales, there are literary pourquoi stories—stories that explain natural phenomena or the way things are. The earliest enduring tales were published by Rudyard Kipling in *Just So Stories* in 1902. Influenced by the Jataka tales of India, he wrote a collection of tales that explain certain animals' features, such as "How the Leopard Got His Spots." "The Elephant Child" gives an explanation of how the elephant got its long trunk in the setting of the "great, gray-green, greasy Limpopo River."

Some stories that use fairy tale themes are spoofs on traditional tales. It is the princess who saves the prince from the dragon in *The Paper Bag Princess* (Munsch). The prince is depicted as vain and haughty, whereas the princess is depicted as strong and resourceful—a real switch from the traditional stereotyped roles.

A master of fairy tale parody is Jon Scieszka, who first captured children's attention with *The True Story of the 3 Little Pigs.* The traditional story is told from the point of view of the wolf, who claims that he was out to borrow a cup of sugar for his granny's birthday cake, and he was framed.

Perhaps Scieszka's best work is the collection of fractured fairy tales titled *The Stinky Cheese Man and Other Fairly Stupid Tales.* The Stinky Cheese Man is made by a lonely old woman from stinky cheese. When she pulls him out of the oven, he runs away, but the little old woman and the little old man do not chase him. In fact, no one wants to chase him. They all run away from his funky smell! Other great stories in this collection include "Little Red Riding Shorts," "Cinderumpelstiltskin," and "Jack's Bean Problem." The author's humor permeates the book to the very end, where in small print on the copyright page he writes, "The illustrations are rendered in oil and vinegar. Anyone caught telling these fairly stupid tales will be visited, in person, by the Stinky Cheese Man."

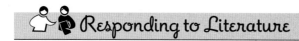

Responding to Literature

Drama   Children love to express themselves through drama, and both traditional fairy tales and literary fairy tales lend themselves especially well to this response. **Spontaneous reenactment** requires no props, costumes, or scripts, but it does require that children be very familiar with the story, so they can spontaneously become characters and recreate story events. Following are steps to prepare your children for dramatizing a story.

- Select one of the literary fairy tales in the preceding discussion and read it several times to your children.
- Divide the children into groups of three or four (depending on the number of characters in the story), and help members of each group decide which parts to take and how the story events will be sequenced.
- Allow each group to freely reenact the story.
- After the drama, have children evaluate themselves to determine if they can improve the next time.

Groups may take turns observing each other—although this kind of reenactment does not require an audience to be an enjoyable experience. Dramatizing promotes purposeful dialogue among children and helps them expand their responses to a story. "Writing in response to drama can provide insights into the complexities of children's perspectives, responses, and thoughts as well as the interplay among their oral, written, textual, and gestural symbol systems" (Crumpler & Schneider, 2002, p. 7).

Animated Object Fantasy

When you were a child, did you talk to your dolls or stuffed animals? If so, did they answer? Many young children fantasize that their dolls and toys are real. Usually children do the talking for both themselves and their toys, but imagine what would happen if the toys could really talk! Authors of animated object fantasy stories bring to life inanimate objects such as a comical doll, a toy boat, a big machine, or a loving tree.

The most common stories in this category are talking toys, usually dolls or stuffed animals with the ability to talk and move about. Hans Christian Andersen's stories "The Brave Tin Soldier" and "The Top and Ball" have main characters that are toys.

One of the first toy fantasy novels to be published was *The Adventures of Pinocchio: The Story of a Puppet* (1883), written by Carlo Lorenzini under the pen name of Carlo Collodi. The book was based on a traditional story Lorenzini heard while growing up in the village of Collodi, Italy. Pinocchio is a wooden puppet who is painstakingly carved by a kindly old man named Geppetto. The puppet comes to life; that is, he can talk and walk, but he wants to be a real flesh-and-blood boy. Because Pinocchio is lazy and selfish, he experiences many unhappy adventures, though the Blue Fairy saves him time and again. He is constantly dishonest, and his nose grows each time he lies. Eventually he learns to be honest, generous, and a hard worker, and the Blue Fairy turns him into a real boy.

Another toy who yearns to be real is *The Velveteen Rabbit* by Margery Williams. A stuffed rabbit is given to a little boy as a Christmas gift, and he eventually becomes the little boy's constant companion. The stuffed rabbit can understand what humans say, and he can talk with the other nursery toys, but he is painfully aware that he is made only of cloth (which is becoming shabby), and he is not able to jump like real rabbits. The boy contracts scarlet fever, and when he recovers, the toy rabbit is put in a bag with contaminated sheets, bedclothes, and other things that must be burned. At this point readers fear that the rabbit may meet the same fate as Andersen's little fir tree—but nursery magic intervenes for a happy ending.

Leo Lionni presents a beautiful tale of two mice, a real one named Alexander and a toy one named Willy, in *Alexander and the Wind-Up Mouse*. When Alexander makes friends with Willy, he is sad because Willy is loved and played with by the child. Alexander has experienced only screams and broom swats from humans. He asks the lizard wizard in the garden to change him into a toy mouse, so he can play and be loved like Willy. But before the moon becomes full and the spell can take effect, Alexander finds the toy mouse in a box of trash; Willy had been discarded when the child got new toys for her birthday. Alexander rushes back to the lizard wizard to ask if the magic can be used to make Willy into a real mouse instead.

A. A. Milne's classic book *Winnie-the-Pooh* began as bedtime stories for Milne's son, Christopher Robin. Christopher and the stuffed animals in his bedroom were the story characters: Winnie-the-Pooh (a naive but loving stuffed bear), Piglet, Kanga, Roo, Eeyore, Tigger, Rabbit, and Owl. The book and its sequel, *The House at Pooh Corner*, contain episodic chapters that center on the antics of the stuffed animals. They live in the Hundred Acre Wood and act much like real animals. For example, Rabbit lives in a hole in the ground (though it does have furniture), and Winnie loves to eat honey.

Don Freeman's lovable *Corduroy* tells the story of a little stuffed bear in a large store who has lost a button on his overalls. He goes through the store searching for his lost button, so he will look good enough for someone to buy. His heart's desire is met when Lisa buys him with the money from her piggy bank, brings him home, and sews on his lost button.

As a child, did you own a copy of *Scuffy the Tugboat* (Crampton)? (My mother bought me one in the grocery store for a quarter.) Literally millions of copies of this book have been sold (Roback, 2001). Scuffy, a little boy's toy boat, is bored floating in the bathtub. When taken outside, he floats away downstream to a large river that takes him into the sea. There he longs for the safety of his home and the little bathtub.

Animated dolls, stuffed animals, and toys have always been favorite subjects of fantasy stories. However, Virginia Lee Burton was a master at bringing larger inanimate objects to life, and her picture books are classics that remain in print. Main characters in her most memorable stories include a lovable steam shovel named Mary Anne in *Mike Mulligan and His Steam Shovel* and a naughty train engine in *Choo Choo: The Story of a Little Engine Who Ran Away*.

Shel Silverstein gives life to a lovely apple tree in *The Giving Tree*. The tree loves the little boy, who plays on and around her until he grows older. Then worldly things and money become the objects of his love. To meet his desires, the boy/man takes and takes from the selfless tree until there is nothing left of her but an old stump. When he is an old man, he returns to the tree, no more contented than when he left. Never does the boy/man say "thank you" in this story. Though this book has been enormously popular, I agree with Jane Yolen (Alter, 1995) that it more rightly should be titled "The Taking Boy."

Silverstein animates imaginary objects in *The Missing Piece* and in the companion book, *The Missing Piece Meets the Big O*. With simple but appealing ink line drawings of circles, triangles, and Pac-Man-like characters, Silverstein depicts characters trying to find the right fit for a relationship to roll along through life. As in his other prose books, there is a story for children on one level and a message for adults on another. By providing some help, you can generate thought-provoking discussion among children about Silverstein's stories.

With similar characters but a very different theme, Leo Lionni tells the story of *Little Blue and Little Yellow*, blobs of color that are best friends. They live with their papas and mamas (who are bigger blobs). They have many friends to play games with, and they go to blob school together. One day, when Little Blue and Little Yellow hug too hard, they turn green, and neither set of parents recognizes them.

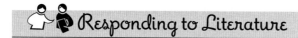 *Responding to Literature*

Puppets   Young children should be encouraged to retell favorite storybooks in their own words. A good way to do this is through simple puppets, such as the ones children make with small paper lunch bags they decorate with construction paper and crayon drawings. With the book *Little Blue and Little Yellow,* help your children retell the story with puppets. Divide the class into groups of four to play the parts of Little Blue, Little Yellow, the mothers, and the fathers. Two children can play the parts of both sets of parents by drawing the Blue parent on one side of the bag and the Yellow parent on the other. Similarly, the puppets for Little Blue and Little Yellow should be colored green on the back, so the children can turn the bag puppets around to show how they turned green when they hugged too hard. The children should retell the story in their own words while they act it out with the puppets.

Human with Fantasy Character

Some fantasy books have an ordinary human and a fantasy creature as main characters. The fantasy creature can be a monster, a strange beast, or even an element of nature. One of Andersen's best-loved stories, "The Little Mermaid," falls in this category with the mythical and memorable mermaid and a human prince as main characters.

Sophie discovers a most unusual creature in *The BFG* (Dahl) when a Big Friendly Giant snatches her from her bed and carries her off in the middle of the night to Giant Land. Though his brothers eat Human Beans, the BFG eats only snozzcumbers. The BFG joins forces with Sophie to stop the other giants from running off to England to "guzzle and swallomp a few nice little chiddlers."

In Mercer Mayer's *There's a Nightmare in My Closet,* a young boy overcomes his fear of the monster in his closet by waiting for him one night and shooting him with a popgun. The boy ends up bringing the monster into bed with him to stop him from crying. (Be cautious if you plan to share this book with very young children to help them overcome their fears. A teacher told me that after she read it to her 3-year-old son, he believed that not only was there a monster under his bed, but now there was one in his closet, too.)

Another young boy finds himself facing a monster in *The Teacher from the Black Lagoon* (Thaler). The title is a spoof on the old movie *The Creature from the Black Lagoon.* The teacher in this book does not come from a lagoon; rather, she shows up the first day of school as Mrs. Green, the boy's new teacher. She's a real monster (literally) with a long green snout and tail. Undoubtedly, this is *the* funniest picture book I have read. However, it may not be appropriate for very young children, as Mrs. Green is prone to munching children for discipline! This book is a great icebreaker on the first day of school. (It makes children wonder what *your* discipline program will be.)

In *Flossie & the Fox* (McKissack), a young girl carries a basket of fresh eggs to Miz Viola's, and she encounters a sly old fox along the way. Because Flossie has never seen a fox, she insists on proof that he is what he says. Flossie skips all the way through the woods while the fox tries to convince her that he *is* a fox and she should be afraid of him. McKissack beautifully captures the language of the pre–Civil War South in her dialogue: "Flossie stopped. Then she turned and say 'I aine never seen a fox before. So, why should I be scared of you and I don't even-now know you a real fox for a fact?'"

Sometimes the fantasy creature is an element of nature, as in *My Life with the Wave* (Paz & Cowan). On a boy's first trip to the seashore, a wave breaks away from the sea and joins him. The boy takes the wave home for a liquid pet, and she floods the house. At first the wave is playful and full of joy, but eventually her mood changes. With the onset of winter storms, she becomes unruly, and when she freezes into an icy statue, the boy and his father return her to the sea. Long after you finish reading, the intriguing illustrations can keep you engrossed in searching for the many hidden figures and images. Careful observers will find a very small mouse in each illustration. Other characters and images to search for include a cat, a dog, a whale, and a sea horse, all of which can be found in most of the illustrations.

The wind is a popular element for fantasy characters. In *Mirandy and Brother Wind* (McKissack), Mirandy wants to catch Brother Wind so he will be her partner in the junior cakewalk, but he skillfully eludes her. In *Old Hannibal and the Hurricane* (Amos), Matt and Sophie help Old Hannibal launch the *Sally Sue* as he describes his encounter with Bellowing Bertha, a hurricane of tremendous fame.

Most books in this category are picture books, so The Spiderwick Chronicles—a series of five short novels by Tony DiTerlizzi and Holly Black—is unique. In the first book, *The Field Guide,* the three Grace children and their mother go to live at Great-Aunt Lucinda's dilapidated Victorian house. But before they can even unpack, Jared Grace notices they are not alone in the house. There's something living there with them. This leads to the discovery of a dark and fascinating notebook, "Arthur Spiderwick's Field Guide to the Fantastical World Around You." It describes fairies and other fantastic creatures, some quite frightening. The children are presented with an even bigger mystery: Did the book have anything to do with the disappearance of Arthur Spiderwick, Great-Aunt Lucinda's father?

Extraordinary Person

Not all fantasy books contain fantasy creatures. Sometimes the characters are humans who are preposterous or extraordinary in some way, such as possessing strange powers or unusual size.

Miniature Humans. The idea of miniature beings has always fascinated children, and there are many good books with miniature human characters. Folklore contains stories of diminutive people, such as "Tom Thumb." However, *Thumbelina* by Hans Christian Andersen was one of the earliest fiction stories about a tiny person.

Mary Norton's *The Borrowers* and its sequels have captivated children for several decades. Pod, Homily, and Arrietty Clock are a family of tiny people no more than two inches tall. They live beneath the floorboards of a quiet country house in England, and they outfit their living quarters as well as meet their other needs by "borrowing" things from the big people. The Borrowers are quite resourceful in the way they recycle trinkets and bits of household objects into clothing, tools, and furnishings. One day the boy of the house spots Arrietty, and the Clock family's adventures begin.

In *George Shrinks* (Joyce), George's parents leave the house early, and while he is still asleep, he dreams he is very small. When he wakes up, he finds it is true! Despite his size, George comically tries to take care of his "little" brother and complete all the tasks his parents have assigned him for the day. When he unwraps a package in the mail and finds a toy airplane, he flies it over the house and into his bedroom window. The family cat swipes the airplane wing, causing it to crash land on George's bed. When it appears the cat is going to eat him, George pops back to his regular size—just before his parents arrive home. In case you were thinking it was all a dream, the author shows the damaged toy airplane in the last three illustrations after George has returned to full size.

Flying People. In fantasy stories people sometimes possess extraordinary powers, such as the ability to fly. These stories are exciting for young children, who often fantasize about flying. In *Abuela* (Dorros) a young girl is feeding a flock of birds in the park with her grandmother. She imagines that the birds pick her up and she can fly. Her grandmother joins her, and they fly over and around New York City.

A similar theme and setting is found in *Tar Beach* (Ringgold), which takes place in New York in 1939. An 8-year-old girl can fly when she thinks about "somewhere to go that you can't get to any other way." From the tar rooftop of her Harlem apartment building, she flies over the buildings of New York City. She especially likes flying over the George Washington Bridge, which she claims as her own.

Talking with Animals. What would our pets tell us if they could talk? The ability to talk with animals is a coveted power. A human character who fluently speaks with all animals is the good country doctor in Hugh Lofting's *The Story of Doctor Dolittle* and *The Voyages of Doctor Dolittle*. In the first book the doctor sails to Africa to treat an epidemic among the monkeys. In the sequel Dolittle and friends journey to Spidermonkey Island in the tropical seas to search for a missing colleague.

Karen Hesse also creates a memorable character in 14-year-old Mila in *The Music of Dolphins*. A feral child is discovered on an unpopulated island, where she has spent the last ten years living with the dolphins who saved her after a wreck at sea. Mila is able to speak with her dolphin family, and she greatly prefers her life among the dolphins to what she experiences living among humans.

Extraordinary Abilities. Fantasy characters possess many other extraordinary abilities. The little girl in *Matilda* (Dahl) uses telekinesis and her genius intellect to annoy and scare off people who are unkind to the schoolchildren.

Another unforgettable character from Roald Dahl is the eccentric Willy Wonka in *Charlie and the Chocolate Factory*. Charlie and other children meet Willy Wonka, creator of the famous and magical chocolate factory that produces the world's greatest candy delights. However, great perils await undeserving children who enter the factory.

Natalie Babbitt's *Tuck Everlasting* leaves readers pondering if they would want to live forever. The Tuck family unknowingly drank water from a spring that prevents them from ever growing older. Every ten years, the family of four meets at the secret spring in a secluded wood. In the 1880s they are observed by 10-year-old Winnie Foster when she is exploring the woods near her house. She learns about their terrible secret, so they prevent her from returning to her home, fearing the ill that would come to the world if anyone else drank from the magic spring.

In *The Lightning Thief* by Rick Riordan, 12-year-old New Yorker Percy Jackson has always had difficulty focusing on his schoolwork and controlling his temper, resulting in his attending six different schools in as many years. After a near fatality at his last school, Percy's mother tells him the truth about the father he has never known. Percy is almost killed by a Minotaur before his mother manages to get him to the safety of Camp Half-Blood (located on Long Island), a summer camp for demigods, where he learns that his father is Poseidon, God of the Sea. Soon Percy is sent to California on a quest with two friends—one a disguised satyr and the other the demigod daughter of Athena. They reach the gates of the Underworld (located in a Hollywood recording studio) and attempt to rectify a feud between Zeus, Hades, and Poseidon.

Lois Lowry's acclaimed trilogy, which starts with *The Giver*, takes place in the future after the world's major societies have been largely destroyed through war and holocaust. Survivors live in villages, which are governed independently and are isolated from one another. Though the first book could be considered science fiction, the other two books include magic and definitely have no advanced technology. The main character in each novel has some extraordinary ability—to see beyond the immediate surroundings, to embroider scenes from the future, and to heal with a touch.

In *The Giver,* Jonas lives in a society of "sameness" that has learned how to control everything—memory, emotion, occupation, marriage, weather, propagation, and who is allowed to live or die. When Jonas turns 12, he is appointed as the next Receiver of Memory and is apprenticed to the current Receiver, who then becomes the Giver (of memory). This person alone holds the memories of the true pain and pleasures of life—because generations ago, the people had all memories (beyond their own generation) removed from the people's consciousness and transferred to the Receiver. This included memories of such horrors as war and famine. Along with the memories, they gave up strong emotions such as love, fear, and pain.

Jonas's father, a Nurturer (caregiver of infants), explains that to avoid confusion, only one identical twin is allowed to live in the community. The newborn twin with the smallest birth weight must be "released." Jonas finally learns the meaning of *release* when the Giver shows him a videotape in which his father is weighing newborn twins. Jonas looks on in horror, and the Giver observes with deep sorrow, as his father dispassionately gives the smaller twin a lethal injection in a scalp vein, saying cheerfully, "I know, I know. It hurts, little guy. But I have to use a vein, and the veins in your arms are still too teeny-weeny. . . . All done. That wasn't so bad was it?" (p. 149). Then he disposes of the lifeless body in a trash chute.

📖 Issues in Fantasy

Should Children Be Able to Read about Violence, Even If It Is Not in the Real World? Many educators believe that *The Giver* is a worthy book (after all, it was awarded the Newbery Medal in 1994) with a profound message: Preventing people from developing memories that allow understanding of both love and pain means preventing them from developing compassion—the virtue that is missing in these futuristic people who use euthanasia to mold their society by culling out the unwanted. If children are shielded from learning about such horrors, could they—like the people in Lowry's futuristic society—be prevented from developing compassion? Or are children prone to generate violence after reading about it and seeing it in television shows, films, and computer games?

Take a stand on whether children under 14 should or should not be allowed to read *The Giver* and the other books in the trilogy. Support your argument with at least three points.

Dav Pilkey created a hilarious character in *The Adventures of Captain Underpants: An Epic Novel.* Two boys hypnotize their principal into thinking he is a superhero—Captain Underpants. When he is put under a spell, he tears off all his clothes except his briefs, yanks off his toupee, ties a red curtain around his neck, and jumps out the school window singing "Tra-la-laaaa!"—his battle cry as he goes out to fight evil forces such as the nefarious Dr. Diaper or the voracious Talking Toilets. (From my experience, do not show this book to a principal; she will want to throw *it* out the school window!)

Enchanted Journey

Many of the classic fantasy stories are **enchanted journeys.** The story begins in the real world, but the main character is soon transported to another world, which is often an enchanted realm. The characters enter the fantasy world by some type of magic. At the end of the story, the protagonist usually returns to the real world, but it is not always by the same manner in which she or he left. In Hans Christian Andersen's "The Snow Queen," Kai is dragged into an icy, magical realm where the beautiful and enticing Snow Queen reigns when his sled is pulled there by the evil enchantress.

Journey to Fantasyland. *Alice's Adventures in Wonderland* by Lewis Carroll is perhaps the earliest example of a novel-length enchanted journey to a fantasyland. Alice is sitting on the riverbank with her sister when a big white rabbit runs past, talking to himself. When he pops down a large rabbit hole, Alice follows him and floats down a long passageway to Wonderland. She experiences many bizarre situations, such as changing sizes and swimming in her own tears, and she meets equally bizarre characters, including the Cheshire Cat, the Mad Hatter, the Mock Turtle, the Queen of Hearts, and the deck of cards that comes to life. Alice returns to the real world when her older sister awakens her.

L. Frank Baum's *The Wonderful Wizard of Oz* was the first modern fantasy novel for children that was written by an American. It begins in Kansas when Dorothy's house is lifted into the air by a cyclone (tornado). When it lands, Dorothy and her dog, Toto, find themselves in the Land of Oz. She desperately wants to return home to her family. The little munchkins advise her to find the great wizard in the wonderful Emerald City of Oz. Along her way, she meets the brainless Scarecrow, the Tin Woodsman, and the Cowardly Lion. Though the wizard turns out to be a humbug, the good witch Glinda tells Dorothy she can return home by clicking the heels of her silver slippers and saying, "Take me home to Aunt Em!" Dorothy finds herself back home in front of the farmhouse Uncle Henry had rebuilt after the storm. Baum wrote thirteen more books about adventures in the Land of Oz.

The beloved story of Peter Pan, the boy who would not grow up, was written first as a play and later as a book by the Scottish novelist and dramatist Sir James Matthew Barrie. Wendy, John, and Michael Darling are children living in London when Peter Pan persuades them to return with him to Neverland, a place where children never grow up. With a little fairy dust, the children fly off to Neverland with Peter and his fairy Tinker Bell, so Wendy can tell stories to the six Lost Boys. During their stay the children encounter the evil pirate Captain Hook, a hungry crocodile, and the Indian Princess Tiger Lily. The Lost Boys beg Wendy to stay and be their mother, but she and her brothers fly back to London and take the boys along instead. Mr. and Mrs. Darling are so happy to have their children back that they adopt the Lost Boys. Peter Pan, however, refuses the offer, saying, "I don't want to go to school and learn solemn things. I don't want to be a man. I want always to be a boy and have fun" (Barrie & Goode, p. 64). (Have you ever known anyone like that?)

In D. J. MacHale's *Pendragon: The Merchant of Death*, 14-year-old Bobby Pendragon learns from his Uncle Press that he is a Traveler, someone who can ride "flumes" through time and space to parallel universes. His first assignment is in Denduron, a medieval world where the gentle Milago are enslaved by the Bedoowan, and it is Bobby's job to free them. He reluctantly teams up with Loor, a girl warrior who is his own age, to accomplish this task. This is a good choice because his lack of martial skills forces him to rely on his wits to free himself from dangerous situations. Bobby recounts his adventures in journals that are magically transported back to his friends Mark and Courtney in Connecticut. At the end of the book, he returns home through the interdimensional flume, an abandoned South Bronx subway station.

There are also excellent picture books of enchanted journeys. In *Where the Wild Things Are* (Sendak), Max is reprimanded for his wild behavior and sent to his room. There a forest grows up with an ocean tumbling by, and Max sails to the land of the Wild Things. When he gets lonely, he sails back the way he came. In case you are thinking his enchanted journey was a dream, Maurice Sendak shows the passage of time by the moon first seen through the bedroom window. When Max leaves, it is a quarter moon; when he returns, it is a full moon.

In *Hey Al* (Yorinks), Al the janitor and his faithful dog Eddie are totally miserable in their dingy Manhattan West Side apartment until a large mysterious bird takes them on a journey to a paradise island in the sky. However, they return home when their comfortable paradise existence threatens to turn them into birds as well.

In *The Polar Express* by Chris Van Allsburg, a boy is awakened by the sound of a train in his front yard on Christmas Eve. He runs outside and catches the Polar Express, a train carrying children to the North Pole. After a trip with fabulous sights, the children meet Santa, who selects the boy to receive the first gift of Christmas. The boy asks for a silver bell from Santa's sleigh, and he is then returned home on the Polar Express; however, he loses his bell on the way. In the morning, the boy finds the silver bell in a small box behind the Christmas tree, but only those who truly believe in Santa can hear its beautiful sound.

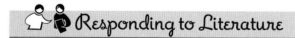 *Responding to Literature*

Story Boxes   A concrete way to respond to literature is with a **story box** (Tompkins & McGee, 1993), also called a *jackdaw* (after the bird that collect trinkets). To make a story box, gather or make things that represent the events, images, characters, or topics of a story or poem and place them in a shoebox. For example, a story box for *The Polar Express* could contain a bedroom slipper, a toy train, a jingle bell, and some Christmas wrapping. Write the title of the book and the names of the author or poet and illustrator on paper taped to the lid of the box. You may also choose to decorate the title paper with a motif from the story. When your children look at the contents, they can make predictions on what the book is about. If they have already read the book, they should be able to recall the story by looking at the various objects.

In another Van Allsburg book, *Jumanji,* Judy and Peter experience a reverse enchanted journey. Playing a mystical board game they find in the park results in their house's being transformed into an exotic jungle that includes a roaring lion, destructive monkeys, and an erupting volcano. Each turn of play plunges them from one perilous predicament into another, but only by finishing the game can they restore their house to normal.

Journey to the Historical Past. An enchanted journey can take the protagonist from the modern world to a real time in the historical past, such as in Jane Yolen's *The Devil's Arithmetic.* Hannah resents the traditions of her Jewish heritage. During a long Seder ceremony in her grandfather's apartment, she is asked to perform the ritual of opening the door for Elijah. When she does, she has opened a door in time that places her in the middle of a small Jewish village in Nazi-occupied Poland. Because the time-travel door closes behind her, she must follow the inevitable course of history, which takes her to a concentration camp. How Hannah reenters her own time makes for a gripping and unforgettable story.

In Jon Scieszka's typical style, he has created a zany series of books called the Time Warp Trio. Three wacky boys—Joe, Sam, and Fred—travel both back and forward in time by means of Joe's magical blue book. The mixture of adventure, comedy, and hocus-pocus makes for fast reading. In the first book, *Knights of the Kitchen Table,* the boys end up in King Arthur's court with a fire-breathing dragon, a belligerent knight, and a vile-smelling giant. They must locate the magical blue book before they can be transported back to their own time. Scieszka does much research for each book in the series, so in addition to being hilarious, the books include historical details, interesting facts, and even some basic math and physics.

Mary Pope Osborne's expansive series of Magic Tree House books starts with *Dinosaurs before Dark.* Jack and his sister Annie discover a tree house that travels through time when they pick a setting from one of the many books stored in the tree house. Their first time-travel adventure takes them back to the Cretaceous period, where their explorations lead to a hungry tyrannosaurus. A pterodactyl comes to their rescue, and they reverse their steps to return in the tree house to their home setting. There are innumerable more (all quite predictable) historic adventures, such as the great hall of a castle in the Middle Ages, the tomb of a long-dead queen of ancient Egypt, and a deserted island with buried treasure and nasty pirates.

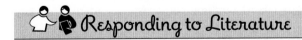 *Responding to Literature*

Dialogue Response Journals   One way to combine children's responses to literature with writing is to keep a **dialogue response journal** with each of your children. In these journals you and the children conduct a written conversation about what they are reading. You read and respond to each entry. (This works particularly well when both you and the child are reading the same book.) One entry a week is generally appropriate for younger children, but older children may write several times a week or even daily. It is important for the child to select the topic of each entry, or else it becomes an essay exam. To achieve maximum expression of ideas, do not correct grammar and spelling. **Invented spelling,** in which children spell words the way they sound, should be encouraged. Children can write their true ideas rather than limiting themselves to words they can spell correctly. Response journals can also be kept between two children.

High Fantasy

Colorful adventure, enchantment, and heroism are the hallmarks of **high fantasy** (Colbath, 1971). The protagonist in high fantasy engages in a monumental struggle against a powerful evil force in the ageless struggle of good and evil. Like enchanted journeys, they may begin in the real world (**primary world**), but the major setting in high fantasy is a self-contained fictional world that is inhabited by imaginary creatures and has its own time frame. These settings are called **secondary worlds.** The setting typically has an aura of medieval times because writers have often drawn from mythology and legends for their characters and settings. In high fantasy books the author develops the secondary world in detail, describing the history, dress, housing, lifestyles, languages, and occupations of the inhabitants. Creators of high fantasy, such as those I'll feature here, typically write a series of books in order to develop the secondary worlds and their inhabitants in depth. Although no short story could contain all the complex elements of high fantasy novels, Hans Christian Andersen's "The Wild Swans" is a lengthy tale that employs a quest into a secondary world, both of which are central to high fantasy novels.

J. R. R. Tolkien and the Lord of the Rings. J. R. R. Tolkien is the writer of high fantasy against whom all other writers in the field are measured (Donelson & Nilsen, 1997). The secondary world he created in his stories, Middle-earth, has been used as a touchstone for all who write high fantasy. Tolkien was a professor at Oxford University in England, specializing in philology, the study of languages. His scholarship is evident in the series of fantasy books that were launched with *The Hobbit,* which grew out of bedtime stories Tolkien told his children. This book was the segue to his celebrated Lord of the Rings trilogy. The trilogy is a sophisticated, complex epic and quite lengthy, making it more suitable for adolescents. In the United Kingdom, a mega-poll indicated that *The Lord of the Rings* is the UK's best-loved book as determined by three-quarters of a million votes cast by readers of all ages (BBC Two, 2004).

Even *The Hobbit* is a challenging read for most elementary children. However, I recommend it for advanced readers who are bored with other books. The story is an adventurous quest set in Middle-earth, which is inhabited by mythical creatures such as hobbits, dwarves, elves, trolls, goblins, the wizard Gandalf, the dragon Smaug, and the disgusting creature Gollum. The protagonist, Bilbo Baggins, is a typical hobbit about three feet tall. Like other hobbits in the Shire, he is plump and has very large and hairy feet that do not require shoes. Bilbo embarks on a quest to help the dwarves, and he confronts the great dragon Smaug—the terror of the countryside. He returns home with a wondrous magic ring that makes the wearer invisible.

C. S. Lewis and The Chronicles of Narnia. C. S. Lewis wrote his Narnia series specifically for children, though adult readers likely understand more of the Christian symbolism that he wove into the books. The land of Narnia gets its magic from the majestic lion, Aslan, who is the Lord of the Wood and son of the great Emperor-Beyond-the-Sea. Unlike the typical heroes of high fantasy, the protagonists of these chronicles are children from earth. They magically make the crossing between our world and the secondary world of Narnia by Aslan's bidding.

The first book to be published was *The Lion, the Witch and the Wardrobe*. Four siblings enter Narnia through a magical wardrobe. Lucy, Edmund, Susan, and Peter find themselves in a mystical land that is under an evil spell: It is always winter, but never Christmas. The children battle the White Witch to rescue the talking beasts of Narnia; meanwhile, the majestic Aslan is drawing near, causing the spell to weaken. Father Christmas arrives, followed by the melting of snow and ice. However, Edmund has crossed over to the side of the White Witch. By the law of the Deep Magic, the White Witch has the right to kill him, but Aslan forgives Edmund and takes on his cruel punishment. The children are despondent when Aslan dies—but the next morning, by the working of the Deeper Magic Before the Dawn of Time, he is resurrected, and the White Witch is defeated.

When Lewis wrote *The Lion*, he probably did not intend to write a series of books. So as he continued to write others one by one, the stories were not in chronological order. Therefore, if you plan to read them all, Lewis recommended that you read them in the order of Narnian chronology, rather than the order in which they were published. The proper sequence follows.

1. *The Magician's Nephew*
2. *The Lion, the Witch and the Wardrobe*
3. *The Horse and His Boy*
4. *Prince Caspian*
5. *The Voyage of the* Dawn Treader
6. *The Silver Chair*
7. *The Last Battle*

Notice that *The Magician's Nephew* is the **prequel** (book that takes place at a time before the action of the preexisting work) to *The Lion, the Witch and the Wardrobe*. It tells how Narnia came to be and how the evil witch entered the land. It explains why the wardrobe was a passageway from earth to Narnia and why the professor was not surprised by the children's story. It even explains the presence of the lamppost in the middle of the wood.

Robin McKinley and the Blue Sword. Though she wrote only two books in the sequence, master storyteller Robin McKinley created an unforgettable mythical world in Damar—the secondary world inhabited by the secretive and magical Hillfolk, the Homelanders, dragons of various sizes, and the captivating wizard Luthe. What makes her saga even more memorable is that the heroes of her books are young women, which is rare in high fantasy. In *The Hero and the Crown*, Lady Aerin of flaming red hair fights to win the birthright and respect due to her as the daughter of the Damarian king and his young wife, a stranger from the mysterious North who died giving birth. With the guidance of Luthe and the magical Blue Sword Gonturan, Lady Aerin sets off to defeat the evil Agsded and return the Hero's Crown to her people.

There is a considerable span of years between *The Hero and the Crown* and *The Blue Sword*. The heroine of the second book is Hari Crewe, an orphaned adolescent who comes to live with her brother, stationed in an outpost on the edge of the Damarian desert. Hari is kidnapped by Corlath, the Hillfolk king, and learns that she has the *kelar*, magical power residing only in the Hillfolk royal family. With intense training and practice, she becomes a King's Rider and carries the Blue Sword Gonturan, which no woman has wielded since the legendary Lady Aerin. Hari knows it will take more than magic and the powerful Blue Sword to defeat Thurra, leader of the less-than-human Northerners who threaten not only the Hillfolk, but her brother's country as well.

J. K. Rowling and Harry Potter. Hogwarts School of Witchcraft and Wizardry and the nearby city of Hogsmeade make up most of the secondary world of Harry Potter and his friends, who have many magical experiences, both good and bad. Rowling states, "I wanted to depict the ambiguities of a society where bigotry, cruelty, hypocrisy, and corruption are rife, the better to show how truly heroic it is, whatever your age, to fight a battle that can never be won" (Geeslin, 2004, p. 2).

The series, which began with *Harry Potter and the Sorcerer's Stone*, has been translated into 64 languages. By the end of 2007, sales of the seven books had reached 375 million—an unprecedented success in the publishing business! However, great controversy surrounds this series because of its positive portrayal of witchcraft. According to Schneider (2002),

> Although children (and adults) all over the world have fallen in love with the Harry Potter stories, the books have been the target of one of the most visible and widely reported censorship/anticensorship campaigns in children's literature. And despite varying opinions on the literary merits of the Potter series, these books have forced many children, parents, educators, and communities to examine and take a stand on issues of censorship. The story lines of Harry Potter books deal with good versus evil, wizardry and witchcraft, magic, and adventure. Consequently, although they are lauded by elementary children, they are simultaneously the target of strong opposition from some people. (p. 137)

In *Harry Potter and the Sorcerer's Stone*, when Harry turns 11, he is informed by a lovable giant that his parents were not killed in a car wreck, as he had been told by his wretched muggle (nonmagical) aunt and uncle. Harry's mother was a witch and his father a wizard. Both were murdered by a sorcerer of such evil magnitude that his name cannot be spoken; however, as an infant, Harry survived the attack. Harry is called to Hogwarts School of Witchcraft and Wizardry to receive his formal training. Nearly all of the wizard masters and wizards-in-training are in awe of

Harry, because he is the only person ever to survive an attack by the unspeakable Lord Voldemort, master of the Dark Arts. However, there are enemies at the school who want Harry to fail. In the beginning, the series presents a humorous look at witchcraft and wizardry, and it pokes fun at the English boarding school system as well. The following excerpt is from a scene in Charms class, where the students are learning how to make objects fly.

> "Now, don't forget that nice wrist movement we've been practicing!" squeaked Professor Flitwick, perched on top of his pile of books as usual. "Swish and flick, remember, swish and flick. And saying the magic words properly is very important, too—never forget Wizard Baruffio, who said 's' instead of 'f' and found himself on the floor with a buffalo on his chest." It was very difficult. Harry and Seamus swished and flicked, but the feather they were supposed to be sending skyward just lay on the desktop. Seamus got so impatient that he prodded it with his wand and set fire to it— Harry had to put it out with his hat. (p. 171)

The seventh and final book in the series was published in 2007. Following is a chronological list:

- *Harry Potter and the Sorcerer's Stone*
- *Harry Potter and the Chamber of Secrets*
- *Harry Potter and the Prisoner of Azkaban*
- *Harry Potter and the Goblet of Fire*
- *Harry Potter and the Order of the Phoenix*
- *Harry Potter and the Half-Blood Prince*
- *Harry Potter and the Deathly Hallows*

Literature Activity: Wizardspeak

How good is your Harry Potter "wizardspeak"? Match the following words to their definitions. Answers are available at www.pearsonhighered.com/anderson3e.

1. Bertie Botts	A. Harry's mean nonwizard relatives
2. Dursleys	B. Harry's best friend
3. Hagrid	C. Giant-size gamekeeper of school grounds
4. Hedwig	D. The evil wizard who killed Harry's parents
5. Hogsmeade	E. The School of Witchcraft and Wizardry
6. Hogwarts	F. An all-wizard village near school
7. Lord Voldemort	G. Station track where students board the express train to school
8. Muggles	H. Harry's pet owl and courier
9. Nearly Headless Nick	I. The school's mischievous poltergeist
10. Peeves	J. The resident ghost of Harry's dorm
11. Platform 9¾	K. Nonmagical people
12. Quidditch	L. A wizard sport with four balls, played on flying brooms
13. Ron Weasley	M. The brand name for every-flavor candy beans

Christopher Paolini and Inheritance. Paolini began writing the series' first book, *Eragon,* when he was only 15. The hero, Eragon, is a young farm boy who finds a marvelous blue stone in a mystical mountain clearing in the secondary world called Alagaësia. The egg hatches into a beautiful sapphire-blue dragon, whom Eragon nurtures and names Saphira. As the dragon matures, Eragon learns that not only can she speak, but also the two can communicate telepathically. With the help of the mysterious storyteller Brom, who gives him a powerful ancient sword, Eragon learns that he is the last of the Dragon Riders, who must side with the humans, elves, and dwarves in the impending war with the cruel King Galbatorix, who is aided by the diabolical Shades and their nonhuman minions the Urgalls. In the first book, the boy and dragon grow in magical powers and in understanding of their relationship and the complex political world into which they have been thrust. Eragon wants only to avenge Galbatorix's brutal murder of his uncle by the marauding Ra'zac, but fate will require much more of him.

Supernatural Fantasy

Supernatural fantasy explores the possibilities offered by the supernatural—for example, by beings that exist outside the natural world (such as ghosts) or by powers that go beyond natural forces (such as telepathy). An early example of supernatural fantasy is Hans Christian Andersen's "The Little Match-Seller," one of his most poignant stories. In the tale, an impoverished little girl sees a number of apparitions, including the spirit of her deceased grandmother, who comes in the middle of a freezing night to take the child to Heaven.

Supernatural Powers. In the humorous adventure *The Dragon of Doom* (Coville), Edward is bored living in the little town of Pigbone until Moongobble the Magician and his talking toad Urk move into a nearby cottage. Edward becomes Moongobble's helper, which is no easy task because Moongobble is new at the profession and not very good (accidentally turning everything into cheese)! When the Society of Magicians threatens to cast Moongobble out, Edward finds himself facing the dreaded Dragon of Doom to save his friend.

A variety of magic tales are contained in *Bruce Coville's Book of Magic: Tales to Cast a Spell on You.* Children can read short stories by eleven authors, including Bruce Coville's "Wizard's Boy" and Jane Yolen's "Phoenix Farm."

In the first book of the Ranger's Apprentice series, *The Ruins of Gorlan* by John Flanagan, 15-year-old Will, an orphan, has always wanted to be a warrior and a knight. However, when his schooling ends, he is disappointingly assigned to be a Ranger's apprentice. The Rangers wear dark cloaks and seem to lurk in the shadows, invisibly. Will soon learns from his grim-faced but benevolent master that the Rangers are the protectors of the kingdom, skillful in surveillance, stealth, woodcraft, and courage in battle. His new skills in wielding a knife and having a heightened awareness of his surroundings become vital to his survival and that of his master. Morgarath, Lord of the Mountains of Rain and Night, is gathering his fierce minions for an attack on the kingdom, and Will is instrumental in the opposition.

Some supernatural powers are passed down from parents to children for generations. Such is the case with *In the Eye of the Tornado* (Levithan). After the death of their parents, Adam and Stieg Atwood fulfill their destiny to use the supernatural power that has been in their family for countless generations. The Atwoods are able to foretell meteorological disasters, and their destiny is to try to save people from these disasters. The government knows that "he who controls the weather, controls the world," and Agent Taggert pursues them—as he pursued their parents, which led to their deaths in the eye of a tornado.

Jenny Nimmo's *Midnight for Charlie Bone* is the first in a series about an unusual group of people—all of whom are endowed with various magical abilities. Ten-year-old Charlie suddenly discovers that he can hear the thoughts of people in photographs. His grim family sends him to Bloor's Academy, an elite boarding school for endowed children—all of whom are descendents of the ancient Red King. Helped by schoolmates with their own special gifts (such as talking with animals or touching a garment to feel the emotions of the last person wearing it), Charlie embarks on a quest to find a mysterious missing girl at the school, whom he learned about from a photograph.

Communication with Spirits. Communicating with spirits or ghosts is a common motif of supernatural fantasy. Rarely do you find picture books in this category, but White Deer of Autumn's *Ceremony—in the Circle of Life* is one. Nine-year-old Little Turtle is a Native American boy who has grown up completely in the mainstream of a large city. In his loneliness and deep sorrow, he is visited by Star Spirit, and the walls in his room become the Earth and Sky. Star Spirit tells him, "I am from a long time past, yet I live today. I have traveled from the Seven Dancing Stars to teach you what many of Earth's people have forgotten" (p. 6). Star Spirit teaches Little Turtle about the Circle of Life, the animals that live in the wild, and the Pipe Ceremony. After offering prayers to the four directions, Star Spirit returns him to his home in the city.

Behind the Attic Wall by Sylvia Cassedy is a serious and compelling story about spirits. When 12-year-old Maggie—orphaned, rejected, and expelled from boarding school—goes to live with her two great-aunts in their gloomy ancestral home, she hears mysterious voices. She searches for the source and in a closet discovers a hidden panel that leads to stairs to the attic. There, shockingly, she finds china dolls inhabited by the spirits of Maggie's ancestors, who built the great house. Maggie frequently visits the dolls, Timothy John, Miss Cristabel, and their dog Juniper, who are forever locked in the time when they tragically died in a fire. She grows to love them, and they are her family. The ending is bittersweet and may move readers to tears.

Karen Hesse's *A Time of Angels* is set in Boston's West End during 1918. Hannah Gold is 14 and, with her two younger sisters, lives with her Tanta (Aunt) Rose while her parents are trapped in Russia because of the war. A deadly influenza epidemic ravishes the city, and Rose dies along with a thousand others. When Hannah is driven out of the tenement building where she lived with her aunt, she becomes ill with the disease. She is guided to safety by a beautiful violet-eyed girl—whom the readers come to realize is an angel who had saved Hannah's life once before. She finds herself in Vermont, being cared for by an old farmer whom the townsfolk shun because of his German heritage. Upon her recovery, she is torn between staying with the kindly old man and finding her family.

Charles Tazewell's *The Littlest Angel* is a classic supernatural fantasy book. The main character is a 4-year-old boy from Jerusalem, who is the youngest angel in heaven. He is quite homesick for earth, and he finds the transition from boy to cherub in the celestial kingdom a difficult one. He tries to fit in and do what is expected of him, but he seems to fail at every attempt. When he is called before the Understanding Angel, he pours out his heart and says he would not be so sad if only he could have his box of beloved possessions from home: a golden butterfly, a sky-blue egg, two white river stones, and the leather collar from his devoted dog. When it comes time for Jesus to be born on Earth, the Littlest Angel is once more sad because he has no gift. Therefore, he adds his precious box to the pile of glorious gifts but worries it is too lowly. However, God is pleased because the Littlest Angel gave what he treasured most, and He transforms the box into the brilliantly shining star of Bethlehem.

Communication with Ghosts. Many elementary children are fascinated with the prospect of ghosts. The plots of ghost stories most often involve a child's encounter with another child from the past.

Pam Conrad's *Stonewords* presents a tale of two girls living in the same house; however, one lives there in the present, and the other lived there more than a hundred years ago. The two girls move in and out of each other's worlds by a back staircase. Eleven-year-old Zoe is determined to discover the nature of her friend's death, so she can alter the tragic event.

On a camping trip with her older sister, 13-year-old Caitlin in *A Taste of Smoke* (Bauer) encounters an oddly dressed boy who is eager to befriend her. Gradually she discovers that he is an orphan who was left behind in a great fire that swept the area a century ago. He literally haunts her, appearing whenever she thinks of him. Desperate to free herself from this ghost, Caitlin must help him find what he is seeking.

Science Fiction

When magic is replaced by advanced technological wonders, a fantasy story is called science fiction. Incredible and inconceivable characters and events are given rational scientific-sounding explanations, which a good science fiction writer makes quite plausible. The time setting in science fiction stories does not have to be the future. It can be the present day with some type of secret advanced technology, or—if you read books that were published some time ago—the setting can even be in the past. For example, Hans Christian Andersen published "Thousands of Years from Now" in 1852. In this science fiction tale, busy Americans see Europe in eight days by flying over it.

Science fiction is based on scientific extrapolation in which speculative scientific developments and discoveries are the reality. Stories extend current scientific developments by starting with what is known today and taking that knowledge one step farther. For example, today surgeons can transplant hearts. In the future, what will happen when they transplant brains? Today scientists can clone cats. In the future, what will happen when humans are cloned?

Some science fiction writers have been prophetic in their literary inventions. What sounded bizarre at the time it was published is now reality. For example, Jules Verne wrote about traveling to the moon in 1865 in *From the Earth to the Moon*. However, because of the technical nature of this genre, very few true science fiction books are written on the elementary level. Although some books for younger children do involve space travel or extraterrestrials, most touch very little on technology, if at all—for example, *The Little Prince* (Saint Exupéry).

Science fiction plots often center on how science and technology affect human life, portraying technology's potential for both good and evil. Readers are drawn to examine the social consequences of technology, and some writers depict a very bleak picture of future societies. *The Crystal Drop* (Hughes) takes place in Canada in 2011, after the destruction of the ozone layer has devastated the land. Megan and her little brother set off to find their uncle after their mother dies.

Madeleine L'Engle's *A Wrinkle in Time* introduces Meg, whose father has learned to travel instantaneously through outer space by means of a tesseract, which is explained only as a mathematical process. In the same manner, Meg and her brother, seeking their lost father, travel to several destinations in space inhabited by strange creatures.

In *Alien Secrets* (Klaus), Puck has been expelled from yet another boarding school, and she is traveling through hyperspace to live with her parents on the planet Shoon where they are doing alien research. She befriends a fellow passenger on the spaceship, a native Showa named Hush, who has lost a national treasure that had been entrusted to him. Puck and Hush become embroiled in an adventure of interstellar crime and sabotage in order to recover the treasure, hidden aboard the craft.

Younger children will enjoy *Cosmo and the Robot* (Pinkney). After Cosmo's beloved robot, Rex, becomes damaged and is taken off to the asteroid dump, his parents try to console him with a Super Solar System Utility Belt with ten supersonic attachments. When he later finds Rex in the dump, his tools come in handy to subdue and then repair the malfunctioning robot, who has gone berserk.

Artemis Fowl (Colfer) is the first in a series of clever fantasy stories that combine folklore and science fiction. Artemis is an ingenious 12-year-old criminal mastermind who plots to restore his family's fortune by divesting the fairy folk of their pot of gold. He kidnaps a fairy and demands ransom. Unfortunately, the victim is the feisty Captain Holly Short of the LEPrecon (Lower Element Police Reconnaissance) Unit. Her senior officer, Commander Root, is a determined elf who will stop at nothing to get Holly back, including using his arsenal of high-tech weaponry.

In science fiction, characters can travel both to the future and to the past; however, travel is accomplished by scientific technology rather than by magic. Richard Peck's *Lost in Cyberspace* is a story of Aaron, a sixth grader who microprocesses himself into cyberspace through cellular reorganization. (He explains it as faxing himself through cyberspace.) He and his friend Josh must deal with unexpected visitors from the past. In the sequel, *The Great Interactive Dream Machine*, Aaron tinkers with the programming of his computer/time machine and accidentally gives it the ability to grant wishes. Unfortunately, the wishes granted are not always those of Aaron and Josh, so they are transported through time and space to some unwanted places.

By far the most popular type of science fiction for elementary children is aliens on Earth. *UFO Diary* (Kitamura) is a picture book narrated by an alien who takes a wrong turn in his dome-shaped rocket ship. He makes an unscheduled stop on Earth, where he visits with a young boy. In *I Was a Sixth Grade Alien* (Coville), two boys tell their stories in alternating chapters on what it is like to be/have an alien from the planet Hevi-Hevi in elementary school. *The Year of the Child: Alien Exchange Students* (Anders & Throop) introduces Meena Biop, a visitor from beyond the stars.

Jeanne DuPrau's *The City of Ember* is a combination science fiction, mystery, and adventure story. The setting is a small community that was built as a last refuge for the human race before the great apocalypse. Except for the floodlights that cast a yellowish glow during daytime hours, the city of Ember exists in complete darkness—no sun, moon, or stars light the sky. The inhabitants have no portable lights (flashlights, candles, or fire)—only the lights run by the ancient underground generator that is powered by a swift flowing river. Beyond Ember is only the pitch-black Unknown Regions, which no one has ever explored. For 240 years, the people lived comfortably because there was plenty of everything in the vast storerooms. Now there are shortages, and sometimes the lights go out when the generator fails. Twelve-year-olds Doon Harrow and Lina Mayfleet seem to be the only people who think there is an Elsewhere. "The Instructions for Egress," the written directions for getting out of Ember, were lost and forgotten, until Lina found them—but only after her baby sister chewed holes in the paper! Lina and Doon work together to decipher the message before the lights go out forever.

Visualize a 14-year-old James Bond, and you have Alex Rider, the daring (and lucky) teenage British spy in Anthony Horowitz's *Stormbreaker,* which is the first in a lengthy series. When his guardian and uncle is mysteriously killed, Alex discovers that his uncle was really a spy for the Special Operations Division of MI6, a top-secret intelligence agency. Government agents want Alex to take over his uncle's last mission—investigating Sayle Enterprises, the makers of a revolutionary computer called Stormbreaker. The company plans to donate one to every school in England, and this raises the agency's suspicions. Alex is first given high-tech gadgets (in lieu of weapons), such as a metal-melting cream and a Game Boy that scans and faxes. Then, posing as a teenage computer whiz who won a Stormbreaker promotional contest, Alex enters the Sayle factory and immediately finds clues from his uncle. Alex's daring allows him to solve the case after experiencing unbelievably dangerous adventures. The second novel, *Point Blanc,* is even more exciting than the first. The high-tech gadgets are even more incredible, and some of the characters are clones!

Uglies by Scott Westerfeld takes place in a futuristic high-tech society that believes its citizens are ugly until age 16 when they undergo a compulsory operation that changes them into pleasure-seeking "pretties." (However, the government surgeons are doing more than an extreme makeover.) Anticipating this transformation, Tally

Youngblood hangs out with Shay, another female ugly. While enjoying hoverboarding and risky pranks together, Shay confides to Tally that she disdains the programmed conformity of their society and plans to run away to The Smoke, a distant rebel settlement of simple-living uglies. When Shay goes missing, a cruel agent from the Department of Special Circumstances coerces Tally to find Shay or forever remain an ugly. Tally sets off on the dangerous journey as a spy. But after finally reaching The Smoke (outside the rusting ruins of what used to be a large city), she has a change of heart when her new friend David reveals the sinister secret behind becoming pretty.

💻 Integrating Literature and Technology

Comparing Technology in Older Books to Present Reality   Read an older science fiction book such as *Danny Dunn and the Homework Machine* (Williams & Abrashkin, 1958). Compare the book's version of futuristic computer technology to what has actually been achieved today. How accurate was the author in predicting the future?

Unlikely Situation

In some fantasy books there is no magic, and none of the characters is a talking animal, live toy, monster, ghost, or other unearthly creature. A book may have all human characters and a realistic setting; however, the characters engage in some totally unrealistic situation that makes the book fantasy rather than realistic fiction. Hans Christian Andersen's "The Emperor's New Suit" falls in this category because there is no magic or superhuman character. Rather, charlatans dupe the emperor into walking naked through his kingdom.

In *The Mysterious Benedict Society* by Trenton Lee Stewart, 11-year-old Reynie Muldoon answers a newspaper ad asking, "Are you a gifted child looking for special opportunities?" Dozens of other children enroll to take the series of challenging tests. In the end, just four unique, gifted children are selected: Reynie, Kate, Constance, and Sticky—all orphans. They call themselves the Mysterious Benedict Society. After being trained by Mr. Benedict and his assistants, the children infiltrate the isolated Learning Institute for the Very Enlightened, which is operated by the criminal mastermind, Mr. Curtin (who turns out to be Mr. Benedict's evil twin). The school broadcasts messages of distrust and blind compliance into the minds of the world's citizens with the goal of Mr. Curtin becoming the world's leader.

The Miss Nelson books by Harry Allard are also good examples. In *Miss Nelson Is Missing,* a teacher with an unruly class disappears, and the vile Miss Viola Swamp becomes their substitute teacher. In *Miss Nelson Is Back,* the children fear they will get Viola Swamp again when Miss Nelson has an operation, so a couple of kids dress up in a Miss Nelson costume and fool the principal. However, The Swamp appears when she finds out what they have done. The Swamp returns once more in *Miss Nelson Has a Field Day,* when the Horace B. Smedley School has the worst football team in the state. As their new coach, The Swamp whips them into shape while

Miss Nelson looks on. Within the last couple of pages of each book, Allard reveals who the real Viola Swamp is.

In Dr. Seuss's first of 44 books, *And to Think That I Saw It on Mulberry Street*, Marco's father tells him to observe carefully what he encounters on the way home from school. The boy sees only a horse and wagon on the street, but his imagination builds as he progressively envisions what *could* be on Mulberry Street: an elephant, giraffes, a wagon full of musicians, a magician, and more.

A hardworking but simple maid goes to work for the Rogers family in *Amelia Bedelia* (Parish). She is great at baking, but she takes her household chores quite literally. When told to dust the furniture, she puts dusting powder on everything. When told to put the lights out, she hangs all the light bulbs on the clothesline for some fresh air. When told to dress the chicken, she sews some green pants and socks to put on it. Peggy Parish has written a number of popular books about the zany Amelia Bedelia.

Petite Madeline and eleven other little girls live "in an old house in Paris that was covered with vines," where they are cared for and tutored by the loving Miss Clavel. In the first book, *Madeline* (Bemelmans), the smallest girl is rushed to the hospital to have her appendix removed. In the sequel, *Madeline's Rescue*, Madeline's daring attempt to walk atop the wall of a bridge lands her in the Seine River, where a brave dog rescues her.

Sara Nickerson's *How to Disappear Completely and Never Be Found* is an unlikely situation book that also presents a mystery. What were the circumstances in which Margaret's father died? She and her younger sister Sophie were only told that he drowned, and yet he had been a championship swimmer. And why does their mother Lizzie appear to own a dilapidated old mansion on a small island? The girls have never seen it before, and yet Lizzie sticks a "For Sale by Owner" sign in the front yard. Lastly, why does Boyd, the boy who lives next door, own a set of hand-drawn comic books—all depicting the old mansion on the cover—by someone named Ratt? The discovery of a reclusive rat-like man hiding in the mansion begins to unravel the mystery.

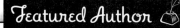

Lemony Snicket

In 1999 Daniel Handler—using the pseudonym Lemony Snicket—launched a wildly popular series (of unlikely situation books) called A Series of Unfortunate Events. Lemony Snicket is the pessimistic—yet personable and well-mannered—narrator of the thirteen-book series. The ruse that Snicket (rather than Handler) is the actual author of the series is perpetuated throughout each book, including the dedication, the author's short biography, and the notes on the back cover. The author even maintains the hoax in his many speaking engagements, saying he is filling in because of some terrible calamity—usually described in detail with props—that has befallen Snicket.

The opening statement of the first book, *The Bad Beginning,* warns, "If you are interested in stories with happy endings, you would be better off reading some other book. In this book, not only is there no happy ending, there is no happy beginning and very few happy things in the middle" (p. 1). In the first chapter, Violet, Klaus, and baby Sunny Baudelaire are met on a beach outing by Mr. Poe, a banker and family friend who informs them their parents have perished when their house mysteriously burned to the ground. As the executor of the parents' will, Mr. Poe is now their legal guardian, and he decides they should live with their distant cousin—the money-grubbing, psychopathic Count Olaf, who subjects them to much misery. In the end, the children expose Olaf's plot to gain the children's inheritance by forcing 14-year-old Violet to marry him! However, Olaf escapes before he can be arrested.

In subsequent books, Olaf—accompanied by his entourage of sinister associates— uses his experience as an actor to reappear in a different guise in each new setting where Mr. Poe places the children. The miserable children soon become resolved that they are surrounded by dim-witted adults, and they continue to experience an unrelenting sequence of catastrophes that require them valiantly to thwart Olaf's many malevolent plots to part them from their considerable inheritance. They survive by use of their various talents: Violet's inventive genius, Klaus's gift for reading and research, and baby Sunny's knack for biting the bad guys at the right time.

Lemony Snicket employs a witty and humorous, mock-Gothic writing style that is unique in its use of satire and sophisticated vocabulary. Helpfully, the narrator always defines unusual words in his intrusive commentaries. For example, "It will be of no interest to you if I describe the action of this insipid—the word 'insipid' here means 'dull and foolish'—play by Al Funcoot, because it was a dreadful play and of no real importance to our story" (pp. 142–143). (The books are great for teachers and parents who enjoy introducing intriguing new words to their children.)

Lemony Snicket's unusual humor, use of irony, and melodramatic literary style make this an unforgettable series. Learn more about these hilarious books at www.lemonysnicket.com/author.html.

Summary

Fiction is literary work that is designed to entertain. However, unlike traditional literature that evolved from countless storytellers, fiction is a product of the imagination of an identifiable author (occasionally two authors). This chapter focused on the first of several subgenres of fiction: modern fantasy—stories with highly fanciful or supernatural elements that would be impossible in real life. Hans Christian Andersen was likely the father of modern fantasy.

Animal fantasy, in which the main character is an animal with human attributes, is the most popular category of fantasy. There are nine additional distinct categories. (1) Literary fairy tales follow the patterns set by the oral tradition of folklore but are written by an identifiable author. (2) Animated object stories bring inanimate objects to life, such as dolls, toys, machines, and trees. (3) Human with fantasy character stories have an ordinary person and a fantasy creature as main characters, such as a monster, strange beast, mythological creature, or an element of nature. (4) Extraordinary person books have main characters with extraordinary powers, such as tiny stature, the ability to fly, the ability to communicate with animals, or great strength. (5) Enchanted journeys start in the real world, but the main character is transported to another world, often an enchanted world or the historical past. (6) High fantasies take place in well-developed secondary worlds, but unlike enchanted journeys that often have humorous tones, the protagonist in high fantasy engages in a monumental struggle against a powerful evil force. (7) Supernatural fantasy plots deal with beings that exist outside the natural world—such as ghosts or spirits—or powers that go beyond natural forces, such as telepathy. (8) Science fiction replaces magic with advanced technological wonders; supernatural characters, items, and occurrences are given rational scientific-sounding explanations. (9) Unlikely situation books contain no magic, but the characters engage in some totally unrealistic situations.

Fantasy Books

Allard, Harry. *Miss Nelson Has a Field Day.* Illus. James Marshall. Houghton Mifflin, 1988.

Allard, Harry. *Miss Nelson Is Back.* Illus. James Marshall. Houghton Mifflin, 1986.

Allard, Harry. *Miss Nelson Is Missing.* Illus. James Marshall. Houghton Mifflin, 1985.

Amos, Berthe. *Old Hannibal and the Hurricane.* Hyperion, 1991.

Anders, Isabel, & Sarah A. Throop. *The Year of the Child: Alien Exchange Students.* Anders Literacy Group, 1999.

Andersen, Hans Christian. *Hans Christian Andersen: The Complete Fairy Tales and Stories.* Trans. Eric Christian Haugaard. Anchor, 1983.

Andersen, Hans Christian. *The Little Match Girl.* Illus. Rachel Isadora. Putnam, 1987.

Andersen, Hans Christian. *Thumbelina.* Illus. Arlene Graston. Doubleday, 1997.

Babbitt, Natalie. *Tuck Everlasting.* Sunburst, 1985.

Barrie, J. M. *Peter Pan and Wendy.* Illus. Scott Gustafson. Viking, 1906/1991.

Bateman, Teresa. *The Ring of Truth.* Illus. Omar Rayyan. Holiday House, 1997.

Bauer, Marion Dane. *A Taste of Smoke.* Yearling, 1995.

Baum, L. Frank. *The Wonderful Wizard of Oz.* Morrow, 1900/1987.

Bemelmans, Ludwig. *Madeline.* Viking, 1958.

Bemelmans, Ludwig. *Madeline's Rescue.* Viking, 2000.

Brett, Jan. *Berlioz the Bear.* Putnam, 1996.

Burton, Virginia Lee. *Choo Choo: The Story of a Little Engine Who Ran Away.* Houghton Mifflin, 1937.

Burton, Virginia Lee. *Mike Mulligan and His Steam Shovel.* Houghton Mifflin, 1939.

Carle, Eric. *The Very Lonely Firefly.* Philomel, 1999.

Carroll, Lewis. *Alice's Adventures in Wonderland.* Random House, 1865/1988.

Cassedy, Sylvia. *Behind the Attic Wall.* HarperTrophy, 1985.

Colfer, Eoin. *Artemis Fowl.* Hyperion, 2001.

Collodi, Carlo. *The Adventures of Pinocchio: The Story of a Puppet.* Illus. Mary Haverfield. Random House, 1883/1992.

Conrad, Pam. *Stonewords.* HarperTrophy, 1990.

Coville, Bruce. *Bruce Coville's Book of Magic: Tales to Cast a Spell on You.* Scholastic, 1996.

Coville, Bruce. *I Was a Sixth Grade Alien.* Aladdin, 1999.

Coville, Bruce. *The Dragon of Doom.* Simon & Schuster, 2003.

Crampton, Gertrude. *Scuffy the Tugboat.* Illus. Tibor Gergely. Golden Books, 1946/1990.

Dahl, Roald. *Charlie and the Chocolate Factory.* Puffin, 1998.

Dahl, Roald. *Matilda.* Puffin, 1998.

Dahl, Roald. *The BFG.* Illus. Quentin Blake. Puffin, 2001.

dePaola, Tomie. *Strega Nona Meets Her Match.* Putnam, 1996.

DiTerlizzi, Tony, & Holly Black. *The Field Guide.* Simon & Schuster, 2003.

Dorros, Arthur. *Abuela.* Illus. Elisa Kleven. Dutton, 1991.

DuPrau, Jeanne. *The City of Ember.* Random House, 2003.

Freeman, Don. *Corduroy.* Viking, 1968.

Hesse, Karen. *A Time of Angels.* Hyperion, 2000.

Hesse, Karen. *The Music of Dolphins.* Scholastic, 1998.

Horowitz, Anthony. *Point Blanc.* Penguin Putnam, 2002.

Horowitz, Anthony. *Stormbreaker.* Penguin Putnam, 2000.

Hughes, Monica. *The Crystal Drop.* Simon & Schuster, 1993.

Joyce, William. *George Shrinks.* HarperTrophy, 2003.

Kipling, Rudyard. *Just So Stories.* Illus. Barry Moser. Chrysalis, 1902/2003.

Kitamura, Satoshi. *UFO Diary.* Farrar, Straus & Giroux, 1991.

Klaus, Annette Curtis. *Alien Secrets.* Random House, 1999.

L'Engle, Madeleine. *A Wrinkle in Time.* Yearling, 1998.

Levine, Gail Carson. *Ella Enchanted.* HarperTrophy, 1998.

Levithan, David. *In the Eye of the Tornado.* Apple, 1998.

Lewis, C. S. *Prince Caspian.* HarperCollins, 1951/1994.

Lewis, C. S. *The Horse and His Boy.* HarperCollins, 1954/1994.

Lewis, C. S. *The Last Battle.* HarperCollins, 1956/1994.

Lewis, C. S. *The Lion, the Witch and the Wardrobe.* HarperCollins, 1950/1994.

Lewis, C. S. *The Magician's Nephew.* HarperCollins, 1955/1994.

Lewis, C. S. *The Silver Chair.* HarperCollins, 1953/1994.

Lewis, C. S. *The Voyage of the* Dawn Treader. HarperCollins, 1952/1994.

Lionni, Leo. *Alexander and the Wind-Up Mouse.* Knopf, 1991.

Lionni, Leo. *Little Blue and Little Yellow.* HarperTrophy, 1995.

Lobel, Arnold. *Frog and Toad Are Friends.* HarperTrophy, 1979.

Lofting, Hugh. *The Story of Doctor Dolittle.* Illus. Michael Hague. Delacorte Press, 1920/1988.

Lofting, Hugh. *The Voyages of Doctor Dolittle.* Grosset & Dunlap, 1922/1998.

Lowry, Lois. *The Giver.* Houghton Mifflin, 1993.

MacHale, D. J. *Pendragon: The Merchant of Death.* Simon & Schuster, 2002.

Mayer, Mercer. *There's a Nightmare in My Closet.* Puffin, 1992.

McGraw, Eloise Jarvis. *The Moorchild.* Aladdin, 1998.

McKinley, Robin. *The Blue Sword.* Puffin, 2000.

McKinley, Robin. *The Hero and the Crown.* Greenwillow, 1985.

McKissack, Patricia. *Flossie & the Fox.* Illus. Rachel Isadora. Dial, 1986.

McKissack, Patricia. *Mirandy and Brother Wind.* Illus. Jerry Pinkney. Dragonfly, 1997.

Milne, A. A. *The House at Pooh Corner.* Dutton, 1928/2001.

Milne, A. A. *Winnie-the-Pooh.* Methuen, 1926/2000.

Munsch, Robert. *The Paper Bag Princess.* Illus. Michael Martchenko. Scholastic, 1999.

Nickerson, Sara. *How to Disappear Completely and Never Be Found.* HarperCollins, 2002.

Nimmo, Jenny. *Midnight for Charlie Bone.* Orchard, 2002.

Norton, Mary. *The Borrowers.* Illus. Beth Krush & Joe Krush. Odyssey Classics, 2003.

Osborne, Mary Pope. *Dinosaurs before Dark.* Random House, 1992.

Paolini, Christopher. *Eragon.* Knopf, 2003.

Parish, Peggy. *Amelia Bedelia.* Illus. Fritz Siebel. HarperTrophy, 1992.

Paterson, Katherine. *The King's Equal.* Illus. Vladimir Vagin. HarperCollins, 1992.

Paz, Octavio, & Catherine Cowan. *My Life with the Wave.* Illus. Mark Buehner. HarperCollins, 1997.

Peck, Richard. *Lost in Cyberspace.* Puffin, 1997.

Peck, Richard. *The Great Interactive Dream Machine.* Puffin, 1998.

Pilkey, Dav. *The Adventures of Captain Underpants: An Epic Novel.* Scholastic, 1997.

Pinkney, Brian. *Cosmo and the Robot.* Greenwillow, 2000.

Ringgold, Faith. *Tar Beach.* Dragonfly, 1996.

Rowling, J. K. *Fantastic Beasts and Where to Find Them.* Scholastic, 2001.

Rowling, J. K. *Harry Potter and the Chamber of Secrets.* Scholastic, 1999.

Rowling, J. K. *Harry Potter and the Deathly Hallows.* Scholastic, 2007.

Rowling, J. K. *Harry Potter and the Goblet of Fire.* Scholastic, 2000.

Rowling, J. K. *Harry Potter and the Half-Blood Prince.* Scholastic. 2005.

Rowling, J. K. *Harry Potter and the Order of the Phoenix.* Scholastic. 2003.

Rowling, J. K. *Harry Potter and the Prisoner of Azkaban.* Scholastic, 1999.

Rowling, J. K. *Harry Potter and the Sorcerer's Stone.* Scholastic, 1998.

Rowling, J. K. *Quidditch through the Ages.* Scholastic, 2001.

Saint Exupéry, Antoine de. *The Little Prince.* Harvest, 1943/2000.

Scieszka, Jon. *Knights of the Kitchen Table.* Illus. Lane Smith. Puffin, 2004.

Scieszka, Jon. *The Stinky Cheese Man and Other Fairly Stupid Tales.* Illus. Lane Smith. Viking, 2002.

Scieszka, Jon. *The True Story of the 3 Little Pigs.* Illus. Lane Smith. Puffin, 1996.

Seeger, Pete. *Abiyoyo.* Illus. Michael Hays. Aladdin, 2005.

Sendak, Maurice. *Where the Wild Things Are.* HarperCollins, 1988.

Seuss, Dr. *And to Think That I Saw It on Mulberry Street.* Random House, 1937/1989.

Silverstein, Shel. *The Giving Tree.* HarperCollins, 1964.

Silverstein, Shel. *The Missing Piece.* HarperCollins, 1976.

Silverstein, Shel. *The Missing Piece Meets the Big O.* HarperCollins, 1981.

Snicket, Lemony. *The Bad Beginning.* HarperCollins, 1999.

Tazewell, Charles. *The Littlest Angel.* Illus. Paul Micich. Ideals, 2007.

Thaler, Mike. *The Teacher from the Black Lagoon.* Illus. Jared Lee. Scholastic, 1989.

Tolkien, J. R. R. *The Hobbit.* Houghton Mifflin, 1937.

Van Allsburg, Chris. *Jumanji.* Scholastic, 1995.

Van Allsburg, Chris. *The Polar Express.* Houghton Mifflin, 1985.

Verne, Jules. *From the Earth to the Moon.* North, 1865/1999.

Westerfeld, Scott. *Uglies.* Simon & Schuster, 2005.

White Deer of Autumn. *Ceremony—in the Circle of Life.* Illus. Daniel San Souci. Beyond Words, 1991.

Williams, Jay, & Raymond Abrashkin. *Danny Dunn and the Homework Machine.* McGraw-Hill, 1958/1964.

Williams, Margery. *The Velveteen Rabbit.* Illus. Michael Green. Avon, 1922/1999.

Yolen, Jane. *The Devil's Arithmetic.* Puffin, 1990.

Yorinks, Arthur. *Hey Al.* Illus. Richard Egielski. Farrar, Straus & Giroux, 1989.

Animal Fantasy

The artist created various types of lines with pen and ink and filled in with watercolors.

From *Frog and Toad Together,* written and illustrated by Arnold Lobel.

📚 *Library locations*   **J (Juvenile) for junior novels; E (Easy) for picture books**

Fantasy stories in which main characters are anthropomorphic animals
that talk, experience emotions, and have the ability to reason like humans

alking animals have always been popular story characters. The earliest were the
fables and talking beast folktales of traditional lore. Animal characters are particularly adapted to expressing ideas about human foibles (Stewig, 1980), and most
likely it was this quality that led ancient storytellers to employ animal characters in
their tales. Whitney (1976) explained that even in contemporary fantasy, animal
tales can be "filled with important truths that might make the child reader uncom-
fortable if presented in realistic terms involving human characters" (p. 133).

In modern **animal fantasy,** the main—and often all—characters are **anthropomorphic
animals** (i.e., animals with human characteristics). They possess human language,
thoughts, and emotions. An effective author of animal fantasy makes the incredible
sound credible while maintaining story logic and is therefore able to create believable
characters and plots. Very young children do not make a clear distinction between
fact and fantasy, so they have little trouble imagining animals with human traits, or
what Russell (1997) called the metaphorical use of animals in human roles. He postulated that animal characters are actually literary symbolism, in which the animals
signify human counterparts. The animals are the vehicles for experiencing human
emotions, values, and relationships. To demonstrate the extent to which readers accept animal characters as substitutes for humans, consider *Arthur's New Puppy*
(Brown), in which an animal (a young aardvark) has a pet animal!

Animal fantasy stories usually do not contain magic (outside of animals that talk
and think like humans). Rather, the most common plots take place in a contemporary setting and focus on everyday issues that mimic human nature, which is in concert with Russell's (1997) theory. However, Nodelman (1996) believes that animal
characters represent the "animal-like" condition of children. He cited the example of
The Tale of Peter Rabbit (Potter), in which Peter is torn between the opposing forces
of his mother's wishes and his natural desire to eat in the garden. Nodelman (1996)
pointed out that whether or not animal characters wear clothing is of significance,
marking them as either more human or more animal. When the characters are more
animal-like, they typically are more focused on their concerns of finding food.

A look through the picture book sections of bookstores and libraries will reveal
how popular animal fantasy is among children's books. I analyzed a HarperCollins catalogue of new children's titles, and animal fantasy books accounted for 31 percent of
the 108 new titles introduced—by far the largest genre when compared to the other genres presented in this textbook: concept books, traditional literature, modern fantasy,
contemporary realistic fiction, historical fiction, biography, informational books, and
poetry. Predictably, the most prevalent characters in these new animal fantasy stories

were dogs and cats. Interestingly, the book covers of 35 percent of the titles that were *not* animal fantasy depicted one or more animals in the illustration.

The popularity of animal fantasy is not a new trend. Peterson (1971) identified fantasy stories about animals as the most prevalent choice of the 745 second graders in his study. Additionally, Lawson (1972) concluded that animal stories were by far the favorite type of reading materials for the 695 fifth graders in her study. In their respective guides to aspiring authors of children's books, both Phyllis A. Whitney (1976) and Jane Yolen (1973) spoke to the popularity of animal stories, and Yolen postulated that animal tales in general are probably the single greatest category in children's books.

More recently, in Mohr's (2002) study, 190 first graders listened to and independently viewed nine picture books over a period of three days. Each was then allowed to select one book to receive as a gift. The nine books represented six genres: one animal fantasy book with dinosaur characters, one informational book about dangerous animals, one concept/alphabet book about zoo animals, one biography, two traditional tales, and three contemporary realistic fiction books. The book about dangerous animals was by far the most popular choice, with 46 percent of the children selecting it. The animal fantasy book was the second most popular choice, and the alphabet book about zoo animals was the third most popular. Even though two of the contemporary realistic fiction books had Latino characters and contained bilingual text, there was no significant difference between the choices of the Latino children (who comprised 30 percent of the subjects) and the rest of the children (all Caucasian) in the study. These results indicate that books about animals, fiction and nonfiction alike, are enormously popular with young children.

Issues in Animal Fantasy

Why Is It Largely Ignored in Other Textbooks?   Clearly animal fantasy stories are popular with children and have been for a long time. The few research studies that have been published in this area indicate that it is young children's top choice, so children certainly know animal fantasy is great. More than 31 percent of the all-time best-selling children's books published in the United States in the past 100 years are animal fantasy (Anderson, 2003), and parents purchased most of these books, so parents know it is popular with young children. Many of the new titles by publishers are animal fantasy books, so publishers obviously know it also. Then why is it largely ignored by other textbook writers? The textbooks I reviewed devoted only three or four pages to animal fantasy.

Why is so little attention given to what acclaimed author Jane Yolen and others believe is the single largest category of children's books?

In this chapter, I first trace some of the milestones in the history of animal fantasy, and then I analyze the characteristics of this genre by dividing it into four main types, citing notable authors and some of their most memorable works. (Stories involving real animals are presented in Chapters 9 and 10, which discuss realistic fiction.)

Evaluating Animal Fantasy

The following questions can guide you as you select animal fantasy books:

- How believable are the anthropomorphic animals?
- Does the protagonist possess an appropriate mix of both animal and human characteristics?
- Does the book tell a good story that children will enjoy?
- Is the plot credible?

Milestones in Animal Fantasy

Animal fantasy has a long, interesting history. I have selected some of the more memorable titles to discuss in the next section. All of these books were immensely popular when first published, and they are still in print today. Their significance comes from their influence on the authors and illustrators who followed them, helping to shape the style of contemporary animal fantasy books.

1877: *Black Beauty: The Autobiography of a Horse* by Anna Sewell

The first significant animal fantasy story was published in England in the nineteenth century and is still in print. *Black Beauty* was not written as a children's book; rather, Sewell wrote it as a protest against the cruel treatment of animals. Its theme is a plea for the humane treatment of horses. The novel is told from the first-person point of view of the thoroughbred Black Beauty, a beautiful horse that is traded to a series of owners, some of whom severely abuse him. When the book was published, people of all ages read and loved it, and it stirred a movement to pass laws against animal cruelty. Today's readers may find the book overly sentimental and overdrawn, but adapted versions are available that target contemporary child readers.

1894: *The Jungle Book* by Rudyard Kipling

The Jungle Book is a collection of seven stories interspersed with seven poems, with settings in the jungles of India. The most popular tale is "Mowgli's Brothers," which features Mowgli, the fearless man-cub who was raised by a family of wolves. His companions include Akela, his wolf father, Baloo the wise brown bear, and Bagheera the sleek black panther, all of whom help him learn the law of the jungle. While Mowgli grows in the language and ways of the jungle animals, the cunning and sinister tiger Shere Khan looms in the darkness, waiting for the right moment to pounce.

Also popular in Rudyard Kipling's collection is "Rikki-Tikki-Tavi," the story of a heroic mongoose that belongs to a small boy. True to his nature, the mongoose stalks and kills the wicked cobra Nag that lives in the garden at the boy's house.

He must then face the female cobra Nagaina; she intends to avenge her mate and protect her unborn babies.

1901/1902: *The Tale of Peter Rabbit* by Beatrix Potter

The Tale of Peter Rabbit was the prototype of children's picture storybooks. In 1901 Potter privately printed the first edition of *Peter Rabbit* after six publishers had turned her down. Frederick Warne and Company published the second edition in color the following year, and Warne continues to publish this and Potter's twenty-two other books. *Peter Rabbit* is a cautionary tale warning children about the serious consequences of not minding their parents. Peter nearly loses his life for nibbling in Mr. McGregor's garden, but he escapes, leaving his jacket and shoes behind. His compliant sisters, Flopsy, Mopsy, and Cottontail, are rewarded with blackberries and milk. The sequel is *The Tale of Benjamin Bunny,* in which Peter and his cousin Benjamin sneak back to Mr. McGregor's garden to retrieve Peter's clothes, which are being used as a scarecrow.

Over the past 100 years, more than 30 million copies of *Peter Rabbit* have been sold worldwide (about one-third of them in the United States). In a Library Association poll conduced in the United Kingdom in 2000, Beatrix Potter ranked second behind only Ernest Hemingway as the favorite author of all time (International Reading Association, 2003a).

1903: *The Call of the Wild* by Jack London

In 1887 and 1889 Jack London participated in the Alaskan gold rush. When he returned to his home in San Francisco, he wrote about his experiences. *The Call of the Wild* is a survival story of a contented pet dog named Buck who is stolen from his California home to work as a rugged sled dog during the Alaskan gold rush. He receives much brutal treatment in the Klondike, and he struggles savagely to survive. When rescued by a miner in the wilderness, he loves the man unconditionally. However, Buck becomes inescapably drawn by the wild cries of a wolf pack nearby. When his beloved master is killed, the dog's long suppressed instincts overtake him. He reverts to the primitive state of his wolf ancestors and is accepted into the pack. Animal lovers will find this adventure book both exciting and heartwrenching.

1908: *The Wind in the Willows* by Kenneth Grahame

The first major animal fantasy novel specifically for children was *The Wind in the Willows*, which became the touchstone for all animal fantasy novels that followed. Kenneth Grahame's bedtime stories—and later his letters—to his son Alastair became the episodes in the book. Grahame had spent much of his childhood living in his grandmother's house on the banks of the Thames River in Berkshire, England, and he used the riverbank as the setting of this book. The good-natured and adventurous Water Rat; the cautious and reflective Mole; the gruff but kindly Badger; and the rich, boisterous, and arrogant Mr. Toad of Toad Hall are all dear and loyal friends.

Mr. Toad's cocky personality and his irrepressible passion for motorcars launch him on wild adventures. Though his friends try to reform him and even manage to take back his ancestral manor house from the evil weasels, the pompous Mr. Toad remains utterly recalcitrant. Themes of warm friendship, sympathetic understanding, and forgiveness are charming features of this book.

The Wind in the Willows was written nearly a century ago in England, and because of its different customs and vocabulary, it is difficult reading for most children. Even my adult students (mostly in their 20s) often find it slow paced, overly sentimental, and difficult to understand. Undoubtedly, the most appealing character is Mr. Toad, and the loose plot of the book concerns mostly his antics. I suggest you read this book aloud to your children starting with Chapters 6, 8, 10, 11, and 12, which describe Mr. Toad's adventures. The rest of the chapters are episodic tales of the other characters.

1929: *Bambi: A Life in the Woods* by Felix Salten

While living in Austria in 1929, Siegmund Salzman—using the pen name Felix Salten—published *Bambi: A Life in the Woods* (translated by Whittaker Chambers). This is the endearing tale of the life of a deer, which opens with the birth of the fawn Bambi in the middle of a forest thicket. As the story unfolds, Bambi learns both the pleasures and the dangers of forest life, such as the bitter winters and the terrors of fire. However, man—the hunter—is the greatest danger. Bambi loses his mother and a childhood friend to hunters, and later he is seriously wounded by gunfire. It is the revered old stag, the Prince of Deer, who rescues him and keeps him alive. This book stirs deep emotions in readers who believe wild animals should not be killed for sport.

1939: *Rudolph the Red-Nosed Reindeer* by Robert L. May

American culture was forever changed by the publication of *Rudolph*. The famous story of Santa's unusual reindeer was born in 1939 when Montgomery Ward & Company asked one of their young copywriters, Robert L. May, to write a book to be used as a Christmas giveaway for the store's customers. May's book, *Rudolph the Red-Nosed Reindeer,* was enormously popular, and Montgomery Ward distributed more than 6 million copies. In 1947 John Marks, a friend of May's, wrote a song about Rudolph. Gene Autry's recording of the song sold millions of copies and quickly rose to the number one spot on the Hit Parade. Although the song about Rudolph became part of the tradition of Christmas, most people do not know *Rudolph* was first a book. This is unfortunate, because May's use of couplets to tell the story is charming.

> "Ha, ha! Look at Rudolph! His nose is a sight!"
> "It's red as a beet!" "Twice as big!" "Twice as bright!"
> While Rudolph just wept. What else could he do?
> He knew that the things they were saying were true!
> Where most reindeer's noses are brownish and tiny,
> Poor Rudolph's was red, very large, and quite shiny.

Young children would surely enjoy this book, especially if the history (printed on the book cover) is shared.

1941: *Make Way for Ducklings* by Robert McCloskey

Robert McCloskey's time-honored classic, *Make Way for Ducklings,* is set in Boston. The reader will see the Charles River, Louisburg Square, Beacon Hill, and the Public Garden from a mallard duck's point of view. The excitement comes when Mrs. Mallard starts to lead her eight little hatchlings from the Charles River to the pond in the Public Garden, which requires the help of Michael the police officer.

1942: *The Poky Little Puppy* by Janette Lowrey

The Poky Little Puppy was named the all-time best-selling children's picture book in the United States by *Publishers Weekly* (Roback, 2001). Nearly 15 million copies of Lowrey's book were sold in the United States alone during the first fifty-eight years of its publication. This cumulative tale is about five puppies who mischievously dig under the fence to explore the outside world. When they smell dinner and dessert, all but the poky puppy run home and are scolded by their mother. The four puppies are sent to bed with no dessert, but the poky puppy returns home after everyone is asleep and eats *all* the dessert. This routine continues for three days. (Somehow the mother never catches on.) But on the third night, the brothers and sisters get up and fill the hole with dirt, shutting the poky puppy outside the fence while they eat dessert.

1952: *Charlotte's Web* by E. B. White

Undoubtedly, *Charlotte's Web* by E. B. White is the most-loved animal fantasy novel of the twentieth century. As the only novel written specifically for children by an American in this list of classics, it has become part of our heritage. It is the all-time best-selling children's paperback book in the United States with more than 11 million copies sold in this country in the first forty-eight years of its publication.

It opens on a farm in Maine, where a girl named Fern lovingly takes care of Wilbur, a runt pig. When Wilbur grows too big, he is sold to Fern's Uncle Zuckerman, whose farm is down the road. Wilbur becomes lonely and dejected in his new location, but Charlotte, the large gray spider who lives in the barn rafters, lovingly befriends him. When he learns from the sheep that he is destined for the dinner table, Wilbur is hysterical. However, the articulate and rational Charlotte, who can read and write, saves his life by weaving words in her web about how terrific Wilbur is. Though Wilbur becomes famous, he is saddened when Charlotte dies of old age, but not before leaving an egg sac under Wilbur's care. The value of true friendship and the cycle of life and death are major themes of this classic.

1957: *The Cat in the Hat* by Dr. Seuss

Dr. Seuss's *The Cat in the Hat* was the prototype of easy-to-read picture storybooks written on a beginning reader's level. In this wildly popular book, two children are bored sitting at home on a rainy afternoon. A cat wearing an odd red-and-white top hat appears, and with hilarious antics he teaches the children some tricks and games, making quite a mess. Everything is amazingly put back in order before the mother returns.

Dr. Seuss

Theodore Seuss Geisel, known to generations of children as Dr. Seuss, debuted as a children's book author in 1937 with *And to Think That I Saw It on Mulberry Street*. He published more than sixty children's books, which were noted for highly imaginative characters and distinct rhyme and meter. In May 1954, *Life* magazine published a report on illiteracy among children, which blamed boring basal readers used for instruction. Dr. Seuss's publisher presented him with a list of 348 high-frequency words and asked him to write a book using no more than 250 of these words. Nine months later, Dr. Seuss completed *The Cat in the Hat*, using only 236 different words, in which a mischievous cat transforms a dull, rainy afternoon into a magical and messy adventure for two bored children. Because of its simplified vocabulary that could be read by beginning readers, it was an international success. This was the birth of the easy-to-read book format.

Dr. Seuss wrote several more notable books. In *Green Eggs and Ham*, Sam-I-Am mounts a determined campaign to convince another Seuss character to eat a plate of green eggs and ham. In *One Fish Two Fish Red Fish Blue Fish*, children read about the activities of such unusual creatures as the Nook, Wump, Yink, Yop, Gack, and the Zeds. *How the Grinch Stole Christmas!* is the saga of the Grinch, who hates Christmas, so he plans to steal all the presents in Who-ville to prevent Christmas from coming. *Fox in Socks* is a collection of amusing tongue twisters that Fox uses to tease his reluctant and exasperated friend Mr. Knox.

Types of Animal Fantasy

In my definition of animal fantasy, I include main characters that are imaginary animals, such as mythological creatures (*The Dragon and the Unicorn*, Cherry), monsters (*Shrek!* Steig), imaginative beings (*How the Grinch Stole Christmas!* Seuss), and recognizable animals with some outstanding feature (*Catwings*, Le Guin). From a content analysis of more than 100 popular animal fantasy books in print, I have identified four major types, as described in the following paragraphs in order of most prevalent (Type I) to least prevalent (Type IV).

Type I: Anthropomorphic Animals in an All-Animal World

In **Type I animal fantasy,** the anthropomorphic animals take the place of humans and exist in a totally animal world. This world may be inhabited by a single species, such as the mice in *Owen* (Henkes), or it may be a world inhabited by various species, as in *Franklin in the Dark* (Bourgeois). The animal characters behave almost entirely like humans, talking in human speech, living in houses, eating human food, wearing clothing, and using various modes of transportation. However, some animal characters may retain a few natural traits, such as their favorite foods. Plots primarily involve the same problems encountered by the stories' child readers, whose lives these characters reflect. Quite often, only the illustrations reveal to readers that the characters are animals.

Arnold Lobel. Arnold Lobel is a master of Type I animal fantasy. Themes of unconditional friendship with sympathetic understanding are prominent in his Frog and Toad series. In the first of the four books, *Frog and Toad Are Friends,* the animals are illustrated in appropriate sizes compared to the other flora and fauna (e.g., Toad sits under a mushroom and is smaller than a sparrow). However, Frog and Toad live in little houses, wear human clothing, walk upright, eat human food, and are able to read and write. Essentially, they do everything that humans do. Because they live in an all-animal world, they are able to communicate with the other woodland creatures—which, interestingly, live in natural habitats and do not wear clothing.

Lobel's stories are easy-to-read books, and each consists of five episodic chapters. My favorite episode is "The Story." One day when Frog is visiting, Toad notices that he does not look well. Toad tucks Frog in his own bed to rest and fixes him a cup of hot tea. Frog asks Toad to tell him a story while he is resting, but Toad cannot think of any, even when he walks up and down the porch for a long time, stands on his head, pours water over his head, and bangs his head against the wall. After that, Frog says he is feeling better and does not need a story.

Frog then tells a story about a sick frog who has a toad friend who cannot think of a story, even after walking up and down, standing on his head, pouring water over his head, and banging his head against the wall. When Frog finishes the story, Toad is asleep.

Lobel wrote several other Type I easy-to-read books, but his book of literary fables gained him the most acclaim. *Fables* consists of twenty brief stories containing important lessons with a variety of animal characters. Each two-page spread has a beautiful full-page illustration facing a one-page story with the moral stated at the end. Because each of these brief stories contains all the elements of story structure, they lend themselves to a variety of activities. They serve as excellent models for children to write their own literary fables, and they are fabulous for story mapping activities (see Figure 2.1). Also, because each story has a narrator and two to three characters with dialogue, they lend themselves well to readers theater.

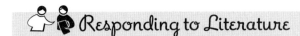 **Responding to Literature**

Readers Theater **Readers theater** is an activity in which children take speaking parts in a brief story and then read it as if it were a radio play. To help your children prepare for readers theater, let them select parts (one part for each character with dialogue, plus the narrator). Have the group practice together until they are ready to read the story like a play. Children should not try to memorize parts, and props are optional. The story can be read from the book, or a script can be written with speaking parts identified for each character and the narrator. The following script is from the novel *The Tale of Despereaux* by Kate Dicamillo.

> **Princess:** Oh, Papa, look, a mouse.
> **Narrator:** The king stopped singing. He squinted. The King was nearsighted; that is, anything that was not right in front of his eyes was very difficult for him to see.
> **King:** Where?
> **Princess:** There.
> **King:** That, my dear Pea, is a bug, not a mouse. It is much too small to be a mouse.
> **Princess:** No, it's a mouse.
> **King:** A bug.
> **Princess:** A *mouse.*
> **Narrator:** As for Despereaux, he was beginning to realize that he had made a very grave error. He trembled. He shook. He sneezed. He considered fainting.
> **Princess:** He's frightened. Look, he's so afraid he's shaking. I think he was listening to the music. Play something, Papa.
> **King:** A king play music for a *bug*? . . .

William Steig. Another excellent Type I animal fantasy author and illustrator, William Steig, creates stories that are unique because he uses magical objects in the plot. In *Sylvester and the Magic Pebble*, little Sylvester (a young donkey) finds a magic red pebble and accidentally turns himself into a rock while trying to hide from a lion. Steig amusingly differentiates between adult and child animals by having only the adults wear clothing. Steig chose an array of species for the characters, but he received criticism when he depicted the police officers as pigs. It is interesting that not all the animals in the story live like humans; some retain natural characteristics—the ducks float on the pond, the lion wants to eat the little donkey, the dogs go sniffing for Sylvester's scent, and the lone wolf howls atop the rock.

 **Responding to Literature**

Literature Webs An interesting way to connect children with stories and encourage their involvement is **webbing:** creating a visual display of information to represent organized relationships. Webbing can be used to foster and record responses to literature. It promotes discussion while helping children construct shared meanings that will extend their understandings and appreciation. Because webs are versatile, they can be used to depict many types of information. The web in Figure 7.1 represents the beginning of a character study on the protagonist in *Sylvester and the Magic Pebble*. Bromley's *Webbing with Literature* (1996) has a treasure trove of ideas on webbing activities. Select another of William Steig's picture books and make a character web of one of the memorable characters.

William Steig also employs magic in *The Amazing Bone*, in which a girl pig finds a talking bone that helps her outwit a band of highway robbers, and in *Zeke Pippin*, in which a boy pig finds a magic harmonica that makes everyone fall asleep when he plays it. (Wouldn't parents find that handy?) In *Doctor De Soto* Steig depicts a variety of species, all of which live in a city and dress and act like humans. This story of a diminutive mouse dentist has only one character that retains natural animal instincts. The large fox plans to eat Doctor De Soto after the dentist fixes his bad tooth.

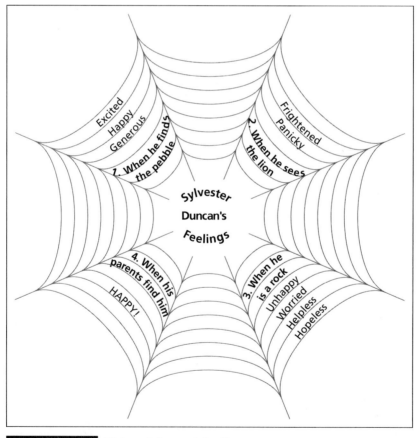

FIGURE 7.1   Web on Sylvester's Feelings

Marc Brown. The plots in Marc Brown's expansive series about Arthur, a young aardvark, center on holidays and issues that young children face, such as the arrival of a new baby, having chicken pox, going to camp, and sleeping over. My favorite is *Arthur's Eyes,* one of the early books, in which Arthur gets eyeglasses and at first the other children laugh at him. Arthur is one of the very few picture book characters with glasses, and in this story Arthur could serve as a positive role model for children who wear glasses.

Other Type I Authors. Young children feel comfortable with familiar story characters, and they enjoy reading many books about them. Several Type I animal fantasy characters are memorialized in book series. Else Holmelund Minarik's stories of the adorable cub first introduced in *Little Bear* have entertained several generations of children with themes of familial relations and friendship. Russell Hoban's Frances, the little badger (sans tail), first appeared in *Bedtime for Frances,* a story about Frances's trouble sleeping because of frightening sounds and objects. In *Franklin in the Dark,* Paulette Bourgeois presented Franklin, the little turtle who drags his shell behind him because he is afraid of crawling into a small dark place.

Gary Soto's *Chato's Kitchen* presents a hilarious tale of Chato (a cat) plotting to eat the *ratoncitos* (little mice) who have moved into the barrio next to his house. He invites them to a dinner of fajitas, frijoles, salsa, enchiladas, and more, but the guests do not know they are intended to be the main course. I must also recognize the large and enormously popular series about the Bear family by Stan and Jan Berenstain. One of their best books came early in the series, *The Berenstain Bears and the Spooky Old Tree.*

Redwall by Brian Jacques is the first in a series of epic adventures with mice characters. Matthias is an ambitious young mouse who must overcome his clumsy ways and prepare to defeat the savage bilge rat, Cluny the Scourge, and his villainous hordes. Matthias determines to find the legendary sword of Martin the Warrior, which he is convinced will help save the ancient realm of Redwall Abbey, the idyllic world of mice. In *Poppy* (Avi) a grumpy porcupine helps Poppy the deer mouse go to battle with Ocax the evil owl after he consumes her fiancé. Poppy then finds a safer home and helps the other mice move.

There are several Type I animal fantasy books appropriate for very young children, especially for bedtime reading. With delightful pictures and minimal text, Little Nutbrown Hare tries to convince Big Nutbrown Hare that he loves him more in *Guess How Much I Love You* (McBratney). In simple rhyming text, another little rabbit goes through his nighttime ritual of telling everything in his bedroom goodnight in *Goodnight Moon* (Brown). In *Olivia* (Falconer) readers learn about a typical day for a little piglet, which ends with Mother reading her three bedtime stories.

From the stories I have shared with you, you can see that a panorama of human emotions can be presented in animal guise. These fantasy stories can give children a new perspective on their own lives by allowing them to see the humor in ordinary mishaps that befall the animal characters.

⌨ Integrating Literature and Technology

Children's Books Forever: www.ChildrensBooksForever.com   When author/illustrator Hans Wilhelm's most popular book series, Tyrone the Terrible, went out of print, he received many e-mails asking how to obtain these books, so he created a website where people can obtain a free full-color download of all his picture books that are now out of print (mostly animal fantasy). They can be printed or viewed in the classroom on a SmartBoard, PowerPoint, or overhead projector. Wilhelm plans to have more than 100 books available on his website, including the soccer-crazy rabbit in *Bunny Trouble*. As a special bonus, the site is free of advertising to ensure the pure enjoyment of books.

Type II: Anthropomorphic Animals Coexisting with Humans

In **Type II animal fantasy,** animals coexist with humans—sometimes in a human-dominated world, as in *Charlotte's Web* (White), where they may or may not be able to speak, and other times in an animal-dominated world where humans only occasionally appear, as in *The Wind in the Willows* (Grahame). In addition, some characters, such as Lafcadio (Silverstein), move from the animal world to the human world and back to the animal world.

Pets. Stories about pet animals are typically set in a human-dominated world where animal and human characters have equal importance. Henry's best friend and constant companion is his dog Mudge in Cynthia Rylant's easy-to-read series on Henry and Mudge. Though Mudge does not speak, the narrator lets the reader know how he is feeling, and the dog typically reflects the boy's mood. For example, in *Henry and Mudge and the Happy Cat*, we learn through text and illustrations that Mudge loves the stray cat, does not mind sharing crackers, and is sad and depressed when the cat goes home. The reader also learns the feelings of the cat, who loves Mudge and likes sleeping in the towel closet. The cat also desires to teach Mudge good manners.

Everyone who owns a dog knows dogs do not like baths, and Gene Zion tells a funny story about baths from the dog's point of view in *Harry the Dirty Dog*. The police officer's pet dog in *Officer Buckle and Gloria* (Rathmann) peps up the officer's boring safety speeches by acting out the consequences on stage. *Clifford the Big Red Dog* (Bridwell) is *really* big—taller than his owner's house! In the first book of the series, readers learn that Clifford must be bathed in a swimming pool and combed with a rake, and he generally wreaks havoc on the neighborhood. In Kevin Henkes's *Kitten's First Full Moon*, an adorable kitten sees the full moon in the sky for the first time and thinks it is a big bowl of milk. She persistently tries to reach it and experiences a night of slapstick mishaps during her struggle.

The dog in *Martha Speaks* (Meddaugh) learns how to talk after eating alphabet soup, and her jabber becomes quite annoying. In *Biscuit* (Capucilli) a little yellow dog wants ever one more thing before he will go to sleep (just like the children who read the story), and at the end he gets what he really wants—to sleep next to the little girl. *How Willy Got His Wheels* (Turner & McHugh) is based on a true story of a handicapped Chihuahua who is rescued from an animal hospital by a kindly woman who helps him gain his independence by fitting him with a small wheelchair.

In a class by itself is *Walter the Farting Dog* (Kotzwinkle & Murray). The book started as a joke between the authors and illustrator, and it ended up on *The New York Times* best-seller list for a couple of years. There's no ignoring that farting makes kids laugh, and Walter—an apologetic-looking dog adopted from the pound—passes gas constantly, no matter what he eats or how hard he tries to hold it! Walter was used as a scapegoat by Uncle Irv, who—if he let one slip—just went and stood near Walter. However, Walter becomes a hero after chasing off would-be burglars with a malodorous explosion. In the sequel, *Walter the Farting Dog: Trouble at the Yard Sale,* Father sells Walter to a man who uses Walter's gas to inflate balloons. He pops them to stun guards during a bank robbery, but Walter escapes to bring justice to the perpetrator.

The rabbit in *Bunnicula* (Howe & Howe) appears to have very strange abilities. In a story that mixes animal fantasy with the supernatural, Chester the household cat has trouble convincing Harold the dog that the rabbit is really a vampire. Bunnicula is a vegetarian vampire who—from his locked cage—mysteriously gets vegetables from the refrigerator and sucks them dry and colorless. In an equally funny sequel, *Howliday Inn,* the family goes on vacation. Bunnicula is left with a neighbor, but Chester and Harold are boarded for a week at Chateau Bow-Wow. Cautious Chester is certain a werewolf is responsible for the eerie howling and the mysterious disappearance of other boarders. In the next book, *The Celery Stalks at Midnight,* Chester and Harold follow a trail of white vegetables after Bunnicula disappears from his cage. Thinking the pale vegetables will become "veggie vampires" after Bunnicula sucks out their juices, they follow with a box of toothpicks for spearing the veggies through their hearts before they can harm others.

Farm Animals. Farm animals in animal fantasy stories are often pigs. Wilbur in *Charlotte's Web* (White) lives on a farm and communicates with the other animals: the comical geese, the wise old sheep, and the disgusting rat Templeton.

Like Wilbur, Daggie Dogfoot in *Pigs Might Fly* (King-Smith) is a runt pig who is unwanted by the farmer. However, Daggie learns to swim and is quite helpful when the farm is flooded. King-Smith's story of another remarkable pig, *Babe: The Gallant Pig*, introduces readers to an unusual pig who was raised by a sheepdog. Using his gracious manners and polite communication, Babe is able to command a herd of sheep, and he becomes a champion sheepherder. The author's many years of farming experience helped him write these humorous fantasies with very realistic settings and situations.

Robert Munsch's *Pigs* is purely humorous. When a farm girl lets a herd of pigs loose, they wreak havoc on her house and the school, not to mention what they do on the principal's shoe. After commandeering a school bus, the pigs drive themselves home.

Minnie and Moo Go to the Moon (Cazet) is a hilarious story about two daring cows who watch the farmer and figure out how to drive his tractor. They even remember to say the magic words when it does not start: "YOU CHEESY PIECE OF JUNK! YOU BROKEN-DOWN, NO-GOOD, RUSTY BUCKET OF BOLTS!" (p. 18). In another hilarious book in this series, *Minnie and Moo and the Potato from Planet X,* the two cows talk about the alien that has just crash-landed in their pasture: " 'See,' said Moo. 'There's the tractor salesman.' 'Moo,' whispered Minnie, 'how many salesmen have green hair, wires in their ears, and bumpy red skin?' 'There's that kid who works in the coffee shop,' said Moo" (pp. 10–11).

In *Click, Clack, Moo: Cows That Type* (Cronin), Farmer Brown's cows find an old typewriter in the barn, and they start making demands. When he does not give them the electric blankets they requested, the cows and chickens go on strike and will not give him any milk or eggs. The duck mediates.

Mice.   Fantasy stories with mice characters are numerous. This is interesting, because mice are decidedly less popular with humans than dogs, cats, birds, and horses. However, the diminutive and vulnerable qualities of mice are attractive to children, who view themselves similarly. Though juvenile novels are uncommon in animal fantasy, several good ones are available with mice characters.

The Tale of Despereaux (Dicamillo) relates the adventures of Despereaux Tilling, a small mouse who reads stories about knights and loves music. He falls in love with a human princess and gets sentenced to death for communicating with humans. Other fully developed characters that have their own story line in this book include the bumbling servant girl Miggery Sow, who longs to be a princess, and the scheming rat Roscuro, who is determined to bring them all to ruin.

Mrs. Frisby and the Rats of NIMH (O'Brien) is a most unusual story in that it combines animal fantasy with science fiction. A group of field rats at the labs of the National Institute of Mental Health (NIMH) has been subjected to experiments that make them highly intelligent. After teaching themselves to read, they find a way to escape. Because of her late husband's bravery, the rats agree to move Mrs. Frisby and her family away from the vegetable garden to safer ground where farmer Fitzgibbon will not plow. However, she must first sprinkle sleeping powder in the food of Mr. Fitzgibbon's house cat.

Beverly Cleary's series on Ralph the Mouse started with *The Mouse and the Motorcycle*. Ralph is a young, impetuous, and adventuresome mouse who lives inside the walls on the second floor of the Mountain View Inn. He becomes enchanted with a young boy's toy motorcycle, which he can ride once he learns how to make the right noise. When the boy, Keith, becomes very ill, Ralph faces danger to find an aspirin tablet to ease his fever. Keith gives him the motorcycle in return. Equally loved are the two books that followed—*Runaway Ralph* and *Ralph S. Mouse*.

In Dick King-Smith's book, the mice characters live in buildings. In the imaginative *Three Terrible Trins*, three young mice living in an old farmhouse learn to play a ball game with the farmer's glass eye. *The Cricket in Times Square* (Selden) has a fast-talking Broadway mouse named Tucker as a central character. He and his sidekick, streetwise Harry the Cat, meet up with a Connecticut country cricket, Chester, who accidentally got transported to the Forty-Second Street subway station in New York via a picnic basket. Chester is taken in by Mario, the son of the kindly Bellinis who run the subway-station newsstand where the three animal friends hang out. Chester's melodious chirping brings attention, and much-needed business, to the Bellinis' newsstand.

Wild Animals. Jan Brett's *Armadillo Rodeo* is a wild tale about a young armadillo who wanders away from his mother and siblings. Thinking a young cowgirl's shiny boot is a bright red armadillo, the nearsighted critter tracks her to a rodeo, where he becomes an unwanted participant. Another story by Brett, *The Umbrella,* is set in the Costa Rican cloud forest, where young Carlos goes for a walk to spot jungle animals. He drops his banana-leaf umbrella to climb a fig tree for a better look, and several animals—from a baby tapir to a hummingbird—climb in, but they all tumble out before Carlos spots them.

In *Don't Let the Pigeon Drive the Bus!* by Mo Willems, a bus driver takes a break from his route, and he asks the reader to look after his vehicle. The pigeon appears and pleads and begs to be allowed to drive the bus. When he can't, he throws a wild temper tantrum!

Diary of a Worm by Doreen Cronin is a humorous day-by-day account of a young worm as he discovers that there are some very good things as well as some bad things about being a worm. For example, he never has to take a bath, but then he can never play the hokey pokey either.

A most intriguing and beautifully constructed book, Dugald Steer's *Dr. Ernest Drake's Dragonology* is an encyclopedic treatment of dragons purportedly written by the famous dragonologist, Dr. Drake. It covers every aspect of dragons, including the different species, natural history, common habitats, typical behaviors, and development of a dragon embryo. On every two-page spread is a foldout, envelope, flap, or cut-out. The cut-outs contain samples of items like dragon skin and dragon dust.

Equally charming is Tomie dePaola's saga of *Bill and Pete*. Bill (a young crocodile) and Pete (his bird friend who picks Bill's teeth clean) have a crazy adventure escaping from The Bad Guy who captures crocodiles and takes them to Cairo to become suitcases. The rear nude picture of The Bad Guy hightailing it out of town gets a lot of laughs.

H. A. Rey created an enduring character in 1941 with his first book about the little monkey, *Curious George*. The man with the big yellow hat captures George in Africa and takes him home on a ship to America. Though George does not talk, he is able to understand speech. He can also do anything humans can (though he always bungles it), such as using the telephone and accidentally calling the fire department. Other adventures include falling overboard, breaking out of jail, and flying over the city with balloons. In the books that follow, George's curiosity continues to get him in trouble. The fast adventure and slapstick humor of this series have made George a favorite for successive generations.

Paleowolf, like Curious George, is able to understand human speech but is not able to speak himself. In *The First Dog* (Brett), when a young wolf and a cave boy in Paleolithic times each face hunger and danger on their journey, they decide to join forces and help each other.

Another character who gets in trouble despite his best intentions is Paddington in *A Bear Called Paddington* (Bond). The Brown family finds a bear wandering about the Paddington train station in London, where he has arrived from darkest Peru. They take him home to be part of their family, and things are never quite the same. Though Paddington desires to help out, he bungles everything—and makes it worse by trying to hide his mistakes.

In his inimitable style, Shel Silverstein created another charming children's book with a profound message for readers of all ages to ponder in *Lafcadio, The Lion Who Shot Back*. While all the other lions in the jungle are fleeing from the hunters, Lafcadio finds one and eats him, keeping the fascinating gun. After a great deal of practice, Lafcadio becomes the greatest shooter in the jungle and is offered a job as a sharpshooter in a circus. As he becomes famous and very rich, he also becomes more like a man. At one time he could sign six autographs at once, using all four paws, his tail, and his teeth.

> But after a while of course he would sign only one at a time with his right front paw because that was more like a man and less like a lion and Lafcadio was becoming more and more like a man all the time. For instance, he stood on his back paws and he learned to sit at the table with his left hand in his lap and his elbows off the table. . . . And he kept his tail curled up and seldom let it hang down except when he forgot himself or he had a little too much buttermilk to drink.

Lafcadio learns to play golf, paint pictures, work out with weights, and many other things that rich and important people do. Eventually he becomes bored and desires something new and exciting, so the circus owner takes him on a hunting trip to Africa. There he is confronted by an old lion who reminds Lafcadio that he is a lion and should be eating the hunters. The hunters tell him he is a man, and he should be shooting the lions. Lafcadio, who is now neither lion nor man, drops his gun and walks away from both.

Type III: Talking Animals in Natural Habitats

The animals in **Type III animal fantasy** stories do not wear clothing or live in houses, and humans are not present. These animals live in natural-type habitats and display many of their animal traits. However, they are able to talk to animals of all species, and they portray human emotions and thoughts.

Eric Carle. Eric Carle is a master of creating unforgettable characters. His illustrations are collages made from transparent tissue papers, which he lightly streaks with paint. His style is so distinctive that you can easily recognize one of his books just by looking at the cover. I have come to expect the unexpected from Carle's books. In *The Very Hungry Caterpillar*, readers will see holes in the varied-size pages where the caterpillar has eaten through. *The Grouchy Ladybug* contains progressively wider pages as the ladybug tries to pick fights with progressively larger animals. The final animal, the whale, is eight pages long and has a movable paper tail that children can flip back and forth, showing how it slaps the ladybug back to land. *The Very Busy*

Spider provides enjoyable tactile experiences as children trace parts of the illustrations embossed on each page: the spider, her web, and the unwary fly that will be the spider's supper.

The Very Quiet Cricket was Eric Carle's first book to use an embedded microchip. A little cricket tries to answer the various animals that greet him, but he is unable to chirp when he rubs his wings. Finally, when he meets a she-cricket and the last page is turned, a chirping sound is heard! Equally enchanting is *The Very Lonely Firefly*, in which a newly hatched firefly is seeking others of his kind. He is attracted to a variety of lights, such as a light bulb and a candle, but at the end he finally finds other fireflies. When the reader turns the last page, eight little fireflies blink on and off via tiny light bulbs powered by a built-in replaceable battery. In *The Very Clumsy Click Beetle*, a small beetle falls on his back but is unable to click and snap back to his feet like the other beetles. Readers will hear an unusual clicking sound that emanates from a fiber-optic microchip with a light sensor powered by a built-in replaceable battery.

In Eric Carle's *Mister Seahorse,* Mrs. Seahorse carefully lays her eggs on Mr. Seahorse's belly, and he conveys them around in his pouch until they hatch. As he happily carries his brood, he meets other male fish who similarly bear the burden of prenatal care such as the tilapia, the nursery fish, and the bullhead catfish. In a number of scenes, Mr. Seahorse swims past camouflaged marine creatures, such as a trumpet fish who is hidden in the reeds. These hidden creatures are revealed when readers turn the colorful overlaying acetate pages.

Leo Lionni. *Inch by Inch* is Leo Lionni's story of a clever inchworm that stays alive by showing the birds how useful he can be in measuring things like bird legs and tail feathers. However, when the nightingale commands him to measure her song (or she will eat him), he inches his way out of sight as she sings. Equally charming is Lionni's book *Frederick,* the story of a mouse that gathers sun rays, colors, and words while the other mice gather food to store for the winter. Frederick's stores are as important as the food when winter comes. In *An Extraordinary Egg,* Jessica the frog finds an egg and brings it home to her two friends, who tell her it is a chicken egg. A few days later, when a baby alligator pops out, the three frogs call him Chicken, although he swims better than they. In *Swimmy,* Lionni uses beautiful seascapes as backdrops for the clever story of how one little fish devises a plan to camouflage himself and his new school of friends.

Janell Cannon. Janell Cannon's book *Stellaluna* was a smash hit. Stellaluna, an adorable baby bat, is parted from her mother during an owl attack. Fortuitously, she ends up in a bird nest. Mama bird accepts Stellaluna but insists that she act like her three baby birds. Stellaluna tries to be like the birds, but the birds want to be like her, and they all hang upside down from the nest. After several adventures, Stellaluna is reunited with her mother. In *Verdi,* a baby green tree python is the protagonist. Verdi loves his bright yellow skin with bold black stripes, and he never wants to turn green like the boring older snakes. In his fast-moving lifestyle, Verdi zips around the rain forest, taking risks. Eventually he injures himself when he discovers he cannot fly from the top of a tree. Using a tree limb as a body splint, Verdi's family helps him recover, and he settles into a more appropriate lifestyle, though not without fun. Cannon's masterpieces include *Crickwing*, the tale of a cockroach with a crooked wing who goes to battle with the ants, and *Pinduli*, the tale of a big-eared hyena who is tired of being picked on by other creatures of the African Savanna.

Erin Hunter. Erin Hunter has authored an expansive series of novels about feral cats, titled Warriors. In the first book, *Into the Wild*, readers learn that for generations, four clans of wild cats have shared the forest according to the laws laid down by their ancestors. Suddenly, the peace among the clans is broken. ShadowClan has banished WindClan from the area, and now they are threatening RiverClan and ThunderClan by insisting on hunting rights within their territories. However, prey is becoming scarce. When one cat kills another, the warrior code is broken, and the ThunderClan believes they are in grave danger. The menacing ShadowClan grows stronger, and more warrior cats die. Then an ordinary young kittypet (house cat) named Rusty goes looking for adventure and stumbles into the ThunderClan's territory. Rusty decides to join the clan, and his bright orange hair and courage earn him the name Firepaw and a place as an apprentice warrior. The next two books in the series are *Fire and Ice* and *Forest of Secrets*.

Kathryn Lasky. In *The Capture*, the first novel in a fifteen-book series called Guardians of Ga'Hoole, a baby barn owl named Soren is pushed from his nest by his nasty older brother. Soren is picked up from the forest floor by mysterious owls and taken to St. Aegolius Academy for Orphaned Owls, where he is held captive. He quickly makes friends with Gylvie, an elf owl, who informs him that the school is actually a training camp where owlets are being brainwashed and groomed for some nefarious plan of the leader. The two friends comfort themselves by retelling the bedtime tales of their parents: legends about the Guardians of Ga'Hoole, knightly owls who would rise each night into the blackness and perform noble deeds. The legends of Ga'Hoole help them to survive, and they are able to escape. When they cannot find their parents, they set off to find Ga'Hoole, where the rest of the series is set. The next two titles in the series are *The Journey* and *The Rescue*.

Type IV: Realistic Animals with Human Thinking Ability

Type IV animal fantasy is set in the real world, so all the animal characters live in appropriate habitats, such as meadows, barnyards, jungles, and stables. They have all the natural habits common to their species, which may include an instinctive fear of humans. Their knowledge of human ways is limited to what they can observe and comprehend. Usually they are able to communicate, but only with animals of the same species—never with people. In Type IV the ability to communicate human-type thoughts (sometimes with human-type speech) is the only element of fantasy. In other words, the setting and characters are very realistic, but the narrator has access to the minds of the animals and lets the readers know what the animals think, feel, and say. The author tells the story through the animals' point of view and, in so doing, assigns some human emotions to the animal characters.

Type IV is a very small subcategory, because it requires that the author engage in painstaking research and keen observation to represent accurately the cultures and habitats of animals, especially animals that live in the wild. The classic example is *Black Beauty* (Sewell), told as the first-person narrative of a horse who reveals his emotions and thoughts to the reader in human language. An equally loved classic is Jack London's *The Call of the Wild*, told from the point of view of Buck, a dog who was stolen and sold as an Alaskan sled dog. The readability level of these two classics is beyond the reach of most elementary children, but they may enjoy listening to the books.

Dogs. Plots in Type IV animal fantasy often show animals in conflict of some kind, usually with nature, as in *The Incredible Journey* (Burnford). Three loyal pets, a young Labrador retriever, a wise old bull terrier, and an adventurous Siamese cat, run away and trek through the Canadian wilderness in search of the family they love. Knowing only that the way home lies to the west, they travel steadfastly. Though they face starvation, exposure, and wild forest animals, they finally make their way home after traveling more than 250 miles. Meindert DeJong's *Hurry Home, Candy* is the story of a small dog that experiences a sad but heroic search for a home and someone to love him. Also by DeJong, *Along Came a Dog* tells of a stray dog that earns a home for himself by protecting a little red hen and her chicks from a preying hawk.

Wolves. Wolves are the main characters in *Julie's Wolf Pack* by Jean Craighead George, the third book in a trilogy about an Alaskan Inuit girl and the wolf pack she loves. The first two books are realistic fiction told through the girl's point of view, and they are discussed in Chapter 9 (Contemporary Realistic Fiction). *Julie's Wolf Pack,* however, is told from the point of view of the Avalik River wolf pack, headed by the young new alpha wolf, Kapu. The wolves display all the customary patterns of behavior of the wolf pack's complex culture—so when an outbreak of rabies threatens the wolves of the tundra, their instinct is to flee the humans who seek to save them through inoculation.

Elizabeth Hall's *Child of the Wolves* is the saga of Granite, a young Siberian husky who escapes from his kennel and is lost in the frozen Alaskan forest. He is taken in by Snowdrift, a great white wolf who is grieving the loss of her pups, which were stolen by human breeders. Because Snowdrift is the alpha male's mate, she is able to keep the puppy in the wolf pack, although he is constantly harassed by the other members because he does not know how to hunt and his short legs prevent fast running. Granite slowly adapts to the pack's way of life, and he is finally accepted when he saves Snowdrift, who has been blinded by a hunter's bullet, from falling off a cliff.

A comparison of the various types of animal fantasy is provided in Table 7.1.

TABLE 7.1 Comparison of Animal Fantasy Types

Fantasy Type	Real-World Setting	All-Animal World	Wear Clothing/ Live in Houses	Coexist with Humans	Communicate with Humans	Possess Human-Type Language and Thoughts
Type I Animals replace humans		Yes	Yes			Yes
Type II Animals coexist with humans			Varies	Yes	Varies	Yes
Type III Animals in natural habitats without humans		Yes				Yes
Type IV Animal viewpoint in a realistic world	Yes			Yes		Yes

Summary

Animal fantasy stories have main characters that are anthropomorphic animals that talk, experience emotions, and have the ability to reason like humans. Some of the milestones in the history of animal fantasy include *Black Beauty, The Jungle Book, The Tale of Peter Rabbit, The Call of the Wild, The Wind in the Willows, Bambi, Rudolph the Red-Nosed Reindeer, Make Way for Ducklings, The Poky Little Puppy, Charlotte's Web,* and *The Cat in the Hat.*

There are four main types of animal fantasy: (1) anthropomorphic animals that exist in an all-animal world, (2) anthropomorphic animals that coexist with humans, (3) talking animals that live in natural habitats, and (4) realistic animals that live in their natural habitats but have human thinking ability.

Animal Fantasy Books

Avi. *Poppy.* HarperTrophy, 1995.

Berenstain, Stan, & Jan Berenstain. *The Berenstain Bears and the Spooky Old Tree.* Random House, 1989.

Bond, Michael. *A Bear Called Paddington.* Illus. Peggy Fortnum. Houghton Mifflin, 2001.

Bourgeois, Paulette. *Franklin in the Dark.* Illus. Brenda Clark. Scholastic, 1986.

Brett, Jan. *Armadillo Rodeo.* Puffin, 2004.

Brett, Jan. *The First Dog.* Voyager, 1992.

Brett, Jan. *The Umbrella.* Penguin Putnam, 2004.

Bridwell, Norman. *Clifford the Big Red Dog.* Scholastic, 1987.

Brown, Marc. *Arthur's Eyes.* Little, Brown, 1986.

Brown, Marc. *Arthur's New Puppy.* Little, Brown, 1993.

Brown, Margaret Wise. *Goodnight Moon.* Illus. Clement Hurd. Harper Festival, 2001.

Burnford, Sheila. *The Incredible Journey.* Illus. Carl Burger. Laurel Leaf, 1995.

Cannon, Janell. *Crickwing.* Harcourt, 2000.

Cannon, Janell. *Pinduli.* Harcourt, 2004.

Cannon, Janell. *Stellaluna.* Harcourt Brace, 1997.

Cannon, Janell. *Verdi.* Harcourt, 1997.

Capucilli, Alyssa Satin. *Biscuit.* Illus. Pat Schories. HarperTrophy, 1997.

Carle, Eric. *Mister Seahorse.* Philomel, 2004.

Carle, Eric. *The Grouchy Ladybug.* HarperTrophy, 1996.

Carle, Eric. *The Very Busy Spider.* Philomel, 1995.

Carle, Eric. *The Very Clumsy Click Beetle.* Philomel, 1999.

Carle, Eric. *The Very Hungry Caterpillar.* Philomel, 1994.

Carle, Eric. *The Very Lonely Firefly.* Philomel, 1999.

Carle, Eric. *The Very Quiet Cricket.* Grosset & Dunlap, 1997.

Cazet, Denys. *Minnie and Moo and the Potato from Planet X.* HarperCollins, 2002.

Cazet, Denys. *Minnie and Moo Go to the Moon.* DK, 1998.

Cherry, Lynn. *The Dragon and the Unicorn.* Harcourt, 1995.

Cleary, Beverly. *Ralph S. Mouse.* HarperTrophy, 1993.

Cleary, Beverly. *Runaway Ralph.* HarperTrophy, 1991.

Cleary, Beverly. *The Mouse and the Motorcycle.* HarperTrophy, 1990.

Cronin, Doreen. *Click, Clack, Moo: Cows That Type.* Illus. Betsy Lewin. Simon & Schuster, 2000.

Cronin, Doreen. *Diary of a Worm.* Illus. Harry Bliss. HarperCollins, 2003.

DeJong, Meindert. *Along Came a Dog.* HarperCollins, 1980.

DeJong, Meindert. *Hurry Home, Candy.* Illus. Maurice Sendak. Harper, 1953.

dePaola, Tomie. *Bill and Pete.* Putnam, 1996.

Dicamillo, Kate. *Tale of Despereaux.* Candlewick, 2003.

Falconer, Ian. *Olivia.* Atheneum, 2000.

George, Jean Craighead. *Julie's Wolf Pack.* Illus. Wendell Minor. HarperTrophy, 1997.

Grahame, Kenneth. *The Wind in the Willows*. Illus. Ernest H. Shepard. Aladdin, 1908/1989.

Hall, Elizabeth. *Child of the Wolves*. Yearling, 1996.

Henkes, Kevin. *Kitten's First Full Moon*. HarperCollins, 2004.

Henkes, Kevin. *Owen*. Greenwillow, 1993.

Hoban, Russell. *Bedtime for Frances*. Illus. Garth Williams. HarperTrophy, 1996.

Howe, Deborah, & James Howe. *Bunnicula: A Rabbit-Tale of Mystery*. Illus. Alan Daniel. Aladdin, 1996.

Howe, James. *Howliday Inn*. Illus. Lynn Munsinger. Aladdin, 2001.

Howe, James. *The Celery Stalks at Midnight*. Illus. Leslie Morrill. Aladdin, 2002.

Hunter, Erin. *Fire and Ice*. HarperCollins, 2003.

Hunter, Erin. *Forest of Secrets*. HarperCollins, 2003.

Hunter, Erin. *Into the Wild*. HarperCollins, 2003.

Jacques, Brian. *Redwall*. Illus. Gary Chalk. Ace, 1998.

King-Smith, Dick. *Babe: The Gallant Pig*. Illus. Mary Rayner. Yearling, 1995.

King-Smith, Dick. *Pigs Might Fly*. Illus. Mary Rayner. Puffin, 1990.

King-Smith, Dick. *Three Terrible Trins*. Illus. Mark Teague. Yearling, 1994.

Kipling, Rudyard. *The Jungle Book*. Illus. Christian Broutin. Viking, 1894/1996.

Kotzwinkle, William, & Glenn Murray. *Walter the Farting Dog*. Illus. Audrey Colman. North Atlantic, 2001.

Kotzwinkle, William, & Glenn Murray. *Walter the Farting Dog: Trouble at the Yard Sale*. Illus. Audrey Colman. Dutton, 2004.

Lasky, Kathryn. *The Capture*. Scholastic, 2003.

Lasky, Kathryn. *The Journey*. Scholastic, 2003.

Lasky, Kathryn. *The Rescue*. Scholastic, 2004.

Le Guin, Ursula K. *Catwings*. Illus. S. D. Schindler. Orchard, 2003.

Lionni, Leo. *An Extraordinary Egg*. Dragonfly, 1998.

Lionni, Leo. *Frederick*. Dragonfly, 1987.

Lionni, Leo. *Inch by Inch*. HarperTrophy, 1995.

Lionni, Leo. *Swimmy*. Dragonfly, 1992.

Lobel, Arnold. *Fables*. HarperTrophy, 1980.

Lobel, Arnold. *Frog and Toad Are Friends*. HarperTrophy, 1979.

London, Jack. *The Call of the Wild*. Aladdin, 1903/2003.

Lowrey, Janette Sebring. *The Poky Little Puppy*. Illus. Gustaf Tenggren. Golden Books, 1942.

May, Robert L. *Rudolph the Red-Nosed Reindeer*. Illus. Michael Emberley. Applewood, 1939/1994.

McBratney, Sam. *Guess How Much I Love You*. Illus. Anita Jeram. Candlewick, 1996.

McCloskey, Robert. *Make Way for Ducklings*. Viking, 1941.

Meddaugh, Susan. *Martha Speaks*. Houghton Mifflin, 1996.

Minarik, Else Holmelund. *Little Bear*. Illus. Maurice Sendak. HarperCollins, 1992.

Munsch, Robert. *Pigs*. Illus. Michael Martchenko. Annick Press, 1989.

O'Brien, Robert. *Mrs. Frisby and the Rats of NIMH*. Aladdin, 1986.

Potter, Beatrix. *The Tale of Benjamin Bunny*. Frederick Warne, 1904/2002.

Potter, Beatrix. *The Tale of Peter Rabbit*. Frederick Warne, 1902/2002.

Rathmann, Peggy. *Officer Buckle and Gloria*. Putnam, 1995.

Rey, H. A. *Curious George*. Houghton Mifflin, 1941/1973.

Rylant, Cynthia. *Henry and Mudge and the Happy Cat*. Illus. Suçie Stevenson. Aladdin, 1996.

Salten, Felix. *Bambi: A Life in the Woods*. Illus. Barbara Cooney. Pocket Books, 1999.

Selden, George. *The Cricket in Times Square*. Illus. Garth Williams. Farrar, Straus & Giroux, 1957.

Seuss, Dr. *Fox in Socks*. Random House, 1965.

Seuss, Dr. *Green Eggs and Ham*. Random House, 1960.

Seuss, Dr. *How the Grinch Stole Christmas!* Random House, 1957.

Seuss, Dr. *One Fish, Two Fish, Red Fish, Blue Fish*. Random House, 1960

Seuss, Dr. *The Cat in the Hat*. Random House, 1957.

Sewell, Anna. *Black Beauty*. Illus. Lucy Kemp-Welch. Grammercy, 1877/2002.

Silverstein, Shel. *Lafcadio, the Lion Who Shot Back*. HarperCollins, 1963.

Soto, Gary. *Chato's Kitchen*. Illus. Susan Guevara. Putnam & Grosset, 1995.

Steer, Dugald A. *Dr. Ernest Drake's Dragonology*. Candlewick, 2003.

Steig, William. *Doctor De Soto*. Farrar, Straus & Giroux, 1990.

Steig, William. *Shrek!* Farrar, Straus & Giroux, 1990.

Steig, William. *Sylvester and the Magic Pebble*. Simon & Schuster, 1988.

Steig, William. *The Amazing Bone*. Farrar, Straus & Giroux, 1993.

Steig, William. *Zeke Pippin*. HarperCollins, 1997.

Turner, Deborah, & Rhonda McHugh. *How Willy Got His Wheels*. Doral, 1998.

White, E. B. *Charlotte's Web*. Illus. Garth Williams. HarperCollins, 1952/1999.

Willems, Mo. *Don't Let the Pigeon Drive the Bus!* Disney, 2003.

Zion, Gene. *Harry the Dirty Dog*. Illus. Margaret Bloy Graham. HarperTrophy, 1976.

Multicultural Literature

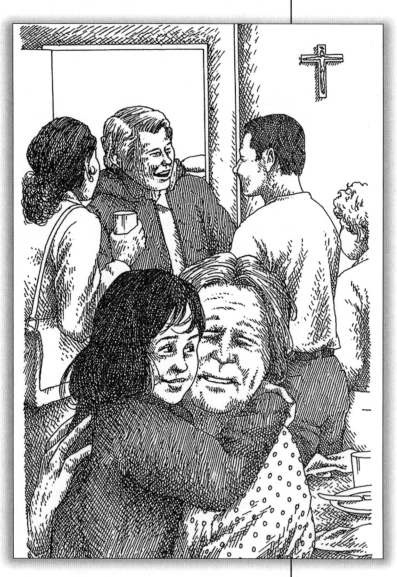

The artist used only pen and black ink to create this illustration.

From *Felita,* written by Nicholasa Mohr and illustrated by Ray Cruz

$\mathcal{L}ibrary\ locations$ **Appears in all genres. Various locations.**

Cross-cultural literature that includes books by and about peoples of *all* cultures

$\mathcal{I}$ remember reading in my elementary school history book about how the United States was made up of people from many nations. The text explained that through intermarriage and assimilation, the different races had been homogenized into what we call Americans. This formulation was called the **melting pot theory.** My textbook even had a cartoon showing people of different races jumping into a huge cooking pot with Uncle Sam stirring them around with a big stick. According to this theory, American people abandoned all their distinguishing cultural characteristics in favor of the dominant white culture.

The melting pot theory permeated the U.S. educational system for many decades. However, there were some serious flaws in this theory. First, not all races melted equally. It is true that people of European descent melted into the dominant pattern; even many Native Americans melted as they were assimilated through intermarriage to European Americans. However, some racial groups, such as people from Africa and Asia, did not homogenize so quickly, and because of this, they were easy targets for discrimination and other forms of racism. A second major flaw to the melting pot theory was that not all people wanted to melt. Some people desired to keep their heritage intact—to preserve the language, religion, customs, and traditions of their parents.

A newer description of the U.S. populace is the **salad bowl theory.** When you toss a salad, all the different vegetables are mixed together. However, they do not melt into some huge veggie fondue; rather, each different vegetable in the bowl retains its own shape, texture, color, and flavor. Each component of the salad makes a contribution, and together they make one great dish.

However, Louise Bell Shuman (personal communication, May 22, 2002) provides an even better analogy.

> I think of American culture as more of a stew. In a stew, ingredients retain their own delicious identities, but each ingredient lends flavor and texture to the whole pot. . . . Each ethnic group that immigrates to American brings its own culture. The cultures do not remain separate. For example, salsa outsold ketchup last year in American grocery stores. Americans are not using less ketchup; they are using more salsa. This demonstrates the extent to which Latino cultures have permeated mainstream American and traditional American meals. The salad bowl theory implies that the cultures are kept separate but are drizzled with some sort of unifying American salad dressing. I do not think this is a very good representation of what is actually happening. My stew has an American broth, which is a blend of all the flavors of the individual ingredients.

Having a variety of vegetables and other ingredients makes both salad and stew more appealing and nutritious. In a like manner, including books about a variety of cultures makes a literature program more interesting and complete. A greater variety also makes it more likely that all children will have access to literature that represents their various backgrounds. Children need to see themselves reflected in stories with positive role models; this tends to increase their self-esteem and pride in their heritage. Also, greater variety in the literature program exposes all readers to the various minority cultures in our country. Vicarious experiences—and ensuing emotional involvement with minority characters in well-written books—have the potential to correct misconceptions about people who are different from the reader. This may help children avoid developing prejudiced attitudes.

One general definition of **culture** is the totality of socially transmitted behavior patterns, arts, beliefs, institutions, and all other products of human work and thought. More specifically, the word *culture* can designate these patterns, traits, and products as the expression of a particular community or population. Cultures can be determined by national origin, ethnic origin, primary language, religion, geographic region, and other factors.

In past decades, children's textbooks and literature focused on white middle-class Americans, but over the years, books have moved toward greater cultural diversity. Keep in mind, however, that European American is also a culture—currently the majority culture in the United States.

Good multicultural books increase readers' appreciation of persons of various cultures and help them overcome stereotypical views. **Stereotyping** is assigning a fixed image or some fixed characteristics to *all* the members of a particular cultural group. This gross overgeneralizing rests on an assumption that something identifiable is shared by *all* members of a group. Groups can be stereotyped based on gender, ethnicity, religion, culture, socioeconomic status, dialect, and other factors. Stereotyping in literature can occur when the author does not develop characters into well-rounded people who have both positive and negative attributes (Houston, 2004).

It is easy to detect and understand how harmful stereotyping can be when the traits are negative, but stereotyping can also be damaging when it relates to positive qualities. Racism in stories can often be subtle, masquerading as a virtue. For example, Native Americans are often stereotyped as being close to nature, but could this be a covert way of saying they are less civilized? Other positive stereotypes have to do with intelligence, athletic ability, and artistic talent. Imagine how children in the cultural group feel when they themselves do not exhibit their group's purported universal traits. To determine whether a multicultural book contains "positive stereotyping," ask yourself questions such as, Are all African American characters portrayed as athletic? Are all Jewish characters portrayed as wealthy? Are all Asian American characters portrayed as highly intelligent? Are all Latino characters portrayed as gregarious? Are all Native American characters portrayed as animal lovers?

Evaluating Multicultural Literature

In evaluating **multicultural literature**, first and foremost ask yourself if it is quality literature supported by a worthy theme. If it is, the following questions will further guide you.

- Is there any cultural stereotyping suggesting that all members of a specific cultural group share the same socioeconomic status, personality traits, facial features, and the like?
- Are the characters multidimensional individuals with lives rooted in their culture?
- Is the language authentic to the background and social environment in which the story takes place?
- Is the portrayal of the culture authentic, reflecting its values and beliefs?
- Are all factual details accurate?
- Are all cultural details authentic and naturally integrated within the story using a modern perspective?
- Are there cultural omissions or distortions that may create misconceptions?
- Are the central issues of the culture realistically portrayed and explored in depth?
- Does the book help children value their own heritage or understand people with other backgrounds?

Categories of Multicultural Books

Bishop (1992) identified three categories of multicultural books, which she classified according to the degree of the cultural understandings they afford readers. Books representative of each of these categories are important in a balanced literature program.

Culturally Neutral Books

Culturally neutral books contain some characters from minority groups or have multicultural faces portrayed within illustrations. However, there is no culturally specific information included. These books' topics contain no real cultural content; nonetheless, their inclusive nature reveals that the authors, illustrators, and publishers value diversity in children's books. These books serve to increase readers' exposure and awareness of diversity. Also, minority children can identify with these books when they belong to the same cultural group as the characters.

Examples of culturally neutral books include *The Egypt Game* (Snyder), in which four children living in a neighborhood play together. Two of the children, a girl and her younger brother, are African American. Were it not for the illustrations and the author's mention of these children's ethnicity early in the book, the reader would not know that the ethnicities of the four children are not the same.

To say a book is culturally neutral does not imply it cannot be useful in helping children understand and accept diversity. For example, *What a Wonderful World* (Weiss & Thiele), a book inspired by a Louis Armstrong song, depicts children of all major U.S. ethnic groups in the illustrations, though no cultural information is given in the text. However, the theme of the book is that the world is wonderful because of its diversity, and no particulars are necessary to understand the value of that message.

Michael Hays took culturally neutral books to a new high when he illustrated *Abiyoyo* (Seeger). The story is set in a small village during past times, much like a folktale. The main characters, a magician and his son, are of African descent. However, all the other characters in the book are from various nations and world religions. For example, the first page shows the main characters with a blond-headed man, a Hindu woman, and an Oriental woman talking around a kitchen table. The illustrations showing all the townspeople together are intriguing for children to look at and try to determine which nationality or religious culture each character represents.

Culturally Generic Books

Culturally generic books focus on characters representing a specific cultural group, but there is little culturally specific information included. The characters in these books are depicted as ordinary people existing within the larger American culture, and the book's themes and plots are generically American. One such book is *Shortcut* by Donald Crews. The cover of this book depicts seven African American siblings, four boys and three girls, standing on a railroad track. In the story the children take a shortcut home by following the tracks. When they hear a freight train approaching, they jump off the tracks onto the steep slopes full of briers. If you did not know that the author was African American and that he wrote about his childhood experiences, only the color of the characters' skin would indicate their ethnicity. Nothing in the children's environment, clothing, or actions reveals they are African Americans. Only on the last page is there a word in the African American vernacular: The book's narrator mentions Bigmama, a common name for grandmother in the African American culture.

Another culturally generic book is *The Lost Lake* by Allen Say, who is Japanese American. The book's characters are young Luke and his father. The illustrations indicate that the father and son are Asian Americans. However, what the narrator relates about the characters is common to many people within the larger American culture. The parents are divorced; the boy becomes bored in the summer; the father and son enjoy a hiking and camping trip; and they eat foods such as salami, dried apricots, beef stroganoff, and coffee on their trip.

Again, it would be a mistake to shrug off culturally generic books with the reaction that "There was nothing to be learned about this culture." On the contrary, these books help readers see past cultural stereotypes and to learn that people of all cultures have many things in common. "Readers see themselves and others as sharing universal experiences" (Temple, Martinez, Yokota, & Naylor, 1998). And indeed, we are all more alike than different.

Culturally Specific Books

Culturally specific books incorporate details that help define the characters as members of a particular cultural group. In these books ethnicity is more than a superficial mask. There is a mix of distinguishing characteristics of the minority cultural group—together with elements that are characteristic of the larger cultural group to which all Americans belong. Specifics of the minority culture include such things as family relationships, religion, language, names, values, attitudes, and interactions with others both inside and outside the cultural group. Illustrations in culturally specific books also portray many cultural details.

In *Felita* by Nicholasa Mohr, the author weaves some of her childhood experiences growing up Puerto Rican in New York City's barrio. The reader learns something about family relationships, language, cuisine, and customs among New York Puerto Ricans (called *Nuyoricans* by Puerto Ricans on the island). The reader also shares the hurt and humiliation young Felita experiences when her family moves to a "better neighborhood," where she receives cruel treatment from the neighborhood children who are not Latinos.

Likewise, readers of *To Walk the Sky Path* (Naylor) will learn about a Mikasuki Seminole family living in a *chickee* on a mangrove island in the Florida Everglades. Billie is the only member of his extended family to go to school and learn how to read, and he sometimes feels he is caught between two worlds. Throughout the book he contrasts the Seminole culture with the mainstream culture of his school and the friends he has made there.

The themes of culturally specific books are usually different from those of other books in realistic fiction. One recurring theme is the mingling of two cultures when a family immigrates to the United States—or when, like the young Seminole boy in *To Walk the Sky Path*, a character enters another culture. Obviously, the differences between the two cultures are pointed out, but frequently this is done in a positive manner, and the similarities among peoples are stressed.

Culturally specific books may contain quite serious themes, such as the persistence of racial oppression in the United States in both historical and contemporary times. Among other themes are the oppression that drove people to leave their homelands and emigrate to the United States, the prejudice the newcomers face in this country, and the challenge of learning to appreciate one's cultural heritage while adjusting to American life. Not all themes involve a major hardship, as in stories about characters who are awakening to the meaning and importance of their heritage.

The folktales from all over the world presented in Chapter 5 demonstrate that traditional literature was the original multicultural literature. Books introduced in this chapter represent a variety of genres, because multicultural literature is published in all genres. I encourage you to move beyond traditional literature in your multicultural readings. I believe that realistic fiction most authentically portrays culture, affording children the greatest opportunities to learn about diversity.

Misrepresentation of Culture

I caution readers to scrutinize older books, especially historical fiction and biography, to determine if they contain **white bias,** a subtle form of racism implying that the mainstream way of life is inherently superior. An example of a biased theme is that minority people achieve success only after giving up the distinctive values and lifestyles of their culture to adopt those of the mainstream society.

However, older books are not the only ones guilty of misrepresentation. One contemporary book that has received much criticism because of its historical and cultural inauthenticity is *Brother Eagle, Sister Sky: A Message from Chief Seattle* by

Susan Jeffers. The book states that the words within are a speech given by the Suquamish Chief Seattle (more accurately, Chief Seathl) at the signing of a peace treaty in 1854. However, Chief Seattle gave the speech in his native language, and a poet named Henry Smith, some thirty-three years after he took notes on the speech, actually wrote the words that appear in the book. Smith published his version of the speech in the October 29, 1887, edition of the *Seattle Sunday Star,* and historians believe that only the gist of the published speech represents Chief Seattle's actual remarks; the poetic language was all Smith's (Museum of History and Industry, 1990).

Not only is the text inauthentic, but Jeffers's illustrations in *Brother Eagle, Sister Sky* also depict cultural aspects of the Plains Indians, not the Suquamish people of the Northwest as the book leads the readers to believe (Scott, 1995). However, the most disturbing aspect of Jeffers's illustrations is that the Native Americans are depicted as ghostlike images—not in a physical form, as is the case with the white family illustrated at the end of the book. It gives the message to readers that Native people are gone, and only their ghosts are left. Native author Cynthia Leitich Smith (2000) says it is shocking "to sit down with a group of second-graders, who tell me that Indians shot arrows, went on warpaths, and lived sometime before the turn of the eighteenth century. From my point of view, just their use of the past tense is chilling" (p. 29).

It is difficult to determine the authenticity of a book that deals with a culture outside one's own. Usually, if the authors and illustrators are of the same cultural group as their characters, this supports their credentials. You can often find short biographical pieces about authors and illustrators on the flaps of hardcover book jackets or in the last few pages of paperback books.

Earlier I introduced the term *white bias.* Native American author David Matheson gives an excellent example in the introduction to his first novel, *Red Thunder* (2002). He tells how outsiders, using typical research methods and interviews, could never tell the story of his people. He expounds how such methods produce analyses of certain aspects of Native life, "but always with a perspective tilted toward some personal experience or dominant views . . . [which] causes misperceptions and even a hidden, coded judgment reflected in their writings" (p. ii). This perception is what I call *white bias,* and it is common in books written about—but not written by—members of a minority group.

My college students sometimes ask me, Are Caucasian/white authors the only ones that write with a bias toward their culture? The answer, of course, is *no.* Authors of all cultures are prone to write with a bias toward their own cultures. Most people with healthy self-concepts are ethnocentric: They believe that their own culture is superior. This is what makes it difficult for people to write about cultures other than their own. In 2007, the Cooperative Children's Book Center (CCBC) analyzed 3,000 newly published books and found that only 6 percent were written by people identified as African, African American, Asian/Pacific Islander, Asian/Pacific Island American, American Indian, or Latino (2007). People from the mainstream culture wrote 94 percent of the books, meaning that white bias is likely very prevalent in children's literature today.

There were fewer books about American Indians than any other ethnic group tracked by the CCBC, as demonstrated by the following figures: 227 books about

African Americans, 124 books about Asian/Pacific Americans, 101 books about Latinos, and only 50 books about American Indians. Latinos are now the largest U.S. minority group, and because the fastest expanding group of Latinos is school-age children, you might expect there would be many books about and for these children; however, in 2007 only 3 percent of the 3,000 newly published books analyzed by the CCBC were about Latinos. Latina author Alma Flor Ada (2003) writes,

> The merit of a book is determined not by the heritage of the author or illustrator, but by their intention, knowledge, sensitivity, responsibility, and artistry. It can be aided by the support given by the editor and publisher. Yet there is an inner look to a culture that is not easily acquired and requires long contact with people of the culture and its environment. The deep experiences of a people can seldom be told authentically from the outside. . . . It is inappropriate when someone from outside the culture looks at the insufficient number of titles about Latinos as an opportunity to publish, and too much of this is happening. It is painful to see that while Latino authors have great difficulty finding supportive publishers, non-Latinos author many of the books about Latinos, particularly the most lavish books. (pp. 36–37)

Native poet and artist John Trudell (King, 2003), who is the former national chairperson of the American Indian Movement, speaks more bluntly. He states, "The non-Native people can't tell our story. They can [only] tell their version of our story" (p. C5). Yet, Marantz and Marantz (2000) revealed the other side of the issue when they wrote regarding authors of international literature, "We can only speculate about whether an author writing in another language translated into English can give a more 'authentic' account than an American writer who has done careful research" (p. 13).

📖 Issues in Multicultural Literature

Who Should Write Books about Minorities?   One of the most controversial topics in children's literature today is whether an author outside a specific culture's social group can write authentically about that group. I raise the following questions:

- Do books by authors outside a particular culture provide a distorted view because of the authors' own cultural biases?
- If authors adequately research another culture, and they write with sensitivity, can they authentically write about that culture?
- Do authors who share the culture of their characters describe them more authentically and convincingly?
- If we purchase books about minorities that are written by authors in the mainstream culture (and call those books multicultural literature), are we making it more difficult for talented minority authors to publish their books?

Select one of these questions to agree or disagree with, and support your opinion with evidence from at least three children's books.

Children from ethnic minority groups need authentic literature that gives them a deeper understanding of their own culture. Leavell, Hatcher, Battle, and Ramos-Michail (2002) explain why this could be critical in minority children's education:

> As educators, we know how important it is to connect instruction to our students' prior knowledge. Sometimes, this link can be difficult to achieve when the student is not from the mainstream school culture. . . . Encountering something that is familiar may also increase . . . students' motivation to participate in learning. (p. 210)

In order to enhance children's cultural pride and a greater appreciation for their minority heritage, the books we share should be void of ethnic stereotyping. Although experienced readers are usually able to recognize obvious stereotypes, how do readers detect the more subtle stereotyping? Checking a book's copyright date may be helpful because older books were not scrutinized for stereotyping, whereas many publishers make some effort to do so today. However, most cases of cultural inauthenticity are revealed only when we read literary critiques and talk to other people who are knowledgeable in multicultural literature.

The authors and illustrators in each of this chapter's cultural sections are members of the designated cultural group. My aim is not to devalue the work of those who write authentic books about characters of another culture; rather, it is to highlight the achievements of sometimes overlooked minority authors and illustrators. Additionally, books written and illustrated by minorities—as well as books about minorities written by people outside the cultural group—are included in each of the genre chapters.

Children's Books Cited in Preceding Sections

Crews, Donald. *Shortcut*. HarperTrophy, 1996.
Jeffers, Susan. *Brother Eagle, Sister Sky*. Dial, 1991.
Mohr, Nicholasa. *Felita*. Puffin, 1999.
Naylor, Phyllis Reynolds. *To Walk the Sky Path*. Sagebrush, 1999.
Say, Allen. *The Lost Lake*. Houghton Mifflin, 1992.
Seeger, Pete. *Abiyoyo*. Illus. Michael Hays. Aladdin, 2005.
Snyder, Zilpha Keatley. *The Egypt Game*. Bantam, 1999.
Weiss, George David, & Bob Thiele. *What a Wonderful World*. Illus. Ashley Bryan. Atheneum, 1995.

Latino Literature

by Alcione N. Ostorga

Latinos represent a variety of rich cultures that draw from traditions of more than twenty nations, including Hispanics (an ethnicity developed through the intermarriage of Spanish and indigenous peoples), who lived in this country for centuries before the U.S. boundaries were finalized. *Latinos* (or the feminine *Latinas*) comprise the descendants of native Hispanic people in the United States, residents of Latin America, and U.S. immigrants (and their descendants) from Latin America—which encompasses all countries in the Western Hemisphere south of the United States: the Caribbean Islands, Mexico, Central America, and South America.

It is important to note that **Latino** is an inclusive term that denotes culture, ethnicity, or nationality—but not language. I was born in Brazil, and my first language is Portuguese. Additionally, many Latinos living in the United States do not speak Spanish, and that is why I point out that language is not a determiner of the Latino culture.

More than half of Latinos living in the United States are of Mexican descent. According to a recent report by the U.S. Census Bureau (2008) based on the American Community Survey Report of 2006, Hispanics are the fastest growing minority group in the United States with an estimate of 40.5 million residents (64% of whom say they are of Mexican origin). Hispanics represent more than 14 percent of the total population and are considered the largest minority group in the United States.

Unfortunately, teachers who work with Mexican American students have found the quality of books for these children to be uneven. The topics were not always culturally relevant, the use of Spanish was frequently inauthentic for Mexican Americans, the syntax of some books was awkward, and the few books they were able to locate were frequently at inappropriate reading levels (Mathis, 2001). Rosemary Brosnan (2000), children's book editor at HarperCollins, believes that a major problem is that bookstore chains underestimate the Latino market and do not carry many books that would appeal to them.

Children from all ethnic and racial groups greatly benefit when they are able to identify with the characters in a book or recognize familiar elements of their culture in what they read and discuss in school. Conversely, the lack of familiar cultural and social elements in children's literature can diminish children's sense of connection to the context of the classroom. In addition to helping children develop a strong cultural identity, books that portray familiar cultural elements can help children connect to the text. Freeman, Freeman, and Freeman (2003) explain how children are more successful in learning to read, and therefore more willing to read, when they make personal connections to books' content. These educators emphasized the critical importance of culturally relevant books for developing proficiency in reading and language.

Undoubtedly, Latino children would benefit from seeing their culture reflected in the books they read, but children (and adults) of all heritages will also benefit greatly. Among the positive effects of multiethnic literature are the expansion of the reader's global awareness, the decrease of negative stereotyping, and the opportunity for learning about the emotional ties and respect that exist within other cultures (Hadaway & Florez, 1990). Therefore, teachers need to infuse multicultural literature in all areas of the curriculum.

Moreover, Latina researcher Marguerite Radencich (1985) contends that books that describe the conflicts and adjustments of immigration and of learning a new language and culture can also be beneficial—not only to the students involved in this transition, but also to their peers who may begin to understand what an individual must endure in adapting to a new country, language, and culture. Children's author and poet Pat Mora (2000) says that "through literature we can cross the borders in our life—religious, age, ethnic, gender—and build community" (p. 56). Mora suggests an interesting response to a book such as *Friends from the Other Side* (Anzaldúa): Have students write about the first immigrants in their families, exploring what they may have experienced. Mora also invites all educators to participate in the annual Dia de los Niños/Dia de los Libros (Children's Day/Book Day) celebrated each April 30th (see page 200 for a website with details).

Before sharing any books with Latino characters—especially those written by non-Latinos—educators and parents should review them critically to ensure they will not perpetuate negative stereotypes or wrongly portray cultural aspects. Avoid books with stereotypic Latino characters who are only depicted as uneducated and impoverished farm workers. Also to be avoided are books whose Latino characters are stereotyped as barefooted, wearing serapes and wide-brimmed hats, and snoozing under a cactus or riding a burro. Latino characters should play active, rather than passive or submissive roles. Murray and Velasquez (1999) suggest using literature with well-developed plots that remain strong when stripped of their cultural elements. Additionally, scrutinize books to ensure they do not depict Latinos as a singular group with no acknowledgment of the vast differences in ethnicities, classes, cultures, religions, and languages. One way to select good literature is to find award-winning books; there are several awards for exemplary Latino children's books (see Latino awards websites list beginning on page 199).

The National Consortium of Latin American Studies Programs sponsors the Américas Award. It is given annually to a children's or young adult book published in the United States that authentically and engagingly presents the experiences of Latinos in Latin America, the Caribbean, or the United States. By including all the Americas, the award reaches beyond both geographic borders and international boundaries, focusing on cultural heritages within the whole hemisphere.

The Tomás Rivera Mexican American Children's Book Award is given annually to the author or illustrator of the most distinguished book for children and young adults that authentically reflects the lives and experiences of Mexican Americans in the southwestern region of the United States. The portrayal of Mexican Americans must be accurate and engaging, avoid stereotypes, and reflect rich characterization. The award is named after Tomás Rivera, the first Mexican American selected as Distinguished Alumnus at Southwest Texas State University, who is remembered as a fine poet, educator, and chancellor of the University of California, Riverside.

The Pura Belpré Award is given biennially to the author and illustrator who best portray, affirm, and celebrate the Latino cultural experience in an outstanding work of literature for children and youth. Unlike the Américas and Tomás Rivera awards, the Pura Belpré Award honors only authors and illustrators of Latino heritage. Pura Belpré was the New York Public Library system's first Latina librarian, as well as a storyteller and an author. She enriched the lives of Puerto Rican children in the United States through her pioneering work of preserving and disseminating Puerto Rican folklore.

Another good selection method is to talk about Latino books with people who are of the same Latino cultural group, keeping in mind that the culture is quite diverse with varied customs. Freeman (2000) suggests involving the classroom children in the process of selection. Ask them if the characters seem realistic, if the events in the story have happened to them (or are likely to happen in their lives), and if the characters speak similarly to them and their family members. Latino children's parents are also valuable resources for evaluating literature. Moreover, they can enrich the literature experience by sharing their own stories or adding information about customs in connection with the books.

Equally critical is the language in which the story is written. Young children whose native language is not English benefit most if they are read to from books written in their first language, which should be used in all initial literacy instruction. Children's competence in their first language will affect how they develop competence in English. Spanish is the native language for most Latinos, so if the teacher does not have a bilingual aide, ask a parent or other student to volunteer to read books written in Spanish. If no one is available, bilingual text can be used—one side of the page has text in English, and the facing page is in Spanish.

Books that make interlingual use of Spanish (i.e., interweave Spanish words and phrases within the English text) are also excellent because language is used to convey more than information; it also conveys feelings and cultural elements that may lose part of their essence when translated. When artfully written, this style can be easily understood by readers/listeners through context and illustrations.

Contemporary Latino authors and illustrators provide realistic and positive portrayals that help Latino readers feel admired and respected and also allow non-Latinos to appreciate these cultures. The following bibliography is a small sample of culturally relevant and authentic Latino children's literature. Titles appearing in both English and Spanish have bilingual text, and many feature the interlingual use of Spanish and English.

Books by Latino Authors and Illustrators

Ada, Alma Flor. *I Love Saturdays and Domingos.* Illus. Elivia Savadier. Aladdin, 2004. This book illustrates a girl's bilingual and bicultural world as she spends Saturdays with her paternal grandparents who speak English and Sundays with her maternal *abuelitos* who are Mexican American and speak with her in Spanish.

Alarcón, Francisco X. *From the Bellybutton of the Moon and Other Summer Poems/Del Ombligo de la Luna y Otros Poemas de Verano.* Illus. Maya Christina González. Children's Book Press, 2005. This collection of poems was inspired by the poet's memories of childhood summers spent in Mexico. The title comes from the meaning of the word *Mexico,* which his grandmother translates as "bellybutton of the moon" in the Aztec language.

Anzaldúa, Gloria. *Friends from the Other Side/Amigos del Otro Lado.* Illus. Consuelo Mendez. Children's Book Press, 1995. Having crossed the Rio Grande into Texas with his mother in search of a new life, Joaquín receives help and friendship from Prietita, a brave young Mexican American girl.

Cisneros, Sandra. *House on Mango Street.* McGraw-Hill, 2000. This collection of vignettes provides glimpses of life in a Latino neighborhood in Chicago as seen through the eyes of

Esperanza. The reading is relatively easy, but some of the stories' themes may be more appropriate for older children.

Delacre, Lulu. *Rafi and Rosi.* HarperCollins, 2004. This joyful tale is about two curious young *coquí* (Puerto Rican tree frogs). Rafi entertains his sister with his magic tricks, but when his pet hermit crab runs away, Rosi is the one who finds it before it sheds its shell.

 Garza, Carmen Lomas. *In My Family/En Mi Familia.* Children's Book Press, 2000. This bilingual book tells the story of the author's childhood in a small Texas community. Her memories are shared in both the enchanting text and the colorful illustrations that portray life in a Mexican American neighborhood.

Garza, Carmen Lomas. *Magic Windows: Cut-Paper Art and Stories/Ventanas Mágicas: Papel Picado y Relatos.* Children's Book Press, 2003. Garza tells stories of herself, her family, her Mexican American community, and her Aztec ancestors through the intricate and beautiful art of *papel picado* (cut-paper).

Deedy, Carmen Agra. *Martina the Beautiful Cockroach.* Illus. Michael Austin. Peachtree, 2007. This is a lively and humorous Cuban folktale about a beautiful cockroach's search for a husband retold by an award-winning storyteller.

Mora, Pat. *A Library for Juana: The World of Sor Juana Ines.* Knopf, 2002. This beautifully illustrated picture book is the biography of a Mexican child, Sor Juana Ines de la Cruz, who grew up to become an internationally renowned scholar and poet of the seventeenth century.

Morales, Yuyi. *Just a Minute: A Trickster Tale and Counting Book.* Chronicle, 2003. This colorful traditional tale relates how Grandma Beetle tricked death (in the form of Señor Calavera), by convincing him to let her finish preparations for her birthday. It is also a humorous counting book that can be used with activities related to the *Día de los Muertos* (Day of the Dead), which is the day after Halloween.

Perez, Amanda Irma. *My Very Own Room/Mi Propio Cuartito.* Illus. Maya Christina Gonzalez. Children's Book Press, 2008. This tale of an 8-year-old Mexican American girl's longing to have her own room (and how her family helps her get it) is a humorous portrait of life in a big family, inspired by the author's own childhood memories.

Rosa-Casanova, Sylvia. *Mama Provi and the Pot of Rice.* Illus. Robert Roth. Aladdin, 2001. When Lucy comes down with chicken pox, her grandmother—who lives on the first floor of a tall apartment building—decides to take a pot of tasty arroz con pollo to her on the eighth floor. As she goes up the seven flights of stairs, she meets a neighbor on every floor, each of whom contributes a special dish, and Mama Provi arrives with a tremendous feast for Lucy.

Ryan, Pam Munoz. *Becoming Naomi León.* Scholastic, 2005. Fifth grader Naomi has been living in California when her long-gone mother reappears to claim her and take her to Las Vegas. As she struggles to find who she really is, she runs away to Mexico with her great-grandmother and brother in search of her missing father and her history. Her journey is one of self-discovery.

 Soto, Gary. *Snapshots from the Wedding.* Illus. Stephanie García. Putnam, 1998. This account of a Mexican American wedding is seen through the eyes of Maya, the flower girl. Illustrations feature photographs of innovative three-dimensional scenes, using clay figures and other assorted objects.

Stevens, Jan Romero. *Carlos and the Squash Plant/Carlos y la Planta de Calabaza.* Illus. Jeanne Arnold. Northland Publishing, 2004. After ignoring his mother's warning about what will happen if he does not bathe after working on his family's farm in New Mexico, Carlos wakes up one morning and finds a squash growing out of his ear!

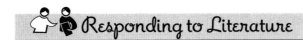
Responding to Literature

Learning about Cultures through Holidays

by Melissa DuBrowa

Discussions focusing on holiday celebrations help students appreciate the lives and rituals of diverse people and can serve to move them beyond an egocentric mindset to valuing the lifestyles of other cultures. January is a good time to discover New Year's celebrations, including the Chinese New Year. *The Dancing Dragon* and *Dragon Dance* are colorful books about the Chinese New Year. *Ten Mice for Tet* is a unique counting book describing the traditions of the Vietnamese New Year.

Inviting parents or community members into the classroom to explain holidays can stimulate discussions. For example, they might read a book to start a discussion on Latino celebrations, such as *Estrella's Quinceanera, Cinco de Mayo,* and *Piñata.*

I also recommend *Hurray for Today,* which shows readers the origin of common holiday rituals from New Year's through Kwanzaa. *Fasting and Dates* explains a Muslim family's celebration of the holy month of Ramadan. Suggestions follow:

Alegria, Mali. *Estrella's Quinceanera.* Simon & Schuster, 2007.
Berger, Gilda. *Celebrate! Stories of the Jewish Holidays.* Scholastic, 2002.
Deitz Shea, Pegi, & Cynthia Weill. *Ten Mice for Tet.* Chronicle Books, 2003.
dePaola, Tomie. *Patrick, Patron Saint of Ireland.* Holiday House, 1992.
dePaola, Tomie. *The Lady of Guadalupe.* Holiday House, 1980.
Emberley, Rebecca. *Piñata.* Little, Brown, 2004.
Holub, Joan, Bernard Huang, & Regan Holub. *Dragon Dance.* Penguin, 2003.
Hoyt-Goldsmith, Diane, & Lawrence Migdale. *Cinco de Mayo.* Holiday House, 2008.
Sabuda, Robert. *Saint Valentine.* Aladdin, 1999.
Vaughan, Marcia, & Stanley W. Foon. *The Dancing Dragon.* Mondo, 1996.
Wade, Mary Dodson, & Nanci R. Vargus. *Cinco de Mayo.* Children's Press, 2003.
Worth, Bonnie, & Aristides Ruiz. *Hurray for Today!* Random House, 2004.
Zucker, Jonny, & Jan Barger Cohen. *Fasting and Dates.* Barron's Educational, 2004.

African American Literature

by Sabrina A. Brinson

African Americans are U.S. citizens who are the descendants of the various indigenous people of the African continent. They have always had a pervasive and important influence on American life. However, as an African American child, I read few books with positive African American characters. In graduate school I looked for what I had missed as a child, searching school and public libraries for children's books with African American characters published before the civil rights movement.

The only books I found published before 1962 were in a large university library, including books like *Little Black Sambo* (Bannerman, 1945) and *The Pickaninny Twins* (Perkins, 1931). My analyses of these books were a sad commentary. The African American characters were typically depicted as a "no 'count natural thief; a flunky happily steppin' and fetchin'; a pitied simpleton; a gargantuan bully; and (ever popular) a poor, helpless, inept underdog scared senseless, a shakin' and a quakin' in his shoes" (Brinson, 1997, pp. 8–9). In addition, many of these characters rattled off unintelligible dialect. Accentuating the text were characters illustrated in charcoal black with out-of-control hair and absurdly overexaggerated features that seemed to leap off the pages!

Although he was not African American, Ezra Jack Keats broke ground when he published *The Snowy Day* in 1962. It is an account of a young African American boy's day of play in the snow in an urban neighborhood. Many other suitable books have followed from individuals both within and outside the cultural group. In my analysis of post–civil rights books, I found a vast difference. Derogatory portrayals of stereotyped African American characters, for the most part, have been eradicated in children's literature. They have been supplanted with portrayals of constructive African Americans using suitable vernacular. Illustrations of characters adorning the text are kaleidoscopic images, representative of the true variations of skin color, hair, and features. The protagonists represent cognizant, autonomous, versatile, productive characters—who incidentally are African American (Brinson, 1997).

To highlight the contributions of African American authors and illustrators, the Coretta Scott King Award is given annually to an African American author and illustrator for their outstanding inspirational and educational books published in the previous year. This award was designed to commemorate the life and foster the ideas of Dr. Martin Luther King Jr., and to honor his widow, Coretta Scott King, for her courage and determination in continuing the fight for racial equity and universal peace. The Ethnic and Multicultural Information Exchange Round Table of the American Library Association sponsors the award.

One of my favorite African American authors is Carole Boston Weatherford; her books include *Juneteenth Jamboree, Sink or Swim: African American Lifesavers of the Outer Banks, The Sound that Jazz Makes Alive* (winner of the Carter G. Woodson Award), *Remember the Bridge: Poems of a People* (winner of the North Carolina Juvenile Literature Award), *Freedom on the Menu: The Greensboro Sit-In* (winner of the North Carolina Juvenile Literature Award), *Dear Mr. Rosenwald, Jesse Owens: Fastest Man Alive, Birmingham, 1963* (winner of the Lee Bennett Hopkins Poetry Award), and *Moses: When Harriet Tubman Led Her People to Freedom*. The latter is my favorite—a soul-stirring profile of Harriet Tubman's strength, ingenuity, and spirituality during her own daring escape, followed by her brave determination during multiple returns to the South to guide numerous others to freedom.

A favorite award-winning illustrator is Kadir Nelson, whose compelling illustrations have accentuated numerous books such as *Salt in His Shoes: Michael Jordan in Pursuit of a Dream, Just the Two of Us, The Village That Vanished,*

Ellington Was Not a Street (winner of the Coretta Scott King Award for illustrations), *Hewitt Anderson's Great Big Life, Moses: When Harriet Tubman Led Her People to Freedom* (winner of the Coretta Scott King Award for illustrations, and a Caldecott Honor Book), and *Henry's Freedom Box: A True Story from the Underground Railroad*. Nelson's talents are further illuminated in books he has both written and illustrated, such as *We Are the Ship: The Story of Negro League Baseball*. In this book, multiple facets of the Negro Leagues are profiled, including the exceptional talents of little-known athletes, victories and defeats on and off the field, dreadful working conditions, and racial discrimination that players conquered to fulfill their dreams to play baseball.

Children who are exposed to alluring stories remember and cherish them through adulthood. Often they model main characters or act out central themes (Brinson, 1997). Stories play an important role in all cultures, weaving words into lessons for daily life (Lilly & Green, 2004). As a result, culturally specific books and illustrations can cultivate positive self-attributes and high ethnic identity in African American children, while also helping children of all backgrounds see African Americans in a positive light. When African American characters are portrayed in a variety of settings and involved in a variety of activities, it accentuates the differences that make us unique, while strengthening the common bonds that join us together. Therefore, as society moves toward greater celebration of our diverse population, it is beneficial to promote African American authors' and illustrators' contributions in children's literature. Multicultural literature is designed to give *all* children a SIP: Strong self-worth, Information/inspiration, and Pleasure (Brinson, 2002).

Children's Books Cited in This Section

Grifaloni, Ann. *The Village That Vanished*. Illus. Kadir Nelson. Dial, 2002.

Jordan, Deloris, & Roslyn M. Jordan. *Salt in His Shoes: Michael Jordan in Pursuit of a Dream*. Illus. Kadir Nelson. Scholastic, 2000.

Keats, Ezra Jack. *The Snowy Day*. Puffin, 1962.

Levine, Ellen. *Henry's Freedom Box: A True Story from the Underground Railroad*. Illus. Kadir Nelson. Scholastic, 2007.

Nelson, Kadir. *We Are the Ship: The Story of Negro League Baseball*. Jump-at-the-Sun, 2008.

Nolen, Jerdine. *Hewitt Anderson's Great Big Life*. Illus. Kadir Nelson. Simon & Schuster, 2005.

Shange, Ntozake. *Ellington Was Not a Street*. Illus. Kadir Nelson. Simon & Schuster, 2004.

Smith, Will. *Just the Two of Us*. Illus. Kadir Nelson. Scholastic, 2001.

Weatherford, Carole Boston. *Birmingham, 1963*. Wordsong, 2007.

Weatherford, Carole Boston. *Dear Mr. Rosenwald*. Illus. R. Gregory Christie. Scholastic, 2006.

Weatherford, Carole Boston. *Freedom on the Menu: The Greensboro Sit-Ins*. Illus. Jerome LaGarrique. Dial, 2004.

Weatherford, Carole Boston. *Jesse Owens: Fastest Man Alive*. Illus. Eric Valasquez. Walker Books, 2006.

Weatherford, Carole Boston. *Juneteenth Jamboree.* Illus. Yvonne Buchanan. Lee & Low Books, 1995.

Weatherford, Carole Boston. *Moses: When Harriet Tubman Led Her People to Freedom.* Illus. Kadir Nelson. Jump-at-the-Sun, 2006.

Weatherford, Carole Boston. *Remember the Bridge: Poems of a People.* Philomel, 2002.

Weatherford, Carole Boston. *Sink or Swim: African American Lifesavers of the Outer Banks.* Coastal Carolina Press, 1999.

Weatherford, Carole Boston. *The Sound That Jazz Makes.* Illus. Eric Valasquez. Walker Books, 2000.

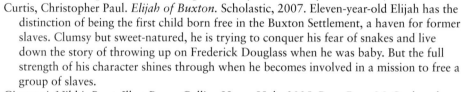

Other Recommended Books by African American Authors and Illustrators

Barnwell, Ysaye M. *No Mirrors in My Nana's House.* Illus. Synthia Saint James. Harcourt, 2005. Nana really knows best, especially when she nurtures her granddaughter's self-esteem. They don't have many material possessions, but she has the privilege of finding life's true treasures—love and beauty—when she views the world through Nana's eyes (includes a compact disc of the song version by Sweet Honey in the Rock).

 Curtis, Christopher Paul. *Elijah of Buxton.* Scholastic, 2007. Eleven-year-old Elijah has the distinction of being the first child born free in the Buxton Settlement, a haven for former slaves. Clumsy but sweet-natured, he is trying to conquer his fear of snakes and live down the story of throwing up on Frederick Douglass when he was baby. But the full strength of his character shines through when he becomes involved in a mission to free a group of slaves.

Giovanni, Nikki. *Rosa.* Illus. Bryan Collier. Henry Holt, 2005. Born Rosa McCauley, she was educated at a teachers college, married to a barber, employed as a seamstress, and served as secretary of the Montgomery branch of the National Association for the Advancement of Colored People. She was dedicated to making a lasting difference, and this led to Rosa McCauley Parks being named the Mother of the Civil Rights Movement.

Green, Michelle Y. *A Strong Right Arm: The Story of Mamie "Peanut" Johnson.* Illus. Kadir Nelson. Dial, 2002. "Batter up"; meet Mamie "Peanut" Johnson, a pitcher with the Negro Leagues' Indianapolis Clowns from 1953 to 1955. The story is enhanced with her own reflections, as well as photographs of Johnson and other players in the league, including Satchel Paige, who taught her how to throw a curveball.

Greenfield, Eloise. *How They Got Over: African Americans and the Call to Sea.* Illus. Jan Spivey Gilchrist. Amistad, 2002. This collection of biographies profiles African Americans who answered the call through a variety of intriguing avenues, from a shipbuilder–businessman during the American Revolution to the first woman and African American to hold the highest-ranking position in the National Oceanic and Atmospheric Administration Commissioned Corps.

Grimes, Nikki. *Talkin' about Bessie: The Story of Aviator Elizabeth Coleman.* Illus. E. B. Lewis. Scholastic, 2002. Coleman's life is uniquely told through family, friends, and admirers. Against all odds, Elizabeth "Bessie" Coleman became the first licensed female pilot of African descent, and later she became known as one of the most daring pilots to perform death-defying stunts in air shows.

Haskins, James. *Delivering Justice: W. W. Law and the Fight for Civil Rights*. Illus. Benny Andrews. Candlewick, 2005. Wesley Wallace Law's allegiance to global enrichment is evident in his enthusiasm as a lifelong mail carrier and in his activism in the community. He helped individuals register to vote, trained protesters in nonviolent methods, and led the Great Savannah Boycott that resulted in equality for all of the city's citizens.

Lyons, Kelly Starling. *One Million Men and Me*. Illus. Peter Ambush. Just Us Books, 2007. On October 16, 1995, African American males of all ages and backgrounds who were devoted to their families and to productivity in their communities gathered at the Lincoln Memorial in Washington, D.C. This account, told through the eyes of a little girl in attendance with her father, sheds additional light on the largest event of its kind in U.S. history.

Medearis, Angela Shelf. *The Freedom Riddle*. Illus. John Ward. School Specialty Publishing, 2003. Based on a true story, this book features a man who literally riddled his way to freedom. Jim, the slave foreman, gets the owner of the plantation to agree to his freedom if he can stump him with a riddle. Time, patience, and brain power are triumphant when the owner can't guess the answer to the riddle cleverly composed by Jim, who gains his freedom.

Rabun, Miles, & William Rabun. *My Grandma's Backyard*. Illus. Tony Moore. Xlibris, 2007. This book is the fabulous result of the young authors' active engagement in learning in a familiar, nurturing environment. A running water pond adorned with frogs and turtles and a wide deck used to recite poems are some of the highlights the brothers include that show how much summer fun they have in their grandmother's backyard.

Shange, Ntozake. *Ellington Was Not a Street*. Illus. Kadir Nelson. Simon & Schuster, 2004. Gifted poet Ntozake Shange reflects on her childhood home and the close group of "world changers" such as Duke Ellington, Kwame Nkrumah, Sonny Tilghman, and W. E. B. Du Bois who often visited her home.

Taylor, Gaylia. *George Crum and the Saratoga Chip*. Illus. Frank Morrison. Lee & Low, 2006. Growing up, George coped with prejudice against his Native and African American heritage. As a young chef in Saratoga Springs his response to a complaint that the french fries were too thick resulted in the creation of the potato chip. The fame of George's tasty sensation spread quickly and he opened his own restaurant where everyone was treated equally.

Thomas, Joyce Carol. *The Gospel Cinderella*. Illus. David Diaz. Amistad, 2004. Enter Queen Rhythm in this musical version of a familiar tale. She is looking for a successor with a special voice because her daughter was swept away in a basket. Hmm . . . With the voice of an angel, a heart of gold, and a hair wreath of pink, orange, and yellow, could she possibly be the Gospel Cinderella?

Woodson, Jacqueline. *Show Way*. Illus. Hudson Talbott. Putnam, 2005. The women in Soonie's family make "Show Ways," quilts with secret meanings that are maps to freedom. Hope of a better place is also passed down through each generation on a South Carolina plantation until it materializes into freedom and land ownership.

Weatherford, Carole Boston. *Champions on the Bench: The Cannon Street YMCA All-Stars*. Illus. Leonard Jenkins. Dial, 2006. In 1955 the Cannon Street team couldn't wait to compete in the state tournament. But all of the state's 61 white teams refuse to play the African American team, eliminating their chance at the Little League World Series. The story is based on true events and includes photographs of the Cannon Street team then and as adults.

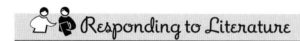

Responding to Literature

Focus Units A **focus unit** is a series of literary experiences that integrate the language arts. It is organized around a central focus such as an author, theme, genre, topic, or literary element. Authors make great subjects for focus units. The following basic procedures illustrate the process.

- With your children, select the author to study.
- Collect multiple titles and copies of books by the author from school and public libraries and personal collections.
- Arrange an attractive bulletin board and display with the books, the author's picture, and any information received from the publisher or the Internet. (Most authors have their own websites where you can download pictures and interesting information.)
- Encourage children to browse through the display and to add books and information they have located.
- Ask the children to collaborate on selecting the book you will read to the class, and form literature circles to discuss the other available books.
- Keep a dialogue response journal with each child, and ask the children to make regular entries about the book you are reading aloud as well as about the book their literature circle is reading. Respond to the journal entries on a regular basis. (Journals can also be kept between pairs of children.)
- Engage the children in meaningful projects that extend the literary experiences, such as grand conversations, webbing, story mapping, and dramatizing.

Asian American Literature

by Ni Chang

Quality children's books can help children understand the lives of Asian Americans, cultivate children's appreciation of other cultures, and transmit societal values, beliefs, ways of life, and patterns of thinking (Lo & Lee, 1993; Lu, 1998). **Asian Americans** are often grouped by the geographical origin of their ancestors:

- East Asian (Chinese, Japanese, and Korean)
- Southeast Asian (Thai, Cambodian, and Vietnamese)
- South Asian (Indian and Pakistani)
- Pacific Islanders (indigenous peoples of Hawaii, Guam, Samoa, and islands in the Pacific Ocean)

I belong to the first group, having been born in China, but many Asian Americans have been in the United States for generations, especially Chinese and Japanese Americans. Others—such as the Hmong, Vietnamese, Laotians, and Cambodians—are relatively new immigrants (U.S. Census Bureau, 2003).

Within the racial group of Asians, there are twenty-nine distinct ethnic categories (Atkinson, Morten, & Sue, 1993). Considerable social and economic variations exist between recent Asian immigrants and people in Asian American communities that have been in the United States for generations (Kim & Yeh, 2002).

In the past, Asian Americans have been negatively stereotyped as inscrutable, submissive, humble, passive, quiet, obedient, physically short with slanted eyes, wearing eyeglasses, and possessing limited communication skills (Kim & Yeh, 2002; Lane, 2004; Lee, 1994; Lee, 1996; Siu, 1996).

Conversely, Asian Americans have been positively stereotyped as intelligent, diligent, persistent, and hardworking—and indeed, many of them have achieved success because of such traits. However, contemporary literature and popular media that only portray Asian Americans with positive stereotypes—as geniuses, overachievers, and math or science whizzes (Lee, 1996)—are also guilty of stereotying. Achievement ordinarily is reaped through one's diligence and persistent mind, which do not belong to any one race. Positive stereotyping can be detrimental to children because it overgeneralizes and misleads. It camouflages individuality and eschews real problems. For example, Lee (1996) reported that Ming, a Cambodian student, was failing his classes. Yet he refused to seek help for his academic difficulties because he believed that admitting academic failure would cause his family to lose face. Trying to stay within the boundaries of the stereotyped Asian child perpetuated his academic problems, and he experienced depression and isolation.

Many other Asian children have various kinds of learning difficulties (Shen & Mo, 1990) and need help to do well in school and to prepare themselves for the labor market. To many new immigrants, the American educational system differs vastly from their own cultures' (Trueba & Cheng, 1993). Understanding this system can be overwhelming or at least challenging (Brand, 1987; Feng, 1994; Trueba & Cheng, 1993). Some Chinese and Korean students experience higher levels of stress because of peer discrimination (called racially insulting names and excluded from activities) than peers who are African American, Latino, and white (Fisher, Wallace, & Fenton, 2000). Other difficulties experienced by Asian American children include attaining support or help from their own parents because they themselves lack knowledge about the U.S. school system or have language barriers, or are even struggling for their immediate survival in a foreign country (Yao, 1988).

The Asian and Pacific Islander population is not homogeneous; it comprises many groups who differ in cultures, customs, languages, religious heritages, ecological adaptations, and ethnic histories. Therefore, it is crucial that books provided for classroom use promote sensitive and accurate portrayals of the various groups. Some appropriate themes include "heritage, battle against racism and discrimination, everyday experiences, urban civilization, friendship and family relationships, growing up" (Hoffman, n.d.).

To assist in selecting appropriate books for children, the Council for Interracial Books for Children (2000) developed criteria for educators and parents to analyze books on Asian Americans. The following criteria should help in selecting culturally authentic children's books about Asian Americans.

- **Reflect the realities and way of life of an Asian American people.** The characters should be depicted as people from a distinct Asian culture whose experiences in the United States have generated new and unique Asian American cultures. The characters should be real people with universal dimensions to whom individuals from other cultural backgrounds can relate. The settings, behavior, speech, clothing, and the like should be depicted accurately for the historical period and cultural context of the story. A story should depict an entire culture rather than merely introduce it as a token (Lo & Lee, 1993).

- **Transcend stereotypes.** Problems should be presented, conceived, and resolved by the Asian American protagonist, rather than by a benefactor from the mainstream culture. Characters should display a full range of human emotions, behaviors, and personality traits. Thus, the reader is able to sense their spirit, individuality, humor, strength, and drive. Characters' occupations should be varied, and their speech should be authentic. Any attempt to demean or ridicule characters due to their race or gender should be avoided.

- **Rectify historical distortions and omissions.** The historical achievements of Asian Americans—such as the Chinese who constructed the transcontinental railroad—should be valued. The internment of more than 110,000 Japanese Americans in camps during World War II should be placed in the historical context of racism, rather than being dismissed as war hysteria.

- **Avoid the model and superminority syndromes.** Characters in the story should be respected on their own terms. Any illustration should preclude indications that Asian Americans gain acceptance and approval only when they exhibit extraordinary qualities, such as excelling in sports and receiving As on their academic work.

- **Reflect an awareness of the changing status of women.** Asian American females should be presented as individuals. Illustrations of females should not be limited to appearing in subservient and passive roles, whereas the males are in leadership and action roles. The achievements of women should be based on their own initiative and intelligence, rather than on their good looks or relationships with male characters.

- **Contain art and photos that accurately reflect racial diversity.** Illustrations should reveal the differences in facial structures between individuals and among groups; Asian Americans do not look the same. For example, there are dissimilarities among Chinese Americans, Filipino Americans, Japanese Americans, and Korean Americans. Faces and skin tones also should be depicted as genuine individuals with distinctive features. Clothing should be appropriate to the activity and occasion, reflecting the historical era (Lo & Lee, 1993). When traditional clothing is called for, it should be appropriate to the culture intended.

Analyze the biographical material on the jacket flap or the back of the book to know what qualifies the author or illustrator to deal with this ethnic group. If the author and illustrator are not Asian or Asian Americans, review their background to see if there is any specific experience or recommendation that qualifies them. The renowned author, Laurence Yep, speaks to the problems that can occur when stories are created by someone whose ethnic background differs from the characters in the book (Baghban, 2000).

> There are so many terrible books written about Chinese Americans by white writers who simply made up whatever they wanted. There is a smaller group of books where an author was conscientious enough to do interviews. Unfortunately, even those authors distorted the data to fit their cultural prejudices and stereotypes. (p. 44)

It is always critical to check the copyright date. Books published before the 1970s are most likely to contain racism and sexism. Therefore, copyright dates can be a clue to how likely the book is to be overtly racist or sexist. Of course, a recent copyright date is no guarantee of a book's relevance or sensitivity because it only signifies the year a book is published. It can take two years or more from the time a manuscript is submitted to the publisher to the time it is actually on the market. Also, sometimes copyright dates tell what year the book was reissued, so look for the original (oldest) copyright date.

Properly selected books can help foster cultural awareness and self-concepts in Asian American children as well as help them with issues of acculturation (Chi, 1993). Authentic multicultural literature allows students in minority groups to read about people from their ancestral backgrounds. They also can assist all children in appreciating Asian American cultures and rejecting the mass media's stereotypical representations (Gerson, 2000; Li, 2000).

The following list annotates authentic stories created by Asian American authors and illustrators. I also suggest you read some of the books honored with the Asian Pacific American Award for Children's and Young Adult Literature by the Asian Pacific American Librarians Association and the Chinese American Librarians Association (see the website list at the end of this chapter).

Chin-Lee, Cynthia (Chinese American). *A Is for Asia.* Illus. Yumi Heo. Orchard, 1997. This alphabet book combines informative text with stylish illustrations to introduce the events, food, animals, crafts, and traditions of many Asian countries.

Choi, Yangsook (Korean American). *The Name Jar.* Dragonfly, 2003. Having just moved from Korea, Unhei (Yoon-Hey) is anxious because no one can pronounce her name. On the first day of school, she announces that she will choose an American name the following week, and her classmates help by filling a jar with names from which she can pick. Did she pick one from the jar?

Hamanaka, Sheila (Japanese American). *All the Colors of the Earth.* Illus. Sheila Hamanaka. HarperCollins, 1999. This book celebrates the colors of children and the colors of love. Poetic text and amazingly light-filled paintings celebrate the earth and its diversity.

Mochizuki, Ken (Japanese American). *Passage to Freedom: The Sugihara Story.* Illus. Dom Lee. Lee & Low, 1997. This is a true story told through the eyes of Hiroki, the son of Sugihara, who was Japanese consul to Lithuania in 1940. Polish Jews fleeing from the Nazis request visas to cross to Japan. Because he is allowed to authorize only a few refugees into Japan, Sugihara appeals three times to his country for permission to issue more, but he is denied. So he secretly issues handwritten visas to thousands of refugees until he and his family are ordered to leave Lithuania.

Na, An (Korean American). *Wait for Me*. Penguin, 2006. Mina, a high school senior, feels obligated to live up to her mother's dream—going to Harvard. She works at her family's dry cleaners and helps to care for her hearing-impaired sister. Then she finds herself caught in lies and secrets after falling in love with a young immigrant worker. She struggles to find a voice of her own.

Namioka, Lensey (Chinese American). *Half and Half*. Delacorte, 2003. Fiona has a Chinese father and Scottish mother. She resembles her father more than her mother. For that reason, she is naturally thought to be interested more in the Chinese culture than the Scottish. Although being biracial had not confused her in the past, she eventually becomes baffled about her identity. Her confusion escalates when both sets of grandparents come to town for folk festivals. Which event is she going to get involved in (both are held at the same time): participating in her grandfather's Scottish dance group or wearing the costume her Chinese grandmother made for her to participate in a talk her father is giving?

Nhuong, Huynh Quang (Vietnamese American). *Water Buffalo Days: Growing Up in Vietnam*. Illus. Jean & Mou-sien Tseng. HarperTrophy, 1999. Nhuong is a young boy growing up in the hills of central Vietnam; his companion is Tank, the family's noble water buffalo. Together, Nhuong and Tank face the dangers of life in the Vietnamese jungle that is their home.

Park, Linda Sue (Korean American). *A Single Shard*. Clarion, 2001. Tree-ear is a 13-year-old orphan living under a bridge in medieval Korea. He longs to learn how to make delicate celadon ceramics after observing Min, a master potter. Min takes Tree-ear on as his helper, and Tree-ear digs and hauls clay and endures Min's irascible temper. Then Tree-ear takes a long solitary journey to Songdo to show Min's work to the royal court. He faithfully continues even after robbers shatter the work, and he has only a single shard to show.

Say, Allen (Japanese American). *Allison*. Houghton Mifflin, 2004. When Allison realizes she does not resemble her American parents, they explain she is adopted from China, and she becomes angry and withdrawn until she finds a stray cat and learns the true meaning of adoption and parental love.

Say, Allen (Japanese American). *Home of the Brave*. Houghton Mifflin, 2002. In dreamlike sequences, a man symbolically confronts the trauma of his family's incarceration in the Japanese internment camps during World War II. This infamous event is made emotionally clear through his meeting a group of children, all with strange name tags pinned to their coats. The man feels the helplessness of the children. He hopes for a time when Americans will be seen as one people—not judged, mistrusted, or segregated because of their individual heritage.

Say, Allen (Japanese American). *Music for Alice*. Houghton Mifflin, 2004. This is the true story of Alice Sumida, whose life is uprooted when World War II breaks out, and she and her young husband are forced to work as farm hands or face life in an internment camp. The book traces her life, while interweaving her continuing love of music and dance, despite the many hardships in her life.

Wong, Janet S. (Chinese–Korean American). *Alex and the Wednesday Chess Club*. McElderry, 2004. Little Alex gives up chess when he loses a game to moldy old Uncle Hooya, but when he gets to third grade, he joins the chess club and becomes obsessed with becoming a champion. Then he finds himself face-to-face with Little Cousin Hooya in the big tournament!

Wong, Janet S. (Chinese–Korean American). *Apple Pie 4th of July*. Illus. Margaret Chodos-Irvine. Harcourt, 2002. A feisty young girl is shocked that her parents are cooking Chinese food to sell in the family store on this all-American holiday. She tries to tell her mother and father how things really are in America as the parade passes by and fireworks light the sky.

Wong, Janet S. (Chinese–Korean American). *The Trip Back Home*. Illus. Bo Jia. Harcourt, 2000. The author recalls a childhood trip with her mother to rural Korea, where they visit her grandparents and aunt in a very traditional household. The daily rhythms of the farming family's way of life are poignantly retold.

Yin, Chris (Chinese American). *Coolies*. Illus. Chris Soentpiet. Philomel, 2001. Shek and Wong are two brothers from Canton, China, who immigrate to America in 1865 and find work as laborers, helping to build the transcontinental railroad from Sacramento to Omaha. Their lives are hard, and they face many dangers during the construction of the railroad.

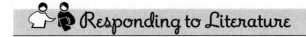 Responding to Literature

Reading Japanese *Manga*

by Suzanne M. Flannery Quinn and Shannon L. Quinn

Manga, the Japanese version of comic books, have a long history in Japan, and they have been popular in their current form for over sixty years. *Manga* are rapidly gaining popularity among preteen and adolescent readers in U.S. and global markets. Young people in the 11- to 21-year-old age range who collect, read, and share *manga* have created a social phenomenon that has sparked a multimillion dollar market worldwide.

Manga are a subgenre of graphic novels, characterized by serialized story lines with dramatic plots and intricate illustrations. Although developed for entertainment, the books are a legitimate form of literature, employing a complex interplay of art and text. Because most *manga* are steeped in Japanese culture and history, readers are building cultural awareness as well as literacy skills (including visual literacy).

Sometimes teachers and parents confuse *manga* with *anime*, which are animated stories based on *manga*. However, *manga* is a print medium, and *anime* (animated) is an electronic medium, which can include video games.

Most *manga* serials are first published in gendered *manga* magazines, such as *Shonen Jump* for boys and *Shojo Beat* for girls. When a series has wide appeal, they are published in a serialized book form approximately 200 pages in length. Typically each story ends with a cliffhanger, creating an incentive for readers to obtain the next book in the series.

Manga are more than simple comic books for children. According to Schodt (1988), they are a literary and social phenomenon with a diversity of style and subject matter, attractive to almost any age group. The text of a *manga* makes use of aesthetic elements, including Japanese style conventions of print, graphic symbols unique to the genre, and literary devices that add texture to the reading experience.

Most *manga* are written according to Japanese conventions of print. They are meant to be read right to left, top to bottom. This is a challenge for people who have never read the genre, but most publishers provide directions for reading. The illustrations are bold and dramatic in multipanel format.

The illustrator relies on visual literacy by making use of graphic symbols as integral components of the storytelling. *Anger veins* appear when a character is exceptionally angry. Veins are composed of four inward curved lines that appear on the face and forehead, and flames might also flare up behind the character. *Sweat drops* can imply annoyance, embarrassment, shock, relief, or confusion, depending on the context. Sweat drops appear on, or float above, the forehead. *Blushing* is depicted by horizontal lines appearing on the cheeks, nose, or whole face, depending on the intensity of the emotion. Blushing indicates embarrassment or strong emotion. *Chibi,* which means small or shrimp, are drawings used to express extreme cuteness or for comic relief. They sometimes take on the form of a kitten or bunny to enhance the effect.

In addition to graphic elements, authors use common literary devices such as flashbacks, soliloquy, climax, and instances of onomatopoeia that are unique to the Japanese language (Ito, 2005).

Many *manga* are designed for teen and adult readers and often contain topics inappropriate for children. Therefore, most publishers provide a rating system on the cover of the books. Only those rated with an *A* (All audiences) or *E* (Everyone) are appropriate for children.

Manga have sparked a cultural phenomenon that involves reading as a social activity, and we highly recommend exploring the following series: *Ultra Maniac* by Wataru Yoshizumi, *Cardcaptor Sakura* by CLAMP, *Kingdom Hearts* by Shiro Amano, *Dragonball Z* by Akira Toriyama, *Yotsuba & !* by Kiyohiko Azuma, *Megaman* by Ryo Takamisaki, and *Kamikaze Kaito Jeanne* by Arina Tanemura.

Read at least one *manga* and tell whether you think it is more like a comic book or a graphic novel.

Native American Literature

For the three previous sections—Latino, African American, and Asian American—I asked a member of each ethnic group to write about her culture's literature. I am writing about Native American literature because my grandfather was Cherokee, and although I was not raised in the culture, I was raised knowing and respecting my heritage. As an adult I have studied about my grandfather's tribe, and in the field of multicultural literature, I have focused on books by and about Native peoples.

Native Americans are the descendants of the original inhabitants of North America. Though many tribes were decimated after the Europeans arrived, today there are still more than 400 tribes of indigenous peoples, each with its own history, religion, and language or dialect. According to noted Native American author, Joseph Bruchac (1997), "American Indians are people with many different native languages and tribal identities, who come from many different "nations." As much as Native Americans from different tribal nations have in common with each other, they also differ as much from one another—including differences in physical appearance, in dress, in traditional dwellings, and in oral traditions. Language is one way that those differences are very evident."

For many decades, informational, biography, and historical fiction books by non-Natives damaged the image of Native Americans. Many of the older books contained demeaning vocabulary and artificial dialogue. Frequently, authors and illustrators stereotyped Native American characters as either cruel savages (*The Matchlock Gun* by Walter D. Edmonds, 1941) or docile, childlike people who were entirely dependent on the mission or reservation for their existence. At best, they were portrayed as annoying barriers to frontier settlement by European Americans.

It is apparent that old stereotypes live on. Too often, non-Native authors and illustrators rely on old images of feathers and buckskin and fail to portray modern Native Americans realistically. Children need to experience books that are void of such stereotypes, so they can learn the realities of how Native Americans live today. Authors should convey that although many Native people maintain their tribal traditions, they also make use of modern technologies. There is a great need for books that authentically reveal the vast diversity among the many tribes.

It is also important for young readers to understand how Native peoples lived in the past. Children need books that portray Native Americans realistically, not as savages as was done in history books for decades, but rather as people who defended their homeland from invaders. Native Americans acted in the same way that Americans would today if the United States were under siege by foreigners. Native Americans should be portrayed realistically within their various civilized and complex cultures, so readers can challenge the stereotypes and distorted misconceptions that many people still hold.

Recently, the American Indian Library Association instituted the American Indian Youth Literature Award (see website on page 199). The first awards for children's books were given to *Crossing Bok Chitto: A Choctaw Tale of Friendship and Freedom,* by Tim Tingle and illustrated by Jeanne Rorex Bridges, and *Counting Coup: Becoming a Crow Chief on the Reservation and Beyond,* by Joseph Medicine Crow.

I have long been concerned that the majority of literature textbooks primarily present books *about* Native Americans rather than books *by* them. Although major publishing houses do publish some traditional stories retold by Native Americans, they often limit their titles by Native authors to this genre. Native authors must often publish their realistic fiction books through small multicultural presses, whose books unfortunately often go out of print more quickly than books by non-Natives produced by the large publishing houses. Nevertheless, there are a number of good children's books by Native Americans, and in the following bibliography, I present fifteen books in a variety of genres that have been written and illustrated by talented people from a variety of tribes.

Bruchac, Joseph (Abenaki). *Squanto's Journey: The Story of the First Thanksgiving.*
    Silver Whistle Books, 2000. This historically accurate account tells of the young Native
    American man who helped the Pilgrims survive their first brutal New England winter,
    though he is later kidnapped and taken to Spain as a slave.
 Bruchac, Joseph (Abenaki). *The Arrow over the Door.* Puffin, 2002. In alternating narra-
    tives, two 14-year-old boys—one Quaker and the other Abenaki—tell the story of what
    led to their memorable meeting in 1777 just prior to the Battle of Saratoga.

Bruchac, Joseph (Abenaki). *The Winter People*. Puffin, 2004. After the British attack his village in 1759, 14-year-old Saxso must track the raiders to try to save his mother and two sisters.

Erdrich, Liselotte (Ojibway). *Sacagawea*. Illus. Julie Buffalohead (Ponca). Carolrhoda, 2003. This biography of Sacagawea, the Shoshone girl who accompanied Lewis and Clark on their expedition to the Pacific coast, covers her life from age 11 when the Hidatsa kidnapped her to the end of her famous journey. It includes speculation about her later life, of which little is known.

Erdrich, Louise (Chippewa). *The Birchbark House*. Hyperion, 2002. Omakayas is an Ojibwa girl who was adopted as an infant after being rescued as the sole survivor of a smallpox epidemic in her village. She tells of her life on an island in Lake Superior in 1847.

Flood, Nancy Bo. *The Navajo Year: Walk through Many Seasons*. Illus. Billy Whitethorne (Navajo). Salina Bookshelf, 2006. The Navajo new year begins in October, and readers follow Coyote through the sights, sounds, and activities associated with each month, such as string games, stories, planting of corn, rodeos, and torrential rains.

Harjo, Joy. *The Good-Luck Cat* (Muskogee–Creek). Harcourt, 2000. A young girl worries when her beloved cat Woogie disappears. She fears that because he has already survived so many narrow escapes from disaster that he is bound to have run out of luck.

Matheson, David (Coeur d'Alene). *Red Thunder*. Media Weavers, 2002. Young Sun Bear, who is growing in the wisdom of his tribe, relates the life of a northwestern Native American family in the early 1700s. The kidnapping of his sister's baby galvanizes the tribe's warriors to make a daring attempt to rescue him from the Blackfeet.

Powell, Patricia Hruby. *Frog Brings Rain*. Illus. Kendrick Benally (Navajo). Salina Bookshelf, 2006. As fire creeps toward the village of the First People, First Man and First Woman must find a way to quench the flames. After the Bird People, the River People, and the Water People decline to help, First Woman asks the mysterious Frog, and he valiantly saves the people and animals.

Ross, Gayle (Cherokee). *How Rabbit Tricked Otter and Other Cherokee Trickster Stories*. Parabola, 2003. This collection of fifteen Cherokee tales brings together the many sides of Rabbit, the trickster who is charming, mischievous, lazy, and sometimes downright mean.

Smith, Cynthia Leitich (Muscogee). *Indian Shoes*. HarperCollins, 2002. Ray and Grandpa Halfmoon, who are living in Chicago, reflect on memories of their Cherokee–Seminole roots in Oklahoma. In one episode, Ray schemes on how to get the money to buy the leather moccasins he saw in the antique store for his grandfather.

Smith, Cynthia Leitich (Muscogee). *Jingle Dancer*. Morrow, 2000. Jenna is a contemporary Creek–Ojibway girl who brings together her jingle dress and dance regalia with the assistance of the women who inspire her—a great-aunt, a cousin, a neighbor, and her grandmother.

Sneve, Virginia Driving Hawk (Lakota). *Enduring Wisdom: Sayings from Native Americans*. Holiday House, 2003. This collection of quotations from American Indians throughout the continent dates from the earliest contact with Europeans to contemporary tribal members.

Sneve, Virginia Driving Hawk (Lakota). *Grandpa Was a Cowboy and an Indian, and Other Stories*. Bison, 2003. Sneve's collection includes tales of contemporary Lakota and Dakota elders, stories set in the turbulent nineteenth century, and ancient Sioux tales about the birth of the universe and deeds of legendary beings.

Tingle, Tim (Choctow). *Crossing Bok Chitto: A Choctaw Tale of Friendship and Freedom*. Illus. Jeanne Rorex Bridges (Cherokee). Cinco Puntos Press, 2006. Martha is a young Choctaw girl who disobeys her mother and crosses the Bok Chitto River in search of blackberries. A tall slave discovers Martha, and a friendship ensues with the slave's family. When the mother learns she is going to be sold, Martha finds a way for them to reach freedom.

Joseph Bruchac

Joseph Bruchac lives in the Adirondack mountain foothills town of Greenfield Center, New York, in the same house where his maternal grandparents raised him. Much of his writing draws on Abenaki ancestry. He and his family have worked extensively in projects involving the preservation of Abenaki culture, language, and traditional Native skills, including performing traditional Abenaki music. Bruchac holds degrees in literature and creative writing and a doctorate in comparative literature. His poems, articles, and stories have appeared in over 500 publications, and he has authored more than 70 books for adults and children. (See a short bibliography below.) In 1999 Bruchac received the Lifetime Achievement Award from the Native Writers Circle of the Americas. As a professional teller of the traditional tales of the Adirondacks and the Native peoples of the Northeastern Woodlands, Bruchac has performed widely in Europe and throughout the United States.

Bruchac, Joseph. *Bearwalker.* HarperCollins, 2007.
Bruchac, Joseph. *Code Talker: A Novel About the Navajo Marines of World War Two.* Puffin, 2006.
Bruchac, Joseph. *Jim Thorpe, Original All-American.* Puffin, 2008.
Bruchac, Joseph. *Sacajawea.* Harcourt, 2008.
Bruchac, Joseph. *The Return of Skeleton Man.* HarperTrophy, 2008.
Bruchac, Joseph. *Whisper in the Dark.* HarperCollins, 2005.

Literature of Religious Cultures

Some cultures, such as religious groups, cross racial lines. Numerous children's books help young readers learn about people who practice various religions.

Christianity

Devon, Paddie. *The Grumpy Shepherd.* Abingdon Press, 1995.
MacKall, Dandi Daley. *Made for a Purpose.* Zonderkidz, 2004.
Stuckey, Denise Lohr. *Jesus, I Feel Close to You.* Paulist Press, 2005.
Wellman, Sam. *C. S. Lewis: Author of Mere Christianity.* Chelsea House, 1998.

Islam

Gnojewski, Carol. *Ramadan: A Muslim Time of Fasting, Prayer, and Celebration.* Enslow, 2004.

Khan, Rukhsana. *Muslim Child: Understanding Islam through Stories and Poems.* Albert Whitman, 2002.

Matthews, Mary. *Magid Fasts for Ramadan.* Clarion, 1996.

Oppenheim, Shulamith Levey. *The Hundredth Name.* Boyds Mills, 1997.

Judaism

Several awards are dedicated to encouraging quality children's books about Jewish experiences. These include the Sydney Taylor Award, the National Jewish Book Award, and the Charles and Bertie G. Schwartz Award. All these awards recognize distinguished children's books that authentically and sensitively express Jewish thought and experiences.

Desnick, Chaim. *The Little Room.* Pitspopany Press, 2004.

Levine, Gail Carson. *Dave at Night.* HarperTrophy, 2001.

Pearl, Sydelle. *Elijah's Tears: Stories for the Jewish Holidays.* Pelican, 2004.

Polacco, Patricia. *Mrs. Katz and Tush.* Yearling, 1994.

Other Religious Traditions

Hahn, Nhat. *The Hermit and the Well* (Buddhism). Paralax, 2003.

Krishnaswami, Uma. *The Broken Tusk: Stories of the Hindu God Ganesha.* Linnet, 1996.

Krishnaswami, Uma. *Chachaji's Cup* (Hindu). Children's Book Press, 2003.

Landaw, Jonathan. *Prince Siddhartha: The Story of Buddha.* Wisdom, 1996.

International Literature

"The nature of the modern world demands that we all become more aware of and sensitive to the diverse cultures found not only in our own nation, but in the world at large" (Russell, 1997, p. 38). What better way to accomplish this than through literature? **International literature** consists primarily of books originally written and published for children living in other lands. However, it also includes books published in the United States that were written by immigrants about their homelands. In addition, some authors write about other countries where they have lived for a period of time or have visited and researched the culture.

International literature promotes social awareness, and it allows readers to consider very different points of view. Gaining an understanding and appreciation of the history and cultures of other countries helps readers attain a global perspective. Quality international literature is "culturally authentic and rich in cultural details and celebrates both diversity and the common bonds of humanity" (Siu-Runyan, 1999, p. 498).

It is not surprising that the international books most widely available in the United States are those that were first published in other English-speaking countries such as the United Kingdom, Canada, and Australia. However, even books written in English undergo some revision to make them appropriate for U.S. readers. To Americanize a book, a publisher may change things such as spelling, punctuation, titles, character names, vocabulary, settings, and cultural allusions. The word *barbie* is a good example. In the United States, Barbie is a doll; in Australia, a barbie is a cookout (short for barbecue). In some cases the changes may be minor; in other instances, authors complain that the intent of the book has been altered, particularly when works are translated from another language.

British author J. K. Rowling discussed the changes that were made to her Harry Potter books before they were marketed in the United States. Changes were made only when both the author and her U.S. editor thought that what was written would create an erroneous picture in an American child's mind. For example, concerning boys' clothing, the word *jumper* was changed to *sweater*. In the title of her first book, the word *philosopher* was changed to *sorcerer* (i.e., *Harry Potter and the Sorcerer's Stone*). The original title, with the term *philosopher's stone*, would have had little meaning to American readers, and it names a very important object in the plot (O'Malley, 1999).

Another example of a title change is Dick King-Smith's *Daggie Dogfoot*. The special little pig in this book has front feet that look more like a dog's than a pig's, and thus he is named Daggie Dogfoot, *dag* being a word for a runt piglet in England. However, U.S. children might think the book was about a dog rather than a pig, so the title of the U.S. edition is *Pigs Might Fly,* an oft repeated phrase in the book.

Several awards honor outstanding international publications. In 1953 the International Board on Books for Young People was established, and in 1956 they initiated the international Hans Christian Andersen Award (discussed in Chapter 2). Also, the Mildred L. Batchelder Award, first declared in 1968, is given to a U.S. publisher by the American Library Association Children's Services Division in recognition of the most noteworthy translated children's book (picture books and folktales excluded) of the year.

International literature generally falls into four categories: traditional tales from other countries, historical fiction set in other countries, contemporary stories set in other countries, and immigrants' experiences that are typically autobiographical, and as such, can encompass historical and/or contemporary settings. Following is a selection of noteworthy international books that includes all four categories.

Africa

Daly, Niki. *Jamela's Dress* (South Africa). Farrar, Straus & Giroux, 2004.
Kurtz, Jane. *Saba: Under the Hyena's Foot* (Ethiopia). Pleasant Company, 2003.
Lekuton, Joseph Lemasolai. *Facing the Lion: Growing Up Maasai on the African Savannah* (Kenya). National Geographic, 2003.
Onyefulu, Ifeoma. *Here Comes Our Bride! An African Wedding Story* (Nigeria). Frances Lincoln Books, 2004.
Stuve-Bodeen, Stephanie. *Babu's Song* (Tanzania). Lee & Low, 2003.

Asia

Brett, Jan. *Daisy Comes Home* (China). Putnam, 2002.
Cha, Dia. *Dia's Story Cloth* (Laos). Lee & Low, 1998.
Dolphin, Laurie. *Our Journey from Tibet*. Dutton, 1998.
Ellis, Deborah. *The Breadwinner* (Afghanistan). Groundwood, 2000.
Yumoto, Kazumi. *The Friends* (Japan). Demco, 1998.

Southern Asia

Khan, Rukhsana. *Ruler of the Courtyard* (Pakistan). Viking, 2003.
Krishnaswami, Uma. *Monsoon* (India). Farrar, Straus & Giroux, 2003.
Krishnaswami, Uma. *Naming Maya* (India). Farrar, Straus & Giroux, 2004.
Staples, Suzanne Fisher. *Shabanu: Daughter of the Wind* (Pakistan). Laurel Leaf, 2003.
Whelan, Gloria. *Homeless Bird* (India). HarperTrophy, 2000.

Caribbean

Alvarez, Julia. *A Cafecito Story* (Dominican Republic). Chelsea Green, 2004.
Gunning, Monica. *Under the Breadfruit Tree* (Jamaica). Wordsong, 1998.
Hanson, Regina. *The Face at the Window* (Jamaica). Clarion, 1997.
Hausman, Gerald, & Ashley Wolfe. *Doctor Bird: Three Lookin' Up Tales from Jamaica*. Philomel, 1998.
Landowne, Youme. *Selavi, That Is Life: A Haitian Story of Hope*. Consortium, 2004.

Central and South America

Lamm, C. Drew. *Gauchada* (Argentina). Illus. Fabian Negrin. Knopf, 2002.
Delacre, Lulu. *Salsa Stories* (Pan American). Scholastic, 2000.
Hernandez, Antonio. *Blanca's Feather* (Mexico). Rising Moon, 2001.
Machado, Ana Maria. *Niña Bonita* (Pan American). Aims, 1996.
Smith, Roland. *Jaguar* (Brazil). Hyperion, 1998.

Europe

Buchholz, Quent. *The Collector of Moments* (Germany). Farrar, Straus & Giroux, 1999.
Funke, Cornelia. *The Thief Lord* (Italy). Scholastic, 2003.
Guettier, Benedicte. *The Father Who Had 10 Children* (Belgium). Dial, 1999.
Morgenstern, Susie. *Secret Letters from 0 to 10* (France). Penguin, 2000.
Orlev, Uri. *Run, Boy, Run* (Poland). Houghton Mifflin, 2003.

Middle East

Carmi, Daniella. *Samir and Yonatan* (Palestine). Scholastic, 2002.
Cottrell, Robert C. *The Green Line: The Division of Palestine*. Chelsea, 2004.
Kaplan, Kathy Walden. *The Dog of Knots* (Israel). Eerdmans, 2004.
McGraw, Eloise Jarvis. *The Golden Goblet* (Egypt). Puffin, 1990.
Orlev, Uri. *The Lady with the Hat* (Israel). Houghton Mifflin, 1995.

Scandinavia

Deedy, Carmen. *The Yellow Star* (Denmark). Franklin Watts, 2002.
Dexter, Catherine. *Safe Return* (Sweden). Candlewick, 1998.
Lindgren, Astrid. *Pippi Longstocking* (Sweden). Puffin, 1997.
Lowry, Lois. *Number the Stars* (Denmark). Houghton Mifflin, 1989.
Reuter, Bjarne. *The Boys from St. Petri* (Denmark). Puffin, 1996.

United Kingdom

Banks, Lynne Reid. *Maura's Angel* (Ireland). Avon, 1999.
Cooper, Susan. *The Boggart and the Monster* (Scotland). Aladdin, 1998.
Cushman, Karen. *The Midwife's Apprentice* (England). Clarion, 1995.
Gray, Elizabeth Janet. *Adam of the Road* (England). Puffin, 1987.
Wynne-Jones, Tim. *The Maestro* (Canada). Demco, 1998.

Integrating Literature and Technology

Finding Multicultural Resources   If you do not have time to go to the book-store or library to locate a resource book on multicultural literature, or if you want information on book awards dealing with minorities and an up-to-date list of the winners, the Internet has a wealth of information at your fingertips (literally—just key in the URLs). Following are some of the most valuable sites I have found.

10 Quick Ways to Analyze Children's Books for Racism and Sexism, by the Council on Interracial Books for Children: www.birchlane.davis.ca.us/library/10quick.htm

American Indian Youth Literature Award, by the American Indian Library Association: www.duluth.lib.mn.us/YouthServices/Booklists/AmerIndLit.html

Américas Award, by the Center for Latin American and Caribbean Studies: www4 .uwm.edu/clacs/aa/index.cfm

Asian American Literature, by Brenda Hoffman: http://falcon.jmu.edu/~ramseyil/ asialit.htm

Asian Pacific American Award for Literature, by the Asian/Pacific American Librarians Association: www.apalaweb.org/awards/awards.htm

Carter G. Woodson Award (for books dealing with ethnic minorities), by the National Council for the Social Studies: www.socialstudies.org/awards/woodson

Coretta Scott King Award (for African American literature), by the American Library Association: www.ala.org

Dia de los Niños/Dia de los Libros: www.patmora.com/dia.htm and www.ala.org/dia

Fakelore, Multiculturalism, and the Ethics of Children's Literature, by Eliot A. Singer: www.msu.edu/user/singere/fakelore.html

Mildred L. Batchelder Award (for translated international books), by the Association for Library Service to Children: www.ala.org/alsc

Multicultural Reading, by Cynthia Leitich Smith: www.cynthialeitichsmith.com

National Jewish Book Award, by the Jewish Book Council: www.myjewishbooks.com/awards03.html

Pura Belpré Award, by the Association for Library Service to Children: www.ala.org/alsc

San Francisco Public Library (Asian Experience Books): http://sfpl.org/sfplonline/kids/booklists/asian.htm

Statistics on Children's Books by and about People of Color Published in the U.S., by the Cooperative Children's Book Center: www.education.wisc.edu/ccbc/books/pcstats.htm

Sydney Taylor Book Award, by the Association of Jewish Libraries: www.jewishlibraries.org/ajlweb/awards/st_books.htm

Tomás Rivera Award, by the Texas State University–San Marcos: www.education.txstate.edu/subpages/tomasrivera

Summary

Multicultural literature is cross-cultural literature consisting of books by and about peoples of all cultures. Some books are culturally neutral; although having some characters from minority groups, there is no culturally specific information included in the text. Other books are culturally generic, featuring main characters from a specific cultural group, but without much culturally specific information included. Culturally specific books incorporate details that help define the characters as members of a particular cultural group.

Older books are more likely to contain white bias, a subtle form of racism that implies that the mainstream way of life is inherently superior. Even newer books can contain white bias if they are written by someone outside the cultural group of the main characters.

Latinos are people from a variety of cultures that include descendants of native Hispanic people in the United States, residents of Latin America, and U.S. immigrants (and their descendants) from Latin America, which encompasses all countries in the Western Hemisphere south of the United States. African Americans are descendants of the various indigenous peoples of the African continent. Asian Americans are descended from the various indigenous peoples of Asian countries such as Cambodia, China, Japan, Korea, Laos, Thailand, and Vietnam. Native Americans are members (or descendants) of the 400 or more tribes of the indigenous peoples of North America.

Contemporary Realistic Fiction

9

The artist used acrylic paints and colored pencils to create this illustrations in the realistic style.

From *Muskrat Will Be Swimming,* by Cheryl Savageau and illustrated by Robert Hynes.

ecall from Chapter 6 that fiction is divided into two major categories—fantasy and realistic fiction. This chapter and the next are devoted to realistic fiction. The division between the contemporary and historical eras is arbitrary, and not all literature specialists agree on where the separation should be made. However, because of the dramatic changes in the United States since the civil rights movement of the 1960s, I have set that era as the dividing point. In this textbook, books with settings prior to the passage of the Civil Rights Act of 1964 are considered historical fiction, and books with settings after are considered contemporary.

Evaluating Contemporary Fiction

The following questions can guide you as you select contemporary realistic fiction.

- Is the topic suitable for the age intended?
- Does the book tell a good story that children will enjoy?
- Is the plot credible?
- Are the characters convincing?
- Does the author avoid stereotyping?
- Does the theme emerge naturally from the story, rather than being stated too obviously?
- Is the theme worth imparting to children?
- Does the author avoid didacticism?

Characteristics of Contemporary Realistic Fiction

The characteristics of **contemporary realistic fiction** are quite different from fantasy. First, the setting is in modern or contemporary times—which I have defined for the purpose of this textbook as any year from 1964 to present day—in a real (or realistic) location. This means that stories take place at real locations in the world, typically the United States. The state is nearly always identified, but the cities may either be real or fictional.

Second, the characters are realistic people. There are no anthropomorphic animals or people with superhuman abilities. Sometimes characters are even based on a real person or a composite of people the author has known, although the names are typically fictional. Expect characters to be described more forthrightly in realistic fiction than with other genres. The stories are frequently narrated in first person by the main character, making them even more realistic.

Because there is no magic or fantasy of any kind in this genre, the plots of contemporary realistic fiction books reflect real-life situations. In some books the tone is light and humorous; in others it is serious and reflects real-life milieus. Plots may deal with subjects such as aging, disability, illness, death, divorce, abandonment, and poverty. Unlike fairy tales, realistic fiction does not always have a happy ending, and often the major problem of the story is not solved, leaving many unanswered questions. However, the protagonist usually finds a way to cope with the problem by the end of the story. Readers who do not care for such equivocal endings can find many good contemporary fiction books with happy endings, often geared for younger children.

Around fourth grade, many children's reading preferences change from fairy tales and fantasy to stories about boys and girls their own age with plots that reflect situations similar to their own lives. Because many intermediate-grade children prefer contemporary fiction, there is an extensive source of books from which to choose.

Censorship

by Jenifer Jasinski Schneider

Censorship of children's literature is a major issue for all genres, but because realistic fiction deals with children's real-life problems, it is usually in the forefront of attacks by parents and political groups who want to control what children have access to read. According to the American Library Association (ALA) Office of Intellectual Freedom (2004c), **censorship** is

> the suppression of ideas and information that certain persons—individuals, groups or government officials—find objectionable or dangerous. Censors try to use the power of the state to impose their view of what is truthful and appropriate, or offensive and objectionable, on everyone else. Censors pressure public institutions, like libraries, to suppress and remove from public access information they judge inappropriate or dangerous, so that no one else has the chance to read or view the material and make up their own minds about it. The censor wants to prejudge materials for everyone.

Censorship of children's literature occurs in various forms and for various reasons. Often the primary goal is to keep children from being exposed to knowledge the censors do not want them to have. In most cases, adults do this out of genuine concern for children's welfare—to protect them from what they see as harmful.

In the journal *Reading Today* (International Reading Association, 2001), the following reasons were most frequently cited for book challenges in schools and libraries:

- Sexual content
- Offensive language
- Topics unsuited for targeted age group
- Occult or Satanist themes

- Violence
- Homosexual themes
- Promoting religious viewpoints
- Nudity
- Racism
- Sex education
- Anti-family themes

Challenges to children's books are widespread, and the most popular books read by children are sometimes the ones that garner the most criticism. The ALA compiles an annual list of the year's most frequently challenged/banned books, and the following children's books were the most frequently challenged in 2007 (ALA, 2008):

- *And Tango Makes Three* by Justin Richardson and Peter Parnell for being anti-ethnic, containing sexism, promoting homosexuality, being anti-family, having a controversial religious viewpoint, and being unsuited to targeted age group
- *Olive's Ocean* by Kevin Henkes for being sexually explicit and containing offensive language
- *The Golden Compass* by Philip Pullman for its religious viewpoint (anti-Christian)
- *The Adventures of Huckleberry Finn* by Mark Twain for racism
- *It's Perfectly Normal* by Robie Harris for being sexually explicit (sex education)

Parents and organizations have strong convictions that guide their attempts to censor particular reading material. However, ignorance is likely to do more harm than knowledge (Nodelman, 1996). In addition, librarians and other educators argue that censorship violates the Constitution's Bill of Rights guarantee of freedom of expression. The ALA (2004d) developed the Library Bill of Rights to help protect this basic freedom and to provide a philosophical basis for opposing censorship. In its Bill of Rights, the ALA affirms that all libraries are forums for information and ideas, and that the following basic policies should guide their services:

- Books and other library resources should be provided for the interest, information, and enlightenment of all people of the community the library serves. Materials should not be excluded because of the origin, background, or views of those contributing to their creation.
- Libraries should provide materials and information presenting all points of view on current and historical issues. Materials should not be proscribed or removed because of partisan or doctrinal disapproval.
- Libraries should challenge censorship in the fulfillment of their responsibility to provide information and enlightenment.
- Libraries should cooperate with all persons and groups concerned with resisting abridgment of free expression and free access to ideas.
- A person's right to use a library should not be denied or abridged because of [the person's] origin, age, background, or views.

- Libraries that make exhibit spaces and meeting rooms available to the public they serve should make such facilities available on an equitable basis, regardless of the beliefs or affiliations of individuals or groups requesting their use (ALA, 2004d).

Selecting versus Censoring

If people find something objectionable in a book, they can keep it away from their own children, but they should not be able to prevent all children from reading the book. As an alternative to censorship, which prohibits children from reading books by removing them from library shelves and bookstores, selection helps readers locate good books among the vast body of works of differing quality. Librarians practice selection when they order books for their libraries and share books with children. Teachers practice selection when they choose books for classroom libraries, to read aloud, and for literature-based lessons. Parents practice selection when they purchase books and check out library books for their children. The author of this textbook practiced selection when she decided which books to include in it. Moreover, children practice selection when they pick books to read on their own.

The difference between censorship and selection is the removal of choice. Censorship removes the "objectionable" materials. Therefore, an individual's ability to choose a book is eliminated. Selection is an individual process of choosing reading material for oneself, one's family, or for readers the individual may serve (in the case of librarians, teachers, and textbook authors). With selection, controversial books are still available, but it is each individual's choice whether to read them.

In schools and classrooms, selection is more complex, because teachers and librarians make decisions that affect many different children. For this reason, books should not be censored or removed, but selected by and for children. The educational organizations listed at the end of this section have created support networks and materials to help educators and parents make informed decisions in their selection of materials. For example, the ALA (2004b) website contains information about the role of libraries in serving children, how librarians select their collections, and how parents can help children and teens make the best use of the library.

The National Council of Teachers of English (NCTE) also provides a website with guidelines for selecting materials in English language arts programs. NCTE suggests that the criteria for selecting materials should include a clear connection to educational objectives and should address the needs of students. By drawing upon these resources, teachers can select diverse books that reflect their students' interests and cultures while maintaining high academic standards. If parents know the reasons behind teachers' choices, they are less likely to challenge them.

However, when proactive selection policies and procedures do not satisfy all parents or organizations, there are other resources available to help teachers oppose censorship restrictions and maintain the academic freedom of their classrooms. For example, the ALA's website contains detailed information on coping with challenges and conducting challenge hearings. In addition, the NCTE website has numerous resources for teachers and schools faced with censorship challenges. It provides guidelines, sample forms, and suggested procedures/approaches for dealing with challenges to literary works, for dealing with censorship of nonprint materials, for defining and defending instructional methods, and for providing rationales for challenged books.

Above all, because the selection of children's literature for the classroom must be an informed process that accounts for children's interests while meeting academic and aesthetic objectives, it is *imperative* that teachers preview all books before recommending them or sharing them with a group of children. Teachers should also develop a rationale for their use of certain books with particular children.

The following organizations are dedicated to securing the open use of literature and nonprint materials for use by children:

- American Booksellers Foundation for Free Expression: www.abffe.org
- American Library Association: www.ala.org
- Freedom to Read Foundation: www.ftrf.org
- National Coalition against Censorship: www.ncac.org
- National Council of Teachers of English: www.ncte.org
- PEN American Center: www.pen.org

Issues in Censorship

Should a Group of Adults Be Able to Control What All Children in a Community Are Able to Read?   Cammie Mannino is a New York bookseller and a strong proponent of First Amendment rights. While she understands that every generation likes the idea of protecting its children, she asserts that society cannot protect children from harsh realities: "They think if their children don't read about it, they won't know about it. And if they don't ever know about it, it won't happen [to them]" (Paulson, 2001, p. 22).

Explain how you do or do not agree that a group of people should have the power to decide what children *cannot* read.

Themes

The themes of contemporary books tend to be abstract concepts that reflect complexities of modern life. Themes often center on people and situations that are in a child's immediate world, such as family, friendship, and school; they also include exciting situations such as adventure and mystery. Some of the more prevalent categories of contemporary themes follow, each of which will be explored in more detail later in this chapter.

- *Family themes* involve plots that focus on family issues. These include stories about loving families, such as *Ramona and Her Father* (Cleary), as well as stories about dysfunctional families.

- *Friendship themes* focus on the lives and adventures of two or more friends, such as *Bridge to Terabithia* (Paterson).

- *Humorous themes* are found in lighthearted books intended to make children laugh at ridiculous situations, such as *How to Eat Fried Worms* (Rockwell).

- *Adventure themes* characterize stories with fast-moving plots and exciting settings, such as *The Haymeadow* (Paulsen). One category of adventure stories consists of *survival stories*, in which a character is pitted against nature, such as *Julie of the Wolves* (George). The settings of survival stories are often exotic places such as oceans, the wilderness, or deserted islands. Another category is *mystery stories*: adventure stories that involve solving a puzzle or crime. These stories often contain unusual characters and clever twists of plot that surprise the readers, as in *Coffin on a Case* (Bunting).

- *Social reality themes* are found in books that involve important issues facing the world today, such as racism, crime, war, poverty, and abuse. One example is *Working Cotton* (Williams), a story of migrant workers and child labor. Sometimes the plots involve characters who learn to cope with their problems or characters who have hope of overcoming their hardship through perseverance—as in *Fly Away Home* (Bunting), the story of a homeless father and his young son who live at an airport.

- *Personal issue themes* focus on an individual character's response to a specific personal problem or situation. Two examples are living with a disability, as in *Tangerine* (Bloor), and the loss of a loved one, as in *Nana Upstairs & Nana Downstairs* (dePaola).

- *Animal themes* focus on a child's relationship with a pet or other beloved animal, as in *I'll Always Love You* (Wilhelm).

When I introduce these topics to my adult students, they often express horror that books for children expose them to the dire situations of modern life. I respond by asking my students if any of their children or young relatives watch television, go to movies, look at the front page of newspapers, or know another child who is experiencing a serious problem. I believe the average child witnesses more violence and is exposed to more harsh realities (both fictional and real) in a few months of watching television than in a lifetime of reading children's books. Even in the case of the few children whose television viewing is curtailed, the realities of the world cannot be hidden.

Driscoll (1999) believes that "we are becoming a nation of mourners and victims. Few communities have not experienced senseless crimes, and media coverage of tragedies perpetuates widespread grief [in all communities]" (p. 17). Most adults underestimate the capacity of children to face serious issues presented in realistic stories. Children need to know about issues that they or their peers may face. To deprive youngsters of knowledge—because we believe their ignorance will keep them safe from the problems of the world—is folly! It has the opposite effect. When children eventually face one of life's painful realities, such as the death of a beloved grandparent, they will be caught off guard. If they do not have the opportunity to think about such situations beforehand and prepare themselves, they may have great trouble coping. Attempting to protect children from painful subjects can ultimately cause them more harm, especially when children are left feeling they are alone in their painful experiences and thoughts.

If adults withhold realistic books, children will find and read them on their own but without an adult to guide them in their selections and responses. There is good reason why middle school and secondary students read contemporary fiction. It reflects their lives and the real world around them. Children soon learn that reading contemporary books can be both entertaining and enlightening.

Reading realistic books can also be therapeutic. **Bibliotherapy** is the process of mending one's life by reading books. The following section was written by Dan T. Ouzts, Professor of Education at the Citadel, and Mark J. Palombo, Information Resource Coordinator for Beaufort Jasper Hampton Comprehensive Health Services. Both are formerly editors of the *Bibliotherapy and Reading Newsletter* of the Special Interest Group, Bibliotherapy and Reading, of the International Reading Association.

Bibliotherapy

by Dan T. Ouzts and Mark J. Palombo

Bibliotherapy (therapy through books) is an effective technique that helps children cope with their problems, thereby promoting mental health. This form of guidance through storybooks is a means for children to identify with a story character who has similar problems. This can improve children's attitudes toward reading when adults guide them to read books that are relevant to problems they are facing. When children who are experiencing difficulties can read about others who have solved similar problems, they may see alternatives for themselves. Beyond this, bibliotherapy is an avenue through which teachers and parents can learn more about their children.

Bibliotherapy addresses the affective dimension of reading by promoting positive attitudes toward reading, self, and others. Carter and Harris (1982) conducted a study using books from the Children's Choices lists, and they identified attributes in children's most popular book selections. *Characterization* was the most frequently mentioned element; many children asserted that a particular book character was "just like me," suggesting that self-identification with story characters is of paramount importance. Additionally, children who have negative attitudes toward reading and learning could, with the help of a knowledgeable teacher or parent, develop more positive attitudes by reading books in which a character overcomes his or her negative attitudes.

The word *bibliotherapy* first appeared in 1930 in an article by G. O. Ireland (Ouzts, 1991). However, two psychiatrists, William and Karl Menninger, were among the first to foster an interest in therapeutic reading as an aid to mental healing (O'Bruba & Camplese, 1983). They encouraged both professional and lay people to use literature to promote coping behaviors that might help people solve problems. The Menningers theorized that the key to successful living is in one's ability to manage aggressions. Their interests focused on neglected and abused children, prisoners, and the threat of nuclear armament.

The process of bibliotherapy used in education today is largely credited to Caroline Shrodes, whose 1949 dissertation on the subject is now a classic (Dreyer, 1993; Grindler, Stratton, & McKenna, 1997). Psychologists, clergy, and educators soon recognized bibliotherapy as a professional tool (Cornett & Cornett, 1980). The American Library Association gave its support to bibliotherapy early in the twentieth century, and since then many college courses, textbooks, research studies, professional publications, and professional conference presentations have promoted the practice. Today, bibliotherapy is recognized as an important discipline in the field of reading (Ouzts, 1991).

The Purpose of Bibliotherapy

Educators need to be concerned with both the emotional and the academic aspects of learning. Bibliotherapy can help to achieve this goal because it has the potential to address the needs of the whole child (Grindler, Stratton, & McKenna, 1997). Through bibliotherapy, children can become sensitive, not only to their own feelings, but to others' feelings as well. Moreover, books allow teachers to intervene with children who are experiencing stress and crises in their lives. Severe stress alters children's behavior and their ability to achieve in school, and it is also evident in the ever-increasing rate of suicide among young people. Today's children face considerable threats, such as drug use, gang violence, homelessness, AIDS, terrorism, and the effects of war. Many of these issues appear in books that educators can promote. (Carefully review your school district's adoption lists to determine which books are acceptable for your grade level.)

There are several compelling reasons for using literature to teach children both how to read and how to cope with any attitudinal or emotional problems that could be barriers to their learning. The right books can offer possible solutions to problems that create children's inner turmoil, so therapy through books could make the difference between an emotionally well-adjusted child and one who may later suffer mental anguish. In addition, reading about a personal situation has the potential to sharpen perception and deepen understanding of others, even if the reader is not experiencing turmoil.

Guidelines for Using Bibliotherapy

Jalongo (1983) recommends initiating bibliotherapy by administering an interest inventory to identify several appealing topics. For specific book titles, your librarian can help you locate a reference book, such as *The Right Book, the Right Time* (Grindler, Stratton, & McKenna, 1997). This book assists educators and parents in matching children facing important issues in their lives with fiction books that feature characters in similar circumstances. Today, however, the majority of people turn to the Internet to find up-to-date information more quickly, and we have described the ways to do this in the next section.

Books need to be carefully selected to match individual children and situations. For example, some books are designed for individual reflection rather than group reading. Whereas a book dealing with a common experience, such as the death of a pet, could be read to a group of children, books dealing with sensitive personal issues, such as sexual abuse, are meant to be read individually.

Huck (1987) affirmed that a book is suitable for bibliotherapy if it has the power to help a reader relieve conscious problems in a controlled manner, *and* it tells an interesting story. Therefore, while you are selecting books that cover possible solutions to children's difficulties, keep in mind that they should also have high literary merit. For this reason, we recommend the Children's Choices and the Teachers' Choices lists, published annually in the October/November issues of *The Reading Teacher*. They provide synopses of books that are excellent resources, dealing with topics such as self-concept, perseverance, relationships, social values, friendship, facing adversity, family values, illness, death, and war (Ouzts, 1998). When teachers and parents select books to address social-emotional skills, it is important to pick books that children find appealing.

In the bibliotherapeutic process, timing and approach are of great importance. Materials should be readily available, but reading choices must be left to individual children. Providing time for class discussion of books is critical; however, no one child should be targeted for responding to questions. Rather, we suggest providing excerpts from a book for children to respond to in dialogue response journals with the teacher. Although there are no formal processes for bibliotherapy, we recommend the following procedures.

- *Before* children listen to or read a book, the teacher should set specific purposes for the activity.
- *During* the guided reading of the book, the teacher should set expectations, guide the discussion, and relate the text to children's experiences in general. (It is critical to guide adequate discussion at this point and to note unusual behaviors or uneasiness exhibited by any of the children.)
- *After* reading the book, evaluate its effects on the children and document any changes in an individual's attitudes or behaviors. Additionally, inventories that note changes in attitudes can be used to document longitudinal effects. (We suggest the *Elementary Reading Attitude Survey*, published by McKenna and Kear, 1990, which is based on the Garfield comic strip character.)

In bibliotherapy, books are usually chosen to assist a child in dealing with his or her current situation. However, books can also be used on a broader scale in socio-emotional therapy—the development of children's social and emotional capacities related to self and others. If children view themselves as failures, they develop irrational ideas about their self-worth and abilities. In addition to dwelling on important tasks they have been unable to perform, they often talk themselves into a corner of ugliness, ineptitude, and unpopularity on many dimensions. Anxiety sets in, and the affected individuals become their own worst enemies.

Children will not develop self-confidence and self-respect if they are burdened with stress. If children have unhappy home situations, academic success will be difficult or even impossible. If we are to teach children well, we need to know them as individuals. It is important to be aware of any changes in behavior and watch for specific types of stress, so you can offer the right book to the right child at the right time. Overcoming a child's risk of failure should be the primary criterion for supplying a special book. Remember that a poor book sets a child back, and a mediocre book leaves a child at a standstill—but a good book will assist in the development of a child's emotions. It is through this beneficial emotional development that children can break attitudinal barriers to learning.

We must add one caveat: Bibliotherapy is not the answer to deeply rooted psychological problems (Grindler, Stratton, & McKenna, 1997). In this case, teachers should refer a child to the school psychologist or counselor. Because teachers are not trained to provide therapy, their emphasis should be on providing books that can show children how to cope with life. While books cannot replace personal interactions in an individual's life, they can provide an added dimension to thoughts and feelings.

We recommend the following resources:

- *Bibliotherapy and Reading* (Newsletter of the Special Interest Group of the International Reading Association): www.citadel.edu/education/academic_programs/reading.html
- Children's Choices and Teachers' Choices: www.reading.org/resources/tools/choices_childrens.html

Integrating Literature and Technology

Searching for Bibliotherapy Resources on the Internet

by Dan T. Ouzts and Mark J. Palombo

Technology makes it easy to locate professional bibliotherapy resources in a matter of moments. Numerous Internet search engines and subject directories are available, such as Google (www.google.com), that can reduce research to a matter of seconds. Familiarity with Internet search tools will improve your success in finding what you want in the shortest amount of time. Start with a simple Google search by keying in a few descriptive words and clicking "Google Search." If you are overwhelmed by the results, refine your search. For example, enter key phrases within quotation marks, so instead of retrieving all the websites that contain your key terms somewhere, it retrieves only those resources that contain the exact phrase within the quotes. If you still have too many choices, further refine your search by entering words or phrases that are more specific, or click the "Advanced Search" link for additional ways to refine your search.

For example, a search using only the term *bibliotherapy* will bring up more than 237,000 websites! This is a daunting number of resources to sift through, so refine the search by entering the key terms *bibliotherapy resources*, which still gives you more than 72,000 websites. You might limit yourself to perusing just the first two screens of results, or you can further delimit your search to resources for elementary children by using *"bibliotherapy resources" and elementary*, where the results are fewer than 74 websites (if you remember to use the quotation marks).

When you are looking for books on a specific topic, try searching within a search. After completing the search for *bibliotherapy resources*, scroll down to the bottom of the screen, and click the "Search within Results" link. Enter a phrase, such as *child abuse*. The result is a list of websites that contains resources on that topic. Some websites are extensive, so to find quickly the resource you need, try searching within a website. Once you have opened a website, click on *Edit* in the top menu and then on *Find (on this page)*. Alternatively, you can hold down the *CTRL* and *F* keys simultaneously on a PC. In the pop-up textbox, enter only the most specific word in your search, in this case *abuse*. This short-cut takes your cursor to the appropriate place (or places, if you repeat the search) within a specific website. Using these techniques will most likely provide the information you are seeking or direct you to additional sites providing you with a bounty of information.

Keep in mind that the Internet is a dynamic resource. Your results will change on a regular basis as new resources are created and existing resources are updated or eliminated. Just remember that searches are made using key words and then refined to narrow your results for specific information. Of course, not every search will locate the exact information you seek.

Families

Few contemporary realistic books have only one theme. For example, a book may have a social issue theme, such as the tragedy of homelessness; however, it must also have a personal issue theme, such as the protagonist's need for a place to live. In this and the following sections, I have grouped books around central themes—but as you read the books, look for other themes the author employs.

Traditional Families

First and foremost to young children are their families and homes. For younger children, happy and humorous books about families abound. Among the most enduring and warmhearted books about traditional families are Beverly Cleary's books about Ramona Quimby, her big sister Beezus, and their family. Two of the most popular of the books are *Ramona and Her Father* and *Ramona Quimby, Age 8*. In the series readers follow Ramona as she grows from a pesky baby sister to a third grader whose antics include accidentally cracking a raw egg atop her head in school. After a fifteen-year break from writing the series, Cleary published *Ramona's World*, in which the exuberant Ramona is 9 years old.

Equally popular is Judy Blume's series about Peter Hatcher, who is constantly tormented by his 2-year-old brother, Fudge. Fudge gets away with everything, including swallowing Peter's pet turtle in *Tales of a Fourth Grade Nothing*. Things worsen in the sequel, *Superfudge*, when Peter's parents announce there is going to be a new baby in the family, and all Peter can think of is a carbon copy of Fudge!

After a twelve-year interval, Judy Blume wrote another amusing tale about the Hatcher family in *Double Fudge*. Peter is in seventh grade, and his younger brother Fudge is obsessed with money, which drives Peter crazy. Things get worse when long-lost relatives, the Howie Hatchers of Honolulu, Hawaii, turn up. Now Peter has to deal with annoying twin cousins—Flora and Fauna, who burst into songs at the drop of a hat—and their weird little brother who turns out to be a miniature Fudge!

In *Big Jimmy's Kum Kau Chinese Take Out* (Lewin), the sights, sounds, and smells of a busy family-owned Chinese take-out restaurant are seen through the eyes of the owner's young son. He describes the hustle and bustle as Uncle Wing is slicing meat, Uncle Loong is chopping mountains of green peppers and broccoli, and his mother and aunty take orders over the phone, while he stuffs each bag with condiments and a fortune cookie.

Judith Viorst's stories stem from her experiences in raising boys. Her funniest account is *Alexander and the Terrible, Horrible, No Good, Very Bad Day,* in which the younger son gives a first-person account of his bad day. It includes waking up with gum in his hair, having his best friend find another best friend, not finding dessert in his lunchbox, and accidentally calling Australia on his father's office phone. In *Alexander, Who's Not (Do you hear me? I mean it!) Going to Move,* he has another bad day when he must help pack for the move to a new home—where he is sure he will never have any friends.

Some books focus on a child's special experience with one parent. In *Tell Me a Story, Mama* (Johnson), a young girl is getting ready for bed, and she and her mother talk about Mama's childhood memories, recounting stories of two generations of an African American family. In *A Perfect Father's Day,* Eve Bunting gives a delightful account of 4-year-old Susie, who treats her father to a series of special activities for Father's Day (activities that happen to be all her own favorites). After a long week of work, a father returns home Friday evening in *Daddy's Lullaby* (Bradman). The baby is the only one awake, and the attentive father cuddles his baby as he checks on his sleeping son and wife. Tiptoeing downstairs, he relaxes in a chair and sings a song, lulling them both to sleep.

Stories about grandparents abound. Tomie dePaola gives a loving account of his Irish grandfather in *Tom*. When Grandpa Tom, the butcher, gives Tommy a pair of chicken feet to play with, he takes them to school and scares the other kids. In *Song and Dance Man* (Ackerman), two boys and a girl delight in their grandfather's performance of his old vaudeville act. *The Wednesday Surprise* (Bunting) is a touching story of 7-year-old Anna, who reads with her grandmother every Wednesday after school. At the end of the story, the reader learns that instead of the grandmother's helping the young girl practice reading, the girl is teaching her grandmother how to read. *Emma* by Wendy Kesselman is a charming account of a grandmother who, after turning 72, begins to paint pictures of all the things she loves.

While learning to make tortillas on her seventh birthday, Magda tries to make perfectly round ones like those made by her grandmother. She is disappointed when hers turn out in a variety of shapes, but her family happily eats them, thinking she is a tortilla artist in *Magda's Tortillas* (Chavarría-Cháirez).

Nontraditional Families

Stories of children living in nontraditional families (i.e., families in which one or both parents are absent) frequently contain themes of serious personal issues.

In many such stories, children are living with one parent. When they live with their fathers, it is frequently because their mothers have died. Eleven-year-old George, his younger brother James, and their widowed father live on Michigan's Dove Island in *The In-Between Days* by Eve Bunting. When George's father begins to spend time with Caroline, who lives on the mainland, George becomes jealous. He becomes angry when 5-year-old James (who does not remember their mother) also becomes fond of Caroline. George plots a prank to show Caroline how much he dislikes her in hopes she will not return.

In *A Chair for My Mother* (Williams), a young girl, her mother, and her grandmother had all their furniture and belongings destroyed in an apartment fire, so family members and neighbors have donated furniture and household goods for them to start over. However, there is nothing comfortable for the mother to sit on when she comes home from waiting tables all day, so they save all their coins in a big jar to buy a soft armchair.

In Beverly Cleary's *Dear Mr. Henshaw,* Leigh's parents are divorced, and his father undertakes a wayfaring life in his tractor-trailer with the family dog. Ten-year-old Leigh is left behind, hurt and confused. In letters to his favorite author, Leigh reveals his problems in coping with his parents' divorce, being the new boy in school, and finding his own place in the world.

Children who live in blended families with a parent and a stepparent face several serious personal issues, such as adjusting to the divorce or death of a parent, resentment in sharing their mother or father with the new spouse, dislike for the stepparent, and the presence of unwanted new siblings. *Two under Par* by Kevin Henkes chronicles 10-year-old Wedge's personal struggle after his mother remarries. They are living over Wedge's stepfather's miniature golf course with the stepfather's drippy son Andrew. To make things worse, there is a new baby on the way. In *The Hideout* by Eve Bunting, 12-year-old Andy runs away from home because he feels unloved by his mother and new stepfather. He hides out in the tower suite of a luxurious San Francisco hotel while trying to contact his father in London.

In some nontraditional families, children live with aunts and uncles or grandparents because parents are deceased or absent. Among the most poignant of these stories is *Missing May* by Cynthia Rylant. Summer was 6 when her mother died and her Great Aunt May and Uncle Ob lovingly took her in. Six years later, when Aunt May dies, Summer grieves and is frightened because Uncle Ob does not want to go on with life. When Cletus, a strange neighbor boy, says he knows someone who can help Ob contact May's spirit, Summer goes along, looking for some sign from Aunt May to ease their sorrow.

In *Our Gracie Aunt* (Woodson), young Johnson and Beebee have been alone in their broken-down apartment for days. A social worker finds and takes them to live with their mother's estranged sister, Gracie. Though skeptical at first, the children soon realize that at their aunt's house, there is always something to eat, and she lovingly tucks them into bed each night. Toward the end of the book, the children visit their mother in a treatment facility, but they return to their secure home with Aunt Gracie, with the hope that their mother will eventually be able to take care of them.

Dysfunctional Families

It's Not the End of the World (Blume) is the story of Karen Newman's family, which is torn apart by the parents' constant fighting. When her father moves out and her mother talks about divorce, Karen tries to think of a way to get them back together. However, when her parents come together briefly, the fighting resumes, and Karen begins to realize that a peaceful single-parent home is not the end of the world.

In *Somewhere in the Darkness* by Walter Dean Myers, Jimmy's father was in prison, so when Jimmy's mother died, he lived with Mama Jean, his mother's best friend. When Crab, his father, suddenly appears to take Jimmy with him to Chicago, the boy is understandably reluctant, and rightly so, because Crab has not been paroled as he tells Mama Jean. Though dying of a kidney disease, he has escaped from the prison hospital to find Jimmy—and to convince him that he is innocent of the crime for which he was convicted.

Abandoned Children

Deep personal turmoil is felt by children whose mothers have abandoned them. When Jeff Green in *A Solitary Blue* (Voigt) was in second grade, his mother vanished, leaving only a goodbye note. Left with his emotionless father, The Professor, Jeff learns that not caring and not feeling is the safest way to live. Five years later his mother, Melody, invites him to spend the summer with her at her grandmother's house, and he begins to open up and love her again. At first he does not recognize her insincere and selfish nature; he overlooks her neglect, which borders on abuse. During a second summer visit in which he sees Melody very little, he realizes he can be alone without being lonely. Upon his return he learns that his father is not without emotion after all, and a true relationship is kindled.

Journey's father deserted the family some time ago, and Journey is 11 when his mother leaves him and his older sister with their grandparents in *Journey* (MacLachlan). The boy is sad and angry and spends the summer looking for clues that will explain why she abandoned them. He sifts through the box of family photos his mother ripped into pieces before she left, looking for answers. Grandfather stays busy taking new photos of the family and their farm to recreate the family's history. Along the way, Journey gains insight that it was his grandfather, not his long departed father or his absent mother, who has always cared for him like a parent.

Walk Two Moons by Sharon Creech is a poignant story of 13-year-old Salamanca's search for her mother, who did not return from a solo vacation. During a trip from Ohio to Idaho with her grandparents in search of her mother, the story of her mother's disappearance is revealed through flashbacks. To pass the time during the long car trip, Sal tells the story of her friend Phoebe, whose mother also disappeared for a while. However, Sal's mother can never return, and the author slowly and tenderly unfolds the story of why the mother did not return to the family she loved.

In *Baby* by Patricia MacLachlan, 12-year-old Larkin finds a baby in a basket in her family's driveway. An anonymous note pleads for the family to take her in, and they do so—trying hard not to love her because the note says the mother will come back for her one day. In the year they care for little Sophie, the family begins to heal from the loss of their own infant, who had died a few months before.

The protagonist of *Pictures of Hollis Woods* by Patricia Reilly Giff was abandoned at birth. Hollis has spent her twelve years living in—and running away from—a half-dozen foster homes, all the while wishing for a family of her own. Her newest guardian is the loving Josie Cahill, a retired art teacher, but Hollis becomes increasingly aware that Josie is forgetful, and Hollis gradually becomes her caregiver. Flashbacks slowly illuminate Hollis's life with her previous family, the Regans, who wanted to adopt her and why she ran away. Artistically talented Hollis preserves memories of this family in her sketchbook. Hollis is fearful that she will be taken away from Josie, so the two of them escape to hide out at the Regans' summer home during the holiday season.

Friendship

A recurring problem in friendship-themed books is the moment when best friends must part. In Patricia Reilly Giff's *Adios, Anna,* Sarah must say goodbye to her best friend, Anna Ortiz, for the summer. Anna is having a great time at camp while Sarah is stuck with two kindergarten babies to watch. Best friends also part in *Ira Says Goodbye* (Waber). When Ira first learns that his best friend, Reggie, is moving, he sadly thinks of all the fun things they have done. Then, when Reggie tells him how excited he is about moving to a city where there are lots of fun things to do, Ira gets mad and thinks about all the things Reggie does that bug him.

Amber Brown Is Not a Crayon by Paula Danziger is the story of Amber and Justin, her best friend since preschool. When Amber finds out in third grade that Justin's family is moving to Alabama, she is devastated. They fall into a silly quarrel, but with some counseling they realize that the true cause of their spat is their dejection about the coming separation.

One of the most moving books about friendship between a girl and a boy is *Bridge to Terabithia* by Katherine Paterson. Though this title is most often remembered because of Leslie's death, it is Leslie's friendship with Jess that the author says is the focus of the book. Leslie moves to a rural Virginia farmhouse adjacent to Jess's at the beginning of their fifth-grade year. Her unique and unconventional manner opens up worlds of imagination and learning that change Jess forever. He is out of town when Leslie falls and strikes her head, and he is disbelieving and numb when he learns of her death. As is characteristic of Paterson's novels, the reader becomes so involved with the characters that it is impossible to remain unmoved by this account, even when forewarned of the death.

ꙮ Responding to Literature

Grand Conversations   Children who love stories love to talk about them. A way to encourage talk is through a **grand conversation**, a collaborative discussion that is much like natural conversation, in which the teacher is a facilitator or participant (not the inquisitor). Grand conversations can occur in a large group, such as the whole class, or in a small group, such as a literature circle. Initially it may be difficult for you to keep from falling into the old role of inquisitor—the role in which you ask a question about a book, call on a child to respond, and then mentally evaluate the child's answer before probing for more information, redirecting the question to another child, or initiating a new question. Table 9.1 contrasts the roles of the teacher and students in traditional discussions and grand conversations. Select a book that you are reading aloud to your children or one they are all reading independently. Conduct a grand conversation, and try to assume the role of facilitator. It usually takes a few times to overcome the traditional inquisitor's role.

TABLE 9.1   **Comparison of Grand Conversations with Traditional Discussions**

☺ Grand Conversations ☺	☹ Traditional Discussions/Inquisitions ☹
Students are encouraged to guide the discussion and to take turns talking when they have something to contribute.	Teacher controls content of discussion and the students' verbal exchanges.
Students' discussion resembles natural conversation with shifting topics.	Students respond to teacher's questions.
Students describe the feelings the text evokes in an exchange that reveals their response to the passage.	Teacher controls what counts as an acceptable interpretation of the passage.
Students collaborate by building on previous comments.	Teacher controls the content and direction of discussion.
Teacher is facilitator and asks open-ended questions.	Teacher asks questions, selects who is to answer, and evaluates each answer according to his or her interpretation of the passage.
Teacher's questions are genuine quests for information or clarification.	Teacher asks questions to assess students' comprehension of a passage.

Humor

Some contemporary realistic books are written primarily for comic relief. Books targeted for primary-grade children often contain slapstick humor, but intermediate-grade children find light sarcasm appealing. Surely children will read more if they can self-select books they are interested in and enjoy. Because of the universal appeal of humorous literature, Klesius, Laframboise, and Gaier (1998) make a special case for using it with **reluctant readers**—children who tend not to choose reading as a pastime. These researchers believe that by offering a good laugh, humorous literature gives nonachievers an authentic reason to read. This can result in better comprehension and the likelihood that reluctant readers will become less reluctant.

Judy Blume's *Freckle Juice* is sure to make readers of all ages laugh. Andrew wants to have freckles like his friend Nicky, because he thinks that then his mother will never notice if his neck is dirty. So he buys Sharon's secret freckle recipe for fifty cents. But when he tries the strange combination of ingredients, he turns green—not freckled.

Thomas Rockwell's *How to Eat Fried Worms* is equally hilarious. Because of a revolting bet, Billy has to eat fifteen worms in fifteen days. The worms are supplied by his opponent, and he is allowed a choice of condiments to help get them down. The gastronomic ordeal takes a new twist each day, making the outcome of this delightfully repulsive story unpredictable.

Gary Paulsen is best known for his adventure stories, but he displays a unique comic vein in *The Schernoff Discoveries*. The hysterically funny antics of two 14-year-old social nerds, who are "easily the most unpopular boys in the entire demographic area encompassing Washington Junior High School" (p. 1), are told in the first-person account of the main character. His best (read: *only*) friend, Harold Schernoff, is a science whiz with a theory for every problem. However, nothing goes according to Harold's plans, especially his scheme on how to act on a first date. The narrator (unnamed) is willing to help Harold test his theories, though they invariably have disastrous results. At the end of the book, readers learn that the narrator is the author, Gary Paulsen—whose aim is to show how a good sense of humor and a faithful friend can help make an outcast succeed. The book is inspiring to readers who fear that adolescent uncoolness might be a permanent state of being.

Books with themes of sibling rivalry are usually humorous—for example, Eloise Greenfield's *She Come Bringing Me That Little Baby Girl*. A little boy's disappointment and jealousy over a new baby sister are gradually dispelled as he becomes aware of the importance of his role as a big brother.

In *Judy Moody* (McDonald), a thoroughly independent and willful Judy starts the first day of third grade in a bad mood. When she gets an assignment to create a collage all about herself, grumpy Judy sets out on a lively and hilarious self-exploration over the next few weeks.

The first book in Barbara Park's expansive Junie B. Jones series is *Junie B. Jones and the Stupid Smelly Bus*. In a running first-person account, Junie B. hilariously describes how she feels about her first day of kindergarten. She hates the bus and the meanies on it, so she decides not to ride it home and hides in the supply closet. After a few adventures exploring the mostly empty school, she is caught by the principal who starts asking her questions.

> "I'm a good hider," I told him.
> Principal acted a little bit grumpy. He said I wasn't allowed to do that anymore. "When you go to school, you have to follow the rules," he said. "What would happen if every boy and girl hid in the supply closet after school?"
> "It would be very smushy in there," I said.
> Then he made his eyes frowny. "But we wouldn't know where anyone was, would we?" he said.
> "Yes," I said. "We would all be in the supply closet." Then Principal looked up at the ceiling. And I looked up, too. But I didn't see anything. . . . (p. 65)

No, David! by David Shannon is illustrated with childlike paintings of a round-headed, sharp-toothed boy who wrecks havoc in his house while his mother vainly yells directives such as, "No, David," during his perilous reach for the cookie jar; "No! No! No!" as he makes the bathtub overflow; and, "Come back here, David!" as he runs naked down the street. Each double-page illustration depicts a different caper that is sure to make young children laugh.

Jeff Kinney's *Diary of a Wimpy Kid* is a hybrid book that falls somewhere between traditional prose and a graphic novel, illustrated with comical line drawings. The narrator is Greg Heffley who chronicles his first year in middle school. The story is told through humorous, sometimes unrelated, episodes, but keep your eye on the piece of moldy cheese on the playground. By the end of the book, it will have you in raucous laughter!

Adventure

Adventure stories typically have fast-moving plots that take place in unusual settings. The quest theme is prevalent: Protagonists in adventure tales often embark on arduous journeys in search of a deeper understanding of themselves. **Survival stories** are adventure stories in which the protagonist is pitted against the elements of nature. In regular adventure stories, the main characters may contend with severe weather in remote locations, but they embark on their adventures by choice, and they can return to a safe haven if they desire. In contrast, the protagonists in survival stories are not in their hostile settings by choice, and they must struggle to survive until they find their way to a safer environment or are rescued. Because of the exciting plots, even reluctant readers used to a steady diet of television can often be induced to read adventure stories with absorbing, breathtaking action. Both Gary Paulsen and Jean Craighead George are well known for their lively adventure stories.

Gary Paulsen draws from many exciting episodes of his own life for background in the survival stories he writes. His own adventures include hunting and trapping in winter as a young person and twice running the Iditarod Trail sled dog race across more than 1,100 miles of grueling Alaskan terrain. Paulsen's experiences with the latter is clearly seen in *Dogsong*, the story of a 14-year-old Eskimo boy, Russel Susskit, who is troubled by the impact of modernity on his life. His longing for the old ways and the songs that celebrated them takes him to the elder, Oogruk, who is the only one in the village who owns a team of dogs. Russel lives and learns with Oogruk and then embarks on an arduous trek by dogsled across the frozen Alaska wilderness. His 1,400-mile journey across ice, tundra, and mountains brings him self-discovery and his own song, as well as an unexpected encounter with another sojourner.

Fourteen-year-old John Barron is the protagonist in *The Haymeadow* (Paulsen). He is asked to spend the summer taking care of the family sheep herd in the ranch's hay meadow, and he is left there alone (except for two horses, four dogs, and 6,000 sheep). John desperately wants to please his father, but a river flood, coyote attacks, and an injured dog make it seem less likely that he will. His resourcefulness, ingenuity, and talent help him survive the summer and to succeed in the rite of passage like his father and grandfather before him.

The Voyage of the Frog (Paulsen) is the story of 14-year-old David Alspeth's ordeal at sea. In the sailboat his uncle left him, David sets out to fulfill his uncle's last wish by scattering his ashes at sea. However, he is caught in a savage storm; when it passes he is lost and becalmed on a windless sea. There is no radio and only a little water and seven cans of food on board the twenty-two-foot boat. As David drifts southward, he experiences a near collision with an oil tanker as well as frightening encounters with sharks and killer whales. How he survives until he is rescued by a whale research ship off the coast of Baja California is a thrilling tale.

Surely Paulsen's best-loved survival story is *Hatchet*. Thirteen-year-old Brian Robeson is stranded in the Canadian wilderness after the single-engine airplane he was on crashes into a lake. Brian is the sole survivor, escaping with nothing but the clothes he is wearing and a hatchet buckled to his belt, which was a parting gift from his mother. Each of his fifty-four days living in the treacherous wilderness is filled with Brian's perseverance in finding food, shelter, and protection from the elements. When part of the wrecked plane finally floats to the surface of the lake, Brian is able to remove a survival pack that includes an emergency transmitter. He unwittingly turns on the transmitter—and it is heard by a fur buyer flying a bush plane with floats, which allow the pilot to land on the lake and rescue Brian.

Gordon Korman is a talented author who writes humorous novels as well as adventure series, such as Island, Everest, and Dive. The first book in his newest adventure series (On the Run) is titled *Chasing the Falconers,* in which he introduces Aidan and Meg Falconer. Their well-respected parents were convicted of treason and sentenced to life in prison. Aidan and Meg are placed in a juvenile detention center for their own protection, but when the place accidentally burns down, the two set out to locate a missing FBI agent whom they believe will exonerate their parents. The fugitives use their wits to make it across country to obtain their first clue while enduring hardship and several thrilling escapes from those who hunt them.

Featured Author

Jean Craighead George

Jean Craighead George, the daughter of an entomologist, had early exposure to natural habitats in the Florida Everglades. Today she is a respected naturalist who travels extensively to observe and report on the behavior of animals in the wild. In her children's books, she blends her profound respect for nature with her deep understanding of the reciprocal relationship between humans and their natural surroundings. She has spent much time in Alaska, where her grandson Luke lives, and has traveled by dogsled far out on the Arctic Sea to climb blue pressure ridges and view the natural settings of the animals in her books.

The protagonist in *Julie of the Wolves* is a 15-year-old Inuit girl named Miyax, whose English name is Julie. She escapes from a dreadful arranged marriage by fleeing across the tundra. She naively thinks she can reach her pen pal in San Francisco, but instead she becomes lost in the Alaskan wilderness without food or a compass. Near starvation, she closely observes an Arctic wolf pack and mimics their behavior until they accept her into the group and provide food. With their help and by drawing upon her father's early training, Julie struggles day by day to survive. She comes to love the wolves as her brothers and is devastated when the leader, Amaroq, is shot from an airplane. After many months of life in the wilderness, she is found by a hunter and taken to her father.

Julie is the sequel to *Julie of the Wolves*. After many years of separation, Julie tries to adjust to living with her father, Kapugen, and her new white stepmother. When Julie finds her father's pilot helmet and goggles, she realizes he is the one who killed the beloved leader of her wolf pack. Kapugen is determined to kill any wolves that appear near the Kangik village's musk oxen herd, even if they are members of Julie's beloved pack. When she hears the calls of her pack nearby, she prepares for a long solitary journey. She finds the pack (now led by Kapu, son of the slain Amaroq), renews their friendship, and regains their confidence. By carrying Kapu's pup in her backpack, she gets the wolves to follow her across the tundra to an area where they can find wild game.

The Talking Earth is possibly George's best portrayal of the reciprocal relationship between humans and nature. The protagonist, 13-year-old Billie Wind, is a Florida Seminole living on the Big Cypress Reservation. When she scoffs at the old legends and beliefs of her people, such as the animal gods who talk, the tribal council decides to punish her by requiring her to spend two days alone in the *pa-hay-okee*, the Everglades. Billie takes her punishment as a challenge, and she willingly prolongs her sojourn in the Everglades for twelve weeks. After surviving a raging forest fire and threats from dangerous animals, she discovers that she must listen to the animals and the land in order to survive.

Mystery

Mystery stories are a special category of adventure tales. They usually involve solving some type of puzzle, which may or may not be a crime. Though Joan Lowery Nixon has written several good murder mysteries for children (such as *A Candidate for Murder*), murder is not typically involved in children's mystery books. However, they do contain unusual characters and clever twists of plot that will surprise readers—unless they have been able to interpret the clues that are interwoven in the story.

Sutherland (1997) described the unique positive effects that reading mysteries can have on young readers. The element of mystery evokes excitement and suspense, so it can rouse the interest of reluctant readers. Because children often speed up their usual reading rate under the stimulus of suspense, mysteries encourage rapid silent reading, a critical skill for fluent readers. In addition, a carefully structured mystery story can help develop logical reasoning.

Responding to Literature

Looking for Mystery Clues   To get the most enjoyment from reading mysteries and to help develop logical reasoning skills, try to solve the mystery in the story before it is revealed to you. Use the following steps:

1. Identify the mystery or puzzle of the book as soon as possible, and write it in a complete sentence in the form of a question (e.g., "Who stole Thomas's money?").
2. List each clue in the plot as it is disclosed by the author.
3. Cross through any clues that turn out to be irrelevant.
4. Using the relevant clues, form one or more possible answers to your question before it is revealed by the author at the end of the story.

Practice this method with one of the short mysteries provided in *Encyclopedia Brown and the Case of the Slippery Salamander* by Donald J. Sobol. Each chapter is a separate mystery, and the solutions are revealed at the end of the book, allowing you to try your skill at solving them yourself.

Since 1962 the Edgar Allan Poe Award has been given yearly by the Mystery Writers of America for the best juvenile novel in the field of mystery, suspense, crime, or intrigue. Authors who have won this award—some of whom are not normally associated with mystery writing—include Robbie Branscum, Eve Bunting, Betsy Byars, Dorothy R. Miller, Phyllis Reynolds Naylor, Joan Lowery Nixon, Willo Davis Roberts, and Susan Shreve. In this section I will touch on books by some of these authors as well as on some of the mystery classics.

Younger children delight in the series of crime-solving stories that started with *Encyclopedia Brown: Boy Detective* by Donald J. Sobol. Leroy Brown's father is the chief of police in Idaville. Leroy's computerlike brain has won him the nickname Encyclopedia, and he helps his father solve the tough cases. Most books in the series consist of ten or so chapters, each with a different crime. The readers are invited to interpret the clues and solve the cases along with Encyclopedia. In the event readers need help, the answers are in the back of the book.

In *Chasing Vermeer* (Balliett), Petra and Calder are brainy sixth graders who are determined to solve the mystery of a missing Vermeer painting, *A Lady Writing*. The thief leaves a trail of public clues via the newspaper, and the kids try to figure out what a set of pentominos (mathematical puzzle pieces) and a mysterious book about unexplainable phenomena have to do with a centuries-old artwork. As a bonus, Brett Helquist hid a secret pentomino message in several of the book's illustrations for readers to decode.

Many residents of Middleburg, Indiana, are already going crazy from the ever-ringing church bells and now, after a bat is spotted in the Bessledorf Hotel run by Bernie's family, they worry that the dangerous Indiana Aztec bat has finally arrived in *Bernie Magruder and the Bats in the Belfry* (Naylor). But who put up all those posters about a species of bat no one has ever heard of? Bernie and his friends Georgene and Weasel set out to answer these questions in this humorous mystery story.

In E. L. Konigsburg's acclaimed book of intrigue *From the Mixed-Up Files of Mrs. Basil E. Frankweiler,* Claudia decides to run away to teach her parents to appreciate her. She invites her brother Jamie, and they take up residence in the Metropolitan Museum of Art. Claudia finds a statue so beautiful that she will not go home until she discovers its maker, but that question has baffled even the experts. They go to the home of the statue's former owner, Mrs. Frankweiler, to find the answer.

The House of Dies Drear by Virginia Hamilton is an absorbing mystery about 13-year-old Thomas and his family, who move into a huge old house with secret tunnels, a cantankerous caretaker, and legends of buried treasure. Thomas senses something strange about the Civil War era house, which used to be a critical stop on the Underground Railroad. Exploring the hidden passageways in and under the house, he pieces together clues in an increasingly dangerous quest for the truth.

In *The Westing Game* (Raskin), sixteen heirs of the eccentric multimillionaire Samuel Westing are assembled in the old Westing house for the reading of his very strange will. To their surprise, the will turns out to be a contest, challenging the group to find out who among them is Westing's murderer. The heirs are paired off and given clues to a puzzle they must solve in order to inherit the money.

Megan's Island by Willo Davis Roberts is the story of 11-year-old Megan Collier's search for her identity. The book opens when, a week before school is out, her mother insists on taking Megan and her younger brother to their grandfather's isolated lake cottage in the middle of the night. Megan is astonished by her mother's actions—and is further disturbed by evidence that they have been followed and are being spied upon by three mysterious strangers.

One of Betsy Byars's funniest books in the Blossom series is *Wanted ... Mud Blossom.* The school hamster that Junior brought home for the weekend is missing; the evidence points to Mud, Pap Blossom's dog, who is hiding under the porch. Meanwhile, old Mad Mary (the Vulture Lady who is Junior's best friend) also has disappeared. Her bag and cane are found by the side of the road, and Junior knows she would never leave them behind voluntarily. The book is full of delightfully comic twists.

Eve Bunting's *Coffin on a Case* features 12-year-old Henry Coffin, the son of a private investigator. When his father is called out of town, Henry helps Lily—a gorgeous high school girl—search for her kidnapped mother. His powers of observation, intuition, and logic help save not only Lily's mother but a valuable art object as well.

In *Search for the Shadowman,* four-time Edgar Allan Poe Award–winner Joan Lowery Nixon combines contemporary and historical fiction in an exciting mystery. Twelve-year-old Andy Thomas delves into his family tree and uncovers a secret kept hidden for generations. Though his own family discourages him and he receives mysterious threats, he is determined to clear the name of the family's black sheep, Coley Joe Bonner.

In *Holes,* a darkly humorous tale of crime and punishment, Louis Sachar tells the story of young Stanley Yelnats, who has been sent to a boys' juvenile detention center at Camp Green Lake, Texas. Though Stanley is innocent of the crime, the camp seems a better alternative than jail. At the waterless camp, Stanley and the other boys must suffer the punishment of digging a hole a day in the hot sun—five feet deep and five feet across—in the hard earth of the dried-up lakebed. Stanley discovers that the wicked warden is really using the boys to dig for loot buried by the Wild West outlaw Kissin' Kate Barlow. The author masterfully weaves a narrative puzzle that tangles and untangles with increasing suspense.

Social Reality

War

Stories that deal with war and its aftermath are less prevalent in contemporary fiction than in historical fiction. However, four great books deal with the aftermath of the Vietnam conflict. *The Wall* by Eve Bunting is a heartrending story of a little boy and his father who travel a great distance to visit the Vietnam Veterans Memorial in Washington, D.C. They find the name of the boy's grandfather, who was killed in the conflict, and make a pencil rubbing of his name. The man says he is the same age his father was when he was killed, and the boy silently wishes that his grandfather could be with them instead of having his name on the wall.

When Vietnam succumbed to Communism, thousands of people had to flee, and they were referred to as Boat People. *Weeping under This Same Moon* by Jana Laiz is a true story that tells of three siblings who make the perilous journey that takes them to New York City. Half the story is narrated by Mei, a 19-year-old woman, and half by Hannah, a 17-year-old American high school student who describes herself as a social misfit with a passion for the environment. When Hannah volunteers to befriend not only Mei but also her other refugee neighbors, it changes the two girls' lives forever.

In *Journey Home* by Laurence McKay, a 10-year-old Vietnamese American girl tells of the journey with her mother to Vietnam to search for her mother's birth family. Mai's mother was left as a baby at an orphanage in Saigon during the Vietnam conflict and was subsequently adopted by a loving American family. Mai's mother locates the man who saw her parents die in the bombing of their village. The old man recounts how he took her from the rubble and carried her through the devastated village to the orphanage.

Katherine Paterson's *Park's Quest* is the story of an 11-year-old boy's search for information about his father, who was killed in Vietnam a decade earlier. Park's mother refuses to speak about his father, but when Park finds he has a grandfather and uncle in rural Virginia, he goes to spend the summer on their farm. Among Park's startling discoveries are that his parents were divorced before his father died and that he has a Vietnamese half sister.

Issues in Contemporary Fiction

Should We Allow Children to Read Books with Social Reality Themes?
In the introduction to this chapter, I emphasized my belief that attempting to keep children ignorant of social realities will not keep them safe from the problems of the world. I do not believe we can hide the realities of the world from children, and I do believe that most children are quite capable of facing serious issues. However, not everyone agrees with this view, and even if you do agree with it, do you have an age limit for which you would draw the line?

Argue for or against the following statement: Attempting to protect children from painful subjects can, among other things, prevent children from understanding the plight of less fortunate people.

Homelessness

Eve Bunting's *Fly Away Home* is the story of a man and his young son, Andrew, who live at the airport because the father's job does not pay enough for a deposit on an apartment. They must avoid detection, so father and son keep to themselves, change terminals every night, sleep sitting up, wash in the rest rooms—and, above all, try not to be noticed. Andrew feels hope when he sees a bird trapped in the terminal find its way to freedom.

The plight of poverty and homelessness is spotlighted when 11-year-old Clay struggles to survive on the street after his father and then his mother abandon him in *Monkey Island* (Fox). He is compelled to stay near the welfare hotel where he and his mother were living. To avoid being taken away by social workers, Clay escapes to the street, where two homeless men, Buddy and Calvin, take him under their wing.

Bye, Bye, Bali Kai (Luger) is the story of a middle-class family's descent into homelessness. Suzie's father loses his job and cannot find another, and her mother's new job does not cover the bills. After eviction from the Bali Kai apartments and a week in a cheap motel, Suzie and her parents sleep in their car behind a dingy abandoned building. Suzie must spend her afternoons in the public library, alone except for Dawn, the school outcast who latches onto her.

Poverty and Child Labor

Working Cotton by Sherley Anne Williams is a somber look at a long workday in the life of a migrant family in which everyone except the smallest child must labor in the fields harvesting cotton. The story is told through the eyes of Shelan, a young girl who works in the fields with her family in central California.

Lupita Mañana by Patricia Beatty is the tale of 13-year-old Lupita, whose father died in an accident near their small Mexican village. Her mother tells Lupita and her older brother Salvador that they must cross the border into the United States to earn enough money to support her and their younger siblings. The children enter California illegally and work at menial jobs, constantly on the watch for *la migra*, the immigration officers who will deport them if found.

In a similar story, Fran Leeper Buss presents the plight of 15-year-old Maria in *Journey of the Sparrows*. Fleeing El Salvador and eager for a new life in the United States, Maria, her pregnant older sister, her little brother, and a stranger endure a terrifying journey nailed inside a crate in the back of a truck that crosses the border and drives on to Chicago. There they find work cleaning, sewing, and washing dishes—always careful to remain invisible so the authorities will not arrest and deport them.

Gangs and Crime

Smoky Night by Eve Bunting is a child's view of the Los Angeles riots, complete with burning buildings and feuding neighbors. The mother explains to her child that rioting happens when people get angry; they only want to smash and destroy because they do not care anymore about right and wrong.

Walter Dean Myers's *Scorpions* is a look at gang life. Twelve-year-old Jamal Hicks is having a tough time at school, with Dwayne always pushing him to fight. Jamal worries about his mother, who is working hard to save enough money for an appeal for his jailed older brother, Randy. Randy was the leader of the Harlem Scorpions, and he wants Jamal to take his place until he gets out, but the gang members, especially Angel and Indian, do not like the idea. The only one who approves is Mack, and he gives a gun to Jamal, who reluctantly takes on the leadership of the gang. Jamal finds that when he carries the gun, his enemies treat him with respect. Then a tragedy occurs. Though Jamal survives the experience, he sacrifices his innocence and his best friend.

In Alice Mead's *Junebug*, Reeve McLain Jr., known as Junebug, is approaching his tenth birthday—the age at which boys in the projects are forced into gangs or ensnared by drug dealers. He dreams that someday he and his younger sister and mother will move away from their awful housing project, where drugs, gangs, and guns are part of everyday life. Before the gangs and drug dealers come after him, he launches his collection of fifty glass bottles, each carrying a message about his desire to be a sailor and his wish for his family to escape their project home.

Racism

Jerry Spinelli's *Maniac Magee* is the story of a remarkable homeless orphan named Jeffrey "Maniac" Magee, who confronts racism in the small town of Two Mills, Pennsylvania. This 12-year-old seeks a home where there is no racism, and he attempts to soothe tensions between rival factions on the tough side of town. The story is presented as an urban legend, extolling Magee's ability to do the unthinkable, such as crossing the boundary between the white West End and the black East End, confronting prejudice and racism head on.

Nicholasa Mohr's *Felita* is a story of the heartache a young Puerto Rican girl in New York experiences when her parents move from *El Barrio* to what they believe is a better neighborhood and school district for their children. Instead of the better future that her father promised, the children are faced with racism and hatred. The kids in the new neighborhood taunt Felita, and her family finally moves back to their old block. In an interesting contrast, Felita also faces prejudice and ridicule from children who are native to Puerto Rico when she goes with her uncle to visit the island in *Going Home.* Among other things, the children laugh at her Spanish and call her a *Nuyorican.*

In Laurence Yep's *Thief of Hearts,* Stacy has always felt comfortable in her suburban middle school. Things begin to go downhill when her family assigns her to escort Hong Ch'un, the new girl from China. When Stacy defends Hong Ch'un against false charges of petty thievery, her friends accuse her of blind loyalty to another culture. When she is called a half-breed, she is shocked and finds herself caught between her Chinese and American heritages. Stacy's mother and great-grandmother take her back to San Francisco's Chinatown, where Stacy learns about their immigrant past and the struggles they faced.

In Judy Blume's *Iggie's House,* an African American family with three children moves into an all-white neighborhood on Grove Street. Eleven-year-old Winnie is the only one who welcomes them, and they soon find a hate sign posted in their front yard: "Go back where you belong. We don't want your kind around here." Winnie learns the difference between being a good neighbor and being a good friend. The author provides a perceptive interpretation of the African American family's reaction.

Personal Issues

Except for books that are strictly humorous, most contemporary realistic books contain one or more personal issues. Frequently the character's personal issue is the major theme of the story. Below is a list of popular contemporary realistic books with personal issue themes that are relevant to elementary school children.

Adoption

Absolutely Normal Chaos (Creech). In 13-year-old Mary Lou's summer journal, she writes about the unexpected visit of Cousin Carl Ray from West Virginia. During his long-term stay, Carl Ray hopes to overcome the anger he felt when he learned his father was not his birth parent, and to search for his biological father, who lives nearby.

Come Sing, Jimmy Jo (Paterson). When his family starts a successful country music group and he becomes the featured singer, 11-year-old James has to deal with big changes. He is not prepared when a stranger approaches and says he is his real father.

Mother Help Me Live (McDaniel). Because she has leukemia, 15-year-old Sarah MacGreggor needs a bone marrow transplant. She is stunned and then angry when her parents tell her they cannot be donors because she is adopted. She searches for and finds her birth mother but is disappointed by the woman's response.

Tell Me Again about the Night I Was Born (Curtis). A small child asks her adoptive parents to tell her again about the night of her birth, demonstrating that it is a cherished tale she knows by heart.

Death

Getting Near to Baby (Couloumbis). Thirteen-year-old Willa Jo and Little Sister must live with Aunt Patty and Uncle Hob until their mother can overcome the grief of Baby's sudden death. Willa Jo and her aunt are constantly at odds, and early one morning, Willa Jo and Little Sister decide to sit on the roof to see the sunrise; then they do not want to come down.

Mick Harte Was Here (Park). Phoebe copes with the painful loss of her 12-year-old brother, who died in a bicycle accident because he was not wearing a helmet. She reminisces about the many happy and funny things they did together.

Nana Upstairs & Nana Downstairs (dePaola). Every Sunday 4-year-old Tommy and his parents visit his grandparents and his 94-year-old great-grandmother, who is always in bed upstairs. Tommy is greatly saddened when his upstairs Nana dies, but his mother comforts him by explaining that she will come back in his memory.

The Wanderer (Creech). An adopted 13-year-old girl has blocked from her memory the death of her parents in a boating accident (in which she survived) and all the foster care she experienced before she was adopted at age 10. Her cousin gently helps her recall the memories.

Determination

Amazing Grace (Hoffman). A classmate tells Grace she cannot play Peter Pan in the school play because she is black and a girl, but Grace discovers that she can do anything she sets her mind to.

Hoot (Hiaasen). The saga of three children's determination to save a colony of endangered burrowing owls from a proposed construction site in Florida makes for lively reading.

The Man in the Ceiling (Feiffer). Jimmy Jibbet may be a disappointment to his father because he is a lousy ball player, but he takes comfort in his conviction that he will one day be a great cartoonist.

Sticks (Bauer). There is only one thing in the world Mickey Vernon really wants—to win the 10- to 13-year-olds' nine-ball championship; but to win he has to beat Buck Pender, who is three years older. An old friend of Mickey's father turns up and offers to coach him, but his mother does not trust the man.

Dilemma

Are You There God? It's Me, Margaret. (Blume). When Margaret's family moves to Farbrook, she learns that everybody belongs to either the Y or the Jewish Community Center, but she does not have a religion because one of her parents was raised Christian and the other Jewish. Margaret has many conversations with God in hope of getting some help in choosing a religion and in coping with the problems of puberty.

Ira Sleeps Over (Waber). When Ira gets ready for his first sleepover, he is torn between taking his teddy bear, Tah Tah, and leaving it home. He has never slept without it before, but his big sister says Reggie will laugh at him.

 Stargirl (Spinelli). A most unusual girl charms the students at Mica High when she first arrives. Initially, everyone finds her unconventional behaviors fascinating. When she persists in cheering when both the home and the opposing team score, her individuality is reviled. Her boyfriend Leo struggles between the need to be accepted by the other students and his love for Stargirl.

Wringer (Spinelli). Palmer LaRue dreads the day he turns 10, when he will be expected to take his place beside the other boys in town and become a "wringer" at the annual Pigeon Day shooting contest. Wringers wring the necks of wounded pigeons, but Palmer is repulsed by the slaughter.

Disability

Joey Pigza Swallowed the Key (Gantos). Joey has attention deficit disorder, and he has trouble sitting still, paying attention, and following the rules—especially when his medication wears off.

Now One Foot, Now the Other (dePaola). When his grandfather suffers a stroke, which results in partial paralysis, Bobby teaches him to walk, just as his grandfather once taught him.

Tangerine (Bloor). Paul Fisher is legally blind, and he has lived most of his life in the shadow of his football star brother, whom he fears. When his family moves to Tangerine County, Florida, Paul gains friends and confidence by playing goalie on the soccer field, and he finally is able to confront his parents to learn the truth about the incident that damaged his sight.

Yellow Bird and Me (Hansen). Doris reluctantly starts helping Yellow Bird, the class clown, with his studies. She finds out that his learning disability makes it difficult for him to learn to read, and in caring for and helping Bird with his reading and learning his part in the school play, she develops a new friend.

Animals

Animal stories most often deal with warm relationships between young people and their animal companions, and stories involving dogs and horses are the most popular. There is much for children to gain by reading these stories. In stories about pets, children can enjoy the "vicarious experience of giving love to and receiving devotion and loyalty from animals" (Huck et al., 1997, p. 496). Stories can also help children learn to breed and raise young animals and can teach lessons about the proper training of pets. Perhaps most important, reading about the nurture and care required for a pet helps children recognize others' needs.

In stories involving wild animals, children can learn about the animals' natural habitats and the impact of predators, weather, and seasons. They can vicariously experience the maturity cycles of animals as they grow and develop, mate, raise young, and die.

Popular animal story plots include children who desire pets but must first convince their parents, or who gain self-confidence and mature along with a beloved pet. Plots can also involve sad but real issues such as the death of a pet or the sorrow a child experiences when a wild baby animal matures and must be returned to its natural habitat. Other serious themes involve humans' cruel treatment of animals and the illegal hunting of wild animals. More often, though, stories for elementary children center on the positive effects of loyalty and devotion between pets and children.

Unlike the animal fantasy stories discussed in Chapter 7, real animal stories portray animals objectively; that is, the author refrains from interpreting behavior or motives for the animals, and the characteristics of animals depicted are true to their species and breed qualities. Also, there should be a balance among the animals' natural world, human beings, and the special bond of friendship with children. Following is a selection of recommended animal stories.

Animal Stories

Because of Winn-Dixie (DiCamillo). Ten-year-old Opal is lonely when she and and her preacher father move to Naomi, Florida. Opal goes into the Winn-Dixie supermarket and comes out with a big, ugly stray dog, whom she dubs Winn-Dixie. Opal is friendless in her new community, but Winn-Dixie is better at making friends than Opal is, and he helps her make friends with the librarian, the blind Gloria Dump, and Otis who owns a pet shop. Because of Winn-Dixie, Opal begins to find her place in the world and let go of some of the sadness left by her mother's abandonment seven years earlier.

I'll Always Love You (Wilhelm). A child's sadness at the death of his beloved dachshund, Elfie, is tempered by his remembrance of saying to it every night, "I'll always love you."

My Life in Dog Years (Paulsen). In eight chapters, one for each of the significant dogs in his life, Paulsen recounts how his canine friends kept him from harm and made his life richer.

Puppies, Dogs, and Blue Northers: Reflections on Being Raised by a Pack of Sled Dogs (Paulsen). This is a tender account of the sled dog Cookie, who was the lead dog when Paulsen ran the Iditarod sled race in Alaska. The story begins with her last litter and continues to her death of old age.

Shiloh (Naylor). When Marty Preston finds a young beagle that is obviously being abused by its owner, his parents insist he return it. When the dog comes back, Marty finds a way to hide him, but lying to his family is extremely difficult.

Summary

Contemporary realistic fiction stories are set in modern times with events that could possibly occur, meaning the settings are realistic, and there are no fantasy elements such as magic, talking animals, or futuristic technology.

Common themes in this genre include (1) families (traditional, nontraditional, dysfunctional, and abandonment), (2) friendship, (3) humor, (4) adventure (including survival and mystery stories), (5) social realities (war, homelessness, poverty and child labor, gangs and crime, and racism), (6) personal issues (adoption, death, determination, dilemma, and disability), and (7) animals.

Censorship is withholding books from children because the censor finds the content or information objectionable or dangerous. Although parents can certainly attempt to censor what their own children read, they should not be allowed to tell other people's children what they can and cannot read.

Bibliotherapy means obtaining therapy through books, or the process of mending one's life by reading certain books that deal with a problem similar to the reader's. Good books assist in the development of children's emotions, and adults can assist children in their selection of books.

Contemporary Realistic Fiction Books

Ackerman, Karen. *Song and Dance Man*. Illus. Stephen Gammell. Dragonfly, 1992.
Balliett, Blue. *Chasing Vermeer*. Illus. Brett Helquist. Scholastic, 2004.
Bauer, Joan. *Sticks*. Putnam, 2002.
Beatty, Patricia. *Lupita Mañana*. HarperCollins, 2000.
Bloor, Edward. *Tangerine*. Scholastic, 2001.
Blume, Judy. *Are You There God? It's Me, Margaret*. Atheneum, 2001.
Blume, Judy. *Double Fudge*. Dutton, 2002.
Blume, Judy. *Freckle Juice*. Illus. Sonia O. Lisker. Sagebrush, 1999.
Blume, Judy. *Iggie's House*. Atheneum, 2004.
Blume, Judy. *It's Not the End of the World*. Atheneum, 2002.
Blume, Judy. *Superfudge*. Berkley, 2004.
Blume, Judy. *Tales of a Fourth Grade Nothing*. Berkley, 2004.
Bradman, Tony. *Daddy's Lullaby*. McElderry, 2002.
Bunting, Eve. *A Perfect Father's Day*. Illus. Susan Meddaugh. Clarion, 1993.
Bunting, Eve. *Coffin on a Case*. HarperCollins, 1992.
Bunting, Eve. *Fly Away Home*. Illus. Ronald Himler. Clarion, 1993.
Bunting, Eve. *Smoky Night*. Illus. David Diaz. Harcourt, 1999.
Bunting, Eve. *The Hideout*. Harcourt Brace, 1993.
Bunting, Eve. *The In-Between Days*. HarperTrophy, 1996.
Bunting, Eve. *The Wall*. Illus. Ronald Himler. Clarion, 1992.
Bunting, Eve. *The Wednesday Surprise*. Illus. Donald Carrick. Clarion, 1991.
Buss, Fran Leeper. *Journey of the Sparrows*. Puffin, 2002.
Byars, Betsy. *Wanted . . . Mud Blossom*. Yearling, 1993.
Chavarría-Cháirez, Becky. *Magda's Tortillas*. Illus. Anne Vega. Piñata Books, 2000.
Cleary, Beverly. *Dear Mr. Henshaw*. Illus. Paul O. Zelinsky. HarperTrophy, 2002.
Cleary, Beverly. *Ramona and Her Father*. Illus. Alan Tiegreen. HarperTrophy, 1999.
Cleary, Beverly. *Ramona Quimby, Age 8*. Illus. Alan Tiegreen. HarperTrophy, 1992.
Cleary, Beverly. *Ramona's World*. Illus. Alan Tiegreen. HarperTrophy, 2001.
Couloumbis, Audrey. *Getting Near to Baby*. Putnam, 1999.
Creech, Sharon. *Absolutely Normal Chaos*. HarperTrophy, 1997.

Creech, Sharon. *The Wanderer*. HarperCollins, 2000.

Creech, Sharon. *Walk Two Moons*. HarperTrophy, 2004.

Curtis, Jamie Lee. *Tell Me Again about the Night I Was Born*. Illus. Laura Cornell. HarperTrophy, 2000.

Danziger, Paula. *Amber Brown Is Not a Crayon*. Putnam, 1994.

dePaola, Tomie. *Nana Upstairs & Nana Downstairs*. Putnam, 2000.

dePaola, Tomie. *Now One Foot, Now the Other*. Putnam, 2005.

dePaola, Tomie. *Tom*. Putnam, 1997.

DiCamillo, Kate. *Because of Winn-Dixie*. Candlewick, 2000.

Feiffer, Jules. *The Man in the Ceiling*. HarperTrophy, 1999.

Fox, Paula. *Monkey Island*. Yearling, 1993.

Gantos, Jack. *Joey Pigza Swallowed the Key*. Farrar, Straus & Giroux, 1998.

George, Jean Craighead. *Julie*. HarperTrophy, 1996.

George, Jean Craighead. *Julie of the Wolves*. HarperTrophy, 2004.

George, Jean Craighead. *The Talking Earth*. Sagebrush, 1999.

Giff, Patricia Reilly. *Adios, Anna*. Illus. DyAnne DiSalvo-Ryan. Gareth Stevens, 1998.

Giff, Patricia Reilly. *Pictures of Hollis Woods*. Random House, 2002.

Greenfield, Eloise. *She Come Bringing Me That Little Baby Girl*. Illus. John Steptoe. HarperCollins, 1993.

Hamilton, Virginia. *The House of Dies Drear*. Sagebrush, 1999.

Hansen, Joyce. *Yellow Bird and Me*. Clarion, 1991.

Henkes, Kevin. *Two under Par*. HarperTrophy, 2005.

Hiaasen, Carl. *Hoot*. Knopf, 2002.

Hoffman, Mary. *Amazing Grace*. Illus. Caroline Binch. Dial, 1991.

Johnson, Angela. *Tell Me a Story, Mama*. Illus. David Soman. Orchard, 1992.

Kesselman, Wendy. *Emma*. Illus. Barbara Cooney. Dragonfly, 1993.

Kinney, Jeff. *Diary of a Wimpy Kid*. Abrams, 2007.

Konigsburg, E. L. *From the Mixed-Up Files of Mrs. Basil E. Frankweiler*. Atheneum, 2002.

Korman, Gordon. *Chasing the Falconers*. Scholastic, 2005.

Laiz, Jana. *Weeping under This Same Moon*. Crow Flies Press, 2008.

Lewin, Ted. *Big Jimmy's Kum Kau Chinese Take Out*. HarperCollins, 2001.

Luger, Harriet Mandelay. *Bye, Bye, Bali Kai*. Harcourt, 2000.

MacLachlan, Patricia. *Baby*. Delacorte, 1995.

MacLachlan, Patricia. *Journey*. Delacorte, 1991.

McDaniel, Lurlene. *Mother Help Me Live*. Bantam, 1992.

McDonald, Megan. *Judy Moody*. Illus. Peter H. Reynolds. Candlewick, 2002.

McKay, Lawrence. *Journey Home*. Illus. Dom Lee & Keunhee Lee. Lee & Low, 1998.

Mead, Alice. *Junebug*. Farrar, Straus & Giroux, 1995.

Mohr, Nicholasa. *Felita*. Puffin, 1999.

Mohr, Nicholasa. *Going Home*. Puffin, 1999.

Myers, Walter Dean. *Scorpions*. HarperCollins, 1996.

Myers, Walter Dean. *Somewhere in the Darkness*. Scholastic, 2003.

Naylor, Phyllis Reynolds. *Bernie Magruder and the Bats in the Belfry*. Atheneum, 2003.

Naylor, Phyllis Reynolds. *Shiloh*. Aladdin, 2000.

Nixon, Joan Lowery. *A Candidate for Murder*. Delacorte, 1991.

Nixon, Joan Lowery. *Search for the Shadowman*. Delacorte, 1996.

Park, Barbara. *Junie B. Jones and the Stupid Smelly Bus*. Random House, 1999.

Park, Barbara. *Mick Harte Was Here*. Random House, 1996.

Paterson, Katherine. *Bridge to Terabithia*. HarperTrophy, 2005.

Paterson, Katherine. *Come Sing, Jimmy Jo*. Puffin, 1995.

Paterson, Katherine. *Park's Quest*. Nelson Thomas, 1991.

Paulsen, Gary. *Dogsong*. Atheneum, 2000.

Paulsen, Gary. *Hatchet*. Atheneum, 1987.

Paulsen, Gary. *My Life in Dog Years*. Illus. Ruth Wright Paulsen. Thorndike, 2003.

Paulsen, Gary. *Puppies, Dogs, and Blue Northers: Reflections on Being Raised by a Pack of Sled Dogs*. Illus. Ruth Wright Paulsen. Yearling, 2002.

Paulsen, Gary. *The Haymeadow*. Delacorte, 1992.

Paulsen, Gary. *The Schernoff Discoveries*. Bantam, 1997.

Paulsen, Gary. *The Voyage of the Frog*. Yearling, 1990.

Raskin, Ellen. *The Westing Game*. Puffin, 2004.

Roberts, Willo Davis. *Megan's Island*. Aladdin, 1990.

Rockwell, Thomas. *How to Eat Fried Worms*. Sagebrush, 1999.

Rylant, Cynthia. *Missing May*. Scholastic, 2004.

Sachar, Louis. *Holes*. Yearling, 2003.

Shannon, David. *No, David!* Blue Sky Press, 1998.

Sobol, Donald J. *Encyclopedia Brown and the Case of the Slippery Salamander*. Delacorte, 1999.

Sobol, Donald J. *Encyclopedia Brown: Boy Detective*. Lodestar, 1963.

Spinelli, Jerry. *Maniac Magee*. Little, Brown, 1999.

Spinelli, Jerry. *Stargirl*. Knopf, 2000.

Spinelli, Jerry. *Wringer*. HarperTrophy, 2004.

Viorst, Judith. *Alexander and the Terrible, Horrible, No Good, Very Bad Day*. Illus. Ray Cruz. Sagebrush, 1999.

Viorst, Judith. *Alexander, Who's Not (Do you hear me? I mean it!) Going to Move*. Illus. Robin Preiss Glasser. Aladdin, 1998.

Voigt, Cynthia. *A Solitary Blue*. Simon Pulse, 2003.

Waber, Bernard. *Ira Says Goodbye*. Houghton Mifflin, 1991.

Waber, Bernard. *Ira Sleeps Over*. Sagebrush, 1999.

Wilhelm, Hans. *I'll Always Love You*. Sagebrush, 1999.

Williams, Sherley Anne. *Working Cotton*. Illus. Carole Byard. Voyager, 1997.

Williams, Vera B. *A Chair for My Mother*. Sagebrush, 1999.

Woodson, Jacqueline. *Our Gracie Aunt*. Hyperion, 2002.

Yep, Laurence. *Thief of Hearts*. HarperCollins, 1995.

Using acrylic paints on a silk canvas, the artist gave the illusion of a variety of textures.

From *The Year of the Perfect Christmas Tree*, by Gloria Houston and illustrated by Barbara Cooney.

Library locations J (Juvenile) for junior novels; E (Easy) for picture books

Realistic fiction in a real-world setting in the historical past,
with events that are partly historical but largely imaginative

*A*s a student, I was never very good at history. It was sooooooo boring! When I
discovered historical fiction books, however, I realized that history is not boring. It
was the way I was taught history that was boring—listening to classmates slowly read
the textbook out loud, one paragraph at a time, and having to memorize names and
dates that meant nothing to me. But when I read about real and realistic people
within the context of a good story set in past times, history came alive and was not
only interesting but often exciting. Because quality **historical fiction** presents an
accurate portrayal of the historical period depicted, it can be woven into the study
of history and can improve children's knowledge and attitudes toward the subject.

Evaluating Historical Fiction

The following questions can guide you as you select historical fiction books.

- Is the story interesting to elementary children?
- Is the setting integral to the story?
- Are there sufficient references to historical events, people, and other clues to
  allow the reader to place the story in the appropriate historical framework?
- Are the characters believable?
- Is the language authentic for the period?
- Is the setting authentic in every detail?
- Are illustrations authentic for the period?
- Has the author avoided any contradictions with real history?
- Are differing points of view on the issues of the time acknowledged?
- After reading the book, do readers believe they know an era or place better?

Characteristics of Historical Fiction

The major difference between historical fiction and contemporary fiction is the time
setting. Both genres can have the same place setting, but they differ in terms of *when*
the story takes place. For the purpose of this textbook, historical fiction settings include any period from prehistory through 1964, when the Civil Rights Act was
passed. Contemporary fiction settings include from 1964 to the present day. As I
mentioned in Chapter 9, this dividing line is arbitrary, and not all literature specialists agree on it. I selected 1964 because laws, attitudes, and opportunities concerning minorities in the United States were very different before that year; this fact needs
to be kept in mind when we read and evaluate historical fiction.

The characters in historical fiction are believable, realistic people whose dialogue reflects the historical period. Main characters are usually fictional. Other characters can be real historical people, but they generally have supporting roles or are only mentioned in passing. For example, it would be difficult to write a book set during the Civil War without mentioning President Lincoln, General Grant, or General Lee. However, it is important for readers to keep in mind that although good historical fiction books are consistent with actual historical evidence, they are *not* history.

Historical fiction stories reflect real-life milieus of past times. Their themes include the basic conflicts of human existence: good and evil, love and hate, peace and war. Plots often deal with events such as war, death, and racial oppression; because of this, authors most frequently write historical fiction with a serious tone. Table 10.1 compares the characteristics of historical and contemporary fiction.

Biographic Historical Fiction

When authors base their stories on events that happened to real people, the books are called **biographic historical fiction.** These books are largely fictional because nearly all the dialogue is fabricated, and the author embellishes the story to fill in unknown details and to make it more interesting. For example, Carol Ryrie Brink based *Caddie Woodlawn* on the life of her grandmother, Caddie Woodhouse. In the introduction, Brink wrote,

> All of the names in the book, except one, are changed a little bit. The names are partly true, partly made up, just as the facts of the book are mainly true but have sometimes been slightly changed to make them fit better into the story. (p. vi)

TABLE 10.1   Comparison of Historical and Contemporary Fiction

Literary Element	Historical Fiction	Contemporary Fiction
Time setting	Before and including 1964	After 1964
Place setting	Anywhere on earth	Anywhere on earth
Characters	Realistic people who may be fictional, based on real people, or real historical people	Realistic people, nearly always fictional
Tone	Most often serious	Serious or light
Themes	Frontier life, war, nostalgia, adventure/survival, racial oppression, social issues of the time	Family, friendship, humor, adventure/survival, mystery, modern social reality, personal issues

Brink spent much time listening to her grandmother's stories about growing up on the Wisconsin frontier in the 1860s. However, not all authors of biographic historical fiction are fortunate enough to have a primary source for their information. Authors who did not know their ancestors must rely on stories handed down through the generations. Even family stories that are handed down by word of mouth tend to become legends, which makes it difficult to separate truth from fiction. There are often gaps of important information in the stories, and—lacking a primary source—the author must research and think of interesting ways to fill in the gaps and weave it all into a good story. One book based on a handed-down story is *Mountain Valor* by Gloria Houston. The author wrote in the endnote:

> *Mountain Valor* is based on a true event. Valor was Matilda Houston. As an adolescent, she rescued her family's livestock when marauders took them during the Civil War. Exactly how she completed her mission is not known. The story of this very courageous young woman has been a part of the folklore of Avery County, North Carolina, for four generations, yet no written documentation . . . exists. (p. 237)

In a personal communication (November 13, 1999), Houston said she researched the period extensively in order to create probable methods for Valor to make the trek across the mountains to bring her family's livestock home and save her family from starvation.

Other biographic historical fiction books are based on stories told to an author by someone outside the family. This makes the writing all the more challenging, because the author has no family resources to provide ideas and details to fill in the gaps. One such book is *Sounder* by William H. Armstrong, which is based on a story told to the author by the person who is the main character in the book, the young African American son of a sharecropper. The author does not name the characters. Only the much-loved family dog, Sounder—a mixture of Georgia redbone hound and bulldog—is named. The absence of names and of a specific setting for the story may have been the author's device to universalize the book's theme of injustice to the poor.

♟ Literature Activity: Determining Time Setting

When settings in books are vague, as in *Sounder*, you can help children sharpen their observation skills by thinking like detectives. Because the family members in the story are sharecroppers, they may have lived in the Deep South—possibly in Georgia (because of the dog's breed). But *when* did the story take place? Here are the clues:

1. The author heard the story fifty years before writing the book (author's note).
2. The book was published in 1969 (copyright page).
3. The sharecropper's son was an older man, perhaps 60 years old, when he told the story (author's note).
4. The story took place when the man was a young boy, perhaps 12 years old (story).

What year, approximately, did the story take place?

In some biographic historical fiction books, authors write about their own childhoods, as in the series by Laura Ingalls Wilder that started with *Little House in the Big Woods*. This book is based on events in Wilder's early childhood, some sixty years prior to its publication. The author was the primary source of information and could glean any needed details from her siblings and family artifacts—letters, diaries, Bibles, and so on. Because of this, the book is most accurate in its depiction of the time period. I am often asked why Wilder's books are considered fiction rather than autobiography. The answer is that in her series, Wilder freely recreated dialogue and filled in any gaps in her memory with fictional details. She also changed the order of events and compressed time; for example, she took incidents that happened over a period of several years and narrated them as if they all happened in one year.

There is a fine line between biographic historical fiction and fictionalized biography, which you will read about in Chapter 11. To determine whether a book is considered fiction or biography, it is best to find out in which genre the author and publisher categorize it. A good indicator of genre is the section of the library in which the book is shelved. Historical fiction is found in the J and E sections with all the other fiction, whereas biography is found in the J900 section. Also, most hardcover books and some paperback books will state the genre near the bottom of the copyright page.

Books that were written as contemporary fiction many years ago and are still in print are also considered historical. One classic example is *Little Women* by Louisa May Alcott, which is set during the Civil War (1861–1865). The book was published in 1868, so Alcott wrote about her own time period; however, the setting is historical for today's readers. Always keep in mind that my 1964 dividing line between historical and contemporary is arbitrary. Therefore, when a book published prior to 1964 has a setting that is incidental to the story, it may still be considered contemporary fiction if there is nothing in the story that points to a specific historical period. An example is *The Snowy Day* by Ezra Jack Keats (1962), in which a young African American boy living in an inner city plays all day in the snow, much the way children today do.

Researching Historical Fiction

Historical fiction is one of the most difficult genres to write and illustrate because most often authors and illustrators are depicting a time period prior to their birth. This requires careful research and travel to the place setting of the book. Authors also must research the language of the period so that dialogue will be appropriate to the time, representing vocabulary and figures of speech common to people of the setting. You read in Chapter 8 about problems with authenticity that can occur when an author does not do adequate research. There are similar results when illustrators do not conduct adequate research.

One of my favorite books is *But No Candy* written by Gloria Houston and illustrated by Lloyd Bloom. Even though Houston was born and raised and has lived most of her life in western North Carolina, where her books are set, she conducts research for each book, using primary sources such as the Appalachian Cultural Center, the Rural Life Museum, and local historians. Imagine her surprise when *But No Candy,* which is set during World War II, was published with anachronistic illustrations! In several illustrations, including the book cover, the characters are shown using a kerosene lamp. In a personal interview, Houston exclaimed, "I never used a kerosene lamp in my life until I was in a hurricane in Florida. My region of North Carolina had electricity in the 1940s, although some rural areas did not."

In addition, the main character Lee and her little brother are illustrated wearing black canvas shoes with rubber soles that look much like Converse All Stars. In the 1940s children did not wear canvas shoes with rubber soles. For one thing, rubber was reserved for military use during World War II, and canvas shoes did not become popular with children until several years after the war. Needless to say, the author and her fans are looking forward to a new edition of the book with new illustrations.

In contrast, Houston's *The Year of the Perfect Christmas Tree* was illustrated by two-time Caldecott Award winner Barbara Cooney. This book is set in the same region of North Carolina, but during World War I. In preparation for writing the book, Houston conducted research using the sources previously listed as well as the Tweetsie Railroad, Inc., Grandfather Mountain, Inc., and Rogers Whitener (columnist for "Folk Ways and Folk Speech"). She also met with local cabin restorers and photographers. Barbara Cooney traveled with the author to the town of Spruce Pine and toured the school, church, cabins, and train station that appear in the illustrations. Cooney worked ceaselessly for six days making notes, sketches, and photographs that she later used for her paintings. She returned to her home in New England armed with dozens of photographs loaned to her by Hugh Morton, a noted photographer of the area, to provide further authenticity. As examples of Cooney's authentic details, the Spruce Pine Church scenes include a period wood-burning stove (complete with the manufacturer's name, "Acme Champion") and the old church pews, which were discovered in the church basement during her visit. It is easy to see why the talented Barbara Cooney is one of the most respected illustrators of historical fiction.

Scott O'Dell Award

The Scott O'Dell Award is a special award given to honor historical fiction books of high literary quality. The award is given annually to a U.S. citizen who has published a distinguished children's historical fiction book with a New World (i.e., North American) setting. The award, established by the noted children's novelist Scott O'Dell, is administered by the Advisory Committee of the Bulletin of the Center for Children's Books. The first award was given in 1984 to Elizabeth George Speare for *The Sign of the Beaver,* which is set in the Maine wilderness in 1768.

Periods Depicted in Historical Fiction

Ancient Times

Children who are fascinated by stories of the Egyptian boy king Tutankhamen will surely enjoy reading Eloise Jarvis McGraw's *The Golden Goblet*. Ranofer, a young

Egyptian boy, longs to become a master goldsmith like his father. However, after his father dies, Ranofer's evil half brother Gebu makes him labor in his stone works. When Ranofer finds a magnificently ornate golden goblet among Gebu's belongings, he knows his brother is a grave robber—a crime punishable by death. Ranofer risks his life to reveal this wicked crime.

The Bronze Bow by Elizabeth George Speare is set in Galilee in the time of Jesus. Daniel Bar Jamin is a young Jewish rebel who is consumed by hate of the cruel Romans who killed his parents. Daniel fights to drive the Romans out of Israel, but he is gradually won over to the gentle teachings of Jesus and learns that love, not hate, is the source of strength.

Medieval Times

Katherine Paterson has written several good young adult books set in feudal Japan, one of which is appropriate for intermediate-grade children. *The Sign of the Chrysanthemum* is set in the twelfth century during the civil wars between the Genki and Heike clans. This story is about a 13-year-old Japanese boy, Muna, who searches for his father, knowing only that he is a samurai warrior with a chrysanthemum tattoo on his arm. Muna travels to the capital city, Kyoto, and works as a servant to the great swordsmith Fukuji while he continues his quest.

Another exciting novel that takes place in twelfth-century Asia, Linda Sue Park's *A Single Shard*, tells the story of Tree-ear, a 13-year-old orphan living under a bridge in medieval Korea. He longs to learn how to make the delicate celadon ceramics after observing Min, a master potter. Min takes Tree-ear on as his helper, and Tree-ear digs and hauls clay and endures Min's irascible temper. Then Tree-ear takes a long solitary journey to Songdo to show Min's work to the royal court. He faithfully continues even after robbers shatter the work, and he has only a single shard to show.

Several good novels for intermediate-grade children are set in medieval Britain and Europe. The backdrop for *Adam of the Road* by Elizabeth Janet Gray is England in the year 1294. Eleven-year-old Adam and his father are minstrels. When Adam goes looking for his stolen red spaniel, Nick, he gets separated from his father. Adam travels the roads alone, searching the fairs and market towns for both his father and his beloved dog.

Marguerite de Angeli's *The Door in the Wall* is the story of Robin, the son of Sir John de Buerford. After his father leaves him in the care of servants, Robin falls ill and his legs become paralyzed. When the servants flee, fearing the plague, Robin is alone and helpless. Brother Luke finds him and takes him to the hospice of St. Mark, where he is lovingly cared for and taught how to walk with crutches. His dreams of becoming a knight are shattered. However, when the great castle of Lindsay is in danger, it is Robin who ingeniously saves the townspeople.

Avi's *Crispin: The Cross of Lead* is an action-packed story of the dangerous flight of a 13-year-old peasant boy across fourteenth-century England. After his mother dies and he is falsely accused of a crime, the timid boy flees his small village—the only home he has ever known—clutching his only possession, a lead cross. Before he escapes, the village priest tells him that his Christian name is Crispin and that his parentage is perplexing (but the cross is a clue). Crispin meets a huge, odd juggler named Bear and reluctantly swears an oath to be his servant. Yet Bear becomes much more than a master—he's Crispin's teacher, protector, and liberator. Readers will learn much about England's brutal feudal system and the ensuing peasant revolt of 1381.

In *The Midwife's Apprentice* by Karen Cushman, a homeless, nameless girl is taken in as a servant by a hot-tempered, snaggletoothed midwife. Eventually, the girl cleans herself up, takes the name Alyce—and, by secretly watching the midwife work, learns to deliver calves and babies. She finds a useful and contented place in the world of fourteenth-century England.

Joseph Bruchac is a prolific writer who is of Abenaki Indian descent. The setting for his acclaimed book, *Children of the Longhouse,* is in the late 1400s in the homeland of the five Nations of the Iroquois, which encompassed what is present-day New York State. In this book, Ohkwa'ri, an 11-year-old Mohawk boy, and his twin sister must deal with a hostile gang of older boys after Ohkwa'ri reveals to the elders the boys' plan to raid a small village of Anen:taks, people with whom the Mohawks had made peace. The boys seek revenge by trying to hurt Ohkwa'ri during the brutal villagewide game of *Tekwaarathon* (lacrosse).

Colonial Times

The vast majority of historical fiction written for American children is set in the United States. Although not all authors supply an exact time setting for their books, I have arranged books discussed in the following sections in chronological order as nearly as possible.

Michael Dorris, a Modoc Indian, wrote a much acclaimed book set in colonial times. *Morning Girl* is the charming but thought-provoking story of a 12-year-old Taino Indian, Morning Girl, and her younger brother, Star Boy. In alternating chapters the two children narrate rich descriptions of their lives on a Bahamian island in 1492. At the end of the book, Morning Girl witnesses the arrival of the first Europeans.

The Cherokee had lived in the Blue Ridge Mountains for hundreds of years before Europeans first saw them in 1539. In *Itse Selu: Cherokee Harvest Festival,* Daniel Pennington recreates a typical Green Corn Festival prior to the European invasion of the Cherokee homelands. In the story Little Wolf watches anxiously as his family and other villagers prepare to celebrate the corn harvest with a feast. Readers will find authentic accounts of the lifestyle, the harvest feast, a traditional folktale, and the sacred corn dance in this book.

Elizabeth George Speare's *The Witch of Blackbird Pond* is the story of Kit Tyler, a high-spirited teenage girl who has grown up in the shimmering Caribbean islands. In 1687 after her parents die, Kit sails to her new home with relatives in the bleak, cold Connecticut colony. There she is lonely and feels suppressed by the narrow-minded ways of the stern Puritan community. Kit befriends a lonely old Quaker woman who lives on Blackbird Pond, and she is subsequently accused of witchcraft.

👥📖 Literature Activity: Separating Fact and Fiction

In reading historical fiction, it is important to help children sort the history from the fiction. Before you start reading a book, make a chart with the two headings: "Historical Fact" and "Fiction." As each new character appears, help readers determine whether he or she is a real historical person (consult reference books if necessary) or a fictional creation. Place the characters' names under the appropriate heading. Similarly, as major parts of the plot unfold, determine which events are historical fact and which are fiction. Information about the setting may also be added.

Adventurous Americans left the relative safety and comfort of the cities and moved westward even in the colonial era, beginning the lengthy process often romanticized as "How the West was won." To the original inhabitants of the land, however, the advancing frontier represented how the West was *lost*.

📖 Issues in Historical Fiction

What is the Native Americans' Point of View?   Most older works of historical fiction, such as Walter D. Edmonds's *The Matchlock Gun* (Putnam, 1941), reflect the Colonial era from only the European American point of view, a point of view that changed little before the civil rights era. This book was based on a real event, which is tragic because it is a prime example of brutal racism. The setting of *The Matchlock Gun* is 1757, a time when the French and Indians are trying to force the pioneers of the British colonies to leave. When young Edward's father is away and his mother is chased by five Indians, Edward fires an old matchlock gun, killing three men and wounding another, who is later killed by his father. In dialogue one might expect to read about a father and son hunting trip, young Edward is commended because he killed more Indians than his father and companions.

Discuss what the Indians' point of view might have been as they tried to prevent white people from taking their ancestral homelands.

Revolutionary Era

Wartime is a popular setting for both children's and adult historical fiction. One of the most unusual books of the Revolutionary period is Gary Paulsen's *The Rifle*. The book is the history of a magnificently crafted rifle that was made in 1768 by a gunsmith named Cornish McManus, who lived near Philadelphia. The accuracy of the rifle makes it a masterpiece, and after John Byam purchases it, he becomes a legendary sharpshooter in the American Revolutionary War. When Byam succumbs to dysentery, the rifle is passed on, but never again fired. The second half of the book traces the history of the rifle through episodic stories of who owns it and how it changes hands over the next 200 years. Since the death of John Byam, no one has ever checked to see if the rifle was loaded. The tragic final episode, set in the present day, reveals that the gun is loaded.

Esther Forbes's *Johnny Tremain* is a novel of a 14-year-old apprentice silversmith who chronicles the beginnings of the Revolution in the American colonies. Johnny is gravely injured while working with molten silver, and his disability prevents him from continuing his apprenticeship. The historic events of Boston in 1773 are presented through Johnny's point of view, and his courageous involvement in the American Revolution makes an exciting adventure story that is both sad and inspiring.

Scott O'Dell's *Sarah Bishop* is based on a true story of one girl's strength and courage during the American Revolution. Sarah's family lives on Long Island, and they have split loyalties during the War for Independence. Her father is a British Loyalist, and her brother is a Patriot. When they both die as a result of the war, Sarah is arrested by British soldiers on false pretense. She escapes to the Connecticut wilderness, where she lives in a cave and fiercely fights for survival.

After Americans won their freedom from the British, they still faced life-threatening disasters that were as horrific as war. Laurie Halse Anderson's *Fever 1793* is the story of how a 16-year-old girl copes with the yellow fever epidemic in Philadelphia. During the summer of 1793, Mattie Cook lives above the family coffee shop with her widowed mother and grandfather. When mosquitoes bring the devastating disease, and people all around quickly succumb to the fever, her mother insists that Mattie flee the city with her grandfather. However, she soon discovers that the sickness is everywhere, and Mattie must learn self-reliance when she is forced to cope with the horrors of a yellow fever epidemic that killed 10 percent of the population of Philadelphia.

Early Frontier Era

Although many adventures took place on the American frontier, the early nineteenth century also saw adventures on the high seas. *The Stowaway* by Kristiana Gregory is based on a historic event in 1818 at Monterey Bay settlement in California. Eleven-year-old Carlito and his family are loyal to Spain, as are most Californians. When the Argentine pirate Hippolyte de Bouchard attacks the settlement, Carlito witnesses the death of his father and vows revenge. In an attempt to sabotage the pirates' ship, Carlito sneaks on board. He is quickly discovered and enslaved by the cruel captain. He finds a friend in fellow stowaway Billy Bumpus, who came aboard searching for his imprisoned father. As the pirates terrorize the Catholic missions along the California coast, Carlito suffers their filthy living conditions and brutal savagery.

Tales of settlement on the American frontier in the early 1800s have both adventure themes and themes of everyday family life. In a picture book format that children of all ages can enjoy, Donald Hall's *Ox-Cart Man* describes a year in the life of a pioneer family. Barbara Cooney's exquisite illustrations depict how each member of the family works hard all year. Each October the father takes whatever they grow or make but do not use to the Portsmouth Market in an oxcart. After he sells all the goods, including the cart and the ox, he buys the things they are unable to make and returns home with the treasures.

Yonder by Tony Johnston has a similar theme. The text, written in free verse, illuminates a family's history for three generations. The beautiful plum tree the first settler planted outside their house is shown changing and growing in each passing season—like the lives of the people in this three-generation farm family.

Sarah, Plain and Tall by Patricia MacLachlan has a warm family theme, based on the author's family history. When Anna and Caleb's widowed father, Jacob, places a newspaper advertisement for a wife and mother, Sarah Wheaton answers. She travels from Maine to their Midwestern prairie home to meet them. Though Sarah falls in love with the family, she misses her seaside home. Jacob, Anna, and Caleb anxiously await her decision, and at the end of the book, a wedding is planned.

A Gathering of Days: A New England Girl's Journal, 1830–32 by Joan W. Blos is the story of 14-year-old Catherine Cabot Hill, told through the journal Catherine keeps over the last two years she lives on the family farm. She records daily events in her small New Hampshire town, as well as the major events of her life: her father's remarriage and the death of her best friend. Catherine comes of age in a time of loss and change.

In her inimitable style, Katherine Paterson presents a compelling story of one girl's determination to reunite her family in *Lyddie*. In 1843 Lyddie Worthen's father abandons his impoverished family on their Vermont farm. Her mother sends her brother and sisters to live with others and hires Lyddie out to earn money to pay her father's debts. Eventually Lyddie goes to Lowell, Massachusetts, to work in the textile mills; she is determined to earn enough money to buy back their old homestead and reunite her family.

Gary Paulsen's *Mr. Tucket* is an adventure story set on the western frontier in 1848. Fourteen-year-old Francis Tucket is heading west on the Oregon Trail, traveling with his family by wagon train. He receives a rifle for his birthday, but when he lags behind to practice shooting, he is captured by Pawnees. A mysterious one-armed trapper named Mr. Grimes helps Francis escape and shows him how to survive the winter by living off the land.

Also set in 1848 is Bruce Clements's *I Tell a Lie Every So Often*. In this rare humorous historical fiction story, two brothers travel 500 miles up the Missouri River by riverboat, mule, and wagon. Fourteen-year-old Henry and his brother Clayton take this unnecessary odyssey because of a lie Henry told about talking to someone who had seen a red-haired girl living with the Indians in the Dakota Territory. Henry's family think the girl might be his cousin, who disappeared nine years before, and they insist the boys look for her. Henry's homespun humor, as he interprets the actions of the bigoted and pretentious characters, makes for fun reading, but it also causes the reader to pause and ponder the treatment of Native Americans in Missouri during the pioneer era.

Both Laurence Yep and Mildred D. Taylor have written historical series in which they follow several generations of a family (though neither author wrote the stories in chronological order). I have included these novels within the appropriate eras in this chapter to trace the history of Chinese Americans and African Americans.

For more than 30 years, Laurence Yep has been writing stories about seven generations of the Young family and their friends, whose ancestors had long lived in the Three Willows village of China. The first Youngs came to America—which they called the Land of the Golden Mountain—because they had no choice: It was the only way for their families in China to survive. The first of nine books in Yep's Golden Mountain Chronicles is *The Serpent's Children.* When the villagers of Three Willows call Cassia and her brother, Foxfire, "the serpent's children," they mean it as an insult. However, a Chinese legend says that once a serpent sets her mind on something, she never gives up, and Cassia is determined to survive when famine, drought, and violence threaten her family's life. Cassia's father is a revolutionary, fighting to free China from the invading Manchus, but her brother Foxfire seeks the mountain of gold in America during the 1849 gold rush. After Foxfire flees to faraway America, Cassia uses all her strength and wisdom to keep her family together and prove she is truly the serpent's child.

The sequel, *Mountain Light,* is set in 1855. Although the Lau and Young families had maintained an age-old blood feud for generations, their relationship changes when they find themselves on the same side of a new struggle against the tyrannical Manchu dynasty. By devoting himself to the revolution, Squeaky Lau wins Cassia's trust and her heart. Then Squeaky must prove his worth as a man—to Cassia, to the village folk, and to himself. He gives up everything and travels to the Land of the Golden Mountain to join Cassia's brother, Foxfire.

Native Americans. Although the 1800s were an exciting and venturesome era for the European and European American pioneers, the frontier era was a time of loss and unwanted change for Native Americans, who were continually forced to move westward as the new Americans usurped their ancestral homelands. Scott O'Dell, for whom the O'Dell Award for historical fiction is named, wrote two interesting books set in this era.

Island of the Blue Dolphins is O'Dell's first book about Karana, an Indian girl living on a rocky island far off the coast of California. Aleuts working for a Russian sea captain invade the island and kill most of the men. In 1835, when the remainder of the tribe is evacuated, 12-year-old Karana is left behind, searching for her missing young brother. After her brother is killed by wild dogs, Karana must lay aside the taboos of her people to survive. She makes weapons, finds food, and fights her enemies, the wild dogs. Eventually she tames one of the dogs, and he and his pups serve as her only companions for the eighteen years she lives on the island.

Zia is narrated by the 14-year-old niece of Karana. Zia and her brother Mando live at the Santa Barbara mission in California, and when they find an eighteen-foot boat washed ashore, they attempt the sixty-mile trip to the island where Karana was left behind. They are unsuccessful, but they do convince people at the mission to search for her. Eventually Karana is rescued from the island and brought to the mission in 1853; however, no one at the mission speaks her language. The padres will not allow Karana's dog, Rontu-Aru, in the dormitory, so she sleeps in the courtyard with him. Later she moves to a cave near the beach and rescues injured animals.

In *Little Woman Warrior Who Came Home,* Evangeline Parsons Yazzie describes how, in 1864, Dzanibaa, her family, and thousands of other Navajos were captured by U.S. soldiers and forced to walk to Fort Sumner in New Mexico, 450 miles from their home in Arizona. Imprisoned in a land where their crops won't grow, the Navajo are reduced to eating bug-infested, rotten food. During the four long years of her incarceration, Dzanibaa reaches puberty, but her mother explains her coming-of-age ceremony must be postponed until they return to their sacred homeland. Finally, in 1868 the Navajo were released from their imprisonment, and Dzanibaa realizes the significance of the clan system and their prayers and songs that helped them survive.

Slavery. Children need to understand one of the most gruesome elements of U.S. history—the institution of slavery. Paula Fox's *The Slave Dancer* gives a horrific but realistic picture of the ghastly transport of Africans to the slave market. In 1840 13-year-old Jessie Bollier is kidnapped off the New Orleans docks and dumped aboard *The Moonlight,* a slave ship bound for Africa to pick up human cargo. On the trip back, Jessie is forced to play his fife during the exercise periods that will maintain the slaves' muscles. Many of the Africans die during the frightful sea voyage. After four months of hazardous sailing with a degraded crew, the ship is wrecked, and Jessie and a young African boy are the only ones to survive.

There are several excellent books set in the 1850s, the era before slavery was abolished by President Lincoln. These stories tell of the abolitionists, the brave Americans who opposed slavery. Many of the abolitionists operated the Underground Railroad, which was neither a railroad nor underground. Rather, it was a secret cooperative network that aided fugitive slaves in reaching sanctuary in the free states or in Canada. It was called a railroad because it had passengers (escaped slaves), conductors (people who led the passengers north), stations (homes of abolitionists who hid them), and stationmasters (leaders of the abolitionists).

Freedom Crossing by Margaret Goff Clark is the story of a 15-year-old girl who is divided in her beliefs about slavery. Following her mother's death, Laura Eastman spends four years in Virginia with an aunt and uncle who are slave owners. After her father remarries, Laura returns home to the family farm in western New York State. She soon learns that their home is a stopover on the Underground Railroad; her father and brother are helping escaped slaves cross the river to Canada. Laura knows that anyone who helps a runaway slave is breaking the law—but when she meets Martin Paige, a 12-year-old slave who would rather die than be sent back, she begins to understand the abolitionists' views.

For beginning readers, F. N. Monjo's *The Drinking Gourd,* set in 1851, tells of a young boy's courage in saving a family of escaped slaves. When Tommy discovers a man and woman and their two children hiding in the barn, his father explains about the Underground Railroad. Little Jeff tells how his family found their way north by following the "drinking gourd," their name for the Big Dipper constellation, which points to the North Star—the guide to Canada and freedom. Later, a U.S. marshal sees Tommy sitting on a wagon full of hay that is covering the fugitives. Tommy's quick thinking and a "righteous lie" divert the marshal's attention and allow his father to take the black family to safety.

Gloria Houston's *Bright Freedom's Song* opens in 1853 in North Carolina's Blue Ridge Mountains. Fourteen-year-old Bright Freedom Cameron discovers that her parents are providing a safe house on the Underground Railroad for fugitive slaves they call "bundles." Her father reveals that he too is a fugitive: He was forced off a farm in Scotland, kidnapped, tricked into signing indenture papers, and ultimately driven to flee from a slaveholder who treated black and white people with equal brutality. Bright comes to understand something of the conditions and convictions that led to the Underground Railroad's formation, and when Pa falls ill, she and Marcus—a former slave who fled bondage with her father—transport the bundles to safety, knowing that a grave punishment for both awaits if they are caught.

Katherine Paterson skillfully weaves a mystery in *Jip: His Story*, set in Vermont in 1855. Jip's background is an enigma. Mysteriously abandoned on a roadside when he was about 2 years old, he was taken to the town poor farm to be raised by the other paupers. When the book opens, Jip is practically running the farm, caring for the animals and doing what he can to care for those around him. Jip is the only one who is not afraid of the "lunatic," an old man who must spend much of his life in a locked cage because of the raging madness that periodically overcomes him. Jip comes to love the old man; he also loves his teacher, who shows him genuine concern. When Jip is stalked by a menacing stranger who claims to be a representative of his father, Jip's teacher (who was the protagonist in Paterson's *Lyddie*) tells him what the Quaker abolitionists have discovered of his background and why he must immediately escape.

Christmas in the Big House, Christmas in the Quarters (McKissack & McKissack) is an unusual book that shows life on a Virginia plantation in 1859. Beginning after the harvest, the narrative describes the preparations for the Christmas season and its many celebrations. The differences in resources, lifestyles, and traditions between the plantation owner's family and the slaves provide a continuous contrast. Although the slaves' hardships are evident, they are not sensationalized, and the slaves' relationships with Massa and Missus in the big house are subtly drawn. The final scenes foreshadow the coming war: While the master tells his young daughter that she will soon be old enough to have her own slave, in the quarters, a mother tells her son not to run away, because she has heard rumors of freedom coming.

Civil War Era

Two books set during the Civil War have young females as protagonists. The first is Patricia Beatty's *Who Comes with Cannons?* Orphaned in 1861, 12-year-old Truth goes to live with her uncle's family in North Carolina. The Civil War breaks out, but Truth and her family, as Quakers, oppose both slavery and war. When a runaway slave seeks refuge on the family's farm, Truth discovers they operate a station of the Underground Railroad. Truth's two cousins are forced into the Confederate Army, and when one of them is captured and imprisoned by the Union Army, Truth goes to Washington via the Underground Railroad to seek a pardon.

Another Civil War heroine is Valor McAimee in *Mountain Valor* (Houston). Valor's father, brothers, and uncle were divided on the issues of the Civil War. The men left to fight on different sides, and 11-year-old Valor, her mother, and her younger cousin Jed must tend the farm. When the farm is robbed by vicious Yankee soldiers, Valor, posing as a boy, infiltrates their camp and manages to recapture and retrieve her family's livestock.

Paul Fleischman's *Bull Run* is a series of brief vignettes, in which the Civil War's first great battle is recounted from the points of view of sixteen participants. The characters include both Northerners and Southerners, men and women, and black and white people. Each vignette focuses on the life and thoughts of a person who participated in some way in the Battle of Bull Run, including a war-fevered boy, a doctor, a slave woman, a lover of horses, and a black man who is determined to become a soldier.

Few picture books tug at the emotions like *Pink and Say* by Patricia Polacco, a story passed down through generations of the author's family. This is the saga of a remarkable wartime friendship between a young white Union soldier, Sheldon Curtis, and a young black Union soldier, Pinkus Aylee. When Pink finds the 15-year-old white boy left for dead, he tends to Sheldon ("Say") and carries him a great distance to his own home. Pink's mother nurses the boy back to health, but she is later shot by marauders while hiding the boys. Before the boys can rejoin the Union troops, they are both captured by Confederate soldiers and taken to Andersonville Prison. Only one will leave alive.

Charley Skedaddle by Patricia Beatty is based on real-life Civil War records and memoirs. During the war a 12-year-old New York Bowery boy, Charley Quinn, joins the Union Army as a drummer, but he deserts in Virginia during his first battle. He encounters a hostile old mountain woman, and he learns that fleeing from his first battle doesn't brand him a coward for life.

Across Five Aprils by Irene Hunt is an unforgettable story of young Jethro Creighton, who grows from a boy to a man when he is left to take care of the family farm in Illinois during the turbulent four years of the Civil War. The book has been acclaimed, both for its historical authenticity and for the warm story it tells of strong family ties.

Carolyn Reeder's *Shades of Gray* takes place after the Civil War, which has left 12-year-old Will Page an orphan. He is forced to leave his city home and live in the Virginia countryside with his Uncle Jed, who refused to fight for the Confederacy. He considers his uncle a traitor and a coward, but a year spent with his aunt and uncle on their hardscrabble farm helps him understand the courage it took to uphold their pacifist principles.

Post–Civil War Frontier Era

Laura Ingalls Wilder used the people, places, and stories of her own life to write a series of books loved by generations of children and adults. A long-running television series titled *Little House on the Prairie* (named after one of the books) was closely based on this series of books. The stories are told through Laura's eyes, and the series spans her life from age 4 to the time she is a young wife and mother. In the first book, *Little House in the Big Woods,* it is the 1870s. Wolves, panthers, and bears roam the deep Wisconsin woods, but the Ingalls family is snug in its little log house. Four-year-old Laura lives with her Pa, Ma, and sisters Mary and Carrie. Pioneer life is hard, and the family must grow or catch all their food. Pa makes bullets, hunts, traps, and cures the meat. Ma makes cheese and maple sugar. Life is also exciting when blizzards and wild animals are encountered.

More Than Anything Else by Marie Bradby is a fictionalized account of the early life of Booker T. Washington. In this heartwarming picture book, 9-year-old Booker leaves his cabin before dawn to work all day shoveling salt with his father and brother in the saltworks of West Virginia. Despite the backbreaking labor, there is a sense of freedom, and the boy longs to learn to read. He meets a man reading a newspaper, and the man shows Booker how to write his name, which is the beginning of his education.

The bulk of children's historical fiction books are juvenile novels geared for readers in the intermediate grades. However, there are two picture books with settings in the late 1800s that primary-grade children will enjoy. *Three Names* (MacLachlan) is what a boy calls his dog, who accompanies him each day as he drives a horse-drawn wagon across the prairie road to and from the one-room school house. *Miss Rumphius* (Cooney) tells of the life of Alice Rumphius. She fulfills her dream to travel the world, then settles in a house by the seaside and makes the world more beautiful by sowing lupine seeds as she walks about the countryside.

In *The Land,* Mildred D. Taylor draws on the family history of her great-grandfather. In a period that spans the 1870s and 1880s, readers learn the story of the Logan family patriarch, Paul-Edward, who is the son of a part-Indian, part-African slave mother and a white plantation owner in Georgia. Paul's father openly acknowledges him and raises him with his other children, but when Paul's beloved white brother betrays him, he runs away to Mississippi. There he marries Caroline, a strong-willed and independent woman. Paul is obsessed with the dream of owning his own land, and he performs backbreaking work to earn the money for it by training and racing horses, laboring as a skilled carpenter, and clearing land for a white man who later cheats him. When the banks refuse Paul credit, he sells his most precious possessions. Finally, with the help of his childhood friend, Mitchell, and a surprise family inheritance, he buys the land of his dreams in the fertile cotton-growing area of northern Mississippi.

Featured Author

Mildred D. Taylor

Taylor was born in Jackson, Mississippi, but grew up in Ohio. Her family visited Mississippi often, and the family accounts she listened to from both her father and her extended family in Mississippi are the basis for her series of books about the Logan family. One of the strongest themes that ran through the family stories was familial strength, and this is evident in Taylor's books. She credits her father's talent at storytelling for her becoming a writer.

Taylor's first major achievement was winning a contest sponsored by the Council on Interracial Books for Children with her manuscript, *Song of the Trees,* narrated by 8-year-old Cassie Logan. Taylor's second book about the Logan family was *Roll of Thunder, Hear My Cry,* which won the Newbery Award in 1977. Taylor said the characters of David Logan (the father) and Stacey Logan (the son) were based on her own father.

Look for descriptions of each of Taylor's books about the Logan family, which are woven into their appropriate era sections in this chapter.

Yep's Golden Mountain Chronicles continue with *Dragon's Gate,* which is set in 1867. When Otter accidentally kills a Manchu soldier, Cassia sends her son to America to join his father Squeaky and his uncle Foxfire. Along with hundreds of other Chinese men, they toil to build a tunnel through the Sierra Nevada Mountains for the transcontinental railroad. In spite of the presence of family, Otter is a stranger among the other Chinese men in this new land. Where he expected to see a land of goldfields, he sees only vast, cold whiteness. Otter's dream is to learn all he can and take the technology back to China's Middle Kingdom and free them from the Manchu empire, but the harsh environment and a family tragedy keep him in America.

Joseph Young, unlike the two generations of Youngs who lived in America before him—was born in America, making him the first American citizen in the family. In *The Traitor* (Yep), life is very tough in Rock Springs, a small town in the Wyoming Territory—not just because of the brutal environment. The rough American miners despise the Chinese, who must work for slave wages in increasingly dangerous conditions. Joseph longs to be considered a real American boy—a dream his father and the other Chinese laborers do not understand. To them, America means nothing but a constant struggle against poverty, deprivation, and hate. The town's growing resentment toward the Chinese explodes in 1885 into one of the worst race riots in American history. Joseph and Michael, an outcast white boy, must trust each other with their lives during this horrifying and cruel event.

By 1903 Chinese American groups had shrunk to a few small enclaves in cities like San Francisco, which is the setting of *Dragonwings* (Yep). Moon Shadow sails from China to join his father, Windrider, who lives in Chinatown and works in the Young's laundry. Though this is his first encounter with his father, Moon Shadow soon loves and respects him. With Moon Shadow's help and the advice of Orville Wright, Windrider achieves his dream of building and flying a biplane, despite the mockery of the other Chinese and the poverty he must endure. Yep was inspired to write this book by a newspaper account of a Chinese immigrant who made a flying machine in the early 1900s. Another historical event, the great earthquake of 1906 that destroyed most of San Francisco, also plays an important part in the plot.

Mildred D. Taylor's saga of the Logan family continues with *The Well.* During a severe drought in 1910, Paul and Caroline Logan share their well water with all neighbors, black and white alike. However, their young sons, David and Hammer, find it hard to share with the Simms family, who torments them because they are black landowners. When the Simms boys poison the Logans' well, all the neighbors suffer.

World War I Era

An enchanting book for younger children is set in 1918, the year World War I ended. *The Year of the Perfect Christmas Tree* by Gloria Houston, like the rest of Houston's historical fiction books, is set in the Appalachian area of North Carolina. When Papa is called to war, little Ruthie and her mother must fulfill his obligation of getting the traditional Christmas tree from the top of Grandfather Mountain to the village church for the holiday celebration. On Christmas Eve Ruthie and her mama climb the rocky crags and return with the perfect Christmas tree. Other books by Houston set in this era are *Littlejim, Littlejim's Gift,* and *Littlejim's Dreams.*

Rosemary Wells's *Mary on Horseback: Three Mountain Stories* is the tale of Mary Breckinridge, who was trained as a nurse during World War I. One day, she rode on horseback into the isolated mountains of Appalachia and never looked back. She spent her life fording icy streams and climbing untracked mountains to bring medical help to those in need. More nurses on horseback joined Mary, and the Frontier Nursing Service was born. This book, based on a real person, tells the stories of three families who were helped by Mary's tender care.

Great Depression Era

After the collapse of the U.S. stock market in 1929, the country was plunged into a profound economic depression that lasted more than a decade: the Great Depression era. At one point about one-quarter of the nation's workforce was unemployed, and jobless workers and their families depended on charity to survive.

Uncle Jed's Barbershop (Mitchell) is set in the segregated South. Sarah Jean's beloved Uncle Jed is the only black barber in the area; he dreams of owning his own barbershop, but he spends his savings to pay for an operation to save Sarah Jean's life. Later his savings are wiped out when the bank fails at the beginning of the Depression; but many years later, when he is 79, Uncle Jed finally achieves his dream.

Karen Hesse's *Out of the Dust* is a unique novel because it is written as a journal in free verse poetry. It is set in the Dust Bowl, the bleak landscape of the Oklahoma Panhandle in 1934, when a severe drought causes the overfarmed soil to literally blow away. A tragic accident is caused when Billie Jo's father leaves a bucket of kerosene near the stove. Her mother's clothing is ignited; Billie Jo tries to beat out the flames, but her mother dies, and Billie Jo's hands are severely scarred, leaving her unable to play her beloved piano to soothe her anguish. However, the quiet strength she displays in taking care of her grieving father during this time of unspeakable loss is inspiring.

In *Leah's Pony* (Friedrich), a young girl makes the ultimate sacrifice when her parents are unable to pay back the bank loan after their crops fail in the Dust Bowl era. Leah sells her beloved pony to buy back her father's tractor when the bank auctions off their livestock and equipment.

In Marissa Moss's *Rose's Journal,* Rose keeps a journal of her family's difficult times on their Kansas farm during the days of the Dust Bowl in 1935. The severe drought has left the fields too dry for crops and farms all around are failing. Because nothing grows, the cattle are so skinny that they have washboard ribs. And there is always the dust to contend with. The family come to the brink of losing their land, but at the last minute, they are saved from foreclosure.

Christopher Paul Curtis's *Bud, Not Buddy* is a funny yet touching account. After a ghastly (though riotous) evening, 10-year-old Bud (not Buddy) Caldwell is on the run from yet another terrible foster home in 1936 in Flint, Michigan. Bud's mother died when he was six, and he wants to find his father, though his mother never told him who he was. Bud believes she left a clue in the form of a blue flier advertising a jazz show with Herman E. Calloway, bandleader and stand-up bass player for the Dusky Devastators. Bud sets off to track down Calloway, toting his few treasures in a battered old suitcase. He gets into hilarious trouble, such as trying to steal a vampire's car, but he also finds kindness—in the charity food line, at the public library, in a Hooverville squatter camp, and on the road.

Grandma Dowdel is an irrepressible character in two of Richard's Peck's most popular books, which span the years of 1929 to 1937. *A Long Way from Chicago* is a series of stories chronicled by Joey, who—with his younger sister Mary Alice—makes annual summer visits to their grandmother. Grandma Dowdel continually astounds them by stretching the boundaries of truth. In Joey's words, "We knew kids lie all the time, but Grandma was no kid, and she could tell some whoppers" (p. 9). Grandma also cheats, trespasses, and contrives to help the town's underdogs outwit the banker and other members of the establishment in their small Illinois town. My favorite chapter is when Grandma defies the sheriff and poaches catfish from a stolen boat, and then has the children help her fry up the fish to feed the Depression drifters. The meal is accompanied by Grandma's (illegal) home-brewed beer—quite a treat during Prohibition!

The Great Depression years are the setting for the bulk of Mildred D. Taylor's Logan Family Saga. In 1931, the Logans' young white friend, Jeremy Simms, relates the account of a horrible bus accident and the black man who helps rescue people from the river in *Mississippi Bridge*. *Song of the Trees* is set in 1932, after Paul-Edward has died. David is now married with four children, and he has gone to Louisiana to lay railroad track to earn enough money to feed his family and to maintain his parents' precious farmland. An unscrupulous white man tries to cheat Caroline Logan (called Big Ma by her grandchildren) out of some of the giant old trees that grow around their home.

If readers experience the Logan Family Saga in chronological order, they will learn of the kind black man, Tom Bee, who saved the life of a young white boy, John Wallace, in the earliest book—*The Land*. Tom had long befriended John, and after John became an adult, he allowed Tom to continue to call him by his first name, a most uncommon practice for blacks at that time. *The Friendship* takes place in 1933 at John Wallace's small general store where the Logan children have gone for medicine. When Tom Bee, now an old man, comes in the store and calls Mr. Wallace by his first name in front of some of the white town folk, the children witness the tragic end of the friendship—ripped apart by racism.

Roll of Thunder, Hear My Cry is by far Mildred D. Taylor's most acclaimed book in the Logan Family Saga. The story is revealed through the eyes of 11-year-old Cassie, who has led a somewhat sheltered life on the family farm, growing up with Big Ma (Caroline Logan), her parents, and her brothers: Stacey, Christopher-John, and Little Man. In order to keep their land during the Depression, Cassie's mother teaches school while her husband, David, works for the railroad in Louisiana. All the blacks in the community face nightriders and burnings, but the Logans' strong ties to one another and to their land give them the strength to defy racism and hold on to their land and the independence it represents.

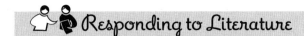

Responding to Literature

Character Mapping   Sometimes young readers lose interest in books like *Roll of Thunder* because the author introduces and develops several major characters at the beginning of the book and, in so doing, creates a slow buildup to the action in the story. **Character mapping** helps maintain children's attention, as well as helping them keep up with the many characters. It also sets a specific purpose for reading, which will enhance readers' comprehension and enjoyment. After you introduce a book, ask your children to read for information that identifies the major characters by name, relationship, age, physical description, personality traits, and other important qualities. Use this information to build a character map children can refer to while reading (see Figure 10.1 on page 257).

At the end of *Roll of Thunder*, readers are left wondering what will happen to Stacey's best friend, T. J., who has been falsely accused of killing John Wallace during a store break-in committed by two white boys. Mr. Logan's desperate thinking diverts the attention of the lynch mob, and T. J. is taken to jail. In the sequel, *Let the Circle Be Unbroken*, T. J. goes on trial with an all-white jury, and the saga of the Logans and the people in their community continues.

In his Golden Mountain Chronicles, Laurence Yep reveals much about the culture and character of the Tang men who came to the United States to work and support their families in China. More than everything else, the Youngs and their friends were adaptable, even organizing their own professional basketball team to leave San Francisco's Chinatown and barnstorm across the country in *The Red Warrior*, which is set in 1939.

World War II Era

The outbreak of war in Europe at the end of the 1930s resulted in a surge of activity in the U.S. economy as the government expanded the national defense system. America entered World War II in 1941 when the U.S. naval base in Pearl Harbor, Hawaii, was bombed by the Japanese air force. The Great Depression ended, and with so many men enlisted in the military, there was a shortage of workers. During this era, many women entered the workforce for the first time. Meanwhile, in Europe, life was a struggle for survival.

With *Milkweed*, Jerry Spinelli presents a compelling portrait of Nazi-occupied Warsaw through the eyes of a young orphan who has no memory other than living on the streets. Because he is naive and kind, he wins the favor of Uri, an older orphan who becomes his protector. Uri gives him the name Misha Pilsudski along with a made-up story about his Gypsy background (so he will not be taken for a Jew). The band of orphans manage to survive, but Misha slips into the ghetto to live with the family of a young Jewish girl who became his friend. Each night, he slips through small holes in the wall and steals food for them. Even while surrounded by the horror of the Holocaust, Misha does not lose his optimism until the train cars arrive to pick up their human cargo.

I only know of one World War II book that describes the plight of German citizens: *The Book Thief* by Markus Zusak. This young adult book would be a difficult read for most children, but they might benefit from listening to a couple of chapters. Certainly teachers and parents could benefit from having an additional viewpoint. This book reveals that not all Germans shared Hitler's beliefs. It also describes the many hardships average Germans endured, such as severe food shortages, the prejudice against non–Nazi Party members, ostracism for any compassion shown to Jews, and the devastating results of the Allied air raids.

Mildred D. Taylor continues her Logan Family Saga with *The Road to Memphis,* which is set in 1941. Cassie is 17 and finishing high school in Jackson, Mississippi, with dreams of becoming a lawyer. Her older brother Stacey is 20 and works in a box factory in Jackson. War has broken out in Europe, and they and their friends often argue about it. When some white boys humiliate Moe and make rude comments about Cassie, Moe lashes out with a tire iron, injuring all three of them. Stacey, Cassie, and Moe embark on a tense three-day trip to Memphis, where Moe can catch a train to Chicago. The road is a perilous one, fraught with even more racist situations. By the time they get to Memphis, Pearl Harbor has been bombed, and Moe must compete with soldiers mobbing the train station to return to their bases. Knowing the war has opened opportunities for black men to serve, Moe swears his love for Cassie and promises to make something of himself.

A number of good books are set during the United States' four-year involvement in World War II, and I will introduce them according to the age of the protagonist. In *But No Candy* (Houston), Lee is 6 years old when her favorite after-school treat, chocolate Hershey bars, become scarce, as certain foods and other goods are designated for troops overseas. She misses the candy—but most of all she misses her Uncle Ted, who is fighting in Europe.

Lois Lowry's *Number the Stars* is set in Copenhagen in 1943. Ten-year-old Ellen Rosen and her family are in danger, because the Jewish people of Denmark are being removed by the Nazis. Ellen moves in with her best friend, Annemarie Johansen, and pretends to be her sister until she is smuggled out of the country in a daring escape.

In San Diego, 11-year-old Foster is deeply affected by the war in *Foster's War* (Reeder). His older brother is shipped to the Pacific as a gunner on a B-26, and his best friend, Jimmy Osaki, and his family are exiled to an internment camp. Foster's bullying father—an air-raid warden with a cold, harsh attitude—makes life even more difficult.

In *Summer of My German Soldier* (Greene), Patty Bergen turns 12 the summer her small Arkansas hometown becomes the site of a prison camp for German soldiers. Although Patty is Jewish, when she stumbles upon a young German escapee, she begins to see him as a lonely frightened person like herself, not as the enemy. Helping him puts her own freedom at risk. This book is moving, and I must warn you it has a tragic ending.

Katherine Paterson's *Jacob Have I Loved* is set on a tiny Chesapeake Bay island off the Maryland shore. Louise is envious of and angry with her fair-haired and talented twin, Caroline, whom everyone adores. Caroline leaves the island to study music, but Louise, to help support her family, is compelled to quit school and work alongside her father as a "waterman" when all the young men go to war. Her friendship with the mysterious Captain Wallace helps her fulfill her dreams and leave the island.

Mary Downing Hahn's *Stepping on the Cracks* is set in 1944 in a small Maryland town. Margaret, a sixth grader whose brother fought and died during the war, and her best friend, Elizabeth, are bullied by Gordy. He grows bolder than ever, and they decide to spy on him. When they discover he is hiding his gentle older brother Stuart, a deserter from the army, they see a new side of Gordy. Slowly they begin to understand Stuart's decision to be a conscientious objector.

Post–World War II Era

A post–World War II novel that will delight younger readers is Bette Bao Lord's *In the Year of the Boar and Jackie Robinson*. In 1947 10-year-old Shirley Temple Wong and her family emigrate from China to Brooklyn. When she first starts at Public School 8, Shirley has no friends, but after earning the friendship of the toughest girl in class, she is included in the playground stickball games. She becomes a loyal fan of the Brooklyn Dodgers and Jackie Robinson.

One of the most inspiring books I have read about teaching is *The Year of Miss Agnes* by Kirkpatrick Hill, which is sent in an Athabascan village in 1948. Previous teachers never lasted more than one year (some far less) in the one-room schoolhouse on the Alaskan frontier. Then one day Agnes Sutterfield arrives. Instead of using the old textbooks, she reads them classics and plays opera music. She teaches basic subjects (especially reading) in relevant ways and teaches them about their own history, land, and culture. She tutors both students and parents in her cabin in the evening and even learns sign language along with her students so a deaf girl can attend school for the first time. The village life is forever changed by Miss Agnes.

Ruth White's *Belle Prater's Boy* is set in the Appalachian town of Coal Station, Virginia, in the 1950s. Belle Prater disappears, and her son, Woodrow—poor and cross-eyed, but brilliant—comes to live with his grandparents. His 12-year-old cousin Gypsy, the town beauty, lives next door and is as curious as the rest of the town about Belle's disappearance. However, Gypsy also ponders the mystery of her own father's death seven years earlier.

Also set in the coal mining area of Virginia is *When I Was Young in the Mountains* by Cynthia Rylant. In this attractively illustrated picture book, the author relates her memories of spending summers with her grandparents who lived in the mountains.

Kira-Kira by Cynthia Kadohata is a story of love and hate, life and death. The Takeshimas' love for their family members is the strongest theme, threading throughout each chapter but exemplified most strongly in Katie's love for her ailing older sister, Lynn. Hate takes the form of post–World War II discrimination against Japanese Americans in a small Georgia town in the 1950s. Life is celebrated every day as Katie strives to show Lynn the *kira-kira* (glittering beauty) all around them. Death is inevitable when Lynn's body succumbs to lymphoma.

Civil Rights Movement

Laurence Yep's Golden Mountain Chronicles continues to trace the lives of the Young family. Eventually, the youngest family members become so Americanized that they lose track of the Chinese part of their identity. *Child of the Owl* is set in the mid-1960s, when 12-year-old Casey is waiting for the day that her father hits it big at the racetrack. When he ends up in the hospital, Casey is sent to live with her grandmother, Paw-Paw. Casey feels lost in Chinatown and is not prepared for the Chinese school and the noisy crowds. Paw-Paw soothes Casey's fears by telling her about her true Chinese name, the mother Casey never knew, and about her family's owl charm. The contradictions and special heritage of being Chinese American is a poignant tale of one child's anxiety about growing up poor and nonwhite in America in the 1960s.

Vaunda Michaeux Nelson's *Mayfield Crossing* is set in 1960, the year children from Mayfield Crossing must attend school in nearby Parkview when their own school is closed. The Parkview children want nothing to do with the Mayfield students and do not allow them to play on Parkview's new baseball field. Things are especially difficult for 9-year-old Meg and her friends Billie and Sherman, all of whom are black. Meg encounters racial prejudice for the first time. Only baseball appears to be a possibility for drawing the students together.

The sequel, *Beyond Mayfield* (Nelson), is set in the early 1960s. Meg lives in Mayfield Crossing, where blacks and whites live together in harmony, but she still attends school in Parkview, where some of her classmates and teachers are bigots. The brother of Meg's white friend Dillon comes home from the navy, and he decides to go south and join the Freedom Riders. When he is killed, Dillon blames Meg's family for talking him into going, and Meg begins to wonder if they are responsible.

Freedom Songs by Yvette Moore is narrated by 14-year-old Sheryl. In 1963 she and her family leave their comfortable Brooklyn home for an Easter visit with Sheryl's grandmother in North Carolina. Sheryl enjoys being with the warm extended family, but she experiences segregation for the first time. Her Uncle Pete joins the Freedom Riders, and when she returns to Brooklyn, she organizes a gospel concert fund-raiser to support their cause.

Christopher Paul Curtis's first book, *The Watsons Go to Birmingham—1963*, is something of a paradox. It is *the* funniest children's novel I have ever read, and yet it slowly builds to a dramatic climax that grips readers' hearts. The story is narrated by Kenny, a fourth grader who is different both because he is smart and because he has a lazy eye. As Kenny relates hilarious stories about his middle-class African American family—The Weird Watsons of Flint, Michigan—the characters come alive, and you feel as if you know them.

Responding to Literature

Story Mapping Complete character and story maps *while* you are reading to your children, rather than providing them beforehand. When you ask children to fill in the parts of the map, they are given a purpose for reading, and this results in enhanced comprehension and enjoyment. A story map of *The Watsons*, including full character maps, is provided in Figure 10.1 as an example of mapping a juvenile novel. (If you plan on reading this novel, do not read past the characters' maps until you finish the book!)

FIGURE 10.1 Story Map of *The Watsons Go to Birmingham—1963* by Christopher Paul Curtis

Setting—Time: Winter 1963
    —Place: Flint, Michigan, and Birmingham, Alabama
Main characters: The Watson family (African American)

Daniel Watson	Wilona Watson	Byron Watson	Kenneth Watson	Joetta Watson
"Dad"	"Momma"	"By"	"Kenny,"	"Joey"
35 years old	gap in front teeth	13 years old	"Square"	kindergartner
clowns around	self-conscious	conceited	fourth grader	softhearted
	caring mother	aloof from	gullible	loves family
	dislikes Michigan	family	good natured	
		mean	lazy (crossed)	
		bad student	eye	
			smart in school	

⇩   ⇩   ⇩   ⇦

Grandma Sands	Buphead	Rufus Fry	Larry Dunn
Momma's mother	Byron's best	Kenny's best	bully of K–4
tiny and old	friend	friend	mean and tough
walks with a cane	14 years old	very poor	has mother with
cackling laugh	mean	wears ragged	a secret
very strict	bad student	clothes	no warm clothes
		skinny	poor
		talks country	

Central problem: Byron constantly disobeys his parents and is becoming a real juvenile delinquent.

Goal: Take Byron to Birmingham to live with Grandma Sands.

Events:
1. The family drives to Birmingham and visits with Grandma Sands.
2. Byron saves Kenny from drowning in the whirlpool.
3. The church where Joetta attends Sunday school is bombed.
4. The family returns home, but Kenny is very depressed because of the tragedy.

Resolution: After arriving at Grandma's, Byron begins to show maturity and realizes how much his family means when he nearly loses Kenny and Joetta. Byron becomes a caring big brother by helping Kenny deal with his emotions.

A good example of Curtis's witty writing is Kenny's account of what happens when he and his best friend, Rufus, encounter the school bully, Larry Dunn, whom they suspect has stolen Kenny's new leather gloves.

> Larry ran up behind us and said, "This is Friday, y'all, time to do the laundry. Who's gonna be first? Country Corn Flake? Cockeye Kenny?" He didn't wait for us to make up our minds and grabbed me first. He said to Rufus, "If you run away during Cockeye's wash I'ma hunt you down and hurt you bad, boy. This ain't gonna take but a minute so just stick around."
>
> Rufus stood there looking worried. Larry wasn't like other bullies; he wasn't happy taking a handful of snow and smashing it in your face and running off. Larry gave what he called Maytag Washes. With a Maytag Wash you had to go through all of the different cycles that a washing machine did, and even though when Larry gave you a Maytag all of the cycles were exactly the same, each part had a different name and the wash wasn't done until you went through the final spin and had snow in every part of your face.
>
> Ever since Larry got these new leather gloves he was giving *Super* Maytag Washes because he could grind a whole lot more snow in your face for a whole lot longer since his hands weren't getting as cold. Larry was tearing me up, I was crying even before the first rinse cycle was done. . . . (p. 57)

Later, Kenny's 13-year-old brother Byron, who is an even bigger bully, takes the gloves from Larry and gives him a unique punishment. However, Byron's bullying and other misdeeds get him in trouble, both in school and out, so the family takes a trip to Birmingham to visit Grandma Sands, the one person who can put Byron in shape. In 1963 the public schools in Birmingham are undergoing forced integration. In retaliation, a black church—Grandma's church—is bombed. True to historical fact, four girls are killed. The readers' emotional involvement with the Watson family makes this historical crime real and devastating.

The Watsons Go to Birmingham is an excellent example of how literature can add a human dimension to the historical facts presented in textbooks. That four girls were killed during Sunday school in Birmingham in 1963 was a sad event, but it happened a long time ago to people and families we did not know. However, when readers discover that Kenny's little sister, Joetta, was attending Sunday school at the church that was bombed, they are pulled into the scene. Readers tensely follow Kenny as, in shock, he searches through the rubble and finds a familiar black patent leather shoe. Readers experience the tragic event as if they were there with Kenny and his family.

Literature is a fascinating way to transmit the story of the past. After all, history is made up of the stories of people—not words in a textbook. The books introduced in this chapter tell interesting stories about fictional and real people who lived in many places during many times. Reading about the people provides insight into, and understanding of, problems people encountered in the past, and it can help readers understand why some of those same problems (such as racism) still exist today. Understanding a problem is the first step in overcoming it.

Enhancing Curriculum with Historical Fiction

by Sharon Smith

Historical fiction is an excellent tool to further readers' understanding of important historical events and time periods. Even though the books are fictional accounts, historical fiction provides a realistic point of view. Therefore, it gives readers a better sense of historical settings, and it provides an intimate look at what life was like for people who lived in the past.

The setting—which includes place and time—plays an essential role in historical fiction, so I recommend using visual aids to enhance children's understanding. I usually introduce a book by describing the exact location of the setting with a globe to indicate the country or state and then a map to provide a closer orientation to the city or area of the setting. As we read the story, children create their own imaginary maps to represent the characters' environment by drawing important components of the setting, such as the main characters' houses, locations where important episodes occur, landmarks, and/or natural environments (river, sea, mountains) that are significant to the story. We also create a timeline of the plot, marking real historical events in red (or boldface if using a word processor) and fictional events in black.

One way to introduce a book that will capture children's interest and make history come alive is to employ storytelling. This is particularly important when they have little or no prior knowledge of the period. For example, before reading *Lyddie* (Paterson), I tell a fictional account of my great-grandmother, who was employed in a fabric mill for a meager salary, working twelve hours a day in stifling heat while continually breathing in lint. I encourage questions as I detail the squalid working conditions in the factory and the paltry living conditions in the boardinghouse. When we begin the story, children make an immediate connection with the main character, the Industrial Revolution, and the reasons the workers became ill.

In building background for a story, do not overlook community resources. For example, when reading *Across Five Aprils* (Hunt) invite guest speakers, such as Civil War re-enactors, artisans, museum curators, local experts, or oral historians.

Making individual scrapbooks or a class collage is another engaging response to historical fiction. Children enjoy collecting items described in the book—such as pictures, mementos, memorabilia, and other artifacts—and artfully arranging them in an album. For example, with *Sarah, Plain and Tall* (MacLachlan), students read about how Papa uses a pitchfork and of Sarah's love of the ocean. They also read about Sarah's cutting the children's hair and scattering the clippings for the birds to use in nest making. Sarah's letters to the family before and after her first visit are also memorable parts of the book. Some examples of artifacts the children could collect would be tiny seashells and a lock of hair (after a trip to the hairdresser—not of their own doing!). They could also write copies of one of the letters using antique-looking paper and a fountain pen. A field trip to a local farm or a museum would be ideal to take pictures of a real pitchfork in use and a hayloft; however, children could always find pictures through a Google search on the Internet. (For ideas on how to make a digital scrapbook, see the next section.)

Historical fiction also offers many opportunities to recreate history. Children learn firsthand about daily living in the past when you organize dramatizations of episodes from historical fiction books. For example, have children dress up like the characters and simulate daily chores—such as making soap, churning butter, or planting corn—in the cumbersome period clothing. (Remind them there was no air conditioning or readily available cold beverages.)

Tasting parties are another way to enhance children's understanding of literature. First, check with students' parents to determine if any have food allergies. Then, with the children's help, prepare a meal using only authentic ingredients that the book describes. Some books, such as the Little House series by Laura Ingalls Wilder, include recipes. Children can also carefully read a book to determine how food was gathered and prepared. For example, in *Island of the Blue Dolphins* (O'Dell), you can prepare fresh fish that has been donated by parents or a local supermarket. (Many children have never tasted fresh seafood, and therefore have difficulty imagining what Karana eats every day.) Use this opportunity to teach about kitchen safety, cleanliness, table etiquette, and nutrition. Serve only bite-size portions of foods, and encourage, but do not force, everyone to taste each food.

Other ideas include using music, song, dance, and art to incorporate multiple literacies in learning about the historical settings of novels. An engaging way to conclude a novel is to conduct a trivia contest. Along with your own review questions, have children write questions about the plot, historical time period, and geography of the book. I hope you will agree that literature is a fascinating way to learn about history, geography, social studies, technology, and the arts when you actively involve children in responding to quality books of historical fiction.

Integrating Literature and Technology

Making a Visual Book Report   A great response to realistic fiction is to make a digital scrapbook of photographs and graphics of people and artifacts that deal with the book's setting and plot. Items may include photographs taken with a digital camera, electronically scanned photographs (taken with any type of camera), and graphics from the Internet (see the section on Searching for Bibliotherapy Resources on the Internet in the previous chapter).

Please be aware that materials from the Internet may be copyrighted. Fair Use—section 110(1) of the U.S. copyright law—allows teachers and students to use protected works in the traditional classroom setting (but *only* in the classroom—not in other settings). You should always include the name of the copyright owner and source under the item (e.g., Retrieved from *The Anderson Family Album* © 2005 by Nancy A. Anderson at http://anderson.com.html).

To capture a graphic from the Internet, follow the directions below:

1. Using the mouse, position your cursor over the graphic you want to capture.
2. Click once with the button on the right side of the mouse.
3. In the menu that opens, scroll to *Save Picture As . . .* and click.
4. In the *Save Picture* popup box that appears, first note the directory at the top where it will be saved (i.e., *Save In: My Pictures*); then at the bottom, supply a descriptive name in the *File name* textbox, and click the *Save* button.
5. Open a word processing document, and position your cursor where you want to insert the graphic.
6. Click on the *Insert* tab at the top of the screen, and then click on *Picture*.
7. An *Insert Picture* popup box appears; in the *Look In* area at the top of the box, first locate the directory where the file was saved; then click on the document file name or icon to insert it in your document.

Arrange the graphics in a colorful digital portfolio, which can be printed as well as saved on disk for other groups of children to view.

Summary

Historical fiction is realistic fiction in a real-world setting in the historical past with events that are partly historical but largely imaginative. It does not have any fantasy elements, nor does it contradict real history. Both the author and illustrator must research the era of the setting in order to represent it authentically. The division between contemporary fiction and historical fiction is arbitrarily set at 1964, the year the Civil Rights Act was passed.

Most historical fiction has purely fictional main characters with real historical figures sometimes mentioned or in minor roles. However, some historical fiction books contain characters that are based on real people (although the names might be changed). This subcategory is called biographic historical fiction.

The Scott O'Dell Award is given yearly to honor historical fiction books of high literary quality that have a New World setting.

For the purpose of analyzing historical fiction books I presented them within major eras of their settings: (1) ancient settings, (2) medieval times, (3) colonial years, (4) revolutionary era, (5) early frontier days, (6) Civil War, (7) post–Civil War frontier, (8) World War I, (9) Great Depression, (10) World War II, (11) post–World War II, and (12) civil rights movement.

Historical Fiction Books

Alcott, Louisa May. *Little Women*. Sterling, 1868/2004.
Anderson, Laurie Halse. *Fever 1793*. Simon & Schuster, 2000.

Armstrong, William. *Sounder*. Illus. James Barkley. Harcourt, 1969/1998.

Avi. *Crispin: The Cross of Lead*. Hyperion, 2002.

Beatty, Patricia. *Charley Skedaddle*. Teacher Created Materials, 1996.

Beatty, Patricia. *Who Comes with Cannons?* HarperCollins, 1992.

Blos, Joan W. *A Gathering of Days: A New England Girl's Journal, 1830–32*. Aladdin, 1990.

Bradby, Marie. *More Than Anything Else*. Illus. Chris K. Soentpiet. Orchard, 1995.

Brink, Carol Ryrie. *Caddie Woodlawn*. Simon Pulse, 1935/1997.

Bruchac, Joseph. *Children of the Longhouse*. Puffin, 1998.

Clark, Margaret Goff. *Freedom Crossing*. Scholastic, 1991.

Clements, Bruce. *I Tell a Lie Every So Often*. Farrar, Straus & Giroux, 2001.

Cooney, Barbara. *Miss Rumphius*. Puffin, 1994.

Curtis, Christopher Paul. *Bud, Not Buddy*. Illus. Trish P. Watts. Laurel Leaf, 2004.

Curtis, Christopher Paul. *The Watsons Go to Birmingham—1963*. Random House, 2001.

Cushman, Karen. *The Midwife's Apprentice*. Clarion, 1995.

de Angeli, Marguerite. *The Door in the Wall*. Doubleday, Laurel Leaf, 1998.

Dorris, Michael. *Morning Girl*. Hyperion, 1999.

Fleischman, Paul. *Bull Run*. Harper & Row, 1993.

Forbes, Esther. *Johnny Tremain*. Houghton Mifflin, 1998.

Fox, Paula. *The Slave Dancer*. Atheneum, 2001.

Friedrich, Elizabeth. *Leah's Pony*. Illus. Michael Garland. Boyds Mills, 1999.

Gray, Elizabeth Janet. *Adam of the Road*. Sagebrush, 1999.

Greene, Bette. *Summer of My German Soldier*. Penguin, 1999.

Gregory, Kristiana. *The Stowaway*. Scholastic, 1995.

Hahn, Mary Downing. *Stepping on the Cracks*. Clarion, 1991.

Hall, Donald. *Ox-Cart Man*. Illus. Barbara Cooney. Sagebrush, 1999.

Hesse, Karen. *Out of the Dust*. Scholastic, 1997.

Hill, Kirkpatrick. *The Year of Miss Agnes*. Simon & Schuster, 2000.

Houston, Gloria. *Bright Freedom's Song*. Harcourt Brace, 1998.

Houston, Gloria. *But No Candy*. Illus. Lloyd Bloom. Putnam, 1992.

Houston, Gloria. *Littlejim*. Illus. Thomas B. Allen. HarperTrophy, 1993.

Houston, Gloria. *Littlejim's Dreams*. Illus. Thomas B. Allen. Harcourt Brace, 1997.

Houston, Gloria. *Littlejim's Gift*. Illus. Thomas B. Allen. Putnam, 1997.

Houston, Gloria. *Mountain Valor*. Illus. Thomas B. Allen. Philomel, 1994.

Houston, Gloria. *The Year of the Perfect Christmas Tree*. Illus. Barbara Cooney. Dial, 1988.

Hunt, Irene. *Across Five Aprils*. Follett, 2002.

Johnston, Tony. *Yonder*. Illus. Lloyd Bloom. Gibbs Smith, 2002.

Kadohata, Cynthia. *Kira-Kira*. Simon & Schuster, 2004.

Lord, Bette Bao. *In the Year of the Boar and Jackie Robinson*. Sagebrush, 1999.

Lowry, Lois. *Number the Stars*. Laurel Leaf, 1998.

MacLachlan, Patricia. *Sarah, Plain and Tall*. HarperTrophy, 1985.

MacLachlan, Patricia. *Three Names*. Illus. Alexander Pertzoff. HarperTrophy, 1994.

McGraw, Eloise Jarvis. *The Golden Goblet*. Puffin, 1990.

McKissack, Patricia C., & Frederick L. McKissack. *Christmas in the Big House, Christmas in the Quarters*. Illus. John Thompson. Scholastic, 2002.

Mitchell, Margaree King. *Uncle Jed's Barbershop*. Illus. James Ransome. Aladdin, 1998.

Monjo, F. N. *The Drinking Gourd*. Illus. Fred Brenner. HarperCollins, 1993.

Moore, Yvette. *Freedom Songs*. Puffin, 1991.

Moss, Marissa. *Rose's Journal: The Story of a Girl in the Great Depression*. Harcourt, 2001.

Nelson, Vaunda Michaeux. *Beyond Mayfield*. Putnam, 1999.

Nelson, Vaunda Michaeux. *Mayfield Crossing*. Puffin, 2002.

O'Dell, Scott. *Island of the Blue Dolphins*. Houghton Mifflin, 1990.

O'Dell, Scott. *Sarah Bishop*. Scholastic, 1991.

O'Dell, Scott. *Zia*. Laurel Leaf, 1996.

Park, Linda Sue. *A Single Shard*. Houghton Mifflin, 2001.

Paterson, Katherine. *Jacob Have I Loved*. HarperTrophy, 1990.

Paterson, Katherine. *Jip, His Story*. Lodestar, 1996.

Paterson, Katherine. *Lyddie*. Puffin, 2004.

Paterson, Katherine. *The Sign of the Chrysanthemum*. Sagebrush, 2001.

Paulsen, Gary. *Mr. Tucket*. Delacorte, 1994.

Paulsen, Gary. *The Rifle*. Harcourt Brace, 1995.

Peck, Richard. *A Long Way from Chicago*. Puffin, 1998.

Pennington, Daniel. *Itse Selu: Cherokee Harvest Festival*. Illus. Don Stewart. Charlesbridge, 1994.

Polacco, Patricia. *Pink and Say*. Philomel, 1994.

Reeder, Carolyn. *Foster's War*. Scholastic, 1998.

Reeder, Carolyn. *Shades of Gray*. Aladdin, 1999.

Rylant, Cynthia. *When I Was Young in the Mountains*. Illus. Diane Goode. Sagebrush, 1999.

Speare, Elizabeth George. *The Bronze Bow*. Houghton Mifflin, 1997.

Speare, Elizabeth George. *The Sign of the Beaver*. Houghton Mifflin, 1983.

Speare, Elizabeth George. *The Witch of Blackbird Pond*. Houghton Mifflin, 2001.

Spinelli, Jerry. *Milkweed*. Random House, 2003.

Taylor, Mildred D. *Let the Circle Be Unbroken*. Puffin, 1991.

Taylor, Mildred D. *Mississippi Bridge*. Beeler, 2004.

Taylor, Mildred D. *Roll of Thunder, Hear My Cry*. Puffin, 2004.

Taylor, Mildred D. *Song of the Trees*. Puffin, 2003.

Taylor, Mildred D. *The Friendship*. Puffin, 1998.

Taylor, Mildred D. *The Land*. Puffin, 2003.

Taylor, Mildred D. *The Road to Memphis*. Puffin, 1992.

Taylor, Mildred D. *The Well*. Penguin, 1998.

Wells, Rosemary. *Mary on Horseback*. Puffin, 2000.

White, Ruth. *Belle Prater's Boy*. Farrar, Straus & Giroux, 1996.

Wilder, Laura Ingalls. *Little House in the Big Woods*. Illus. Garth Williams. HarperTrophy, 1932/2004.

Wilder, Laura Ingalls. *Little House on the Prairie*. Illus. Garth Williams. HarperTrophy, 1935/2004.

Yazzie, Evangeline Parsons. *Little Woman Warrior Who Came Home: A Story of the Navajo Long Walk*. Illus. Irving Toddy. Salina Bookshelf, 2005.

Yep, Laurence. *Child of the Owl*. HarperTrophy, 1990.

Yep, Laurence. *Dragon's Gate*. HarperTrophy, 1995.

Yep, Laurence. *Dragonwings*. Sagebrush, 1999.

Yep, Laurence. *Mountain Light*. HarperTrophy, 1997.

Yep, Laurence. *The Red Warrior*. HarperCollins, 2005.

Yep, Laurence. *The Serpent's Children*. HarperTrophy, 1996.

Yep, Laurence. *The Traitor*. HarperTrophy, 2004.

Zusak, Markus. *The Book Thief*. Knopf, 2005.

Biography and Autobiography

11

The artist used various shading techniques with colored pencils and watercolors to create optical texture; note the use of scale to give the illusion of distance in the background.

From *Cleopatra,* by Diane Stanley and Peter Vennema and illustrated by Diane Stanley.

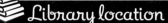

𝓛𝒾𝒷𝓇𝒶𝓇𝓎 𝓁𝑜𝒸𝒶𝓉𝒾𝑜𝓃	J920, alphabetical under *subject's* last name

(May also be in other 900 locations; picture book biographies may be in E section)

Biography: A nonfiction work describing the life—or part of the life—of a real individual

Autobiography: A person's own life story

This and the next two chapters are devoted to nonfiction. You may recall from Chapter 1 that **nonfiction** includes traditional literature, biography, informational books, and poetry. All the genres of fiction and picture books (Juvenile and Easy sections) make up only 27 percent of a typical library's holdings of children's books. The remaining books are nonfiction, of which informational books make up the bulk. Nonfiction is located in the numbered sections of the library (see Box 1.3).

Biography is one of the most interesting nonfiction genres, because it deals with the lives of interesting people. Most biographies are shelved in the J920 section. (If you are in a public library, make sure you are looking in the J section and not the adult 920 section.) Biographies and autobiographies are shelved together, and the books are arranged in alphabetical order by the *subject*'s (not the author's) last name. This is very handy when you are looking for books about an individual, because you will find most of the available biographies about that person together. In some libraries, partial biographies are located in other areas of the 900 section; and brief biographies in picture book format are sometimes located in the E section with other picture books.

Children more easily remember similar words if their derivations are explained. The word **biography** is derived by adding the prefix *bio-,* which means *life,* to *-graphy,* which comes from the Greek for *to write.* A biography, therefore, is a written work about someone's life. Add the prefix *auto-,* meaning *self,* and the word **autobiography** is formed: a work about one's own life. However, unless otherwise stated, when I refer to biographies in this chapter, I am including autobiographies.

Well-written autobiographies often read like a conversation with a familiar friend, as the author draws you into his or her life. They are nearly always written in a narrative style and in the first person. Because children are very familiar with narrative writing (from reading storybooks), autobiographies are especially good for introducing this genre, particularly when children are allowed to select a contemporary person they admire. However, not many people write their own life stories. The vast majority of life stories are written by an author who may or may not have known the person who is the subject of the book. These biographies are typically written from an objective (third-person) point of view, and they are most likely to be written in an expository (informative or explanatory) format.

Because historical fiction can contain some real historical personages, it is important to help children differentiate between it and biography. Explain that if a book has *any* fictional characters, it cannot be biography. It also helps to remind children that historical fiction is shelved in the unnumbered sections (J and E) of the library, whereas biography is in the 900 section (history) of nonfiction.

When working on school assignments, children too often turn to encyclopedias that give only the bare, dry facts. Unfortunately, biographies are often an untapped source of rich and diverse reading. This genre has changed a great deal since I was in elementary school. Today many well-written biographies make their subjects come alive. The bibliography at the end of this chapter contains titles of engaging books written on various reading levels. These books encourage readers to identify with the subjects and make a human connection. As each book unfolds, readers can watch an interesting person advance through several stages of life—growing, learning, achieving, and sometimes failing.

As with historical fiction, the writing of exemplary biographies requires authors to conduct extensive research, utilizing primary sources where available. A good biographer does not assume young readers have the necessary background knowledge to comprehend and enjoy the book. If the subject lived a long time ago (and to elementary children, that often means any period before they were born), readers need some understanding of the times and places in which the person lived. The author must provide a context for ideas, language, daily life, and the social issues that affected the subject's life.

Responding to Literature

Timelines   After reading an autobiography, construct a timeline of your own life, using strips of poster board. Also add events that you think or hope will happen in your life, such as graduating from college, embarking on a career, getting married, purchasing a house, and having children.

Evaluating Biography

The following questions can guide you as you select biography books.

- Is the book of high literary merit, presenting the subject in an interesting manner?
- Is it rich in factual content that conveys the historical period and geographical place in which the subject lived?
- Is it accurate and authentic, conveying the true nature of the subject?
- Is there evidence of careful research, such as reference notes, bibliographies, maps, or timelines?
- Is there a balance between the subject's achievements and strengths and his or her weaknesses?
- Are any archaic or specialized words explained in the text?
- Is the author qualified to write about this subject?

Reading Biographies for Pleasure

Many children never select biographies for pleasure reading because they view this genre as something to read for a school assignment rather than something to enjoy. However, biographies can be a source of both information and enjoyment, particularly when readers are allowed to select the individuals who interest them.

Athletes and Entertainers

Youthful readers have youthful interests. They want to read about people such as athletes and entertainers, whose names are familiar to them—some of whom may be controversial or unconventional people. Following is a list of books about people who are popular with young readers. (Full information for this and other lists in this chapter can be found in the end-of-chapter bibliography.)

Ashley Tisdale: Life Is Sweet! by Grace Norwich
George Lopez: Latino King of Comedy by Lila Guzman
Gloria Estefan by Michael Benson
Harry Houdini by Vicki Cobb
Jim Thorpe, Original All American by Joseph Bruchac
On the Field with Derek Jeter by Matt Christopher
On the Mound with Curt Schilling by Matt Christopher
Oprah Winfrey: "I Don't Believe in Failure" by Robin Westin
Pele by James Buckley
Tiger Woods: A Biography for Kids by Libby Hughes
Toby Keith by Amie Leavitt

Authors and Illustrators

Children who love reading will love to read about their favorite authors and illustrators. Often these books are coming-of-age stories that tell how the individuals were attracted to careers in writing and illustrating. Learning about their lives can provide a deeper understanding of their books. Also, look for introductions to fiction books that have a brief autobiographical statement by the author. These are often the impetus that prompts children to search for a full autobiography.

Bad Boy: A Memoir by Walter Dean Myers
Bowman's Store (autobiography) by Joseph Bruchac
Beatrix Potter: A Journal by Beatrix Potter
I Am Scout: The Biography of Harper Lee by Charles J. Shields
Isabel Allende: Award-Winning Latin American Author by Mary Main
J. K. Rowling by Colleen Sexton
Laura Ingalls Wilder by William Anderson
The Poet Slave of Cuba: A Biography of Juan Francisco Manzano by Margarita Engle

Well-Known Men and Women

Children also are curious about the people whose names they hear regularly at school and at home. Reading about political and social leaders—both past and present—will help them better understand the global society in which they live.

Abraham Lincoln: From Pioneer to President by Ellen Blue Phillips
Amelia Earhart by Tanya Stone
Annie Oakley by Charles M. Willis
Benjamin Franklin: An American Genius by Kay M. Olson
Bill Gates by Jeanne M. Lesinski
Chief Tecumseh by Anne M. Todd
Eleanor Roosevelt by Kem Knapp Sawyer
George Washington: An American Life by Laurie Calkhoven
Helen Keller: A Photographic Story of a Life by Leslie Garrett
John McCain by Barbara Jane Feinberg
Keeping the Rope Straight: Annie Dodge Wauneka's Life of Service to the Navajo by
    Carolyn Niethammer
Maria Von Trapp: Beyond the Sound of Music by Candice F. Ransom
Martin Luther King, Jr. by Amy Pastan
Nelson Mandela by Lenny Hort
Pocahontas by Nancy Polette
Vera Wang, Queen of Fashion by Ai-Ling Louie
Yes We Can: A Biography of Barack Obama by Garen Thomas

Types of Biography

Biography is written in diverse formats. Some biographers adhere faithfully to the facts; others add some fictional elements, such as dialogue, to make the book more closely resemble a story. Some books trace the full life of an individual from birth to death; others cover only one period, such as the subject's childhood or most significant life achievement. Some biographies are primarily text, whereas others are in picture book format.

Authentic Biography

Authors who write **authentic biography** are very concerned with accuracy. In their books they carefully distinguish between fact and supposition. They limit information about a person's life to the events that are verifiable. Dialogue is included only if substantiated by reliable personal recollections or historical documents, such as letters and diaries. As part of their research, authors of authentic biography often travel to the places where the subject lived and worked, locating public documents and interviewing people for unpublished information. Authentic biographies are more likely to be written with a balanced perspective, in which the author includes the negative or unfortunate aspects of a person's life as well as the successes.

Jean Fritz provides an honest portrayal of Theodore Roosevelt, twenty-sixth president of the United States, in *Bully for You, Teddy Roosevelt!* In the book Fritz writes of what happened when Roosevelt's beloved wife, Alice Lee, died shortly after giving birth to their only child—who was also named Alice.

> He believed that anything painful in the past should be left in the past, and of course he had to run to keep ahead of the pain. After the first stages of grief, Teddy never mentioned Alice's name again. He put away her pictures and her letters, and years later, when he wrote his autobiography, he never mentioned that once there had been an Alice Lee in his life. Furthermore, he never told young Alice anything about her mother. Not once. (p. 41)

Another example of an honest portrayal is Doris Faber's *Eleanor Roosevelt: First Lady of the World*. Eleanor Roosevelt was married to Franklin D. Roosevelt (Theodore Roosevelt's cousin), thirty-second president of the United States. Faber attributes Eleanor's lifetime of tireless public work to her husband's unfaithfulness.

> [Eleanor] found another reason why she *needed* work. Unpacking Franklin's luggage on his return from a trip, she noticed some letters in a familiar handwriting. Her own pretty secretary, Lucy Mercer, had written them. A glance showed her that these were love letters. To a woman like Eleanor Roosevelt, who had the strictest of moral standards, it was impossible just to forgive Franklin. But when he promised never to see Lucy again, Eleanor coldly said that, for the sake of their children, she would continue living with him. As much as Franklin had hurt her, though, she could not help blaming herself. . . . She simply could not go on day after day—unless she did some work that would make her stop feeling entirely useless. (pp. 30–31)

Authentic biographies can usually be recognized because the text contains little (if any) dialogue, and because a list of information sources is included at the end of the book. An excellent example of authentic biography is *Cleopatra* by Diane Stanley and Peter Vennema. There is no dialogue in the text, and the few quotes were taken from primary sources. Illustrations on the book cover and throughout were exquisitely painted by Stanley in the style of Alexandrian mosaics. Coins with Cleopatra's profile (the only existing examples of her image) were models for the illustrations of the Egyptian queen. The copyright page contains an *acknowledgment* of the specialists in art history and ancient history who advised the authors. Information sources include a *preface* that gives the necessary historical background, a *note on ancient sources* about information obtained in Plutarch's books, and an explanation of why so little information survived about Cleopatra. A two-page spread shows a *map* of Egypt, the Roman Provinces, and surrounding regions in 51 B.C. The text covers the life of Cleopatra from age 18 to 39, when she killed herself, and it is followed by an *epilogue* that explains what happened to Egypt and Cleopatra's children after she died. Also included is a *pronunciation guide* for all the names. At the end of the book is a *reference list* of the eleven books the authors consulted while writing and illustrating the book.

Another important characteristic of an authentic biography is that it is written by a qualified author. Usually there is a note by or about the author on the inside flaps of the book jacket, or at the beginning or end of the book. After reading the note, ask yourself the following questions to judge the author's qualifications.

- Is there a statement that the author faithfully adhered to facts?
- Is the author well known for writing authentic biographies?
- What is in the author's education or life experience that qualifies her or him to write an authentic biography about the subject?
- Has the author written biographies about others who lived during the same time?
- Did the author know or personally interview the subject?

Featured Author

Jean Fritz

One of the best-known authors of authentic biography is Jean Fritz, whose humanizing details and amusing tone make her books good reading. Among her many books is a series about founders of the United States—Sam Adams, Benjamin Franklin, John Hancock, Patrick Henry, and Paul Revere. Though her research is scrupulous, she writes with a unique perspective. Her merger of careful research and a strong sense of story with humorous overtones results in both informative and pleasurable reading. Part of Fritz's unique writing style is weaving little-known details about the subject into each book.

The first half of *What's the Big Idea, Ben Franklin?* is devoted to Franklin's childhood, in which the author lays the foundation for the scientific curiosity that led to Franklin's discovery that lightning was electricity. Fritz describes one of his early experiments, performed while he swam in his favorite pond.

> Then he tried lying on his back, holding a kite string, and letting the kite act as a sail and pull him across the pond. This was a great success. There was only one trouble. In those days boys went swimming naked. And if Benjamin didn't want to go home naked, he had to get a friend to carry his clothes to the other side of the pond. (It had to be a good friend because the pond was a mile wide.) (p. 19)

At the end of the book, in a list of notes that are referenced by page number, Fritz adds some interesting details she did not include in the text. For example, she wrote that no one (except Franklin and the woman involved, of course) knew the identity of the mother of his oldest child, William Temple, who went to live with Franklin when he got married. When his son sided with England during the American Revolution, Franklin suffered his greatest disappointment. Fritz's illumination of ordinary events produces a lively interpretation of history, without compromising standards by adding fabricated dialogue and other forms of fictionalization.

In her author's note, Megan Stine gives the following information about her subject in *The Story of Malcolm X, Civil Rights Leader*.

In reading and writing about Malcolm X, I have found that there are often different versions of the "truth" about many events in his life. Some of these differences are big, and some are small. In his autobiography, for instance, Malcolm remembers some of the dates incorrectly—probably because the stories he was remembering had all happened so many years before. In other places Malcolm changed the names of people he knew, maybe to protect their privacy. Sometimes Malcolm told the stories from his childhood exactly as they were told to him—regardless of whether he actually thought they were true. Sometimes it is hard to know what is true and what is not. . . . (p. 1)

This passage points out some of the problems with the accuracy of autobiography. Autobiographers may not believe it necessary to research certain facts and may rely only on their sometimes faulty memories. Also, autobiographers may omit or change certain information to protect others or to portray themselves more favorably. However, we cannot assume biography is any more accurate than autobiography, because "truth" is subject to interpretation. Biographies about the same subject can have major discrepancies. In comparing Stine's biography of Malcolm X with Arnold Adoff's *Malcolm X*, I found the following major discrepancies:

1. Adoff wrote that Malcolm and his brothers sometimes hunted for rabbit, which they took home for supper (p. 6). However, Stine wrote that Malcolm's mother would not cook or eat pork or rabbit, even when her children were starving (p. 12).

2. Adoff wrote that during the years Malcolm was in prison, he and Elijah Muhammad, the leader of the Nation of Islam, wrote numerous letters to each other (pp. 20, 25). However, Stine wrote that Malcolm and Muhammad exchanged letters only once (p. 41).

3. Adoff wrote that Malcolm married his wife, Betty, after a courtship (p. 32). However, Stine wrote that Malcolm took Betty out one time (to a museum), had her meet with Elijah Muhammad, and then proposed to her over the telephone months later.

4. Adoff wrote that Malcolm and his wife had four daughters (p. 32). Stine wrote that Malcolm and Betty had six daughters, and she listed their names and birth dates (p. 65).

📖 Issues in Biography

Which Is a More Accurate Source of Information: Biography or Autobiography?   Do you believe an autobiography would be more accurate because the author is the primary source of information? Or, do you believe a biography would be more accurate because the author is more objective? For example, would former president Richard Nixon's autobiography be more accurate than a biography written by someone not personally associated with him?

Give three reasons that you believe autobiography would or would not be more accurate than biography.

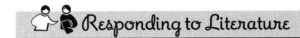
Responding to Literature

Comparing Biographies Read a historical person's autobiography and one biography (or two authentic biographies) of the person. Take note of any contradictions in the books. What would account for the contradictions? In reference to this activity, explain what is meant by "Truth is subject to interpretation."

Fictionalized Biography

Most elementary children prefer fiction to nonfiction. Because of this, many children's biographers write in a narrative style that reads much like a novel, called **fictionalized biography.** This requires the author to provide speculative or imagined scenes and details, which often include invented dialogue and **interior monologue**—a device that lets readers know what the subject is thinking. The rationale for fictionalizing biography is that it results in an appealing introduction to a genre that otherwise turns off many children. Adding dialogue contributes to the readers' identification with the subject, and interest increases when readers are sympathetic. Following is an excerpt from *Louis Braille, the Boy Who Invented Books for the Blind* (Davidson):

> Soon [books for the blind] was all Louis could think—or talk—about. And his friends got good and tired of it.
> "Do shut up, Louis," they begged.
> "But it's so important!" Louis tried to explain. "Don't you see? Without books we can never really learn! But just think what we could grow up to be if only we could read. Doctors or lawyers or scientists. Or writers even! *Anything* almost."
> "All right," one of the boys snapped. "We want to read too. Find us a way, if you're so smart."
> "I can't," Louis cried. "I'm blind!" (pp. 35–36)

In this excerpt, the conversation between Louis and his schoolmates was invented by the author to more fully portray Braille's passion for finding a way for blind people to read. Braille's speech is more effective in relating this passion than an expository statement such as "Louis Braille passionately wanted books that blind people could read."

Even autobiographies can be fictionalized. In the introduction to *Homesick: My Own Story,* Jean Fritz wrote:

> Since my childhood feels like a story, I decided to tell it that way, letting the events fall as they would into the shape of a story, lacing them together with fictional bits, adding a piece here and there when memory didn't give me all I needed. I . . . use conversation freely. . . . So although this book takes place within two years . . . the events are drawn from the entire period of my childhood. . . . Strictly speaking, I have to call this book *fiction,* but it does not feel like fiction to me. (p. 7)

Attempting to achieve the emotional engagement of the familiar storytelling format in a biography often results in a book of **faction**—a merger of fact and fiction.

However, some critics argue that to add *any* element of fiction automatically excludes a book from the category of nonfiction. Nonetheless, you will find numerous books in the children's biography section that are fictionalized in some way. Obviously, fictionalized biography is not as reliable historically, and some authors are even guilty of distorting history with books that read more like legends.

In presenting a dramatic narrative to bring subjects to life through the familiar devices of storytelling, some authors step over the line to *biographical fiction,* fiction that is based on the life of a real person. Recall from the last chapter on historical fiction that in writing biographical fiction, the author uses considerable invention and takes great liberties with the facts about a real person. A prime example is *Amos Fortune, Free Man,* in which Elizabeth Yates invented a story about a former slave, using only his gravestone epitaph and some old legal documents. Yet this book is nearly always shelved in the nonfiction section, because the publisher said it was nonfiction!

Sometimes fictionalized biography and biographical fiction are difficult to differentiate. It is even hard to remember which term is which. It is easier to help children keep the terms straight if you explain that the adjective (first word) is the type, and the noun (second word) is the *genre.*

- Fictionalized *biography* is biography in which the author has included invented elements, such as dialogue (considered nonfiction).
- Biographical *fiction* is a fiction story based on the life of a real person or persons (considered fiction).

Forms of Biography

Biography, like other genres, has several categories: complete, partial, childhood, picture book, and collective biographies.

Complete

Some biographies span the entire life of the subject, from cradle to grave, and are called **complete biographies.** To do justice to their subjects, these books are understandably long and therefore geared for more able readers, such as intermediate-grade children. These are the books most children select or are assigned for biography book reports. Older books often contain only text with no photographs or illustrations. For example, *Invincible Louisa* (Meigs) has 247 pages of small print with no photographs and only one illustration on the book's cover. Cornelia Meigs traces the life of Louisa May Alcott, the author of *Little Women,* from the day she was born in 1832 until 1888, when she died two days after her father's death. The author covers her life so thoroughly that the reader learns not only about Louisa, but about her parents and sisters as well.

Sometimes, when authors try to write a complete biography for less able readers, the result is a stripped-down version whose briefness does not portray the personality of the subject. When a person's life is reduced to a series of facts that convey no sense of the spirit of the individual, it is no wonder children lose interest in this genre.

Partial

Partial biographies focus on one part or one aspect of a subject's life; this category, of course, includes biographies of living people. Young readers are interested in the childhood and adolescent experiences of admirable people. Often, childhood biographies focus on the influences that led to the subject's achievements later in life. This is particularly interesting if the person had to overcome adversity (such as poverty, a physical impairment, or the early loss of a parent). *Albert Einstein* by Ibi Lepscky is an interesting childhood biography that focuses on Einstein's unique and inquisitive nature. Readers will be amazed to learn that Einstein, though a genius, did not do well in school—because he was interested only in arithmetic and refused to do his other lessons!

Childhood Biographies and Autobiographies

Anne Frank by Wil Mara
Bindi Irwin by Sarah Tieck
Jack: The Early Years of John F. Kennedy by Ilene Cooper
Sadako and the Thousand Paper Cranes by Eleanor Coerr
Through My Eyes (autobiography) by Ruby Bridges

Some childhood biographies are sad, because the subject did not live to reach adulthood. In the fictionalized biography, *Sadako and the Thousand Paper Cranes,* Eleanor Coerr writes about Sadako Sasaki, who died at the age of 12 from leukemia as a result of radiation from the bomb dropped on Hiroshima, Japan. Also very moving is the partial autobiography of a 13-year-old Jewish girl, Anne Frank. She kept a diary for two years while hiding from the Nazis in a secret building annex in Holland. She and her family were captured and sent to concentration camps, where all but her father perished. Her diary was later found in the annex, and her father published it under the title *Anne Frank: The Diary of a Young Girl.*

Some partial biographies focus on the most important event in a person's life. For example, in *And Then What Happened, Paul Revere?* Jean Fritz focused on Revere's life as a Patriot and his famous ride to warn the colonists that the British were coming. Little is said about Revere's childhood, and even less about his life after the Revolutionary War.

The Glorious Flight: Across the Channel with Louis Blériot, July 25, 1909 (Provensen & Provensen) also focuses on the most significant part of a person's life. Blériot's fascination with flying machines produced the Blériot XI, which in 1909 became the first heavier-than-air machine to fly the English Channel. In selecting partial biographies, take care to avoid watered-down versions that leave out facts that are essential for a balanced portrayal. When these essential facts are omitted, the reader often sees a distorted view of history.

Picture Book

A more recent format is **picture book biography.** Some picture book biographies zoom in on a childhood incident of a well-known person, such as *Richard Wright and the Library Card* (Miller), a fictionalized account of an important one-year period (based on his autobiography). During the mid-1920s, Wright is working to save money to move north. He convinces a white man to lend him his library card, because blacks cannot check out books. During that year, Wright reads many classics that inspire him to become one of the first great African American authors.

The picture book biographies by Robert Quackenbush are enjoyable reading for elementary children. There is no dialogue in the text; however, Quackenbush keeps a running commentary, often humorous, through the speech bubbles of cartoon characters he illustrates on each two-page spread. For example, in *Once upon a Time! A Story of the Brothers Grimm,* the book tells of the brothers' fortunate encounter with a genuine storyteller, Frau Viehmann, who "settled for rolls and coffee in exchange for her stories" (p. 22). Underneath the text a cartoon shows Jacob saying in a speech bubble, "Quick! Frau Viehmann is coming! Are there any rolls in the house?" Wilhelm answers, "Will egg rolls do?" Quackenbush is successful in maintaining children's interest through dialogue and humor in his illustrations without compromising the standards of authentic biography in the text.

Picture Book Biographies

A Picture Book of George Washington Carver by David Adler
Cesar Chavez: Fighting for Farmworkers by Eric Braun
Chief Red Cloud: 1822–1909 by Judy Monroe
Diamond in the Sky: A [Shinichi] Suzuki Biography by Jerlene Cannon
James and Dolly Madison and Their Times by Robert M. Quackenbush
Selena by Barbara J. Marvis
Sitting Bull and the Battle of Little Bighorn by Dan Abnett

Collective

Collective biographies examine the lives of several people who are linked by a common thread, such as occupation, ethnicity, or achievement. In collective biographies, photographs or illustrations abound, and brief biographical sketches are provided for each individual. For example, *The Buck Stops Here* by Alice Provensen devotes one or two pages to each of the presidents through George Bush. Interesting illustrations with meaningful symbols adorn the pages, and a short description of each president's term with biographical information is located at the back. Sometimes a collective biography such as this will pique a child's interest, and the child will seek a longer biography of one of the subjects to read.

American Women Inventors by Carole Ann Camp
Back-to-Back: Super Bowl Champions Peyton and Eli Manning by Hugh Hudson
Dare to Dream! 25 Extraordinary Lives by Sandra McLeod Humphrey
Jammin' with the Jonas Brothers by Lexi Ryals
The Beatles by Jeremy Roberts

Integrating Biography with the Study of History

Like historical fiction, biography can enliven the study of history by revealing what it was like to live in another time. History is enhanced when books give readers "the chance to reflect on events from one individual viewpoint, to step off the beaten track and into fresh territory" (Wilms, 1978, p. 218). When readers closely connect with the subject of a biography, the evocation experience is analogous to walking around in the skin of someone who lived in another place at another time. Biography is unique in its potential to enhance children's understanding of the true significance of past events and of the people involved.

Enhancing Curriculum with Biography

by Sharon Smith

Biographies and autobiographies offer readers the opportunity to see history or contemporary society through the eyes of one individual. This genre often captures elementary children's interest because—unlike historical fiction—the main character is a real person, someone to whom readers can often relate. However, a biography also provides factual insight into the times and places in which the person lived, a perfect compliment to the study of history. This genre is uniquely versatile in that readers can take either an aesthetic or an efferent stance while reading, and enjoy it equally well. Biography books easily enhance all subject areas because they are written about people from all fields and occupations.

Good biographers bring their subjects to life, and you can enhance this lived-through experience by having children become the subject for an interview. After reading about a memorable figure (for example, Benjamin Franklin, Marie Curie, or Jim Henson), a child can assume the persona of that subject by dressing in costume and pretending to be him or her. While the rest of the class prepares interview questions, explain to the child what it means to stay in character. Before responding to questions, the child will need to think how the subject might have answered. The other children then may interview the subject and learn about a well-known person in a fun and interesting way. Sometimes colleges have instructors or contacts who are enactors of people from past eras, such as the Civil War, and a visit from one of them would certainly set the stage for this activity.

Another activity is to have several children assume the personas of a variety of famous people from different eras but within the same field. Then you may present a panel of scientists, musicians, or politicians who converse with one another. What would Thomas Jefferson have to say to Harry Truman or Ronald Reagan? And what would be the focus of a conversation among Mozart, Glenn Miller, and Ray Charles? In this activity, not only could students learn about the lives of well-known people, but also how the eras in which they lived affected their thoughts and actions.

Children can also portray subjects of autobiographies they have read. After reading an autobiography of a contemporary person, students can locate more reading material about him or her, such as newspaper articles, magazine features, and websites. Then children can review videos or audio recordings of the subject (from films, television, online sources, or radio) and prepare brief first-person accounts, telling the audience why they should read their autobiographies. Students might also give their presentations to classes of younger children to spark their interest in reading nonfiction. Likewise, the children's librarian at a local library might allow some of the children to give their presentations during story hour. Presentations should include reading an excerpt from the autobiography and answering questions from the audience.

Another activity to deepen children's understanding of a biography is to create a keepsake box for the subject, gathering items that are associated with that person or things the person might have collected. For example, a box for Sacagawea might include a pair of baby booties, leaves from a medicinal plant, fishing hook and line, some dried corn, and seashells from the Pacific Ocean. Keepsake boxes should be labeled with the person's name, lined inside with scraps of fabric, and decorated outside with colorful scenes from significant episodes in the person's life. Children then use the keepsake boxes and their contents to tell others about the person whose life it represents, much as the story boxes mentioned in Chapter 6 tell about a storybook.

When children give book talks on biographies, you will want to steer them away from reporting just the obvious facts, such as when the subject was born, what they accomplished, and when they died. Before assigning the class to read and report on a biography, intrigue them by saying they are going to be detectives. With a magnifying glass in one hand and a notepad in the other, model how to select three or four intriguing facts from a biography that would interest their classmates. For example, read some of the items from the back pages of *What's the Big Idea, Ben Franklin?* (Fritz). While reading their selected biographies, children should be encouraged to make notes about the little known, but interesting, facts as well as the common information to present to their classmates. Instead of a book talk, children might create a missing person's report using their notes but not the subject's name. They would have to include sufficient description in order for classmates to guess the identity of the person.

Today, many well-known people such as movie stars, professional athletes, musicians, and authors have websites with e-mail addresses where fans can contact them. After children read an autobiography, encourage them to do an Internet search to find a website where they may e-mail questions or comments to the celebrity. You may be surprised by e-mailed responses, especially from authors and illustrators with whom a class of children might carry on a lively discussion.

Biographies and autobiographies offer readers interesting and unique perspectives on other people's lives. Many describe people who are good role models for young children, and certainly all can be used to enhance some areas of the curriculum from science to music.

Integrating Literature and Technology

Making Biography Newspapers After reading one biography to your class, for example, *The Story of Sacajawea: Guide to Lewis and Clark,* have children perform extensive research and reading of other sources on this person, such as textbooks, reference books and CD-ROMs, periodicals, Internet sites, and other biographies. Children should become thoroughly familiar with the person and his or her family, as well as with political and social issues of the era in which the person lived.

Using a scanner and a computer with a publishing program, such as Microsoft Publisher, help the class create a fictional newspaper for a significant date in the subject's life using the information the students have gleaned. In the above example, this might be a day in September 1806 when the Corps of Discovery returned to St. Louis, Missouri. The newspaper should include the following elements:

- Masthead that reflects the style of the time and place
- Lead story that is an account of a significant episode in the person's life with at least one scanned picture (photograph, graphic, or drawing)
- Editorials reflecting opinions—substantiated with historical facts and statistics—on moral or social issues that were important to the subject
- Classified ads for jobs, services, and products that reflect the economic structure of the era
- Obituary of at least one real person who died during the subject's life (including a picture)
- Advertisement of at least one item invented during the subject's life, including at least one picture
- Entertainment notices of songs, plays, books, or films that were popular during the subject's life
- Reading list of printed sources and websites used for developing the newspaper

This teaching idea is based on Marianne Rossi's Historical Fiction Newspaper project, described in "Classroom Spotlight on Technology: Fiction Based on Fact" in *Reading Today* (February/March 2003), p. 10.

Summary

A biography is a nonfiction work that describes the life (or part of the life) of a real person. When someone writes his or her own life story, it is called an autobiography. To encourage children to read biographies for pleasure, allow them to pick their own subjects, and many will select books about their favorite entertainer or athlete. In addition, many authors and illustrators write autobiographies, which are of interest to children.

Two major types of biographies exist. Authentic biography limits information about the subject to events that are verifiable, and for this reason, it rarely contains dialogue. Fictionalized biography includes speculative or imagined scenes and details, which often includes invented dialogue or interior monologue.

Four forms of biographies are identified. A complete biography spans the entire life of the subject from birth through death. A partial biography focuses on one part or one aspect of a subject's life, such as his or her childhood or most significant achievement. Picture book biographies are only 32 to 64 pages long, and the account is partially revealed though pictures. Collective biographies examine the lives of several people who are linked by a common thread.

Biography Books

Abnett, Dan. *Sitting Bull and the Battle of Little Bighorn.* PowerKids, 2006.
Adler, David. *A Picture Book of George Washington Carver.* Holiday House, 2000.
Adoff, Arnold. *Malcolm X.* Illus. John Wilson. HarperCollins, 2000.
Anderson, William. *Laura Ingalls Wilder.* Collins, 2007.
Benson, Michael. *Gloria Estefan.* Lerner, 2000.
Braun, Eric. *Cesar Chavez: Fighting for Farmworkers.* Capstone, 2006.
Bridges, Ruby. *Through My Eyes.* Scholastic, 1999.
Bruchac, Joseph. *Bowman's Store.* Lee & Low, 2001.
Bruchac, Joseph. *Jim Thorpe, Original All American.* Dial, 2006.
Buckley, James. *Pele.* DK, 2007.
Calkhoven, Laurie. *George Washington: An American Life.* Sterling, 2007.
Camp, Carole Ann. *American Women Inventors.* Enslow, 2004.
Cannon, Jerlene. *Diamond in the Sky: A Suzuki Biography.* Alfred, 2002.
Christopher, Matt. *On the Field with Derek Jeter.* Little, Brown, 2000.
Christopher, Matt. *On the Mound with Curt Schilling.* Little, Brown, 2004.
Coerr, Eleanor. *Sadako and the Thousand Paper Cranes.* Puffin, 2004.
Cooper, Ilene. *Jack: The Early Years of John F. Kennedy.* Dutton, 2003.
Davidson, Margaret. *Louis Braille, the Boy Who Invented Books for the Blind.* Scholastic, 1991.
Engle, Margarita. *The Poet Slave of Cuba: A Biography of Juan Francisco Manzano.* Henry Holt, 2006.
Faber, Doris. *Eleanor Roosevelt: First Lady of the World.* Puffin, 1996.
Feinberg, Barbara Jane. *John McCain.* Millbrook, 2000.
Frank, Anne. *Anne Frank: The Diary of a Young Girl.* Doubleday, 1952.
Fritz, Jean. *And Then What Happened, Paul Revere?* Illus. Margot Tomes. Putnam, 1998.

Fritz, Jean. *Bully for You, Teddy Roosevelt!* Illus. Mike Wimmer. Putnam, 1991.

Fritz, Jean. *Homesick: My Own Story.* PaperStar, 1999.

Fritz, Jean. *What's the Big Idea, Ben Franklin?* Illus. Margot Tomes. Sagebrush, 1999.

Garrett, Leslie. *Helen Keller: A Photographic Story of a Life.* DK, 2004.

Guzman, Lila. *George Lopez: Latino King of Comedy.* Enslow, 2008.

Hort, Lenny. *Nelson Mandela.* DK, 2006.

Hudson, Hugh. *Back-to-Back: Super Bowl Champions Peyton and Eli Manning.* Price, Sloan, Stern, 2008.

Hughes, Libby. *Tiger Woods: A Biography for Kids.* Genesis Press, 2007.

Humphrey, Sandra McLeod. *Dare to Dream! 25 Extraordinary Lives.* Prometheus, 2005.

Leavitt, Amie. *Toby Keith.* Mitchell Lane, 2008.

Lepscky, Ibi. *Albert Einstein.* Illus. Paolo Cardoni. Barron's Educational, 1993.

Lesinski, Jeanne M. *Bill Gates.* First Avenue Editions, 2006.

Louie, Ai-Ling. *Vera Wang, Queen of Fashion.* Dragoneagle, 2007.

Main, Mary. *Isabel Allende: Award-Winning Latin American Author.* Enslow, 2005.

Mara, Wil. *Anne Frank.* Children's Press, 2007.

Marvis, Barbara J. *Selena.* Mitchell Lane, 2003.

Meigs, Cornelia. *Invincible Louisa.* Little, Brown, 1933.

Miller, William. *Richard Wright and the Library Card.* Illus. Gregory Christie. Lee & Low, 1997.

Monroe, Judy. *Chief Red Cloud: 1822–1909.* Blue Earth, 2003.

Myers, Walter Dean. *Bad Boy: A Memoir.* Amistad, 2002.

Niethammer, Carolyn. *Keeping the Rope Straight: Annie Dodge Wauneka's Life of Service to the Navajo.* Salina Bookshelf, 2006.

Norwich, Grace. *Ashley Tisdale: Life Is Sweet!* Price Stern Sloan, 2006.

Olson, Kay M. *Benjamin Franklin: An American Genius.* Capstone, 2006.

Pastan, Amy. *Martin Luther King, Jr.* DK, 2004.

Phillips, Ellen Blue. *Abraham Lincoln: From Pioneer to President.* Sterling, 2007.

Potter, Beatrix. *Beatrix Potter: A Journal.* Warne, 2006.

Provensen, Alice. *The Buck Stops Here.* HarperCollins, 1990.

Provensen, Alice, & Martin Provensen. *The Glorious Flight: Across the Channel with Louis Blériot.* Sagebrush, 1999.

Quackenbush, Robert M. *James and Dolly Madison and Their Times.* Pippin, 1992.

Quackenbush, Robert. *Once upon a Time! A Story of the Brothers Grimm.* Robert Quackenbush Studios, 1999.

Ransom, Candice F. *Maria Von Trapp: Beyond the Sound of Music.* Carolrhoda, 2002.

Roberts, Jeremy. *The Beatles.* Learner, 2001.

Ryals, Lexi. *Jammin' with the Jonas Brothers.* Price, Sloan, Stern, 2008.

Sawyer, Kem Knapp. *Eleanor Roosevelt.* DK, 2006.

Sexton, Colleen. *J. K. Rowling.* First Avenue Editions, 2007.

Shields, Charles J. *I Am Scout: The Biography of Harper Lee.* Henry Holt, 2008.

Stanley, Diane, & Peter Vennema. *Cleopatra.* Illus. Diane Stanley. Morrow, 1994.

Stine, Megan. *The Story of Malcolm X, Civil Rights Leader.* Parachute Press, 1994.

Stone, Tanya. *Amelia Earhart.* DK, 2007.

Thomas, Garen. *Yes We Can: A Biography of Barack Obama.* Fiewel & Friends, 2008.

Tieck, Sarah. *Bindi Irwin.* Buddy Books, 2008.

Todd, Anne M. *Chief Tecumseh.* Heinemann, 2004.

Westin, Robin. *Oprah Winfrey: "I Don't Believe in Failure."* Enslow, 2005.

Willis, Charles M. *Annie Oakley.* DK, 2007.

THE DIFFERENCE BETWEEN A FROG AND A TOAD

A FROG

MOST LIVE IN OR
NEAR WATER

LARGE, ROUND
EAR MEMBRANES

NARROW BODY

RIDGES DOWN BACK

SMALL TEETH IN
UPPER JAW

LONG LEAPS

LONG HIND LEGS

SMOOTH, MOIST
SOFT SKIN

CLUMPS OF EGGS
IN WATER

**The artist used pen and ink to outline the
shapes before filling in with watercolors.**

From *Frogs,* written and illustrated by Gail Gibbons.

Library locations — Informational books

Informational books: Literature whose primary purpose is to inform the reader by providing an in-depth explanation of factual material

000–099	General Works Computers
100–199	Philosophy and Psychology Personal improvement
200–299	Religion Christianity, Islam, Judaism, other religions
300–399	Social Sciences Family, government, community life, conservation, transportation, law, holidays, costumes, etiquette
400–499	Language English, other languages
500–599	Natural Sciences and Mathematics Mathematics, astronomy, physics, chemistry, earth science, dinosaurs, trees, flowers, animals
600–699	Applied Sciences, Useful Arts, and Technology Medicine, health, diseases, human body, safety, space and aeronautics, gardening, building, pets, sewing, manufacturing, machines, and inventions
700–799	Fine Arts, Sports, and Recreations Architecture, drawing, handicrafts, painting, music, performing arts, games, sports, photography, hobbies, coins, magic, "how-to" books
800–899	Literature
900–999	History, Geography, and Travel Travel, world history, United States history, geography

The amount of information available to humans doubles every few years. Some futurists have predicted that in about two decades, available information will double every few months! Consequently, it should be no surprise that **informational books** constitute approximately one-half of the books in most libraries' juvenile collections. Children have inquiring minds and want to learn about themselves and their own world, as well as about things and places they have never seen. Informational books help satisfy this natural inquisitiveness and spark new curiosity.

Like biography, informational books are nonfiction. However, they should not be confused with **textbooks,** which are written on various grade levels and are marketed to school districts (but typically not found in libraries). Whereas textbooks present a breadth of information on a discipline, such as history, informational books present an in-depth look at a particular topic within a discipline, such as the U.S. Constitution's Bill of Rights (e.g., *In Defense of Liberty: The Story of America's Bill of Rights,* Freedman)—a topic that might be covered in one page in a textbook. Also, the genre of informational books does not include **reference books:** dictionaries, encyclopedias, almanacs, atlases, or any other books that are not intended to be read in their entirety. Like the other genres presented in this textbook, informational books are literature and are therefore considered **trade books,** which are primarily marketed to libraries, wholesale booksellers, retail bookstores, and book clubs.

There is an interesting phenomenon in the publishing of nonfiction books that does not exist with fiction: There are two types of publishers. **Institutional publishers,** such as Children's Press and Usborne, specialize in nonfiction literature books for classrooms and public and school libraries. These publishers primarily produce series rather than individual titles, such as a series of biographies of influential African Americans or a series of books about various Native American tribes. Institutional publishers typically do not attempt to market to bookstores, which are less likely to purchase nonfiction series books. To attract a volume of sales, these books are usually priced lower than other trade books.

In contrast, trade book publishers present a broad range of titles and cater to the more lucrative retail market. Because these publishers pay their authors and illustrators more, "trade books are more likely to be written by an author with more knowledge and experience than the institutional books are" (Patent, 1998). Additionally, trade book illustrations are usually of higher quality and are more appealing.

Evaluating Informational Books

The following questions can guide you as you select informational books.

- Is the information accurate and up to date with current research data (with no significant omissions)?
- Is the content organized in a logical sequence to lead the reader from the familiar to the new?
- Is the text clear and interesting, containing appropriate vocabulary for elementary children?
- Is there a glossary with concise definitions of specialized terminology or are terms explained clearly in text?
- Does the author clearly distinguish among fact, theory, and opinion?
- Are both text and illustrations free from stereotypes?
- Is there evidence of careful research, such as bibliography, references, and endnotes?
- Are appropriate reference aids included, such as headings, index, and recommended additional readings?

- Is the visual format uncluttered and appealing?
- Are there full-color visual aids, such as photographs, illustrations, maps, charts, graphs, diagrams, original documents, and reproductions of artwork?
- Are the visuals and their captions accurate, and do they clarify and extend the text?

The importance of excellent visual aids cannot be overemphasized. Visual representation of abstract concepts and information outside readers' prior knowledge is essential for children's comprehension and enjoyment of informational books.

Characteristics of Informational Books

Whereas fiction books present stories, informational books present facts and concepts in an in-depth look at a specific topic (or, in younger children's books, a brief overview of a topic). "How-to" books are also included in this genre, for example, how to make string figures (*Cat's Cradle,* Johnson). In addition to basic information that children might need to include in a school report, informational books contain many interesting details and lesser-known facts.

Responding to Literature

"How-To" Books   From the 700 section of the library, select a book on a sport you want to learn (or learn to play better), such as tennis, golf, basketball, or football. Demonstrate a new technique that you learned from the book.

Unlike fiction, which employs dialogue and narrative language, most informational books utilize **expository language,** the language that is used in textbooks, newspapers, magazines, and nonfiction books. Good informational books are organized with a logical presentation of information, such as simple-to-complex or chronological order. Often, full-color photographs are included to provide authenticity.

When you are selecting informational books, it is important to check copyright dates. Recent books are most likely to contain accurate, up-to-date information. In particular, books on science and technology become outdated quickly. Scientists, researchers, and technologists are constantly making new discoveries, developing new technology, and revealing new facts.

And even in disciplines such as history, knowledge advances and attitudes toward interpreting and reporting information change. Newer books are less likely to contain the racism, sexism, and ageism that characterized some older books—sometimes in the form of omissions, which are often more difficult to detect than blatant bias. According to Tunnell (1992), history-related trade books are "one of the best sources for teaching students history, for they place the human experience in the forefront. In the end, understanding history is indeed a matter of understanding human perspectives" (p. 247).

Modern informational books are colorful and have pleasing, uncluttered designs, often falling within a range of thirty-two to sixty-four pages. Many attractive full-color photographs, illustrations, and other graphics adorn the pages. For example, in *Hidden World: Human Body* (Delafosse), viewers can use a "magic" paper flashlight that comes in the back of the book to view internal organs, inspect X-rays, and view a developing baby in the colorful illustrations. Also, because informational books are primarily about people, places, events, and ideas, writers increasingly use a narrative framework to convey information—much as I have by writing with the first-person point of view in this textbook.

Informational books may present straightforward information about their topics, either through a single-topic treatment such as *Wild Weather: Lightning!* (Hopping) or in a potpourri such as *Insects* (Mound). However, some authors treat their subjects, such as the ecology issue, from a particular slant or viewpoint. "Issue books" in science present interesting or relevant phenomena, topics, or trends in relation to developments that pose a threat to our world; an example is *Monteverde: Science and Scientists in a Costa Rican Cloud Forest* (Collard). Rather than trying to persuade readers, exemplary issue books present data directly, so readers can make up their own minds about issues. This can encourage children's belief in their abilities to effect positive change in the world (Collard, 1998).

Issue books are not restricted to scientific topics such as the environment. According to Tunnell (1992), "children's trade books present history from varying perspectives and invite discussion that leads to making judgments about issues of morality. The conflicting information found in various trade books can have a positive effect on children's attention, curiosity, and interest" (p. 245).

In order to promote and recognize excellence in the field of nonfiction writing for children, the National Council of Teachers of English established the Orbis Pictus Award in 1989. The annual award honors the most outstanding nonfiction (informational and biography) trade books published each year in the United States. The award was named in commemoration of the book *Orbis Pictus* by Johann Comenius, which was first published in 1657 and is considered the first informational book written specifically for children.

Other nonfiction awards include the Boston Globe/Horn Book Award, the Carter G. Woodson Book Award, the Children's Book Guild Nonfiction Award, the Christopher Awards, the Eva L. Gordon Award for children's science literature, and the Robert F. Silbert Informational Book Award. Sometimes an award a book has received will be printed on the book's cover or jacket. In other cases you will need to look at the back cover or on the jacket flaps for a listing of any awards presented to the book's author.

Enhancing Curriculum with Informational Books

Content area textbooks, such as science and social studies, are usually much too difficult for the majority of children in the intended grade level to read independently. This is a result of the books' specialized vocabulary and unfamiliar content, as well as readers' lack of experience reading expository text. Additionally, many textbooks bore children with their dull tones and arid writing. In contrast, the tone of informational books is often exciting, and these books often provide more interesting details and descriptions than textbooks. Children's informational books can supplement and even substitute for traditional textbooks because they strongly support content area learning. Informational books support children's learning across the curriculum. Following are some of the many benefits children can gain from reading informational books:

- Children experience authentic learning as they investigate their own questions and topics of interest.
- Children inquire and solve problems.
- Children see connections and interrelationships among content and concepts.
- Children's critical thinking skills are fostered as they compare and contrast books on the same topic, noting authors' various points of view and what information is included (or omitted).
- Children learn about faraway places, past times, and new ideas and concepts.
- Children begin to view the world as changing and evolving.
- Children acquire new vocabulary and broader background knowledge.
- Children develop critical reading skills for comprehending all nonfiction text structures.

Some educators believe that as a result of these benefits, students perform better on standardized tests, which are increasingly used to measure and compare the performance of students, teachers, schools, school districts, and state education systems. Higher standardized test scores can benefit students by increasing their opportunities for placement in advanced classes, scholarships, and entrance to universities. Also, many large companies screen applicants through standardized tests, so a good test-taking ability could result in more career options.

Unlike textbooks, which are written on a single reading level for a particular grade, informational books on many topics are available on a variety of levels, for beginning through advanced readers. "When you have a variety of trade books available, children can select books they are comfortable reading and can focus their attention on learning new content area material" (Freeman & Person, 1998, p. xiii). Offering informational books is an important way to help children read independently and acquire and apply knowledge in our ever-changing world.

Many educators teach through thematic units that explore a topic in an interconnected way via the various language arts of listening, speaking, reading, writing, viewing, and dramatizing. Instead of organizing instruction around subject areas such as math, science, or geography, a thematic unit is organized around a theme or topic, such as the ocean or mammals. Thematic instruction encourages inquiry through active participation, and it promotes higher-level thinking because it stresses conceptual learning and integration of knowledge. Literature can support the content and concepts targeted in thematic units. Trade books can be read aloud by the teacher or independently by children. Children can consult trade books for reference as they seek answers to questions and investigate topics. The books also serve as models for children's own expository writing across the curriculum.

Many teachers introduce a unit of study by reading aloud from an informational book. This serves to stimulate interest and activate the children's prior knowledge of the topic as well as building schemata for new knowledge. Often this process includes identifying specialized vocabulary to define and post on a bulletin board. It is not necessary to read an entire book to your students. You can choose the sections you think will interest and inform them best. Or you can give a two-minute book talk on each of several books, showing the cover and one or two illustrations and telling students what the book is about. The books can then be placed in the reading center for children to select during reading time. Likewise, children should not be required to finish each book they start. They will find some too difficult or too easy (or too dull). They need an opportunity to browse through several books to find the ones that answer their questions on an appropriate reading level (Grolier, 1995).

Informational books are not only for research and curriculum enhancement. Like other trade books, they are intended for pleasure reading. Their attractive formats, reasonable lengths, and interesting topics are inviting to young readers—but only if children are made aware that these books exist. That is the responsibility of parents, teachers, and librarians.

Building a Foundation for Content Area Reading

Around the fourth grade, many children who previously had no reading difficulties begin to lag behind in their comprehension of textbooks. This occurs because after third grade, children are increasingly required to engage in independent reading of textbooks and other nonfiction material. If children reach the intermediate grades unfamiliar with both the content of textbooks and the frameworks of expository text, reading difficulties can result (Gillet & Temple, 1986). To help protect your children from this pitfall, I suggest you regularly expose them to nonfiction books after they reach first grade.

Nonfiction (expository) text differs vastly from fictional text. All fiction stories follow the highly predictable story structure (characters, setting, problem, goal, events, and resolution). Experienced readers can predict what will happen next in a story based on other stories they have read and even their own life experiences. However, nonfiction is written in a variety of text structures—none of which are very predictable. Text structures can be thought of as organizational patterns for arranging and connecting ideas in expository text (Freeman & Person, 1998). When both the text structure and the topic are unfamiliar, children are unable to relate the new knowledge to their existing schemata, and their comprehension is minimal. Children learn story structure by listening to, reading, and writing stories, so it makes sense that they will learn expository text structures by the same means—listening to, reading, and writing expository text. Therefore, it is *critical* for parents and educators to include nonfiction in their reading time with primary-grade children.

Following are descriptions and examples of the six most common **nonfiction text structures.**

1. *Description:* The author describes the topic by listing characteristics, as in *Giant Dinosaurs of the Jurassic* by Gregory Wenzel.
2. *Chronology:* The author presents events in the order in which they happened, as in *The Day We Walked on the Moon* by George Sullivan.
3. *Explanation:* The author provides causes, effects, or reasons for various phenomena and events, as in *Earthquakes* by Seymour Simon.
4. *Comparison/Contrast:* The author compares and contrasts two things (such as events, concepts, organisms, or phenomena), as in *A Whale Is Not a Fish and Other Animal Mix-Ups* by Melvin Berger.
5. *Definition:* The author defines the components of the topic and gives examples, as in *My Five Senses* by Aliki.
6. *Problem/Solution:* The author identifies a problem and its causes, and then delineates a solution, as in *Where Have All the Pandas Gone? Questions and Answers about Endangered Species* by Melvin Berger and Gilda Berger.

Graphic Organizers

Graphic organizers help children learn more effectively by letting them categorize information visually. Organizers serve as linkages among topics and subtopics in a book or chapter, and this helps children organize their new knowledge into existing schemata (Grolier, 1995). The character and story map presented in Chapter 10 is a graphic organizer for a fiction book; similarly, graphic organizers exist for nonfiction.

One of the best graphic organizers for nonfiction is the **KWL chart.** The letters stand for Know, Want to know, and Learned. The KWL activity can be done individually or with the whole class. On the board or chart paper, draw three columns, and label them "What I Know," "What I Want to Know," and "What I Learned." See Table 12.1 for an example on *Frogs* (Gibbons). The steps are easy to follow:

- First, before reading a nonfiction book, ask children to brainstorm what they already know about the subject, and write the items in the first column, "What I Know."
- Second, ask them to form several questions about the subject, and write these in the second column, "What I Want to Know."
- Third, after reading the book, ask children to tell you the answers to their questions, and write them in the third column, "What I Learned."
- Next, add additional information children say they learned from the book in the third column, "What I Learned."
- Last, check the items in the first column, "What I Know," to see if there were any misconceptions and make corrections as necessary.
- Extend the activity by asking children to identify and list any questions from the second column, "What I Want to Know," that were not answered in the book. At the bottom add a new section, "What Else I Want to Know," and list new questions they thought of while reading the book. Encourage children to do further reading on the topic to find answers to their new questions.

| TABLE 12.1 | KWL Chart for *Frogs* (Gibbons) |

FROGS		
What I Know	**What I Want to Know**	**What I Learned**
• They are amphibians. • They live in water. • They swim and hop. • If you touch one, you get warts. [*No, the book did not say this was true.*]	• What do they eat? • How long do they live? • What do baby frogs look like? • Where do frogs go in the winter? • Are toads frogs?	• Tadpoles eat algae, and frogs eat insects and worms. • They live several years. • Tadpoles look like fish and swim underwater. • They hibernate underground. • No, toads live on land. • Some frogs have poison glands in their skin. • Snakes, rats, and birds eat frogs.

What Else I Want to Know

• Can poisonous frogs harm people and pets?

• How do frogs breathe when they hibernate underground?

• What are the different colors of frogs?

Examples of other graphic organizers for informational books are depicted in Figures 12.1 through 12.4.

- *Spider maps* (Figure 12.1) are useful for books on a single topic with attributes that can be categorized.
- *Cycle maps* (Figure 12.2) lend themselves to science topics that have a cyclical nature, such as the life cycle.
- *Timelines* (Figure 12.3) are helpful for books on historical topics.
- *Venn diagrams* (Figure 12.4, p. 292) can be used to compare and contrast two things. One circle is devoted to each of the two items. The different attributes are written in the outside left and right circles, and the shared attributes are written in the center where the two circles overlap.

It is essential to start graphic organizers *before* reading the book (or near the beginning) and have children add to the organizer *during* the reading. Displaying a completed organizer before reading will not actively engage children in the book. Asking

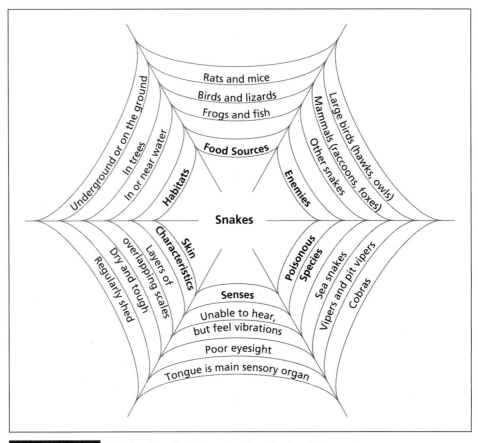

FIGURE 12.1   Spider Map for *Take a Look at Snakes* (Maestro)

children to complete a whole organizer independently after finishing the book constitutes a test of their memories, rather than a learning experience. However, completing an organizer with children while (and immediately after) reading a book gives them a purpose for listening as they actively anticipate the next bit of information to add to the organizer. Children's comprehension is greatly enhanced when they see the information visually unfold. They do not have to tax their memories in order to see how all the information is interrelated, and they can more easily develop new schemata on the topic.

A teacher may develop a graphic organizer with the whole class or a small group. Once children become comfortable with a strategy such as the KWL, they can complete it individually with their self-selected books. Organizers are also very useful when children are gathering information for writing reports.

In addition to completing graphic organizers, discussion helps children recall, synthesize, and summarize new knowledge. Discussion also assists in the reflection process that needs to accompany the reading of all genres, including informational books. Some sample discussion questions follow:

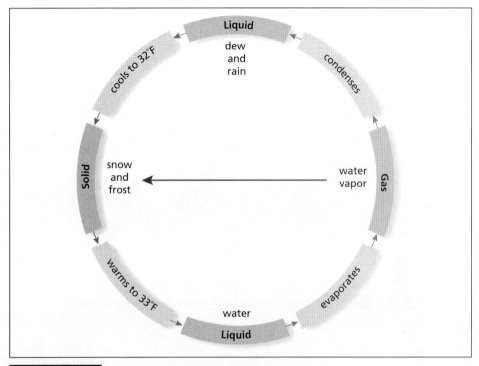

FIGURE 12.2   Cycle Map for *A Drop of Water* (Wick)

1955	1960	1965	1970	1975	1980	1985	1990

USSR
launches
Sputnik

First
space
walk

Skylab
station
launched

First flight
of space
shuttle

Hubble
launched

First
humans
in space

Armstrong
walks on
moon

Voyager 1
launched

Challenger
explodes

FIGURE 12.3   Timeline of Space Exploration for *The Day We Walked on the Moon* (Sullivan)

- What information did you enjoy reading about the most?
- What new information do you plan to share with someone else?
- Which photograph or illustration was the most interesting? Why?
- What else would you like to find out about this topic?
- What questions would you like to ask the author?
- What did you learn that could help you in school? Outside of school?

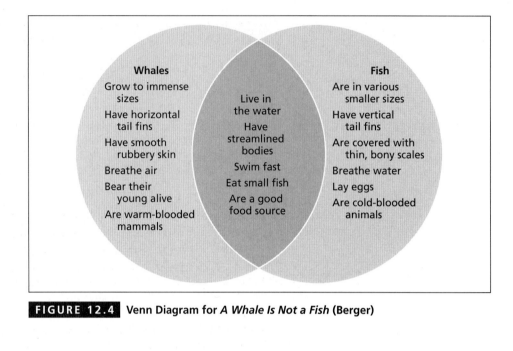

Whales
Grow to immense sizes
Have horizontal tail fins
Have smooth rubbery skin
Breathe air
Bear their young alive
Are warm-blooded mammals

Live in the water
Have streamlined bodies
Swim fast
Eat small fish
Are a good food source

Fish
Are in various smaller sizes
Have vertical tail fins
Are covered with thin, bony scales
Breathe water
Lay eggs
Are cold-blooded animals

FIGURE 12.4 Venn Diagram for *A Whale Is Not a Fish* (Berger)

Issues in Informational Books

Are Informational Storybooks Fiction or Nonfiction?   As I have remarked throughout this textbook, not all literature books fall neatly into one and only one genre. There are many good books, such as *The Magic School Bus* series by Joanna Cole and books by Lynne Cherry that deal with ecological issues, such as *The Great Kapok Tree: A Tale of the Amazon Rain Forest*. These books certainly inform readers about topics, yet they also have some elements of fiction—for example, characters, dialogue, anthropomorphic animals, and other fantasy elements. They are not really fiction because the purpose of a fiction book is to entertain, rather than to inform readers. I use the term *informational storybooks* to describe books in which the primary purpose is to inform but which contain some of the entertaining elements of fiction. Informational storybooks can be very useful for presenting facts and concepts to young children, and they often attract readers who otherwise pass up informational books for storybooks. However, because they are written in the familiar story structure, they will not help less experienced readers make the transition to expository text. Some educators include informational storybooks within the genre of informational books, but others say that informational books are nonfiction and therefore cannot contain *any* element of fiction.

Argue for or against including informational storybooks within the genre of informational books.

Integrating Literature and Technology

Finding Content Information with www.MarcoPoloSearch.org After you finish reading an informational book to your children, and they are eager to learn more about the topic, you can quickly find related information by doing a MarcoPolo search. MarcoPolo provides high-quality, standards-based Internet content with a search engine that draws from nine dynamic databases developed by the organization's partners:

- *ARTSEDGE,* John F. Kennedy Center for the Performing Arts
- *EconEdLink,* National Council on Economic Education
- *EDSITEment,* National Endowment for the Humanities
- *Illuminations,* The National Council of Teachers of Mathematics
- *Literacy Network,* National Center for Family Literacy
- *ReadWriteThink,* International Reading Association and the National Council of Teachers of English
- *Science NetLinks,* American Association for the Advancement of Science
- *Smithsonian History Explorer,* National Museum of American History
- *Xpeditions,* National Geographic Society

MarcoPolo's basic search engine allows you to search by primary (K–2), intermediate (3–5), and middle (6–8) grades, as well as by the following subjects: arts, economics, foreign language, geography, language arts, mathematics, philosophy and religion, science, and social studies. Their advanced search engine allows you to designate the subject, database, specific grade level, and format, which includes application, audio, images, text, and video.

Featured Author

Russell Freedman

Russell Freedman does extensive research when writing his nonfiction books. This involves going to libraries, museums, historical societies, and monuments. He must thoroughly understand his topic before he starts writing. He has written on many topics, but his favorite ones are historical eras, historical people, and animal lives and behaviors. He has been given many awards, the most prestigious being the 1988 Newbery Medal for *Lincoln: A Photobiography.* He is also the recipient of three Newbery Honors, the Silbert Medal, and the Laura Ingalls Wilder Award.

About half of Freedman's nonfiction works are biography, but following are some of his best-selling informational books: *Immigrant Kids, Children of the Great Depression, Who Was First Discovering the Americas?, Freedom Walkers: The Story of the Montgomery Bus Boycott, In Defense of Liberty: The Story of America's Bill of Rights,* and *Give Me Liberty: The Story of the Declaration of Independence.*

Summary

Informational books are literature books whose primary purpose is to inform the reader by providing an in-depth explanation of factual information in areas such as government, mathematics, astronomy, plants, animals, sports, painting, history, and geography. Because there are so many topics to cover, informational books make up about half of libraries' holdings. Informational books should not be confused with textbooks or reference books such as dictionaries or encyclopedias.

Unlike fiction that employs narrative and dialogue language written in the highly predictable story structure, informational books use a variety of text structures, which most children find more difficult to comprehend. Six of the most common nonfiction text structures are (1) *description*—author describes the topic by listing characteristics, (2) *chronology*—author presents events in the order in which they happened, (3) *explanation*—author provides causes, effects, or reasons for various phenomena and events, (4) *comparison/contrast*—author compares and contrasts two things (such as events, concepts, organisms, or phenomena), (5) *definition*—author defines the components of the topic and gives examples, and (6) *problem/solution*—author identifies a problem and its causes and then delineates a solution.

Graphic organizers enhance children's comprehension of nonfiction books. One of the most versatile organizers is the KWL Chart, which helps readers activate their prior knowledge and then pose questions they hope to be answered by reading the book. Other graphic organizers include (1) *spider maps*, which are useful for books on a single topic with attributes that can be categorized, (2) *cycle maps*, which lend themselves to science topics that have a cyclical nature, such as the life cycle, (3) *timelines*, which are helpful for books on historical topics, and (4) *Venn diagrams*, which can be used to compare and contrast two or more things.

Recommended Informational Books

Aliki. *My Five Senses*. Sagebrush, 1999.

Berger, Melvin. *A Whale Is Not a Fish and Other Animal Mix-Ups*. Illus. Marshall Peck. Scholastic, 1995.

Berger, Melvin, & Gilda Berger. *Is a Dolphin a Fish? Questions and Answers about Dolphins*. Scholastic, 2002.

Berger, Melvin, & Gilda Berger. *Where Have All the Pandas Gone? Questions and Answers about Endangered Species*. Scholastic, 2002.

Bishop, Nic. *Spiders*. Scholastic, 2007.

Blumberg, Rhoda. *York's Adventures with Lewis and Clark: An African-American's Part in the Great Expedition*. HarperCollins, 2004.

Boyer, Allen B. *Patriot School: The United States Military Academy at West Point*. Perfection Learning, 2005.

Cartlidge, Cherese. *Alternative Energy*. Erickson Press. 2008.

Cobb, Vicki. *I Face the Wind*. HarperCollins, 2003.

Cole, Joanna. *Hungry, Hungry Sharks*. Random House, 2003.

Collard, Sneed B. *Animals Asleep*. Houghton Mifflin, 2004.

Collard, Sneed B. *Monteverde: Science and Scientists in a Costa Rican Cloud Forest.* Franklin Watts, 1997.

Davies, Nicola. *Surprising Sharks.* Candlewick, 2003.

Delafosse, Claude. *Hidden World: Human Body.* Scholastic, 1999.

Donnelly, Judy. *The Titanic: Lost and Found.* Random House, 2003.

Freedman, Russell. *Children of the Great Depression.* Clarion Books, 2005.

Freedman, Russell. *Freedom Walkers: The Story of the Montgomery Bus Boycott.* Holiday House, 2006.

Freedman, Russell. *Give Me Liberty: The Story of the Declaration of Independence.* Holiday House, 2002.

Freedman, Russell. *Immigrant Kids.* Scholastic, 2006.

Freedman, Russell. *In Defense of Liberty: The Story of America's Bill of Rights.* Holiday House, 2003.

Freedman, Russell. *Who Was First Discovering the Americas?* Clarion, 2007.

Fritz, Jean. *The Lost Colony of Roanoke.* Putnam, 2004.

Gibbons, Gail. *Frogs.* Holiday House, 1993.

Giblin, James Cross. *Secrets of the Sphinx.* Scholastic, 2004.

Gifford, Clive. *Soccer: The Ultimate Guide to the Beautiful Game.* Kingfisher, 2002.

Hoose, Phillip. *The Race to Save the Lord God Bird.* Farrar, Straus & Giroux, 2004.

Hopkinson, Deborah. *Shutting Out the Sky: Life in the Tenements of New York, 1880–1924.* Orchard, 2003.

Hoppenstedt, Elbert M. *Aerial Gunners of World War II.* Perfection Learning, 2005.

Hopping, Lorraine Jean. *Wild Weather: Lightning!* Illus. Jody Wheeler. Sagebrush, 2001.

Jackson, Donna. *ER Vets: Life in an Animal Emergency Room.* Houghton Mifflin, 2005.

Jenkins, Steve. *Actual Size.* Houghton Mifflin, 2004.

Johnson, Anne Akers. *Cat's Cradle: A Book of String Figures.* Klutz, 1993.

Jordan, Shirley. *The Seven Wonders of the Ancient World.* Perfection Learning, 2004.

Layden, Joe. *National Football League Super Bowl.* Scholastic, 2004.

Leedy, Loreen, & Pat Street. *There's a Frog in My Throat! 440 Animal Sayings a Little Birdie Told Me.* Holiday, 2003.

Maestro, Betsy. *Take a Look at Snakes.* Scholastic, 1997.

Mann, Elizabeth. *Empire State Building: When New York Reached for the Skies.* Mikaya Press, 2003.

Montgomery, Sy. *Quest for the Tree Kangaroo: An Expedition to the Cloud Forest of New Guinea.* Houghton Mifflin, 2006.

Mound, Laurence A. *Insects.* Dorling Kindersley, 2004.

Murphy, Jim. *An American Plague: The True and Terrifying Story of the Yellow Fever Epidemic of 1793.* Clarion Books, 2003.

Murphy, Jim. *Inside the Alamo.* Delacorte, 2003.

O'Brien, Patrick. *Duel of the Ironclads: The Monitor vs. the Virginia.* Walker, 2003.

Simon, Seymour. *Earthquakes.* Sagebrush, 1999.

Singer, Marilyn. *Venom.* Darby Creek, 2007.

Sis, Peter. *The Wall.* Foster/Farrar, 2007.

Siy, Alexandra, & Dennis Kunkel. *Mosquito Bite.* Charlesbridge, 2005.

Sullivan, George. *The Day We Walked on the Moon.* Scholastic, 1992.

Thimmesh, Catherine. *Team Moon: How 400,000 People Landed Apollo 11 on the Moon.* Houghton Mifflin, 2006.

Wenzel, Gregory. *Giant Dinosaurs of the Jurassic.* Charlesbridge, 2004.

Wick, Walter. *A Drop of Water.* Scholastic, 1997.

Winters, Kay. *Voices of Ancient Egypt.* Illus. Barry Moser. National Geographic, 2003.

Poetry and Verse 13

The artist used only positive space to create this illustration in the impressionist style.

From *Thirteen Moons on Turtle's Back*, written by Joseph Bruchac and Jonathan London and illustrated by Thomas Locker.

Library locations   **J808, J811, and J821**

Verse: A composition having strong rhythm and a rhyming pattern

Poetry: Verse in which word images are selected and expressed to create powerful, often beautiful impressions (may or may not rhyme)

𝒫oetry is multifaceted; it can tell a story, describe something in a fresh and novel way, make a comment on humanity, draw a parallel to aspects of your life, or make you laugh. It can also flash a sharp image to your mind, delight your ear, or make you experience strong emotions. Reading poetry allows you to view the world through a new lens. Amazingly, poetry does all this while using far fewer words than any other form of writing. Another unique aspect of poetry is that although most people (above primary grades) will read a book only once, children as well as adults love to hear their favorite poems again and again. Perhaps this is because poets are able to take the feelings that are inside all of us and put them into meaningful words.

For many children the traditional Mother Goose rhymes are their first exposure to verse. Dr. Seuss's rhyming text is also a common introduction to verse for the very young. Note that I did not call these works poetry, for there is an important distinction. **Verse** is any composition that has a strong rhythm and a rhyming pattern. Because of its uniqueness, **poetry** is not so easily defined. Indeed, it is a class of text in itself. If a piece of writing is not poetry, it is considered **prose**. All the other genres we have studied so far—fiction and nonfiction—are prose. This classification makes it easy to recognize what is *not* poetry, but it does not define what poetry is. It is difficult to define because it has many forms and can mean something different to each person. Also, drawing the line between verse and poetry is difficult.

Although poetry is verse, certainly not all verse is considered poetry, which is the more sophisticated form of the two. Cullinan (1989) called poetry the distilled language that captures the essence of an idea or experience, appealing to the ear as well as the mind and emotions. In order for poetry to appeal to the ear, you must read it aloud. Beatrice Schenk de Regniers explained,

> To my mind, a poem is not completed until it is read aloud . . . it seems to me that the full power of a poem—the jazzy rhythms, the lyrical cadence, the dance of language, the sheer pleasure of fooling around with sound and meaning—can be fully appreciated only if the poem is read aloud. This would be particularly true for children. (1988, p. xvii)

So, unless you are sitting in class while you read this chapter, I suggest you read each poem aloud as you come to it in order to experience the full effect of the rhythm and rhyme.

Evaluating Poetry and Verse

The following questions can guide you as you select poetry.

- Is the poem appealing to children?
- Is the poem free from didacticism, sentimentality, and patronizing language?
- Does the rhyme scheme sound natural?
- Will children be able to understand and appreciate any figurative language, such as similes and metaphors?
- Does the poem help the listener view the topic in a new way?

Characteristics of Poetry and Verse

Rhythm and Rhyme

Verse must contain **rhythm.** If you are knowledgeable about music, think of rhythm in language as the same as *meter* in music. For the rest of us, rhythm is the pattern of stressed and unstressed syllables in a line that gives poetry its beat or tempo. Read aloud the following limerick line, and listen for the stressed syllables, which are in boldface type. (I divided the two-syllable word.)

There **was** an old **man** from Pe – **ru.**

In the classic limerick, the rhythm is highly structured. Using a dash for unstressed syllables and a slash for stressed syllables, the pattern for this line is

$- / - - / - - /$

Verses also have a rhyming pattern. Probably everyone knows what rhyme is, although few people know how to define it. Children will tell you it means "words that sound alike." However, the words *two, too,* and *to* sound alike, but are not considered rhymes because each word represents the exact same combination of sounds. These words are **homophones,** words that are pronounced the same but have different meanings, such as *blue* and *blew.*

A **rhyme** is made up of two or more words with the same *ending sounds* (containing at least one vowel sound) but different beginning sounds. In verse, rhymes most frequently appear at the ends of lines. The ends of rhyming words need not be spelled alike, as you can see from the following verse.

What is a word that rhymes with blue?
I think it could be either new or canoe.

Now, can you complete this one?

What is a word that rhymes with orange?
I think it could be either _____.

(Not all words have rhymes.)

Sometimes a writer will exercise **poetic license,** which is a deviation from conventional form to achieve a desired effect. In the following example, the writer added some syllables to achieve the rhyme scheme.

> There was an old man from Florida,
> Whose sight was simply horrid-a.
>> While crossing the street,
>> He was knocked off his feet.
> And now the poor man is no more-ida.

Language

Compare a page of poetry with a page of prose, and you will see there is more **white space**—areas without print—on a page of poetry. The lines do not run flush with the right margin, and there is extra space between groups of lines. Many poets use space creatively. For example, a poet could have only one or two words per line. This is more than a visual effect; it also adds to the meaning of the poem. Additionally, poets use punctuation differently than authors of prose, and this too can enhance the meaning of a poem.

The language of poetry is both condensed and distilled—compacted and purified. The essence of the subject is captured in a few words that cause the reader to recall memories or experience strong reactions. Good poetry contains no extraneous words. Each word contributes to the total effect of the rhythm, rhyme, and message that readers experience. I have heard that the renowned poet Eve Merriam once said that a poem is like a can of frozen juice—add three cans of water and you get prose.

Part of the impact of poetry is created by the poet's extensive use of **figurative language** to create imagery in the mind of the reader. Poets use comparisons to vividly describe a thing, emotion, or experience. A **simile** is a comparison of two things that are unlike, and it typically uses the connective words *like* or *as*—for example, "hands *as* cold *as* ice" and "legs *like* steel rods." A **metaphor** is a comparison that is implied through analogy by stating that one thing *is* another, for example, "her eyes *were* bright diamonds." Images can also be developed through **personification,** which is the representation of animals, ideas, and things as having human qualities—for example, "I heard the wind call my name." These are some of the ways poets use words to create mental images.

Sound patterns make listening to poetry enjoyable. **Alliteration** is the repetition of initial consonant sounds in neighboring words or stressed syllables. Listen for the /s/ sound (spelled with both *s* and *c*) in the title "Sarah Cynthia Sylvia Stout Would Not Take the Garbage Out" (Silverstein). **Assonance** is the repetition of vowel sounds within words. Listen for the short /o/ sound in the title "Saucy Little Ocelot" (Prelutsky). Prelutsky repeats this sound throughout the poem. His use of assonance, alliteration, rhyme, and a fast tempo make listening to this poem enjoyable.

Forms of Poetry

Poetry appears in clearly discernible forms that are determined by their **stanzas,** groups of lines in a poem with an identifiable pattern of rhyme or rhythm (or both). Some forms that are commonly found in books of poetry for children follow.

Narrative poems tell a story, usually with setting, characters, events, and climax. Because of this, they are most frequently longer poems. One common rhyming scheme for its stanza is A B C B, with each letter representing a line of poetry; lines represented by the same letters rhyme. In the following two stanzas from the narrative poem *The Night before Christmas,* attributed to Clement C. Moore, lines two and four rhyme.

'Twas the night before Christmas,	A
when all through the house	B
Not a creature was stirring,	C
not even a mouse.	B
The stockings were hung	A
by the chimney with care,	B
In hopes that St. Nicholas	C
soon would be there.	B

Limericks are humorous five-line verses with a rhyming scheme of A A B B A. They are thought to have originated in the city of Limerick, Ireland, and were first popularized in print by Edward Lear in *A Book of Nonsense.* Limericks are highly structured, typically with a syllable count of 8, 8, 6, 6, 8. Count the syllables in each line of the verse that follows.

There was an old man from Peru	A
Who dreamed he was eating his shoe.	A
He awoke in the night	B
In a terrible fright	B
And found it was perfectly true!	A

In **concrete poems,** words are arranged to form a pictorial representation of the subject. Concrete poems are not written in stanzas, and they may or may not rhyme. They are fun to read but challenging to write, because the poet must select a subject that can easily be made into a recognizable shape. See Figure 13.1 for an example.

FIGURE 13.1   Concrete Poem

Lyric poems focus on a single experience, describing the feeling of a moment. They come in a multitude of stanza forms. Much contemporary poetry for children is lyrical. A good example is the following poem by Oliver Herford.

I Heard a Bird Sing

I heard a bird sing
In the dark of December
A magical thing
And sweet to remember:
"We are nearer to Spring
Than we were in September,"
I heard a bird sing
In the dark of December.

If you have helped children write poetry, you know they often concentrate on rhyme and give little attention to meter or conveying a message. What they end up with is not poetry at all, but silly verses that are not very cohesive. For example, once I asked children to write a poem about their pet or another favorite animal. One girl wrote the following verse.

I had a dog
whose name was Spot.
Once he ran around the tree all day,
and he got very, very hot.

Well, it has two rhyming words, but the meter is uneven and the message is nonexistent, especially in view of the fact that the girl had a cat named Muffin but could not think of anything to rhyme with that name.

Removing the necessity of rhyme allows poets more freedom in capturing beautiful or interesting messages in their words.

Free verse can be either rhymed or unrhymed. It is called "free" because it has irregular rhythmic patterns and line lengths. Poets who write in this style aim to recreate the free rhythms of natural speech. The following poem by Langston Hughes is written in free verse.

April Rain Song

Let the rain kiss you.
Let the rain beat upon your head with silver liquid drops.
Let the rain sing you a lullaby.

The rain makes still pools on the sidewalk.
The rain makes running pools in the gutter.
The rain plays a little sleep-song on our roof at night—
And I love the rain.

Haiku is a Japanese form of poetry that consists of seventeen syllables arranged in three lines of five, seven, and five syllables. In the true Japanese style, the subject is something in nature. However, many American haiku are about other subjects. The following haiku follows the traditional format.

The full moon's bright light,
Casting shadows in the snow
Like the noonday sun.

Literature Activity: Poem Mobiles

Select a favorite poem that consists of three to five stanzas. After writing the poem on construction paper, cut the stanzas apart and suspend them from a mobile made of a coat hanger and yarn. Stanzas should be hung at the appropriate length, so they can be read in order from top to bottom. Add illustrations of the poem, and suspend the mobile from the ceiling.

Poetry in Our Culture

After you graduated from traditional nursery rhymes, did you have the opportunity to read any of the classics of children's poetry? Several generations of children and adults have enjoyed the timeless poetry in the following list. If you missed these books as a child, I encourage you to read them now, so you can select some classic poems for your children to enjoy.

- Robert Browning's *The Pied Piper of Hamelin* (1842)
- Clement C. Moore's [attributed] *The Night before Christmas* (1849)
- Henry Wadsworth Longfellow's *Paul Revere's Ride* (1863)
- Kate Greenaway's *Under the Window* (1879)
- Robert Louis Stevenson's *A Child's Garden of Verses* (1885)
- Alfred Noyes's *The Highwayman* (1906)
- A. A. Milne's *When We Were Very Young* (1924) and *Now We Are Six* (1927)

Poetry is an integral part of our culture, and we can hear and read it in places other than books of poetry. For example, have you considered that most songs are poetry set to music? In Peter Spier's *The Star-Spangled Banner,* you can thoughtfully read the words of this beautiful poem. For children (and adults) who do not know what the words mean, Spier's detailed, colorful illustrations bring them to life.

And the rocket's red glare,
    the bombs bursting in air,
Gave proof through the night
    that our flag was still there.

Some ancient scripture is poetry and may have originally been sung. *The Song of Three Holy Children* (Baynes) is from the Apocrypha. This joyous hymn of praise was sung by Shadrach, Meshach, and Abednego, young Jewish captives in Babylon who refused to worship King Nebuchadnezzar's idol.

O ye Children of Men, bless the Lord:
praise him, and magnify him for ever.
O let Israel bless the Lord:
praise him, and magnify him for ever.

Speeches can also be poetic. Perhaps the most beautiful and powerful poetic speech is that of Dr. Martin Luther King Jr., given in Washington, D.C., on August 28, 1963, to an interracial crowd of more than 250,000 people. Scholastic's edition of this speech, titled *I Have a Dream,* is illustrated by fifteen artists who have won the Coretta Scott King Award or Honor—among them Ashley Bryan, Floyd Cooper, Leo and Diane Dillon, Jan Spivey Gilchrist, Brian Pinkney, James Ransome, and Kathleen Atkins Wilson. Throughout his speech, King conveyed strong imagery with his use of metaphors and figures of speech.

NCTE Award for Excellence in Poetry for Children

In 1977 the National Council of Teachers of English (NCTE) established an award titled Excellence in Poetry for Children. The award was given annually from 1977 to 1982, and since 1982, it has been given every three years to honor the lifetime contribution to children's poetry of a living U.S. poet. Winners include Arnold Adoff, John Ciardi, Barbara Juster Esbensen, Eloise Greenfield, Mary Ann Hoberman, X. J. Kennedy, Karla Kuskin, Myra Cohn Livingston, David McCord, Eve Merriam, Lilian Moore, and Valerie Worth.

Developing Love (or Hate) for Poetry

Most young children love poetry. Even when they are too young to understand the words, they will listen to nursery rhymes because they delight in the sounds and rhythm. Often children will reread favorite poems until they have memorized them. With a little encouragement, young children begin to create their own poems. However, by the middle grades, many children begin to lose interest in poetry or even develop a strong dislike for it. Why does this happen?

Ways to Teach Kids to Hate Poetry

For several years I have asked my adult students if they developed a dislike for poetry as they grew older. Those who said they did supplied me with the following prescription for turning children off of poetry:

- Read children sentimental poems that you think are wonderful.
- Make them all memorize the same poem, and then make each kid recite it in front of the class.

- Require the children to write poems, and then make each child read his or her poem to the entire class.
- Require the kids to write poems, grade them, and display *all* of them on the bulletin board.
- Tediously analyze the scheme of each poem read.
- Discuss a poem until everyone in the class gets the same meaning as you.
- Spend a whole month teaching haiku.

Did any of you experience these teaching methods when you were a child? I did, and it had the same effect on me as it did on some of my students; so I hope you do *not* follow any of those negative examples.

Ways to Encourage Kids to Love Poetry

Here are several ways to ensure that children continue to love poetry as they get older.

- Keep in mind that children have different tastes in poetry, and allow them to help you select the poems to share with the class. (Generally, avoid overly sentimental or abstract poems, which appeal more to adults.)
- Ask children to recite favorite poems that they have memorized. (Even then, they should be allowed to have the poem written on a card in case they get nervous and forget.)
- Encourage volunteers to share poetry they have written, and post poems only with children's permission.
- Ask children to respond to poetry, but avoid picking each line apart, which kills the listener's enjoyment.
- Occasionally analyze a component of a poem to demonstrate the poet's techniques, but avoid analyzing each stanza of each poem, which becomes drudgery.
- Allow listeners to express their own interpretations because a poem will mean something a little different to each listener.
- Share poetry regularly in small measures. Brief daily or weekly experiences with poetry are preferable to a monthlong unit, which makes children weary of the genre.
- Keep a variety of poetry books available at all times.

Have you ever thought of encouraging reluctant readers to read poetry? It is an excellent genre for children who have limited reading ability, or who simply do not like to read. The minimal amount of print on each page of poetry is not as overwhelming as a page of prose. Poet Janet S. Wong explains that "when they look at a poem of mine, a short poem, they see all that white space around it, and it's not intimidating. It doesn't scare them. They look at it and say, 'That's only ten lines. I can read that'" (Yokota & Sanderson, 2000, p. 58). Wong tells of a 13-year-old girl who read one of her books of poetry in an hour. The girl's grandmother said it was the first time she had ever read a whole book.

In selecting poems for all children, look for those that involve a universal experience or message, written both on the emotional level and on the intellectual level of the listeners. As for the forms of poetry, children often say they prefer poems that rhyme. In particular, they like limericks, narrative poems, and lyric poems that are funny or about familiar experiences. It has been my experience that their least popular forms of poetry are unrhymed poems and haiku, as well as poems that are overly sentimental or abstract.

Surely one of the best loved authors of humorous verse for children is the versatile Shel Silverstein—poet, author, illustrator, and song lyricist. His poems have been described as "mischievous and charmingly tasteless." Some adults believe his work is unsuitable for children, claiming much of it is risqué or presents poor role models. However, this has not prevented children of several generations from reading his books and loving the way he makes them laugh. I find his work clever and uproariously funny. Read the poem that follows—which I selected because it has been attacked by parents and educators—and make your own judgment.

They've Put a Brassiere on the Camel

They've put a brassiere on the camel,
She wasn't dressed proper, you know.
They've put a brassiere on the camel
So that her humps wouldn't show.
And they're making other respectable plans,
They're even insisting the pigs should wear pants,
They'll dress up the ducks if we give them the chance
Since they've put a brassiere on the camel.

They've put a brassiere on the camel,
They claim she's more decent this way.
They've put a brassiere on the camel,
The camel had nothing to say.
They squeezed her into it, I'll never know how,
They say that she looks more respectable now,
Lord knows what they've got in mind for the cow,
Since they've put a brassiere on the camel.

📖 Issues in Poetry

Should Children Read the Poems by Shel Silverstein?   Read the poetry collection *A Light in the Attic* by Shel Silverstein, which has been banned from some schools. Two of the poems that have been criticized are "Prayer of the Selfish Child," which parodies a traditional bedtime prayer, and "Something Missing," which tells of a man who forgot to put on his pants. The latter is comically illustrated by Silverstein in pen and ink (with a rear view, of course).

Take one of the following positions and defend it, citing examples from the book:

- Silverstein's poems are offensive and should not be shared with children.
- Silverstein's poems are funny and harmless, and I intend to share them with my children.

Types of Poetry Books

Some books contain only one poem, which may or may not be a narrative poem. The poem may be from a previously published collection, or it may be written specially as the text of a picture book. Often *single-poem books* are found in the picture book section of the library instead of with longer poetry books.

When one poet publishes several poems in one book, it is called a *poetry collection.* However, a selection of poems by a number of different poets published in one book is called a *poetry anthology.* Often poetry anthologies are themed, with all the poems dealing with a certain topic, such as a season or animals. The person who selects the poems is called the *anthologist,* and her or his name appears in the place of an author. Anthologists must carefully select poems that will complement the others while being diverse, which is more challenging when the book has a specific theme. Once the poems are selected and permissions to reproduce are obtained, the anthologist must then decide the order in which the poems will appear to optimize the presentation.

The Value of Poetry in the Classroom

by Georgann C. Wyatt

When I teach the children's literature course to undergraduate students, I receive mixed reactions when we first discuss poetry. Some students say, "Poetry is a waste of time. I have never liked it, and I never will!" Yet others in the class respond that they have always loved poetry. There is no other genre that elicits such strong—and opposing—feelings as poetry does. I believe this is because of the way poetry was taught to them when they were in school. (See the earlier section on Developing Love [or Hate] for Poetry.) To those who say they dislike poetry, I point out the various types of poetry and verse that are part of their daily lives, such as song lyrics (including rap) in the music they listen to, as well as the catchy advertising jingles on TV and radio commercials.

Poetry has the power to reach into a person's innermost being and touch each facet of life, including the emotional, intellectual, social, physical, and spiritual. After the tragedy of September 11, 2001, the members of the U.S. Congress gathered to sing "God Bless America." This was a powerful example of how poetry and melody together touched both those who were singing and those who viewed them on television. There was a great need for people in the United States to express their intense emotions, and this song met the need for many that day.

Poetry, whether spoken or sung, has the ability to unite people in a common cause, establish an emotional connection, reveal a spiritual conviction or inspiration, and convey joy or grief (and every emotion in between). Poetry touches the imagination and the emotions in ways that prose does not. Poetry distills the essence of an experience, idea, or feeling. It can paint with broad strokes on a large canvas, or it can focus on specific details. It uses metaphors and sensory images to create pictures in readers' minds and gives insights into their life experiences. Poetry, in its various forms, surrounds our daily lives, and if readers are matched with the right poems at the right time, a deep appreciation may develop.

Poetry is too precious to ignore in the classroom because it can enhance the lives of children as well as adults. However, it is critical to match poems with children's developmental levels, and to find out what types of poems they enjoy (and dislike). Too often adults promote only the poems they enjoy, and these may be abstract, nostalgic, sentimental, or didactic. These are the types of poems that most kids dislike. Poetry needs to relate to children's everyday experiences to be meaningful to them. Children should be allowed to respond to poems with their imaginations, emotions, and physical senses. As children's knowledge of the world increases, their tastes in poetry will expand. The key concept here is that appreciating poems is more important than analyzing them, writing them, or (worse) being required to memorize them.

In addition to the affective growth children can achieve from reading poetry, there is also an opportunity for cognitive growth. Steinbergh (1994) points out that poetry helps develop language skills. Children's own language develops as they become aware of the sounds and the precision of poetic language. This makes it a powerful tool with children who are English language learners as well as children who are native English speakers. Furthermore, poetry enhances higher-level thinking. Reading poetry requires children to think on a symbolic level as they encounter figures of speech such as metaphors. When they write poetry, they have an opportunity to express complex and abstract thoughts that are infrequently used in prose writing.

When adults show their own interest and excitement in well-selected poems, children develop an appreciation for poetry. At the end of my children's literature course, most of the students who first said they disliked poetry have realized that it was not the genre of poetry they disliked, but rather the way it was taught to them and the poems they were required to read and memorize. My students are then open to see some of the beauty and benefits of this unique genre.

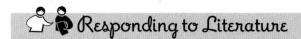 *Responding to Literature*

Writing Poetry

by Mary Lou Morton

Have you ever thought that it was impossible for you to write a good poem? I can show you how to write one in just a few minutes, and it is just as quick and easy to teach your children to do so. A poem is really a set of words that are intertwined to convey a special meaning. It is the special arrangement of those words that allows the writer to express the images and feelings that make poetry such a powerful genre. But how do you come up with the special words?

- First, choose a familiar setting to write about. It can be a special place, an ordinary place, or a dream-like place as long as it is familiar and vivid to you. For this example, I chose my kitchen.
- Next, make a list of items (nouns) that you can see in this place. (It is best to do the activity in the actual setting, but you can also picture the setting in your mind.)

- Then brainstorm a list of three or four adjectives for each item, using all five senses to think of what you might see, hear, smell, taste, and feel (with both hands and heart).

Faucet	shiny, dripping, slender
Soap	white, bubbly, slippery, sudsy
China cabinet	glass, tall, overflowing
Table	wooden, round, brown
Tablecloth	brightly-colored, flower-designed, round
Silverware	shiny, sharp, clinking
Chairs	brown, silvery-legged, cracked
Pots and pans	noisy, messy, heavy
Oven	yummy-smelling, hot, white
Toaster	burnt-smelling, black, hot
Dishwasher	clean, loud, white, swirling
Towel	pretty, dirty, wet

- Last, select the best words to arrange into a pleasant-sounding order.

My Kitchen

Wooden table,
Brightly colored tablecloth,
Clinking silverware,
Overflowing china cabinet,
Yummy-smelling oven,
Silvery-legged chairs,
Loud, swirling dishwasher,
Slippery soap,
Pretty hand towel,
Shiny faucet,
Drip! Drip!

Can you visualize my kitchen? If so, then I have been successful in conveying the image of my kitchen. Try it yourself in the setting where you are sitting right now or visualize a setting that is special to you.

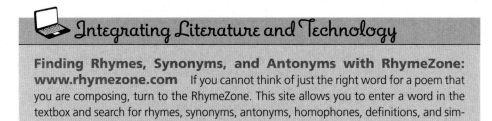

Integrating Literature and Technology

Finding Rhymes, Synonyms, and Antonyms with RhymeZone: www.rhymezone.com If you cannot think of just the right word for a poem that you are composing, turn to the RhymeZone. This site allows you to enter a word in the textbox and search for rhymes, synonyms, antonyms, homophones, definitions, and similar sounding words (for alliteration). For example, a search for the word *light* revealed the following rhyming words (among many others): bite, bright, fight, flight, fright, height, kite, might, night, plight, quite, right, sight, spite, tight, white, and write. Because *light* is a multiple meaning word, the search also revealed numerous definitions and synonyms, and it also revealed several antonyms, including *dark, heavy,* and *extinguish.* The search for similar sounding words allowed me to compose the following alliterative sentence: *All my life, I have liked light limejuice—no lie!*

Featured Author

Francisco X. Alarcón

Francisco X. Alarcón has an international reputation as poet, educator, scholar, and activist. He was born in California but lived in Guadalajara, Mexico, as a child; he returned to California when he was 18. He considers himself a binational, bicultural, bilingual poet and educator, and his children's collections of poetry paint vivid pictures of Latino culture, family, flavor, and fun. His book of bilingual poetry for children, *Laughing Tomatoes and Other Spring Poems,* was awarded the Pura Belpré Honor Award by the American Library Association and also awarded the National Parenting Publications Gold Medal. He also received the Pura Belpré Honor Award for *From the Bellybutton of the Moon and Other Summer Poems.* His most recent book of bilingual children's poetry is *Animal Poems of the Iguazu.* Alarcón is a member of the board of directors of Children's Book Press, which has published multicultural books for children for more than twenty-five years. He currently teaches at the University of California, Davis, where he directs the Spanish for Native Speakers Program.

Summary

Verse is a composition having strong rhythm and a rhyming pattern. Poetry is verse in which word images are selected and expressed to create powerful, often beautiful mental images. Poetry may or may not rhyme. If a piece of writing is not poetry, it is considered prose. The language of poetry is both condensed and distilled, and it makes extensive use of figurative language such as simile, metaphor, and personification. The language also includes alliteration and assonance to present a pleasing sound. Forms of poetry include narrative, concrete, lyric, free verse, limerick, and haiku. Types of poetry books include single-poem books, collections, and anthologies.

Recommended Poetry Books

Adoff, Arnold. *Touch the Poem.* Illus. Lisa Desimini. Blue Sky Press, 2000.

Alarcón, Francisco X. *Angels Ride Bikes and Other Fall Poems.* Illus. Maya Christina Gonzalez. Children's Book Press, 2005.

Alarcón, Francisco X. *Animal Poems of the Iguazu.* Illus. Maya Christina Gonzalez. Children's Book Press, 2008.

Alarcón, Francisco X. *From the Bellybutton of the Moon and Other Summer Poems.* Illus. Maya Christina Gonzalez. Children's Book Press, 2005.

Alarcón, Francisco X. *Iguanas in the Snow and Other Winter Poems.* Illus. Maya Christina Gonzalez. Children's Book Press, 2005.

Alarcón, Francisco X. *Laughing Tomatoes and Other Spring Poems.* Illus. Maya Christina Gonzalez. Children's Book Press, 2005.

Alarcón, Francisco X. *Poems to Dream Together.* Illus. Paula Berragan. Lee & Low, 2005.

Begay, Shonto. *Navajo: Visions and Voices across the Mesa.* Scholastic, 1995.

Berry, James (Ed.). *Around the World in Eighty Poems.* Illus. Katherine Lucas. Chronicle, 2002.

Bruchac, Joseph, & Jonathan London. *Thirteen Moons on Turtle's Back.* Illus. Thomas Locker. Philomel, 1992.

Fleischman, Paul. *Big Talk: Poems for Four Voices.* Illus. Beppe Giacobbe. Candlewick, 2000.

George, Kristine O'Connell. *Hummingbird Nest: A Journal of Poems.* Illus. Barry Moser. Harcourt, 2004.

Greenfield, Eloise. *In the Land of Words: New and Selected Poems.* Illus. Jan Spivey Gilchrist. Amistad, 2003.

Grimes, Nikki. *Tai Chi Morning: Snapshots of China.* Illus. Ed Young. Cricket, 2004.

Harrison, Michael, & Christopher Stuart-Clark. *One Hundred Years of Poetry for Children.* Oxford University Press, 2007.

Hughes, Langston. *Poetry for Young People.* Sterling, 2006.

Jacobs, Frank (Ed.). *Loony Limericks.* Dover, 1999.

Katz, Bobbi (Ed.). *Pocket Poems.* Illus. Marilyn Hafner. Dutton, 2004.

Kennedy, Caroline. *A Family of Poems: My Favorite Poetry for Children.* Hyperion, 2005.

King, Martin Luther, Jr. *I Have a Dream.* Illus. Ashley Bryan et al. Scholastic, 1997.

Kurtz, Jane. *River Friendly, River Wild.* Illus. Neil Brennan. Simon & Schuster, 2000.

Lear, Edward. *The Owl and the Pussycat.* Kids Can Press, 2007.

Lindbergh, Reeve (Ed.). *In Every Tiny Grain of Sand: A Child's Book of Prayers and Praise.* Candlewick, 2000.

Maher, Ramona. *Alice Yazzie's Year.* Illus. Shonto Begay. Tricycle, 2003.

Martin, Bill, Jr. *The Bill Martin Jr. Big Book of Poetry.* Simon & Schuster, 2008.

Myers, Walter Dean. *Blues Journey.* Illus. Christopher Myers. Holiday House, 2003.

Nash, Ogden. *The Adventures of Isabel.* Sourcebooks, 2008.

Nye, Naomi Shihab (Ed.). *Salting the Ocean: 100 Poems by Young Poets.* Illus. Ashley Bryan. Greenwillow Books, 2000.

Paschen, Elise. *Poetry Speaks to Children.* Sourcebooks, 2005.

Perry, Andrea. *Here's What You Do When You Can't Find Your Shoe.* Illus. Alan Snow. Simon & Schuster, 2003.

Prelutsky, Jack. *Awful Ogre Running Wild.* Illus. Paul O. Zelinsky. Greenwillow, 2008.

Prelutsky, Jack. *Be Glad Your Nose Is on Your Face and Other Poems*. Illus. Brandon Dorman. Greenwillow, 2008.

Prelutsky, Jack (Ed.). *The 20th Century Children's Poetry Treasury*. Illus. Meilo So. Knopf, 1999.

Sidman, Joyce. *Meow Ruff: A Story in Concrete Poetry*. Illus. Michelle Berg. Houghton Mifflin, 2006.

Silverstein, Shel. *A Light in the Attic*. Harper & Row, 2002.

Silverstein, Shel. *Falling Up*. HarperCollins, 1996.

Silverstein, Shel. *Runny Babbit: A Billy Sook*. HarperCollins, 2005.

Silverstein, Shel. *Where the Sidewalk Ends*. HarperCollins, 2002.

Spier, Peter. *The Star-Spangled Banner*. Dragonfly, 1992.

Wong, Janet S. *Minn and Jake*. Farrar, Straus & Giroux, 2003.

Wong, Janet S. *The Rainbow Hand: Poems about Mothers and Children*. Simon & Schuster, 1999.

Yolen, Jane. *O, Jerusalem: Voices of a Sacred City*. Illus. John Thompson. Scholastic, 1996.

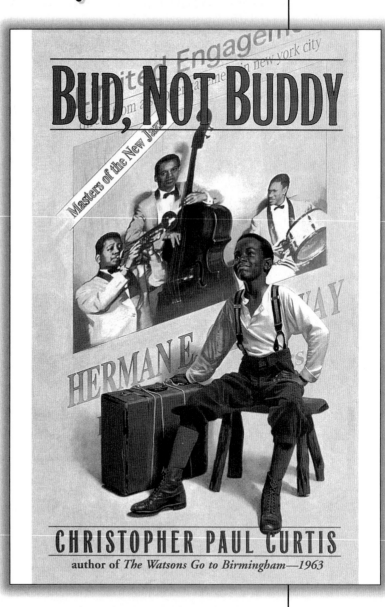

With oil paints, the artist used the elements of dimension and optical texture to create a very realistic-looking boy.

From *Bud, Not Buddy,* written by Christopher Paul Curtis and illustrated by Trish P. Watts.

$\mathcal{I}$f you have been reading children's books along with this textbook, you should now be quite knowledgeable about children's literature. What can you do with your knowledge—besides sharing with others the excitement and beauty of books? I have talked about how historical fiction, biography, and informational books can give a much-needed transfusion to the study of history, and how informational books can be used to teach and learn about virtually every subject. In this final chapter, I demonstrate how to tie together everything you know to use literature in teaching children to read.

Reading Aloud to Children

There is a positive correlation between being read to—both at home and in school—and reading achievement (Anderson, Hiebert, Scott, & Wilkinson, 1985). Some of the benefits of reading to children follow.

- It stimulates and broadens children's interest in quality literature in a variety of genres.
- It allows children to experience books that are too difficult for them to read independently.
- It gives children the opportunity to hear excellent literature they might never read for themselves, such as great books with slow beginnings and books above their reading ability.
- It broadens children's background experiences, which builds their schemata.
- It introduces children to a wide range of written language, which helps them expand their vocabulary and their repertoire of sentence patterns.
- It shows children that adults enjoy reading, thereby encouraging reading as a lifetime activity.

I have stressed that children will benefit greatly if their parents read to them daily (or at least several times a week) from the time they are born until they tell you they want to read for themselves (or they want to read to *you*). Unfortunately, many parents do not read to their children. They do not have the time, or they simply do not see the need. Therefore, teachers often must supplement (or substitute for) the reading of parents throughout the elementary school years. I recommend that teachers devote a minimum of fifteen minutes a day to reading aloud from literature. This should be a regular part of the daily curriculum; it should not be used as a reward when the children finish all their work, or omitted as a punishment when they misbehave.

Select books and poems that you like and that you think will appeal to children. Fiction books should generally be fast-paced and contain well-developed characters and generous dialogue. Let children help you select the books to read aloud, making sure that all genres are represented within the school year. When reading to children, let them have a good look at the picture on the page before reading the text. Allowing children to study the illustration *before* listening to the text will encourage them to make mental predictions that will aid their comprehension and enjoyment of the book.

Questioning Guidelines

Asking children questions before, during, and after reading a book or chapter enhances their comprehension (or lets you know when they do not comprehend). Two important guidelines:

- Avoid asking questions that can be answered by *yes* or *no*. They require almost no thinking because the answer is usually phrased in the question. For example:

  Yes or no question: "Do you think Sylvester will ever make wishes with a magic pebble again?"
  Answer: No
  Divergent question: "What do you think Sylvester will do if he ever finds another magic pebble?"
  Possible answers: Ignore it, bury it, throw it in the lake, tell his parents

- Avoid asking only memory-level questions that can be answered by *who, what, when, where,* and *why*. These literal questions require very little thinking and give you little information about children's comprehension. For example:

  Memory-level question: "What happened when Sylvester saw the lion?"
  Answer: He got scared, so he wished he were a rock.
  Divergent question: "What could Sylvester have done to be safe from the lion?"
  Possible answers: He could wish he could fly away, wish he were invisible, wish he were a bigger lion, wish the lion would not be hungry, or wish the lion fell asleep.

The answers to higher-thinking-level questions will contain the who, what, when, where, and why of the story, but they also require the listener to move beyond the memory level. See Box 14.1 for ideas on phrasing questions that require a variety of thinking skills.

It is not necessary to ask questions in a hierarchy (i.e., from category I through category VII). What is desirable is to ask children questions that require varied thinking. For example, see the questions in Box 14.2 (p. 316).

Listening–Prediction Activity

When you read a fiction book to a group of children for the first time, the type of questions you ask should be different from those you ask when you are reading a nonfiction book or a familiar story. New stories lend themselves well to prediction questions. An excellent activity that will engage children in divergent thinking while they are listening to a new story is the **listening–prediction activity.** This can be done with either a picture book or a chapter in a juvenile novel; however, the book must

---

Box 14.1

Levels of Questioning

I. Memory level

Who is . . . ?
What is . . . ?
Where was . . . ?
What did . . . ?
How many . . . ?
When did . . . ?

II. Translation level

In your own words, tell. . . .
How else might you say . . . ?
Which picture shows . . . ?
Describe. . . .
Tell how. . . .

III. Interpretation level

Compare. . . .
Tell what you think. . . .
Is . . . greater than . . . ?
Why is it called . . . ?
Explain why. . . .
What caused . . . ?
What conclusions have you reached
     about . . . ?

IV. Application level

When might you . . . ?
Where could you . . . ?
Which would you use if . . . ?
How will this affect . . . ?
Suggest two possible ways to. . . .

V. Analysis level

Why is . . . ?
What evidence is there that . . . ?
In what way might . . . ?
Give some instances in which. . . .
Which of these would . . . ?

VI. Synthesis level

How many ways can you think of to . . . ?
What would happen if . . . ?
Devise a plan to. . . .
How can you explain . . . ?

VII. Evaluation level

Should . . . be permitted to . . . ? Why?
Is . . . accurate? Why do you think this?
Was it wrong/right for . . . ? Why do you
     think so?
How well did . . . ?
What is the most important . . . ? Why?
What are the chances that . . . ?
Which of the following . . . ?

Source: DeHaven, Edna P. *Teaching and Learning the Language Arts,* published by Allyn & Bacon, Boston, MA. Copyright © 1979 by Pearson Education. Reprinted by permission of the publisher.

---

have a predictable plot that follows the story structure of characters, setting, problem, goal, events, and resolution.

The prediction activity is effective only when the listeners have not previously heard or read the story. Therefore, after selecting a predictable book, the first step is to read the title and show the book cover or first illustration and ask, "Has anyone heard or read this book?" If several of the children are familiar with the book, select an alternate book. If only one or two have heard it, tell them, "Now, I know *you* will

---

Box 14.2

Sample Questions for "The Lobster and the Crab" from *Fables* by Arnold Lobel

- Who is getting ready to set sail in his boat? *(memory level)*
- Compare the way the Lobster acted to the way the Crab acted during the storm. *(interpretation level)*
- Describe how the Crab felt when the boat capsized and sank. *(translation level)*
- Why is the Lobster really not afraid of the ocean? *(analysis level)*

- Was it wrong for the Lobster to let the Crab come with him when he knew the boat was full of holes? Why do you think so? *(evaluation level)*
- Suggest a possible way that they might have kept the boat from sinking. *(application level)*
- What would happen if *you* were in a boat that sank? *(synthesis level)*

---

know all the answers to the questions I am going to ask, so for this story, I want you to zip up your lips, and see if the other children can figure out what you already know." (Usually, those children will attentively—and smugly—listen to hear whether the others give appropriate answers.)

After reading the title and showing the book cover or first illustration, engage the children in a discussion to build background schemata for understanding the topic of the story, being sure to introduce any unfamiliar words. Then, ask children to predict what *might* happen in the story. (It is important not to say, "What *will* happen in the story," because that gives kids the idea that this is a "guess-the-right-answer" activity.)

Let children record their predictions in their **literature journals** (special logs they keep to record the books they have read and their responses to the books). You may also want to write a few of their predictions on the board. After recording predictions, read a few pages of the story, and then stop and ask listeners to confirm, reject, or revise their predictions, explaining why they made their choices.

Read a few more pages, and just before something important or interesting happens, ask children to predict what *might* happen next. Ask them to justify their predictions, and listen to determine whether they are logical answers. The objective is for children to make plausible predictions based on story structure, on what has happened so far in the story, and on their prior knowledge—not for them to guess the right answer.

Read a page or two until the episode occurs; then ask listeners to confirm or reject their predictions. Repeat the last two steps (no more than three times in one session). After completing the book, ask the children to predict what might happen to the characters if the author wrote a sequel.

Children have much to gain from a prediction activity. It encourages creative divergent thinking and the use of logic, while heightening curiosity and interest in stories (Temple & Gillet, 1989). Box 14.3 summarizes the steps of this activity.

Box 14.3

Steps of the Listening–Prediction Activity

1. Select a predictable book children have not heard.
2. Read the title and show the book cover (or first illustration), and engage listeners in a discussion to build background.
3. Ask, "What *might* happen in this story?" Record predictions.
4. Read a few pages, and ask children to confirm, reject, or revise their predictions, explaining why.
5. Read a few more pages, and just before something important or interesting happens, ask,

"What *might* happen next?" Ask listeners to justify their predictions.

6. Read a page or two until the episode is revealed, and then ask children to confirm or reject their predictions.
7. Repeat the last two steps (no more than three times in one session).
8. After completing the book, ask, "If the author writes a sequel, what *might* happen to the characters next?"

Sustained Silent Reading

In addition to listening to you read, children need to engage in **sustained silent reading** (SSR) of literature each day. This practice should start in first grade (perhaps ten minutes a day) and continue through the elementary grades; children may read for at least thirty minutes in the upper grades. This free reading period should be over and above the time allotted to reading instruction. There should be no talking or other interruptions during this time. In some classrooms, even the teacher reads a book during SSR. Children should select their own books, but they may need some guidance and motivation from you.

Readers mentally respond to good literature, both during and following their reading. You can encourage reflections by asking children to tell you their opinions of the books they are reading or to retell their favorite parts. Children can write a few sentences daily in their literature journals to record their thoughts. However, requiring children to answer comprehension questions (including those on a computer) or to do a book report or worksheet will quickly reduce this activity to drudgery.

Reading Instruction with Trade Books

Basal reading programs with graded sets of textbooks and workbooks are still the most common method of teaching reading in this country. However, many teachers supplement the basals with trade books—and some teachers use only trade books to teach reading. Necessary vocabulary and reading skills are taught with passages from the literature book rather than with workbooks and worksheets. This is a very effective way to teach children to read. Children are more motivated to read real books than to read the excerpts from books or the stories from picture books (minus most of the pictures) that they encounter in basal readers.

Children learn to read by reading—not by completing workbooks, worksheets, board work, and textbook exercises (whether done on paper or on a computer). Money that schools target for expensive workbooks and duplication of worksheets could be used to buy literature books. The countless hours teachers spend on grading the workbooks and worksheets and preparing board work could be spent on listening to children read and respond in genuine reading experiences. Surely this would be a better investment of both time and money.

When teachers decide to use trade books in lieu of basals, some of their first concerns are, How do I select which books to use (see Williams & Bauer, 2006)? And how do I obtain enough copies? There are many factors to consider in selecting a literature book for reading instruction. Some of the factors you should consider in reviewing prospective books are

- Quality of story
- Number of pages
- Amount and size of print
- Difficulty of vocabulary
- Sentence complexity
- Concept complexity
- Sophistication of content
- Quality of illustrations
- Age of main character

If your school does not have sufficient copies of a single book, that is not a problem. The range of reading abilities and interests in any classroom of children is vast. For example, in a class of thirty third graders, you will most likely have children whose reading abilities range from low first grade through sixth grade. Children's reading interests are just as broad. Therefore, it is often more effective to have six copies each of five different titles. This is the method used in literature circles, in which children decide on the books they will read.

Children sometimes select a book that is too difficult for them (perhaps because they want to be in the same group with a friend). However, they will soon become frustrated with a book that is beyond their reading ability. A quick way for a child to determine whether a book is too difficult is the **five-finger method,** developed by William Powell. When a child is reviewing a book to see if she or he would like to read it, have the child follow these steps:

- Open the book near the center to a page that is full text (no illustrations).
- Read the page to yourself.
- When you come to a word whose meaning you do not know, put up one finger. (Proper nouns, such as names of particular people, places, and things, do not count.)
- At the end of the page, if you have raised five or more fingers, the book is probably too difficult for independent reading.

Children's Oral Reading

As I have reinforced throughout this book, children learn to read by reading. They have very little to gain from listening to other children read aloud who are at or below their own reading level. Most children's oral reading is slow and fairly expressionless, as they are striving to say all the words correctly. This is especially true when they have not been allowed to read the passage silently first, which would have allowed them to decode most of the unfamiliar words. On top of that, many children are required to read material that is far beyond their ability.

The all-time biggest waste of instructional time in schools is when one child reads while the rest of the class (supposedly) listens! Actually, most of the other children will count paragraphs to determine which one they are going to read, so they can spend the rest of the time dreaming and scheming. Some good readers will read ahead in the book to keep from dying of boredom. They will quickly finish the story or chapter and perhaps start the next. In fact, some will even finish the whole book long before the rest of the class. However, if they are called on to read aloud and they do not know what page the teacher is on, they are scolded for not paying attention! They actually get in trouble for *reading* during reading class instead of *listening* to someone else stumble and bumble along! Can you see the ridiculous irony of this?

Individual Oral Reading

The majority of children's reading time should be spent in guided silent reading. However, teachers (but not the whole class) need to listen to each child read orally at least once a week. This can be accomplished in about thirty minutes a day while the rest of the class is reading silently. Divide the class into five groups of about six students each. During the course of a week, meet with one group a day. First guide them in reading several pages silently. Then have the children take turns rereading a paragraph or page orally with the goal of reading fluently and with good expression.

The following week, call individual children to your desk while the other students are reading silently (about six students a day for five minutes each). This is an excellent time to take running records to determine children's progress during the year. During this time ask each child to read the *next* page in the book (one that has not yet been read), so you can assess what strategies the child uses to decode unknown words. You can also determine whether children are monitoring their own comprehension by going back to reread a sentence where an error was made that changed the meaning. By alternating each week between the small groups and the individual meetings, you will be able to listen to every child read every week by devoting only thirty minutes a day.

Cunningham (1995) offers six critical guidelines for children's oral reading.

   1. **Except when assessing, ALWAYS have a child read a book or passage silently before reading it orally.** Readers comprehend more when they read silently because they can focus on comprehension rather than on saying every word correctly. Beginning

readers who have not learned to read silently will benefit when they are allowed to quietly "mumble read" a passage to themselves before reading it orally.

2. Oral reading should be with a book or passage that is fairly easy. If readers do not recognize at least 95 percent of the words in a passage, their ability to use context in conjunction with the way an unfamiliar word is spelled (phonics) will dramatically drop because they will make too many errors to make sense of the passage.

3. Children who are listening should NEVER correct another reader's mistakes! When they do, it robs the reader of learning to self-correct and monitor her or his own comprehension. Also, children should never be allowed to blurt out a word while a reader is trying to figure it out, because this prevents the reader from using her or his decoding skills. If the reader looks to you for help on an unknown word, ask her or him to reread the beginning of the sentence, skip the unknown word, and read to the end of the sentence or paragraph. Then the child can go back and try to decode the word with the use of context and the way it is spelled. This is known as the **read–skip–read strategy.**

4. Ignore errors that do not change meaning. *All* good readers make small, non-meaning-changing errors when they read aloud. It indicates that their eyes are ahead of their voices. Fluent readers have a well-developed **eye–voice span** (the distance between where our eyes are and where our voice is) of about four or five words. They read by phrases rather than word by word.

5. When the reader makes a meaning-changing error, WAIT! To encourage children to develop comprehension monitoring, wait until a reader finishes the sentence (or paragraph) to see if she or he self-corrects after reading the words that follow the error.

6. If waiting does not work, give sustaining feedback. If the reader continues, stop her or him and say something like, "That didn't make sense. You read, . . . [Read the sentence exactly the way the child did.] Does that word make sense here? What word do you know that makes sense in this sentence and is spelled with these letters?" Always stress that when they are figuring out an unknown word, it must have the right letters *and* make sense.

Group Oral Reading

Repeated oral reading of a selection helps children achieve fluency, and there are several activities that allow all children to participate.

Choral Reading. In choral reading, a group of children read together. In the beginning, you may want to lead the reading until your children learn how to begin and end at the same time—and how to use their soft reading voices, so the teacher next door will not complain. Also, when you lead, you are modeling fluency and good intonation. Choral reading is especially effective with poetry or a favorite rhyming picture book, but it can be used for any situation in which oral reading is called for. Solve the problem of who gets to read the directions in the textbook by letting a row or table group read the directions together. Of course, you will want to ensure that all groups get to read an equal number of times.

Readers Theater. Many fiction books lend themselves well to readers theater. This activity gives children an opportunity to achieve fluency by rereading a piece multiple times until it can be read like a radio play. (See Chapter 7 for a sample script.) The following steps will guide you through this activity.

- In groups of about four, children select a story or a passage from a book. The selection should contain ample dialogue of three or more characters.
- Children select the parts of the characters and the narrator and engage in repeated readings of the passage. First they chorally read the entire piece. Then each practices reading his or her part until all have achieved fluency.
- Children present their piece to the rest of the class. They do not use costumes, scenes, or complex props. Rather, they use varying tones of their voices and gestures to convey the characters' lines. Simple props found in the school can be used.

Story Theater. A related activity is **story theater,** which involves both reading and dramatizing.

- In groups of about six, children select a story with lots of action. This could be a picture book or a chapter from a juvenile novel.
- Half the group serve as readers, and the other half are mimes and act out the scene.
- Readers practice reading the selection multiple times until they achieve fluency. Concurrently, the mimes prepare their pantomime of the story.
- Groups take turns presenting their stories to the class.
- For the next story theater, the readers and mimes trade places.

Guided Silent Reading

The majority of reading instructional time should be spent in guided silent reading. This can be implemented differently for fiction and nonfiction books.

Reading–Prediction Activity

Just as the prediction activity is an excellent method for guiding children through listening to a new fiction story, it is also an excellent method for guiding children through reading a new fiction story. The procedures of the **reading–prediction activity** are much the same as the listening–prediction activity, except that children read the story instead of listen to it. Because this is a prediction activity, it will not work if children have already been exposed to a story, because their answers will then be based on simple memory recall rather than divergent thinking. Therefore, it is best to use this strategy when introducing the first chapter of a new book. (Thereafter, if children have access to the book, many will read ahead.)

The steps of the reading–prediction activity follow.

1. Distribute the books and tell students to read the title and view the book cover or first illustration. Then ask, "What do you think this book might be about?" Engage students in a discussion to build background for the book, and present any new vocabulary.

2. Ask students, "What might happen in this story?" Have students write predictions in their literature journals, and then ask several to share what they have written. Write a few on the board.

3. Ask all students to read silently the first two pages, then stop. Readers who finish first should write in their journals whether they confirm, reject, or need to revise their predictions. They should be encouraged to reread the first two pages and study the illustrations to help make their decisions. When all have finished reading, ask for volunteers to tell you whether they confirmed, rejected, or revised their predictions, and ask them to justify their answers.

4. Have students read a set number of pages and stop and write predictions on what might happen next. Then have them finish reading the section and confirm or reject their predictions. After everyone has finished reading, discuss the predictions and whether they were logical (rather than "correct") based on their own background experiences and what they have read so far. (This step can be completed more than once, as long as you tell students where to stop reading to make a prediction. A sticky note in each book is a good reminder of where to stop.)

5. After completing a book, ask students, "If the author writes a sequel, what do you think might happen to the characters next?"

Guided Reading Activity

Prediction activities are effective only for unfamiliar fiction stories. For other books, I recommend the **guided reading activity**. It is effective with nonfiction, such as informational books and biography; with fiction books that do not have a full plot (and are therefore unpredictable); and with fiction stories that many of the children are familiar with (for example, when children have read ahead in the book). The guided reading activity has three parts: prereading, guided reading, and postreading.

I. Prereading. Distribute the books and ask children to read the title and view the book cover or first illustration. Ask them, "What do you think you might learn from this book/selection? What information does the book cover (or first illustration) give you about the contents?" Draw children into a discussion about the topic to build background schemata. Be sure to introduce any words you think are unfamiliar.

II. Guided Silent Reading. Children read with better comprehension when they read for a purpose. Therefore, set the purpose for reading each section (two to four pages) by telling the group, "Read this section to find out _____" (something they will read in the section). For example, "Read this section to find out why water holds together in drops." Monitor children while they are reading to be sure they stay on task, and help them with any unfamiliar words. When all children have finished reading the section, ask someone to answer the purpose-setting question, and then ask related comprehension questions. Repeat this process for each section of two to four pages. Readers who finish the section first can write the answer to the purpose-setting question in their literature journals.

III. Postreading. When all children have finished reading, ask for their reactions. Be accepting of responses, whether they liked or did not like the reading selection; however, ask children to justify their answers. For example, "I liked this book because George made me laugh," or "I didn't like this book because George doesn't talk, and in animal fantasy the animals are supposed to talk." Next, ask comprehension questions to determine whether the children understood what they read. (For fiction books, I recommend you use questions such as the ones in Box 14.1.) It is also appropriate to ask questions after each section of two to four pages during the guided silent reading stage. Regardless of whether the questions are asked during the reading or after the group finishes the selection, children should always be allowed to keep their books open and reinspect the text. Otherwise, you will be checking children's memory rather than their comprehension.

Recall from Chapter 2 that the primary response mode of readers is internal thought. You tap into that by asking for children's reactions after they finish reading. If you also ask them to write an entry in their literature journals, they will have further cause to reflect. By recording their thoughts about a book, children have a source to refer to later when they have read more books and are making comparisons among them.

Sometimes teachers extend a reading lesson with a writing project. For example, with a fiction book, children could rewrite the ending, write a letter to a story character, write a diary entry in the voice of one of the characters, write another story following the same pattern, or write a readers theater script from an episode. The steps in the guided reading activity are summarized in Box 14.4.

The guided reading activity can easily be adapted to a **guided listening activity**. In this strategy the teacher, rather than the students, does the reading. This activity would be appropriate when the teacher has selected a nonfiction book, such as an informational book or a biography, to share with the class during the teacher read-aloud time. Table 14.1 presents a comparison of the four strategies I have described.

Box 14.4

Steps in the Guided Reading Activity

I. Prereading

- Ask children to read the title and view the book cover or first illustration; then ask the following questions:

    "What do you think you might learn from this book/selection?"

    "What information does the book cover (or first illustration) give you about the contents?"

  Build background schemata and introduce new words.

II. Guided Silent Reading

- Set the purpose for reading each section of two to four pages by saying, "Read this section to find out _____."

- Monitor children while they are reading to ensure they stay on task, and help them with any unfamiliar words.
- When children have finished with the section, ask someone to answer the purpose-setting question, and ask other related comprehension questions as appropriate.
- Repeat this process for each section.

III. Postreading

- Ask for children's reactions to the selection, and have them justify their answers.
- Ask comprehension questions, and allow children to reinspect the text for answers when necessary.
- Conduct literature response activities.

TABLE 14.1 **Comparison of Reading and Listening Activities**

Strategy	Type of Text	Children's Task	Type of Questions	Timing of Questions
Listening–Prediction Activity	New fiction	Listen	Prediction	Before something important happens
Reading–Prediction Activity	New fiction	Read	Prediction	Before something important happens
Guided Listening Activity	Nonfiction and familiar fiction	Listen	Comprehension	After something important happens
Guided Reading Activity	Nonfiction and familiar fiction	Read	Comprehension	After something important happens

Implementing a Yearlong Literature Program

Teachers who use only trade books to teach reading need a plan for organizing their instruction. Two popular ways are by genres and by thematic units.

Organizing Reading Instruction by Genres

Organizing instruction by genres involves devoting a month to each of the major genres and highlighting one or more authors and illustrators noted for their work in the targeted genre. An example of organizing reading selections by genre and author/illustrator follows.

- *September:* Traditional literature and Ed Young
- *October:* Fantasy and Lemony Snicket
- *November:* Animal fantasy and Dr. Seuss
- *December:* Contemporary fiction and Jean George
- *January:* Historical fiction and Mildred Taylor
- *February:* Biography and Jean Fritz
- *March:* Informational books and Russell Freedman
- *April:* Poetry and Francisco Alarcón
- *May:* Multicultural literature and Joseph Bruchac

For each genre, it is important to select books on a variety of reading levels, including picture books, juvenile novels, and a few adolescent novels for the gifted readers in your class. Book lists in each of the genre chapters in this textbook cover a range of reading levels. A quick way to find titles for specific authors and illustrators is to look in the Name and Title Index at the end of this book. Your school and public librarians will be able to help you locate the books they own by the featured authors and illustrators.

If you are able to locate multiple copies of a variety of books (for example, six copies each of five titles), **literature circles** are an excellent way to organize this reading program. Recall from Chapter 2 that literature circles are small temporary discussion groups of children who have chosen to read the same book. Children select which of the five books they would like to read first. (If you do not have enough copies for all children to get their first choice, make sure they get it on the next cycle.) Groups meet on a regular schedule, perhaps twice a week. They discuss their reading and bring their literature journals, in which they have kept notes about their reading, to guide their discussion. Discussion topics are initiated by the children, and the responsibility for starting the discussion rotates. Group meetings should consist of open, natural conversations about books. Personal connections are encouraged, and open-ended questions are welcomed. After the teacher has initially explained the process and modeled the students' roles, he or she serves as a *facilitator,* not as a group member or instructor.

✎ Responding to Literature

Book Talks   *Book talks* are a good way for readers to get others interested in books they really like. Book talks should not be confused with book reports or reviews, which cover an entire book and give away the ending. Rather, book talks cover *no more* than the first half of the book in order to entice others to read it. The following instructions will help children prepare a book talk:

- Select a book you have read that is hilarious, exciting, scary, mysterious, heartrending, or just terrific. (It can be fiction, nonfiction, or poetry.)
- Prepare a two- to three-minute talk, but do not try to memorize anything.
- Write the main characters' names, the setting, and notes about the first half of the book on a sticky note inside the back cover for reference in case you forget.
- Stand up, face your audience, and state the title and author, showing the book cover.
- Speak clearly and with enthusiasm; conveying admiration for the book gets others interested in reading it. Talk about the book—but only enough to entice them.
- Last, read a paragraph or half page of something that is especially interesting, funny, or exciting, and show a couple of your favorite illustrations.

Organizing Reading Instruction Thematically

Many teachers choose to teach reading through thematic units that focus on one book and draw in other subjects such as language arts and social studies. Instruction is organized around a theme or topic, such as the Civil War, the ocean, the rainforest, or the Great Depression. During the read-aloud period, the teacher shares a book related to the unit. All children read the selected focus novel during the class's reading instruction time. During sustained silent reading and for homework, they also read at least one other novel and one nonfiction book (informational or biography). In addition, they view at least one Internet site. There are five major steps in guiding children through experiencing a novel in a thematic unit.

1. **Select the focus novel and related books.** In addition to selecting the novel that the whole class will read, locate other books with the same theme. Select five to ten titles for each of the following:

- Supplemental novels to be read individually
- Picture books for enrichment
- Informational books to build background
- Biographies to supplement background
- Internet sites

2. **Introduce the novel.** Provide necessary background to help children comprehend and appreciate the novel, while piquing their interest in the subject.

- Show illustrations and read short excerpts from one or more related informational books.
- Engage students in a discussion to activate prior knowledge.
- Introduce the meanings of important words and concepts.
- Distribute books, and lead students through the *prereading schema-building process* (introduced in Chapter 1).
- Guide children in reading the first section of the novel using the reading–prediction activity.

3. **Guide readers in experiencing the novel.** Select one of the resource books for your daily read-aloud session. Children will select from the other resource books or Internet sites for their daily sustained silent reading period and keep notes in their literature journals. For the focus novel, a general guideline is to complete one chapter a day.

- Use the reading–prediction activity or the guided reading activity to guide students in reading the focus novel silently.
- Students make daily entries into their literature journals to record their predictions and their reactions to what they have read.
- The teacher guides the students in completing a story map and character maps for each of the main characters, and these are posted and added to throughout the unit.

4. **Guide readers in responding to the novel.** There is a variety of highly motivating ways students can respond to the focus novel during and after reading the book. These include

- Grand conversations
- Language charts
- Dramatization
- Webbing
- Story boxes

During the unit, students should also be called on to give book talks on the supplemental books they have read. Notes made in their literature journals can guide them in their presentations.

5. **Guide students in analyzing the novel.** Literature responses named in the preceding step should be continued for at least one day after the children finish the focus novel, giving children an opportunity to develop their internal responses to the story. After that time, the teacher can facilitate a grand conversation in which the students make a final analysis of the book. Some of the things students analyze are a book's content, literary elements, and structural design. Also, comparisons can be made to books previously read.

An innovative way to guide students in comparing novels in a thematic unit is through **language charts** (Roser, Hoffman, Labbo, & Farest, 1995). A language chart is constructed from a large piece of butcher paper that is ruled as a matrix. One axis contains the titles and authors of several books in the unit that a group will read. The second axis is made up of questions, invitations for reflection, and additional prompts for book discussions. After the discussion of each book, the teacher records the children's responses on the chart. However, the chart is "not intended to replace the natural book talk that accompanies and follows book sharing with children; rather, it is intended to focus thinking *after* book conversations have ranged freely" (p. 83).

One of the most valuable functions of the charts is to stimulate children's recall of previously read stories, so they can analyze all the stories, finding connections in the form of similarities and differences. Some other functions of language charts are

- To make a record of classroom literacy experiences
- To stimulate children's expression of personal responses to literature
- To encourage children to reflect upon a literary experience
- To serve as a springboard for other responses to literature (Stoodt, Amspaugh, & Hunt, 1996)

Even if you are teaching reading with conventional basal textbooks, supplemental activities with literature can help children develop specific reading abilities. Box 14.5 is a recommended list of activities for developing several essential reading abilities.

I hope those of you who are (or will be) parents read to your children every day. For parents who want to incorporate reading instruction into their daily reading period, Box 14.6 presents a simple and effective routine. Teachers may reproduce this section as a handout for parents if the source citation at the bottom is included.

Box 14.5

Developing Reading Abilities with Literature

Developing listening comprehension (potential for reading comprehension)

Listening–prediction activity
Retelling stories after listening
Summarizing and paraphrasing nonfiction text after listening

Developing reading comprehension

Reading–prediction activity
Story maps, webbing, and other graphic organizers
Retelling a book or passage after reading

Developing sight vocabulary

Reading pattern books
Repeated reading of familiar books
Echo and choral reading with a fluent reader
Shared reading with a partner

Developing fluency

Repeated readings of short passages
Choral reading of poetry with a small group
Practice reading a picture book to read aloud
Readers theater
Story theater

Box 14.6

Teaching Reading in Thirty Minutes a Night

Would you like to greatly enhance your child's reading ability? If so, are you willing to give up a thirty-minute television show every night and read with your child? The following routine will help your child learn to read to his or her full potential.

Nightly Routine Summary

I. (ten minutes) Read to your child and ask prediction questions (six nights a week), or write a **language experience account** (LEA) (one night a week).

II. (fifteen minutes) Listen to your child read without overcorrecting.

III. (five minutes) Reread previously written LEAs (six nights a week), or read through the word bank (one night a week).

Part I

Read to your child six nights a week from a book he or she is not able to read independently but can understand when you read it aloud. When reading a book for the first time, ask prediction questions, for example, "From looking at the cover (or first illustration) and listening to the title, what do you think might happen in this story?" After reading a few pages, ask, "What do you think might happen next?" Repeat this question every few pages, and let your child predict what might happen next in the story. Prediction questions are asked only with new books. After reading a familiar book, ask your child to retell the story as if he or she were telling it to a friend who had never heard it before. Spend about ten minutes reading to your child each session.

On the seventh night, have your child dictate an account of something he or she has experienced, such as a trip to the park, a movie, a favorite television show, a visit from a relative, a family pet, something done with a friend, or something that happened at school. Write each sentence after it is dictated. When your child has finished dictating, read the whole paragraph back, pointing *under* each word as you say it. Next, have your child read it *with* you. Then have your child read it alone. This is called a language experience account, or LEA.

Part II

Listen to your child read from a book that is fairly easy. Do not correct every error your child makes. If an error *does not change* the meaning, ignore it, and let your child continue to read. If the error *does change* the meaning, wait until your child reads to the end of the sentence to see whether he or she will go back and self-correct. If not, ask your child to stop; then read the sentence exactly the way he or she did. For example, if your child substitutes the word *green* for the word *great* and does not self-correct by the end of the sentence, say, "Wait a minute. Let me read that sentence to you the way you read it to me: 'Trigger was a green horse.' Does that make sense?" Point to the word missed, and ask your child to think of another word that *would* make sense in the sentence. This will help your child develop use of context clues for decoding unknown words.

When your child is reading and comes to an unknown word, wait at least five seconds to see whether he or she can figure it out from the context and the way the word is spelled. (I suggest counting slowly to yourself to resist the urge to blurt it out.) If your child does not say the word correctly after five seconds, say the word and let him or her continue to read. *Avoid saying, "Sound it out"!* This discourages your child from using context to help decode unknown words. If your child is able to sound it out, he or she will do so without your prompting, which actually distracts your child from thinking.

With beginning readers or reluctant readers, use support reading with pattern books or easy-to-read books. Support reading takes three forms:

- **Echo reading:** You read a sentence (or line) while pointing *under* each word. Next, your child reads the same sentence (or line) while pointing.
- **Choral reading:** You and your child read the story together, with you setting the pace and modeling good intonation.
- **Paired reading:** Sit with your child to your right. You read the left-hand pages of the book, and your child reads the right-hand pages. Then switch sides and reread the book.

Spend about fifteen minutes listening to your child read each session.

Part III

Construct a word bank of sight words your child has mastered from books and LEAs. These can be written on index cards and stored alphabetically in a file box. The last five minutes of each session should be spent in rereading LEAs (six nights a week) or reviewing the words in the word bank (one night a week).

If you faithfully devote thirty minutes a night to reading with your child, his or her reading ability can be greatly enhanced. (Or, you can go back to watching *Seinfeld*.)

Integrating Literature and Technology

Enhancing Literacy Skills

by B. Ruth Sylvester

In the last decade, the Internet has become integral to American culture. The majority of businesses and even many individuals have websites. People with common interests can converse online in chat rooms. Electronic commerce has become commonplace. E-mail provides an easy and speedy means of communication. Students read websites that complement their textbooks. Because homes, workplaces, and schools have been transformed by technology, it is a logical venue for literacy development.

The Internet is an excellent medium for helping children to learn about books' authors. This helps readers contextualize the book they are reading by learning interesting information, such as the author's experiences that initiated the work. Some authors' websites also provide background information on the issues and times relevant to a book. Often, author websites allow students to participate in electronic discussions, view video clips of the author discussing his or her work, read reviews of other books by the author, and enroll in an electronic mailing list for notices about new books. A great site for information on authors is the Fairrosa Cyber Library at www.fairrosa.info/cl.authors.html.

Not only can the Internet extend children's knowledge of authors and their works, but it can also be a useful tool to gain background knowledge to better comprehend and enjoy books. For example, before children read *The Cricket in Times Square* by George Selden, the teacher may present websites about New York City, its subway system, and

Times Square. Readers can view the fascinating world beneath New York City at www.nationalgeographic.com/features/97/nyunderground. This site depicts the systems found at various levels below the city. Much of *The Cricket in Times Square* takes place in a subway station, with which many students have no first-hand knowledge. A photo tour of the subway, as well as a "Transportation" link, provide much background information on the operation of subways. Because the unique insect characteristics of Chester Cricket are significant to the plot, children can read how crickets make their chirping sounds at www.insecta-inspecta.com/crickets/field. Children can listen to WAV audio files of real crickets at http://new.wavlist.com/soundfx/014. For teacher activities on scores of other good children's books, go to the Cyberguides website at www.sdcoe.k12.ca.us/score/cyk3.html.

Software companies, such as Living Books, produce electronic versions of popular children's books on CD-ROM. Children may simply listen to the book, read along, echo read, or read the dialogue of just one character. The text is highlighted as the story is read to help listeners keep place with the recorded voice. Readers may also click on individual words to hear them. The stories are attractively illustrated and have animations and sound effects to keep readers' attention and aid comprehension. Children who have multiple encounters with the book make gains in comprehension, fluency, and sight word recognition.

Some children have limited access to printed books: low-budget schools often have small library collections; rural areas may have no nearby public libraries, or children may be homebound because they have no transportation to a library. However, online books are as close as a computer with an Internet connection. Online literature collections include traditional tales (see www.rickwalton.com/folktale/folktale.htm), classic works in the public domain, stories authored by children, and other original works that have been self-published on the Internet. Newer, simplified authoring software allows even novice users to write and illustrate their own works. Online bookstores such as Amazon.com now sell eBooks that are downloaded from their website.

Project Gutenberg (www.gutenberg.net) claims to add one hundred eBooks a week to their already voluminous online library. Most online books are text only; however, as multimedia authoring becomes more user-friendly, many self-published books are multimodal presentations that include graphics, audio, video, and links to related websites. A great advantage to eBooks is that they can be read on screen or printed on paper to read later. They can also be saved and transferred to a portable eBook reader (see Chapter 1). In all cases, if the format is a common word processing program, the user can manipulate the electronic text in a variety of ways. The text can easily be reformatted by changing margins, font color, and font style and size—which can be made larger (for easier reading) or smaller (to reveal more words per page). In addition, if you lose your place or just want to reread a favorite section, use the search function to find a key word or phrase to take you to a particular place within the text.

Technology expands learning environments by allowing children access to primary sources to obtain information, thereby providing experiences with people and places otherwise unavailable. It also makes some stories and books more accessible. However, it can never replace parents, teachers, and hard copy books in children's literacy development.

Summary

Instead of using basal readers (reading textbooks), teachers and parents can use literature to teach children to read. I encourage modeling fluent reading by reading aloud to your children daily and asking appropriate questions. For a new fiction book, prediction questions are appropriate. For familiar fiction or nonfiction, comprehension questions that require thinking on a variety of levels are appropriate. Children should also be allowed to read silently—without interruption—each day.

Children need experience reading aloud, but the whole class does not need experience listening to one child at a time read aloud. However, the teacher can ask children to come individually to read aloud for assessment purposes. Most of children's reading time should be spent reading silently. The teacher can use the reading–prediction activity or the guided reading activity to guide their reading.

Using about six copies of five different titles, teachers can use literature circles to build children's reading ability. A yearlong literature program can be planned around genres or by themes. Using genres, devote one month to each genre, and highlight one or two authors who are well known in that genre. Using themes, select a focus book with a strong theme and bring in other reading material on the same topic, such as supplemental novels, picture books, informational book, biographies, and Internet sites.

Direct links to all Internet sites cited in this book can be accessed by visiting the companion website at www.pearsonhighered.com/anderson3e.

Happy reading!

—N. A. A.

acrylic paint   An artistic medium made of liquid acrylic plastic (polymer) that is used to bind color pigment, producing brilliant colors

aesthetic stance   The response a reader assumes when he or she is reading for entertainment, often resulting in an evocation (a lived-through experience)

African Americans   Americans who are descendants of the various indigenous people of the African continent

airbrushing   An art form in which an atomizer using compressed air sprays paint on a surface

alliteration   The repetition of initial sounds in neighboring words or stressed syllables

alphabet book   A concept book that presents the letters of the alphabet (also called an ABC book)

alternating point of view   A story that is told in first person accounts by two or more characters

animal fantasy   Fantasy stories in which main characters are anthropomorphic animals who talk, experience emotions, and have the ability to reason as humans

animal fantasy, Type I   Anthropomorphic animals take the place of humans and exist in a totally animal world that may be inhabited by a single species or by various species

animal fantasy, Type II   Anthropomorphic animals coexist with humans, sometimes in a human-dominated world (where they may or may not be able to speak) and other times in an animal-dominated world where humans only occasionally appear

animal fantasy, Type III   Anthropomorphic animals do not wear clothing and live in natural-type habitats without humans; they display many of their animal traits, but are able to talk to animals of all species and portray human emotions and thoughts (usually written in a fanciful tone)

animal fantasy, Type IV   Anthropomorphic animal characters live in the real world of humans in appropriate habitats and have all the natural habits common to their species, but

communicate among their own species with an animal viewpoint in the realistic world (usually written in a serious tone)

anthologist   A person who selects poems by several poets for inclusion in a book called an anthology (also applies to genres such as short stories or essays)

anthropomorphic animals   Animal characters that can talk, experience emotions, and have the ability to reason as humans

anthropomorphism   Giving human characteristics to animals, plants, and objects

Asian Americans   Americans descended from the various indigenous peoples of Asian countries such as Cambodia, China, Japan, Korea, Laos, Thailand, and Vietnam

assonance   The repetition of identical vowel sounds within neighboring words

authentic biography   Biography in which information about a person's life is limited to the events that are verifiable; dialogue is included only if substantiated by reliable personal recollections or historical documents, such as letters and diaries

autobiography   A person's written account of his or her own life story

backdrop setting   A setting that is relatively unimportant to the story, often used in traditional literature and fantasy

ballads   Traditional stories that were sung as narrative poems

basal readers   Textbooks used to teach reading

beast stories   Traditional tales with anthropomorphic animals as characters

bibliotherapy   Using books to help oneself gain self-awareness or solve personal problems

big book   A book that is enlarged to about four times its normal size, used by a teacher with a group of children

biographic historical fiction   A fictional story based on the life of a real person or persons (considered historical fiction)

biography   A nonfiction work describing the life (or part of the life) of a real individual

333

board book A book for very young children, usually consisting of twelve to thirty-two sturdy cardboard pages that have a glossy wipe-off finish

book format The way a book is put together or the way it looks, such as picture book, hardcover, and paperback

book talk A two- to three-minute talk about a book that covers no more than the first half of the book in order to entice others to read it

cartoon An artistic style in which drawings are reduced to their essentials with simple lines and primary colors

censor To examine books or other published materials with the purpose of removing what the examiner finds objectionable

censorship The process of removing or suppressing books or other media that the censor considers morally, politically, or otherwise objectionable

chaining tale A cumulative tale in which each part of the story is linked to the next

chapter book A book with sufficient amount of text to require organization of chapters

character mapping An activity in which readers identify and chart the major characters by name, relationship, age, physical description, personality traits, and other important qualities

characters Who a story is about

children's classics Books children read more than one hundred years ago that are still in print today (many not specifically written for children)

children's literature All books written for children (excluding works such as comic books, joke books, cartoon books, and reference books)

choral reading An oral reading activity in which a group of children read a selection simultaneously, often several times to achieve fluency

choral reading strategy A supported reading strategy in which the adult and child read a book together with the adult setting the pace and modeling good intonation

circular plot A story with the same components as linear plots, but the resolution or end of the story shows that the characters are in the same situation as when the story started

collage An art form in which shapes are cut or torn from materials such as paper and fabric and are assembled and glued on a surface

collective biography A biography that examines the lives of several people who are linked by a common thread, such as occupation, ethnicity, or achievement

color The variety of hues that are the different parts of the spectrum, achieved through pigments and light

complete biography A biography that spans the entire life of the subject from birth to death

composition In an illustration, the combination and arrangement of the elements such as space, line, shape, color, and texture

concept book A picture book that presents numerous examples of a particular concept such as the alphabet, numbers, colors, shapes, and opposite words

concept of word A child's recognition that a written word is a string of letters bounded by spaces

concepts of print The format of written language; for example, a page is read from top to bottom, lines are read from left to right, and books are read from front to back

concrete poem A poem not written in stanzas, but rather with words arranged to form a pictorial representation of the subject

conflict The opposition of two forces in a story, which results in tension; can be a character against self, a character against another character, a character against society, or a character against nature

contemporary realistic fiction Fictional stories set in modern times with events that could possibly occur

counting book A concept book that presents the counting numbers (also called number books)

cultural literacy The ability to interpret an analogy that employs a word or phrase taken from the canon of literature of one's culture

culturally generic book A book that focuses on characters representing a specific cultural group, but with little culturally specific information included

culturally neutral book A book that contains some characters from minority groups or has multicultural faces portrayed within illustrations; however, the book's topic contains no real cultural content

culturally specific book   A book that incorporates details that help define the characters as members of a particular cultural group

culture   The totality of socially transmitted behavior patterns, arts, beliefs, institutions, and all other products of human work and thought; these patterns, traits, and products are the expression of a particular community or population

cumulative plot   A story that contains repetition of phrases, sentences, or events with one new aspect added with each repetition

cumulative tale   Traditional stories told in a cumulative manner with repetition of actions and verbal patterns

Dewey decimal system   Method for organizing the location of books in a library

dialogue response journal   A journal that records a written conversation between an adult and a child about what they are reading

dimension   The use of shading to represent the variations of reflected light from an object's surface to make a flat shape appear to have depth

directed listening activity   A reading strategy that uses the same steps as the directed reading activity with the exception that the students listen to a book rather than read it themselves

drawing   A linear art technique made with instruments such as pencil, pen and ink, charcoal, marker, or crayon

dynamic character   A character who undergoes change in response to life-altering events in a story as opposed to a static character who undergoes no change in personality

easy-to-read book   A book written specifically on the level of a beginning reader

echo reading   A supported reading strategy in which the adult reads a sentence (or line) while pointing under each word, and then the child reads the same sentence (or line)

efferent stance   The response a reader assumes when she or he is focused on information, facts, or instructions, and on what will be retained after the reading (employed with

textbooks, reference books, informational books, and biographies)

enchanted journey   A fantasy story that begins in the real world, but the main character is soon transported to another world, which is an enchanted realm

endpapers   Sturdy pages of a hardcover book that are glued to the inside of the front and back covers to hold the book together; sometimes colorfully decorated with the story's motif

episodic plot   A story in which the characters and setting are usually the same throughout, but there is no central problem that permeates the book; rather, each chapter has a miniplot complete with introduction, problem, events, and resolution

evocation   A lived-through experience, which is a reader's response in aesthetic reading

exposition   An element of plot in which the narrator briefly tells (rather than recreates in scenes) what has happened before the story opens

expository language   Informative or explanatory language found in nonfiction works

expressionist   An artistic style that leans toward the abstract, focusing on depicting emotions; variations include cubism, fauvism, and art deco

eye–voice span   When reading orally, the distance between where the reader's eyes are focused and the word he/she is saying aloud (in fluent readers, a lag of about four or five words)

fables   Very brief traditional stories that teach a lesson about behavior, usually with animal characters

faction   A story that is a merger of fact and fiction—for example, fictionalized biography

fairy tales   Traditional stories written to entertain with tales of supernatural events in a wonderland setting filled with magic and fantastical characters

fiction   A literary work designed to entertain, the content of which is produced by the imagination of an identifiable author

fictionalized biography   Biography written in a narrative style that includes speculative scenes and details, invented dialogue, and interior monologue

figurative language   Language, such as similes and metaphors, that creates imagery in the mind of the reader

first-person point of view   Story narration by one of the characters who refers to himself or herself as "I" and "me"

five-finger method   A strategy whereby a child holds up one finger each time an unknown word is encountered on a single page; more than five such words indicates the book may be too difficult

flashback   An element of plot in which the narrator relates an earlier scene to give the reader background information

flat character   A supporting character who exhibits only one side of his or her personality (also known as a static character)

focus unit   A series of literary experiences that integrate the language arts, organized around a central focus such as an author, theme, genre, topic, or literary element

folk art   An artistic style that is based upon designs and images peculiar to a specific culture

folklore   The historic oral version of folk literature

folktales   Stories passed from one generation to the next in the oral tradition; includes myths, fables, ballads, and fairy tales

foreshadowing   An element of plot in which the narrator hints at a forthcoming event in the story

formula books   A series that relates highly predictable events, suggesting that the author was following a fixed pattern

free verse   Poems with irregular rhythmic patterns and line lengths; may be rhymed or unrhymed

frontispiece   An illustration in a book that precedes the title page

genre   Categories of literature, such as fantasy and poetry

grand conversation   A collaborative student discussion that is much like natural conversation, in which the teacher is a facilitator

graphic novels   Novels whose stories are told through a combination of text and illustrations in panels similar to comic books

graphic organizer   Diagrams that outline the important concepts in a piece of expository text, including KWL charts, spider maps, cycle maps, timelines, and Venn diagrams

grocery store books   Books about cartoon, comic book, TV, and movie characters that are typically sold in grocery stores and large chain stores

guided listening activity   Follows the procedures for the guided reading activity, but instead of reading a book, children listen to an adult read a book to them

guided reading activity   A reading strategy used with either fiction or nonfiction that guides the reader though a selection during prereading, guided reading, and postreading stages with discussion and comprehension questions

haiku   A Japanese form of poetry that consists of 17 syllables arranged in three lines of 5, 7, and 5 syllables, typically with a subject that deals with nature

hero's quest   A theme in which the protagonist embarks on a long journey, fraught with trials and impossible tasks, in which he or she searches for something of great importance or value

high fantasy   A fantasy story with colorful adventure, enchantment, and heroism in which the protagonist engages in a monumental struggle against a powerful evil force

historical fiction   Realistic story in a real-world setting in the historical past with events that are partly historical but largely imaginative

homophones   Words that are pronounced the same but have different meanings, such as *blue* and *blew*

hue   Pure color (without the addition of black or white)

illustrated book   A book in which the illustrations are extensions of the text and may add to the story but are not necessary to understand it

impressionist   An artistic style that employs an interplay of color and light created with splashes, speckles, or dots of paint (as opposed to longer brush strokes) to create a dreamlike, romantic effect

informational book   A trade book with the primary purpose of informing the reader by providing an in-depth explanation of factual material

informational story   A trade book that is designed to inform readers, yet has some of the elements of fiction books, such as characters, dialogue, and fantasy

institutional publisher   A company that specializes in publishing nonfiction literature books for schools and libraries; primarily produces series rather than individual titles

integral setting   A story setting that is essential, meaning the story could not have taken place anywhere but the one specified by the author

interior monologue   An author's device that lets readers know what a character is thinking

international literature   Books originally written and published for children living in other lands; also books published in the United States that were written by immigrants about their homeland

invented spelling   Spelling words the way they sound when the standard spelling is not known

juvenile novel   A novel written specifically for children; also called junior novels

KWL chart   A graphic organizer for nonfiction; the name stands for Know, Want to know, and Learned

language chart   A strategy to guide students in analyzing novels in a thematic unit by stimulating children's recall of previously read stories in order to determine similarities and differences

language experience account (LEA)   A child's dictated account of something he or she has experienced, recorded by an adult and used for reading instruction

lap reading   An experience in which a child sits on an adult's lap, and they look at a book together

Latinos (feminine *Latinas*)   People from a variety of cultures that include descendants of native Hispanic people in the United States, residents of Latin America, and U.S. immigrants (and their descendants) from Latin America—which encompasses all countries in the Western Hemisphere south of the United States

legends   Traditional stories or epic poems that are a combination of history and myth, based in part on real characters or historical events, such as the tales of King Arthur, Robin Hood, and Joan of Arc

letter–sound correspondence   Knowledge of which letter (or letter cluster) represents specific language sounds

limerick   A humorous five-line verse with a rhyming scheme of A A B B A

limited omniscient point of view   A story that unfolds through the viewpoint of only one of the characters

line   In an illustration, the horizontal, vertical, angled, or curved mark made by a tool across a surface

linear plot   A story that unfolds logically, containing a beginning that introduces the characters and the central problem, a middle in which the main character attempts to overcome the problem and usually meets with obstacles, and the end where the problem is either resolved or the main character learns to cope with it

listening–prediction activity   A comprehension activity in which children listen to a story and make predictions about what might happen next (used with unfamiliar stories with a strong plot)

literary elements   The various parts that make up a fiction story: characters, point of view, setting, plot, theme, style, and tone

literary fairy tale   A fantasy work that follows the patterns set by the oral tradition of folklore, yet written by an identifiable author; can be any subgenre, such as literary ballad, literary fable, or literary myth (also called literary folktale)

literature circles   Small temporary discussion groups that have chosen to read the same book in a classroom

literature journals   Logs students keep to record the books they have read and their responses to them

lyric poem   A poem that focuses on a single experience, describing the feeling of a moment; does not have a specific stanza form

melting pot theory   A theory that, through intermarriage and assimilation, the different ethnic groups that emigrated to the United States have been homogenized by abandoning their distinguishing cultural characteristics in favor of a dominant white culture

merchandise books Book that are published to promote sales of theme park or movie tickets and the merchandise associated with them such as dolls and toys

metaphor An implied comparison that one thing is another, for example, "her eyes were bright diamonds"

modern fantasy A fiction story with highly fanciful or supernatural elements that would be impossible in real life

Mother Goose A name often attributed to nursery rhymes of British origin

motif A recurring element within traditional stories that occurs in various combinations across stories and cultures, such as magic objects or helpers, tests of character or strength, and transformations (human to animal or animal to human)

multicultural literature Cross-cultural literature that includes books by and about peoples of all cultures

mystery story An adventure story that usually involves solving some type of puzzle, which may or may not be a crime

myths Traditional stories, religious in nature, that provide an explanation for otherwise unexplainable events such as night and day; usually have deities as major characters

narrative poem Poem that tells a story; usually contains setting, characters, events, and climax

Native Americans Members (or descendants) of the 400 or more tribes of the indigenous peoples of North America

negative space See **space**

nonfiction The Dewey decimal classification for the genres of traditional literature, biography, informational books, and poetry (i.e., the genres that are not considered fiction)

nonfiction text structures Organizational patterns for arranging and connecting ideas in expository text, including description, chronology, explanation, comparison/contrast, definition, and problem/solution

novel An extended fictional narrative that allows the author to provide fuller character and plot development than in short stories and picture books; typically divided into chapters

nursery rhymes Traditional verses intended for very young children

objective point of view A story narration that presents the facts with no comment or interpretation of what is happening (reader learns about characters only through their actions and speech)

oil paint An artistic medium made by combining color pigment with a linseed oil base and turpentine or other thinners, producing opaque colors

omniscient point of view A story narration by an all-knowing and all-seeing voice who can relate events that are occurring simultaneously

oral tradition The method of passing stories from one generation to the next by word of mouth

paired reading A supported reading strategy in which an adult sits next to a child and they alternate reading pages of the book

partial biography A biography that focuses on one part or one aspect of a subject's life

pastels Soft-colored chalks for drawing; can also be applied by hand in a powdered form

pattern book A picture book containing repetitive words, phrases, questions, or some other structure that makes it predictable

pen and ink A drawing technique accomplished with a pen as the instrument and ink (usually black) as the medium

personification The representation of animals, ideas, and things as having human qualities, for example, "I heard the wind call my name."

perspective In an illustration, the vantage point from which the viewers are looking at the objects or events depicted

phonemes The smallest unit of speech that distinguishes one word sound from another, such as the *c* in *cat*

picture book A book that conveys its message through a series of pictures with only a small amount of text (or none at all)

picture book biography A biography in picture book format that typically zooms in on a childhood incident of a well-known person

picture storybook A picture book that contains a plot with the text and illustrations equally conveying the story line

plot The sequence of events showing characters in action (i.e., what happens in a story); can be cumulative, linear, episodic, or circular

poetic license A deviation from conventional writing form to achieve a desired effect

poetry Verse in which word images are selected and expressed to create strong, often beautiful impressions (may or may not rhyme)

poetry anthology A book (often themed) containing a number of poems by several poets

poetry collection A book containing several poems by a single poet

point of view The perspective from which an author presents a story: first person, alternating, omniscient, limited omniscient, and objective

positive space See **space**

pourquoi tale A traditional tale that explains the ways things are, particularly natural phenomena; often has animal characters (not to be confused with myths that have gods and goddesses as main characters)

prequel In a series, a book that takes place at a time before the action of a preexisting book

prereading schema-building process A process whereby readers construct their own schema before reading, consisting of three parts: begin at the end, cover the cover, and finish at the front

primary world In fantasy, the real world

prose Any composition that is not poetry

protagonist The central character of a story

prototype The first of its kind—for example, a book in a new category

public domain Status of works not protected by copyright laws, usually because of age

reader response theory A belief that meaning is not inherent in the text; rather, the reader creates meaning in an active mental process when the reader and text converge

readers theater An activity in which children take speaking parts in a brief story and then read it as if it were a radio play

reading–prediction activity A comprehension activity in which children read a story and make predictions about what might happen next (used with unfamiliar stories with a strong plot)

read–skip–read strategy A reading strategy used when an unknown word is encountered in text; the sentence is reread from the beginning, the unknown word is skipped, and then the rest of the sentence is read to see whether the reader can use context to decode an unknown word or infer meaning

realistic art An artistic style that depicts objects realistically with recognizable shapes, realistic color, and proper perspectives and proportions

reference books Dictionaries, encyclopedias, almanacs, atlases, and other informative books that are not intended to be read in their entirety, but rather to be referred to for specific information

reluctant reader A person who is able to read but does not select reading as a pastime

rhyme Two or more words with the same ending sounds (containing at least one vowel sound) but different beginning sounds

rhythm The pattern of stressed and unstressed syllables in a line that gives poetry its beat or tempo

round character A well-developed character

salad bowl theory A theory that people from different ethnic groups retain many of the socially transmitted behavior patterns, arts, beliefs, institutions, etc., and all contribute to the larger culture known as American

schema A system of cognitive structures stored in memory that are abstract representations of events, objects, and relationships in the world; also referred to as background experience or prior knowledge

schemata Plural of schema

science fiction A work of fiction in which magic is replaced by advanced technological wonders

secondary world In high fantasy, a self-contained fictional world that is inhabited by imaginary creatures and has its own time frame

sequel A book that is a continuation of a previous book

series books A number of books that have some unifying element, such as characters or theme

setting Where and when a story takes place

shades Variations of colors that are produced when differing amounts of black are added to a single hue

shape In an illustration, the two dimensions of height and width arranged geometrically; created when spaces are contained by a combination of lines

simile A stated comparison that uses connective words such as *like* or *as*—for example, "hands as cold as ice"

simpleton A character in traditional literature who is not very smart; also called noodle head, droll, or numskull

social reality theme A book theme that involves important issues facing the world today such as racism, crime, war, poverty, and abuse

space In an illustration, the areas that objects take up (**positive space**) and the white or blank areas that surround shapes and forms (**negative space**)

speech-to-print match The ability to match spoken words to their written counterparts

spine The part of a book that shows when it is on the shelf, containing the title and author's last name

spontaneous reenactment Dramatization of a story without the use of props, costumes, or scripts in which children spontaneously become characters and recreate story events

stanza Groups of lines in a poem with an identifiable pattern of rhyme or rhythm (or both)

stereotype character A flat character who possesses only the traits considered typical of her or his particular group—for example, stepmothers

stereotyping Assigning a fixed image or some fixed characteristics to all the members of a particular cultural group

story box A box containing items that represent the events, images, characters, or topics of a story or poem

story mapping An activity in which the readers name the plot components of a book

story theater An oral reading activity in which children practice a selection using the readers theater strategy while other children dramatize it

style The manner in which writers express their ideas to convey a story

subgenre A smaller category within a major genre; for example, ballads are a subgenre of traditional literature

superminority syndrome The use of stereotype characters that need outstanding abilities, skills, or talents in order to gain approval and esteem

surrealist An artistic style that distorts and plays with images, depicting a fantasy quality

survival story An adventure story in which the protagonist is pitted against the elements of nature

suspense A sense of anxiety readers experience when they are uncertain of the outcome of a story

sustained silent reading A period in the school day in which everyone in the classroom is reading silently without interruption

tall tales Exaggerated stories with gigantic, extravagant, restless, and flamboyant characters, such as Paul Bunyan and Pecos Bill

tempera An artistic medium made by mixing pigment with egg yolk or a gelatinous or glutinous substance, producing brilliant hues

textbooks Instructional books that are written on various grade levels and are marketed to school districts (typically not found in libraries)

texture In an illustration, the illusion of a tactile surface

theme The central idea or underlying message the author is conveying to the reader; can be explicit (stated directly by the narrator or a story character) or implicit (readers have to infer the meaning from what happens in the story)

tints Variations of color that are produced when differing amounts of white are added to a single hue

tone The author's attitude toward the book's subject, characters, and readers; includes serious, humorous, moralistic, hopeful, sympathetic, and satirical

trade book Any literature book that is marketed to libraries, wholesale booksellers, retail bookstores, and book clubs

traditional literature Stories, songs, and rhymes with unknown authorship that were passed down orally from one generation to the next before being written down; also known as folk literature

traditional rhymes Traditional verses intended for very young children

trickster A character in traditional literature who is able to outsmart others because he is cunning, shrewd, or deceptive

trilogy A group of three books related in subject or theme

two-page spread Two facing pages in a book

Venn diagram A graphic organizer consisting of two overlapping circles, used to compare and contrast two things

verse A composition having strong rhythm and a rhyming pattern

visual literacy The ability to interpret graphic stimuli

visual scale The apparent relative size of objects that indicates their proximity; used to create the illusion of depth (or distance) on a two-dimensional plane

watercolor An artistic medium made by combining water with either a dry form of pigment or pigment bound with a water-soluble solution of gum arabic and glycerin, producing a transparent look

webbing Creating a visual display of information to represent organized relationships, often used to foster and record responses to literature

white bias A subtle form of racism that implies the mainstream way of life is superior

white space Any area on a page of text that does not contain print

wonder story A folktale that includes enchantments, supernatural beings, and magical objects

woodcut An art medium in which the artist cuts away the background of a picture, applies ink or color to the surface, and then presses it against paper

wordless picture book A book in which the story is revealed through a sequence of illustrations with no—or a very few—words (also known as textless books)

young adult literature Literature written for youth ages 13 through 18 (also called adolescent literature)

Ada, A. F. (2003). *A Magical Encounter: Latino Children's Literature in the Classroom* (2nd ed.). Boston: Allyn & Bacon.

Alter, G. (Ed.). (1995). Touching Magic with Jane Yolen. *Social Studies and the Young Learner, 8*(2), 29–32.

American Library Association. (2004a). *Coping with Challenges: Kids and Libraries, What You Should Know.* Chicago: Author. Retrieved September 16, 2004, from www.ala.org/alaorg/oif/kidsandlibraries.html

American Library Association. (2004b). *Intellectual Freedom and Censorship Q & A.* Chicago: Author. Retrieved September 16, 2004, from www.ala.org/alaorg/oif/intellectualfreedomandcensorship.html#ifpoint3

American Library Association. (2004c). *Library Bill of Rights.* Chicago: Author. Retrieved September 16, 2004, from www.ala.org/work/freedom/ lbr.html

American Library Association. (2008). *Children's Book on Male Penguins Raising Chick Tops ALA's 2007 List of Most Challenged Books.* Retrieved July 15, 2008, from www.ala.org/ala/pressreleases2008/may2008/penguin.cfm

Anderson, N. A. (1995). Developing and Assessing Emergent Literacy through Children's-Literature. In M. D. Collins & B. G. Moss (Eds.), *Literacy Assessment for Today's Schools* (pp. 227–234). College Reading Association.

Anderson, N. A. (2003). *The Books Children Really Read—100 Years of Publishing Trends.* Paper presented at the California Reading Association Conference, San Diego, CA.

Anderson, R. C., Hiebert, E. H., Scott, J. A., & Wilkinson, I. A. G. (1985). *Becoming a Nation of Readers: The Report of the Commission on Reading.* Pittsburgh, PA: National Academy of Science.

Atkinson, D. R., Morten, G., & Sue, D. W. (Eds.). (1993). *Counseling American Minorities: A Cross-Cultural Perspective* (4th ed.). Madison, WI: Brown & Benchmark.

Baghban, M. (2000). Conversations with Yep and Soentpiet: Negotiating Between Cultures. *The Dragon Lode, 18*(2), 41–51.

BBC Two. (n.d.). *The Big Read.* Retrieved August 22, 2004, from www.bbc.co.uk/arts/bigread/

Bishop, R. S. (1992). Multicultural Literature for Children: Making Informed Choices. In Violet J. Harris (Ed.), *Teaching Multicultural Literature in Grades K–8* (pp. 37–53). Norwood, MA: Christopher-Gordon.

Blount, R. H., Jr., & Webb, M. V. (1997). *Art Projects Plus.* Grand Rapids, MI: Instructional Fair.

Brand, D. (1987, August). The New Whiz Kids. *Time, 130*(9), 42–51.

Brinson, S. A. (1997). Literature of a Dream: Portrayal of African American Characters before and after the Civil Rights Movement. *The Dragon Lode, 15*(3), 7–10.

Brinson, S. A. (2002). *Start Early: Using Multiethnic Literature in P–3 Classrooms.* Paper presented at the National Council of Teachers of English Conference, Atlanta, GA.

Bromley, K. D. (1996). *Webbing with Literature: Creating Story Maps with Children's Books* (2nd ed.). Boston: Allyn & Bacon.

Brosnan, R. (2000, March 13). Latino Books for Children. Message posted to Cooperative Children's Book Center listserv (CCBC-Net), archived at http://ccbc.education.wisc.edu/ccbd-net/mar2000.text

Brown, J. E., & Stephens, E. C. (1995). *Teaching Young Adult Literature: Sharing the Connection.* Belmont, CA: Wadsworth.

Bruchac, J. (1997). *Lasting Echoes: An Oral History of Native American People.* Orlando, FL: Harcourt Brace.

Carter, B., & Harris, K. (1982). What Junior High Students Like in Books. *Journal of Reading, 26,* 42–46.

Cefali, L. (1995). Alphabet Books Revisited. *Book Links, 5*(7), 36–41.

Chamberlain, J., & Leal, D. (1999). Caldecott Medal Books and Readability Levels: Not

Just "Picture Books." *The Reading Teacher, 52,* 898–901.

Chi, M. M. (1993). Asserting Asian-American Children's Self and Cultural Identity through Asian-American Children's Literature. *Social Studies Review, 32*(2), 50–55.

Chisholm, M. (1972). Mother Goose—Elucidated. *Elementary English, 49,* 1141–1144.

Cianciolo, P. J. (1973, April). Use Wordless Picture Books to Teach Reading, Visual Literacy, and to Study Literature. *Top of the News* (American Library Association), *29,* 226–234.

Coffin, T. P. (1999). *Encarta Encyclopedia 99.* Microsoft Corporation.

Colbath, M. L. (1971). Worlds as They Should Be: Middle-earth, Narnia, and Prydain. *Elementary English, 48,* 937–945.

Collard, S. B. (1998). Sharing the Passion of Science. *Book Links, 8*(5), 30–34.

Cooperative Children's Book Center. (2008). Children's Books By and About People of Color Published in the United States. Madison, WI: University of Wisconsin. Retrieved June 3, 2008, from www.education.wisc.edu/ccbc/books/pcstats.htm

Cornett, C. E. (1999). *The Arts as Meaning Makers.* Upper Saddle River, NJ: Merrill.

Cornett, C. E., & Cornett, C. F. (1980). *Bibliotherapy: The Right Book at the Right Time.* Bloomington, IN: Phi Delta Kappa Educational Foundation.

Council on Interracial Books for Children. (1976). How Children's Books Distort the Asian American Image. *Interracial Books for Children Bulletin, 7*(2), 3–23.

Crumpler, T., & Schneider, J. J. (2002). Writing with Their Whole Being: A Cross Study Analysis of Children's Writing from Five Classrooms Using Process Drama. *Research in Drama Education, 7*(1), 61–79.

Cullinan, B. E. (1989). *Literature and the Child* (2nd ed.). San Diego: Harcourt Brace Jovanovich.

Cullinan, B. E. (1992). *Read to Me: Raising Kids Who Love to Read.* New York: Scholastic.

Cunningham, P. M. (1995). *Phonics They Use.* New York: HarperCollins.

D'Angelo, K. (1981). Wordless Picture Books and the Young Language-Disabled Child. *Teaching Exceptional Children, 4*(1), 34–37.

Daniels, H. (1994). *Literature Circles: Voice and Choice in the Student-Centered Classroom.* York, ME: Stenhouse.

DeCasper, A. J., Lecanuet, J. P., Busnel, M. C., & Granier-Deferre, C. (1994). Fetal Reactions to Recurrent Maternal Speech. *Infant Behavior & Development, 14,* 159–164.

DeHaven, E. P. (1979). *Teaching and Learning the Language Arts* (pp. 112–113). Boston: Little, Brown.

de Regniers, B. S. (Ed.). (1988). *Sing a Song of Popcorn: Every Child's Book of Poems.* New York: Scholastic.

Donelson, K. L., & Nilsen, A. P. (1997). *Literature for Today's Young Adults* (5th ed.). New York: Longman.

Dreyer, S. S. (1993). *The Bookfinder.* Circle Pines, MN: American Guidance Services.

Driscoll, S. (1999). Coping with Violence. *Book Links, 9*(9), 17–19.

Eitelgeorge, J. S., & Anderson, N. A. (2004). The Work of Hans Christian Andersen—More Than Just Fairy Tales. *Bookbird: A Journal of International Children's Literature, 42*(3), 37–44.

Evslin, B., Evslin, D., & Hoopes, N. (1966). *The Greek Gods.* New York: Scholastic.

Feng, J. H. (1994). *Asian-American Children: What Teachers Should Know.* Retrieved June 2, 2008, from www.ericdigests.org/1994/teachers.htm

Fisher, C. B., Wallace, S. A., & Fenton, R. E. (2000). Discrimination Distress during Adolescence. *Journal of Youth and Adolescence, 29*(6), 679–695.

Freeman, A. (2000). *Selection of Culturally Relevant Text.* Tucson: University of Arizona Press.

Freeman, E. B., & Person, D. G. (1998). *Connecting Informational Children's Books with Content Area Learning.* Boston: Allyn & Bacon.

Freeman, Y., Freeman, A., & Freeman, D. (2003). Home Run Books: Connecting Students to Culturally Relevant Texts. *NABE News, 26*(3), 5–12.

Gambrell, L. B. (1996). Creating Classroom Cultures That Foster Reading Motivation. *The Reading Teacher, 50,* 14–25.

Gambrell, L. B. (1997). *Creating Classroom Cultures That Foster Motivation to Read.* Paper presented at the Southwest International Reading Association Regional Conference, Tucson, AZ.

Gardner, H. (1999). *Intelligence Reframed: Multiple Intelligences for the 21st Century.* New York: Basic Books.

Geeslin, C. (2004, Spring). Along Publishers Row. *The Author's Guild Bulletin, 92,* 2.

Gerson, L. (2000). Modern China in Fiction. *Book Links, 9,* 19–22.

Gillet, J. W., & Temple, C. (1986). *Understanding Reading Problems: Assessment and Instruction* (2nd ed.). Boston: Scott Foresman.

Glazer, J. I. (1997). *Introduction to Children's Literature* (2nd ed.). Upper Saddle River, NJ: Merrill.

Grindler, M. C., Stratton, B. D., & McKenna, M. C. (1997). *The Right Book, the Right Time.* Boston: Allyn & Bacon.

Groff, P. (1974, April). Children's Literature versus Wordless "Books." *Top of the News* (American Library Association), *30,* 294–303.

Grolier Classroom Publishing. (1995). *Using Nonfiction Effectively in Your Classroom.* New York: Children's Press.

Gunning, T. G. (1998). *Best Books for Beginning Readers.* Boston: Allyn & Bacon.

Hadaway, N. L., & Florez, V. (1990). Teaching Multiethnic Literature, Promoting Cultural Pluralism. *The Dragon Lode, 8*(1), 7–13.

Harris, T. L., & Hodges, R. E. (Eds.). (1995). *The Literacy Dictionary: The Vocabulary of Reading and Writing.* Newark, DE: International Reading Association.

Hillman, J. (1999). *Discovering Children's Literature* (2nd ed.). Upper Saddle River, NJ: Merrill.

Hirsch, E. D., Jr. (1987). *Cultural Literacy: What Every American Needs to Know.* Boston: Houghton Mifflin.

Hoffman, B. (n.d.) Asian-American Literature: History, Classroom Use, Bibliography and WWW Resources. Retrieved August 1, 2004, from http://falcon.jmu.edu/~ramseyil/asialit.htm

Houston, G. (2004). *Literature for Young Readers.* Spring Hill, NC: Sunny Brook.

Huck, C. S. (1987). *Children's Literature in the Elementary School* (4th ed.). New York: Holt, Rinehart & Winston.

Huck, C. S., Hepler, S., Hickman, J., & Kiefer, B. Z. (1997). *Children's Literature in the Elementary School* (6th ed.). Madison, WI: Brown & Benchmark.

International Reading Association. (2001, February). Censorship in the Cyber Age. *Reading Today,* 22–23.

International Reading Association. (2003a, January). A Rabbit's Tale. *Reading Today,* 42.

International Reading Association. (2003b, February/March). Classroom Spotlight on Technology: Fiction Based on Fact. *Reading Today,* 10.

Ito, K. (2005). The History of *Manga* in the Context of Japanese Culture and Society. *Journal of Popular Culture, 38*(3), 456–475.

Jalongo, M. (1983). Bibliotherapy: Literature to Promote Socioemotional Growth. *The Reading Teacher, 36,* 796–802.

Kim, A., & Yeh, C. J. (2002). *Stereotypes of Asian American Students.* ERIC Clearinghouse on Urban Education New York. (ERIC Document Reproduction Service No. ED462510)

King, F. J., III. (2003). A *Native Voice* Visit: Activist/Actor/Artist John Trudell. *The Native Voice, 2*(23), C5.

Klesius, J., Laframboise, K. L., & Gaier, M. (1998). Humorous Literature: Motivation for Reluctant Readers. *Reading Research and Instruction, 37,* 253–261.

Knell, S. E. (1999). *Assessing a Second-Grade Student's Motivation to Read.* Unpublished doctoral dissertation, University of Arkansas.

Lamme, L. L., Fu, D., & Allington, R. (2002). "Is This Book an AR Book?" A Closer Examination of a Popular Reading Program. *The Florida Reading Quarterly, 38*(3), 27–32.

Lane, B. (2004). 10 Quick Ways to Analyze Children's Books for Racism and Sexism.

The Council on Interracial Books for Children. Retrieved June 3, 2008, from www.birchlane.davis.ca.us/library/10quick.htm

Lawson, C. V. (1972). *Children's Reasons and Motivation for the Selection of Favorite Books.* Doctoral dissertation, University of Arkansas.

Leavell, J. A., Hatcher, B., Battle, J., & Ramos-Michail, N. (2002). Exploring Hispanic culture through Trade Books. *Social Education, 64,* 210–215.

Lechner, J. V. (2004). *Anthology of Traditional Literature.* Boston: Allyn & Bacon.

Lee, S. J. (1994, December). Behind the Model-Minority Stereotype: Voices of High- and Low-Achieving Asian American Students. *Anthropology & Education Quarterly, 25*(4), 413–429.

Lee, S. J. (1996). *Unraveling the "Model Minority" Stereotype: Listening to Asian American Youth.* New York: Teachers College Press.

Li, S. (2000). Mulan and More: Heroines of Chinese Folklore in Picture Books. *Book Links, 10,* 15–18.

Lilly, E., & Green, C. (2004). *Developing Partnerships with Families through Children's Literature.* Upper Saddle River, NJ: Pearson Merrill Prentice Hall.

Lo, S., & Lee, G. (1993). Asian Images in Children's Books: What Stories Do We Tell our Children? *Emergency Librarian, 20*(5), 14–19.

Lu, M. Y. (1998). *Multicultural Children's Literature in the Elementary Classroom.* (ERIC Document Reproduction Service No. ED423552)

Lukens, R. J. (1999). *A Critical Handbook of Children's Literature* (6th ed.). New York: Longman.

Lurie, A. (2004). Was Cinderella Blonde? *Muse, 8*(4), 9–17.

Lynch-Brown, C., & Tomlinson, C. M. (1999). *Essentials of Children's Literature* (3rd ed.). Boston: Allyn & Bacon.

Marantz, S., & Marantz, K. (2000). Picture Books Peek behind Cultural Curtains. *Book Links, 10*(1), 13–16.

Mathis, J. B. (2001, November). *Literacy Possibilities of Mexican-American Children's Literature: Publishers, Scholars, and Readers Respond.* Paper presented at the College Reading Association Conference, Orlando, FL.

May, J. P. (1980). Film Productions of Children's Books: Weston Wood Studios and Disney. *Catholic Library World, 51,* 210–214.

McKenna, M., & Kear, D. (1990). Measuring Attitude toward Reading: A New Tool for Teachers. *The Reading Teacher, 43,* 626–638.

Mesmer, H. A. (1998). Goosebumps: The Appeal of Predictability and Violence. *The New Advocate, 11,* 107–118.

Mohr, K. A. J. (2002). *Children's Choices: A Comparison of Book Preferences between Hispanic and Non-Hispanic First-Grade Students.* Paper presented at the College Reading Association Conference, Philadelphia.

Mora, P. (2000). The Seeds of Stories. *The Dragon Lode, 18*(2), 55–59.

Murray, Y. I., & Velasquez, J. (1999). *Promoting Reading among Mexican American Children.* (ERIC Document Reproduction Service No. ED 438150)

Museum of History and Industry. (1990). *Chief Seattle.* Retrieved August 22, 2004, from www.synaptic.bc.ca/ejournal/muhisind.htm

National Council of Teachers of English. (1996). Standards for the English Language Arts. Retrieved August 22, 2004, from www.ncte.org/about/over/standards/110846.htm

Nodelman, P. (1996). *The Pleasures of Children's Literature* (2nd ed.). White Plains, NY: Longman.

Northrup, M. (2004). Multicultural Cinderella Stories. *Book Links, 13*(5), 41–46.

Norton, Donna E. (1999). *Through the Eyes of a Child* (5th ed.). Englewood Cliffs, NJ: Merrill.

O'Bruba, W., & Camplese, D. (1983). Beyond Bibliotherapy. In K. VanderMeulen (Ed.), *Reading Horizons: Selected Readings, 2.* Kalamazoo: Western Michigan University.

Oldrieve, R. M. (2003, April). The Series Books Phenomenon: The Case of "How Do Beginning Readers Graduate to Real Books?" *Reading Today, 18.*

O'Malley, J. (1999). Talking with J. K. Rowling. *Book Links, 9*(7), 32–36.

Ouzts, D. (1991). The Emergence of Bibliotherapy as a Discipline. *Reading Horizons, 31,* 199–206.

Ouzts, D. (1998). *An Examination of the International Reading Association's Children's Choices, Teachers' Choices, and Young Adults' Choices as Related to Bibliotherapy.* Paper presented at the College Reading Association Conference, Myrtle Beach, SC.

Ouzts, D. T., & Palombo, M. J. (2006). Children's Books Chosen by Children. In L. K. Elksnin & N. Elksnin (Eds.), *Teaching Social-Emotional Skills at School and Home* (p. 292). Denver, CO: Love Publishing.

Patent, D. H. (1998). Science Books for Children: An Endangered Species? *The Horn Book, 74,* 309–314.

Paulsen, Ken. (2001, Winter). Speaking Freely about Children's Book Censorship. *The Authors Guild Bulletin, 89,* 14–25.

Peterson, G. C. (1971). *A Study of Library Books Selected by Second Grade Boys and Girls in the Iowa City, Iowa, Schools.* Doctoral dissertation, University of Iowa.

Radencich, M. C. (1985). Books That Promote Positive Attitudes toward Second Language Learning. *The Reading Teacher, 38,* 528–530.

Richards, J. C. (2002). Arts at Every Opportunity: Weaving It All Together. In J. P. Gipe (Ed.), *Multiple Paths to Literacy: Classroom Techniques for Struggling Readers* (pp. 355–375). Upper Saddle River, NJ: Merrill.

Richards, J. C., & Anderson, N. A. (2003). What Do I See? What Do I Think? What Do I Wonder? (STW): A Visual Literacy Strategy to Help Emergent Readers Focus Attention on Storybook Illustrations. *The Reading Teacher, 65,* 442–444.

Richards, J. C., & McKenna, M. C. (2003). *Integrating Multiple Literacies in K–8 Classrooms: Cases, Commentaries, and Practical Applications.* Mahwah, NJ: Lawrence Erlbaum.

Roback, D. E. (2001). All-Time Bestselling Children's Books. *Publishers Weekly, 248*(51), 24–32.

Rosenblatt, L. M. (1993). The Transactional Theory of Reading and Writing. In R. B. Rudell, M. R. Rudell, & H. Singer (Eds.), *Theoretical Models and Processes of Reading* (4th ed., pp. 1057–1092). Newark, DE: International Reading Association.

Rosenblatt, L. M. (1995). *Literature as Exploration* (5th ed.). New York: Modern Language Association.

Roser, N. L., & Martinez, M. G. (1995). *Book Talk and Beyond: Children and Teachers Respond to Literature.* Newark, DE: International Reading Association.

Roser, N. L., Hoffman, J. V., Labbo, L. D., & Farest, C. (1995). Language Charts: A Record of Story Time Talk. In N. L. Roser & M. G. Martinez (Eds.), *Book Talk and Beyond: Children and Teachers Respond to Literature.* Newark, DE: International Reading Association.

Rothlein, L., & Meinbach, A. M. (1996). *Legacies: Using Children's Literature in the Classroom.* New York: HarperCollins.

Russell, D. L. (1997). *Literature for Children: A Short Introduction.* New York: Longman.

Schneider, J. J. (2002). Censorship and Harry Potter. In N. A. Anderson (Ed.), *Elementary Children's Literature: The Basics for Teachers and Parents* (p. 137). Boston: Allyn & Bacon.

Schodt, F. (1988). *Manga! Manga! The World of Japanese Comics.* Tokyo: Kodansha International.

Schulman, J. (Ed.). (1998). Foreword to *The 20th Century Children's Book Treasury.* New York: Knopf.

Scott, J. C. (1995). *Native Americans in Children's Literature.* Phoenix, AZ: Oryx Press.

Shen, W., & Mo, W. (1990). *Reaching Out to Their Cultures: Building Communication with Asian-American Families.* (ERIC Document Reproduction Service No. ED351 435)

Singer, E. A. (2001). *Fakelore, Multiculturalism, and the Ethics of Children's Literature.* Retrieved August 22, 2004, from www.msu.edu/user/singere/fakelore.html

Siu, S. F. (1996). *Asian American Students at Risk: A Literature Review.* Report No. 8.

Baltimore, MD: Johns Hopkins University, Center for Research on the Education of Students Placed At Risk. (ED 404 406)

Siu-Runyan, Y. (1999). 1998 Notable Books for a Global Society: A K–12 List. *The Reading Teacher, 52,* 498–504.

Smith, C. L. (2000). Native Now: Contemporary Indian Stories. *Book Links, 9*(12), 29–32.

Steinbergh, Judith. (1994). *Reading and Writing Poetry: A Guide for Teachers Grades K–4.* New York: Scholastic.

Stewig, J. W. (1980). *Children and Literature.* Chicago: Rand McNally.

Stonehill, B. (Ed.). (1998). The On-Line Visual Literacy Project. Retrieved August 22, 2004, from www.pomona.edu/Academics/course related/classprojects/Visual-lit/intro/intro .html.

Stoodt, B. D., Amspaugh, L. B., & Hunt, J. (1996). *Children's Literature: Discovery for a Lifetime.* Scottsdale, AZ: Gorsuch Scarisbrick.

Sutherland, Z. (1997). *Children and Books* (9th ed.). New York: Longman.

Temple, C. A., & Gillet, J. W. (1989). *Language Arts: Learning Processes and Teaching Practices.* Boston: Little, Brown.

Temple, C. A., Martinez, M., Yokota, J., & Naylor, A. (1998). *Children's Books in Children's Hands: An Introduction to Their Literature.* Boston: Allyn & Bacon.

Tompkins, G. E., & McGee, L. M. (1993). *Teaching Reading with Literature: Case Studies to Action Plans.* Upper Saddle River, NJ: Merrill.

Trueba, H. T., & Cheng, L. (1993). *Myth or Reality: Adaptive Strategies of Asian Americans in California.* Bristol, PA: Falmer Press.

Tunnell, M. O. (1992). Books in the Classroom: Columbus and Historical Perspective. *The Horn Book, 68,* 244–248.

U.S. Census Bureau. (2003). *The Asian and Pacific Islands. Population in the United States: March 2002.* Washington, DC: U.S. Department of Commerce—Economics and Statistics Administration.

U.S. Census Bureau. (2008). Hispanics in the United States. A presentation created by the Ethnicity and Ancestry Branch—Population Division of the U.S. Census Bureau. Retrieved June 3, 2008, from www.census.gov/ population/www/socdemo/hispanic/ reports.html

U.S. Department of Education. (1994). *National Standards for Art Education.* Washington, DC: Office of Educational Statistics.

Warner, M. (1991). The Absent Mother: Women against Women in Old Wives' Tales. *History Today, 41*(4), 22.

Warren, J. S., Prater, N. J., & Griswold, D. L. (1990). Parental Practices of Reading Aloud to Preschool Children. *Reading Improvement, 27,* 41–45.

Whitney, P. A. (1976). *Writing Juvenile Stories and Novels.* Boston: The Writer.

Wilburn, M. H. (1998). *Buffalo Dreams: Using Native American Creation Legends to Stimulate Writing.* Paper presented at the International Reading Association Conference, Orlando, FL.

Williams, N. L., & Bauer, P. T. (2006). Pathways to Affective Accountability: Selecting, Locating, and Using Children's Books in Elementary School Classrooms. *The Reading Teacher, 60*(1), 14–22.

Wilms, D. M. (1978). An Evaluation of Biography. *Booklist, 75,* 218–220.

Wolf, D., & Blalock, D. (1999). *Art Works! Interdisciplinary Learning Powered by the Arts.* Portsmouth, NH: Heinemann.

Wolkomir, R., & Wolkomir, J. R. (2004). Who Wrote "Cinderella"? *Muse, 8*(4), 20–26.

Yao, E. L. (1988). Working Effectively with Asian and Immigrant Parents. *Phi Delta Kappan, 70*(3), 223–225.

Yokota, J., & Sanderson, S. (2000). Talking with Janet S. Wong. *Book Links, 9*(1), 57–61.

Yolen, J. (1973). *Writing Books for Children.* Boston: The Writer.

Yolen, J. (1981). *Touch Magic: Fantasy, Faerie, and Folklore in the Literature of Childhood.* New York: Philomel.

Name and Title Index

Aardema, Verna, 34, 45, 56, 60, 101, 102
Abboreno, Joseph F., 92
Abiyoyo, 117, 142, 172, 176
Abnett, Dan, 275, 279
Abraham Lincoln: From Pioneer to President, 268, 280
Abrashkin, Raymond, 137, 143
Absolutely Normal Chaos, 33, 45, 227, 231
Abuela, 122, 141
Ackerman, Karen, 213, 231
Acosta, Cristina, 92
Across Five Aprils, 248, 259, 262
Actual Size, 295
Ada, Alma Flor, 44, 68, 104, 175, 179
Adam of the Road, 199, 240, 262
Adelita: A Mexican Cinderella Story, 104
Adios, Anna, 216, 232
Adler, David, 275, 279
Adoff, Arnold, 58, 60, 271, 279, 303, 310
Adventures of Captain Underpants: An Epic Novel, The, 14, 25, 124–125, 142
Adventures of Huckleberry Finn, The, 204
Adventures of Isabel, The, 310
Adventures of Pinocchio: The Story of a Puppet, The, 6, 24, 119, 141
Adventures of Tom Sawyer, The, 2, 6, 25
Aerial Gunners of World War II, 295
Aesop, 84
Aesop's Fables (Caxton), 93
Aesop's Fables (Pinkney), 94
Aesop's Fables (Santore), 93, 94
Aigner-Clark, Julie, 64
A Is for Asia, 189
Alarcón, Francisco X., 179, 309, 310, 325
Albert B. Cub & Zebra: An Alphabet Storybook, 66, 68, 69
Albert Einstein, 274, 280
Alcott, Louisa May, 6, 24, 238, 261, 273
Alegria, Mali, 181
Alexander and the Terrible, Horrible, No Good, Very Bad Day, 213, 233
Alexander and the Wind-Up Mouse, 59, 61, 119, 141
Alexander, Who's Not (Do you hear me? I mean it!) Going to Move, 213, 233

Alex and the Wednesday Chess Club, 190
Alice's Adventures in Wonderland, 1, 4, 5, 6, 7, 24, 54, 60, 115, 125, 140
Alice Yazzie's Year, 310
Alien Secrets, 135, 141
Aliki, 288, 294
Allard, Harry, 8, 24, 137–138, 140
Allen, Thomas B., 262
Alligators All Around, 67, 69
Allington, Richard L., 77
Allison, 190
All the Colors of the Earth, 189
Along Came a Dog, 163, 165
Alphabatics, 67, 69
Alphabet, 69
Alphabet Adventure, 58, 61
Alphabet City, 68
Alphabet from A to Y with Bonus Letter Z!, The, 69
Alphabet of Dinosaurs, An, 68
Alter, Gloria, 120
Alternative Energy, 294
Alvarez, Julia, 198
Amano, Shiro, 192
Amazing Bone, The, 154, 167
Amazing Grace, 228, 232
Amber Brown Is Not a Crayon, 216, 232
Ambush, Peter, 185
Amelia Bedelia, 138, 142
Amelia Earhart, 268, 280
American Plague: The True and Terrifying Story of the Yellow Fever Epidemic of 1793, 295
American Tall Tales, 97, 98
American Women Inventors, 276
Amos, Berthe, 122, 140
Amos Fortune, Free Man, 273
Amspaugh, Linda B., 328
Ananse and the Lizard, 102
Anaya, Rudolfo, 104
Ancona, George, 58
Anders, Isabel, 136, 140
Andersen, Hans Christian, 29, 87, 113–115, 116, 118, 121, 122, 125, 128, 132, 134, 137, 140
Anderson, Laurie Halse, 243, 261
Anderson, Linda, 95

Anderson, Nancy A., 52, 75, 114, 146, 329–330
Anderson, Richard C., 313
Anderson, William, 267, 279
Andrews, Benny, 185
And Tango Makes Three, 204
And Then What Happened, Paul Revere?, 274, 279
And to Think That I Saw It on Mulberry Street, 138, 142, 151
Angels Ride Bikes and Other Fall Poems, 310
Animalia, 68
Animal Poems of the Iguazu, 309, 310
Animals Asleep, 294
Animals of the Bible, 28, 45
Animorphs: The Andalite's Gift, 33, 45
Anne Frank, 274, 280
Anne Frank: The Diary of a Young Girl, 274, 279
Annie Oakley, 268, 280
Annie's abc, 66, 69
Anno, Mitsumasa, 52, 56, 60, 62, 67, 68, 70, 71
Anno's Alphabet, 68
Anno's Counting Book, 52, 56, 60, 62, 70, 71
Anzaldúa, Gloria, 178, 179
Applegate, Katherine A., 33, 45
Apple Pie, 4th of July, 190–191
"April Rain Song," 301
Arabian Nights, or Tales Told by Sheherezade, The, 82
Arai, Tomie, 96
Archambault, John, 64, 69
Arctic Fives Arrive, 70, 71
Arenson, Roberta, 105
Are You There God? It's Me, Margaret, 32, 34, 45, 228–229, 231
Armadillo Rodeo, 159, 165
Armstrong, William H., 35, 45, 237, 262
Armstrong-Ellis, Carey, 71
Arnold, Jeanne, 180
Around the World in Eighty Days, 6, 25
Around the World in Eighty Poems, 310
Arrow over the Door, The, 193
Arrow to the Sun, 88, 89
Arroz con Leche: Popular Songs and Rhymes from Latin America, 95
Artemis Fowl, 135, 140
Artemis Fowl: The Graphic Novel, 14, 24
Arthur's Eyes, 155, 165
Arthur's New Puppy, 145, 165
Art Projects Plus, 59

Arts as Meaning Makers: Integrating Literature and the Arts throughout the Curriculum, The, 59
Art Works! Interdisciplinary Learning Powered by the Arts, 59
Asbjørnsen, Peter Christen, 83, 84, 105
Ashanti to Zulu: African Traditions, 66, 68, 69
Ashley Tisdale: Life Is Sweet!, 267, 280
Ashpet: An Appalachian Tale, 102
At Home with Beatrix Potter: The Creator of Peter Rabbit, 8, 25
Atkinson, Donald R., 187
August, Louise, 105
Austin, Michael, 180
Avi, 33, 45, 155, 165, 240–241, 262
Awful Ogre Running Wild, 310
Azuma, Kiyohiko, 192

Baba Yaga and the Wise Doll, 105
Baba Yaga and Vasilisa the Brave, 105
Babbitt, Natalie, 37, 45, 123, 140
Babe: The Gallant Pig, 157, 166
Baboushka and the Three Kings, 105
Babushka Baba Yaga, 101, 105
Babu's Song, 197
Baby, 216, 232
Babymouse: Heartbreaker, 14, 25
Baca, Maria, 104
Back-to-Back: Super Bowl Champions Peyton and Eli Manning, 276, 280
Bad Beginning, The, 139, 142
Bad Boy: A Memoir, 267, 280
Baer, Gene, 54, 60
Baghban, M., 189
Balliett, Blue, 223, 231
Bambi: A Life in the Woods, 149, 166
Bang, Molly, 70, 71
Banks, Lynne Reid, 199
Bannerman, Helen, 182
Barbour, Karen, 94
Barkley, James, 262
Barnwell, Ysaye M., 184
Barnyard Dance!, 64, 65
Barrie, Sir James Matthew, 125–126, 140
Base, Graeme, 68
Bateman, Teresa, 117, 140
Battle, J., 176
Bauer, Joan, 228, 231

Bauer, Marion Dane, 134, 140
Bauer, Patricia T., 318
Baum, L. Frank, 6, 24, 125, 140
Baxter, Robert, 89
Baynes, Pauline, 302–303
Beall, Pamela Conn, 74
Bear Called Paddington, A, 160, 165
Bearwalker, 195
Beatles, The, 276, 280
Beatrix Potter: A Journal, 267, 280
Beatty, Patricia, 226, 231, 247, 248, 262
Beautiful Blackbird, 102
Beauty and the Beast, 101, 104
Because of Winn-Dixie, 230, 232
Bechstein, Ludwig, 84
Becoming Naomi León, 180
Bedtime for Frances, 155, 166
Bees, Snails, & Peacock Tails: Shapes Naturally, 73
Begay, Shonto, 103, 310
Be Glad Your Nose Is on Your Face and Other Poems, 311
Behind the Attic Wall, 133, 140
Belle Prater's Boy, 255, 263
Belpré, Pura, 178
Bemelmans, Ludwig, 138, 140
Benally, Kendrick, 103, 194
Benjamin, Floella, 109
Benjamin Franklin: An American Genius, 268, 280
Benson, Michael, 267, 279
Bentley, Dawn, 64, 71, 72
Berenstain, Janice, 73, 74, 155, 165
Berenstain, Stanley, 73, 74, 155, 165
Berenstain Bears and the Spooky Old Tree, The, 155, 165
Berg, Michele, 311
Berger, Gilda, 90, 181, 288, 294
Berger, Melvin, 288, 292, 294
Berkes, Marianne, 71
Berlioz the Bear, 116, 140
Bernie Magruder and the Bats in the Belfry, 223, 232
Berragan, Paula, 310
Berry, Holly, 95
Berry, James, 310
Best Books for Beginning Readers, 19
Best Word Book Ever, 74
Beyond Mayfield, 256, 263
BFG, The, 121, 141

Big Jabe, 98
Big Jimmy's Kum Kau Chinese Take Out, 213, 232
Big Talk: Poems for Four Voices, 310
Bill and Pete, 159, 165
Bill Gates, 268, 280
Billions of Bats: A Buzz Beaker Brainstorm, 14, 25
Bill Martin Jr. Big Book of Poetry, The, 310
Billy Beg and His Bull, 103, 106
Binch, Caroline, 59, 60, 232
Bindi Irwin, 274, 280
Birchbark House, The, 194
Birmingham, 1963, 182, 183
Biscuit, 156–157, 165
Bishop, Nic, 294
Bishop, Rudine Sims, 171
Black, Holly, 122, 141
Black Beauty: The Autobiography of a Horse, 6, 25, 147, 163, 167
Black Bull of Narroway: A Scottish Tale, The, 104
Black? White? Day? Night?, 74
Blair, Eric, 101, 104
Blake, Quentin, 141
Blalock, D., 59
Blanca's Feather, 198
Bliss, Harry, 165
Bloom, Lloyd, 238–239, 262
Bloor, Edward, 207, 229, 231
Blos, Joan W., 244, 262
Blount, R. Howard, 59
Blue Fairy Book: Selected Tales from the Collection, The, 84
Blues Journey, 310
Blue Sword, The, 130, 141
Blumberg, Rhoda, 294
Blume, Judy, 32, 34, 38, 45, 212–213, 215, 218, 227, 228–229, 231
Boggart and the Monster, The, 199
Bolster, Rob, 71
Bond, Michael, 160, 165
Book of Nonsense, A, 300
Book Talk and Beyond: Children and Teachers Respond to Literature, 39
Book Thief, The, 254, 263
Borrowers, The, 122, 142
Bossy Gallito, The, 104
Bourgeois, Paulette, 152, 155, 165
Bowman's Store, 267, 279
Boyer, Allen B., 294

Boynton, Sandra, 64, 65

Boys from St. Petri, The, 199

Boy Who Had a Dream: A Nomadic Folk Tale from Tibet, The, 103

Bradby, Marie, 248–249, 262

Bradman, Tony, 213, 231

Braekstad, H. L., 105

Brand, D., 187

Branscum, Robbie, 222

Braun, Eric, 275, 279

Breadwinner, The, 198

Brennan, Neil, 310

Brenner, Fred, 262

Brett, Jan, 94, 101, 104, 116, 140, 159, 165, 198

Bridges, Jeanne Rorex, 193, 194–195

Bridges, Ruby, 274, 279

Bridge to Terabithia, 207, 216, 233

Bridwell, Norman, 156, 165

Briggs, Raymond, 77

Bright Freedom's Song, 246–247, 262

Brimner, Larry Dane, 98

Bringing the Rain to Kapiti Plain, 101, 102

Brink, Carol Ryrie, 236, 262

Brinson, Sabrina A., 181–185

Broken Tusk: Stories of the Hindu God Ganesha, The, 196

Bromley, Karen D'Angelo, 154

Bronze Bow, The, 240, 263

Brooks, Felicity, 96

Brosnan, Rosemary, 177

Brother Eagle, Sister Sky: A Message from Chief Seattle, 173–174, 176

Broutin, Christian, 166

Brown, Jean E., 2, 31, 34, 36

Brown, Marc, 145, 155, 165

Brown, Marcia, 19, 24, 29, 36, 45, 93, 94, 104, 106

Brown, Margaret Wise, 64, 155, 165

Brown, Ruth, 105

Brown Bear, Brown Bear, What Do You See?, 64

Browne, Anthony, 102, 104

Browning, Robert, 302

Bruce Coville's Book of Magic: Tales to Cast a Spell on You, 132, 141

Bruchac, Joseph, 54, 60, 103, 193–194, 195, 241, 262, 267, 279, 296, 310, 325

Bryan, Ashley, 102, 176, 303, 310

Buchanan, Yvonne, 184

Buchholz, Quentin, 198

Buckley, James, 267, 279

Buck Stops Here, The, 275, 280

Bud, Not Buddy, 53, 56, 60, 251–252, 262, 312

Buehner, Mark, 142, CI-3

Buffalohead, Julie, 194

Bull Run, 247–248, 262

Bully for You, Teddy Roosevelt!, 269, 280

Bunnicula: A Rabbit-Tale of Mystery, 157, 166

Bunny Trouble, 156

Bunting, Eve, 207, 213, 214, 222, 224, 225, 226, 231

Burger, Carl, 165

Burkert, Nancy Ekholm, 53, 59, 60, 104

Burnett, Frances H., 6, 24

Burnford, Sheila, 163, 165

Burton, Virginia Lee, 95, 120, 140

Busnel, M. C., 18

Buss, Fran Leeper, 226, 231

But No Candy, 238–239, 254, 262

Butterfly Butterfly: A Book of Colors, 72

Butterfly Counting Book, The, 70, 71

Byard, Carole, 233

Byars, Betsy, 222, 223–224, 231

Bye, Bye, Bali Kai, 225, 232

Caddie Woodlawn, 236, 262

Cafecito Story, A, 198

Cahoon, Heather, 64, 71, 72

Caldecott, Randolph, 7, 27

Calkhoven, Laurie, 268, 279

Call of the Wild, The, 148, 163, 166

Cardcaptor Sakura, 192

Camp, Carole Ann, 276

Camplese, D., 208

Candidate for Murder, A, 222, 232

Cann, Helen, 92

Cannon, Janell, 161–162, 165

Cannon, Jerlene, 275, 279

Canyon, Jeanette, 71

Captain Stormalong, 98

Capture, The, 162, 166

Capucilli, Alyssa Satin, 156–157, 165

Cardoni, Paolo, 280

Carle, Eric, 8, 24, 29, 55, 56, 59, 60, 64, 69, 70, 71, 72, 73, 74, 75, 116, 140, 160–161, 165

Carlos and the Squash Plant / Carlos y la Planta de Calabaza, 180

Carlson, Melody, 64

Carmi, Daniella, 199
Carrick, Donald, 231
Carroll, Lewis, 1, 4, 5, 6, 24, 54, 60, 115, 125, 140
Carter, B., 208
Cartlidge, Cherese, 294
Cassedy, Sylvia, 133, 140
Castagnetta, Grace, 95
Cat and Rat: The Legend of the Chinese Zodiac, 107
Cat in the Hat, The, 12, 25, 150–151, 167
Cat's Cradle: A Book of String Figures, 284, 295
Catwings, 151, 166
Caxton, William, 93
Cazet, Denys, 158, 165
Cefali, Leslie, 67
Celebrate! Stories of the Jewish Holidays, 90, 181
Celery Stalks at Midnight, The, 157, 166
Cendrillon: A Caribbean Cinderella, 105
Cepeda, Joe, 104
Ceremony—in the Circle of Life, 133, 142
Cesar Chavez: Fighting for Farmworkers, 275, 279
Cha, Dia, 198
Chachaji's Cup, 196
Chair for My Mother, A, 214, 233
Chalk, Gary, 166
Chamberlain, Julia, 12
Chamberlain, Margaret, 103
Champions on the Bench: The Cannon Street YMCA All-Stars, 185
Chang, Ni, 186–191
Chanticleer and the Fox, 93, 94
Chapman, Jane, 75
Charley Skedaddle, 248, 262
Charlie and the Chocolate Factory, 123, 141
Charlotte's Web, 33, 45, 150, 156, 157, 167
Chasing the Falconers, 220, 232
Chasing Vermeer, 223, 231
Chast, Roz, 69
Chato's Kitchen, 155, 167
Chaucer, Geoffrey, 93, 94
Chavarría-Cháirez, Becky, 213, 231
Chen, Ju-Hong, 103
Cheng, Lilly, 187
Cherry, Lynne, 59, 60, 151, 165, 292
Chi, Marilyn Mei-Ying, 189
Chicka Chicka ABC, 64
Chicka Chicka Boom Boom, 69
Chicka Chicka 1 2 3, 71

Chief Red Cloud: 1822–1909, 275, 280
Chief Tecumseh, 268, 280
Child, Francis James, 94
Child of the Owl, 256, 263
Child of the Wolves, 163, 166
Children of the Great Depression, 293, 295
Children of the Longhouse, 241, 262
Child's Garden of Verses, A, 302
Chin, Charlie, 96
China's Bravest Girl: The Legend of Hua Mu Lan, 96
Chin-Lee, Cynthia, 189
Chisholm, Margaret, 108
Chizuwa, Masayuki, 71
Chodos-Irvine, Margaret, 190–191
Choi, Yangsook, 189
Choo Choo: The Story of a Little Engine Who Ran Away, 120, 140
Christelow, Eileen, 64, 70, 71
Christie, R. Gregory, 183, 280
Christmas Carol, A, 5, 6, 25
Christmas in the Big House, Christmas in the Quarters, 247, 262
Christopher, Matt, 267, 279
Chronicles of Narnia, The (series), 129
Cianciolo, Patricia Jean, 76
Ciardi, John, 303
Cinco de Mayo (Hoyt-Goldsmith & Migdale), 181
Cinco de Mayo (Wade & Vargus), 181
Cinderella, 104
Cinderella and Other Tales by the Brothers Grimm, 104
Cinderella, or the Little Glass Slipper, 106
Cisneros, Sandra, 179–180
City of Ember, The, 136, 141
Claire, Elizabeth, 105
CLAMP, 192
Clark, Brenda, 165
Clark, Margaret Goff, 246, 262
Claybourne, Anna, 96
Cleary, Beverly, 28, 33, 45, 158, 165, 206, 212, 214, 231
Clemens, Samuel (*see* Twain, Mark)
Clements, Bruce, 244, 262
Cleopatra, 56, 61, 264, 269, 280
Click, Clack, Moo: Cows That Type, 158, 165
Clifford the Big Red Dog, 156, 165
Climo, Shirley, 94, 105

Cobb, Vicki, 267, 294
Code Talker: A Novel About the Navajo Marines of World War Two, 195
Coerr, Eleanor, 274, 279
Coffin, Tristram Potter, 94, 99
Coffin on a Case, 207, 224, 231
Cohen, Caron Lee, 101, 103
Cohen, Jan Barger, 181
Colbath, Mary Lou, 128
Cole, Joanna, 292, 294
Colfer, Eoin, 14, 24, 135, 140
Collard, Sneed B., 285, 294–295
Collector of Moments, The, 198
Collier, Bryan, 184
Collodi, Carlo, 6, 24, 119, 141
Colman, Audrey, 166, CI-6
Color Dance, 72
Comenius, Johann, 285
Come Sing, Jimmy Jo, 227, 233
Complete Fairy Tales of Charles Perrault, 104
Compton, Joanne, 102
Compton, Kenn, 102
Conrad, Pam, 134, 141
Coolies, 191
Cooney, Barbara, 45, 50, 61, 94, 109, 166, 232, 234, 239, 243, 249, 262, CI-5
Cooper, Floyd, 303
Cooper, Ilene, 274, 279
Cooper, Susan, 199
Corduroy, 119, 141
Cornell, Laura, 232, CI-4
Cornett, C. F., 209
Cornett, Claudia E., 59, 209
Cosmo and the Robot, 135, 142
Cottrell, Robert C., 199
Couloumbis, Audrey, 228, 231
Count and See, 70, 71
Counting Coup: Becoming a Crow Chief on the Reservation and Beyond, 193
Counting Crocodiles, 71
Count with the Very Hungry Caterpillar, 71
Coville, Bruce, 132, 136, 141
Cowan, Catherine, 121, 142, CI-3
Coyote Stories for Children: Tales from Native America, 100, 103
Crampton, Gertrude, 16, 25, 119–120, 141
Crane, Lucy, 86, 88
Crane, Walter, 7

Creech, Sharon, 33, 45, 215–216, 227, 228, 231–232
Crews, Donald, 71, 172, 176
Crews, Nina, 58, 60, 109
Cricket in Times Square, The, 158–159, 167, 330–331
Crickwing, 162, 165
Crispin: The Cross of Lead, 240, 262
Cronin, Doreen, 158, 159, 165
Crossing Bok Chitto: A Choctaw Tale of Friendship and Freedom, 193, 194–195
Crumpler, T., 118
Cruz, Ray, 50, 56, 61, 168, 233
Crystal Drop, The, 135, 141
C. S. Lewis: Author of Mere Christianity, 195
Cubes, Cones, Cylinders & Spheres, 58, 61
Cullinan, Bernice E., 19, 101, 297
Cummings, Pat, 102
Cunningham, Patricia M., 319–320
Curious George, 159, 166
Curtis, Christopher Paul, 53, 56, 59, 60, 184, 251–252, 256–258, 262, 312
Curtis, Jamie Lee, 228, 232, CI-4
Cushman, Karen, 199, 241, 262

Daddy's Lullaby, 213, 231
Daggie Dogfoot, 197
Dahl, Roald, 121, 123, 141
Daisy Comes Home, 198
Daly, Niki, 197
Dancing Dragon, The, 181
D'Angelo, Karen, 76
Dangerous Alphabet, The, 68
Daniel, Alan, 166
Daniels, H., 42
Danny Dunn and the Homework Machine, 137, 143
D'Antonio, Sandra, 95
Danziger, Paula, 216, 232
Dare to Dream! 25 Extraordinary Lives, 276, 280
Dasent, George Webbe, 105
Dave at Night, 196
Davidson, Margaret, 272, 279
Davies, Nicola, 295
Davy Crockett Saves the World, 98
Day, Alexandra, 77
Days of the Blackbird: A Tale of Northern Italy, 105

Days with Frog and Toad, 4, 25
Day We Walked on the Moon, The, 288, 291, 295
de Angeli, Marguerite, 240, 262
Dear Mr. Henshaw, 33, 45, 214, 231
Dear Mr. Rosenwald, 182, 183
DeCasper, Anthony J., 18
Deedy, Carmen Agra, 180, 199
Deep Blue Sea: A Book of Colors, The, 72
Defoe, Daniel, 5, 25
DeHaven, Edna P., 315
Deitz Shea, Pegi, 181
DeJong, Meindert, 29, 163, 165
Delacre, Lulu, 95, 104, 180, 198
Delafosse, Claude, 285, 295
Delivering Justice: W. W. Law and the Fight for Civil Rights, 185
Denyer, Susan, 8, 25
dePaola, Tomie, 49, 55, 60, 75, 85, 88, 90, 100, 104, 105, 108, 109, 117, 141, 159, 165, 181, 207, 213, 228, 232, CI-3
de Regniers, Beatrice Schenk, 297
Desimini, Lisa, 58, 60, 310
Desnick, Chaim, 196
Devil's Arithmetic, The, 3, 25, 38, 45, 127, 143
Devon, Paddie, 195
Dexter, Catherine, 199
Diamond in the Sky: A Suzuki Biography, 275, 279
Diary of a Wimpy Kid: A Novel in Cartoons, 13, 14, 25, 219, 232
Diary of a Worm, 159, 165
Dia's Story Cloth, 198
Diaz, David, 185, 231
Dicamillo, Kate, 153, 158, 165, 230, 232
Dickens, Charles, 5, 6, 25
Dillon, Diane, 34, 45, 47, 56, 60, 102, 303
Dillon, Leo D., 34, 45, 47, 56, 60, 102, 303
Dinosaurs before Dark, 127, 142
DiSalvo-Ryan, DyAnne, 232
DiTerlizzi, Tony, 122, 141
Dive (series), 220
Doctor Bird: Three Lookin' Up Tales from Jamaica, 105, 198
Doctor De Soto, 154, 167
Dodge, Mary Mapes, 6, 25
Dodgson, Charles (*see* Carroll, Lewis)
Dodson, Peter, 68
Dog of Knots, The, 199
Dogsong, 220, 233

Dolphin, Laurie, 198
Donelson, Kenneth L., 2, 128
Donkin, Andrew, 14, 24
Donnelly, Judy, 295
Don't Let the Pigeon Drive the Bus!, 159, 167
Doorbell Rang, The, 75
Door in the Wall, The, 240, 262
Dorman, Brandon, 311
Dorris, Michael, 241, 262
Dorros, Arthur, 122, 141, CI-6
Dots, Spots, Speckles, and Stripes, 73
Double Fudge, 213, 231
Doudna, Kelly, 74
Dragon and the Unicorn, The, 151, 165
Dragonball Z, 192
Dragon Dance, 181
Dragon of Doom, The, 132, 141
Dragon's Gate, 250, 263
Dragonwings, 250, 263
Dr. Ernest Drake's Dragonology, 159, 167
Dreyer, Sharon S., 209
Drinking Gourd, The, 246, 262
Driscoll, Sally, 207
Drop of Water, A, 291, 295
Dr. Seuss's ABC, 67, 69
Drummer Hoff, 46, 54, 56, 61, 75
DuBrowa, Melissa, 181
Duel of the Ironclads: The Monitor vs. the Virginia, 295
Duffy and the Devil, 101–102, 104
DuPrau, Jeanne, 136, 141
Dyer, Jane, 64

Each Orange Had 8 Slices, 71
Earthquakes, 288, 295
East of the Sun and West of the Moon and Other Norwegian Fairy Tales, 105
Eating the Alphabet: Fruits & Vegetables from A to Z, 66, 68
Ed Emberley's ABC, 66, 68
Edmonds, Walter D., 193, 242
Egypt Game, The, 171, 176
Egyptian Cinderella, The, 105
Ehlert, Lois, 54, 60, 66, 68, 69, 71, 72
Eitelgeorge, J. S., 114
Eleanor Roosevelt, 268, 280
Eleanor Roosevelt: First Lady of the World, 269, 279

Elementary Reading Attitude Survey, 210
Elijah of Buxton, 184
Elijah's Tears: Stories for the Jewish Holidays, 196
Elijah's Violin & Other Jewish Fairy Tales, 106
Ella Enchanted, 116, 141
Ellington Was Not a Street, 183, 185
Ellis, Deborah, 198
Emberley, Barbara, 46, 61, 75
Emberley, Ed, 46, 54, 55, 56, 61, 66, 68, 75
Emberley, Michael, 166
Emberley, Rebecca, 181
Emma, 213, 232
Emperor and the Kite, The, 107
Empire State Building: When New York Reached for the Skies, 295
Encyclopedia Brown and the Case of the Slippery Salamander, 222, 233
Encyclopedia Brown, Boy Detective, 222–223, 233
Enduring Wisdom: Sayings from Native Americans, 194
Engle, Margarita, 267, 279
English Fairy Tales, 84
Enormous Carrot, The, 105
Eragon, 132, 142
Erdrich, Liselotte, 194
Erdrich, Louise, 194
Eric Carle's Opposites, 74
Erie Canal, The, 95
ER Vets: Life in an Animal Emergency Room, 295
Esbensen, Barbara Juster, 303
Estrella's Quinceanera, 181
Everest (series), 220
Evetts-Secker, Josephine, 92
Evslin, Bernard, 91
Evslin, Dorothy, 91
Extraordinary Egg, An, 161, 166

Faber, Doris, 269, 279
Fables, 152, 166, 316
Face at the Window, The, 198
Facing the Lion: Growing Up Maasai on the African Savannah, 197
Falconer, Ian, 64, 155, 165
Falling Up, 311
Family of Poems: My Favorite Poetry for Children, A, 310
Fantastic Beasts and Where to Find Them, 142
Farest, Cindy, 327–328

Farolitos for Abuelo, 104
Fasting and Dates, 181
Father and Son Tales, 92
Father Who Had 10 Children, The, 198
Faulkner, Matt, 103
Favorite Norse Myths, 92
Feiffer, Jules, 228, 232
Feinberg, Barbara Jane, 268, 279
Felita, 56, 61, 168, 173, 176, 227, 232
Feng, Jianhua, 187
Fenton, R. E., 187
Fever 1793, 243, 261
Finch, Mary, 105
Field Guide, The, 122, 141
Finding Buck McHenry, 34, 45
Fire and Ice, 162, 166
First Dog, The, 159, 165
Fish, Helen Dean, 28, 45
Fisher, C. B., 187
Fisher, Leonard Everett, 96
Five Little Monkeys Jumping on the Bed, 64, 70, 71
Flanagan, John, 132
Fleischman, Paul, 77, 247–248, 262, 310
Flood, Nancy Bo, 194
Florczak, Robert, 105
Florez, V., 177
Flossie & the Fox, 121, 141
Fly Away Home, 207, 225, 231
Flying with the Eagle, Racing the Great Bear: Stories from Native North America, 103
Fool of the World and the Flying Ship, The, 88, 89, 100, 105
Foon, Stanley W., 181
Forbes, Esther, 35, 45, 243, 262
Ford, Pamela Baldwin, 105
Forest of Secrets, 162, 166
Fortnum, Peggy, 165
Foster's War, 254, 263
Four Corners of the Sky, The, 92
Four Hungry Kittens, 77
Fourth Question: A Chinese Tale, The, 102, 103
Fox, Mem, 64
Fox, Paula, 29, 225, 232, 246, 262
Fox in Socks, 151, 167
Franco, Betsy, 73
Frank, Anne, 274, 279
Franklin in the Dark, 152, 155, 165
Freckle Juice, 218, 231

Frederick, 38, 45, 161, 166
Freedman, Russell, 29, 283, 293, 295, 325
Freedom Crossing, 246, 262
Freedom on the Menu: The Greensboro Sit-In,
    182, 183
Freedom Riddle, The, 185
Freedom Songs, 256, 262
Freedom Walkers: The Story of the Montgomery
    Bus Boycott, 293, 295
Freeman, A., 177, 179
Freeman, D., 177
Freeman, Don, 119, 141
Freeman, Evelyn B., 286, 287
Freeman, Y., 177
Friedrich, Elizabeth, 251, 262
Friends, The, 198
Friends from the Other Side / Amigos del Otro
    Lado, 178, 179
Friendship, The, 252, 263
Fritz, Jean, 29, 269, 270, 272, 274, 277,
    279–280, 295, 325
Frog and Toad All Year, 33, 36, 45
Frog and Toad Are Friends, 13, 25, 116, 141,
    152, 166
Frog and Toad Together, 34–35, 36, 37, 45, 61, 144
Frog Brings Rain, 103, 194
Frog Goes to Dinner, 77
Frog Prince, The, 101, 104
Frogs, 55, 61, 281, 288–289, 295
Frog Went A-Courtin', 95
From Acorn to Zoo: And Everything in Between
    in Alphabetical Order, 66, 67, 68, 69
From the Bellybutton of the Moon and Other
    Summer Poems / Del Ombligo de la Luna y
    Otros Poemas de Verano, 179, 309, 310
From the Earth to the Moon, 135, 142
From the Mixed-Up Files of Mrs. Basil E.
    Frankweiler, 223, 232
Fu, D., 77
Fu, Shelly, 92
Funke, Cornelia, 198
Funny Little Woman, The, 103

Gaber, Susan, 105
Gaier, Mary, 218
Gaiman, Neil, 68
Galdone, Paul, 70, 71, 101, 103
Galland, Antoine, 82, 84, 113

Gambrell, L. B., 77, 78
Gammell, Stephen, 231
Gantos, Jack, 229, 232
García, Stephanie, 57, 61, 180, CI-2
Gardner, H., 58
Garland, Michael, 262
Garrett, Leslie, 268, 280
Garza, Carmen Lomas, 180
Gathering of Days: A New England Girl's
    Journal, 1830–32, 244, 262
Gathering the Sun: An Alphabet in Spanish and
    English, 68
Gauchada, 198
Geeslin, C., 130
Geisel, Theodore Seuss (see Seuss, Dr.)
George, Jean Craighead, 163, 165, 207, 219,
    221, 232, 325
George, Kristine O'Connell, 310
George Crum and the Saratoga Chip, 185
George Lopez: Latino King of Comedy, 267, 280
George Shrinks, 122, 141
George Washington: An American Life, 268, 279
Gergely, Tibor, 25, 141
Gerson, L., 189
Getting Near to Baby, 228, 231
Giacobbe, Beppe, 310
Giant Dinosaurs of the Jurassic, 288, 295
Gibbons, Gail, 55, 60, 281, 288–289, 295
Giblin, James Cross, 295
Giff, Patricia Reilly, 216, 232
Gifford, Clive, 295
Giganti, Paul, 71
Gilchrist, Jan Spivey, 184, 303, 310
Gillet, Jean Wallace, 287, 316
Gingerbread Boy, The, 101, 103
Giovanni, Nikki, 184
Give Me Liberty: The Story of the Declaration of
    Independence, 293, 295
Giver, The, 37, 45, 123–124, 141
Giving Tree, The, 120, 142
Glasser, Robin Preiss, 77, 233
Glazer, Joan I., 13, 31
Gloria Estefan, 267, 279
Glorious Flight: Across the Channel with Louis
    Blériot, July 25, 1909, 274, 280
Gnojewski, Carol, 196
Going Home, 227, 232
Going to Bed Book, The, 64, 65

Golden Compass, The, 204

Golden Goblet, The, 199, 239–240, 262

Golden Mountain Chronicles (series), 245, 250, 253, 255–256

Goldilocks and the Three Bears, 104

Golem, 97

Gonzales, Edward, 104

Gonzalez, Lucia M., 104

González, Maya Christina, 179, 180, 310

Goode, Diane, 263, CI-5

Good-Luck Cat, The, 194

Good Night, Garden Gnome, 77

Good Night, Gorilla, 64

Goodnight Moon, 64, 155, 165

Good Night, Sweet Butterflies: A Color Dreamland, 64, 72

Gordon, Jeffie Ross, 70, 71

Gospel Cinderella, The, 185

Graham, Margaret Bloy, 167

Grahame, Kenneth, 148–149, 156, 166

Grandmother's Nursery Rhymes / Las Nanas de Abuelita, 109

Grandpa Was a Cowboy and an Indian, and Other Stories, 194

Grandpre, Mary, 49, 51, 54, 61, 111

Granier-Deferre, C., 18

Graston, Arlene, 115, 140

Gray, Elizabeth Janet, 199, 240, 262

Great Interactive Dream Machine, The, 135–136, 142

Great Kapok Tree: A Tale of the Amazon Rain Forest, The, 59, 60, 292

Greaves, Margaret, 103

Green, Connie R., 183

Green, Jen, 92

Green, Michael, 143

Green, Michelle Y., 184

Greenaway, Kate, 7, 26, 49, 302

Greene, Bette, 254, 262

Greene, Ellin, 103, 106

Green Eggs and Ham, 151, 167

Greenfield, Eloise, 184, 218, 232, 303, 310

Green Line: The Division of Palestine, The, 199

Gregory, Kristiana, 243, 262

Gregory Cool, 59, 60

Griego, Margot C., 109

Grifaloni, Ann, 183

Grimes, Nikki, 184, 310

Grimley, Gris, 68

Grimm, Jacob, 82, 84, 104, 113

Grimm, Wilhelm, 82, 84, 104, 113

Grindler, Martha C., 209, 211

Griswold, Diane L., 16

Groff, Patrick, 76

Grolier Classroom Publishing, 287, 288

Grouchy Ladybug, The, 160, 165

Grover, Eulalie Osgood, 109

Grumpy Shepherd, The, 195

Guardians of Ga'Hoole (series), 162

Guess How Much I Love You?, 64, 155, 166

Guettier, Benedicte, 198

Guevara, Susan, 167

Gulliver's Travels, 5, 25

Gunning, Monica, 198

Gunning, Thomas G., 19

Gustafson, Scott, 140

Guzman, Lila, 267, 280

Hadaway, N. L., 177

Hafner, Marilyn, 310

Hague, Michael, 141

Hahn, Mary Downing, 255, 262

Hahn, Nhat, 196

Haley, Gail E., 102

Half and Half, 190

Hall, Donald, 36, 45, 243, 262, CI-5

Hall, Elizabeth, 163, 166

Hamanaka, Sheila, 189

Hamilton, Virginia, 29, 102, 223, 232

Handler, Daniel (*see* Snicket, Lemony)

Hans Brinker or the Silver Skates, 6, 25

Hans Christian Andersen: The Complete Fairy Tales and Stories, 115, 140

Hansel and Gretel, 102, 104

Hansen, Joyce, 229, 232

Hanson, Regina, 198

Hare and the Tortoise, The, 94

Harjo, Joy, 194

Harris, Joel Chandler, 84, 88, 99, 102

Harris, K., 208

Harris, Robie H., 204

Harris, Theodore L., 20

Harrison, Michael, 310

Harry Houdini, 267

Harry Potter and the Chamber of Secrets, 131, 142

Harry Potter and the Deathly Hallows, 131, 142

Harry Potter and the Goblet of Fire, 131, 142
Harry Potter and the Half-Blood Prince, 131, 142
Harry Potter and the Order of the Phoenix,
    131, 142
Harry Potter and the Prisoner of Azkaban, 131, 142
Harry Potter and the Sorcerer's Stone, 37, 45, 54,
    61, 111, 130–131, 142, 197
Harry the Dirty Dog, 156, 167
Harwayne, Shelley, 72
Haskins, James, 185
Hastings, Selina, 96
Hatcher, B., 176
Hatchet, 22, 25, 34, 37, 45, 220, 233
Haugaard, Eric Christian, 115, 140
Hausman, Gerald, 105, 198
Haverfield, Mary, 141
Hawkes, Kevin, 77
Haymeadow, The, 207, 220, 233
Hays, Michael, 142, 172, 176
Hector Protector and As I Went over the Water,
    108, 109
Heidi, 6, 25
Helen Keller: A Photographic Story of a Life,
    268, 280
Heller, Linda, 106
Heller, Ruth, 105
Helquist, Brett, 231
Henkes, Kevin, 152, 156, 166, 204, 214, 232
Henry and Mudge and the Happy Cat, 156, 166
*Henry and Mudge: The First Book of Their
    Adventures,* 13, 25
*Henry's Freedom Box: A True Story from the
    Underground Railroad,* 183
Henterly, Jamichael, 77
Heo, Yumi, 189
Hepler, Susan, 5, 11, 85, 229
*Here Comes Our Bride! An African Wedding
    Story,* 197
*Here's What You Do When You Can't Find Your
    Shoe,* 310
Herford, Oliver, 301
Hermit and the Well, The, 196
Hernandez, Antonio, 198
Hero and the Crown, The, 130, 141
*Her Stories: African American Folktales, Fairy
    Tales, and True Tales,* 102
Hesse, Karen, 123, 133, 141, 251, 262
Hewitt Anderson's Great Big Life, 183

Hey Al, 126, 143
*Hey Diddle Diddle and Other Mother Goose
    Rhymes,* 108, 109
Hiaasen, Carl, 228, 232
Hickman, Janet, 5, 11, 85, 229
Hidden World: Human Body, 285, 295
Hideout, The, 214, 231
Hiebert, E. H., 313
Highwayman, The, 302
Hill, Kirkpatrick, 255, 262
Hillenbrand, Will, 71
Hillman, Judith, 2, 5, 18
Himler, Ronald, 231
Hirsch, Eric Donald, Jr., 91, 93
*History of Little Goody Two Shoes,
    The,* 5, 25
Hoban, Russell, 155, 166
Hoban, Tana, 58, 61, 70, 71, 73
Hobbit, The, 128–129, 142
Hoberman, Mary Ann, 95, 303
Hodges, Margaret, 96, 97
Hodges, Richard E., 20
Hoffman, B., 187, 232
Hoffman, James V., 327–328
Hoffman, Mary, 228
Hogrogian, Nonny, 101, 105
Holes, 224, 233
Holm, Jennifer L., 14, 25
Holub, Joan, 181
Holub, Regan, 181
Homeless Bird, 198
Home of the Brave, 190
Homesick: My Own Story, 272, 280
Hoopes, Ned, 91
Hoose, Phillip, 295
Hoot, 228, 232
Hopkinson, Deborah, 295
Hoppenstedt, Elbert M., 295
Hopping, Lorraine Jean, 285, 295
Horacek, Petr, 72
Horowitz, Anthony, 136, 141
Horse and His Boy, The, 129, 141
Hort, Lenny, 268, 280
House at Pooh Corner, The, 119, 142
*Household Stories from the Collection of the
    Bros. Grimm,* 86, 88
House of Dies Drear, The, 223, 232
House on Mango Street, 179–180

Houston, Gloria, 35, 40–42, 45, 50, 59, 60, 93, 170, 234, 237, 238–239, 246–247, 250–251, 254, 262
Howard, Kim, 104
Howe, Deborah, 157, 166
Howe, James, 157, 166
Howell, Troy, 92
Howliday Inn, 157, 166
How Rabbit Tricked Otter and Other Cherokee Trickster Stories, 194
How the Grinch Stole Christmas!, 151, 167
How They Got Over: African Americans and the Call to Sea, 184
How to Disappear Completely and Never Be Found, 138, 142
How to Eat Fried Worms, 207, 233
How Turtle's Back Was Cracked: A Traditional Cherokee Tale, 100, 103
How Willy Got His Wheels, 157, 167
Ho Yi the Archer and Other Classic Chinese Tales, 92
Hoyt-Goldsmith, Diane, 181
Huang, Bernard, 181
Huck, Charlotte S., 5, 11, 85, 104, 210, 229
Hudson, Hugh, 276, 280
Hughes, Langston, 301, 310
Hughes, Libby, 267, 280
Hughes, Monica, 135, 141
Hulme, Joy N., 70, 71
Hummingbird Nest: A Journal of Poems, 310
Humphrey, Sandra McLeod, 276, 280
Hundredth Name, The, 196
Hungry, Hungry Sharks, 294
Hunt, Angela Elwell, 102
Hunt, Irene, 248, 259, 262
Hunt, Jane, 328
Hunter, Erin, 162, 166
Hurd, Clement, 64, 165
Hurray for Today!, 181
Hurry Home, Candy, 163, 165
Hutchins, Pat, 73, 74, 75
Hyman, Trina Schart, 97, 104
Hynes, Robert, 201

I Am Scout: The Biography of Harper Lee, 267, 280
I, Doko: The Tale of a Basket, 107
I Face the Wind, 294

Iggie's House, 227, 231
Iguanas in the Snow and Other Winter Poems, 310
I Have a Dream, 303, 310
"I Heard a Bird Sing," 301
I Know an Old Lady Who Swallowed a Fly, 95
I'll Always Love You, 207, 230, 233
I Love Saturdays and Domingos, 179
I Love You as Much . . ., 64
Immigrant Kids, 293, 295
In-Between Days, The, 214, 231
Inch by Inch, 161, 166
Incredible Journey, The, 163, 165
In Defense of Liberty: The Story of America's Bill of Rights, 283, 293, 295
Indian Shoes, 194
In Every Tiny Grain of Sand: A Child's Book of Prayers and Praise, 310
Inheritance (series), 132
In My Family / En Mi Familia, 180
Insects, 285, 295
Inside, Outside, Upside Down, 73, 74
Inside the Alamo, 295
Integrating Multiple Literacies in K–8 Classrooms: Cases, Commentaries, and Practical Applications, 59
In the Eye of the Tornado, 133, 141
In the Land of Words: New and Selected Poems, 310
In the Time of Drums, 97
In the Year of the Boar and Jackie Robinson, 255, 262
Into the Wild, 162, 166
Invention of Hugo Cabret: A Novel in Words and Pictures, The, 14, 25
Invincible Louisa, 273, 280
Ira Says Goodbye, 216, 233
Ira Sleeps Over, 229, 233
Ireland, G. O., 208
Isabel Allende: Award-Winning Latin American Author, 267, 280
Is a Dolphin a Fish? Questions and Answers about Dolphins, 294
Isadora, Rachel, 115, 140, 142
Ishi, Last of His Tribe, 2, 21, 25
Island (series), 220
Island of the Blue Dolphins, 245, 260, 263
I Spy: An Alphabet in Art, 69
I Spy Shapes in Art, 73

361

It Could Always Be Worse: A Yiddish Folk Tale, 106

I Tell a Lie Every So Often, 244, 262

Itse Selu: Cherokee Harvest Festival, 241, 263

It's Not the End of the World, 215, 231

It's Perfectly Normal, 204

Ivanhoe, 20, 25

I've Been Working on the Railroad, 95

I Was a Sixth Grade Alien, 136, 141

Jack and the Beanstalk, 103

Jackson, B., 16, 25

Jackson, Donna, 295

Jackson, K., 16, 25

Jack: The Early Years of John F. Kennedy, 274, 279

Jacob, Murv, 103

Jacob Have I Loved, 254, 263

Jacobs, Frank, 310

Jacobs, Joseph, 84

Jacques, Brian, 14, 25, 155, 166

Jaffe, Nina, 105

Jaguar, 198

Jalongo, M., 209

Jamela's Dress, 197

James, Helen Foster, 68

James and Dolly Madison and Their Times, 275, 280

Jammin' with the Jonas Brothers, 276, 280

Jaramillo, Nelly Palocio, 109

Jason and the Golden Fleece, 88, 89

Jataka Tales, The, 93

Jay, Alison, 71

Jeffers, Susan, 173–174, 176

Jenkins, Leonard, 185

Jenkins, Steve, 73, 77, 295

Jeram, Anita, 64, 166

Jesse Owens: Fastest Man Alive, 182, 183

Jesus, I Feel Close to You, 195

Jia, Bo, 191

Jim Thorpe, Original All-American, 195, 267, 279

Jingle Dancer, 194

Jip: His Story, 247, 263

J. K. Rowling, 267, 280

Joey Pigza Swallowed the Key, 229, 232

John Henry, 97

John McCain, 268, 279

Johnny Appleseed, 98

Johnny Tremain, 35, 45, 243, 262

Johnson, Angela, 213, 232

Johnson, Anne Akers, 284, 295

Johnson, Janet P., 98

Johnson, Steven T., 68

Johnston, Tony, 244, 262

Jonas, Ann, 72

Jones, Malcolm, 84, 88

Jonke, Tim, 102

Jordan, Deloris, 183

Jordan, Roslyn M., 183

Jordan, Shirley, 295

Journey (MacLachlan), 215, 232

Journey, The (Lasky), 162, 166

Journey Home, 224–225, 232

Journey of the Sparrows, 226, 231

Journey to the Center of the Earth, 5, 6, 25

Joyce, William, 122, 141

Juan Bobo Goes to Work: A Puerto Rican Folktale, 100, 104

Judge, Lita, 68

Judson, Clara Ingram, 28

Judy Moody, 218, 232

Julie, 221, 232

Julie of the Wolves, 207, 221, 232

Julie's Wolf Pack, 163, 165

Jumanji, 127, 142

Jump Again! More Adventures of Brer Rabbit, 88, 99, 102

Jump! The Adventures of Brer Rabbit, 88

Junebug, 226, 232

Juneteenth Jamboree, 182, 184

Jungle Book, The, 6, 25, 147–148, 166

Junie B. Jones and the Stupid Smelly Bus, 218, 232

Just a Minute: A Trickster Tale and Counting Book, 180

Just So Stories, 117, 141

Just the Two of Us, 182, 183

Kadohata, Cynthia, 255, 262

Kamikaze Kaito Jeanne, 192

Kaplan, Kathy Walden, 199

Katin, Miriam, 105

Katz, Bobbi, 310

Kear, D., 210

Keats, Ezra Jack, 56, 61, 182, 183, 238

Keelboat Annie: An African-American Legend, 98

Keeping the Rope Straight: Annie Dodge Wauneka's Life of Service to the Navajo, 268, 280

Kellogg, Steven, 98
Kemp-Welch, Lucy, 167
Kennedy, Caroline, 310
Kennedy, X. J., 303
Kesselman, Wendy, 213, 232
Khala Maninge: An African Fable—The Little Elephant That Cried a Lot, 94
Khan, Rukhsana, 196, 198
Kidd, Ronald, 95
Kidnapped, 6, 25
Kiefer, Barbara Z., 5, 11, 85, 229
Kightley, Rosalinda, 72, 73
Kim, Angela, 187
Kimmel, Eric A., 92
King, F. J., III, 175
King, Martin Luther, Jr., 303, 310
King Arthur & His Knights, 96
Kingdom Hearts, 192
King's Equal, The, 117, 142
King-Smith, Dick, 157, 158, 166, 197
Kinney, Jeff, 13, 14, 25, 219, 232
Kipling, Rudyard, 6, 25, 117, 141, 147–148, 166
Kira-Kira, 255, 262
Kitamura, Satoshi, 66, 67, 68, 69, 136, 141
Kitchen, Bert, 94
Kitten's First Full Moon, 156, 166
Klaus, Annette Curtis, 135, 141
Klesius, Janell, 218
Kleven, Elisa, 141
Knee-Knock Rise, 37, 45
Knell, Susan E., 42–44, 77–79
Knights of the Kitchen Table, 127, 142
Konigsburg, E. L., 223, 232
Korman, Gordon, 220, 232
Kotzwinkle, William, 157, 166, CI-6
Kovalski, Maryann, 74, 75
Krebs, Laurie, 71
Krishnaswami, Uma, 196, 198
Kroeber, Theodora, 2, 21, 25
Krush, Beth, 142
Krush, Joe, 142
Kunhardt, Dorothy, 16, 25, 64
Kunkel, Dennis, 295
Kurtz, Jane, 197, 310
Kuskin, Karla, 303

Labbo, Linda D., 327–328
Lady of Guadalupe, The, 181

Lady with the Hat, The, 199
Lafcadio, the Lion Who Shot Back, 160, 167
La Fontaine, Jean de, 84, 93
Laframboise, Kathryn L., 218
LaGarrique, Jerome, 183
Laiz, Jana, 224, 232
Lamb, Christine, 103
Lamb, Susan Condie, 61
Lamm, C. Drew, 198
Lamme, L. L., 77
Land, The, 249, 252, 263
Landaw, Jonathan, 196
Landowne, Youme, 198
Lane, B., 187
Lang, Andrew, 84
Langstaff, John, 95
Language of Birds, The, 105
Lasky, Kathryn, 162, 166
Last Battle, The, 129, 141
Lathrop, Dorothy, 28, 45
Laughing Tomatoes and Other Spring Poems, 309, 310
Laura Ingalls Wilder, 267, 279
Lawson, Cornelia V., 146
Layden, Joe, 295
Leah's Pony, 251, 262
Leal, Dorothy, 12
Lear, Edward, 300, 310
Leavell, J. A., 176
Leaves! Leaves! Leaves!, 56, 61, CI-2
Leavitt, Amie, 267, 280
Lecanuet, J. P., 18
Lee, Dom, 189, 232
Lee, Fran, 92
Lee, Ginny, 186, 188
Lee, Jared, 142
Lee, Keunhee, 232
Lee, Stacy J., 187
Leedy, Loreen, 295
Leeson, Robert, 105
Legacies: Using Children's Literature in the Classroom, 32
Le Guin, Ursula K., 151, 166
Lehman, Barbara, 77
Lekuton, Joseph Lemasolai, 197
L'Engle, Madeleine, 135, 141
Lent, Blair, 103
Lepscky, Ibi, 274, 280

Lesinski, Jeanne M., 268, 280
Lester, Julius, 84, 89, 97, 103
Let the Circle Be Unbroken, 253, 263
Levine, Ellen, 183
Levine, Gail Carson, 116, 141, 196
Levithan, David, 133, 141
Lewin, Betsy, 165
Lewin, Ted, 213, 232
Lewis, C. S., 34, 45, 129, 141
Lewis, E. B., 184
Li, S., 189
Library for Juana: The World of Sor Juana Ines, The, 180
Light in the Attic, A, 305, 311
Lightning Thief, The, 123
Lilly, Elizabeth, 183
Lincoln: A Photobiography, 293
Lindbergh, Reeve, 310
Lindgren, Astrid, 199
Lion and the Mouse and Other Aesop's Fables, The, 94
Lionni, Leo, 35, 38, 45, 56, 59, 61, 119, 120, 141, 161, 166
Lion, the Witch and the Wardrobe, The, 34, 45, 129, 141
Lisker, Sonia O., 231
Literacy Assessment for Today's Schools, 75
Literature Circles: Voice and Choice in the Student-Centered Classroom, 42
Little Bear, 12, 25, 155, 166
Little Black Sambo, 182
Little Blue and Little Yellow, 120, 141
Little Brown Jay: A Tale from India, The, 105
Little House in the Big Woods, 238, 248, 263
Little House on the Prairie, 33, 34, 45, 263
Littlejim, 251, 262
Littlejim's Dreams, 251, 262
Littlejim's Gift, 251, 262
Little Lord Fauntleroy, 6, 24
Little Match Girl, The, 115, 140
Little Prince, The, 135, 142
Little Red Ant and the Great Big Crumb: A Mexican Fable, The, 94
Little Red Riding Hood and Other Stories, 104
Little Room, The, 196
Littlest Angel, The, 134, 142, CI-1
Little Woman Warrior Who Came Home: A Story of the Navajo Long Walk, 245–246, 263

Little Women, 6, 24, 238, 261, 273
Livingston, Myra Cohn, 303
Lloyd, Sam, 72
Lo, Suzanne, 186, 188
Lobel, Anita, 74, 104
Lobel, Arnold, 4, 13, 25, 33, 34–35, 36, 37, 45, 49, 61, 116, 141, 144, 152, 166, 316
Locker, Thomas, 54, 60, 296, 310
Lofting, Hugh, 123, 141
London, Jack, 148, 163, 166
London, Jonathan, 54, 60, 296, 310
Longfellow, Henry Wadsworth, 302
Long Way from Chicago, A, 252, 263
Lon Po Po: A Red-Riding Hood Story from China, 54, 56, 61, 80, 103, 107
Looking Down, 77
Loony Limericks, 310
Lord, Bette Bao, 255, 262
Lord of the Rings, 128
Lorenzini, Carlo (see Collodi, Carlo)
Lost Colony of Roanoke, 295
Lost Horse, The, 107
Lost in Cyberspace, 135, 142
Lost Lake, The, 172, 176
Louie, Ai-Ling, 268, 280
Louis Braille, the Boy Who Invented Books for the Blind, 272, 279
Love Letters, 58, 60
Lowrey, Janette Sebring, 16, 25, 150, 166
Lowry, Lois, 37, 45, 123–124, 141, 199, 254, 262
Lu, Mei-Yu, 186
Lucas, Katherine, 310
Luger, Harriet Mandelay, 225, 232
Lukens, Rebecca J., 35
Lund, Gary, 103
Lupita Mañana, 226, 231
Lurie, A., 106
Lyddie, 244, 247, 259, 263
Lynch-Brown, Carol, 14, 31
Lyons, Kelly Starling, 185

MacDonald, Suse, 67, 69
MacGregor, Ellen, 2, 25
Machado, Ana Maria, 198
MacHale, D. J., 14, 25, 126, 141
MacKall, Dandi Daley, 195
MacLachlan, Patricia, 215, 216, 232, 244, 249, 259, 262

MacMillan, Eric G., 94
MacMillan, Ian C., 94
Made for a Purpose, 195
Madeline, 138, 140
Madeline's Rescue, 138, 140
Maestro, Betsy, 290, 295
Maestro, The, 199
Magda's Tortillas, 213, 231
*Magical Encounter: Latino Children's Literature
    in the Classroom, A*, 44
Magician's Nephew, The, 129, 141
Magic School Bus, The (series), 292
*Magic Windows: Cut-Paper Art and Stories /
    Ventañas Magicas: Papel Picado y Relatos*, 180
Magid Fasts for Ramadan, 196
Maher, Ramona, 310
*Maiden of Northland: A Hero Tale of Finland,
    The*, 105
Main, Mary, 267, 280
Make Way for Ducklings, 150, 166
Malcolmson, Anne, 95
Malcolm X, 271, 279
Mama Provi and the Pot of Rice, 180
Maniac Magee, 226–227, 233
Man in the Ceiling, 228, 232
Mann, Elizabeth, 295
Mara, Wil, 274, 280
Marantz, K., 175
Marantz, S., 175
Marcellino, Fred, 104
Maria Von Trapp: Beyond the Sound of Music,
    268, 280
*Marriage of the Rain Goddess: A South African
    Myth*, 92
Marshall, James, 24, 29, 140
Martchenko, Michael, 142, 166
Martha Speaks, 156, 166
Martin, Bill, Jr., 64, 69, 71, 75, 310
Martin, Justin McCory, 74
Martin, Rafe, 105
Martin, Steve, 69
Martina the Beautiful Cockroach, 180
Martinez, Miriam, 39, 174
Martin Luther King, Jr., 268, 280
Marvis, Barbara J., 275, 280
Mary on Horseback: Three Mountain Stories,
    251, 263
Matchlock Gun, The, 193, 242

Matheson, David, 174, 194
Mathis, J. B., 177
Matilda, 123, 141
Matthews, Mary, 196
Maura's Angel, 199
May, J. P., 16
May, Robert L., 149–150, 166
Maya's Children: The Story of La Llorona, 104
Mayer, Marianna, 97, 105
Mayer, Mercer, 77, 121, 141
Mayfield Crossing, 256, 263
McBratney, Sam, 64, 155, 166
McCally, Emily Arnold, 77
McCloskey, Robert, 150, 166
McCord, David, 303
McCurdy, Michael, 98
McDaniel, Lurlene, 227, 232
McDermott, Gerald, 88, 89, 91, 92
McDonald, Megan, 218, 232
McGee, Lea M., 126
McGraw, Eloise Jarvis, 116–117, 141, 199,
    239–240, 262
McHugh, Rhonda, 157, 167
McKay, Lawrence, 224–225, 232
McKenna, Michael C., 59, 209, 210, 211
McKinley, Robin, 129–130, 141
McKissack, Fredrick L., 247, 262
McKissack, Patricia C., 121, 122, 141, 247, 262
McMillan, Bruce, 58
McNeil, Carla Speed, 14, 25
Mead, Alice, 226, 232
Meddaugh, Susan, 156, 166, 231
Medearis, Angela Shelf, 185
Medicine Crow, Joseph, 193
Mediopollito / Half-Chicken, 104
Meeker, Clare Hodgson, 103
Megaman, 192
Megan's Island, 223, 233
Meigs, Cornelia, 273, 280
Meinbach, Anita Meyer, 31, 32, 47
Melmed, Laura Krauss, 64
Meltzer, Milton, 29
Mendez, Consuelo, 179
Menninger, Karl, 208
Menninger, William, 208
Meow Ruff: A Story in Concrete Poetry, 311
*Merchant of Death: Pendragon Graphic Novel,
    The*, 14, 25

Merriam, Eve, 299, 303
Mesmer, Heidi Anne, 17
Metaxas, Eric, 98
Micich, Paul, 142, CI-1
Mick Harte Was Here, 228, 232
Micklethwait, Lucy, 69, 73
Midnight for Charlie Bone, 133, 142
Midsummer Knight, 14, 25
Midwife's Apprentice, The, 199, 241, 262
Migdale, Lawrence, 181
Mike Fink, 98
Mike Mulligan and His Steam Shovel, 120, 140
Milkweed, 253, 263
Miller, Dorothy Reynolds, 222
Miller, William, 275, 280
Milne, A. A., 119, 142, 302
Minarik, Else Holmelund, 12, 25, 155, 166
Minn and Jake, 311
Minnie and Moo and the Potato from Planet X, 158, 165
Minnie and Moo Go to the Moon, 158, 165
Minor, Wendell, 165
Mirandy and Brother Wind, 122, 142
Misoso: Once Upon a Time Tales from Africa, 102
Missing May, 214, 233
Missing Piece, The, 120, 142
Missing Piece Meets the Big O, The, 120, 142
Mississippi Bridge, 252, 263
Miss Nelson Has a Field Day, 137–138, 140
Miss Nelson Is Back, 137, 140
Miss Nelson Is Missing, 8, 24, 137, 140
Miss Pickerell Goes to Mars, 2, 25
Miss Rumphius, 249, 262
Mitchell, Margaree King, 35, 45, 251, 262
Mo, Weimin, 187
Mochizuki, Ken, 189
Moe, Jorgen, 83, 84, 105
Mohr, Kathleen A. J., 146
Mohr, Nicholasa, 56, 61, 168, 173, 176, 227, 232
Monjo, F. N., 246, 262
Monkey Island, 225, 232
Monroe, Judy, 275, 280
Monsoon, 198
Montes, Marisa, 100, 104
Monteverde: Science and Scientists in a Costa Rican Cloud Forest, 285, 295
Montgomery, Sy, 295
Moo Baa La La La, 64, 65

Moon, Sarah, 104
Moorchild, The, 116–117, 141
Moore, Clement C., 300, 302
Moore, Lilian, 303
Moore, Tony, 185
Moore, Yvette, 256, 262
Mora, Francisco X., 94
Mora, Pat, 177–178, 180
Morales, Yuyi, 180
More Tales of Uncle Remus: Further Adventures of Brer Rabbit, His Friends, Enemies, and Others, 89
More Than Anything Else, 248–249, 262
Morgenstern, Susie, 198
Morning Girl, 241, 262
Morrill, Leslie, 166
Morrison, Frank, 185
Morten, George, 187
Morton, Mary Lou, 307–308
Mosel, Arlene, 101, 103
Moser, Barry, 88, 102, 141, 295, 310
Moses: When Harriet Tubman Led Her People to Freedom, 182, 183, 184
Mose the Fireman, 98
Mosquito Bite, 295
Moss, Marissa, 251, 262
Mother Help Me Live, 227, 232
Mound, Laurence A., 285, 295
Mountain Jack Tales, 102
Mountain Light, 245, 263
Mountain Valor, 237, 247, 262
Mouse and the Motorcycle, The, 158, 165
Mouse Shapes, 73
Moxley, Sheila, 109
Mr. Lunch Takes a Plane Ride, 58, 61
Mr. Seahorse, 75, 161, 165
Mrs. Frisby and the Rats of NIMH, 158, 166
Mrs. Katz and Tush, 196
Mr. Tucket, 244, 263
Mud Pony, The, 101, 103
Mufaro's Beautiful Daughters: An African Tale, 102
Munsch, Robert, 117, 142, 157, 166
Munsinger, Lynn, 166
Murphy, Chuck, 73
Murphy, Jim, 295
Murray, Glenn, 157, 166, CI-6
Murray, Y. I., 178
Musgrove, Margaret, 66, 68, 69

Music for Alice, 190
Music of Dolphins, The, 123, 141
Muskrat Will Be Swimming, 201
Muslim Child: Understanding Islam through Stories and Poems, 196
Muth, Jon J., 104
Myers, Christopher, 310
Myers, Walter Dean, 215, 226, 232, 267, 280, 310
My First Book of Money: Counting Coins, 71
My Five Senses, 288, 294
My Grandma's Backyard, 185
My Great-Aunt Arizona, 59, 61
My Life in Dog Years, 230, 233
My Life with the Wave, 121, 142, CI-3
My Sister Shahrazad: Tales from the Arabian Nights, 105
Mysterious Benedict Society, The, 137
Myths of Ancient Greece, 92
My Very First Book of Numbers, 70, 71, 72
My Very First Book of Shapes, 72, 73
My Very Own Room / Mi Propio Cuartito, 180

Na, An, 190
Naden, Corinne J., 88, 89
Name Jar, The, 189
Naming Maya, 198
Namioka, Lensey, 190
Nana Upstairs & Nana Downstairs, 207, 228, 232
Napping House, The, 75, CI-4
Nash, Ogden, 310
National Football League Super Bowl, 295
Navajo: Visions and Voices across the Mesa, 310
Navajo Year: Walk through Many Seasons, The, 194
Naylor, Alice, 172
Naylor, Phyllis Reynolds, 173, 176, 222, 223, 230, 232
Negrin, Fabian, 198
Neighborhood Mother Goose, The, 58, 60, 109
Nelson, Kadir, 98, 182–183, 184, 185
Nelson, Vaunda Michaeux, 256, 263
Nelson Mandela, 268, 280
Never Mind! A Twin Novel, 33, 45
Newbery, John, 5, 25, 27
Nhuong, Huynh Quang, 190
Nickel, Scott, 14, 25
Nickerson, Sara, 138, 142

Niethammer, Carolyn, 268, 280
Night before Christmas, The, 300, 302
Nilsen, Alleen Pace, 2, 128
Nimmo, Jenny, 133, 142
Niña Bonita, 198
Nipp, Susan Hagen, 74
Nixon, Joan Lowery, 222, 224, 232
Noah's Ark, 77
No, David!, 219, 233
Nodelman, Perry, 54, 145, 204
Nolen, Jerdine, 98, 183
No Mirrors in My Nana's House, 184
Northrup, M., 106
Norton, Donna E., 11, 81
Norton, Mary, 122, 142
Norwegian Fairy Tales and Folklore, 83
Norwegian Folk Tales, 83, 105
Norwich, Grace, 267, 280
Now One Foot, Now the Other, 229, 232
Now We Are Six, 302
Noyes, Alfred, 302
Number the Stars, 199, 254, 262
Nursery and Household Tales, 82
Nye, Naomi Shihab, 310

O'Brien, Patrick, 295
O'Brien, Robert, 158, 166
O'Bruba, W., 208
O'Dell, Scott, 29, 243, 245, 260, 263
Officer Buckle and Gloria, 156, 166
Oh My Oh My Oh Dinosaurs!, 65
O, Jerusalem: Voices of a Sacred City, 311
Old Hannibal and the Hurricane, 122, 140
Old MacDonald Had a Farm, 95
Oldrieve, R. M., 17
Olive's Ocean, 204
Olivia, 155, 165
Olivia's Opposites, 64
Olson, Kay M., 268, 280
O'Malley, Judy, 197
Once a Mouse . . . : A Fable Cut in Wood, 36, 45, 93, 94
Once upon a Time! A Story of the Brothers Grimm, 275, 280
One Duck Stuck, 75
One Fine Day, 101, 105
One Fish Two Fish Red Fish Blue Fish, 151, 167
One Hundred Hungry Ants, 70, 71

One Hundred Ways to Get to 100, 71
One Hundred Years of Poetry for Children, 310
One Lighthouse, One Moon, 74
One Million Men and Me, 185
1-2-3: A Child's First Counting Book, 71
On the Field with Derek Jeter, 267, 279
On the Mound with Curt Schilling, 267, 279
On the Run (series), 220
On Top of Old Smoky: A Collection of Songs and Stories from Appalachia, 95
Onyefulu, Ifeoma, 197
Oppenheim, Shulamith Levey, 196
Oprah Winfrey: "I Don't Believe in Failure," 267, 280
Oram, Hiawyn, 105
Orbis Pictus, 285
Orgel, Doris, 94
Original Volland Edition of Mother Goose, The, 109
Orlev, Uri, 198, 199
Osborne, Mary Pope, 92, 97, 98, 127, 142
Ostorga, Alcione N., 176–180
Our Gracie Aunt, 214–215, 233
Our Journey from Tibet, 198
Out of the Dust, 251, 262
Ouzts, Dan, 208–212
Over in the Jungle: A Rainforest Rhyme, 71
Over in the Meadow, 70, 71
Owen, 152, 166
Owen, Ann, 95
Owen, Annie, 66, 69
Owl and the Pussycat, The, 310
Ox-Cart Man, 36, 45, 243, 262, CI-5

Pain and the Great One, The, 34, 45
Pallotta, Jerry, 68, 69, 70, 71
Palombo, Mark J., 208–212
Panchatantra, The, 93
Panda Bear, Panda Bear, What Do You See?, 75
Paolini, Christopher, 132, 142
Paper Bag Princess, The, 117, 142
Parish, Peggy, 138, 142
Park, Barbara, 17, 218–219, 228, 232
Park, Linda Sue, 190, 240, 263
Parks, Van Dyke, 84, 88, 99, 102
Park's Quest, 225, 233
Parms, Clifford Alexander, 92
Parnell, Peter, 204

Parzival: The Quest of the Grail Knight, 97
Paschen, Elise, 310
Passage to Freedom: The Sugihara Story, 189
Pastan, Amy, 268, 280
Patent, Dorothy Henshaw, 283
Paterson, Katherine, 29, 97, 117, 142, 207, 216, 225, 227, 233, 240, 244, 247, 254, 259, 263
Patrick, Patron Saint of Ireland, 181
Patriot School: The United States Military Academy at West Point, 294
Pat the Bunny, 16, 25, 64
Paul Bunyan, 98
Paul Revere's Ride, 302
Paulsen, Gary, 22, 25, 34, 37, 38, 45, 207, 218, 219–220, 230, 233, 242–243, 244, 263
Paulsen, Ken, 206
Paulsen, Ruth Wright, 233
Paz, Octavio, 121, 142, CI-3
Pearl, Sydelle, 196
Peck, Marshall, 294
Peck, Richard, 135–136, 142, 252, 263
Pecos Bill, 98
Pele, 267, 279
Pendragon: The Merchant of Death, 126, 141
Penguins ABC, 69
Pennington, Daniel, 241, 263
People Who Hugged the Trees, The, 105
Percy, Bishop Thomas, 94
Perez, Amanda Irma, 180
Perfect Father's Day, A, 213, 231
Perkins, Lucy Fitch, 182
Perrault, Charles, 82, 84, 104, 106, 113
Perry, Andrea, 310
Persian Cinderella, The, 105
Person, Diane Goetz, 286, 287
Pertzoff, Alexander, 262
Peter Pan and Wendy, 125–126, 140
Petersham, Maud, 108, 109
Petersham, Miska, 108, 109
Peterson, Gordon Charles, 146
Phelps, Ethel J., 105
Phillips, Ellen Blue, 268, 280
Pickaninny Twins, The, 182
Picture Book of George Washington Carver, A, 275, 279
Pictures of Hollis Woods, 216, 232
Pied Piper of Hamelin, The, 302
Pigs, 157, 166

Pigs Might Fly, 157, 166, 197
Pilkey, Dav, 14, 25, 124–125, 142
Piñata, 181
Pinczes, Elinor J., 70, 71
Pinduli, 162, 165
Pink and Say, 248, 263
Pinkney, Brian, 97, 135, 142, 303
Pinkney, Jerry, 25, 49, 89, 94, 97, 103, 142, CI-1
Pippi Longstocking, 199
Planet without Pronouns, The, 74
Planting a Rainbow, 72
Pocahontas, 268
Pocket Poems, 310
Poems to Dream Together, 310
Poetry for Young People, 310
Poetry Speaks to Children, 310
Poet Slave of Cuba: A Biography of Juan Francisco Manzano, The, 267, 279
Poky Little Puppy, The, 16, 25, 150, 166
Point Blanc, 136, 141
Polacco, Patricia, 101, 105, 196, 248, 263
Polar Express, The, 126, 142
Polette, Nancy, 268
Pollock, Penny, 103
Poppy, 155, 165
Potter, Beatrix, 7, 8, 25, 47, 61, 145, 148, 166, 267, 280
Powell, Patricia Hruby, 103, 194
Powell, William, 318
Prater, Norma Jean, 16
"Prayer of the Selfish Child," 305
Prelutsky, Jack, 299, 310–311
Prince Caspian, 129, 141
Prince Siddhartha: The Story of Buddha, 196
Princess Mouse: A Tale of Finland, The, 105
Pronouns, 74
Provensen, Alice, 274, 275, 280
Provensen, Martin, 274, 280
Pullman, Philip, 204
Puppies, Dogs, and Blue Northers: Reflections on Being Raised by a Pack of Sled Dogs, 230, 233
Puppy Trouble, 77
Puss in Boots: A Fairy Tale, 104
Puzzling Shapes: A Puzzle Book, 64

Quackenbush, Robert, 275, 280
Quest for the Tree Kangaroo: An Expedition to the Cloud Forest of New Guinea, 295
Quidditch through the Ages, 142
Quinn, Shannon L., 191–192
Quinn, Suzanne M. Flannery, 191–192

Rabun, Miles, 185
Rabun, William, 185
Race to Save the Lord God Bird, The, 295
Radencich, Marguerite Cogorno, 177
Radio Man, CI-6
Rafi and Rosi, 180
Ragtime Song and Dance: Traditional Black Music, 95
Rainbow Crow: A Lenape Tale, 101, 103
Rainbow Hand: Poems about Mothers and Children, The, 311
Ralph S. Mouse, 158, 165
Ramadan: A Muslim Time of Fasting, Prayer, and Celebration, 196
Ramona and Her Father, 206, 212, 231
Ramona Quimby, Age 8, 212, 231
Ramona's World, 212, 231
Ramos-Michail, N., 176
Ranger's Apprentice (series), 132
Ransom, Candice F., 268, 280
Ransome, Arthur, 88, 89, 100, 105
Ransome, James, 45, 262, 303
Rapunzel, 104
Raschka, Chris, 92
Raskin, Ellen, 223, 233
Rathmann, Peggy, 64, 156, 166
Raven: A Trickster Tale from the Pacific Northwest, 91, 92
Rayner, Mary, 166
Rayyan, Omar, 140
Read to Me: Raising Kids Who Love to Read, 19
Real Mother Goose, The, 109, CI-2
Reasoner, Charles, 98
Red Book, The, 77
Red Thunder, 174, 194
Redwall, 14, 25, 155, 166
Red Warrior, The, 253, 263
Reeder, Carolyn, 248, 254, 263
Remember the Bridge: Poems of a People, 182, 184
Rescue, The, 162, 166
Return of Skeleton Man, The, 195
Reuter, Bjarne, 199
Rey, H. A., 159, 166
Reynolds, Peter H., 232

Richards, Janet C., 52, 58–59
Richardson, Frederick, 109
Richardson, Justin, 204
Richard Wright and the Library Card, 275, 280
Rifle, The, 34, 45, 242–243, 263
Right Book, the Right Time, The, 209
Ring of Truth, The, 117, 140
Ringgold, Faith, 123, 142
Rinpoche, Ringu Tulku, 103
Riordan, Rick, 123
Rivera, Tomás, 178
River Friendly, River Wild, 310
Road to Memphis, The, 254, 263
Roback, Diane E., 119
Robbins, Ruth, 105
Roberts, Jeremy, 276, 280
Roberts, Willo Davis, 222, 223, 233
Robinson Crusoe, 5, 25
Rocket in My Pocket: The Rhymes and Chants of Young Americans, A, 108, 109
Rockwell, Anne, 66, 68, 69
Rockwell, Thomas, 207, 218, 233
Rogers, Gregory, 14, 25
Rojankovsky, Feodor, 95
Roll of Thunder, Hear My Cry, 249, 252–253, 263
Rooster Crows, The, 108, 109
Root, Kimberly Bulcken, 103
Root, Phyllis, 75
Rosa, 184
Rosa-Casanova, Sylvia, 180
Rose, Deborah Lee, 71, 105
Rosenblatt, Louise M., 40–41, 58
Roser, Nancy L., 39, 327–328
Rose's Journal: The Story of a Girl in the Great Depression, 251, 262
Rosie's Walk, 73, 74
Ross, Gayle, 100, 103, 194
Rossi, Marianne, 278
Roth, Robert, 180
Rothlein, Liz, 31, 32, 47
Rowling, J. K., 17, 37, 45, 54, 61, 111, 130–131, 142, 197
Rubber Duckies, The, 71
Rudolph the Red-Nosed Reindeer, 149–150, 166
Ruffins, Reynold, 102
Ruins of Gorlan, The, 132
Ruiz, Aristides, 181
Ruler of the Courtyard, 198

Runaway Bunny, The, 64
Runaway Ralph, 158, 165
Runny Babbit: A Billy Sook, 311
Rumpelstiltskin, 104
Run, Boy, Run, 198
Russell, David L., 31, 39, 50, 66, 145, 196
Ryals, Lexi, 276, 280
Ryan, Pam Munoz, 180
Rylant, Cynthia, 13, 25, 156, 166, 214, 233, 255, 263, CI-5

Saba: Under the Hyena's Foot, 197
Sabuda, Robert, 181
Sacagawea (Erdrich), 194
Sacajawea (Bruchac), 195
Sachar, Louis, 224, 233
Sadako and the Thousand Paper Cranes, 274, 279
Safe Return, 199
Saggy Baggy Elephant, 16, 25
Saint Exupéry, Antoine de, 135, 142
Saint George and the Dragon: A Golden Legend, 96, 97
Saint James, Synthia, 184
Saint Valentine, 181
Salsa Stories, 198
Salten, Felix, 149, 166
Salting the Ocean: 100 Poems by Young Poets, 310
Salt in His Shoes: Michael Jordan in Pursuit of a Dream, 182, 183
Salzman, Siegmund (*see* Salten, Felix)
Samir and Yonatan, 199
Sampson, Michael, 71
Sanderson, Stephanie, 304
San Souci, Daniel, 143
San Souci, Robert D., 102, 103, 105, CI-1
Sarah Bishop, 243, 263
"Sarah Cynthia Sylvia Stout Would Not Take the Garbage Out," 299
Sarah, Plain and Tall, 244, 259, 262
"Saucy Little Ocelot," 299
Savadier, Elivia, 109, 179
Savageau, Cheryl, 201
Sawyer, Kem Knapp, 268, 280
Sawyer, Ruth, 28
Say, Allen, 172, 176, 190
Scarry, Richard, 74
Schaefer, Jack, 3, 25

Schafer, Kevin, 69

Schanzer, Rosalyn, 98

Schernoff Discoveries, The, 218, 233

Schindler, S. D., 166

Schneider, Jenifer Jasinski, 118, 130, 203–206

Schnetzler, Pattie L., 69, 71

Schodt, Frederik, 191

Schories, Pat, 165

Schulman, Janet, 18–19

Schwartz, Howard, 106

Scieszka, Jon, 34, 45, 117–118, 127, 142

Scorpions, 226, 232

Scott, J. A., 313

Scott, J. C., 174

Scott, Sir Walter, 20, 25

Scuffy the Tugboat, 16, 25, 119–120, 141

Search for the Shadowman, 224, 232

Sea Squares, 70, 71

Secret Letters from 0 to 10, 198

Secret Room, The, 101, 106

Secrets of the Sphinx, 295

Secrets of the Vine for Little Ones, 64

See and Spy Counting, 64

Seeger, Pete, 117, 142, 172, 176

Seeger, Laura Vaccaro, 74

Seibold, J. Otto, 58, 61

Selavi, That Is Life: A Haitian Story of Hope, 198

Selden, George, 158–159, 167, 330–331

Selena, 275, 280

Selznick, Brian, 14, 25

Sendak, Maurice, 25, 29, 47, 67, 69, 108, 109, 126, 142, 165, 166

Series of Unfortunate Events, A (series), 138–139

Serpent's Children, The, 245, 263

Seuss, Dr., 12, 25, 28, 55, 67, 69, 138, 142, 150–151, 167, 297, 325

Seven Blind Mice, 93, 94, 107

Seven Wonders of the Ancient World, The, 295

Sewell, Anna, 6, 25, 147, 163, 167

Sexton, Colleen, 267, 280

Shabanu: Daughter of the Wind, 198

Shades of Gray, 248, 263

Shane, 3, 25

Shange, Ntozake, 183, 185

Shannon, David, 219, 233

Shapes, 72, 73

Shapes: Slide 'n' Seek, 73

She Come Bringing Me That Little Baby Girl, 218, 232

She'll Be Coming Round the Mountain, 95

Shen, Wenju, 187

Shepard, Aaron, 105

Shepard, Ernest H., 142, 166

Shields, Charles J., 267, 280

Shiloh, 230, 232

Shojo Beat, 191

Shonen Jump, 191

Shortcut, 172, 176

Show Way, 185

Shrek!, 151, 167

Shreve, Susan, 222

Shrodes, Caroline, 209

Shulevitz, Uri, 89, 101, 105, 106

Shuman, Louise Bell, 169

Shutting Out the Sky: Life in the Tenements of New York, 1880–1924, 295

Sidewalk Circus, 77

Sidman, Joyce, 311

Siebel, Fritz, 142

Siegel, Siena Cherson, 14, 25

Siegelson, Kim, 97

Sierra, Judy, 71

Sign of the Beaver, The, 239, 263

Sign of the Chrysanthemum, The, 240, 263

Silver Chair, The, 129, 141

Silverman, Jerry, 95

Silverstein, Shel, 55, 120, 142, 160, 167, 299, 305, 311

Simon, Seymour, 288, 295

Singer, Marilyn, 295

Single Shard, A, 190, 240, 263

Sing, Pierrot, Sing: A Picture Book in Mime, 75

Sink or Swim: African American Lifesavers of the Outer Banks, 182, 184

Sip of Aesop, A, 94

Sir Gawain and the Loathly Lady, 96

Sis, Peter, 295

S Is for S'Mores: A Camping Alphabet, 68

Sitting Bull and the Battle of Little Bighorn, 275, 279

Siu, Sau-Fong, 187

Siu-Runyan, Yvonne, 196

Six Sleepy Sheep, 70, 71

Siy, Alexandra, 295

Skip across the Ocean: Nursery Rhymes from around the World, 109

Slave Dancer, The, 246, 262

Sleeping Beauty, 104

Slote, Alfred, 34, 45
Smith, Cynthia Leitich, 174, 194
Smith, Lane, 45, 142
Smith, Roland, 198
Smith, Sharon, 259–260, 276–278
Smith, Will, 183
Smoky Night, 226, 231
Snapshots from the Wedding, 57, 61, 180, CI-2
Snicket, Lemony, 138–139, 142, 325
Sneve, Virginia Driving Hawk, 194
Snow, Alan, 310
Snowman, The, 77
Snow-White and the Seven Dwarfs, 53, 59, 60, 104
Snowy Day, The, 56, 61, 182, 183, 238
Snyder, Zilpha Keatley, 171, 176
So, Meilo, 311
Sobol, Donald J., 222–223, 233
Soccer: The Ultimate Guide to the Beautiful Game, 295
Soentpiet, Chris K., 191, 262
Solitary Blue, A, 215, 233
Soman, David, 232
"Something Missing," 305
Somewhere in the Darkness, 215, 232
Song and Dance Man, 213, 231
Song of Robin Hood, The, 95
Song of the Trees, 249, 252, 263
Song of Three Holy Children, The, 302–303
Sorensen, Henri, 64
Soto, Gary, 57, 61, 155, 167, 180, CI-2
Sounder, 35, 45, 237, 262
Sound That Jazz Makes Alive, The, 182, 184
Speare, Elizabeth George, 29, 239, 240, 241, 263
Spiders, 294
Spiderwick Chronicles, The (series), 122
Spier, Peter, 77, 95, 302, 311
Spinelli, Jerry, 37, 45, 226–227, 229, 233, 253, 263
Spyri, Johanna, 6, 25
Squanto's Journey: The Story of the First Thanksgiving, 193
Stanley, Diane, 50, 51, 56, 61, 264, 269, 280
Staples, Suzanne Fisher, 198
Stargirl, 229, 233
Star-Spangled Banner, The, 302, 311
Steer, Dugald, 159, 167
Steig, William, 151, 153–154, 167
Steinbergh, Judith, 307
Stellaluna, 161, 165
Stephens, Elaine C., 2, 31, 34, 36

Stepping on the Cracks, 255, 262
Steptoe, John, 99, 102, 232
Stevens, Jan Romero, 180
Stevenson, Robert Louis, 6, 25, 302
Stevenson, Suçie, 25, 166
Stewart, Don, 263
Stewart, Donna, 59–60
Stewart, Trenton Lee, 137
Stewig, John Warren, 48, 76, 145
Sticks, 228, 231
Stine, Megan, 270–271, 280
Stinky Cheese Man and Other Fairly Stupid Tales, The, 117–118, 142
Stone, Tanya, 268, 280
Stonehill, B., 49, 51
Stone Soup, 19, 24, 104
Stonewords, 134, 141
Stoodt, Barbara D., 328
Stories or Tales from Past Times with Morals, 82
Stormbreaker, 136, 141
Story, a Story: An African Tale, A, 102
Story of Doctor Dolittle, The, 123, 141
Story of Jumping Mouse: A Native American Legend, The, 99
Story of Malcolm X, Civil Rights Leader, The, 270–271, 280
Story of Mankind, The, 27, 45
Story of Sacajawea, Guide to Lewis and Clark, The, 278
Stowaway, The, 243, 262
Stratton, Beverly D., 209, 211
Strauss, Susan, 92, 100, 103
Street, Pat, 295
Strega Nona, 85, 88, 100, 105
Strega Nona Meets Her Match, 117, 141
Strong Right Arm: The Story of Mamie "Peanut" Johnson, A, 184
Stuart-Clark, Christopher, 310
Stuckey, Denise Lohr, 195
Stuve-Bodeen, Stephanie, 197
Suba, Susanne, 109
Sue, Derald Wing, 187
Sullivan, George, 288, 291, 295
Summer of My German Soldier, 254, 262
Superfudge, 212, 231
Surpising Sharks, 295
Sutcliff, Rosemary, 82, 89
Sutherland, Zena, 49, 222
Swedish Fairy Tales, 105

Swift, Jonathan, 5, 25
Swimmy, 35, 45, 161, 166
Swiss Family Robinson, The, 5, 6, 25
Sword and the Circle, The, 82, 89
Sylvester, B. Ruth, 57, 330–331
Sylvester and the Magic Pebble, 153–154, 167

Tai Chi Morning: Snapshots of China, 310
Tails, 64
Takamisaki, Ryo, 192
Take a Look at Snakes, 290, 295
Talbott, Hudson, 185
Tale of Benjamin Bunny, The, 148, 166
Tale of Despereaux, 153, 158, 165
Tale of Peter Rabbit, The, 7, 8, 25, 47, 61, 145, 148, 166
Tale of Three Trees: A Traditional Folktale, The, 102
Tale of Two Rice Birds: A Folktale from Thailand, A, 103
Tales of a Fourth Grade Nothing, 212, 231
Tales of Uncle Remus: The Adventures of Brer Rabbit, The, 89, 103
Talkin' about Bessie: The Story of Aviator Elizabeth Coleman, 184
Talking Earth, The, 221, 232
Talking Eggs: A Folktale from the American South, The, 102, 103, CI-1
Tanemura, Arina, 192
Tangerine, 207, 229, 231
Tar Beach, 123, 142
Taste of Smoke, A, 134, 140
Tattercoats, 103
Tatterhood and Other Tales: Stories of Magic and Adventure, 105
Taylor, Gaylia, 185
Taylor, Mildred D., 244, 249, 250, 252–253, 254, 263, 325
Tazewell, Charles, 134, 142, CI-1
Teacher from the Black Lagoon, The, 121, 142
Teaching and Learning the Language Arts, 315
Teague, Mark, 166
Team Moon: How 400,000 People Landed Apollo 11 on the Moon, 295
Tell Me Again about the Night I Was Born, 228, 232, CI-4
Tell Me a Story, Mama, 213, 232
Temple, Charles A., 172, 287, 316

Tenggren, Gustaf, 166
Ten Little Dinosaurs, 69, 71
Ten Little Rubber Ducks, 71
Ten Mice for Tet, 181
Tenniel, Sir John, 1, 7, 24, 49–50, 54, 60
Ten, Nine, Eight, 70, 71
Ten Suns: A Chinese Legend, 92
Thaler, Mike, 121, 142
There's a Frog in My Throat! 440 Animal Sayings a Little Birdie Told Me, 295
There's a Nightmare in My Closet, 121, 141
"They've Put a Brassiere on the Camel," 305
Thief Lord, The, 198
Thief of Hearts, 227, 233
Thiele, Bob, 171, 176
Thimmesh, Catherine, 295
Thirteen Moons on Turtle's Back, 54, 60, 296, 310
Thomas, Garen, 268, 280
Thomas, Joyce Carol, 185
Thompson, John, 262, 311
Three Billy Goats Gruff, The, 105
Three Names, 249, 262
Three Terrible Trins, 158, 166
Throop, Sarah A., 136, 140
Through My Eyes, 274, 279
Through the Looking-Glass and What Alice Found There, 5, 6, 24
Thumbelina, 115, 122, 140
Thump, Thump, Rat-a-Tat-Tat, 54, 60
Tieck, Sarah, 274, 280
Tiegreen, Alan, 231
Tiger Woods: A Biography for Kids, 267, 280
Tikki Tikki Tembo, 101, 103
Time for Bed, 64
Time of Angels, A, 133, 141
Tingle, Tim, 193, 194–195
Tiny Tyrant, 14, 25
Titanic: Lost and Found, The, 295
Toby Keith, 267, 280
To Dance: A Ballerina's Graphic Novel, 14, 25
Todd, Anne M., 268, 280
Toddy, Irving, 263
Tolkien, J. R. R., 128–129, 142
Tom, 49, 60, 213, 232, CI-3
Tomes, Margot, 280
Tomie dePaola's Book of Bible Stories, 90
Tomlinson, Carl M., 14, 31
Tompkins, Gail E., 126

Tootle, 16, 25
Toriyama, Akira, 192
Tortillas Para Mama and Other Rhymes in Spanish and English, 109
Touch the Poem, 310
To Walk the Sky Path, 173, 176
Town Mouse, Country Mouse, 94
Traitor, The, 250, 263
Treasure Island, 6, 25
Trip Back Home, The, 191
Trivas, Irene, 45
Trondheim, Lewis, 14, 25
Trudell, John, 175
Trueba, Henry T., 187
True Story of the 3 Little Pigs, The, 34, 45, 117, 142
Tseng, Jean, 190
Tseng, Mou-sien, 190
Tuck Everlasting, 123, 140
Tuesday, 55, 61, 77, CI-5
Tunnell, Michael O., 284, 285
Turkey Girl: A Zuni Cinderella Story, The, 103
Turner, Deborah, 157, 167
Twain, Mark, 2, 6, 25, 204
Twelve Days of Kindergarten, The, 71
20th Century Children's Poetry Treasury, The, 311
Twenty Thousand Leagues under the Sea, 6, 25
Two Under Par, 214, 232
Tyrone the Terrible (series), 156

UFO Diary, 136, 141
Uglies, 136, 142
Ultra Maniac, 192
Umbrella, The, 159, 165
Uncle Jed's Barbershop, 35, 45, 251, 262
Uncle Remus, His Songs and Sayings, 84
Under the Breadfruit Tree, 198
Under the Window, 26, 302
Underwater Alphabet Book, The, 68, 69

Vagin, Vladimir, 105, 142
Vail, Rachel, 33, 45
Valasquez, Eric, 183, 184
Van Allsburg, Chris, 47, 126–127, 142
Van Fleet, Matthew, 64, 69
Van Laan, Nancy, 100, 103
van Loon, Hendrik Willem, 27, 45
Vargus, Nanci R., 181
Vaughan, Marcia, 181

Vega, Anne, 231
Velasquez, J., 178
Velveteen Rabbit, The, 119, 143
Vennema, Peter, 56, 61, 264, 269, 280
Venom, 295
Vera Wang, Queen of Fashion, 268, 280
Verdi, 161–162, 165
Verne, Jules, 5, 6, 25, 135, 142
Very Busy Spider, The, 160–161, 165
Very Clumsy Click Beetle, The, 161, 165
Very Hungry Caterpillar, The, 8, 24, 59, 60, 69, 160, 165
Very Lonely Firefly, The, 116, 140, 161, 165
Very Quiet Cricket, The, 161, 165
Vidal, Beatriz, 102, 103
Village That Vanished, The, 182, 183
Viorst, Judith, 213, 233
Voices of Ancient Egypt, 295
Voigt, Cynthia, 215, 233
Voyage of the Dawn Treader, The, 129, 141
Voyage of the Frog, The, 22, 23, 25, 220, 233
Voyages of Doctor Dolittle, The, 123, 141

Waber, Bernard, 216, 229, 233
Wade, Mary Dodson, 181
Wait for Me, 190
Walk Two Moons, 215–216, 232
Wall, The (Bunting), 224, 231
Wall, The (Sis), 295
Wallace, Nancy Elizabeth, 56, 61, CI-2
Wallace, S. A., 187
Walsh, Ellen Stoll, 73
Walsh, Vivian, 61
Walter the Farting Dog, 157, 166, CI-6
Walter the Farting Dog: Trouble at the Yard Sale, 157, 166
Wanderer, The, 228, 232
Wang, Rosalind C., 102, 103
Wanted . . . Mud Blossom, 223–224, 231
Ward, Helen, 94
Ward, John, 185
Warner, Marina, 87
Warren, Janet S., 16
Warriors (series), 162
Water Buffalo Days: Growing Up in Vietnam, 190
Watsons Go to Birmingham—1963, The, 59, 60, 256–258, 262
Watts, Trish P., 49, 53, 56, 60, 262, 312

Way Meat Loves Salt: A Cinderella Tale from the Jewish Tradition, The, 105
We All Went on a Safari: A Counting Journey through Tanzania, 71
We Are the Ship: The Story of Negro League Baseball, 183
Weatherford, Carole Boston, 182, 183, 184, 185
Webb, Martha Venning, 59
Webbing with Literature: Creating Story Maps with Children's Books, 154
Wednesday Surprise, The, 213, 231
Weeping under This Same Moon, 224, 232
Wee Sing & Learn Opposites, 74
Weill, Cynthia, 181
Weiss, George David, 171, 176
Weitzman, Jacqueline Preiss, 77
Well, The, 250, 263
Wellman, Sam, 195
Wells, Rosemary, 251, 263
Wenzel, Gregory, 288, 295
Westerfeld, Scott, 136, 142
Westin, Robin, 267, 280
Westing Game, The, 223, 233
Whale Is Not a Fish and Other Animal Mix-Ups, A, 288, 292, 294
What a Wonderful World, 171, 176
What Color Is Your Underwear?, 72
What's Cooking?, 72
What's the Big Idea, Ben Franklin?, 270, 277, 280
Wheeler, Jody, 295
Wheels on the Bus, The, 64, 74, 75
Whelan, Gloria, 198
When I Was Young in the Mountains, 255, 263, CI-5
When We Were Very Young, 302
When Woman Became the Sea: A Costa Rican Creation Myth, 92
Where Have All the Pandas Gone? Questions and Answers about Endangered Species, 288, 294
Where the Sidewalk Ends, 311
Where the Wild Things Are, 126, 142
Whisper in the Dark, 195
White, E. B., 28, 33, 45, 150, 156, 157, 167
White, Ruth, 255, 263
White Deer of Autumn, 133, 142
Whitethorne, Billy, 194
Whitney, Phyllis A., 145, 146

Who Comes with Cannons?, 247, 262
Who Was First Discovering the Americas?, 293, 295
Why Mosquitoes Buzz in People's Ears, 34, 45, 56, 60, 102
Wick, Walter, 291, 295
Wiesner, David, 55, 61, 77, CI-5
Wijngaard, Juan, 96
Wilburn, Medicine Hawk, 100
Wilder, Laura Ingalls, 28, 33, 34, 45, 238, 248, 260, 263
Wild Weather: Lightning!, 285, 295
Wilhelm, Hans, 156, 207, 230, 233
Wilkinson, Bruce H., 64
Wilkinson, I. A. G., 313
Willems, Mo, 159, 167
Williams, Garth, 45, 166, 167, 263
Williams, Jay, 137, 143
Williams, Margery, 119, 143
Williams, Nancy L., 318
Williams, Sherley Anne, 207, 226, 233
Williams, Vera B., 214, 233
William Tell, 96
Willis, Charles M., 268, 280
Wilms, Denise M., 276
Wilson, John, 279
Wilson, Kathleen Atkins, 303
Wimmer, Mike, 280
Wind in the Willows, The, 148–149, 156, 166
Winnie-the-Pooh, 119, 142
Winter People, The, 194
Winters, Kay, 295
Wishing on a Star: Constellation Stories, 92
Wisniewski, David, 97
Witch of Blackbird Pond, The, 241, 263
Withers, Carl, 108, 109
Wolf, D., 59
Wolfe, Ashley, 105, 198
Wolfson, Margaret Olivia, 92
Wolkomir, J. R., 106
Wolkomir, R., 106
Women Warriors: Myths and Legends of Heroic Women, 97
Wonderful Wizard of Oz, The, 6, 24, 125, 140
Wong, Janet S., 190–191, 304, 311
Wood, Audrey, 58, 61, 72, 75, CI-4
Wood, Bruce, 72
Wood, Don, 58, 75, CI-4

Woodson, Jacqueline, 185, 214–215, 233
Working Cotton, 207, 226, 233
Worth, Bonnie, 181
Worth, Valerie, 303
Wright, Blanche Fisher, 109, CI-2
Wringer, 37, 45, 229, 233
Wrinkle in Time, A, 135, 141
Wyatt, Georgann C., 306–307
Wynne-Jones, Tim, 199
Wyss, Johann, 5, 6, 25

Xuan, Yongsheng, 92

Yah-Shen: A Cinderella Story from China, 103
Yankee Doodle, 95
Yao, E. L., 187
Yates, Elizabeth, 273
Yazzie, Evangeline Parsons, 245–246, 263
Year of Miss Agnes, The, 255, 262
Year of the Child: Alien Exchange Students, The, 136, 140
Year of the Perfect Christmas Tree, The, 35, 45, 50, 61, 234, 239, 250–251, 262
Yeh, Christine J., 187
Yellow Bird and Me, 229, 232
Yellow Star, The, 199
Yep, Laurence, 29, 189, 227, 233, 244–245, 250, 253, 255–256, 263

Yes We Can: A Biography of Barack Obama, 268, 280
Yin, Chris, 191
Yokota, Junko, 172, 304
Yolen, Jane, 3, 25, 38, 45, 81, 94, 120, 127, 132, 143, 146, 311
Yonder, 244, 262
Yorinks, Arthur, 126, 143
York's Adventures with Lewis and Clark: An African-American's Part in the Great Expedition, 294
Yoshizumi, Wataru, 192
Yotsuba & !, 192
You Can't Take a Balloon into the Museum, 77
Young, Ed, 51, 54, 56, 61, 80, 93, 94, 103, 107, 310, 325
Yumoto, Kazumi, 198

Zaidi, Nadeem, 64
Zeitlin, Steve, 92
Zeke Pippin, 154, 167
Zelinsky, Paul O., 64, 104, 231, 310
Zemach, Harve, 101–102, 104
Zemach, Margot, 104, 106
Zia, 245, 263
Zion, Gene, 156, 167
Zucker, Jonny, 181
Zusak, Markus, 254, 263

Subject Index

Activities (*see* Literature responses and activities)
Adolescent literature (*see* Young adult literature)
Aesthetic stance, 40, 59, 276
African American literature, 174–175, 181–185, 227, 256–257
  authors and illustrators, 183–185
  award for, 182, 200, 303
  biographies, 237, 270, 275, 294
  civil rights era, 184–185, 256, 270
  historical fiction, 249–250, 252, 254
  traditional tales, 84, 98, 99, 102
Alliteration, 67, 299, 308
Alphabet books, 7, 9, 65–69, 189
Andersen, H. C., influence on fantasy, 29, 87, 113–116, 118, 121–122, 125, 128, 132, 134, 137
Animal fantasy, 144–167
  characteristics, 116, 145
  comparison of types, 164
  evaluation criteria, 147
  history of, 147–151
  types of, 151–164
Animal stories (*see also* Animal fantasy)
  fantasy, 144–167
  informational, 292
  realistic fiction, 207, 221, 229–230
  traditional literature, 86, 92–93, 99
Anthropomorphic animals, 86, 92, 98–99, 116, 145, 152, 156 (*see also* Animal fantasy)
Art and text, union of, 47
Artistic elements, 48–52
  color, 49–50
  composition, 51–52
  lines, 49
  point of view, 51–52
  scale and dimension, 51
  shape, 49
  space, 48
  texture, 51
Artistic media, 55–57
  drawing, 56
  painting, 55–56
Artistic styles, 52–55
Asian and Asian American literature, 186–191
  authors and illustrators, 189–191

  award for, 189
  evaluating, 188
  historical fiction, 240, 244–245, 250, 253, 255–256
  international, 198
  traditional tales, 82, 103
Assonance, 299
Autobiography, 265, 271, 277 (*see also* Biography)
Awards, general
  Caldecott, 7, 27–28, 106–107, 183
  Children's Choices, 29–30, 208, 210–211
  Newbery, 5, 27–28, 124, 249, 293
  Teachers' Choices, 29–30, 205, 210–211
Awards, genre specific (*see also* Awards, nonfiction)
  Edgar Allan Poe (mystery), 222, 224
  Mildred L. Batchelder (international literature), 197, 200
  NCTE for Excellence in Poetry, 303
  Scott O'Dell (historical fiction), 239, 245
Awards, lifetime contributions
  Hans Christian Andersen, 29, 107, 197
  Laura Ingalls Wilder, 28–29, 293
Awards, minority/ethnic
  Américas (Latino), 178, 199
  Asian Pacific American, 189, 199
  Carter G. Woodson (minority), 182, 199, 285
  Charles and Bertie G. Schwartz (Jewish), 196
  Coretta Scott King (African American), 182–183, 200, 303
  National Jewish Book, 196, 200
  Pura Belpré (Latino), 178, 200, 309
  Sydney Taylor (Jewish), 196, 200
  Tomás Rivera (Latino), 178, 200
Awards, nonfiction
  Carter G. Woodson, 182, 199, 285
  Orbis Pictus, 30, 285

Ballads and folk songs, 9, 94–96
Basal readers, 19–20, 151, 317–318, 328
Best-selling books, 13, 64, 146, 150
Bibliotherapy, 208–212
Big books, 43, 75
Biographic historical fiction, 236–238

Biography, 264–280
  authentic, 268–270
  award, 285
  collective, 275–276
  complete, 273–274
  Dewey decimal location, 265
  enhancing curriculum with, 276–278
  evaluation criteria, 266
  fictionalized, 272–273
  partial, 274
  picture book, 275
  pleasure reading, 267
Board books, 63–65
Book talk, 39, 78, 277, 287, 326–328

Censorship, 130, 203–206
Chapter books, 12, 14
Character continuum activity, 31–32
Character mapping, 253, 257
Characters, stereotyped, 31, 85, 170, 188
Characters, types, 31
Children's classics, 5–6
Children's literature
  defined, 2–4
  history of, 4–8
  value of, 18–20
Classroom library, developing, 42–44
Cinderella-type stories, 84, 106
Comprehension monitoring, 319–320
Concept books, 64–74
  alphabet, 65–69
  counting, 69–71
  other, 72–74
Concept of word, 74
Concepts of print, 75
Conflict in plots, 36–37
Contemporary realistic fiction, 201–233
  characteristics, 202–203
  evaluation criteria, 202
  themes
    animals, 229–230
    adventure, 219–222
    families, 212–216
    friendship, 216
    humor, 218–219
    mystery, 222–224
    personal issues, 227–229
    social reality, 224–227

Counting books, 52, 64, 69–71, 95, 180–181
Cultural literacy, 14, 91, 93, 95, 110
Culture, 169–170, 173–176
Cumulative tale, 35, 87, 101
Curriculum, enhancing
  with biography, 276–278
  with historical fiction, 259–260
  with informational books, 285–287

Dewey decimal system, 9–11, 63, 81, 112, 145,
  202, 236, 265, 282, 297
Drama, 78, 118, 186, 260, 273, 321

Early childhood books, 62–79
Easy-to-read books, 12–13, 36, 150, 152, 156
Efferent stance, 40, 276
Elements
  literary, 30–39
  visual arts, 48–52
Evaluation criteria
  animal fantasy, 147
  biographers, 270
  biography, 266
  contemporary realistic fiction, 202
  historical fiction, 235
  illustrations, 47
  informational books, 283
  modern fantasy, 112
  multicultural literature, 170
  poetry, 298
  traditional literature, 81
Evocation, 40–41, 276
Exposition, 36
Eye–voice span, 320

Fables, 92–94
Fairy tales, 98–106
  beast stories, 99
  Cinderella stories, 106
  cumulative tales, 101
  pourquoi tales, 100–101
  realistic tales, 101
  simpleton tales, 100
  trickster tales, 99–100
  wonder stories, 101–102
Fantasy (*see* Modern fantasy)
Fiction, 111–167, 201–261
Five-finger method, 318

Flashback, 36, 192, 215–216
Focus units, 186
Folk literature (*see* Traditional literature)
Folklore (*see* Traditional literature)
Folktales, 89–106
Foreshadowing, 36
Formats, book, 11–18
Formula books, 17–18

Genres, 8–9
Grand conversation, 217, 327
Graphic novels, 13–14, 191–192, 219
Graphic organizers, 37, 288–292
    character map, 253, 256–257
    cycle map, 289, 291
    KWL chart, 288–289
    spider map/web, 153–154, 289–290
    story map, 36–37, 256–257, 328
    timeline, 259, 266, 289, 291
    Venn diagram, 6, 289, 292
Great Depression era, 251–253, 293
Grocery store books, 15–19, 119

High fantasy, 113, 128–132
Historical fiction, 235–263
    award, 239
    biographic historical fiction, 236–238
    characteristics, 235–236
    enhancing curriculum with, 259–260
    evaluation criteria, 235
    periods of, 239–258
    researching, 238–239

Illustrated books, 7, 13, 63
Informational books, 281–295
    awards, 285
    benefits of, 286
    characteristics, 284–285
    content area reading and, 287–288
    Dewey decimal locations, 282
    evaluation criteria, 283–284
    "how to" books, 284
Informational stories, 292
Institutional publishers, 283
International literature, 196–199
Issues in literature
    animal fantasy, 146
    biography, 271

    book awards, 30
    censorship, 206
    contemporary fiction, 225
    fantasy, 124
    graphic novels, 14
    historical fiction, 242
    illustrations/artwork, 58
    informational books, 292
    multicultural literature, 175
    picture books, 76
    poetry, 305
    series books, 18
    traditional literature, 109

Journals
    dialogue response, 127–128, 186, 210
    literature, 316–317, 322–323, 325, 327

KWL chart, 288–289

Language
    expository, 265, 272, 284, 286–287, 292
    figurative, 38, 298–299
    narrative, 33, 284, 294
    poetic, 299, 307
Language chart, 327–328
Language experience account (LEA), 76, 329
Latino literature, 176–180
    authors and illustrators, 179–180
    awards, 178
    international, 198
    traditional, 104
Legends, 96–97
Letter–sound correspondence, 67–68
Listening activities
    guided listening activity, 323–324
    listening–prediction activity, 314–317, 324,
        328
Literary fairy tales, 87, 114–118
Literature and technology (*see* Technology and
    literature)
Literature circles, 42, 186, 217, 318, 325
Literature responses and activities (*see also*
    Technology and literature; Issues in
    literature)
    biographies, comparing, 272
    book and movie versions of a classic,
        comparing, 6

Literature responses and activities *(continued)*
  book cover art, making predictions
    from, 54
  book covers, drawing, 59–60
  book talks, 326
  character continuum, 31–32
  character mapping, 253
  cultural artifacts, locating, 106
  cultural literacy (of mythology), testing
    your, 91
  dialogue response journals, 127
  drama, 118
  fact and fiction, separating, 242
  focus units, 186
  grand conversations, 217
  holidays, learning about cultures through, 181
  "how-to" books, 284
  illustrations in folktales, comparing, 48
  manga, reading, 191
  motifs in Cinderella stories, comparing, 106
  mystery clues, looking for, 222
  optical textures, analyzing, 50
  picture and text clues, finding, 35
  poem mobiles, 302
  poetry, writing, 307
  points of view, changing, 34
  Potter's illustrations, analyzing, 8
  puppets, 120
  readers theater, 153
  series books, analyzing, 18
  schema building, 24
  story boxes, 126
  story mapping, 256
  storytelling, 83
  themes of Lionni's books, determining, 38
  timelines, 266
  time setting, determining, 237
  webbing, 153
  What Do I See? (STW), 52
  wizardspeak (Harry Potter), 131

Manga, 13, 191
Merchandise books, 16–17
Metaphor, 299
Modern fantasy, 111–143 (*see also* Animal
    fantasy)
  animated object, 118–120
  characteristics, 112

enchanted journey, 125–127
  evaluation criteria, 112–113
  extraordinary person, 122–125
  high fantasy, 128–132
  history, 113–115
  human with fantasy character, 121–122
  literary fairy tale, 116–118
  supernatural fantasy, 132–134
  science fiction, 134–137
  types, 115–116
  unlikely situation, 137–139
Mother Goose (*see* Traditional rhymes)
Motif, 106, 114, 133
Multicultural literature 168–200 (*see also* African
      American literature; Asian and Asian
      American literature; Latino literature;
      Native American literature)
  culturally generic, 172
  culturally neutral, 171–172
  culturally specific, 172–173
  evaluation criteria, 170–171
  misrepresentation in, 173–175
  resources, 199–200
  themes, 173
Mystery stories, 207, 222–224
Myths, 89–92

Native American literature, 192–195
  authors and illustrators, 193–195
  award, 193
  historical fiction, 242, 245–246
  misrepresentation in, 173–175, 242
  traditional, 100, 103
Nonfiction, 264–280
  awards, 285
  Dewey decimal locations, 282
  text structures, 287–288
Novels, juvenile
  Dewey decimal location, 11
  history of, 4–5
  teaching reading through, 317–318,
    325–328
Nursery rhymes, 89, 107–109

Pattern picture books, 35, 74–75, 328, 330
Personification, 299
Phonemes, 67
Phonemic awareness, 67

Picture books, 11–12 (*see also* Concept books; Pattern picture books; Wordless picture books)
  Dewey decimal location, 112
  history of, 7–8, 11–12, 47–48, 112–113,
Picture storybooks, 7–8, 11–13, 47–48, 63, 148, 150
Plot, 35–37
Poetry, 296–311
  anthologies, 306
  award, 303
  characteristics, 298–299
  classics of, 302–303
  collections, 306
  concrete, 300
  Dewey decimal locations, 297
  developing love for, 303–305
  evaluation criteria, 298
  free verse, 301
  haiku, 301–302, 304–305
  humorous, 300, 305
  limericks, 298, 300, 305
  lyric, 301
  narrative, 300
  rhythm, 298
  single poem books, 306
  value of, 306–307
Point of view, 31–34
  alternating, 33
  in animal fantasy, 117, 147, 150, 156, 163
  in art, 51–52
  in biography, 265
  first person, 32–33
  limited omniscient, 33
  objective, 33
  omniscient, 33
Pourquoi tales, 100–101
Prequel, 129
Prereading schema-building process, 20–24, 327
Prose, 297, 299, 304, 306–307
Prototypes of children's literature, 5, 8, 82, 114, 148, 150
Public domain, 6, 57, 95, 331

Questions
  comprehension, 41
  grand conversation, 217
  guidelines for asking, 314–316

  illustrations, 47
  informational books, 291
  levels of, 315
  multicultural issues, 175
  prediction, 21, 324
  story themes, 38
  style of author, 38

Racism, 170, 173–174, 188–189, 199, 204, 226–227, 242
Reader response theory, 20, 40–42, 47, 58
Readers theater, 152–153, 321, 323, 328
Reading, 312–332
  aloud, 313–314
  choral, 320–321
  content area, 287–288
  developing ability with literature, 328
  echo, 328, 330–331
  genres, instruction by, 325
  guided reading activity, 322–324
  lap, 74–75
  motivating children, 77–79
  oral, 319–321
  paired, 330
  parents teaching, 329–330
  prediction activity, 321–322, 324, 328
  read-skip-read strategy, 320
  silent, 317, 321–322
  teaching with trade books, 317–318
  thematic instruction, 326–328
Reading levels, 3–4, 319, 325
Reference books, 3, 10, 40, 43, 283
Religion
  Dewey decimal location, 10, 89
  expression of, 90
  literature about, 90, 195–196
Reluctant readers, 17, 77, 218–219, 222, 304, 330
Responding to literature, 38 (*see also* Literature responses and activities)
Rhyme, 298–299
Rhythm, 298–299

Schema/schemata, 20–24, 65, 287–288, 290, 316 (*see also* Prereading schema-building process)
Science fiction, 113, 116, 134–137
Secondary worlds, 113, 128–132

Sequel, 17, 316
Series books, 17–18, 283
Setting, 34–35
Sight words, 330–331
Simile, 298–299
Speech-to-print match, 75
Spine, book, 11, 15, 84, 112
Spontaneous reenactment, 118
Stanza, 95, 300–302, 304
Stereotyping (*see* Characters, stereotyped)
Story boxes, 126, 277, 327
Story mapping, 36–37, 76, 152, 256–257, 328
Story structure, 75–76, 152, 287, 292, 315–316
Story theater, 321, 328
Style, literary, 38
Survival stories, 34, 148, 207, 219–221, 236
Suspense, 36, 222

Tall tales, 39, 97–98
Technology and literature
    Association for Library Services to Children, 28
    bibliotherapy resources, 211
    biography newspapers, creating, 278
    Children's Books Forever, 156
    content information, 293
    eBook readers, 7
    Gayle's Preschool Rainbow, 71
    KIDiddles Musical Mouseum, 95
    illustrating scenes from storybooks, 57
    literacy skills, enhancing, 330
    multicultural resources, finding, 199
    older books, comparing technology in, 137
    rhymes, synonyms, and antonyms, 308–309
    visual book report, 260
Textbooks, 283–287, 317–318, 328
Thematic instruction, 66, 286, 326–328

Themes, 37–38
    of contemporary realistic fiction, 206–207
    of historical fiction, 236
    of multicultural literature, 173
    of traditional literature, 87–88
Tone, literary, 39
Trade books, 19, 283, 317–318
Traditional literature, 80–110
    characteristics, 84–87
    Dewey decimal location, 81
    evaluation criteria, 81
    history, 82–84
    subgenres, 89–109
    themes, 87–88
    violence in, 109–110
Traditional rhymes, 107–109
Trickster characters, 88, 91, 99–100, 107, 180, 194
Trilogy, 17, 123, 128, 163

Verse, 297
Visual art and literature, 58–59
Visual literacy, 47–48, 52, 76, 191–192

Wars
    Civil, 10, 223, 238, 247–248
    Revolutionary, 242–243, 274
    Vietnam, 190, 224–225
    World War I, 239, 250–251
    World War II, 188, 190, 238–239, 253–254, 295
Webbing (*see* Graphic organizers)
White space, 12, 299, 304
Wordless picture books, 11, 75–77

Young adult literature, 2–4, 53, 178, 189, 240, 254

by the estate of Langston Hughes. Used by permission of Alfred A. Knopf, a division of Random House, Inc.

"They've Put a Brassier on the Camel" on p. 305 is from *A Light in the Attic* by Shel Silverstein, copyright © 1981 by Evil Eye Music, Inc. Used by permission of HarperCollins Publishers.

Illustration on p. 312 is from *Bud, Not Buddy* (jacket cover) by Christopher Paul Curtis, copyright © 1999. Used by permission of Random House Children's Books, a division of Random House, Inc.

Color Insert Credits

Illustration on p. CI-1 (top) is from *The Talking Eggs* by Robert D. San Souci, pictures by Jerry Pinkney, copyright © 1989 by Jerry Pinkney, pictures. Used by permission of Dial Books for Young Readers, a division of Penguin Young Readers Group, a member of Penguin Group (USA) Inc., 345 Hudson Street, New York, NY 10014. All rights reserved.

Illustration on p. CI-1 (bottom) is from *The Littlest Angel* by Charles Tazewell. Illustration by Paul Micich, copyright © 1991 by Children's Press. Used by permission of Ideals Publications.

Illustration on p. CI-2 (top) is from *The Real Mother Goose* illustrated by Blanche Fisher Wright. Reprinted by permission of Scholastic, Inc.

Illustration on p. CI-2 (right) is from *Snapshots from the Wedding* by Gary Soto, copyright © 1997 by Gary Soto, text. Used by permission of G. P. Putnam's Sons, a division of Penguin Young Readers Group, a member of Penguin Group (USA) Inc., 345 Hudson Street, New York, NY 10014. All rights reserved.

Illustration on p. CI-2 (bottom) is from *Leaves! Leaves! Leaves!* copyright © 2003 by Nancy Elizabeth Wallace, reprinted with permission of Marshal Cavendish.

Illustration on p. CI-3 (top) is from *Tom* by Tomie dePaola, copyright © 1993 by Tomie dePaola. Used by permission of G. P. Putnam's Sons, a division of Penguin Young Readers Group, a member of Penguin Group (USA) Inc., 345 Hudson Street, New York, NY 10014. All rights reserved.

Illustration on p. CI-3 (bottom) is from *My Life with the Wave,* translated and adapted by Catherine Cowan. Illustrations copyright © 1997 by Mark Buehner. Used by permission of HarperCollins Publishers.

Illustration on p. CI-4 (top) is from *Tell Me Again about the Night I Was Born* by Jamie Lee Curtis. Illustrations copyright © 1996 by Laura Cornell. Used by permission of HarperCollins Publishers.

Illustration on p. CI-4 (bottom) is from *The Napping House,* copyright © 1984 by Audrey Wood; illustrations copyright © 1984 by Don Wood. Reprinted with permission of Heacock Literary Agency, Inc.

Illustration on p. CI-5 (top) is from *When I Was Young in the Mountains* by Cynthia Rylant, copyright © 1982 by Cynthia Rylant, text. Used by permission of Dutton Children's Books, a division of Penguin Young Readers Group, a member of Penguin Group (USA) Inc., 345 Hudson Street, New York, NY 10014. All rights reserved.